S0-ABO-593

Pervasive Prejudice?

A volume in the series

STUDIES IN LAW AND ECONOMICS
EDITED BY *William M. Landes and J. Mark Ramseyer*

Pervasive Prejudice?

Unconventional Evidence of Race and Gender Discrimination

IAN AYRES

THE UNIVERSITY OF CHICAGO PRESS
CHICAGO AND LONDON

IAN AYRES is the William K. Townsend Professor of Law at Yale Law School. He is coauthor of *Responsive Regulation: Transcending the Deregulation Debate* (1992, with John Braithwaite) and *Studies in Contract Law* (5th ed. 1997, with Edward J. Murphy and Richard E. Speidal), and *Voting with Dollars: A New Paradigm for Campaign Finance* (forthcoming, with Bruce Ackerman).

The University of Chicago Press, Chicago 60637
The University of Chicago Press, Ltd., London
© 2001 by The University of Chicago
All rights reserved. Published 2001
Printed in the United States of America
10 09 08 07 06 05 04 03 02 01   1 2 3 4 5

ISBN: 0-226-03351-1 (cloth)

Library of Congress Cataloging-in-Publication Data

Ayres, Ian.
    Pervasive prejudice? : unconventional evidence of race and gender discrimination / Ian Ayres.
        p.   cm—(Studies in law and economics)
    Includes bibliographical references and index.
    ISBN 0-226-03351-1 (cloth : alk. paper)
    1. Race discrimination—United States. 2. Sex discrimination—United States. 3. Discrimination—Economic aspects—United States. 4. Markets—United States. I. Title. II. Series.

JC599.U5 A97 2001
305—dc21

                                                        2001027514

♾ The paper used in this publication meets the minimum requirements of the American National Standard for Information Sciences—Permanence of Paper for Printed Library Materials, ANSI Z39.48-1992.

This book is dedicated to

Anna and Henry Ayres-Brown
and to
the memory of John Pace and the Fellowship House Bridge Group

CONTENTS

ACKNOWLEDGMENTS

Crunching numbers is hard work. In what follows, much of the heavy lifting was done by my coauthors—Peter Siegelman, Laura Dooley, Robert Gaston, Joel Waldfogel, and Peter Cramton. Their ownership of the ensuing chapters rests both on their sweat equity in estimating many of the regressions as well as on their identifying the core tests that made these studies possible.

Crunching numbers is also expensive. Throughout my career, I have been blessed by the generous financial support of several institutions. Grants from the National Science Foundation and Yale's Initiative for Public Interest Law supported the bail bond research that is reported in chapter 6. I also thank the deans of the law schools where I have been lucky enough to teach—Robert Bennett (Northwestern), Paul Brest (Stanford), and Guido Calabresi and Anthony Kronman (Yale)—for the time off from teaching and the hiring of many research assistance and testers.

The support of the American Bar Foundation deserves special mention. The A.B.F. invested hundreds of thousands of dollars in the car empiricism that forms the basis of four chapters of this book. The director of the A.B.F., Bill Fellstiner, and the chair of the board, Robert Bennett, were instrumental in guiding my controversial request for funding past the sometimes contradictory objections of board members ("We don't need to fund this study, because the market doesn't discriminate"; "We don't need

to fund this study, because we already know the market discriminates";
"We don't need to fund this study, because it's not about the law."). But
beyond the generous funding (and the half-time teaching load!), my time
at the A.B.F. transformed me into an empirical recidivist. Had I begun
teaching elsewhere, it would have been all too easy for me (like many of
my colleagues in the legal academy) to generate ungrounded theory pieces.
I still write such pieces (and find some ineffable value in them). But my
time at the A.B.F. transformed me irrevocably into an empirical scholar,
and for that I am grateful.

I also thank my research assistants—several of whom are now profes-
sors or soon will be—who contributed to the diverse projects that make
up this book: Dan Ackerberg, Todd Cleary, George Comer, Calita Elston,
Kathie Heed, Akilah Kamaria, Darrell Karolyi, Kristin Madison, Rebecca
Mitchells, Gideon Parchomovsky, Franklin Parlamis, Ravi Pherwany, Patti
Steeves, Cathy Sharkey, and Fred Vars.

In addition, I received very helpful comments from Lori Andrews, Jen-
nifer Arlen, Steve Bainbridge, Lynn Baker, Bob Bennett, Paul Brest, Guido
Calabresi, John Caskey, Jay Casper, Morgan Cloud, Peter Cramton, Rich-
ard Craswell, Carolyn Craven, J. Michael Dennis, John Donohue, E. Don
Elliot, Richard Epstein, Dan Farber, William Felstiner, Owen Fiss, Robert
Frank, Mayer Freed, Alan Friedman, Rob Gertner, Mark Grady, James
Heckman, Michael Horvath, John Jefferies, Mark Kelman, Dan Kessler,
Al Klevorick, Lewis Kornhauser, Niki Kuckes, John Langbein, Ruth Mar-
cus, Stephen Marks, Bob Mnookin, Dan Ortiz, Tom Palay, A. Mitchell
Polinsky, Eric Rasmussen, Marty Redish, Deborah Rhode, Carol Rose,
Dan Rubinfeld, Len Rubinowitz, George Rutherglen, Carol Sanger, Peter
Schuck, Stewart Schwab, Ken Scott, Roger Shechter, Peter Siegelman, Eric
Talley, Joe Tracy, Bill Turnier, Daryl Warder, Deborah Young, and David
Van Zandt.

I am grateful to several publishers for permission to reprint portions
of previously published essays. Chapter 2 is drawn from Fair Driving: Gender and Race Discrimination in Retail Car Negotiations, 104 Harv. L. Rev.
817 (1991), reprinted by permission of the Harvard Law Review, and from
Race and Gender Discrimination in Negotiation for the Purchase of a New
Car, 84 Am. Econ. Rev. 304 (1995) (with Peter Siegelman), reprinted by
permission of the American Economic Association. Chapter 3 is drawn
from Further Evidence of Discrimination in New Car Negotiations and
Estimates of Its Cause, 94 Mich. L. Rev. 109 (1995), reprinted by permission of the Michigan Law Review. Chapter 6 is drawn from Unequal Racial
Access to Kidney Transplantation, 46 Vand. L. Rev. 805 (1993) (with

Laura Dooley and Robert Gaston), reprinted by permission of Vanderbilt Law Review. Chapter 7 is drawn from A Market Test for Race Discrimination in Bail Setting, 46 Stan. L. Rev. 987 (1994) (with Joel Waldfogel), © 1994 by the Board of Trustees of the Leland Stanford Junior University. And chapter 8—on FCC spectrum auctions—is drawn from Pursuing Deficit Reduction through Diversity: How Affirmative Action at the FCC Increased Auction Competition, 48 Stan. L. Rev. 761 (1996) (with Peter Cramton), © 1996 by the Board of Trustees of the Leland Stanford Junior University.

Finally, I would like to thank Jennifer Gerarda Brown—my coauthor and friend—for reading over these chapters many times and for noticing when I start to behave like my evil uncle Wendell.

New Haven, 2000

CHAPTER 1

"Untitled" Discrimination

In a comedy sketch broadcast some years ago on *Saturday Night Live,* black comedian Eddie Murphy disguised himself to appear white. He soon discovered that white consumers were treated radically better than black consumers. At one point in the sketch, the seemingly white Murphy attempts to buy a magazine at a store only to be told by the storekeeper that there is no need to pay so long as black customers are not around. The skit played off a deep suspicion of people of color—that they could uncover pervasive discrimination if only they were privy to how whites are treated.

A *PrimeTime Live* segment broadcast several years ago had a similar punch line. The television news magazine separately sent two "testers"— a white male and black male—to shop in a variety of retail stores along with a hidden camera to record how each was treated. The video depicted several different types of race discrimination. A car salesman quoted the black tester a higher price; in an empty shoe store a clerk forced the black male to wait for fifteen minutes before assisting him; and in a record store a clerk conspicuously trailed the black tester as he browsed, while the white tester was allowed to shop without scrutiny.

In the *Saturday Night Live* sketch, the whites knew about the discrimination and blacks were kept in the dark. But I believe the *PrimeTime Live* segment suggests the opposite is closer to the truth. Several white colleagues and students who have seen the segment have remarked how it opened their eyes to the reality of quotidian discrimination in retail markets.[1] People of color have better insights into what is and what is not normal service and hence are better attuned to the possibility of race discrimination. But knowledge about how other similarly situated people are treated is a crucial barrier to learning whether (and the extent to which) discrimination exists. Consumers usually know how they are treated, but often lack information on how other consumers are treated. Equality of treatment can thus be what economists call a "credence attribute"—that is, a characteristic of consumption that the consumer does not learn about either at the time of sale or through consumption of the product or service itself.[2] Just as a manufacturer's claim that its lightbulbs have an expected life of two thousand hours, a car dealer's explicit or implicit claim that it does not discriminate on the basis of race or gender may be difficult for consumers to verify through their individual experiences.

Of course, there are many types of discrimination about which consumers would readily learn if they systematically occurred. For example, if a McDonald's franchise set a higher hamburger price for Hispanics than Anglos, it is likely that customers waiting in line would observe the disparate treatment.[3] We should not expect hamburger price discrimination to persist in a competitive market place.

1. While visually compelling, the *PrimeTime Live* segment suffered from the important methodological failure to clarify whether or not the images of discrimination depicted were representative of the overall testing. Particularly the producers failed to indicate in what proportion of cases the black tester was treated worse—as well as what proportion of the time the white tester was treated worse. This failing is particularly egregious because such a disclosure would have taken only a few seconds of air time and because the producers were on explicit notice that such a representation was necessary. The *PrimeTime Live* segment was inspired by the news coverage surrounding my car discrimination work, discussed in chapter 2. The producers of the segments telephoned me and asked for my input *before* conducting the tests but ignored my suggestions about "representativeness," both with regard to the initial race testings and also with regard to subsequent tests concerning gender and age discrimination.

2. Credence attributes of products are usually distinguished from "search attributes" (which consumers learn about before they purchase the product) and "experience attributes" (which consumers learn as they consume the product). See, e.g., Richard Craswell, Interpreting Deceptive Advertising, 65 B.U. L. Rev. 657 (1985).

3. Posted prices facilitate comparison. Minorities would immediately know if they were asked to pay more than the posted price and would probably be able to observe if whites ahead of them in line were asked to pay less than the posted price.

Some French restaurants, however, list higher prices on their menus translated into English than on the bill of fare written in French. So long as English-speaking tourists don't ask to see a French menu as well, they are likely to be unaware of the price discrimination.

Indeed, there seems to be a widespread, implicit belief (at least among white males) that race and gender discrimination is not a serious problem in retail markets. The civil rights laws of the 1960s focused on only a handful of nonretail markets—chiefly concerning employment, housing, and public accommodation services.[4] Indeed, the most gaping hole in our civil rights law concerns retail gender discrimination. No federal law prohibits gender discrimination in the sale of goods or services. A seller could flatly refuse to deal with a potential buyer of a car or a paperclip because of her gender. And while the civil rights laws of the 1860s prohibited race discrimination in contracting, the civil rights laws a century later only prohibited sex discrimination in a narrow range of "titled" markets. The thousands of other markets that make up our economy are completely unregulated with regard to gender (as well as to religion and national origin) discrimination and only somewhat more regulated with regard to race.[5] And only a handful of cities and states (chief among them California) make up for this failing by prohibiting gender discrimination in contracting generally.

The nonregulation of retail discrimination seems to be premised on a vague coterie of assumptions: (1) retail discrimination does not exist because retailers have no motive to discriminate; (2) retail discrimination does not exist because competition forces retailers not to discriminate; and (3) any retail discrimination that does occur does not have serious consequences because of effective counterstrategies by potential victims. It is also argued that any discrimination in the sale of goods or services is less important than the potential effects of discrimination in the markets for employment and housing. But without denying the primacy of employment, the current regulatory regime leaves approximately 66 percent of the dollars we spend—and 35 percent of the dollars we earn—unregulated (with respect to gender discrimination) or less regulated (with respect to race discrimination).[6]

---

4. The last category, public accommodations, is most elastic, see chapter 2, but traditionally has included only producers who were regulated as "common carriers"— such as hotels, restaurants, and means of public transportation.

5. Sections 1981 and 1982 prohibit only "intentional discrimination" on account of race, while Title VII and its counterparts also regulate conduct that has an unjustified disparate racial impact.

6. These admittedly heuristic percentages were calculated by crudely dividing the national income and expenditure accounts into covered and uncovered categories. For example, with regard to expenditures, I assumed that "meals and beverages, purchased," "barbershops, beauty parlors, baths, health clubs," "housing" (by far the largest), and "admission to spectator amusements" (including movie theaters, and so on) were cov-

In this book, I contest the idea that race and gender discrimination in the retail sale of goods is nonexistent or unimportant. My thesis is that race and gender discrimination is neither a thing of the past nor is it limited to the narrow set of "titled" markets regulated by the civil rights legislation of the 1960s (Title VII, Title II, and so on). The book's primary contribution is empirical, but let me begin with a few theoretical reasons why we should take the possibility of retail discrimination seriously.

Retailers May Have a Motive to Discriminate

The argument that discrimination in the sale of goods and services does not exist because retailers lack any disparate treatment motive is itself premised on the twin ideas that discriminating against economically marginal groups would not be profitable and that racial animus would not manifest itself in discrete retail transactions. The latter idea is that while animus might cause race discrimination in the more relational settings— employment, apartment rental, and restaurants—which civil rights laws regulate, regulated retail transactions are sufficiently discrete that seller and/or customer prejudice would not induce disparate treatment. There are, however, several problems with this theory. First, as pointed out by Ian MacNeil, many contractual arrangements are not as discrete as initially appear.[7] Barbers may have much more tactile and repeated contact with their customers than one-time sellers of a house, but the law much more vigorously regulates the latter transaction. Second, the thought that prejudice is less likely to be acted upon in discrete transactions is premised on a narrow theory of what might be called "associational" animus—that is, that bigots don't like associating with particular groups. But, as I discuss in chapter 3, there are other types of animus that might persist even in discrete markets. For example, if sellers enjoy extracting an extra dollar of profit from people of color more than from whites, we might expect to see disparate racial treatment in pricing or quality of service. Finally, appreciating the pervasive discretion given to employees as agents opens

---

ered. In 1995, $877 billion out of $2.6 trillion in personal consumption expenditures (34 percent) fell into covered categories. Statistical Abstract of the United States 1997 (table 710). The income percentage was derived analogously by dividing personal income into covered categories (chiefly "wage, salary and other labor income") and uncovered categories (all other income). Id. at table 711.

7. See Ian MacNeil, *The New Social Contract* 10 (1980).

up the possibility that even profit-maximizing principals will by necessity countenance some disparate treatment by their subordinates.

Discriminating retailers may also be actuated by profit. Sellers may have a profit-maximizing incentive to price discriminate against minorities and women—even if sellers believe that members of these groups are on average poorer. It has long been known that "statistical discrimination" might cause rational, profit-maximizing sellers to charge more to groups that on average cause sellers to incur higher costs. Thus, as a theoretical matter, the drivers of taxis might discriminate against African American men if the drivers perceive a higher chance of being robbed by such passengers.[8] But, more provocatively, focusing on the example of new car sales, I argue that profit-maximizing sellers may engage in "revenue-based" race and gender disparate treatment. Dealerships may discriminate not because they expect higher costs but because they expect to be able to extract higher revenues. This is a surprising possibility because, as an empirical matter, people of color have a substantially lower ability to pay for new cars. But profit-maximizing sellers care far more about the variability in willingness to pay than in the mean willingness. The presence of a few minority members who are willing to pay a large markup can make it rational for the dealership to offer higher prices to all members of the group—even if group members are on average poorer.

It is correct and useful to ask whether sellers would plausibly be motivated to engage in a particular type of discrimination. But treating this issue seriously opens up a variety of dimensions where discrimination in

8. I emphasize that the theoretical possibilities of cost-based statistical discrimination on the part of cab drivers should not imply that observed discrimination is consonant with rational inference. For example, there are numerous anecdotes of discrimination (particularly, refusals to pick up) against older African American men and women dressed in suits and giving other indicia of low crime potential. See Cornel West, *Race Matters* xiv–xv (1993); see also Stanley E. Ridley et al., *Taxi Service in the District of Columbia: Is it Influenced by Patrons' Race and Destination?* (1989) (a report available from the Washington Lawyers' Committee for Civil Rights under the Law). There are other potential statistical rationales for drivers' disparate treatment of blacks, including the "revenue-based" possibility that drivers believe they "will have a harder time finding a return fare from predominantly black neighborhoods that are the likely destination of black passengers." Peter Siegelman, Race Discrimination in "Everyday" Commercial Transactions: What Do We Know, What Do We Need to Know, and How Can We Find Out, *in National Report Card on Discrimination in America: The Role of Testing* 69 (Michael Fix & Margery Austin Turner eds., 1999). An initial pilot study completed by Suzanne Perry and me also suggests that black taxi patrons may leave substantially lower tips than whites, controlling for a host of other variables (including destination and length of trip). See also Farrell Bloch, *Antidiscrimination Law and Minority Employment: Recruitment Practices and Regulatory Constraints* 30 (1994).

the retail sale of goods and services could be a plausible seller strategy for either profit or non-profit-based reasons.

Competition May Not Drive Out Retail Discrimination

Nobel-prize winning economist Gary Becker emphasized how competition could provide a much-needed antidote for the disease of discrimination.[9] Nondiscriminating sellers could earn higher profits by picking up the sales of those minorities and/or women excluded from equal access to the discriminating sellers. One problem with this theory is that it focuses on the ability of competition to drive out discriminating sellers, but competition may not be as effective at driving out the preferences of discriminating customers. If fixed costs of production limit the number of firms selling and if a substantial number of, say, white customers prefer dealing with a firm that discriminates against (by excluding or offering inferior service to) people of color, then firms may decide that it is more profitable to exclude minorities than to lose the patronage of whites.

As an empirical matter, however, my guess is that most firms would not find overt race or gender discrimination to be a profit-maximizing strategy. While Lester Maddox may have increased his sales by excluding African Americans,[10] in most markets a "whites only" or "males only" policy or overtly charging higher prices to particular demographic groups would lead to a general negative consumer reaction—by both minorities and progressive white consumers.

A more important limitation on competition is consumer information. In order for discrimination to cause the competitive shift of consumers toward nondiscriminatory sellers, consumers must know which sellers are discriminating and which are not. There is thus an important informational prerequisite for competition to have the predicted Beckerian effect. But as described above, there are many aspects of treatment where consumers may not be able to compare how sellers treat similarly situated counterparts. Retail discrimination is most likely to persist where consumers do

---

9. See Gary Becker, *The Economics of Discrimination* 14–15, 39–54 (1957).

10. Lester Maddox gained national publicity shortly after passage of the 1964 Civil Rights Act when he distributed ax handles to supporters in order to prevent blacks from patronizing his Atlanta restaurant, the Pickrick. Ex-Governor Lester Maddox of Georgia Has Heart Surgery, Reuters, Apr. 1, 1991; Maddox to Campaign in Carolinas against Dukakis, UPI, Oct. 17, 1988.

not learn the benchmark treatment of fellow consumers. Thus, while there is little opportunity for a single fastfood franchise to charge different prices for hamburgers, it is possible for a dealership to charge different prices to potential buyers of cars. Since bargained prices diverge from the list price, it is very difficult for a consumer to know whether she has received a non-discriminatory price. And it will be more difficult for a nondiscriminatory seller to credibly market itself on the basis that the race or gender of customers do not influence its bargaining strategy.[11]

Markets in which price or other terms of trade are individually bargained for provide much greater opportunities for race or gender discrimination than markets with homogeneous product attributes and posted prices. However, even retailers that sell standardized products at posted prices might discriminate on the basis of race or gender with regard to discretionary aspects of service. Anyone watching the *PrimeTime* segment could vividly see that record and department stores could substantially increase the "transaction costs" of minority customers. This is not just an issue of whether the retailer provides "service with a smile" but, as in the *PrimeTime Live* testing, whether the retailers make minority customers wait substantially longer before being served (or whether the minority customers are conspicuously shadowed to scrutinize whether they are shoplifting).

Retailers may also discriminate in their willingness to accommodate private and somewhat idiosyncratic consumer requests. For example, Jane Connor is currently testing retailers in Binghamton, New York, to see whether there are racial differences in their willingness to accede to a request to use a restroom or a request to return a sweater without a receipt. Economists (and others) tend to ignore or downplay the harms of such discrimination. But nontrivial injury may be visited on people of color in terms of both higher transactions costs and taking more precaution to comply strictly with retailer policies. One audit study showed that African Americans in Washington, D.C., had to wait 27 percent longer to hail a cab.[12] If this seems a minor inconvenience, white readers should try to imagine what their life would be like if *every* (or even just many) transactions took 27 percent longer. Even a single incident can impose real psychological costs. Consider, for example, Patricia Williams's story of being

---

11. An important exception is the example of no-haggle dealerships, discussed in chapter 5.

12. Ridley et al., *supra* note 8.

denied entrance to an open Benneton store by a gum-chewing, buzzer-wielding store clerk?[13]

While the term *public accommodations* refers to particular types of markets covered by antidiscrimination laws, Connor's research suggests that retailers' willingness to make "private accommodations" may be an important locus of disparate racial or gender treatment. Because such retailer accommodations are either made privately or arise in nonstandard circumstances, it is unlikely that competition will be an effective palliative. By the one-off nature of these transactions, it is difficult to infer whether a particular retailer action is motivated by the requesting consumer's race or gender, and consequently it will be difficult for nondiscriminating retailers to market themselves as such to people of color and/or women.

The point here is that imperfect consumer information about whether a particular retailer discriminates can impede the competitive responses necessary to drive out discrimination. Ironically, one of the world's leading econometricians, Nobel-prize winning James J. Heckman, has recently criticized audit testing itself because of an analogous problem:

> [T]he evidence acquired from [audit pair tests] is less compelling than is often assumed. Inferences from such studies are quite fragile to alternative assumptions about unobservable variables . . . .[14]

In essence, Heckman is arguing that because social scientists are not able to observe all the factors that might plausibly motivate a decisionmaker, it is unwarranted to infer that disparate treatment was due to a tester's race or gender as opposed to some other unobservable factor. However, if it is difficult for social scientists to discover discrimination in purposive, controlled, and systematic testing, it will be all the harder for a consumer to acquire such information. I disagree with Heckman that the results of such studies are "quite fragile" to alternative assumptions (and Heckman provides no citations to support this claim). Particularly in retail settings, it is possible for social scientists to control for the most plausible attributes

---

13. See Patricia J. Williams, *The Alchemy of Race and Rights* 44–51 (1991). In an unpublished manuscript Devon Carbado lists twenty-six "privileges" that men and whites "enjoy" throughout their lives. Devon W. Carbado, Straight Out of the Closet (1999) (unpublished manuscript on file with author) .

14. James J. Heckman, Detecting Discrimination, 12 J. Econ. Perspectives 101 (1998).

that could credibly affect seller behavior.[15] In the next chapter, I discuss the details of my audit test at new car dealerships in which I controlled for a host of different testing attributes—including not just speech, clothing, and physical attractiveness of the testers, but also the type of car that the testers used to approach the dealership. Of course, Heckman is right that I cannot be sure the testers blinked their eyes at the same rate, but I doubt that results are so fragile when it comes to controlling for other factors. There is, however, an important point of agreement in Heckman's and my analyses, which is that imperfect information about whether discrimination exists can insulate the practice from either public or private responses.

Victims Self-Help May Not Eradicate the Injury

Even if competition is not strong enough to drive discriminatory treatment from the market, the ability of potential victims to purposively select the retailer from which they will purchase may importantly mitigate the harm from discrimination that people of color bear in equilibrium. Again, Heckman has championed this point:

> [Audit evidence of disparate racial treatment] is entirely consistent with
> little or no market discrimination at the margin. Purposive sorting
> within markets eliminates the worst forms of discrimination. There
> may be evil lurking in the hearts of firms that is never manifest in con-
> summated market transactions.[16]

Heckman is clearly correct as a theoretical matter that purposive sorting can mitigate the effects of disparate treatment by individual retailers. But the quoted assertions inappropriately transform—without the benefit of any data—theoretical predictions into descriptions of empirical fact. There is simply no evidence on the degree to which purposive sorting mitigates the harms of disparate treatment, and, indeed, I provide evidence in chap-

15. Heckman's primary concern was with audit pair testing of employers in deciding whether to hire. Unobservable factors related to applicant productivity may be much more salient than in the retail context because of the more relational character of the employment contract and because the employee's promise of labor is much less standardized than a consumer's promise of money.

16. Heckman, *supra* note 14, at 103; see also Richard A. Epstein, *Forbidden Grounds: The Case against Employment Discrimination Laws* 52 (1992).

ter 4 that disparate racial treatment does persist in "consummated market transactions" when I examine actual car sales.

Moreover, there is a deep tension between Heckman's previous assertions that social scientists are unable—even with the aid of controlled audit tests—to identify which retailers are discriminating and his assertion that consumers can purposively shift to retailers they know to be nondiscriminatory. The same unobservable factors that make identifying discrimination difficult for social scientists will impede consumer self-help.

■ ■ ■

At the beginning of this chapter, I suggested that—counter to the Eddie Murphy skit—blacks who have better information about "normal" treatment are likely to have a better inkling than whites about the degree of disparate treatment occurring in particular retail markets. It is instructive to note that in a 1997 Gallup study, 30 percent of blacks surveyed said that they had experienced discrimination while "shopping" within the previous thirty days.[17] By way of contrast, the figure for experiences of discrimination while "dining out" (including bars, theaters, and other entertainment) was only 21 percent. This suggests that discrimination in the purer "public accommodation" markets may be less severe than the "untitled" retail markets generally. But having a better inkling about the existence of discrimination is different than knowing, first, whether a particular instance of treatment is inferior to that of other customers and, second, whether that disparate treatment is caused by your race. Retailers may still be able to maintain "plausible deniability" about whether a failure to accommodate a particular request is an aberration or a manifestation of systematic discrimination. With regard to idiosyncratic or infrequent accommodations, it will be hard even for minority consumers to know the true basis of their treatment and the true benchmark. Retailers can compete on price, but it will be much harder for them to compete on "service with a smile" and even harder to compete on implicit promises of nondiscrimination. Just as health maintenance organizations (HMOs) have difficulty competing against one another with respect to whether they will aggressively treat

17. See the *Gallup Poll Social Audit on Black/White Relations in the United States* (June 10, 1997) at 30–31 <www.gallup.com/poll/special/race.htm>. The poll was based on telephone interviews with a representative sample of 1,269 blacks and 1,680 whites who were interviewed in early 1997. The margin of error for a percentage estimate for blacks is approximately ± 5 percentage points. See id. at 5–6.

cancer,[18] it is difficult for retailers to compete with respect to whether you will be treated well if you lose a receipt or if your toddler needs to use the employee bathroom.

My objective in this book is not to deny that either profit-motived sellers or purposively sorting consumers can be powerful forces against private discrimination. Instead, I hope to show that taking theories of motive and knowledge seriously allows us better to predict where discrimination can persist as well as situations where it cannot. The book's title—*Pervasive Prejudice?*—is not meant to imply that race and gender discrimination pervades all aspects of market behavior, but instead is meant to indicate that discrimination *may* occur in a wide range of retail markets. Notwithstanding competition, race and gender discrimination can persist not just in the "titled" markets, but in any of the "untitled" retail markets where minority consumers have imperfect information about how their white counterparts are treated. The question mark in the title should also be emphasized. To demonstrate empirically that race or gender discrimination occurs in a wide range of markets would require amassing evidence from hundreds of different product or service markets. This book does not accomplish this task but instead provides a more intensive investigation of a smaller set of markets. Peter Siegelman and John Yinger have written separately the two most comprehensive review articles on retail discrimination.[19] My hope is that providing detailed evidence of race and gender discrimination in specific geographic and product markets—particularly with

18. See Russell Korobkin, The Efficiency of Managed Care "Patient Protection" Laws: Incomplete Contracts, Bounded Rationality, and Market Failure, 85 Cornell L. Rev. 1 (1999).

19. The most systematic survey of discrimination in consumer markets is Siegelman, *supra* note 8. See also John Yinger, Evidence of Discrimination in Consumer Markets, 12 J. Econ. Perspectives 23 (1998). Gender and race discrimination have been uncovered in a variety of markets. For example, several dry cleaners in Washington, D.C., have discriminated against female customers by charging higher prices for women's blouses than for men's shirts. See Carol Matlack, Experts on Call, 21 Nat'l J. 2549, 2549 (1989). Historically blacks have been discriminated against in the sale of many goods and services. In 1959, black consumers and businesses associated with the National Association for the Advancement of Colored People (NAACP) were at times unable to buy such goods as milk, bread, groceries, gas, credit, fertilizer, seed, insecticides, and farm machinery. See American Friends Serv. Comm., *Nat'l Council of Churches of Christ & S. Regional Council, Intimidation, Reprisal, and Violence in the South's Racial Crisis* (1959), *reprinted in* Civil Rights—1959: Hearings before the Subcomm. on Constitutional Rights of the Senate Comm. on the Judiciary, 86th Cong., 1st Sess. 1573 (1959); see also Perry v. Command Performance, 913 F.2d 99 (3d Cir. 1990) (involving the refusal by a beauty salon hairdresser to serve a black woman).

regard to automobile sales in the Chicago area—will make the pervasiveness claim a more plausible policy concern.

The book's subtitle—*Unconventional Evidence of Race and Gender Discrimination*—also deserves comment. The empirical tests reported in this book are nonconventional in both method and subject matter. While civil rights testing has traditionally focused on employment, housing, and public accommodations, this book provides evidence of discrimination in a variety of "unconventional" markets, including retail car sales, kidney transplantation, bail bonding, and Federal Communication Commission (FCC) licensing. The four major empirical findings are:

1. Chicago car dealerships charge black and/or female customers significantly higher markups than similarly situated white male customers.
2. Federal transplantation rules have an unjustified disparate racial impact, making it much more difficult for African Americans to receive a kidney for transplant (without promoting transplant success).
3. New Haven judges unjustifiably set higher bail for minority male defendants.
4. Allowing women and minorities to pay 50 cents on the dollar when bidding for thirty FCC paging licenses *increased* the government's revenue by $50 million.

My approach to investigating these markets is also somewhat "unconventional" in that I introduce new econometric and game-theory procedures for analyzing civil rights issues. The three major methodological contributions of the book are:

1. The bail chapter (chapter 7) offers two methodological innovations in civil rights empiricism. First, it shows how the reaction of secondary markets can be used to econometrically "price" probable cause. The rates that bail bond dealers charge is shown to be an individualized estimate of the probability that a defendant will fail to appear. Second, and more importantly, the chapter develops an "outcome" test of disparate impact. As applied to this particular setting, the chapter shows why the willingness of bond dealers to charge minority defendants lower rates provides evidence that judges' bail setting criteria had an unjustified disparate impact on minority defendants. The outcome tests are the first civil rights re-

gressions to avoid the "omitted variables" problem that plagues traditional disparate treatment tests. The method is also unique in that it provides evidence of both traditional legal elements (disparate impact and the absence of justification) in a single regression. The chapter argues that this new "outcome" testing is important—not only because it sheds light on bail bonding in particular—but also because it can be the basis for new tests in other contexts.

2. Even though the basic car empiricism is based on the traditional audit pair methodology, the data ultimately collected is used in chapter 3 to estimate the underlying parameters of an explicit game-theoretic bargaining model. This estimation procedure helps distinguish among five different explanatory theories of discrimination and provides the first quantitative estimates of what causes race and gender discrimination in retail car negotiations.

3. Game theory is also used in chapter 8, concerning FCC licensing, to show how granting substantial bidding subsidies to women and minority bidders can actually *increase* government revenue by inducing nonsubsidized firms to bid more aggressively.

Together, these last two points suggest that game theory is an underutilized tool for civil rights practitioners that can help predict how different causal theories (animus versus statistical discrimination) and different government remedies (affirmative action quotas versus bidding credits) affect private behavior.

The book is divided into three parts—concerning disparate treatment, disparate impact, and affirmative action, respectively. The first part provides an intensive exploration of race and gender disparate treatment in new car sales. Chapter 2 describes the basic audit finding of discrimination. Chapter 3 explores alternative causal explanations for the disparate treatment. Chapter 4 contrasts the audit results with subsequent evidence of discrimination in consummated transactions, and Chapter 5 discusses legal implications of the analysis.

The book's second part provides two contrasting tests of disparate racial impact. Chapter 6 provides traditional evidence that the government's kidney transplantation "point system" has had an unjustified disparate impact on African Americans. It shows first that the point system disproportionately excluded African Americans as transplantation recipients and then separately demonstrates that the point system was not justified in terms of enhancing the expected transplant success rate. In contrast,

Chapter 7 uses the "outcome" test to show that the criteria used by New Haven judges in setting bail bonds has had an unjustified disparate impact on black male defendants. The market evidence that black male defendants have a lower probability of flight suggests that the criteria for setting the amount of bail bonds disproportionately overdeters these defendants relative to white males.

Finally, the third part uses game theory to inform its tests of how affirmative action bidding credits affected the ultimate sale price in recent FCC narrowband spectrum auctions. The concluding chapter focuses on information and motives as a fruitful way of grounding future empirical scholarship and policymaking in our continuing struggle to identify and eliminate discrimination from our economy.

Although five of the book's nine chapters are based on research that originally appeared in article form,[20] it is not merely a compilation of my previously published empirical articles on race and gender discrimination. Rather, wherever possible I have tried to update the original findings with additional testing (as with chapter 4's new analysis of dealer discrimination in consummated transactions) and to provide broader theoretical implications for the methodology (as with chapter 9's extended discussion of outcome tests of unjustified disparate impact).

In three of the chapters (chapter 5 concerning car discrimination, chapter 6 concerning kidney transplantation, and chapter 8 concerning FCC auctions), I explicitly respond to critics of the original articles. In these chapters, I also discuss how subsequent regulation (for example, of kidney transplantation and of radio spectrum auctions) or technological innova-

---

20. Chapters 2 and 3—on discrimination in new car sales—rely on Fair Driving: Gender and Race Discrimination in Retail Car Negotiations, 104 Harv. L. Rev. 817 (1991); Race and Gender Discrimination in Negotiation for the Purchase of a New Car, 84 Am. Econ. Rev. 304 (1995) (with Peter Siegelman); and Further Evidence of Discrimination in New Car Negotiations and Estimates of Its Cause, 94 Mich. L. Rev. 109 (1995). Chapter 6—on kidney transplantation—relies on Racial Equity in Renal Transplantation: The Disparate Impact of HLA-Based Allocation, 270 J. Am. Med. Ass'n 1352 (1993) (with Robert Gaston, Laura Dooley, and Arnold Diethelm); Response to letters-to-the-editors, 271 J. Am. Med. Ass'n 269 (1994); Unequal Racial Access to Kidney Transplantation, 46 Vand. L. Rev. 805 (1993) (with Laura Dooley and Robert Gaston); and HLA Matching in Renal Transplantation, 332 New Eng. J. Med. 752 (1995) (with Robert Gaston and Mark Deierhoi). Chapter 7—on bail bond setting—relies on A Market Test for Race Discrimination in Bail Setting, 46 Stan. L. Rev. 987 (1994) (with Joel Waldfogel). And chapter 8—on FCC spectrum auctions—relies on Pursuing Deficit Reduction through Diversity: How Affirmative Action at the FCC Increased Auction Competition, 48 Stan. L. Rev. 761 (1996) (with Peter Cramton); and Aid Diversity, and the Treasury, N.Y. Times, at F13 (May 21, 1995) (with Peter Cramton).

tion (such as the emergence of the Internet in car sales) has changed the opportunities for discrimination. At times I have chosen to retain some of the text of the original articles—both so that readers can get a sense of the original arguments that provoked the subsequent criticism and so that readers will understand the technological and regulatory constraints that potential discriminators faced at the time of their decisionmaking. While doing so, however, I endeavor to make clear what information was available at the time of the decisions being studied and how this information may have subsequently changed.

PART I

DISPARATE TREATMENT

This part of the book intensively tests for disparate treatment in a single market: the retail sale of new automobiles. The next four chapters present evidence from audit and nonaudit sources of race-contingent dealer behavior. I examine possible causes for this discrimination, test whether the racially disparate pricing persists in consummated transactions (after consumers have taken self-protective counterstrategies), and lay out possible legal remedies to promote equity and efficiency in this important but notoriously dysfunctional market.

CHAPTER 2

Gender and Race Discrimination

in Retail Car Negotiations

IAN AYRES AND PETER SIEGELMAN

O f the "untitled" retail markets, the new car market is particularly ripe for civil rights scrutiny for three reasons. First, it is an important market. The acquisition of a new car is a substantial purchase: apart from buying a home, new car purchases represent for most Americans their largest consumer investment.[1] Moreover, the transportation that automobiles provide is often necessary for a number of other major life activities (such as driving to work). Second, competition among sellers and purposive sorting by buyers may not be effective in driving out discrimination. As discussed in chapter 1, the private results of the individualized negotiations might prevent consumers from discovering whether dealers discriminate, thus giving dealers the discretion to do so. Third, controlled audit testing is relatively straightforward. The fact that new cars (in contrast to, say, Persian rugs) are relatively standardized and homogenous products facilitates interretailer comparison.

---

1. See Bureau of Economic Analysis, U.S. Dep't of Commerce, *The National Income and Product Accounts of the United States, 1929–82*, at 105 (1986) (table 2.3) (showing annual personal expenditures on cars consistently to be one of the largest categories of expenditures); see also Bureau of the Census, U.S. Dep't of Commerce, *Statistical Abstract of the United States* 465 (119th ed. 1999) (same, with respect to 1990–97). In 1997, for example, American consumers spent $86.2 billion on new cars. See id.

This chapter reports the results of using audit testing[2] to examine whether new car dealerships in the Chicago area discriminated in negotiating against women and minorities. More than four hundred independent negotiations at more than two hundred dealerships were conducted in 1990 to examine how dealerships bargain. Testers of different races and genders entered new car dealerships separately and bargained to buy similar new cars, using a uniform negotiation strategy. The focus of the study was whether automobile retailers would react differently to this uniform strategy when potential buyers differed only by gender or race.[3]

2.   Since the Fair Housing Act of 1968 outlawed discrimination in the sale and rental of housing, numerous studies have tested whether minorities and whites are treated differently in the housing market. See sources cited in chapter 5, note 22. The empirical analysis in this chapter broadly borrows the methodology of fair housing audit tests, in which a black tester and a white tester separately approach a real estate agent or seller and express an interest in the same housing. The test of discrimination is simply whether they are treated similarly: Are they shown the same houses, in the same neighborhoods, for the same prices?

3.   This study is the first to focus on whether sellers discriminate on the basis of race or gender when customers bargain similarly. Other studies, in contrast, have focused solely on the existence of race- or gender-based differences in bargaining techniques. See, e.g., Dean G. Pruitt & Peter J. Carnevale, Gender Effects in Negotiation: Constituent Surveillance and Contentious Behavior, 22 J. Experimental Soc. Psychol. 264 (1986); Edward E. Sampson & Marcelle Kardush, Age, Sex, Class, and Race Differences in Response to a Two-Person Non-Zero-Sum Game, 9 J. Conflict Resol. 212 (1965). In 1959, Professor Allen F. Jung of the University of Chicago Business School studied whether testers who utilized different bargaining processes obtained different price quotations from identical new car dealers. See Allen Jung, Price Variations among Automobile Dealers in Chicago, Illinois, 32 J. Bus. 315 (1959). In a five-page article based on the same study, Jung argued that women were not treated significantly differently from men. See Allen Jung, Interviewer Differences among Automobile Purchasers, 10 Applied Stat. 93, 96–97 (1961). However, Jung's own explanation of the equal bargaining results belies his interest in carrying out a controlled test: "The natural business acumen of the men and the beauty and charm of the ladies must be considered offsetting factors as far as obtaining lower automobile prices." Id. at 96. Jung made no attempt to test for racial discrimination.

More recent testing has focused on whether the knowledgeability or aggressiveness of consumers affects the outcome of car negotiation. Guenter Mueller and Withold Galinat's field experiment found that consumers fared better when they initiated the bargaining processes with a "tough" strategy. See Guenter Mueller & Withold Galinat, Bargaining Efficiency in Real-Life Buyer-Seller-Interaction: A Field Experiment, in *Aspiration Levels in Bargaining and Economic Decision Making* 80, 85 (Reinhold Tietz ed. 1982). Christina Taylor and Sharon Dawid sent testers to Ford dealerships in Connecticut and New York and found that testers who appeared knowledgeable obtained lower prices than testers who seemed naive. See Christina Taylor & Sharon Dawid, Bargaining for a New Car: The Knowledgeable versus the Naive Consumer, 59 Psychol. Reps. 284, 285–86 (1986).

The tests revealed systematic disparate treatment.[4] Dealerships offered white males significantly lower prices than blacks and women. As detailed below, the average prices offered white women were more than $200 higher than the offers to white men, the offers to black women were more than $400 higher than those to white men, and the offers to black men were more than $900 higher.

A central purpose of the Civil Rights Act of 1866[5] was to guarantee that "a dollar in the hands of a Negro will purchase the same thing as a dollar in the hands of a white man."[6] As discussed in chapter 1, the standard argument against vigorous enforcement or extension of our civil rights laws to retail consumer markets has been grounded in the conviction that the impersonal forces of market competition will limit race and gender discrimination to the traditionally protected markets, in which there is significant interpersonal contact.[7] The results of this study, however, challenge such an unquestioning faith in competition: in stark contrast to congressional objectives, blacks and women simply could not buy the same car for the same price as could white men using identical bargaining strate-

---

4. We use "discrimination" or "disparate treatment" interchangeably to refer to the evidence that black and female testers were treated differently from white male testers. The term *discrimination,* although surely a literal characterization, unfortunately connotes to many the notion of animus (even though in antitrust, for example, "price discrimination" is not taken to imply any hatred by sellers). "Disparate treatment," in contrast, connotes to some a strictly technical legal meaning developed in civil rights case law. For our purposes, the terms *discrimination* and *disparate treatment* are both used to refer to the result that sellers' conduct was race- and gender-dependent; in other words, sellers took race and gender into account and treated differently testers who were otherwise similarly situated. Paul Brest has similarly defined race discrimination in terms of "race-dependent decisions and conduct." Paul Brest, The Supreme Court, 1975 Term—Foreword: In Defense of the Antidiscrimination Principle, 90 Harv. L. Rev. 1, 6 (1976). These terms are not meant to imply that salespeople harbored any animus based on race or gender.

5. 14 Stat. 27, *reenacted by* Enforcement Act of 1870, § 18, 16 Stat. 144 (*codified at* 42 U.S.C. §§ 1981, 1982 [1988]).

6. Jones v. Alfred H. Mayer Co., 392 U.S. 409, 443 (1968).

7. The increasingly accepted conception of "relational contract," Ian Macneil, The New Social Contract 10 (1980), runs counter to the notion that all unprotected markets are discrete exchanges and therefore immune to animus-based discrimination. Indeed, it is difficult at a theoretical level to see why retail purchases of personal property involve less personal contact than many public accommodations. Although the uniform pricing of many consumer goods eliminates the possibility of price discrimination, the ongoing relational nature of exchange may allow gender-based or racial animus to be reflected along other dimensions of product or service quality. And as described in chapter 1, even in markets with more discrete exchanges, women and minorities can be disadvantaged when there is gender- or race-based product differentiation.

gies. The fact that different prices were quoted by the car dealers to con-sumers following identical scripts implicates basic notions of equity and indicates that the scope of the civil rights laws has been underinclusive. The process of bargaining, already inefficient in many ways,[8] becomes all the more problematic when it works to the detriment of traditionally disad-vantaged members of our society.

Much, however, has changed since 1990 when this testing was origi-nally conducted. Chapters 4 and 5, respectively, examine more recent data sets and discuss the important movements toward no-haggle and Internet sales. These developments will be particularly important in thinking about potential legal implications of the analysis.

The first section of this chapter describes how the tests of race and gender discrimination were conducted. The second section reports the re-sults of the tests. Section three compares the results of this audit with the results of an earlier pilot study conducted in 1989.

I. Methodology of the Test

This study used an audit technique in which pairs of testers (one of whom was always a white male) were trained to bargain uniformly and then were sent to negotiate for the purchase of a new automobile at ran-domly selected Chicago-area dealerships.[9] The goal was to have the testers

8. For example, the necessity of bargaining dramatically increases the search costs of buying a good and may therefore engender transactional inefficiencies as well. The so-cial utility of bargaining is generally addressed in Ian Ayres & F. Clayton Miller, "I'll Sell It to You at Cost": Legal Methods to Promote Retail Markup Disclosure, 84 Nw. U. L. Rev. 1047, 1062–70 (1990).

9. The testers did not inform the salespeople that they were participating in a test. This lack of disclosure raises significant ethical concerns, as the salesperson's time is spent without chance of a sale. The study has several features designed to mitigate the problem of wasting the salespersons' time during the negotiation process. Most impor-tant, the testers visited the dealerships during the least busy times of the week (from the hours of 9:00–12:00 and 1:00–5:00 Monday through Friday). During these times few people shop for cars, and there are often several salespeople without customers to serve. In addition, testers were instructed that if all the salespeople of a dealership were busy, they should return to the dealership at another time. In only 1 of more than 180 visits did the testers have to discontinue the test because of crowding. Steps were also taken to minimize the time that the testers spent with the salespeople. The test itself was de-signed to be completed in ten to fifteen minutes and the testers were instructed to spend no more than an hour at a dealership.

The Federal Judicial Center Advisory Committee on Experimentation in the Law has proposed guidelines for limiting the use of deception in legal experimentation. The

differ only by race and/or gender (that is, present an otherwise uniform appearance and uniform behavior) so that any systematic differences in treatment could be attributed to the dealers' race- and/or gender-dependent decisionmaking.[10] The white male results provide a benchmark against which to measure the disparate treatment of the other (nonwhite, nonmale) testers. Thirty-eight testers (eighteen white males, seven white females, eight black females, and five black males) bargained for approximately four hundred cars comprising nine car models[11] at 242 dealerships.[12] Dealerships were selected randomly, testers were assigned to deal-

---

committee concluded that "[d]eception requires (1) that the concealment itself be indispensable to the validity of experimental results, and (2) that the burden of justification for the practice concealed not merely be met, but met by a clear and convincing margin." Advisory Comm. on Experimentation in the Law, Fed. Judicial Center, *Experimentation in the Law* 46 (1981). The first requirement is easily met: asking salespeople if they could be tested for race and gender discrimination would certainly change their behavior. Whether the study meets the secondary burden of justification is a closer question. As reported below, blacks in this study were often forced to pay two to three times the markup of white males. If similar measurements of discrimination hold for all sales in the United States, blacks annually would pay $150 million more for new cars than do white males. The benefits from documenting such potentially significant discrimination seem to meet the burden of justification. The tests have been given approval by the Human Subject Research Committees of both the American Bar Foundation and Northwestern University. See Letter from Northwestern University Institutional Review Board (June 12, 1989); oral approval from American Bar Foundation (May 1988).

Deceptive tests of new car sales have been conducted by other researchers. See *supra* note 3. In other fields, social scientists have feigned to be, among other things, cancer patients in hospitals and potential buyers in shoe stores. See, e.g., Eric Schaps, Cost, Dependency, and Helping, 21 J. Personality & Soc. Psychol. 74 (1972) (involving accomplices posing as shoe store customers). The Supreme Court itself has condoned similar deception by giving fair housing testers standing. See, e.g., Havens Realty Corp. v. Coleman, 455 U.S. 363 (1982).

10. Some commentators have had difficulty accepting that testers could be controlled. For example, see the discussion in chapter 5 of Mike Royko's criticism of the pilot study.

11. The nine models ranged from compacts to standard cars, and included both imports and domestic makes. Human-subject review committees—seeking to protect the privacy of the dealers as human subjects in these tests—prevented us from disclosing the car models.

12. Because of discarded tests and scheduling difficulties, 98 of the 404 observations are unpaired negotiations in which only one tester visited a particular dealership. Sample selection problems are always a concern in such situations. Chow tests on the two regression equations reported in table 2.1 cannot reject pooling the paired and unpaired observations, however, so there is little reason to believe that the unpaired audits are systematically different from the paired audits. See Ian Ayres & Peter Siegelman, Race and Gender Discrimination in Bargaining for a New Car, 85 Am. Econ. Rev. 304 (1995) (finding similar results from analysis of paired data alone).

erships randomly, and the choice of which tester in the pair would first enter the dealership was made randomly.[13]

Each tester followed a bargaining script designed to frame the bargaining in purely distributional terms: the only issue to be negotiated was the price.[14] The script instructed the tester to focus quickly on a particular car[15] and offer to provide his or her own financing.[16] After eliciting an initial price from the dealer,[17] the tester waited five minutes before responding with an initial counteroffer that equaled an estimate of the dealer's marginal cost.[18] As discussed later, making an initial offer at the dealer's cost reveals to the dealer that the tester is a fairly sophisticated buyer.

13.   That is, the white male tester was at times the first tester and at times the second tester to bargain at a dealership. The paired testers usually visited the dealership on the same day (and within at most four days of each other).

14.   This distributional context removes collaboration and problem solving as measures of effective bargaining. See Roger Fisher & William Ury, *Getting to Yes* 73–79 (1981). For example, the bargaining was structured so that the players (the testers and salespeople) could not collaboratively bargain over financing to enhance the gains from trade. In many real-world bargaining contexts, collaborative or "win–win" solutions do not exist. See James White, The Pros and Cons of "Getting to Yes" (Book Review), 34 J. Legal Educ. 115, 116 (1984). The bargaining instead resembles the classic "split-the-dollar" game in which two contestants can share a dollar if they can agree on how to divide it between them. See Eric Rasmusen, *Games and Information* 227–29 (1989).

15.   If the salesperson showed the tester more than one car, the script instructed the tester: "[W]ithin two or three minutes focus your attention on the car with the lowest sticker price. This will be the car that you will then bargain over. You should indicate this by saying: 'I'm interested in buying this car.'" Tester Script 4 (Nov. 8, 1990).

16.   Testers were instructed to respond to questions such as "Will you need help with a loan?" by saying, "No, I can provide my own financing." Id. at 11.

Initially, some testers were instructed to volunteer that they would be moving to California in the coming month. This representation, suggested by Mitch Polinsky, sought to reduce dealers' inferences about repeat sales, referral sales, or repair service. However, dealers encountering two customers moving to California looking for the same car on the same day were more likely to suspect that the two consumers were shopping in tandem. Because of the dealer expressions of suspicion, the California representation was quickly abandoned and the tests in which the representation was made were discarded. This example illustrates a general tension between increased controls and maintaining verisimilitude so as not to alert dealers that they were being tested.

17.   If the salesperson failed to quote an initial price, testers would ask, "How much would the car cost me to buy it [sic] today, including taxes and other fees?" Id. at 5.

18.   Because sellers will seldom sell below their marginal cost, the marginal cost counteroffer established an initial position that approximated the seller's reservation price (the minimum amount for which a seller could sell to make any profit). Estimates of dealer cost were obtained from *Consumer Reports Auto Price Service* (Mar. 2, 1990) (computer printout) and *Edmund's 1990 New Car Prices* (Nov. 1990).

After the tester's initial counteroffer,[19] the salesperson could do one of three things: (1) accept the tester's offer, (2) refuse to bargain further, or (3) make a lower offer. If the salesperson attempted to accept the tester's offer or refused to bargain further, the test was over (and the tester left the dealership). If the salesperson responded by making a lower offer, the test continued, with the tester's next counteroffer scripted in one of two ways. At some dealerships, the pairs of testers used a "split-the-difference" strategy in which the tester's counteroffer was raised so as to halve the difference between the dealer's offer and the tester's last offer.[20] At other dealerships, the testers used a "fixed-concession" strategy in which the testers' counteroffers were independent of the sellers' behavior. Testers began, as before, by making their first counteroffer at marginal cost. Regardless of how much the seller conceded, each of the tester's subsequent counteroffers increased his or her previous offer by 20 percent of the gross markup.[21]

Under either bargaining strategy, each tester continued to alternate offers with the dealer until the dealer either (1) attempted to accept the tester's offer, or (2) refused to bargain further. Testers jotted down each offer and counteroffer, as well as options on the car and the sticker price. Upon leaving the dealership, the testers completed a survey recording information about the test.[22]

19. It should be noted that the testers did not make legally binding counteroffers. The testers were carefully trained not to sign anything so that they would be protected by the statute of frauds. See U.C.C. § 2-201 (1987) (invalidating oral contracts for more than $500). Moreover, the testers did not make actual counteroffers but merely invited additional offers by saying: "Would you sell me this car today for $ . . . ?" Tester Script, *supra* note 15, at 6.

20. Consider, for example, a seller who initially offers to sell a car for $13,000. The tester counters at $10,000 (an estimate of the car's marginal cost). If the salesperson lowered the initial offer to $12,000, the tester would wait five minutes and split the difference by offering $11,000 [(12,000 + 10,000) / 2]. The split-the-difference strategy was identical to the script used in the pilot study. See Ian Ayres, Fair Driving: Gender and Race Discrimination in Retail Car Negotiations, 104 Harv. L. Rev. 817 (1991).

21. That is, if the car had a sticker price of SP and the tester's last offer was LO, then the tester's next offer would be LO + 0.2 × (SP − LO). Because the gross margin (SP − LO) decreases as the bargaining continues, the fixed-concession strategy produced smaller concessions in each subsequent round. The testers did not have to calculate the fixed-concession offers. The appropriate sequence was supplied to them in advance.

22. In addition to the types of factors described above, the script also controlled ancillary aspects of the bargaining. For example, testers waited in the center of the showroom to be approached by a salesperson. Significantly, the script allowed the testers to be steered to different cars and different salespeople. Forcing the second tester to seek out the same car or the same salesperson as the first tester would have introduced nonuniformity in the testers' bargaining strategies. Moreover, the study was designed to test for disparate treatment using the car dealership as the unit of analysis. Allowing testers to bar-

This design produced results that permit two tests for discrimination. The first, "short test" of discrimination simply compares the dealer's response to the testers' initial question, "How much would I have to pay to buy this car?" The "long test" of discrimination, on the other hand, compares instead the final offers given to testers after the multiple rounds of concessionary bargaining. By focusing on the initial offer, the short test is well controlled because salespeople had little information about the prospective buyers from which to draw inferences. By focusing on the final offer, the long test isolates more accurately the price a real consumer would pay, but it increases the risk that individual differences among the testers influenced the results.

In order to minimize the possibility of nonuniform bargaining, particular attention was paid to issues of experimental control. A major part of the study was choosing uniform testers and training them to behave in a standardized manner. Testers were chosen to satisfy the following criteria for uniformity:

1. Age: All testers were twenty-four to twenty-eight years old.
2. Education: All testers had three or four years of college education.
3. Dress: All testers were dressed similarly during the negotiations. Testers wore casual sportswear: the men wore polo or button-down shirts, slacks, and loafers; the women wore straight skirts, blouses, minimal makeup, and flats.
4. Transportation: All testers drove to the dealerships in similar used rental cars of the same model and year. Using similar modes of transportation prevented the dealers from making inferences based on the kind of car the tester drove or the way the tester reached the dealership.[23]

---

gain with different salespeople afforded a test of whether dealerships engage in more sophisticated forms of discrimination by steering classes of testers to particular kinds of cars or particular kinds of salespeople. See *infra* notes 58–59 and accompanying text.

For ethical reasons, the testers did not tape the bargaining sessions. Because the individual testers were the only observers of the field bargaining sessions, there are two potential types of experimental error in the results. First, the testers may have failed accurately to observe and describe their own behavior; second, the testers may have failed accurately to observe and describe the behavior of the salesperson. The training and initial tester observation were used to minimize both types of errors.

23. In the pilot study, all the testers parked their cars out of the dealership's sight and approached the dealership on foot. See Ayres, *supra* note 20, at 824 n.27. Some dealers remarked to testers that it was unusual, especially in the suburbs, for customers to walk onto a dealership lot. Again, this experience points to a more general tension between the degree of audit control and the degree of verisimilitude. See *supra* note 16.

5. Economic Class: Testers volunteered that they could finance the car themselves.

6. Occupation: If asked by a salesperson, each tester said that he or she was a young urban professional (for example, a systems analyst for First Chicago Bank).

7. Address: If asked by the salesperson, each tester gave a fake name and an address in an upper-class, Chicago neighborhood (Streeterville).

8. Attractiveness: Applicants were subjectively ranked for average attractiveness.

The testers were trained for two days before visiting the dealerships. They were not told that the research was intended to test for race and gender discrimination.[24] Nor did they know that another tester would be negotiating at each of the dealerships. The testers were told only that the research was investigating how dealers negotiate. The training included not only memorizing the tester script but also participating in mock negotiations designed to help testers gain confidence and learn how to negotiate and answer questions uniformly. The training emphasized uniformity in cadence and inflection of tester response. In addition to spoken uniformity, the study sought to achieve tester uniformity in nonverbal behavior.[25]

The script was also designed to promote tester uniformity through silence. The testers volunteered very little information and were trained to feel comfortable with periods of silence. The script anticipated that the salespeople would ask questions and gave the testers a long list of contingent responses to questions that might be asked.[26] The study sought to let the salespeople completely control the bargaining process without letting them know they had such control.[27] At the beginning and end of the testing

24. In the pilot study the testers knew the study's purpose, and it is possible that this knowledge affected their expectations or behavior. See Ayres, *supra* note 20, at 824–25 n.27. Both studies, however, yielded similar results.

25. Testers were sensitized to issues of body language and nonverbal cues. For example, they were told to avoid eye contact and not to cross their arms.

26. The script provided an all-purpose default or residual response for questions not otherwise anticipated. For example, if the salesperson asked the tester a detailed question about the tester's career or personal background, the tester was instructed to respond: "I don't mean to be rude, but I'm kind of pressed for time, and would rather just talk [about] buying a car." Tester Script, *supra* note 15, at 12.

27. This aspect of the script can be analogized to the party game in which one person is told to leave the room so that the group can make up a story about him or her. When the person returns to the room, he or she asks yes or no questions in order to construct the story. The trick to the game is that the group never constructs a story,

process, project coordinators accompanied the testers to dealerships and observed how the testers bargained to determine whether they were following the script and accurately reporting the bargaining process.

Despite these attempts to control for uniform tester behavior, some differences between testers undoubtedly remained. Salespeople may have, for example, offered certain testers a higher price not because of their race or gender, but because they blinked more often or opened the car door more quickly. Two important questions about such residual differences must then be asked. First, are they likely to be correlated with race or gender? If not, the remaining nonuniformity should not influence our conclusion that it is race and gender that generate different outcomes for the testers. Second, are the residual differences large enough to explain the *amount* of discrimination that is reported below? Readers should focus, therefore, not merely on statistical significance but also on the amount of the reported discrimination.[28] Although perfect control of such complex bargaining is impossible, the amounts of discrimination reported in the next section of this chapter cannot be plausibly explained by race- or gender-correlated divergences from the uniform bargaining behavior called for in our script.

II. Results of the Test

A. Price Discrimination

Table 2.1 reports regressions testing whether dealers treated testers differently. Because the testers were trained to follow an identical bargaining script, any statistically significant difference in the offers made to distinct race–gender types can be ascribed to disparate treatment by the dealers. In particular, the regressions—after controlling for the effects of

---

but simply decides to answer "yes" to any question ending in a vowel (and "no" to any question ending in a consonant). The questioner in the game thus effectively constructs a story revealing what's on his or her own mind.

28. Statistical significance measures how probable it is that the observed result occurred purely by random chance. To say, for example, that the average final offers sellers made to black and white testers are statistically different at a 5 percent significance level means that the differences would only be produced randomly 5 percent of the time (one out of twenty times). If a sample size is large enough, even small absolute differences in price (of, say, $5) will be statistically significant. Cf. 29 C.F.R. § 1607.4(D) (1990) (generally defining adverse impact for purposes of an Equal Employment Opportunity Commission (EEOC) finding of employment discrimination as existing only when disparities are both statistically significant and proportionally large).

Table 2.1   Regressions Evaluating Effects of Testers' Race/Gender Type and Control Variables on Dealers' Initial and Final Profits[a] (N = 404; t-statistics in parentheses)[b]

	Initial Profit ($)	Final Profit ($)
Constant	724.61*	417.52*
	(7.23)	(6.62)
Tester Race–Gender		
White female	209.62	215.69
	(1.54)	(1.85)
Black male	962.32*	1,132.59*
	(6.75)	(9.28)
Black female	470.05*	446.30*
	(3.90)	(4.32)
Control Variables[c]		
Split	−240.19	−262.59
	(−1.55)	(−1.97)
Tester experience	4.76	3.41
	(0.66)	(0.55)
First	88.23	138.48
	(0.91)	(1.67)
Unpaired	−100.62	−161.02
	(−1.00)	(1.87)
Summary Statistics		
Adjusted R^2	0.27	0.33
SSR $\times 10^{-3}$	263,758	193,706

* Significantly different from zero at the 5 percent level.
[a] None of the coefficients of the MODEL, DAY, WEEK, and TIME variables, see *infra* note 29, were statistically significant. These variables were omitted from table 2.1 to save space.
[b] The ratio of the coefficient to the standard error of the estimate is called the t-statistic. As a rule of thumb, a t-statistic greater than two suggests there is less than a 5 percent chance that the observed effect occurred purely by chance.
[c] For variable definitions, see *infra* note 29.

several variables that varied across the audits[29]—test whether the dealers' initial and final offers to black and/or female testers were higher than offers to white male testers.

The final offer of each test was the lowest price offered by a dealer

---

29.   Beside the three tester race and gender dummy variables—WHITE FEMALE, BLACK MALE, and BLACK FEMALE—the regression attempted to discover what aspects of the bargaining caused dealers to demand a particular level of profit in their initial and final offers. In particular, the regression focused on the relationship between the profits the dealers would have made on their offers and the following variables:

SPLIT	=	1, if tester used split-the-difference negotiating strategy, or 0, if fixed-concession strategy
MODEL$_j$	=	dummy variables for each different model type
DAY$_k$	=	dummy variables for each day of the week
WEEK$_l$	=	dummy variables for each week of the month
TIME	=	number of days since start of testing
EXPERIENCE	=	number of prior tests by this tester
FIRST	=	1, if tester was the first in the pair to visit dealership, or 0, otherwise
UNPAIRED	=	1, if test was an unpaired observation, or 0, if test was part of a paired audit

The regression equation took the following form:

$$\text{PROFIT} = \text{CONSTANT} + \sum_i \beta_i (\text{TESTER RACE/GENDER TYPE}_i)$$
$$+ \sum_j \gamma_j \text{MODEL}_j + \sum_K \delta_K \text{DAY}_K + \sum_L \eta_L \text{WEEK}_L$$
$$+ \theta \text{TIME} + \nu \text{SPLIT} + \lambda \text{EXPERIENCE} + \mu \text{FIRST} \qquad (2.1)$$
$$+ \nu \text{UNPAIRED} + \epsilon$$

where epsilon is an error term that is assumed to be independent and identically distributed.

Although a thorough review of econometric theory is beyond the scope of this chapter, a few concepts may be of use to the reader. The ordinary least square (OLS) regression technique produces estimates for the CONSTANT and the greek-letter coefficients, β, γ, and so on in the regression equation, except for the error term. A "dummy variable" resembles an on-off switch, assuming values of 0 or 1. By assigning dummy variables to all but one category, we can compare differences between any two categories. Thus, for the group of four mutually exclusive and exhaustive tester race–gender types, we assign a dummy variable to three of these four categories, and the regression provides us with the estimated coefficients for each variable; white men form the benchmark omitted category. The estimated dummy coefficients represent the amount by which membership in the associated category increases or decreases the dependent variable as compared to the benchmark category. See Ian Ayres & Joel Waldfogel, A Market Test for Race Discrimination in Bail Setting, 46 Stan. L. Rev. 987, 1009 n.84 (1994). For example, the $962 coefficient in table 2.1 associated with the BLACK MALE dummy variable suggests that the dealer profit on initial offers made to black male testers was $962 higher than the profit on initial offers made to white male testers, the omitted benchmark category.

after the multiple rounds of bargaining.[30] By comparing these initial and final offers with independent estimates of dealer cost,[31] it was possible to calculate the dealer profit associated with each type of offer (for example, initial profit equals initial offer minus dealer cost).

The regressions reported in table 2.1 show that dealer profits for both initial and final offers were substantially lower for white male testers than for other race–gender groups.[32] While the estimates from these two regres-

30. The lowest price offered by a dealer could come either when the dealer attempted to accept a tester's final offer or when a dealer refused to lower his last offer. See *supra* text at note 22.

31. The cost estimate, obtained from *Consumer Reports* and *Edmund's*, see *supra* note 18, is one of marginal cost, in that the dealer's fixed and overhead costs are not included. These cost estimates ignore "hold backs," "incentives," and other types of manufacturer refunds that reduce the dealer's net marginal cost. Domestic car manufacturers traditionally (and foreign car manufacturers recently) have periodically refunded approximately 3 percent of the dealer's original cost as a so-called holdback. See Remar Sutton, *Don't Get Taken Every Time* 23 (1986). In addition, manufacturers at times will institute "dealer incentives"—additional refunds to dealers for sales. See, e.g., Weekly Incentive Survey, *Automotive News*, Mar. 5, 1990, at 38. Because the exact size of these hold backs and incentives is not public knowledge, the cost estimates were not discounted to reflect these amounts.

32. Ancillary tests of discrimination also buttress the results reported in this chapter. Three research assistants joined the author of this book in a "beat the boss contest" in the actual purchase of an automobile. The research group consisted of one white male (the author), one black male, one white female, and one black female. Members of the group individually bargained for a specific car model at Chicago dealerships. I offered my research assistants a prize of $50 or half the amount by which they could undercut my best offer, whichever was greater. The contest lacked the controls of this chapter's study but had other advantages: the testers were bargaining for an actual sale and thus had real financial incentives to get the best deal.

The results of the contest are largely consistent with the results of the larger study:

	Results of Research Group Contest	
	Dealership Profits	
Tester Type	Best Offer ($)	Average Offer ($)
White male	139	548
White female	439	806
Black male	879	1,051
Black female	878	1,185

The contest produced the same ordinal ranking of discrimination, but there seem to be returns to the greater sophistication of the bargainers who were not constrained to follow a script.

A controlled phone survey of dealerships was also conducted. A white male tester and a black female tester each called more than one hundred dealerships and, following a uniform script, bargained for cars over the phone. The results of the phone survey dissions (reported in the two right-hand columns of table 2.1) may look forbidding, they are easily explained. The estimates for the CONSTANT represent the amounts of profit that white male testers were asked on average to pay: $725 and $418 on initial and final profits, respectively. Dealerships asked black males, however, to pay much more than white males: an extra $962 on initial offers and a whopping additional $1,133 on final offers, after controlling for other variables. Black males in essence were asked to pay more than double the markup of white males initially ($1,687 versus $725) and almost four times the markup offered to white males in the dealers' final offers ($1,550 versus $418).

The numbers reported in the parentheses underneath each of the coefficient estimates test whether the estimate is statistically different than zero. These "t-statistics" measure the number of standard deviations that the estimated coefficient is from zero. Estimates that are more than two standard deviations from zero (either > 2 or < -2) are generally considered to be statistically significant. These black male/white male differentials (represented by BLACK MALE coefficients) are thus highly statistically significant: six to nine times their standard errors.[33] This means that as a statistical matter, we can reject the hypothesis that the difference in prices offered was merely the by-product of the random variation of the sample.

Table 2.1 also shows that dealers' initial and final offers to black females were roughly $470 and $446 higher than comparable offers to white males. Black female testers were asked initially to pay a markup that was

---

close a different form of disparate treatment. The black female tester had greater success in eliciting initial offers (95 percent versus 79 percent) and on average received lower final offers. These results, however, may have been caused by the dealers' greater willingness to quote "low-ball" prices to the female tester over the phone. Dealers make low-ball or below-cost prices to induce potential customers onto the car lot, where it may then be possible to "bump" the price quoted over the phone. When dealers quoted prices below cost, they quoted lower prices to the female tester. When they quoted prices above cost, they quoted higher prices to the female tester:

Dealership Profits Based on Telephone Survey		
	Average Dealership Profits	
Tester Type	Offers above Cost ($)	Offers below Cost ($)
Female tester	940	−732
Male tester	290	−383

Thus, it seems that dealers implement one of two strategies against female customers— either quoting them large markup prices or very low "low-ball" prices.

33. Recall that a ratio greater than two is considered statistically significant. See table 2.1 note b.

65 percent higher than white males' initial markup, and finally asked to pay a markup that was more than twice the white male final markup ($864 versus $418). These coefficients are again highly significant in both regressions.

The disparate treatment of white females, in comparison, is less pronounced. Dealers' initial and final offers to white females were roughly $200 more than to white males. The dealers in effect asked white females to pay an initial markup almost 29 percent higher, and ultimately demanded a markup more than 50 percent higher ($633 versus $418). The initial profit differential, however, is not statistically significant and the final profit differential is only marginally significant ($p < 0.065$).[34]

The discrimination encountered by black female testers cannot be allocated to race or gender discrimination in a nonarbitrary way. It is impossible to say to what extent dealerships treated them differently because of their race or gender. Consequently, it is impossible to estimate a pure race or gender discrimination effect. Rather, consonant with modern scholarship,[35] it is more productive to think of black females as a separate group that is exposed to discriminatory treatment distinct from either white females or black males.

The statistically significant differences in the dealerships' initial offers provides particularly strong evidence of disparate treatment. Even if the final price offered is the more relevant measure of economic harm, the analysis of initial offers, as noted above, provides a "short test" of disparate treatment because the dealer's behavior is tested at the beginning of the negotiation—when there have been fewer opportunities for testers to deviate from the script.

The reliability of these results is buttressed by an analysis of the relative unimportance of individual tester effects. The average dealer profits on the nonwhite, nonmale testers were statistically different from the average profits on the white males at a 5 percent significance level. The average initial and final profits for the eighteen individual white males were, however, not significantly different from each other. This last result lends sup-

---

34. The WHITE FEMALE coefficient on the intial profit regression had a p-value equaling 0.124.

35. See, e.g., Tonya M. Evans, Comment, In the Title IX Race toward Gender Equity, the Black Female Athlete Is Left to Finish Last: The Lack of Access for the "Invisible Woman," 42 Howard L.J. 105, 1078 (1998); Kimberle Crenshaw, Mapping the Margins: Intersectionality, Identity Politics, and Violence against Women of Color, 43 Stan. L. Rev. 1241 (1991).

port to the proposition that the idiosyncratic characteristics of at least the white male testers did not affect the results.[36]

The regressions in table 2.1 also tested the success of several procedural controls. For example, we expected the coefficients on the EXPERIENCE, FIRST, and UNPAIRED variables not to be statistically different from zero.[37] The table shows that none of these coefficients was significant at the traditional 5 percent level and that additional tester experience added a trivial amount ($3.41) to dealers' final offers. But the size of the FIRST coefficient in the final profit regression is troubling even though not statistically significant: it suggests that a dealer's final offer to the first tester in a pair was $138 higher than to the second tester. This result might mean that some dealers realized a test was being conducted and artificially lowered the offer to the second testers.[38]

We also expected that the tester's use of a split-the-difference strategy or a fixed-concession strategy would not affect the dealer's initial offer, for the simple reason that the tester elicited the dealer's initial offer before the tester began implementing either one of these counteroffer strategies. The SPLIT coefficient was unexpectedly negative, indicating that dealers'

36.   See Ayres & Siegelman, *supra* note 12, at 311. The training and selection of the testers were designed to eliminate as much intertester variation as possible. Thus, we would expect to find little or no evidence of individual-tester effects in our data. For reasons described above, however, we cannot test for the presence of individual-tester effects that are correlated with testers' race or gender. A fixed-effects specification with one dummy variable for each individual tester is equivalent to subtracting the tester-specific mean for each variable. This means that any variables that do not vary over time for each individual tester (including the tester race and gender dummies) are indistinguishable from the individual-tester fixed effect and cannot be used.

37.   If testers faithfully followed the script, those who had previously completed more tests would not be treated differently. If the testers were successful at concealing the auditing, we would not expect the first tester to receive systematically different treatment than the second tester bargaining at the same dealership. Finally, if the unpaired audits were representative of the larger sample, we would not expect systematically different results from these tests.

38.   Manufacturers, rival dealers, and U.S. Census officials at times audit dealerships to determine the real cost of purchasing a new car. Telephone Interview with Margerie Yonsura, Wordsmith Relations (Sept. 1, 1992). Alternatively, the dealer may have lowered its offer after failing to sell to the initial tester.

We were also concerned that the dealers' final offers on the unpaired bargaining sessions were $161 lower than the final offers on bargaining sessions that were paired. This finding suggests that the dealership conditions that caused one of the tests to fail may have affected the results of the other, now unpaired, tester who was included in the regression sample. To control for this possible flaw, we reran the regression using only the paired data and found that the amount and significance of discrimination was not affected.

initial offers to testers using the split-the-difference-strategy were $240 less than the initial offers to testers using a fixed-concession strategy, but again this difference was not statistically significant.

The data also confirmed that the finding of discrimination is not merely an artifact of the split-the-difference negotiation strategy. When testers' counteroffers split the difference, discrimination in early rounds may force dealers' final offers to be discriminatory as well. For example, if the dealer's second offer to a black male includes a $1,000 profit while the dealer's offer to a white male includes only a $400 profit, then any subsequent bargaining will reflect discrimination because under a split-the-difference strategy the black male tester will counter with a price based on a $500 profit that is higher than the dealer's earlier $400 profit offer to the white male.

We found, however, that dealers continued to discriminate even when the testers adopted a fixed-concession strategy.[39] Table 2.1 in fact suggests that the split-the-difference approach might be the more effective of the two strategies because it led to dealer final offers that were $262 lower than the fixed-concession strategy, even though this result was not quite statistically significant at the 5 percent level.[40]

We also investigated whether our findings of race and gender discrimination might be linked to the fact that the dealerships' final offers were sometimes refusals to bargain further and sometimes acceptances of tester offers.[41] By adding an ACCEPT dummy (= 1 if the seller attempted to accept a tester offer) to the regressions reported in table 2.1, we found that sessions ending in attempted acceptances had an approximately $400 lower final profit than those that ended in a refusal to bargain (and this result was statistically significant). The size of this acceptance effect, however,

---

39. Separate regressions found no difference in the amount of discrimination for the fixed-concession negotiations. See *supra* note 21 (describing the fixed-concession strategy).

40. A 5 percent level of significance would require a t-statistic with an absolute value greater than 1.98. As shown in table 2.1, the coefficient estimate for the SPLIT variable has a t-statistic of 1.97 and so is almost significant at the standard 5 percent level.

41. In a parallel effort, we examined whether our results were affected by the fact that sellers sometimes made unsolicited initial offers and sometimes needed to have offers elicited by the testers. Logit regressions indicated that dealers were less likely to make an unsolicited initial offer to white males than to other tester types, but that this difference was not statistically significant. Solicited initial offers were significantly larger than unsolicited initial offers, but there was no statistical difference in final offers between tests that began with elicited initial offers and those that began with unsolicited offers by the seller.

was the same for all testers; interacting the ACCEPT dummy with the tester type yielded small and insignificant coefficients.[42] The willingness of dealers to offer lower prices to white males was reflected in a greater willingness to continue bargaining until an acceptable tester offer was made. When the tester was a white male, 25.6 percent of the tests ended in an attempted seller acceptance; this figure was only 14.9 percent for the other tester types. The fact that sellers are more likely to accept offers from white males actually biases our estimates *against* finding discrimination, however, because acceptances only provide an upper bound for sellers' reservation prices. That is, in those cases where dealers attempted to accept an offer from a white male tester, the dealers might have been willing to make an even lower offer, which would have increased our measure of discrimination. Overall, our findings of discrimination do not seem to be sensitive to the fact that most negotiations did not end in an attempted seller acceptance.[43]

In addition to the linear regressions in table 2.1, nonparametric tests also strongly support the finding of disparate treatment. If race or gender were unrelated to the prices quoted to testers, we would expect that the benchmark white male testers would get lower offers than their audit partners half the time, while faring worse than their counterparts in the remaining half of the tests. As table 2.2 indicates, however, this was not the case. Overall, white males did better than others in roughly two-thirds of the paired tests (for both initial and final offers). A likelihood-ratio test reveals that the differences from 50 percent were all statistically significant at the 5 percent level.

The disparities are even larger in dollar terms. In paired tests in which white male testers received the lower final offer, on average they did $897 better than their counterparts. Where the nonwhite males did better, they beat white males by only $167.[44] Moreover, in 43.5 percent of the tests, white males received an *initial* offer that was lower than the *final* offer made to the nonwhite male testers.

42. The ACCEPT variable may not be exogenous in these regressions, because higher profitability may cause the dealer to accept a tester's offer.

43. The game-theoretic parameterization in chapter 3 analyzes the subsample of our negotiations that end in dealer refusals to bargain.

44. Wilcoxon signed-ranks tests similarly reveal that the median final and initial profits with white males were significantly lower than those with the other tester types. For a description of such tests, see Morris H. Degroot, *Probability and Statistics* 573–76 (2d ed. 1986). This suggests that white males did better on average not simply because a few of them received very low offers, but because the entire distribution of offers to white males was lower than the distributions for the other tester types.

Table 2.2   Percentage of Tests in Which White Males Obtained the Better Result

	Initial Profits	Final Profits
White males vs. all others (153 pairs)	68.0	66.7
White males vs. white females (53 pairs)	58.4	56.6
White males vs. black males (40 pairs)	87.5	85.0
White males vs. black females (60 pairs)	63.3	61.7

Note: All values are significantly different from 50 percent at the 1 percent level using a likelihood ratio test $\chi_{(1)}^2$.

B. Non–Price Discrimination

Another potentially important form of disparate treatment concerns the sellers' willingness to bargain. Consumers are hurt if sellers either refuse to bargain[45] or force the consumers to spend more time bargaining to achieve the same price. Critics might argue that the black and female testers would not have received a higher price if, at the end of the test, they had given the dealership a "take it or leave it" price. But why should black and female consumers have to expend additional effort to gain the same lower price that our white male testers received without screwing up their courage to make a "take-it-or-leave-it" ultimatum? It may be that black and female testers could also have received the price quoted to white males if they had executed twenty push-ups during the course of bargaining. If so, the fact that white male testers did not have to execute the push-ups to receive the better price would clearly constitute discrimination.

Our testing uncovered very little evidence of outright refusals to bargain and no evidence that dealerships were less likely to bargain with non-white male testers. Indeed, as summarized in table 2.3, if anything the dealers displayed a willingness to bargain longer with black male and white female testers—in terms of both number of bargaining rounds and number

45.   In the sale of housing, for example, sellers generally discriminate in order to discourage blacks from purchasing. See Rose Helper, *Racial Policies and Practices of Real Estate Brokers* 42–46 (1969). Refusals to bargain and the steering of black consumers are the classic methods of achieving this end. Even in the sale of housing, however, there are numerous cases detailing discrimination with the intent to sell at a higher price, and such discrimination was explicitly outlawed by the Fair Housing Act, 42 U.S.C. § 3604(b) (1988). See, e.g., United States v. Pelzer Realty Co., 484 F.2d 438, 442–43 (5th Cir. 1973) (finding illegal a realtor's requirement that black home buyers either bring the realtor additional business or pay higher prices). See generally Robert G. Schwemm, *Housing Discrimination Law* 155–56 (1983) (summarizing the requirements of § 3604(b)'s prohibition on discriminatory terms).

Table 2.3 Differences in Rounds

	Average Number of Rounds	Average Length of Test (Minutes)	Average Length per Round (Minutes)
White Male	2.75	36.2	13.2
White female	2.98	49.1	16.5
Black male	2.96	39.7	13.4
Black female	2.71	35.2	13.0

of minutes.[46] Although black male testers clearly had to pay the most for cars, it was not because dealers refused to spend time bargaining with them.

Indeed, the sellers' insistence on bargaining longer with black men may be an indirect attempt to enhance their market power by reducing their potential competition. If the hourly costs to consumers of searching for a car increase with the time spent searching, then the longer a dealership keeps customers bargaining in its showroom, the less likely they will visit other dealerships. In other words, dealers may intentionally try to bargain for more rounds with certain types of consumers, if doing so is particularly likely to reduce the chance that they will visit other dealerships.[47] This data on willingness to bargain (particularly the time spent negotiating) is used in chapter 3 together with the basic data on initial and final offers to help distinguish between different causal theories.

The initial pilot study conducted in 1989 also examined other ways in which sellers may have treated the testers differently. Although these data are not as authoritative (based as they are on a smaller sample of only approximately 180 negotiations), they illuminate ancillary ways that deals can facilitate price discrimination. Moreover, these comparisons suggest

46. These black male, black female, and white female averages were statistically different from the white male average ($p < 0.1$). A chi-square analysis failed to reject a joint test that the number of rounds was the same for different tester types ($p = 0.1465$), but did reject the null hypothesis that the average length of bargaining was the same for different tester types and length was the same for different tester types ($p = 0.00003$).

47. Using ordered statistics, one can estimate the expected gains that different testers would experience by searching for the minimum price at additional dealerships. The more prices vary from dealer to dealer, the more likely it becomes that a search will turn up better offers. See George Stigler, *The Organization of Industry* 173–75 (1968).

something about the racial and sexual perceptions that determine the behavior of salespeople. In the pilot study, the testers recorded how often they were asked specific types of questions. Statistical tests were then conducted to evaluate whether sellers asked nonwhite, nonmale testers certain questions significantly more or less often than white male testers. These tests indicated the following:

- Sellers asked black female testers more often about their occupation, about financing, and whether they were married.
- Sellers asked black female testers less often whether they had been to other dealerships and whether they had offers from other dealers.
- Sellers asked black male testers less often if they would like to test drive the car, whether they had been to other dealerships, and whether they had offers from other dealers.
- Sellers asked white female testers more often whether they had been to other dealerships.
- Sellers asked white female testers less often what price they would be willing to pay.

These differences may indicate ways that dealers try to sort consumers in order to price discriminate effectively. For example, the fact that salespeople asked black testers less often about whether they had been to other dealerships (or had other offers) may indicate that salespeople do not think that interdealer competition is as much of a threat with black customers as with white customers. Because the price that sellers are willing to offer any customer may be sensitive to that customer's responses, the disparity among whom is questioned may facilitate a seller's attempt to price discriminate.

In the pilot study, the testers also recorded the different tactics that the salespeople used in trying to sell the car. Test statistics were calculated to evaluate whether particular sales tactics were used significantly more or less often with white male testers than with their nonwhite, nonmale counterparts. These tests indicated the following:

- Salespeople tried to sell black female testers more often on gas mileage, the color of the car, dependability, and comfort, and asked them more often to sign purchase orders.
- Salespeople tried to sell white female testers more often on gas mileage, the color of the car, and dependability.

Table 2.4   Disclosure of Cost Data

Tester Type	Percentage of Salespeople Disclosing Cost Figure
All Testers	35
White male	47
White female	42
Black male	25
Black female	0

- With black male testers, salespeople more often offered the sticker price as the initial offer and forced the tester to elicit an initial offer from the seller. Salespeople asked black male testers to sign a purchase order less often.

These tests suggest that salespeople believe women are more concerned than men with gas mileage, color, and dependability. The tests also indicate that salespeople try to "sucker" black males into buying at the sticker price by offering the sticker price or refusing to make an initial offer until asked.

Finally, the script for the pilot study also elicited information about the dealers' willingness to reveal their marginal cost to consumers. In half of the bargaining sessions, the testers were told to ask the seller (at the end of the test) what the dealer had paid the car manufacturer. Thirty-five percent of the sellers represented a specific dollar cost in response to the testers' inquiries. These disclosures, however, were not evenly distributed across the tester groups. Disaggregated by tester type, the disclosure rates indicated that salespeople were less willing to disclose cost data to black testers, especially black female testers, as shown in table 2.4.

Instead of disclosing their cost information to black testers, the salespeople were more likely to dissemble and claim that they did not know the car's cost. To the extent that such cost disclosure is valuable,[48] the failure to disclose costs to black buyers would undermine their ability to bargain as effectively as whites and thus facilitates price discrimination based on race. Based on this sample, however, it is unclear whether such disclosure would actually put white testers at a competitive advantage. When the seller did reveal his cost, the represented cost was substantially

48. Consumers rationally value information concerning a seller's costs in "thin markets," in which the infrequency of transactions makes the competitive price hard to determine. See Ayres & Miller, *supra* note 8, at 1059–60.

Table 2.5   Seller Misrepresentation
of Cost Data

Tester Type	Average Misrepresentation ($)
White male	849
White female	1,046
Black male	752
Black female	—

higher than independent estimates of seller cost for the same models, as seen in table 2.5. Thus, although salespeople are more likely to disclose cost figures to white testers, they systematically overstate their costs. The greatest misrepresentations were made to white female testers.

III. Contrasts with the Pilot Study

The core evidence of disparate treatment reported in table 2.1 confirms the original pilot study's findings that offers to black males and black females are significantly higher than those made to white males.[49] The ordering of discrimination, however, changed: while in the pilot study the final offers to black females were $500 higher than the final offers to black males,[50] in the current study (as seen in table 2.1) black males received final offers that were $686 higher than those black females received.[51] This

49.   The results of the pilot study were also consistent with regard to white female testers. Initial offers made to them were not statistically different than the offers made to white male testers. But in the pilot as well as in table 2.1, the final offers displayed substantially more discrimination with regard to white female testers that was (at least marginally) statistically significant.

50.   The average dealer profits for final offers made to different classes of testers in the pilot study were:

Tester Type	Average Dealer Profits on Final Offers ($)
White male	362
White female	504
Black male	783
Black female	1,283

See Ayres, *supra* note 20, at 828.

51. $1,133.6 − $446.3 = $686.3.

changed ordering of discrimination suggests that individual characteristics
of testers may have biased the results of the pilot study. Because there was
only one black male tester and only one black female tester in that original
study, any systematic deviations by these testers from the script could have
biased the test results. As noted in the pilot study: "The black male tester
in the initial experiment, for example, was himself a former car salesperson
and is currently a law student. It is possible that the lower offers he received
in the initial experiment were by-products of his overly aggressive deviations from the script."[52] This explanation for the ordering in the earlier
study, however, is not completely satisfying. In the larger study, the black
female testers experienced much less discrimination than the single black
female in the initial study. For example, the final offer differential with
white males decreased more than $800. Unlike our expectation for the
black male in the initial study, there is no reason to suppose that the black
female tester in the initial study was less aggressive than the subsequent
black female testers.

Because of our concern with potential individual tester effects, we
tested for the presence of individual tester effects by using what econometricians call a "random effects" regression specification.[53] Using this more
sophisticated specification,[54] we found no evidence that any individual testers encountered idiosyncratic treatment—that is, treatment that differed
from the treatment of other testers of the same race and gender. And even
after controlling for potential individual effects, we found race and gender
effects of the same size and statistical significance as in table 2.1.[55]

The results of the current study also differed from the pilot study with
regard to customer steering. In both studies, the script allowed dealerships
to steer testers to different types of salespeople or different types of cars.
Neither study found evidence that testers were steered to different types
of cars, but the pilot study did find that testers were steered to salespeople

52. Ayres, *supra* note 20, at 828 n.36.

53. See, e.g., William E. Griffiths et al., Learning and Practicing Econometrics
456–57 (1993).

54. Because we have multiple observations for each of the thirty-eight testers (and
testers were not paired with a single, fixed partner), we were also able to test for the
presence of individual-tester effects. To do this, we reorganized the panel data by individual testers (for example Profit$_{it}$ = dealer profit on the ith test for the tth tester) and computed a standard random effects regression. This estimation procedure allowed us to estimate the variance of the individual-specific error. If this estimated variance is
significantly greater than zero, it is evidence of individual tester effects.

55. See Ayres & Siegelman, *supra* note 12, at 311–12.

of the same race and gender. White male sellers were more likely to serve white male testers; white female sellers were more likely to serve white female testers; and black male sellers were more likely to serve black testers. This evidence of steering was surprisingly combined with the result that testers systematically received higher offers from salespeople of the same race and gender.[56] In short, testers in the pilot were steered toward salespeople of their same race and gender who then tended to offer them higher prices. (To be clear, all salespeople tended to charge black male testers higher prices, but black male salespeople offered even higher prices.) This intragroup bargaining effect is not predicted by the social psychology literature. Several studies, for example, have shown that parties tend to bargain more cooperatively with someone of their own race and gender than with a person of a different race or gender.[57] The pilot study's contrary finding suggests, however, that salespeople may try to take strategic advantage of consumers' perceptions. Salespeople of the same race and gender may feel that they are better judges of prospect or may feel that they can exploit the consumer's misplaced intraracial or intragender trust. The result is more plausible when combined with the pilot study's finding that testers were systematically steered to salespeople of the same race and gender.

In the larger and more authoritative study, however, neither the salesperson steering nor the intragroup discrimination result persisted. The race and gender of the testers and the sellers were independent of each other.[58] And the amounts of discrimination encountered by different tester types

56. The interaction effects of salesperson type and tester type were jointly significant, but the individual interactions were not statistically significant—possibly because in the pilot study there was a relatively small proportion of salespeople who were not white males (16.8 percent).

57. See, e.g., Jeffrey Z. Rubin & Bert R. Brown, *The Social Psychology of Bargaining and Negotiation* 163 (1975).

58. For the paired sample of 306 negotiations, the distribution of tester and seller types broke down as follows:

Tester	Seller			
	White Male	White Female	Black Male	Black Female
White male	123	11	17	2
White female	37	4	11	1
Black male	46	6	7	1
Black female	29	5	6	0

A chi-square test[9] = 5.64, p = 0.78, which fails to reject a null hypothesis of independence.

was independent of the race and gender of the salesperson. Black testers did no worse when buying from white salespersons, and women were not quoted higher final prices when the salesperson was male.[59]

In sum the regressions reveal strong evidence of disparate racial treatment. By following the audit script, the testers projected similar personal characteristics except for their race and gender, and all the tests of procedural irregularity were, as expected, statistically insignificant.[60] Dealers demanded a final markup to white women that was 50 percent higher than that offered to white males ($633 versus $418), although this result was only significant at the 6.5 percent confidence level. In contrast, there was a consistent and highly significant pattern of racial discrimination, with white male testers receiving substantially lower offers than either type of black tester. Black females were ultimately asked to pay a markup that was more than twice the white male markup ($864 versus $418), and black males were ultimately asked to pay almost four times the white male markup ($1,550 versus $418). Indeed, the initial offer white male testers received was lower than the final offer 43.5 percent of nonwhite males received.[61] That is, without any negotiating at all, two out of five white males obtained a better offer than their counterparts achieved after bargaining on average for more than forty minutes.

59. The one exception was that black women did seem to get worse deals when buying from black salesmen. F tests for the joint significance of the tester-seller interactions were also uniformly insignificant, with the exception of black females in the final markup equation. See table 3.2.

60. As discussed in the text, however, the size of some of these insignificant coefficients gives us some residual concern about the effect of unpaired testers on final profits, first testers on final profits, and using the split-the-difference strategy on initial profits.

61. See Ayres & Siegelman, *supra* note 12, at 313.

CHAPTER 3

Toward Causal Explanation

The results reported in chapter 2 established the existence of discrimination but not its cause. The evidence of disparate racial treatment was not only statistically significant but also surprisingly pronounced. This chapter explores possible explanations for why dealers would discriminate in this manner. Only with an accurate understanding of the reasons for dealer behavior can regulators hope to determine what, if any, governmental intervention might effectively protect black and/or female customers.

Two types of evidence are deployed to infer cause. First, using multivariate regression analysis, I explore what dealership characteristics are associated with the most extreme types of disparate treatment. Such regressions are a traditional method to indirectly test for animus. For example, finding that dealerships owned by minorities discriminated less than dealerships owned by whites might be evidence that the discrimination was motivated by the animus of the owner rather than by a general profit-making opportunity.[1] Second, I use a game-theoretic analysis of sellers' pricing negotiation strategy to infer the causes of the seller's demonstrated race and gender discrimination.

---

1. Other interpretations, however, are possible. It might be that racial discrimination was generally profitable but that minority-owned dealerships refused to avail themselves of this possibility, or that the minority dealerships by not discriminating supplied a segment of the market consumers that searched to avoid discrimination.

At first blush, it would seem difficult to use evidence of higher offers to distinguish between different possible causes of discrimination. Because either animus or statistical inference might cause a dealer to make a higher offer, it would seem impossible to infer from a higher offer whether the dealer was motivated by hatred or by profits.[2] This reasoning holds true if the dealer only makes a single offer to each buyer. It is possible, however, to infer more about the causes of discrimination when the dealer makes multiple offers. The dealer's choice of an initial offer, the size of concessions, and the speed of concessions can be expected to vary by causal story. For example, sellers might offer a higher initial price to black customers either because they believe that the black consumers are averse to bargaining or because the sellers have a particular desire to disadvantage black consumers.[3] But game theory suggests that these two causes of discrimination will give rise to different concession rates—in particular, a desire to disadvantage blacks would cause sellers to hold out longer for a high price, implying a slower concession rate than if sellers offer high initial prices because they believe black consumers are averse to bargaining.[4] Our evidence of the dealers' initial offers and willingness to make concessions can thus be used to distinguish among different causal theories.

Game-theoretic analysis of bargaining predicts that a seller's strategy will be a function of the seller's beliefs about certain variables, including the buyer's reservation price,[5] and the buyer's and seller's costs of bargaining. Although these variables in theory determine the buyer's and sell-

2. Indeed, I originally wrote that one needs to look beyond the seller's offers themselves—to explore "ancillary" evidence—to assess the cause of the higher prices: "The fair driving tests, like their fair housing analogues, were designed primarily to identify the existence of disparate treatment—not to determine its cause. As a result, ancillary evidence must be used to determine which of the . . . competing theories best explains seller behavior." Ian Ayres, Fair Driving: Gender and Race Discrimination in Retail Car Negotiations, 104 Harv. L. Rev. 817, 845 (1991).

3. We refer to these two motivations, respectively, as "cost-based statistical discrimination" and "consequential animus." See *infra* text at note 51.

4. See *infra* note 50 and accompanying text.

5. A buyer's reservation price is his or her willingness to pay. Dealers attempting to extract the maximum amount of revenue from each consumer will attempt to assess "the consumer's firm-specific reservation price—that is, how much the consumer is willing to pay for a car from a particular dealership." Ayres, *supra* note 2, at 844. Dispute resolution theorists alternatively refer to a reservation price as a person's "BATNA," which stands for "best alternative to negotiated agreement." See Roger Fisher & William Ury, *Getting to Yes* 104–11 (1991) (1981); Jennifer Gerarda Brown & Ian Ayres, Economic Rationales for Mediation, 80 Va. L. Rev. 323, 331 & nn.26–27 (1994).

er's negotiation strategies,[6] to date no one has estimated the actual effect of these variables in real-world negotiations.[7] This chapter provides a first attempt to derive numerical estimates of these structural parameters.[8] Evidence about the sellers' initial offers, final offers, and the lengths of the negotiation are used to estimate crudely the sellers' beliefs about buyers' reservation prices, the buyers' costs of bargaining, and the sellers' costs of bargaining.

This process is repeated to estimate the sellers' beliefs with regard to each race–gender tester type. The goal is to use the evidence about sellers' beliefs to distinguish among four different causal theories of discrimination:

1. Sellers may have higher costs per period negotiating with certain buyer types—"associational animus."
2. Sellers may desire to disadvantage certain buyer types—"consequential animus."
3. Certain buyer types may have higher per-period negotiating costs—"cost-based statistical discrimination."[9]
4. Certain buyer types may have higher reservation prices—"revenue-based statistical discrimination."

Estimating the sellers' beliefs about different buyer types can thus "nest" these four causal tests of discrimination in a single parameterization that allows the sellers' own conduct to reveal their motives.[10]

The estimates of the buyers' and sellers' cost of bargaining and of the buyers' reservation price are based on a number of extreme assumptions

6. See, e.g., Anat R. Admati & Motty Perry, Strategic Delay in Bargaining, 54 Rev. Econ. Stud. 345 (1987); Peter C. Cramton, Dynamic Bargaining with Transaction Costs, 37 Mgmt. Sci. 1221 (1991).

7. Bargaining experiments have explored how student subjects change their behavior as the costs of negotiation delay increase. See, e.g., Elizabeth Hoffman & Mathew Spitzer, The Coase Theorem: Some Experimental Tests, 25 J.L. & Econ. 73 (1982).

8. Prior efforts to estimate the underlying parameters of game-theoretic models of bargaining have been constrained by the quality of the empirical data. See, e.g., Peter C. Cramton & Joseph S. Tracy, Strikes and Holdouts in Wage Bargaining: Theory and Data, 82 Am. Econ. Rev. 100 (1992).

9. As discussed *infra* note 38, this chapter uses a slightly different definition of "cost-based discrimination" than in Ayres, *supra* note 2.

10. A model can "nest" different hypotheses if forms of each hypothesis occur for distinct parameter values of the model.

that are not only literally false but probably fail to capture important parts of reality. The estimates are at best a heuristic exercise to guide us imperfectly toward determining the causes of discrimination. But given that virtually no other quantitative evidence about the causes of discrimination in this or any other market exists[11] and given the usefulness of estimating the basic determinants of negotiation strategies, these estimates of the sellers' beliefs may shed some additional light on a relatively dark corner of the civil rights landscape.

With these important caveats, this parameterization of the bargaining game suggests three primary conclusions:

1. Sellers discriminate against different buyer types for different reasons. Cost-based inferences may explain part of sellers' discrimination against black females while consequential animus may explain part of sellers' discrimination against black males.
2. The sellers' bargaining behavior is inconsistent with associational animus but supports—especially regarding black males—consequential animus as a partial cause of the sellers' discrimination.
3. The sellers' bargaining behavior is broadly consistent with revenue-based statistical inferences as a partial cause of the sellers' discrimination.

These conclusions are also generally consistent with ancillary regression evidence about the causes of discrimination. As suggested in the pilot study, revenue-based discrimination explains at least part of sellers' behavior.[12] The game-theoretic parameterization, with all its limitations, however, suggests a less monolithic explanation.

I. Competing Causal Explanations

Before developing the explicit bargaining model, it is useful to step back and contrast competing causal explanations for disparate treatment. Most basically, it is helpful to distinguish between animus-based and statistical-based (or profit-based) theories of discrimination.

---

11. But see John Yinger, Measuring Racial Discrimination with Fair Housing Audits: Caught in the Act? 76 Am. Econ. Rev. 881 (1986).

12. Ayres, *supra* note 2, at 843–45, 847–52.

A. Animus-Based Theories of Discrimination

Animus theories of discrimination posit that a certain group is treated differently because that group is disliked or hated. The discriminatory behavior is not motivated by a desire to increase profits and indeed may cause company profits to decline. It is useful to distinguish among different sources and types of animus. As to sources, a variety of market participants can interject animus into a market. A dealership, for example, might charge blacks more because the dealership's owner dislikes blacks, because the dealership's employees dislike blacks, or because the dealership's other customers dislike blacks.[13] As originally formulated by Gary Becker, these sources of bigotry could induce sellers to charge blacks higher prices as an animus-compensating tax.[14] The source of bigotry might partially determine the specific form that animus-based discrimination takes. For example, in the fair housing context, consumer animus has led to steering and refusals to bargain.[15]

Law and economics scholars have too narrowly defined the types of potential discriminatory preferences. Becker's theory focused on a single type of what I term "associational" animus. In the employment context, he showed that if a bigoted employer dislikes spending time (associating) with members of a particular group, the employer may offer members of the group a lower wage to compensate the employer for her associational animus.[16]

But animus-based discrimination can arise from very different preferences. Bigots—instead of wanting to avoid association with a particular group—may gain pleasure by mistreating the disliked group. I refer to this type of discriminatory motive as "consequential animus" because the seller dislikes the consequence of contracting with disfavored groups on equal terms.[17] Indeed, in order to succeed in mistreating the disliked group, it

13. Holzer and Ihlanfeldt have found in four large U.S. metropolitan areas that "the racial composition of an establishment's customers has sizable effects on the race of who gets hired, particularly in jobs that involve direct contact with customers and in sales or service occupations." Harr J. Holzer & Keith R. Ihlanfeldt, 111 Q.J. Econ. 835 (1998).

14. See Gary Becker, *The Economics of Discrimination* 14–15, 39–54 (1957).

15. For a discussion of refusals to bargain in the sale of houses, see Yinger, *supra* note 11.

16. Becker, *supra* note 14.

17. Consequential animus may take many other forms as well. For example, if sellers enjoy seeing blacks and women expend time bargaining, this form of animus would also have the effect of decreasing sellers' net costs of bargaining with these groups. At a

may be necessary for the bigot to associate with members of that group. In the "fair driving" context, consequential animus of employees against blacks or women might cause salespeople to bargain harder (because an additional dollar of profit extracted from a minority is more valuable than a dollar extracted from a white male). Because testers, as described in chapter 2, visited the dealerships during the least busy times of the day, bigoted dealers—with nothing better to do with their time—might have gained satisfaction in frustrating or wasting the time of women or blacks.[18]

While this chapter focuses primarily on associational and consequential theories of animus, it is worth emphasizing that other discriminatory preferences are possible. For example, we could imagine "role-based" varieties of either associational or consequential animus. Dealers might dislike buyers who acted in ways that diverged from the dealer's expectation of how that race–gender type should act. Female testers could have faced prejudice for speaking with "a male voice."[19] black testers could have faced prejudice for not "staying in their place." A role-based bigot might not want to associate with or might take pleasure in disadvantaging group members who violate expected roles.

The possibility of role-based prejudice calls into question the appropriateness of using a uniform buyer strategy to test for discrimination. Different consumer types may have "different paths" to the same price. As a theoretical matter, comparing the treatment of uniform testers might therefore overstate the price disparity for most black consumers who may adopt different but equally efficient bargaining strategies. Partly for this reason, it would be useful to combine the results of this study with uncontrolled studies of actual sales. Chapter 4 provides this very analysis by considering whether consummated sales exhibit similar racial disparities in pricing. The

---

more subtle level, the sellers' motive may not be to disadvantage other groups, but to advantage their own group. Richard McAdams has previously explored the possibility that relative group preferences might provide a more compelling explanation of many types of discrimination. See Richard H. McAdams, Cooperation and Conflict: The Economics of Group Status Production and Race Discrimination, 108 Harv. L. Rev. 1003 (1995); see also John J. Donohue III, Prohibiting Sex Discrimination in the Workplace: An Economic Perspective, 56 U. Chi. L. Rev. 1337 (1989). Although the bargaining model analyzed in the text begins with individual preference as the foundational cause of discrimination, McAdams's work explores the social underpinnings of these preferences.

18. In addition, consumer animus might cause salespeople to encourage blacks to leave the dealership quickly to cater to bigoted white customers. The testing indicates, however, that such refusals were rare.

19. Cf. Price Waterhouse v. Hopkins, 490 U.S. 228 (1989) (involving alleged discrimination based on sexual stereotyping); Susan D. Carle, Gender in the Construction of the Lawyer's Persona, 22 Harv. Women's L.J. 239 (1999) (exploring role of gender in lawyering).

short answer is that they do. Even if women and other minority members *could* avoid discrimination by acquiescing in not violating their expected roles, however, forcing black or female consumers to conform to a particular societal stereotype as a prerequisite for receiving equal treatment represents a powerful form of discrimination.[20]

B. Statistical Theories of Discrimination

Theories of statistical discrimination predict that disparate treatment stems not from a distaste for particular consumer groups, but rather from a seller's desire to maximize profits.[21] Applied to the results from chapter 1, a theory of statistical discrimination would posit that salespeople treat people of different races or gender differently only because salespeople make rational statistical inferences about average differences among the groups. Statistical theories of discrimination can be further subdivided into those which are cost-based inferences and those which are revenue based.[22]

Cost-based statistical discrimination in the car market is theorized to stem from sellers' inferences that certain types of consumers tend to impose additional costs on a dealership. For example, sellers might treat consumer groups differently if they perceive that certain groups are greater credit risks. By charging high-risk groups a higher markup, the dealership seeks to cover its higher default risk with a higher average profit per customer.[23] Profit-

20. The commission structure of car sales might mitigate the effects of employer animus. Nonbigoted salespeople would not want to sacrifice their commissions just to satisfy an employer's bigoted preferences. Conversely, profit-maximizing employers, eager for their employees to generate sales, would have incentives to prevent employees from indulging their bigotry.

21. See Edmund S. Phelps, The Statistical Theory of Racism and Sexism, 62 Am. Econ. Rev. 659, 659 (1972) (arguing that individuals may discriminate based on their previous statistical experience with a group—such as blacks or women—rather than judge people on an individual basis); Stewart Schwab, Is Statistical Discrimination Efficient?, 76 Am. Econ. Rev. 228 (1986); Jody David Armour, Race Ipsa Loquitor: Of Reasonable Racists, Intelligent Bayesians, and Involuntary Negrophobes, 46 Stan. L. Rev. 781 (1994). See also Jody David Armour, *Negrophobia and Reasonable Racism: The Hidden Costs of Being Black in America* (1997).

22. Richard Posner makes this distinction when he suggests that either revenue-based or cost-based statistical discrimination may cause disparate pay for male and female employees. See Richard Posner, An Economic Analysis of Sex Discrimination Laws, 56 U. Chi. L. Rev. 1311, 1319–20 (1989).

23. In the study, however, this basis for disparate treatment was removed, because the testers volunteered that they could finance their own purchases, thereby relieving the dealers of any default risk. If the dealers did not believe the testers' representations that they could finance the purchases, however, statistical discrimination based on

maximizing dealers would also make inferences about the ancillary costs
and profits that are likely to flow from a particular sale. For example, dealers
might offer different prices to consumer groups that have different tendencies to service their cars at the dealership. If postsale servicing is profitable,
and female buyers were more likely to have servicing done at the original
dealerships, then dealers might rationally give better offers to women.[24]

In addition to such cost-based inferences, dealers may also have incentives to make inferences about the potential revenue from different types of
consumers. Revenue-based statistical discrimination results when dealers
make inferences about how much consumer groups on average are willing
to pay for a car. Revenue-based price discrimination is found in a variety of
markets. Airlines, for example, do not charge businesspeople higher fares
because of animus or higher costs; the difference in fares represents an
attempt to charge higher-valuing consumers a higher price.[25] In the retail
car market, the dealer's ultimate goal is to maximize profits by charging
each consumer his or her reservation price—that is, the maximum amount
the consumer is willing to pay. Under this theory, race and gender serve
as proxies to inform sellers about how much individual consumers would
be willing to pay for the car.[26]

---

inferred default risk might exist. If salespeople distrust a tester's stated interest in "purchasing a car today," they may be unwilling to enter into serious negotiations.

The inferences sellers draw from customer representations may vary with the context. For example, federal agents have charged Maryland car dealerships with knowingly
aiding the drug trade by accepting cash payments for cars—indicating that at least one
dealership took buyers who claimed they could "buy a car today" very seriously. See
Lynne Duke, U.S. Seizes 48 Cars in P. G. Raid, *Wash. Post,* July 22, 1989, at A1, col. 2.

24.   Similarly, if warranty service were unprofitable, statistical discrimination
would dictate that dealerships prefer those consumer groups that made fewer warranty
claims. Dealers may also discriminate between consumer groups because of statistical inferences that one group is more likely to make repeated purchases or more likely to refer other consumers to the same dealership. Inferences about the profits from such ancillary sales of other cars or services might alternatively be characterized as cost-based
statistical discrimination because the disparate treatment stemming from those inferences
will not be eliminated by dealership competition in the new car market.

25.   Revenue-based price discrimination persists in other consumer markets as
well. For example, universities force undergraduate and graduate students to assist financial aid offices in estimating their ability to pay tuition. See Ian Ayres, Colleges in
Collusion, *New Republic,* Oct. 16, 1989, at 19.

26.   Revenue-based statistical discrimination is a form of what Pigou called "third-degree" price discrimination. Arthur Cecil Pigou, *The Economics of Welfare* 240–56 (1920).
Under regimes of third-degree price discrimination, the seller divides "customers into two or
more independent groups, each of which has its own continuous demand function reflecting
quantities sold to that group at alternative prices." Frederick M. Scherer, *Industrial Market
Structure and Economic Performance* 316 (2d ed. 1980) (footnote omitted).

Initially, a revenue-based theory seems to be at odds with the revealed pattern of discrimination. Given the current econnomic demographic of Chicago, it is difficult to believe that dealers would infer that women and blacks had a greater ability to pay for a car than white males.[27] Yet, to understand a more refined version of revenue-based discrimination, it is necessary to differentiate between a consumer's general willingness to pay and his or her willingness to pay at a specific dealership.[28] For example, a consumer who needs transportation might be willing (and able) to pay up to $30,000 to acquire a car. A number of factors—such as her transportation needs and the price of alternative goods—establish the consumer's marketwide reservation price. This price may have been especially sensitive to her ability to pay, which in turn depended on her wealth and credit opportunities. The amount this consumer is willing to pay at a particular dealership, however, depends much more on what she believes competing dealerships would offer. Moreover, as emphasized below, a consumer's willingness to pay at a particular dealership may be a function of how "motivated" the consumer is to purchase (quickly) or how averse she is to protracted bargaining. Even though she values having a car at $30,000, she will not be willing to pay a particular dealership $15,000 if she believes she could buy from another dealership at $10,000. Or she may be willing to "cave in" and accept an $18,000 dealer offer if her subjective costs of bargaining are relatively high.

From the perspective of a dealer trying to implement revenue-based statistical discrimination, the crucial variable is the consumer's *firm-specific* reservation price—that is, how much the consumer is willing to pay for a car from that particular dealership. A consumer's firm-specific reservation price is more sensitive to competitive characteristics of the market than to his or her general willingness to pay. In particular, both the consumer's costs of searching for a better price and knowledge of the market play a larger role in determining the price a consumer is willing to pay at a particular dealership. As the costs of bargain-hunting increase, a consumer's firm-specific reservation price approaches his or her marketwide valuation. Revenue-based statistical discrimination against women and blacks

27. A consumer's willingness to pay cannot be larger than his or her ability to pay.

28. The distinction between market demand and firm-specific demand is common to law-and-economic analysis. See, e.g., William Landes & Richard Posner, Market Power in Antitrust Cases, 94 Harv. L. Rev. 937, 947–52 (1981) (discussing the relationship between market demand, firm-specific demand, and market power). For individual consumers, this is the distinction between a market reservation price and a firm-specific reservation price.

may still be possible (notwithstanding their relative poverty), because the price a consumer is willing to pay at a particular dealership is at times substantially below his or her ability to pay. Thus, revenue-side statistical discrimination seeks to discover not the consumer's general valuation of a car, but how much he or she would be willing to pay a particular dealership. If a dealership can infer that a black or a woman is less likely to search at other dealerships, it may rationally attempt to charge him or her more. If a consumer's cost of searching at more than one dealership is prohibitively expensive, the dealership may realize that, as far as that consumer is concerned, it has a virtual monopoly.[29] Thus, profit-maximizing dealers may rationally make not only higher initial offers, but also lower concessions when bargaining against members of consumer groups who the dealer believes cannot afford to shop elsewhere.[30]

Finally, in making revenue-based inferences, dealerships are not so much interested in assessing a particular consumer group's average willingness to pay as they are in assessing the likelihood that some members of that group will be willing to pay a high markup. As discussed below,[31] if a larger proportion of minorities are willing to pay a high markup, it might be rational for the dealership to demand high prices from that entire group of consumers. Revenue-based discrimination becomes more theoretically plausible—notwithstanding the average greater poverty of minorities—because consumers' willingness to pay a specific dealership will be largely disconnected from their ability to pay, and profit-maximizing dealers will care much more about the upper tail of the "willingness to pay" distribution than about its average.[32]

29. The process of bargaining may reveal information to dealers about a particular consumer that facilitates revenue-based discrimination. For example, if a consumer's distaste for bargaining is correlated with his or her willingness to pay, the process of bargaining could allow low-valuing consumers to "signal" their lower reservation prices by bargaining longer. In the language of game theory, this signal can be "credible" because the high-valuing consumers face, by assumption, larger costs of signaling. See Eric Rasmusen, *Games and Information* 205 (1989); Ian Ayres, Playing Games with the Law, 42 Stan. L. Rev. 1291, 1304–5 (1990). Such signaling does not, however, require sellers to treat one class of buyers differently from another. A seller could choose a uniform concession rate and then let the different-valuing consumers separate themselves by the way in which they bargain.

30. Game-theory models of bargaining suggest that a seller will charge higher prices to groups with higher bargaining costs. See Rasmusen, *supra* note 29, at 234; John Sutton, Non-Cooperative Bargaining Theory: An Introduction, 53 Rev. Econ. Stud. 709, 711 (1986).

31. See *infra* note 53 and accompanying text (discussing this "search for suckers" phenomenon).

32. It is dangerous to extrapolate knowledge about an average to knowledge about the extreme of a distribution. Thus, while it may be appropriate to conclude that African

II. A Game-Theoretic Model of Animus and Statistical Discrimination in Bargaining

It is particularly difficult to distinguish among these competing causal hypotheses without an explicit model of how bigotry or cupidity might influence sellers' bargaining behavior. For example, though both animus and profit-maximizing statistical theories of discrimination might explain why dealers offer black testers higher initial prices, it is unclear that either of these theories helps explain the size or rate of the dealers' concessions when buyers and sellers take time to haggle.

Game theory suggests, however, that different sources of discrimination will cause dealers to choose different initial offers, different concession rates, and different concession amounts. For example, sellers might offer a higher initial price to a black customer either because they believe that black consumers are averse to bargaining or because the sellers have a particular desire to disadvantage black consumers. But game theory suggests that these two causes of discrimination will give rise to different concession rates: in particular, a desire to disadvantage blacks will cause sellers to hold out longer for a high price, implying a lower concession rate than when the seller believes that black consumers are averse to bargaining.[33] My evidence of the dealers' initial offers and willingness to make concessions can thus be used to distinguish among competing causal theories. To empirically identify the dealers' motive for discrimination, therefore, I derive a bargaining model that allows me to treat different causes of discrimination as special cases of a single bargaining game. For example, in this model certain parameter values produce a pure animus-based form of discrimination while other parameter values give rise to a pure profit-maximizing-based form of discrimination. The results of chapter 2's audits are then used to infer which causal theories best fit the data.

Americans have a lower average ability to pay than white consumers, it is not safe to say that whites are more likely to be willing to pay "home run" profits to a dealer. This issue of blacks' willingness to pay arises again in Chapter 7's discussion of the market for bail bonds. Mike Royko (in a column attacking the original pilot study) makes the converse mistake of extrapolating from evidence about the extreme of a distribution to evidence about the mean. Royko, in an irrelevant and offensive aside, concludes "being a white guy is terrific, even if we run slow." Mike Royko, Color Not an Option in Best New-Car Deal, *Chi. Trib.*, Dec. 17, 1990, C3 (1990). But even if it is true that the fastest male runners are disproportionately of African descent, this provides a rather flimsy basis for concluding that white males generally are slower—especially if by using the term *we* he intends to include sedentary oldsters. See also the discussion of Royko's article in chapter 5.

33. See *infra* at note 70 and accompanying text.

I begin by developing a model of bargaining that will allow me to nest competing theories of animus and statistical discrimination.[34] To reproduce the scripted bargaining procedure used in collecting the data, the buyer and seller in the model make alternating offers, beginning with an offer from the seller. The model also conforms to the data in that the seller can choose how long to delay before making an offer.[35] The buyer and seller each incur costs per unit of time spent bargaining, equal to c_b and c_s, and these costs are assumed to be common knowledge.[36]

The seller's reservation price is assumed to be its marginal cost, and this amount is assumed to be common knowledge as well.[37] For expositional convenience, the seller's reservation price is normalized to zero, which means that in looking at our results, the seller's profit equals the price, and the gains from trade are equal to the buyer's reservation price.

The buyer, however, is assumed to have private information about her reservation price, although the distribution of that price is common knowledge. To solve the model, I assume that the buyers' reservation prices are distributed uniformly between zero and some maximum value, h.[38]

34. The model is based on a bargaining game designed by Peter Cramton. See Cramton, *supra* note 6.

35. Cramton's original model also allowed the buyer to choose how long to delay before making an offer. Even though testers following the script made their offers five minutes after a new dealer offer, the script's timing restriction does not affect the seller's equilibrium strategy because the model predicts that the seller's strategy will be independent of the buyer's bargaining strategy. See *infra* note 44.

36. The model also assumes a second type of transaction cost in that all traders discount future payoffs at a common rate, r. Alternatively, r can be interpreted as the probability, per unit of time, that the negotiations will exogenously break down. The importance of r as an underlying determinant of the bargaining equilibrium is discussed *infra* notes 65–66 and accompanying text.

37. Both of these assumptions are reasonable: a seller's marginal cost is often a good proxy for its reservation price, see Ian Ayres & F. Clayton Miller, "I'll Sell It to You at Cost": Legal Methods to Promote Retail Markup Disclosure, 84 Nw. U. L. Rev. 1047 (1990), and the testers quickly indicated that the sellers' cost was common knowledge by setting their first counteroffer equal to this cost. See chapter 2, note 18 and accompanying text. The model also assumes that the dealer's marginal cost of selling a car is the same for all tester race–gender types. This is reasonable because the testers' script was explicitly structured to eliminate cost-based differences among the testers. For example, the testers volunteered that they did not need financing. See Ayres, *supra* note 2, at 846. The pilot study used the term *cost-based discrimination* to refer to the possibility that dealers would offer different prices if they believed there were different costs of selling to specific tester types. Here, the term is used to refer to the possibility that dealers would offer different prices if they believed that certain tester types had higher per-period costs of bargaining.

38. The assumption that the distribution of buyers' reservation prices has a lower support of zero is not restrictive. As shown *infra* note 44, the sellers' optimal bargaining

These assumptions give rise to a "signaling" equilibrium because the buyer's option to delay allows buyers with low reservation prices to signal this fact by their willingness to delay.[39] The dealer's equilibrium strategy is contingent upon three underlying parameters: the buyer's and the seller's per period cost of bargaining (c_s and c_b) and the buyer's maximum reservation price (h). Given particular values of these parameters, the chapter appendix shows that a simple concession curve summarizes a seller's equilibrium strategy. For example, figure 3.1 depicts a concession curve when $c_s = c_b = \$100/\text{hour}$, and $h = 3{,}000$.[40] The concession curve shows the offer that the seller is willing to make at any particular time. A seller's equilibrium concession strategy has the following characteristics:

> The seller starts by making the initial offer, depicted at time 0 on the concession curve;[41] if the buyer makes a counteroffer on or above the concession curve, the seller accepts;[42] if the buyer makes a counteroffer below the curve, the seller rejects and offers the price on the concession curve for the elapsed amount of time.[43]

The model predicts that sellers will make a series of decreasing offers, but that at some point rationally will refuse to make any further concessions.[44]

---

strategy is independent of this lower support—so, at least in the case of a uniform distribution, rational buyers only need to infer the location of the upper support.

39. Because the gains from trade are discounted by a common discount rate, r, buyers with low reservation prices have lower costs of delay and hence can use delay as a credible signal. See Admati & Perry, *supra* note 6. Unlike screening models, this model has the attractive feature that the equilibrium does not depend critically on a minimum time between offers.

40. The example also assumes that the discount rate for both parties is 0.5. See *infra* notes 65–66 and accompanying text.

41. In figure 3.1, the seller's initial offer is $1,000.

42. For example, in figure 3.1, if the buyer offers $800 after a quarter of an hour, the seller would accept.

43. Again taking figure 3.1 as an example, if the buyer offers $600 after a quarter of an hour, the seller would reject the offer and immediately offer $789. The model's prediction that sellers would immediately counter any buyer offer lower than the concession curve was somewhat contradicted by tester experience, however, as testers reported that sellers would at times delay before making subsequent offers.

44. As shown in figure 3.1, after 0.6 hours, the seller refuses to make any further concessions below $400. Sellers know that buyers with a reservation price below some critical value cannot credibly signal their valuation because the transaction costs of delay are greater than the buyer's expected gains from trade. Sellers infer that these low valuers will not find it worthwhile to begin bargaining, and sellers consequently choose not to make offers to buyers with these low valuations. See the chapter appendix. The model also predicts that a seller's offers will be independent of the buyer's previous

Fig. 3.1   Dealer concession curve

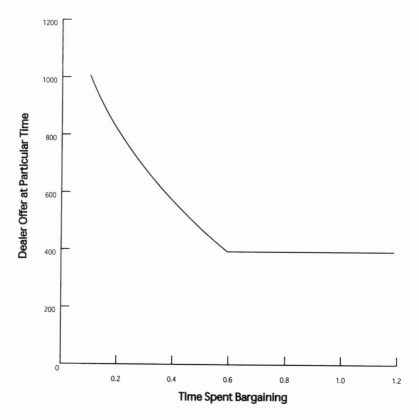

If dealers' beliefs about the underlying parameters (c_s, c_b, and h) differ according to tester type, the model predicts that dealers will use different concession curves when bargaining with these different tester types. Thus, if a dealer experiences a higher cost of bargaining with a particular type of buyer, or believes that a particular type of buyer has a higher willingness to pay or has higher costs of bargaining, the model predicts how these differences will affect the dealer's behavior.[45]

---

counteroffers. For example, in figure 3.1 the seller's strategy after a quarter of an hour is to offer to sell for $725, regardless of whether the buyer's last counteroffer was $150 or $700. This prediction of independence finds at least weak support in the data: as reported in chapter 2, sellers' final offers when testers used a fixed-concession strategy were not significantly different from sellers' final offers when testers used a split-the-difference strategy. See chapter 2, text after note 41. The difference in the offers, however, was unexpectedly high and almost achieved 5 percent statistical significance. See id.

45.   The details of the model are worked out in the chapter appendix.

The next section shows how dealers' beliefs about these three variables correspond to traditional causal theories of discrimination. I then use evidence of the dealers' actual concession curves to infer which of the causal theories best explains the data.

A. Nesting Four Causal Theories within the Model

The bargaining model derived above can accommodate four competing explanations as to why dealers would offer higher prices to a disfavored group than to white males:

1. Sellers may have higher costs of bargaining with a disfavored group—"associational animus"—reflected in higher values of c_s.[46]

2. Sellers may desire to disadvantage a disfavored group—"consequential animus"—reflected in lower net values of c_s.

3. Sellers may believe that a disfavored group has higher costs of bargaining—"bargaining cost-based" discrimination—reflected in higher values of c_b.

4. Sellers may believe that a disfavored group has higher reservation prices—"reservation-price-based" discrimination—reflected in higher h.

First, consider associational animus. A seller's dislike of spending time with a particular group (associational animus) can be naturally captured by an increase in the seller's costs per period (c_s) of associating (when negotiating) with testers from the disfavored group. In our bargaining model, associational animus yields a startlingly perverse result: black consumers can benefit from the presence of bigotry. One of the robust results of bargaining theory is that higher bargaining costs tend to reduce one's bargaining power.[47] Higher per period costs of negotiating with black consumers should lower sellers' bargaining power and induce them to make lower offers to black buyers.[48] Thus, even before we formally estimate the model,

---

46. This chapter also examines the possibility that different discount rates might give rise to disparate treatment. See *infra* note 105 and accompanying text.

47. See Martin J. Osborne & Ariel Rubinstein, *A Course in Game Theory* 117–31 (1994).

48. Sufficiently large associational costs could reverse the market power story by causing a seller to terminate the negotiations if the buyer does not accept what is in effect a take-it-or-leave-it initial offer. See Cramton, *supra* note 6, at 1222–23. However, given that the dealers were willing to spend a substantial amount of time bargaining with all testers, and dealers bargained longer with black men than with white men, see

theory suggests that associational animus against black customers will not be able to explain why, in a bargaining context, dealers offered black testers higher prices.

The perverse result that seller bigotry might benefit blacks suggests that allowing animus to take only the form of an associational tax (a higher c_s) does not account for all possible forms of bigotry. For example, bigoted sellers might alternatively enjoy extracting a high profit more from black or female customers than from white males. The chapter appendix shows that disproportionately valuing profits from disfavored groups has the effect of reducing the seller's effective, per-period cost of bargaining.[49] Sellers motivated by consequential animus act as if they had lower per period costs of bargaining: they are willing to bargain longer for a high price because they attach a higher value to extracting profits at the expense of a disfavored group. Unlike associational animus, consequential animus, by reducing the seller's effective costs of bargaining, enhances a seller's bargaining power and is compatible with blacks' or women's receiving higher offers than white males.

The model can also capture two types of revenue-based discrimination stemming respectively from sellers' statistical inferences about a group's cost of bargaining and from its dealer-specific willingness to pay.[50] "Bargaining-cost-based" discrimination could occur if a seller believed that a disfavored group is on average more averse to bargaining. Bargaining aversion or impatience might cause buyers to act as if they had higher bargaining costs. The sellers' statistical inference about a group's cost of bargaining might cause profit-maximizing sellers to quote higher prices to all members of this group because sellers would believe that members of this

---

chapter 2, table 2.3 and table 3.1, it is unlikely that this extreme form of associational animus could explain our results.

49. For example, a seller's payoff might increase by $a > 1$ for each additional dollar secured in negotiations with a disfavored consumer group. This form of consequential animus has the effect of lowering the seller's effective cost of bargaining, so that $c_s = c_s/a$. See the chapter appendix.

50. One car-salesman-turned-consumer-advocate described the general tendency of dealers to make statistical inferences based on gender: "Salesmen . . . categorize people into 'typical' buyer categories. During my time as a salesman I termed the most common of these the 'typically uninformed buyer.' . . . [In addition to their lack of information, these] buyers tended to display other common weaknesses. As a rule they were indecisive, wary, impulsive and, as a result, were easy to mislead. Now take a guess as to which gender of the species placed at the top of this 'typically easy to mislead' category? You guessed it—women." Darrell Parrish, *The Car Buyer's Art: How to Beat the Salesman at His Own Game* 3 (1989).

group on average have less bargaining power. The model captures the possibility of such bargaining-cost-based discrimination by allowing sellers to form different beliefs about the bargaining costs (c_b) of specific tester race–gender types.[51]

Finally, we can use the model to examine "reservation-price-based" statistical inferences founded on perceived differences in the distribution of reservation prices among consumer groups.[52] If sellers believe that blacks or women have different distributions of reservation prices than white males—for example, distributions with higher means or greater variances—this could lead dealers to offer higher prices to members of these groups.

The bargaining model used in this chapter formalized the assertion of the pilot study that revenue-based discrimination will often become a "search for suckers":

> From a dealer's perspective, bargaining for cars is a "search for suckers"—a search for consumers who are willing to pay a high markup.
> . . . In their quest to locate high-markup buyers, dealers are not guided by the amount that the *average* black woman is willing to pay. Rather, they focus on the proportion of black women who are willing to pay close to the sticker price.[53]

51. Within the precise confines of the model, the dealers' inferences about tester cost are not statistical in the typical sense. The model assumes that the testers' cost of bargaining (c_b) is commonly known by both the tester and the dealer. Normally, statistical discrimination is modeled as a process whereby a decisionmaker uses gender or some other observable characteristic as a proxy for some unknown characteristic. See Phelps, *supra* note 21. But a belief that blacks have higher bargaining costs based on common knowledge would induce dealers to charge blacks higher prices just as a belief based on statistical inference would.

52. In the real world, statistical discrimination might be based on any "primitive" variables other than buyers' reservation prices that might affect bargaining. For example, in contrast to this model, buyers' bargaining costs are typically not known to sellers; sellers could thus use race or gender to make inferences about the costs of negotiations for different buyer types. Or, in models with search costs, sellers could use race or gender to infer buyers' search costs. In this model, buyers' reservation prices are the key variable that is unknown to sellers, and are thus the focus of statistical discrimination. See Jennifer Gerarda Brown, The Role of Hope in Negotiation, 44 UCLA L. Rev. 1661 (1997) (cataloging underlying bargaining primitives including "hope").

53. Ayres, *supra* note 2, at 854–55 (citations omitted). The pilot study emphasized that the term *sucker* should not be taken to imply that high-markup buyers are irrational or uninformed because high search costs or a high aversion to bargain could make it rational to pay a high markup. Id. at 854 n.109.

The game-theoretic model starkly replicates this result because profit-maximizing sellers do not care about a group's average willingness to pay; rather, revenue-based discrimination turns solely on the seller's belief about the maximum amount any given group member would be willing to pay.[54] The dealers' exclusive interest in estimating the "upper tail" of the buyer's willingness-to-pay distribution is an artifact of the uniform distribution assumption. However, the intuition that dealers' behavior will be more attuned to their beliefs about high-markup buyers rather than the average buyer still holds true under less restrictive assumptions.[55] Therefore, even if blacks have a lower average willingness to pay than whites, profit-maximizing sellers might nevertheless make higher offers to blacks so long as a sufficient number of black consumers are willing to pay an especially high markup.

The model is not structured, however, to allow for the possibility of what I earlier referred to as "cost-based" discrimination. In contrast to bargaining-cost-based discrimination (which is a type of revenue-based discrimination in which the dealer believes it can extract more revenue from consumers who are averse to bargaining), under a cost-based theory, dealers discriminate because they expect it to be more costly to sell to certain consumer types. Profit-maximizing sellers might use race or gender to make inferences not only about the expected revenues, but also about the expected costs of selling a car to a particular buyer—including, for example, the expected costs of default on car loans.

We have excluded the possibility of cost-based discrimination, however, because of the way the audit tests were structured. The testers' script was explicitly structured to eliminate cost-based differences among the testers. The testers volunteered that they did not need financing—potentially an important source of disparate dealer costs. But even though all testers volunteered this information, dealers might disparately assess its

54. Notice that the lower bound of the support of buyers' reservation prices (l) does not appear in the seller's first order condition, equation (3.3). More generally, the seller's strategy does not depend on l_i unless l_i is so high that the seller finds it optimal to make an initial offer that is acceptable to all type i buyers. See Cramton, *supra* note 6. This did not occur in our data.

Penelopi Goldberg has developed a similar point. She emphasizes that it might be rational for dealers to discriminate between groups that have identical mean reservation prices but different variances. See Penelopi Goldberg, Dealer Price Discrimination in New Car Purchases: Evidence from the Consumer Expenditure Survey, 104 J. Pol. Econ. 622, 643 (1996), and chapter 4 (discussing Goldberg's empiricism).

55. Even under general assumptions about distributions, a linear mean-preserving spread of buyers' reservation prices will shift a seller's offers upward for any given period of delay. See Cramton & Tracy, *supra* note 8.

credibility depending on the gender and race of the tester. If statistically valid, this inference could form the basis for cost-based statistical discrimination.[56] As an empirical matter, however, differences in net dealership cost simply do not explain why black female testers paid over three times the markup of white male testers. George Stigler has considered whether price dispersion in cars could be attributed to cost-based differences in the provision of service. He concluded that "it would be metaphysical, and fruitless, to assert that all dispersion is due to heterogeneity."[57] Because of the specific way the audit tests were structured, we conclude that cost-based theories of statistical discrimination are perhaps the weakest causal explanation.

This section has shown that the traditional game-theoretic determinants of bargaining behavior—that is, the buyer's and seller's costs of bargaining and inferences about the buyer's willingness to pay—can capture four different explanations of discrimination. On theoretical grounds, we have been able to reject "associational animus" as a plausible explanation for higher prices encountered by minority and/or female testers. On structural grounds, we have excluded cost-based statistical discrimination as a plausible explanation for the discrimination. In the next section we empirically evaluate the remaining three hypotheses.

Although the next section's estimates of the model's parameter values are an important first step in quantifying evidence of the causes of discrimination, our simple bargaining model cannot capture a number of powerful and more foundational explanations for discrimination. The model cannot distinguish between rational statistical inference and irrational stereotyping, for example, or identify the cause of the irrationality.[58] In the end, it

56. Profit-maximizing dealers might also make inferences about the profits from ancillary sales, so dealers' inferences about the likelihood of repeat purchases, referrals, or repair service could also cause statistical discrimination. To dampen the importance of such inferences, we initially had testers volunteer to salespeople that they were moving out of the state within a month. Having more than one tester make this representation at a single dealership, however, increased the likelihood that dealers would suspect a test, and so we discontinued it. See chapter 2, note 16.

57. George Stigler, *The Organization of Industry* 172 (1968).

58. The model can similarly capture whether dealers bargain as if they disproportionately enjoy disadvantaging minority buyers, but estimates of the sellers' bargaining cost cannot begin to tell us why sellers have such preferences. In part, this is because the model proceeds from an atomistic conception of dealers and dealer behavior: social influences on preferences are taken as exogenous. See McAdams, *supra* note 17; Anthony D. Taibi, Banking, Finance, and Community Economic Empowerment: Structural Economic Theory, Procedural Civil Rights, and Substantive Racial Justice, 107 Harv. L. Rev. 1463 (1994) (criticizing the incompleteness of economic theories of discrimination).

may prove impossible to parse out the various elements of animus and irrational stereotypes from rational inferences. No single causal theory may be adequate to explain discrimination against both blacks and women. With these caveats, we now explore whether car dealers' disparate racial and gender treatment of consumers flow from different causes.

B. Estimating the Parameters of the Model

This section uses data on the sellers' actual concessions to estimate which seller beliefs give rise to the measured bargaining behavior. I have shown how in theory the model predicts that three underlying parameters (c_s, c_b, and h) will determine how sellers bargain. Now I work backward, using evidence of how sellers in fact bargained with particular tester types to infer the underlying parameters that would be consistent with the sellers' bargaining behavior.

In particular, we calculated three measures of seller behavior when bargaining with each of the four tester types: the sellers' average initial offer (p_I), the sellers' average final offer (p_F), and average time spent bargaining (Δ_F).[59] These averages, shown in panel A of table 3.1 give crude information about the shape of sellers' concessions curves when bargaining with different tester types.

We can use these three observations about a seller's concession curve to estimate the seller's beliefs about the three parameters of interest: the sellers' and buyers' bargaining costs (c_s and c_b) and the upper bound of buyers' reservation prices (h).[60] This inferential process would be an inter-

---

59. The average final offer and the time spent bargaining were calculated using only those test sessions that ended with the seller's refusal to bargain further. Otherwise the seller's attempted acceptance might have occurred at a point above the concession function. Moreover, the fact that negotiations ended with sellers refusing to bargain further allows us to identify buyer costs. See the chapter appendix.

60. The inferential process is straightforward because the underlying parameters (c_s, c_b, and h) can be expressed as algebraic functions of the seller's initial and final offer and the time spent bargaining (p_I, p_F, and Δ_F).

$$c_s = \frac{r(p_I D_F - p_F)}{(1 - D_F)}, \tag{3.1}$$

$$c_b = \frac{r D_F^2 (p_I - p_F)}{(1 - D_F)}, \tag{3.2}$$

$$h = \frac{[p_I(8 + 5D_F - D_F^2) - p_F(5 + 2D_F - D_F^2)]}{3} \tag{3.3}$$

where $D_F = \exp[-r\Delta_F]$. See the chapter appendix. These explicit formulas are derived from Cramton, *supra* note 6; see also the chapter appendix. While these expressions seem algebraically formidable, they capture the strategic intentions of the model. For ex-

Table 3.1 Parameterization of the Bargaining Model by Tester Type[a]

	White Males	White Females	Black Females	Black Males
A. Data on Seller Concessions				
Number of observations	198	63	81	53
Average of initial price, P_I	1,076.9	1,145.9	1,360.8	1,709.6
Average final price, P_F	687.8	740.0	951.2	1,468.1
Average time (in hours) spent bargaining, Δ_F	0.60	0.77	0.59	0.66
B. Estimated Value of Underlying Parameters (holding r constant)[b]				
Seller's bargaining cost (per hour), c_s	560.46	433.11	578.84	207.16
Buyer's bargaining cost (per hour), c_b	592.60	469.53	635.35	331.36
Buyer type's maximum valuation, h	2,868.85	3,017.93	3,462.39	3,792.68
C. Estimated Value of Underlying Parameters (holding c_s constant)[c]				
Discount rate (per hour), r	0.63	0.46	0.52	0.17
Buyer's bargaining cost (per hour), c_b	365.5	308.7	437.0	309.8
Buyer type's maximum valuation, h	2,580.0	2,750.6	3,172.5	3,722.3

[a] For tests that ended in refusal to bargain only.
[b] Calculated by evaluating the function for each individual and averaging the results across all individuals. Assumes that the discount rate is 0.1 per hour for all tester types.
[c] Calculated by evaluating the function for each individual and averaging the results across all individuals. Assumes that the discount rate is set so that the seller's cost is equal to $100 per hour for all tester types.

esting exercise in empirical game theory if it were done once simply to evaluate the general determinants of seller behavior. But as we have shown, by repeating the process with regard to each buyer race–gender type, we can also evaluate alternative causal theories of discrimination. Our estimates of c_s, c_b, and h are shown in panel B of table 3.1 and figures 3.2–3.4 for each of the different buyer groups.

The estimates in table 3.1 stand on a much weaker statistical footing than the regression estimates in table 2.1. The "parameterization" method is extremely crude: in theory, all of the points on the sellers' concession

ample, longer bargaining hours (D_F) imply lower seller costs (c_s) because sellers with lower costs would be willing to haggle longer. This is captured algebraically in equation (3.1) because the derivative of c_s with respect to Δ_F is positive (as shown in equation [3.4]).

$$\frac{dc_s}{dD_F} = \frac{r(p_I - p_F)}{(1 - D_F)^2} > 0. \tag{3.4}$$

curve could be used to identify the sellers' beliefs, but the estimation in table 3.1 uses only three pieces of information about the curve, and even those are only averages. However, because the model makes strong predictions about seller behavior, these three observations (for each tester type) are sufficient to make crude inferences about three seller beliefs. In econometric terms, however, there are no additional degrees of freedom, so it is impossible to assess whether our estimates are statistically significant.

These results should also be interpreted very cautiously because three of the model's assumptions are suspiciously artificial. First, the model makes extremely strong assumptions about the buyer's and seller's knowledge: namely, that the buyer's and seller's per period bargaining costs (c_b and c_s), the discount rate (r), the seller's reservation price ($\$0$) and the distribution of buyer reservation prices (uniformly distributed between zero and h) are all common knowledge.[61] This assumption would fail, for example, if buyers did not know sellers' per-period cost of negotiation. Common knowledge assumptions, however, are often used to solve bargaining games of this type.[62]

Second, the model's assumption that buyer reservation prices are uniformly distributed is highly restrictive. For example, if reservation prices followed a normal, bell-curve distribution, profit-maximizing sellers would need to make more complicated inferences about both the mean and variance of reservation prices.[63] Our use of only three pieces of seller information, however, limits our ability to identify the parameters of other, more complicated, distributions.[64]

Third, the model assumes that the buyer and the seller discount their

---

61. This implies not only that the seller and buyer each knows these values, but that each knows that the other knows, and each knows that the other knows that the other knows, ad infinitum. See Ian Ayres & Barry Nalebuff, Common Knowledge as a Barrier to Negotiation, 44 UCLA L. Rev. 1631 (1997); John Geanakoplos, Common Knowledge, J. Econ. Persp., fall 1992, at 53.

62. See, e.g., Ayres & Nalebuff, *supra* note 61; Cramton, *supra* note 6. But see Robert H. Gertner & Geoffrey P. Miller, Settlement Escrows, 25 J. Legal Stud. 87 (1995) (applying an asymmetric information bargaining model to settlement negotiations).

63. See *supra* text accompanying note 55. As a theoretical matter, the sticker prices on the cars could limit the maximum amount that dealers could use for their initial offer and add another determinant of dealer behavior. But because the average dealer offer was substantially below the average sticker price even for black male testers, sticker prices probably were not a binding constraint.

64. Three observations about the sellers' concession curve cannot be used to identify four underlying parameters—as in trying, for example, to infer both the mean and variance of the buyer reservation price distribution as well as the buyer and seller per period cost.

Fig. 3.2   Estimates of sellers' per-period cost (c_s) of negotiating with different tester race–gender types for varying discount rates (r)

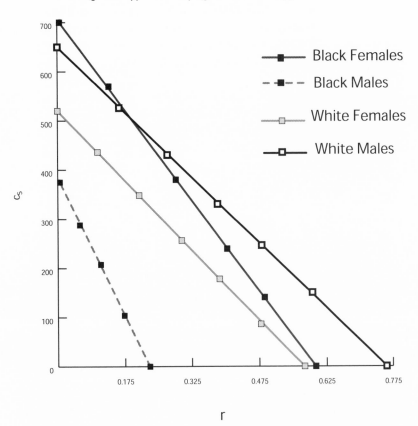

future gains from trade at the same rate.[65] This assumption is suspect because buyers and sellers may have different discount rates. Moreover, as we explore below,[66] it is possible that the seller has different discount rates for particular tester types. Without placing some restriction on the relative values of the discount rate, however, our information about the seller concession curve cannot identify the other underlying parameters.

Because of the nonstatistical estimation procedure and the model's re-

65.   Panel B of table 3.1 assumes a discount rate of 10 percent per hour while figures 3.2–3.4 show the values of c_s, c_b and h for various discount rate values. These discount rates are substantially higher than the pure time value of money, but may be reasonable because they also include the risk that the bargaining could end at any time. See *supra* note 36.

66.   See *infra* note 105 and accompanying text.

strictive assumptions, the estimates of the underlying parameters in table 3.1 and figures 3.2–3.4 cannot be reliably interpreted as unbiased estimates of, for example, the seller's actual dollar cost of bargaining per hour. The parameter estimates, however, may provide some evidence to ordinally rank the sellers' beliefs about different tester types. Ordinal rankings are still useful in assessing the causes of the discrimination. For example, a finding that sellers have *lower* costs of bargaining with black men would point toward consequential animus as a causal theory. Even these ordinal inferences, however, may be fraught with error. The results should be viewed cautiously as a first heuristic step, but along with ancillary regression results (reported below) they provide some insights into why sellers discriminate.

1. Animus-Based Discrimination

Figure 3.2 suggests that sellers have lower per-period costs of negotiating with black males than with any other tester type. Table 3.1 shows that at a discount rate of 10 percent per hour sellers act as if their cost is $560 per hour when bargaining with white males but only $207 when bargaining with black males. Figure 3.2 shows that except when bargaining with black males, the seller bargaining costs with other tester types are basically similar.[67] The sellers' bargaining costs with black males are estimated to be relatively low because sellers made the smallest concessions to black male testers but bargained with them for longer than average. The model predicts that higher bargaining costs would have led sellers to make quicker and more substantial concessions.[68]

These results are inconsistent with associational animus as the cause of discrimination because the sellers are acting as if the cost of associating with white males was highest or second highest among all tester types. These estimates of c_s are, however, consistent with the theory that consequential animus is at least partially responsible for the higher prices offered to black males. As discussed above, disproportionately valuing profits extracted from black males would lead dealers to act as if they had lower "net" costs of negotiation: sellers would hold out longer and make smaller concessions. Indeed, the sellers' slow and small concessions to black males

67. Sellers act as if their cost of bargaining with white females might also be lower. See figure 3.2.

68. In our larger sample, salespeople spent nearly 13 percent longer negotiating with the "minority" testers than with the white males, which casts doubt on salesperson animus as the source of price differences. The average test by a white male lasted 36.2 minutes. The average for the other testers was 40.8 minutes. A t-test reveals that these differences are statistically significant at the 0.001 level.

are consistent with the hypothesis that sellers enjoyed extracting dollars from black males twice as much as extracting dollars from white males.[69]

These estimates of seller bargaining cost provide some evidence of consequential animus, but without more data they cannot identify precisely whose animus influences the seller's behavior. To explore the source of animus—especially the consequential animus that would produce higher offers for black males—we estimated regressions designed to reveal whether the race of a dealership's owner, salesperson, or customers influenced the amount of discrimination. If we assume that black market participants are less likely to have animus against other blacks,[70] then by comparing the effect of, say, the salesperson's race on the amount of discrimination we may be able to isolate the source of the animus. The results of these regressions are reported in table 3.2.

(a) Owner Animus

Table 3.2 includes a dummy variable for minority-owned dealerships as well as an interaction dummy equaling one when both the tester and the owner were black. Neither of these had coefficients that were significant in any of the regressions, indicating that the owner's race did not influence the bargaining outcome and that black testers did not fare better at black-owned dealerships.[71]

---

69. As shown in the chapter appendix, if sellers value black male profits α times more than white male profits, they will act as if their cost of bargaining is $c_{bm} = c_{wm}/\alpha$ (where c_{bm} and c_{wm} are the sellers' cost of bargaining with black males and white males, respectively). The estimates for c_{bm} and c_{wm} in table 3.1 can be used to calculate an estimate for α equaling 2.7 (in other words, 560.46/206.16).

70. For a variety of social reasons, African Americans may also act as if they harbor associational or consequential animus against other African Americans. For example, the bigotry of white consumers might be one reason black male testers were quoted higher prices by black salesmen. If white consumers are reluctant to buy from black salesmen, then to "make their profit quota" black salesmen may be forced to try to earn higher profits from sales to blacks. An economic system of discrimination may thus enlist the victimized class to participate in the discriminatory behavior. See Ayres, *supra* note 2, at 840–41, 847.

71. I used as sources the "Black Pages," an analogue of the Yellow Pages in which firms that are more than 50 percent black owned voluntarily list their businesses, supplemented by a City of Chicago listing of minority-owned businesses. Listing in either source is voluntary, so I may have excluded some black-owned dealerships. I was unable to find any female-owned dealerships in analogous sources. Because there were only nine black-owned dealerships in our sample, these dealerships might have been able to "free-ride" on the market discrimination by charging their black customers a price that reflects the discriminatory premium at white-owned dealerships. It is also theoretically possible that black owners dislike dealing with blacks, but at a minimum this would implicate a nontraditional form of discrimination.

Table 3.2 Regressions of Initial and Final Profits and Markups on Control Variables, Race–Gender Dummies, and Interaction Effects[a] (N = 404; t-statistics in parentheses)

	Initial Profit ($)	Final Profit ($)	Initial Markup (%)	Final Markup ($)
Tester Race–Gender Dummies				
White female (WF)	193.78	225.44	1.79	2.02*
	(1.30)	(1.76)	(1.43)	(2.00)
Black male (BM)	886.18*	889.01*	6.72*	7.06*
	(3.23)	(3.82)	(2.93)	(3.79)
Black Female (BF)	399.67	169.70	3.06	0.98
	(1.60)	(0.79)	(1.47)	(0.58)
Neighborhood Variables				
Suburb (1 = suburb)	−230.04	−221.91	−1.64	−1.51
	(−1.58)	(−1.78)	(−1.34)	(−1.52)
Suburb × black tester	63.64	263.76	0.95	2.61
	(0.25)	(1.22)	(0.45)	(1.53)
Household income × 10⁻³	4.50	−0.08	0.03	−0.001
	(0.79)	(−0.02)	(0.60)	(−0.02)
Percent black in neighborhood	−30.74	117.92	−0.29	0.88
	(−0.12)	(0.54)	(−0.14)	(0.51)
Percent black × black tester	−916.89	−540.93	−7.30	−3.76
	(−1.85)	(−1.27)	(−1.76)	(−1.12)
Other controls				
Tester experience	7.05	5.95	0.05	0.04
	(0.95)	(0.95)	(0.83)	(0.80)
Split	−253.10	−252.93	−1.71	−1.37
	(1.58)	(−1.83)	(−1.28)	(1.25)
First	50.82	127.96	0.17	1.11
	(0.52)	(1.52)	(0.20)	(1.65)
Seller and Interaction Effects				
Minority owner (1 = yes)	446.74	472.22	2.89	3.53
	(1.00)	(1.24)	(0.78)	(1.18)
Minority owner × black tester	−165.10	12.05	−0.17	0.70
	(−0.28)	(−0.02)	(−0.03)	(0.18)
Tester WF, seller WF	−69.39	368.58	−0.89	2.18
	(−0.15)	(0.94)	(−0.23)	(0.70)
Tester WF, seller BM	76.56	−129.69	0.19	−1.22
	(0.26)	(−0.51)	(0.08)	(−0.61)

$Household income × 10^{-3}$

Table 3.2 *(Continued)*

	Initial Profit ($)	Final Profit ($)	Initial Markup (%)	Final Markup ($)
Tester BM, seller WF	427.90	243.44	4.13	2.58
	(1.06)	(0.71)	(1.22)	(0.94)
Tester BM, seller BM	379.60	80.02	3.41	0.92
	(0.95)	(0.23)	(1.02)	(0.34)
Tester BF, seller WF	190.31	248.60	2.02	2.46
	(0.59)	(0.91)	(0.75)	(1.13)
Tester BF, seller BM	464.32	673.29*	3.30	5.54*
	(1.42)	(2.41)	(1.21)	(2.50)
Summary Statistics				
Adjusted R^2	0.26	0.33	0.29	0.39
SSR $\times$ 10^{-3}	256859	187741	17.96	11.78
F-Tests				
White female effect $F(3,367)$[b]	0.78	1.66	0.83	1.79
Black male effect $F(6,367)$	8.07*	14.72*	7.77*	16.64*
Black female effect $F(6,367)$	2.99*	4.12*	3.06*	4.62*

* Significantly different from zero at the 5 percent level.
[a] Other variables included in regression but not shown to save space: constant term, model dummies, Time, day-of-week dummies, and week-of-month dummies.
[b] The numbers in parentheses are the degrees of freedom for the F-test.

There is additional evidence against the importance of owner animus in explaining discrimination. Bigoted owners should be more likely to discriminate against their own employees, with whom they presumably have to associate quite closely over an extended period of time, than against their customers. Given that owners frequently hire nonwhite male salespersons, who comprised 21.3 percent of the salespeople in our sample, it seems implausible that these owners would need a $800 higher markup to compensate them for selling to black male customers.

(b) Salesperson Animus

Salespeople are another possible source of animus. The interaction effects in table 3.2 attempt to test whether the gender and race of the salesperson influenced the amount of discrimination our testers experienced.

The coefficients were largely insignificant, casting doubt on both consequential and associational employee animus as a source of discrimination. As noted earlier, black testers did no worse when buying from white salespersons, and women did not get worse deals when the salesperson was male. In fact, the only statistically significant tester–salesperson interaction suggests black women were systematically quoted higher final prices when buying from black salesmen.[72]

We did find some direct evidence of animus in the form of explicitly racist or sexist statements by salespeople. However, salespeople were more likely to use hostile language when bargaining with white males than with other testers. Salespeople made hostile or demeaning statements in about 4 percent of the white male tests and in just under 3 percent of the nonwhite male tests. And, again, demanding more than $800 seems an implausibly high figure as compensation for having to associate with black male customers.[73] Consequential animus is the more credible theory.

(c) Customer Animus

A dealership's customers should also be considered as a potential source of associational animus against black or women consumers. John Yinger has concluded that in the housing market, for example, discrimination against blacks is motivated by realtors' perceptions that other renters or house buyers dislike having a black neighbor.[74] Similarly, the car dealers' effective per-period cost, c_s, could be higher for black or female consumers if their presence in the showroom made it less likely that others, whites or men, would shop there.

The evidence for associational animus on the part of customers, how-

72. F-tests for the joint significance of the tester–seller interactions were also uniformly insignificant, with the exception of black females in the final markup equation. As mentioned in chapter 1, the pilot study found that women and blacks received higher offers when negotiating against a salesperson of the same race and gender, and that testers were steered toward salespeople of the same race and gender as themselves. See chapter 2, at note 59; Ayres, supra *note* 2, at 819, 840. I detected, however, no evidence of such steering in the larger study.

73. This $800 represents a total "compensation" for animus that is split between the salesperson and the dealership owner. Consider, for example, a scenario in which the salesperson's compensation is $800c$ per hour, where c ($0 < c < 1$) is the salesperson's commission rate. If the disparate treatment were exclusively predicated upon salesperson associational animus, the associational compensation for the salesperson is determined by this commission rate. Yet even for values of c as low as 0.10, it still seems unlikely that the salesperson would demand $80 per hour more for selling to (associating with) a black female than a white male.

74. Yinger, *supra* note 11.

ever, is weak. Concerns about the reactions of other customers should lead dealers to shepherd blacks and women out of the showroom as rapidly as possible to avoid their being seen by other potential customers. Yet white male testers had almost the shortest average negotiating sessions.

There is some evidence of neighborhood-based consequential animus. One-third of Chicago dealerships are located in neighborhoods with a greater than 90 percent black population. Black testers buying in a predominantly black neighborhood might encounter less customer-based consequential animus than in a more racially mixed neighborhood. Table 3.2 estimates that black testers did receive lower final offers when shopping in black, rather than white, neighborhoods. The coefficients on these interaction variables were large, in the range of −$540 to −$900, but were statistically insignificant.[75] Although the signs of the coefficients are consistent with consequential animus, there are compelling theoretical reasons to exclude consequential animus by consumers as a cause of disparate treatment by dealers. Most consumers do not have information about the prices other consumers have received, so they are not in a position to take pleasure in others' misfortune, which is the definition of consequential animus.

2. Bargaining-Cost-Based Statistical Discrimination

Differences in buyers' costs of bargaining (c_b) might also induce seller discrimination. One group of buyers might have high bargaining costs relative to another either because their opportunity costs (lost wages, for example) are high, or because they have a greater dislike for the process of bargaining.[76] The key question in the present context is whether these bargaining costs are correlated with race or gender.

Figure 3.3 depicts our estimates of the buyers' costs of bargaining for

75. Neighborhoods are defined by what the City of Chicago calls "community areas." Each contains thirty to sixty thousand people. "Community areas are defined by the City of Chicago as groups of census tracts. They were first identified in the 1930s by the Social Science Research Council of the University of Chicago. They correspond roughly to informally recognized neighborhoods such as Lakeview and Hyde Park. The boundaries have changed very little since their inception . . . ." City of Chicago, *Chicago Statistical Abstract* 281 (1992).

76. Research in social psychology has yet to reach a firm conclusion about whether there are racial or gender differences in aversion to bargaining. See Jeffrey Z. Rubin & Bert R. Brown, *The Social Psychology of Bargaining and Negotiation* 162–65, 169–74 (1975). Some dealers have suggested that middle-class black males associated the need to bargain with poverty and were thus reluctant to bargain. See Warren Brown, Who Gets the Best Deals on Wheels? *Wash. Post*, Dec. 14, 1990, at F1.

Fig. 3.3   Estimates of the per-period cost of negotiating for different tester race–
gender types (c_b) for varying discount rates (r)

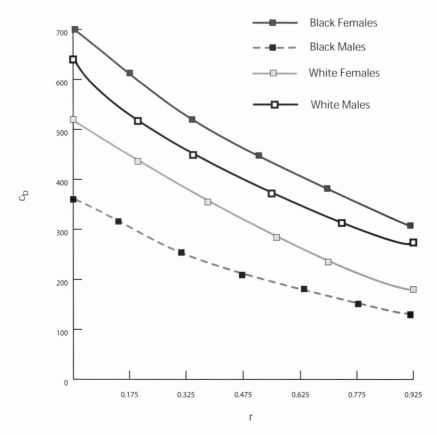

each buyer type. For all discount rates, the ordering of buyers' transaction costs remains stable: black males have the lowest costs and black females have the highest. See panel B of table 3.1(B) for calculations at a representative discount rate.

Figure 3.3 thus provides some evidence that the race and gender discrimination was caused by the sellers' perceptions of differences in buyers' bargaining costs. The higher offers to black female testers might be partially attributable to their higher costs of bargaining. White female and black male testers also had lower estimated bargaining costs (c_b) than white male buyers, which by themselves would have produced lower offers. But our parameter estimates tell us that despite their own lower bargaining costs, white females and black males also faced lower seller bargaining costs as well as less favorable distributions of reservation prices. On balance, the seller bargaining costs and reservation price effects dominated.

Ancillary evidence also suggests that dealers may have attempted to take advantage of women's and blacks' greater aversion to bargaining by making it procedurally harder for these buyer types to purchase a car. First, black males were more often asked to sign purchase orders (40.2 percent versus 27.6 percent for white males)[77] and to put down a deposit (37.7 percent versus 25.6 percent for white males).[78] Black testers were also much more likely than white males to be "bumped"—that is, to have the manager raise a salesperson's offer (7.0 percent versus 1.5 percent).[79]

3. Reservation-Price-Based Statistical Discrimination

A revenue-based explanation for race and gender discrimination is supported by the dealers' general practice of making revenue-based inferences about any customer's willingness to pay. Salespersons have their own term for a kind of statistical discrimination, which they call "qualifying the buyer." "Qualifying" is the process of estimating on the basis of direct observation how much the buyer is willing or able to pay. Sellers make inferences from how the buyer is dressed and what kind of car she is currently driving, and ask the buyer such questions as for example, "How did you get to the dealership?" and "Have you visited other dealerships?" Disparate treatment may stem from the fact that dealers use race and gender as the basis for drawing inferences about consumers' dealer-specific willingness to pay and, more particularly, as the basis for drawing inferences about the potential dealer competition for black and female customers (which as emphasized above has such a strong influence on a consumer's willingness to pay).[80]

---

77. This difference was statistically significant: $\chi_{(1)}^2 = 7.14$.

78. This difference was statistically significant: $\chi_{(1)}^2 = 6.78$.

79. This difference was statistically significant: $\chi_{(1)}^2 = 7.66$.

80. Consumers who "fall in love" with a particular car signal the dealership that it has a monopoly with regard to their business and can charge accordingly. Consumer advocates stress the importance of being able to conceal interest in a particular car. See "How to Buy a New Car and Avoid Dealer Scams" <http://www.carbuyingtips.com/car3.htm> (visited, August 7, 2000); Remar Sutton, *Don't Get Taken Every Time* 84–87 (1986).

One dealer, interviewed informally, espoused a desire to close his showroom in the evening, if his competitors would follow suit. Although forcing consumers to purchase at inconvenient times would seem to reduce the demand for cars, the dealer felt that restricting showroom hours would also reduce the amount of search that buyers undertake. Thus, the dealer believed that although he might not attract as many people to his showroom, he would have less competition for those who did arrive. The Federal Trade

Fig. 3.4 Estimates of reservation price (h) for different tester race–gender types for varying discount rates (r)

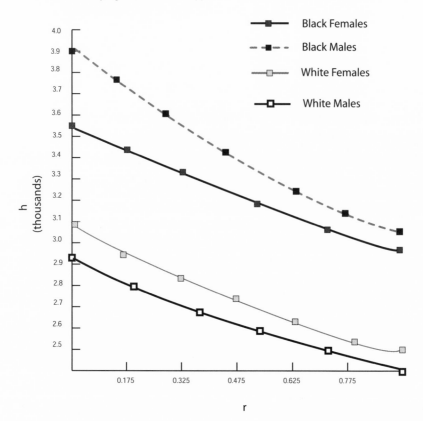

Figure 3.4 estimates sellers' beliefs about tester reservation prices, particularly the implied highest-valuing buyer for each of the different buyer types.[81] For all discount rates, there is a stable ordering of reservation prices

Commission in fact has ruled that "an agreement among car dealers in the Detroit metropolitan area to close dealer showrooms on Saturdays and on three weekday evenings is an unlawful restraint of trade." Detroit Auto Dealers Ass'n, No. 9189 (F.T.C. 1989) (1989 FTC LEXIS 10, *84).

81. That is, the figure depicts implicit seller beliefs about the upper bound (h_i) of buyer reservation prices for each buyer type. Because sellers' behavior does not depend on the other characteristics of the uniform distribution (such as the mean or the lower bound), it is not possible to estimate these parameters using test buyers.

that matches the ordering of initial and final seller offers: sellers believe that black males are willing to pay the most, and white males to pay the least.

Even though the average black person is poorer than the average white male, the upper tail of the valuation distribution for blacks could be higher or fatter because of differences in information or higher costs of search.

(a) Search Costs

Dealership inferences about a consumer's cost of searching will have an important influence on the dealer's assessment of a consumer's willingness to pay. If the dealer believes that a consumer's cost of search are so high that she is unlikely to compare prices at a competitor, then the dealer in effect can infer that it is a monopolist with regard to this consumer and is likely going to be able to extract a much larger revenue (which is to say, price).

Sellers might perceive that race and gender are related to buyers' search costs for several reasons. For example, black consumers might have higher search costs because they are less likely than whites to own a car at the time they are shopping for a new one, and therefore might have more difficulty traveling to multiple dealerships.[82]

The data provide some evidence that sellers considered search costs to be differentially important for different groups of testers. Nonwhite male testers were more than 2.5 times as likely as white males to be asked how they got to the dealership, suggesting that dealers show particular interest in determining whether nonwhite males have substantial opportunities to search. In addition, testers who revealed that they did not own a car had to pay $127 higher markup while those who indicated that they

---

82.   Fred Mannering & Clifford Winston, Brand Loyalty and the Decline of the American Automobile Firms, Brookings Papers on Econ. Activity—Microeconomics 67 (1991). There is a large, uneven, and largely dated marketing literature that does seem to support the notion that "variation in prepurchase search behavior is related to racial differences." See, e.g., Carl E. Block, Prepurchase Search Behavior of Low-Income Households, 48 J. Retailing, spring 1972, at 3, 9. Laurence Feldman and Alvin Starr also conclude that there are differences in search behavior by race although they find that these diminish after controlling for income. Laurence Feldman & Alvin Starr, Racial Factors in Shopping Behavior, *in* A New Measure of Responsibility for Marketing 216 (Keith Cox & Ben M. Enis eds., 1968). For a survey of studies examining differences in car ownership rates by race that concludes that blacks are less likely to own a car than whites, even after controlling for income, see Raymond A. Bauer & Scott M. Cunningham, *Studies in the Negro Market* 156–78 (1970).

had visited other dealerships saved $122, although these results were only significant at a 20 percent level.[83]

The evidence, however, does not uniformly support a search cost explanation. If sellers are sensitive to buyers' search costs in setting prices, we would expect black testers to receive better deals in the suburbs than at urban dealerships. By traveling the substantial distance from Chicago's inner city to the suburbs, where very few blacks live, blacks are in effect signaling to suburban dealers that they are willing and able to undertake an extensive search for a car. Yet contrary to this theory, the regression estimates that blacks negotiating in suburbs faced initial and final offers that were $64 and $264 higher, respectively, than offers given them at city dealerships, although these differences were statistically insignificant.[84] Moreover, initial and final offers for black testers in all-white neighborhoods were $916 and $540 higher than in all-black neighborhoods (but again, this result was statistically insignificant).[85] The presence of black customers in white neighborhoods did not signal a willingness to search that translated into lower dealer offers. But customer animus and search-cost theories of discrimination may not be independent. Neighborhoods with few black residents probably also have stronger animus against black customers, and it is precisely by venturing into such hostile neighborhoods that blacks could most effectively signal that they have low search costs. Thus, the animus effect might swamp, or at least confound, the signaling effect and cause blacks bargaining in such neighborhoods to pay higher prices.

(b) Consumer Information

Dealership inferences about consumer information may also play a role in their assessing a consumer's willingness to pay. If the dealership infers that the consumer does not know the dealer's own cost or what a reasonable markup would be, or even more important that the consumer does not know that it is possible to pay less than the sticker price, then the dealer is likely to infer that the consumer will have a higher (dealer-specific) willingness to pay.

83. These figures were derived by constructing dummy variables for the tests where this information was revealed and including them in the final profit regression in table 3.1. Testers revealed this information only when asked, however, and the dealer's decision to ask the question might not be exogenous to the dealer's final offer.

84. The t-statistics for these coefficients were 0.25 and 1.22, respectively.

85. The t-statistics were only 1.85 and 1.28.

Race or gender may also be correlated with buyers' information about the car market. For example, a Consumer Federation of America survey found that 37 percent of respondents did not believe that the sticker price on a car was negotiable.[86] More important for our purpose is the fact that there were wide differences in consumer knowledge by race and gender. Sixty-one percent of blacks surveyed believed the price was not negotiable compared to only 31 percent of whites. Women were more likely than men to be misinformed about the willingness of dealers to bargain, although the disparities were not as great as between blacks and whites.[87] Because the survey respondents were not limited to people who were actually interested in buying a car, the survey may overstate racial differences in information among the car buying public if nonbuying blacks are relatively less informed than nonbuying whites. But social scientists have found statistically significant "differences in consumer knowledge, skills and attitudes between blacks and whites"—even after controlling actual purchase behavior.[88]

Sellers in our study may have been motivated in part by such informational disparities in quoting higher prices to blacks and women. Dealers were somewhat more likely to volunteer information about the cost of the car to white males than to the other testers, possibly because they believed that white males already had such information. White males were given unsolicited cost information in 55 percent of their tests while all other testers were given such information in 48 percent of tests. The difference was not statistically significant at the 5 percent level, however.

86.   Consumer Fed'n of Am., U.S. *Consumer Knowledge: The Results of a Nationwide Test* (1990); see also Ayres, *supra* note 2, at 856 n.115. Similarly, during interviews conducted in confidential litigation research unrelated to this study, prospective jurors were asked whether "most people pay sticker price for their cars." Twenty percent of those surveyed responded "yes."

But as discussed in chapter 5, increased use of the Internet for research may enhance the quality of consumer information. See, e.g., Gregory L. White, "General Motors to Take Nationwide Test Drive on Web," *Wall Street J.* B4 (Sept. 28, 1998).

87.   See Consumer Fed'n of Am., *supra* note 86, at 8; see also Ayres, *supra* note 2, at 856 n.115. Women were 7.2 percent more likely to answer questions about automobile purchases incorrectly. See Consumer Fed'n of Am., *supra* note 86, at 9.

A belief among black consumers that the sticker price is not negotiable would not be erroneous if black consumers have found that dealers are actually unwilling to bargain with them. The tests conducted in this study, however, indicate that most dealers were willing to make at least some price concessions to black testers.

88.   George Moschis & Roy Moore, Racial and Socioeconomic Influences on Adolescent Consumer Behavior, *in* Proceedings of the American Marketing Association 261 (1981).

What is more significant is that dealers used the sticker price as their first offer to 29 percent of nonwhite males, but to only 9 percent of white male testers.[89] This suggests that sellers believed white males were more knowledgeable than other testers about the possibility of paying less than the sticker prices.

C. The Reinforcing Role of Dealer Competition

Many commentators have argued that competition among sellers will tend to eliminate certain forms of race and gender discrimination against buyers.[90] The following discussion examines how market competition among dealerships may in fact reinforce the opportunities for statistical discrimination.

As a first intuition, competition should be expected to quickly eliminate revenue-based statistical discrimination (because rival dealers would immediately move to undercut any supracompetitive prices offered to high-valuing car buyers);[91] to slowly eliminate animus-based discrimination (because bigoted sellers would be at a competitive disadvantage and so would eventually be driven out of the market); and to never eliminate cost-based statistical discrimination (because no dealer would have a market-based incentive to offer prices that fall below the best estimates of that dealer's actual costs).[92]

---

89. This difference was statistically significant: $\chi_{(1)}^2 = 25.9$.

90. See, e.g., Becker, *supra* note 14, at 38, 70–71 (arguing that competition drives inefficient, bigoted producers from the market). For an enlightening exchange on whether civil rights laws tend to enhance or retard these competitive forces, see John J. Donohue III, Is Title VII Efficient? 134 U. Pa. L. Rev. 1411 (1986); Richard Posner, The Efficiency and the Efficacy of Title VII, 136 U. Pa. L. Rev. 513 (1987); and John J. Donohue III, Further Thoughts on Employment Discrimination Legislation: A Reply to Judge Posner, 136 U. Pa. L. Rev. 523 (1987) [hereinafter cited as Donohue, Further Thoughts].

91. Competition should generally cause sellers to charge a uniform price equal to their cost. Price dispersion and supracompetitive pricing has been observed as a persistent phenomenon in some markets with multiple sellers. See Mark Kelman, Trashing, 36 Stan. L. Rev. 293, 316–17 (1984) (noting that similar Palo Alto gas stations charged disparate prices for full service and that similar Washington, D.C., photographers charged disparate prices for passport photos).

92. Even if car dealers found it to be more "expensive" on average to enter into transactions with black customers (because, for example, of a higher default risk), it might be socially inefficient to allow dealers to discriminate in that cost-based manner. Cost-based statistical discrimination imposes a "tax" on all black consumers regardless of their actual individual characteristics and might discourage blacks from efficiently investing in creditworthiness. See Donohue, Further Thoughts, *supra* note 90, at 533–34; Stewart Schwab, Is Statistical Discrimination Efficient? 76 Am. Econ. Rev. 228, 233 (1986).

The preceding analysis, however, tentatively suggested just the opposite causal ordering. Cost-based statistical discrimination is the least plausible explanation, and revenue-based statistical discrimination is the most plausible. The simple competitive story thus poses a major challenge to the assertion that revenue-based statistical discrimination caused the disparate treatment. In a large city such as Chicago, with hundreds of car dealerships, how could rival dealerships successfully charge individual consumers significantly more than dealership marginal costs?

Intuitively it would seem that the first dealership to advertise fixed prices with reasonable markups should increase its profits because its sales volume would dramatically increase; that dealership should have a competitive advantage. By advertising its (relatively low) fixed prices, the dealership should attract the customers who were (or were about to be) victims of revenue-based statistical discrimination.[93] Chapter 5 recounts the rise (and partial decline) of no-haggle pricing (sometimes also referred to as the "no-dicker sticker") that occurred in the mid-1990s—as well as the current shift toward Internet research and sales. But at the time of this testing in 1990 only a few "mail order" dealerships (such as the National Auto Brokers)[94] advertised and sold at fixed prices. The vast majority of local dealerships almost universally preferred bargaining methods of sale.

As is also more fully explored in chapter 5, there are strong structural reasons why the haggling norm has proven to be so resilient (even when faced by the entrance of no-haggle mavericks). Most important, the incentives for dealers to opt for a high-volume, standard "stated" price strategy may be discouraged by the tendency of dealership profits to be concentrated in a few sales. Price dispersion in new car sales necessarily concentrates dealer profits in a few car sales.[95]

Anecdotal evidence suggests that at some dealerships up to 50 percent of the profits can be earned on just 10 percent of the sales.[96] Profit concen-

---

93. Consumers might also prefer going to a dealership with "stated prices" because they could avoid the costs of bargaining for a car.

94. See, e.g., *Edmund's 1990 New Car Prices* 188–89 (Nov. 1990) (reprinting an advertisement).

95. If homogeneous products are sold without price dispersion, a seller's profits are distributed equally across goods sold. Price dispersion implies, however, that some products are sold for a higher profit. Price dispersion causes a seller's profits to be disproportionately concentrated in its high-markup sales.

96. This evidence comes primarily from confidential conversations with car dealers and salespeople. Chapter 4, however, provides some confirmation based on the concentration of profits in consummated transactions.

trations of this magnitude are crucial in understanding why competition does not eliminate revenue-based price discrimination. From a dealer's perspective, bargaining for cars is a "search for suckers"—a search for consumers who are willing to pay a high markup for whatever reasons.[97] Notwithstanding standard competitive theory, the dealerships are willing to force the majority of consumers to endure frustrating and socially wasteful bargaining in hopes of finding those few high-profit sales that disproportionately contribute to their bottom line.[98] For the dealers, the competitive incentive to move away from bargaining to a stated-price system simply may not be compelling because dealerships would thereby lose the profits from sucker sales. As long as the expected profits from the additional sales at a low markup are less than the profits from high-markup sales, dealers will prefer the bargaining regime.

Even if individual dealers could profitably replace bargained sales with stated price sales, manufacturers may prefer a sales process that allows their dealers as a class to extract the most money from consumers.[99] The manufacturer can powerfully discourage individual dealers from moving to stated-price competition simply by limiting that dealership's supply of cars. Such limitations destroy dealer incentives to commit to a fixed, low-profit markup because stated-price competition is more profitable than the alternative only if a dealership can significantly increase its sales volume.[100]

97. The term *sucker* does not imply that high-markup buyers are irrational or even uninformed. As argued above, see *supra* note 53, a willingness to pay a high markup may be rational given high search costs or a high aversion to bargaining. Echoing the explicit sexual language they used among themselves to talk about female customers, some salesmen use the term *lay-downs* to refer to women who are willing to pay the sticker or near sticker price. See Brown, Sexism in the Showroom? *Wash. Post,* Feb. 12, 1989, at H1, col. 1.

98. See Ayres & Miller, *supra* note 37, at 1068–70.

99. This is especially true if the additional stated-price sales are drawn from the manufacturer's other dealers. In general, manufacturers should prefer the dealer sales process that extracts the largest amount of consumer surplus, because manufacturers should be able to capture those dealership profits through higher wholesale car prices and higher franchise fees. Although it would seem that manufacturers charging a fixed price to dealers would want to encourage dealers to sell a high volume of cars, manufacturers may find that they can reap higher overall profits by charging higher prices to dealers under a relatively low volume bargaining regime than under a higher volume stated-price regime.

100. The reaction of rival dealerships could also reduce the profitability of advertising a stated price. Dealerships that "will not be undersold" could simply match their rivals' advertised price. The first dealership to advertise lower prices might be providing a public service, but if consumers merely use its advertisements to receive matching offers at other dealerships, the first dealership's advertising strategy might not generate a sufficient increase in sales volume to be profitable for that dealership.

The dealers' reliance on high-markup buyers lends additional credibility to the notion that dealership disparate treatment of consumers might be a form of revenue-based statistical discrimination. The dealers' search for high-markup buyers may be tailored to focus on specific racial or gender groups. In their quest to locate high-markup buyers, dealers are not guided by the amount that the average black woman is willing to pay. Rather, they focus on the proportion of black women who are willing to pay close to the sticker price.[101] Even a small difference in the percentage of high-markup buyers represented by consumers of any one race or gender class may lead to large differences in the way dealers treat that entire class.[102] Thus, the previous explanations of racial- or gender-based differences in search costs, information, or aversion to bargaining need not be true for the average members of a consumer group in order for those differences to generate significant amounts of revenue-based disparate treatment. As discussed above, women and minority men not only are more poorly informed than white males, but there is more heterogeneity of "informedness" within nonwhite, nonmale groupings.[103] This higher variance of knowledge within the minority and white female tester groups by itself could explain at least part of the sellers' disparate treatment. Profit-maximizing dealers may rationally quote higher prices to blacks even if the average black consumer in fact has a lower willingness to pay.

101. Although statistical theories of discrimination are often couched in terms of inferences about group means, inferences can also be made about aspects of the probability distribution for a group that can rationally affect behavior. Pedestrians' aversion to young male drivers, for example, need not be based on a belief that the average male youth drives recklessly; the recklessness of merely 5 percent of such drivers would make pedestrians rationally leery of them all. This "search for suckers" analysis is similar to models in which seller behavior turns on the proportion of comparison shoppers in the population. See, e.g., Alan Schwartz & Louis L. Wilde, Intervening in Markets on the Basis of Imperfect Information: A Legal and Economic Analysis, 127 U. Pa. L. Rev. 630, 647–51 (1979).

102. The sensitivity of sellers to the characteristics of a small percentage of high-markup consumers is analogous to the results of game-theory models. See, e.g., David Kreps, Paul Milgrom, John Roberts & Robert Wilson, Rational Cooperation in the Finitely Repeated Prisoners' Dilemma, 27 J. Econ. Theory 245, 245–47 (1982) (explaining that a firm might be rationally sensitive to a low probability that rivals will adopt an irrationally competitive stance). As Eric Rasmusen has summarized:

> The beauty of [this] model is that it requires only a little incomplete information: a small probability [of irrationality]. It is not unreasonable to suppose that a world which contains Neo-Ricardians and McGovernites contains a few mildly irrational tit-for-tat players, and such behavior is especially plausible among consumers, who are subject to less evolutionary pressure than firms.

Rasmusen, *supra* note 29, at 118.

103. See *supra* note 87 and accompanying text.

Although basic economic theory suggests that dealer competition should quickly eliminate price dispersion, dealers in the market for new cars nevertheless sell the same car for different prices. Highly concentrated profits give dealers incentives to search for high-markup buyers through the process of bargaining.[104] In particular, the dealers' search for high-markup buyers may reinforce incentives to discriminate on the basis of race or gender. The concentration of profits is a central pathology of retail car sales and one to which we return in chapter 4.

Conclusion

In sum, this game-theoretic exercise of estimating the causes of discrimination has shown that the sellers' bargaining behavior is broadly consistent with revenue-based statistical inference as a partial cause of the sellers' discrimination: sellers' differential beliefs about the testers' reservation prices track the sellers' initial and final offers. This exercise has also shown that sellers may discriminate against different buyer types for different reasons. Figure 3.4 shows that sellers' discrimination against black females may in part stem from a belief that black females are more averse to bargaining than white males, and figure 3.2 suggests that consequential animus may explain part of sellers' discrimination against black males.

These results, however, must be interpreted cautiously. In order to identify the relationship between the sellers' concessions and the underlying parameters, I have had to make strong assumptions. Under alternative assumptions, the concession data are susceptible to alternative interpretations. Instead of assuming that the discount rate is the same for each buyer type, for example, we might assume a constant seller bargaining cost for the four kinds of testers, and allow the discount rate to vary. Panel C of table 3.1 shows that when we assume a constant seller bargaining cost of $100 per hour, the implicit discount rate for negotiations with black male

104. The pattern of discrimination uncovered in this chapter also creates an opportunity for a different kind of competitive response: entrepreneurs might profitably offer to negotiate on behalf of consumers who might otherwise be forced to pay high markups. This study suggests, for example, that a white male consumer would have a competitive advantage in attaining a lower offer. Several types of transaction costs, however, inhibit the viability of such negotiation services. Consumers may not know the extent to which they might be subject to high markups. Entrepreneurs attempting to market their negotiation services may have a hard time credibly communicating both that a problem exists and that their service provides a solution. After all, a consumer using the service would have difficulty verifying that he or she received a competitive price.

testers is substantially lower than the discount rate for white males—0.17 percent versus 0.63 percent.[105] Even assuming a constant seller bargaining cost, the model's estimates of reservation prices and buyer cost retain the same ordinal ranking, which suggests that our conclusions about statistical discrimination are robust to this alternative assumption.

The argument that revenue-based discrimination best explains the data thus remains impressionistic. The results might best be described as a set of facts in search of a more complete causal theory. Indeed, it may be that simple causal theories of discrimination fail to capture the mutually enforcing nature of multiple causes. To take just one example, greedy but unbigoted salespeople may rationally decide to parrot the discrimination of bigoted salespeople. Thus, if the majority of salespeople in a geographic market charge blacks higher prices because of bigotry, a nonbigoted salesperson might be able profitably to increase his or her commission by matching (or only slightly undercutting) the discriminatory overcharge.

In the end, it may prove impossible to parse out the various elements of animus and rational inferences from irrational stereotypes. No single causal theory may be adequate to explain discrimination against both blacks and women. Whatever its causes, however, the discrimination revealed in this study stands squarely in the face of earlier analysis that rejected the need for discrimination laws concerning the sale of goods. The search for a causal theory, therefore, is not merely an academic exercise. Finding an answer is important because effective governmental intervention should ideally grow out of an accurate theory of market failure.

Appendix 3.A

Peter Cramton shows that the seller's equilibrium strategy can be characterized by a concession function indicating the offers (p) that he would be willing to make (or counteroffers he would be willing to accept) for any given delay (Δ):

$$p(\Delta) = e^{-r\Delta}\left(xb_l + \frac{c_s}{r}\right) - \frac{c_s}{r}, \tag{3A.1}$$

---

105. Because the discount rate can be thought of as the probability that bargaining will exogenously terminate, this might be interpreted to mean that black males have a considerably lower probability of exogenous termination than the other tester types. Under this interpretation, dealers would be willing to hold out longer for a high price with black males because the dealers believe there is a low chance the bargaining will be terminated.

where b_I is the buyer type that is indifferent about accepting the seller's initial offer, and x equals the seller's share of the gains from trading with a buyer of type b_I:[106]

$$x = \frac{1}{2} + \frac{(c_b - c_s)}{2rb_I}. \tag{3A.2}$$

b_I is determined by the first-order condition that maximizes the seller's expected payoff. Assuming that buyers' reservation prices follow a uniform distribution on the interval $[0,b]$, this first order condition is:

$$p_I = xb_I = \frac{3(b - b_I)}{2} - \frac{3(2c_b)^{1/2}(c_b/3 - c_s)}{(2r)^{3/2}(xb_I + c_s/r)^{1/2}} - \frac{c_s}{r}. \tag{3A.3}$$

The buyers' participation constraint completes the model. Buyers whose reservation price is below some critical value, b_F, cannot profitably signal their type, because the transaction costs of delay produce negative buyer payoffs. Anticipating that any gains from trade will more than be consumed in bargaining, these low-valuing buyers will refuse to participate in the game. Sellers can calculate the maximum delay, Δ_F (and associated b_F), after which a rational buyer would be unwilling to bargain:

$$\Delta_F = -\frac{\ln[2c_b/(rb_I + C)]}{2r},$$

where $C = c_s + c_b$. Buyer offers made after Δ_F thus represent out-of-equilibrium behavior (which occurred because our testers followed a bargaining script and were not subject to the same participation constraint). We assume that any seller receiving an offer after a delay greater than Δ_F would believe with probability one that the buyer's reservation price is b_F. Sellers should therefore refuse to make further concessions once the delay reaches Δ_F. The buyers' participation constraint can thus help explain the fact that sellers at times refused to make further concessions when negotiating with our testers.

Combining equations (3A.2) and (3A.3) with the facts that the initial

---

106. See Cramton, *supra* note 6. The term *gains from trade* refers to the amount by which the buyer's value exceeds the seller's. The division of gains under symmetric information was first derived by Rubinstein and is often referred to as the buyer's and seller's "Rubinstein share." Ariel Rubinstein, Perfect Equilibrium in a Bargaining Model, 50 Econometrica 97 (1982).

price $p_I = p(\Delta = 0) = xb_I$ and the final price $p = p(\Delta = \Delta_F)$, it is possible to solve for c_s, c_b and h as functions of the observable variables and r (as shown in equations [3.1]–[3.3], *supra* at note 60).

Consequential Animus. If a seller's payoff might increase by $\alpha > 1$ for each additional dollar secured in negotiations with a disfavored consumer group, the seller will bargain as if her effective per-period cost of bargaining was lower so that $c'_s = c_s/\alpha$. Resolving for the Rubinstein shares, the expression for x in equation (3A.2) would become:

$$x' = (1/2) + (c_b - c'_s)/2rb_I.$$

An increase in consequential animus (rise in α) would thus be reflected in a lower c'_s and a higher seller share of the gains from trade.

CHAPTER 4

Discrimination in Consummated Transactions

Anumber of authors have questioned whether the disparate treatment found in the audit study of dealership offers, reviewed in chapters 2 and 3, provides much evidence of the economic injury born by blacks who in equilibrium might in a variety of ways mitigate its impact. Richard Epstein, for example, has argued:

> [I]n open markets customers are free to select not only their bargaining strategies but also the dealerships they visit. If blacks or women know that they are apt to get a good deal from some small fraction of the market, then they can avoid other, less receptive dealerships and their unattractive offers. How much of the differential found by Ayres would thus have disappeared is hard to say. In addition it may be possible for a buyer to reduce the differentials even further by bringing along a friend, by eliciting a rival offer from another dealer over the telephone. . . . These tactics are of course also open to white males, but given the lower bids that they are able to elicit, they are likely to yield better returns when adopted by others who anticipate that they will be offered higher prices.[1]

1. Richard A. Epstein, Standing Firm, on Forbidden Grounds, 31 San Diego L. Rev. 1, 52–53 (1994).

Epstein is somewhat agnostic (it's "hard to say") about the extent to which consumers might be able to avoid the effects of discrimination by patronizing dealerships that they know to be nondiscriminating, but James Heckman makes a more far-reaching claim:

> [Audit evidence of disparate racial treatment] is entirely consistent with little or no market discrimination at the margin. *Purposive sorting within markets eliminates the worst forms of discrimination.* There may be evil lurking in the hearts of firms that is never manifest in consummated market transactions.[2]

Without benefit of any empirical evidence, Heckman argues a theoretical possibility as an established fact. In essence, Heckman and Epstein are arguing that victim self-help can produce an equilibrium that is "as if" discrimination did not exist. Blacks could receive (almost) the same prices as whites.[3]

---

2. James J. Heckman, Detecting Discrimination, 12 J. Econ. Persp. 101, 103 (1998) (emphasis added). The importance of these kinds of general equilibrium concerns has long been recognized in the labor market context. See, e.g., Peter Siegelman, Racial Discrimination in "Everyday" Commercial Transactions: What Do We Know, What Do We Need to Know, and How Can We Find Out?, *in A National Report Card on Discrimination in America: The Role of Testing* 69 (Michael Fix & Margery Austin Turner eds., 1999); Christopher Flinn & James J. Heckman, Are Unemployment and Out of the Labor Force Behaviorally Distinct States? 1 J. Lab. Econ. 65 (1983); Harriet Orcutt Duleep & Nadja Zalokar, The Measurement of Labor Market Discrimination When Minorities Respond to Discrimination, *in New Approaches to Economic and Social Analyses of Discrimination* 181 (Richard Cornwall & Phanindra Wunnava eds., 1991). John Yinger, Cash in Your Face, 42 J. Urb. Econ. 339 (1997), formalizes the intuition that discrimination by sellers reduces the benefits of additional search by buyers, causing them to accept higher prices or lower quality than they otherwise would. Yinger applies this methodology to the housing market, and finds that the costs of discrimination are roughly $4,000 per minority household per search.

3. Epstein has also criticized the audit approach for the small proportion of observations in which dealers attempted to accept a tester offer:

> [I]n [Ayres'] sample there were apparent contracts (i.e., a verbal agreement on the price that was not binding) in only 25 percent of the cases with white males, and in 15 percent of the cases with the remainder of his sample. The market would be in a state of perpetual turmoil if huge percentages of potential buyers were unable to buy cars at all. A technique of testing that leaves so many incomplete transactions cannot be an accurate replica of a functioning market.

Epstein, *supra* note 1, at 34. This criticism ignores the structure of the audit. The testers were instructed to bargain until the dealership refused to negotiate further or attempted to accept one of their offers. The test focused on the lowest offer the dealer was willing to make either before refusing to negotiate further or in accepting the tester's predetermined offer. We could have had 100 percent of the observations end in a nonbinding verbal agreement (which would have satisfied Epstein's definition) had we merely in-

The audit tests themselves provide powerful evidence that African Americans cannot protect themselves from the effects of discrimination by merely searching for and shifting their consumption to nondiscriminating dealers. An important finding of the audit regression concerns the pervasiveness of discrimination across dealerships. The regressions suggest that black consumers could not protect themselves simply by patronizing minority- or woman-owned dealerships or by striving to bargain with minority and/or women salespeople. At most, there were some statistically insignificant point estimates suggesting that black consumers might reduce the amount of race discrimination they encountered by avoiding suburban dealerships or dealerships located in neighborhoods with a low percentage of minority residents. The point estimates of the regression in table 3.2 indicated that the race discrimination over final offers was $264 worse in the suburbs. But this result was statistically insignificant.[4] And the same regression also suggested that suburban dealerships generally make final offers that are $221 lower than city dealerships.[5] So blacks could only protect themselves against suburban race discrimination by choosing to patronize urban dealerships that discriminate less but charge on average more. Similarly, the regressions suggested that final offers for black testers in all-white neighborhoods were $540 higher than in all-black neighborhoods. But again, this result was statistically insignificant[6] and combined with a point estimate that final offers at dealerships in all-black neighborhoods were generally $118 dollars higher than all-white neighborhoods. As Penelopi Goldberg concluded:

---

structed the testers to accept the dealer's last and lowest offer at the point the salesperson refused to bargain further.

As discussed in chapter 3, we also investigated whether our findings of race and gender discrimination might be linked to the fact that the dealership's final offers were sometimes refusals to bargain further and sometimes acceptances of tester offers. We found that sessions ending in attempted acceptances had an approximately $400 lower final profit than those that ended in a refusal to bargain (and this result was statistically significant). The size of this acceptance effect, however, was the same for all testers. But the fact that sellers are more likely to accept offers from white males actually biases our estimates *against* finding discrimination, however, because acceptances only provide an upper bound for sellers' reservation prices. That is, in those cases where dealers attempted to accept an offer from a white male tester, the dealers might have been willing to make an even lower offer, which would have increased our measure of discrimination.

4. The t-statistic was only 1.22.
5. The t-statistic was only −1.78.
6. The t-statistics were only 1.85 and 1.28.

[The audit] experiment offers some direct evidence on the issue [of whether purposive sorting by testers mitigated the effect of dealership disparate treatment]: testers in the controlled experiment visit various dealerships in the Chicago area, some of which are located in poorer areas or in black neighborhoods, yet there is no evidence of any difference in the treatment minorities receive in such locations.[7]

In short, our testing of over four hundred dealerships in Chicagoland found pervasive prejudice. There were no statistically significant "safe harbor" dealerships where our black testers could confidently go and uniformly bargain for a deal as good as white testers received.[8]

Still the audit does not exclude the possibility that minority purchasers might have been able to get a better deal at the same dealership if they had employed a different bargaining strategy. It is important to emphasize that forcing these minorities to use a different type of negotiation might itself represent an important type of race discrimination. This is especially true if the alternative path to a good deal was significantly more onerous. If whites need only bargain for four hours to negotiate a low markup, but blacks must negotiate for eight hours, then a finding that blacks in equilibrium did not pay more for cars would not mean that blacks were uninjured by the dealerships' disparate treatment. However, it might as a theoretical matter be possible that the dealership does not require more onerous bargaining but merely different bargaining by blacks and whites: whites may be penalized if they speak in a black voice and vice versa. This "separate but equal" possibility would still be a form of disparate racial treatment, but the harms from discrimination would be more contestable.[9]

Accordingly, it is useful to test whether blacks pay more in actual consummated transactions. Actual sales of course are not controlled tests and while multivariate regressions might control for a handful of purchaser characteristics, it is, as a practical matter, impossible to econometrically control after the fact for the myriad ways that purchasers might bargain. An analysis of consummated transactions, therefore, does not provide in-

7. Penelopi Goldberg, Dealer Price Discrimination in New Car Purchases: Evidence from the Consumer Expenditure Survey, 104 J. Pol. Econ. 622, 643 (1996).

8. A possible exception to this might be the so-called no-haggle dealerships, discussed in chapter 5.

9. The social meaning of separate but equal regimes still can work substantial injury on traditionally subordinated people. See Jed Rubenfeld, Textualism and Democratic Legitimacy: The Moment and the Millennium, 66 Geo. Wash. L. Rev. 1085 (1998).

dependent evidence of disparate treatment. A finding that blacks pay more than whites does not—by itself—indicate that dealerships engage in race-based bargaining. Dealerships might bargain uniformly with all potential customers—conceding at a uniform rate against all potential purchasers—with white customers on average holding out for better deals than black customers. Instead, a finding of disparate transaction prices would at a minimum be evidence that the dealerships' decision to haggle (as opposed to the no-haggle policies of Saturn and others discussed in chapter 5) have a disparate impact on black purchasers. But when combined with the proceeding evidence of disparate treatment in dealership offers, a finding that black purchasers pay more on average than white purchasers suggests that neither (1) purposive searching nor (2) alternative (and possibly more onerous) bargaining nor (3) dropping out of the market eliminates the effects of racially disparate dealership offers.

This chapter analyzes two different data sets of consummated transactions. In the first section, I respond to Penelopi Goldberg's analysis of the Census Bureau's Consumer Expenditure Survey (CES) of approximately thirteen hundred new car purchasers drawn randomly from the nation. In the second section, I analyze approximately nine hundred new car purchasers from the Sutherlin Mazda new car dealership in Atlanta. The CES data has the advantage of being based on a national sample of purchasers, but, I will argue, suffers from severe errors in the measurement. The Atlanta data measures more directly the dealerships' underlying profits on financing and the vehicle itself, but is limited to a single dealership in a single city (and, as discussed below, may be subject to various sample selection problems because of its production as part of adversarial litigation).

The chapter's thesis is that the consummated transaction data sets are consistent with audit study findings that dealerships offer higher prices to black consumers. Both the CES and Atlanta data on actual purchases shows that whites pay lower average prices than blacks. Moreover, the size of the differentials are broadly similar. While the racial price differences are not statistically significant in Goldberg's analysis of the CES data, I argue that this is a function of the noisiness of the data. In the less noisy audit studies and in the less noisy Atlanta purchases data, we observe similar coefficients and smaller standard errors, which allow us to statistically identify the racial differentials as being statistically significant. After discussing the CES and Atlanta data sets in turn, the chapter concludes with a meta-analysis of the consummated purchases and audit data sets.

Consumer Expenditure Survey

Spurred by the initial publication of the audit data presented in chapter 2, Penelopi Goldberg used data from the Consumer Expenditure Survey (CES) to undertake the first analysis of racially disparate treatment in consummated transactions. The CES data set is created by the Bureau of Labor Statistics to compute the Consumer Price Index. Each quarter around forty-five hundred households are interviewed and asked questions about their income and expenditures—including questions about their purchases of cars. For the years 1983–87, Goldberg created a data set of approximately thirteen hundred reliable new car purchases. She constructed a measure of the discount from the dealer's sticker price and regressed this variable on a host of consumer characteristics including race and gender. The results of her core regressions using race and gender as coefficients are shown in table 4.1.

Goldberg interprets these coefficients as offering no evidence of racial price disparities: "The results are quite different from the ones reported in Ayres [the pilot study] and Ayres and Siegelman [reported in chapter 2].

Table 4.1   Estimated Price Premium over White Males by Purchaser Demographic Group

Demographic Group	National CES Consummated Sales (Goldberg)
White females	129
	(117)
	[244]
"Minority" females	426
	(525)
	[28]
"Minority" males	$274
	(263)
	[39]
Adjusted R^2	0.14

Source: Goldberg, *supra* note 7, table 2, col. 1. Standard errors in parentheses. Number of observation in brackets. A number of other right-hand variables are not reported to save space.

Variables referring to race and sex have no explanatory power."[10] Goldberg, however, does not interpret the results as casting doubt on the audit findings of disparate treatment. Moreover, she expressly rejects the Epstein/Heckman hypothesis that purposive searching could eliminate the impact of disparate treatment by even a large majority of dealerships. As noted above, Goldberg accepts the audit evidence that there were no "safe harbor" dealerships for blacks to patronize in order to avoid discrimination. Her attempt rather is to reconcile the audit and the CES results by proposing a bargaining explanation based on racial differences in the variance of reservation prices:[11]

> [I]f the reservation price distribution for blacks is more spread out than the corresponding distribution for whites, then certain plausible parameter values generate a bargaining process with the following characteristics: (1) First-round offers are higher for blacks than for whites. (2) At the equilibrium, low-value blacks receive lower final offers than low-value whites. (3) High-value blacks receive higher final offers than high-value whites.[12]

Under this theory, dealers may still offer black consumers initially higher prices and still produce an equilibrium where the average prices paid by blacks and whites are the same. Goldberg supports her reservation price variance theory by showing that in the CES data minority purchasers have a statistically significant higher variance of sticker discounts than nonminorities.[13] She also uses 10 percent and 90 percent quantile regressions to show that minority purchasers have more dispersed prices than nonminorities. Under the reservation price variance theory, the dealers still engage in disparate racial treatment, but the race-conscious selling strategy favors blacks with low reservation prices (relative to whites) while harming blacks with relatively high reservation prices.

While Goldberg's attempt to reconcile the two results is admirable, I believe a simpler and more persuasive explanation is that the noisiness of her data and its small sample size did not allow her to identify the statistical

10. Goldberg, *supra* note 7, at 624.

11. As discussed in note 5 of chapter 3, a buyer's reservation price is the maximum amount she would be willing to pay a particular dealership for a particular type of car.

12. Goldberg, *supra* note 7, at 645.

13. The variance of minority discounts is 1.45 times larger than the variance of whites. Id. at 646.

significance of positive increments by which minority prices exceeded white prices. Even though Goldberg claims that her results are "quite different" from both the pilot audit and the regressions reported in chapter 2, the size and sign of the coefficients are instead quite similar. Goldberg estimates that white women pay $129 more than white men, while in chapter 2 (table 2.1) we estimated a $216 coefficient for the white female differential on final profits—and the original *American Economics Review (AER)* article (which uses a slightly restricted sample of paired observations) by coincidence reports the exact same differential of $129.

Later in her article, Goldberg claims that "[o]nly the parameter estimates referring to white females seem to be in line with Ayres & Siegelman's findings,"[14] but the coefficients for black females are also of similar magnitude. Goldberg estimates the black female differential to be $426, while in chapter 2 the differential is estimated to be $465 (and the original *AER* estimate was $404). The only difference with regard to the minority female coefficients in these studies is not their sign or size, it is merely that Goldberg's coefficient is not statistically different than zero, while the audit coefficient is. But Goldberg is wrong to characterize this result as being very different from the ours. She certainly cannot reject the hypothesis that her estimate of $426 is the same as either of our audit estimates. Failing to reject that the differential is zero does not imply that the true differential is more likely to be zero than the audit estimate. Indeed, her data suggest the opposite is true: there is more evidence in favor of the hypothesis that black women pay $400 more than white males than for the hypothesis that they pay the same amount.

The only estimated differential that is of a different magnitude concerns black males. Goldberg estimates a $274 differential (above white males), while chapter 2 reports a $1,133 differential (and the *AER* reported a $1061 differential). But her claim that her results are different than both the *AER and* the pilot study runs into a little trouble, because the pilot study reported a similar black male differential of $283. The difference in pilot study and full audit in estimating the black male differential is a troubling issue discussed in chapter 2 (and discussed later in this chapter in connection with the Atlanta results). But what is clear is that the point estimates for minority purchasers are consistently hundreds of dollars above the white males. What is crucial for Goldberg's interpretation is that the minority male and minority female differentials are not statistically

14. Id. at 641.

significant from zero. This is what drives her to characterize her results as "quite different" from the audit study.

But a close analysis of the quality of CES data indicates instead that Goldberg's estimates may not be statistically different than zero simply because her data is too imprecise to accurately measure the racial differentials. Orley Ashenfelter was the first to suggest this alternative interpretation. He concluded that

> [Goldberg's article] basically has results similar to yours—except with much larger sampling errors, which is unsurprising given the noisy data set she uses. Early on I suggested that she send the paper to the *AER* as a confirmation of your results![15]

The remainder of this section takes a closer look at Goldberg's methodology and her results to argue that Ashenfelter's "noisy data" hypothesis is a more persuasive way to reconcile the CES and the audit data.

First, Goldberg's tests suffer from aggregating different racial groups together. While the audit study tested for disparate treatment of blacks, the CES data allowed Goldberg to test only whether "minorities" paid higher prices. And for this purpose, a "minority" was defined to be black, American Indian, Aleut, Eskimo or other. Whites, Asians, and Pacific Islanders were grouped together as "White" and there is some uncertainty whether Hispanics were included in the minority definition as "Other" or as part of the "White" definition.[16] If different racial groups encounter different degrees of discrimination, then the aggregation of these groups by itself would increase the sampling error of estimating a single "minority" coefficient. Thus, from the outset there is an important difference in comparing black (male and female) differentials with "minority" (male and female) differentials.

Second, there were very few minorities in the CES data set. While Goldberg's car purchases data set contained a total of 1,279 observations, only 3 percent of the purchasers were minority males and only 2 percent were minority females. Moreover, it is unclear what percentage of these were black. In a footnote, Goldberg reports that "[i]n other regressions, the minority variable was split into the various race categories reported in

---

15. Letter from Orley Ashenfelter to Ian Ayres (July 17, 1996).

16. My information on the racial composition of the CES data was generously provided by Goldberg.

the CES, with no change in the results."[17] But with so few observations on the individual races, it is hardly surprising that Goldberg was unable to produce statistically significant results. Indeed, the aggregation of multiple races combined with the small number of minority observations by itself could easily explain Goldberg's inability to produce statistically significant minority coefficients.

Third, Goldberg's data is based on "head of household" surveys that "were collected as long as 3 months after the actual transaction took place, and are subject to errors of recall or memory that add noise to the price and other variables of interest."[18] Although the CES are *derived* from actual transactions, they are not true "transactions prices," but are based on household heads' recollections of what was paid for the car. But the survey respondent may not know or remember how much was paid, or may intentionally coverup having paid too much. And as Goldberg acknowledges, her approach assumes that the race and gender of the household head is the same as the race and gender of the person(s) who bargained for the car itself.

Fourth, Goldberg uses a necessarily imprecise measure of dealership profits. Unlike the audit data that used markup estimates (comparing actual dealership offers written contemporaneously by testers with detailed estimates of dealership cost), Goldberg estimates the discount from the sticker price. This is a Herculean task that requires the manipulation of ten underlying estimates:

$$\text{Discount} = [\text{Base Model List Price} + \text{Option List Price} + \text{Destination Fees}$$
$$+ \text{Dealer Prep Fees} + \text{Other Dealer Specific Costs}]$$
$$- [(\text{Down Payment} + \text{Principle Borrowed} - \text{Extra Charges})/$$
$$\text{Sales Tax Rate} + \text{Trade-In Allowance}]$$

The first bracketed term on the right-hand side is Goldberg's estimate of the dealer's sticker price and it is plagued by errors in identifying the base model and particular car options (which are often unobservable).[19] The

17. Goldberg, *supra* note 7, at 637 n.18.

18. Siegelman, *supra* note 2.

19. Goldberg explains that her approach "treats unobserved options as part of the error term. To the extent that the purchase of these additional features is uncorrelated with the explanatory variables on the right-hand side, the estimation results are consistent." Goldberg, *supra* note 7, at 630. But, of course, if blacks tend to buy no frills cars with fewer unreported options, Goldberg will underestimate black list prices and, consequently, the amounts of discrimination.

second bracketed term is Goldberg's convoluted estimate of the net transaction price; if anything it is even noisier than the estimate of dealer sticker. Goldberg implicitly assumes that both financing and trade-ins were at cost. This is important because 83 percent of the CES car purchasers financed their cars through the dealership, and 50 percented traded in a used car in conjunction with the new car purchase. If the dealers systematically packed transaction profits into minority financing or trade-ins, then Goldberg's results could understate the amount of discrimination. Or more neutrally, if the dealerships sometimes shifted a constant profit into the finance or the trade-in component of the deal, then we might see larger standard errors in the CES than were seen in the audit study (where trade-ins and dealer financing were expressly taken off the table by the tester script).[20]

An analysis of regression results also suggests the noisiness of the data. To begin, Goldberg reports an adjusted R-squared of only 14 percent, while the audit studies can explain more than twice the variance in the regressor (with adjusted R-squared's ranging from 33–44 percent).[21] And Goldberg's finding that first-time buyers receive systematically "better deals" is suspect. Anecdotal evidence and theory strongly suggest that such buyers are easy marks for salespeople. Indeed, analysis of the pilot study suggests that testers who revealed (under direct questioning) that they did not own a car were asked to pay $337 more,[22] but Goldberg estimates that such first-time buyers were asked to pay $444 less (and the result was statistically significant). It is also surprising that in such a large data set that none of the financial or demographic variables (value of financial assets, after-tax income, college education) were statistically significant. A small part of this may also be due to the author's decision to report white heteroskedastic-consistent errors that are systematically larger than normal ordinary least squared (OLS) estimates and thus tend to reduce the tests of significance.

Goldberg's own "reservation price variance" theory emphasizes that the regression residuals for minority purchasers are larger than for white

20. Because the CES data does not disclose the purchaser's residence, Goldberg was also forced to use a tax rate that was the probabilistic (weighted average) tax rate for the region.

21. It should also be noted that Goldberg's graphs indicate that a substantial proportion of her observations have negative discounts—indicating that the car was sold above its original sticker price. This suggests some errors in measurement as well.

22. See Ian Ayres, Fair Driving: Gender and Race Discrimination in Retail Car Negotiations, 104 Harv. L. Rev. 817, 848 (1991). The result was statistically significant at the 8 percent level.

purchasers. She contends that this great variance can explain both why the audits show initial higher offers to minorities and why minorities may not pay more on average. But reservation cost variance theory does not do a good job explaining why discrimination against minorities persisted throughout the bargaining process in the audit tests. The audit data uncovered not just initial higher offers but higher final offers. The tested dealerships—contrary to the reservation price variance theory—were not willing under either the split-the-difference or the fixed-concession strategy to let the black testers bargain down to the lower price. Furthermore, contrary to the prediction of the reservation price variance theory, the dealers were more likely to end the negotiation by refusing to bargain further when bargaining with black testers. But if the dealers believed blacks to have more variable reservation prices, we would expect dealerships to be willing to bargain longer with blacks to allow low-valuing blacks to credibly signal their reservation price.[23]

A more convincing interpretation is simply that the differences in the statistical significance of the CES and auditing data arises because, although we are both measuring the same underlying parameter(s), Goldberg is doing so with data that are substantially noisier than the audit studies. She acknowledges this possibility herself:

> The possibility that measurement error is responsible for the standard errors of race and gender parameters cannot be eliminated, yet it is hard to explain why measurement error would make all socioeconomic characteristics insignificant while most of the parameter estimates referring to market, transactions or model specific variables have the expected signs and are highly significant.[24]

As already noted, first-buyer dummy does not have the expected sign; the insignificance of the financial variables and the low R-squared are all indicia of measurement errors. More important is that the imprecision in the very aggregated definition of "minority" when combined with the paucity of observations combine to make the measurement error hypothesis especially compelling.

Still the difference in magnitude of the black male coefficient is trou-

---

23. It should be also noted that while Goldberg claims her theory works for "plausible" parameter values, she does not fit her data to a model as was done in chapter 3.

24. Goldberg, *supra* note 7, at 642–43.

bling. Fortunately, I have gained access to another data source on transaction prices from an individual dealership in Atlanta that allows an alternative look into the actual workings of the retail car market. It is to this data that I now turn.

II. Atlanta Dealership Transaction Prices

Just as Goldberg's article in part was a response to my previously published *American Economics Review* article, the data analyzed in this section was created in part because of a previous publication in *Harvard Law Review* concerning the original pilot study. An Atlanta attorney, Edward D. Buckley III, in the course of interviewing former car salespeople of Sutherlin Mazda in Conyers, Georgia (a suburb of Atlanta), was told that the dealership was pressuring the salespeople to discriminate against African American customers. Buckley remembered reading press accounts of the original *Harvard Law Review* article, which he then proceeded to read for himself. Buckley ended up filing a class action lawsuit on behalf of black customers against the dealership. As part of his case preparation, Buckley collected sales and commission receipts from the dealership's salespeople for more than eight hundred car sales.[25] This transaction data forms the core of this section's analysis.[26]

The sales and commission data from the Atlanta-area car dealer has several advantages over the CES data. It expressly states not only the total vehicle profit, but breaks down this profit stemming from dealership financing and the profit coming from the vehicle sale itself. It expressly states the transaction price for the vehicle sale as well, making it possible to deduce the dealership's vehicle cost.[27] The data also indicates whether there was a trade-in but (as with the CES data) not the dealership's profit (or loss) on the trade-in. The Atlanta data also has a much higher percentage of black purchasers: 49 percent of the purchasers are black (and 46 percent are female)—so there is much more information about the experience of black purchasers in this sample.

Although the data set has information on sales for a number of years (1990–95), that information is from only a single dealership in a single

25. See Tim O'Reiley, Race-Based Car Pricing Charged: Buyers Attempt Class Action against Sutherlin, *Fulton County Daily Rep.*, May 8, 1996, at 1.

26. I discuss the legal implications of the suit in chapter 5.

27. Dealership cost = sale price − vehicle profit.

city. Moreover, the data was produced by potentially biased salespeople (who were also pursuing a lawsuit against the dealership). The salespeople might have censored the data to produce more discriminatory results. More important, salespeople provided the race of the consumers from memory, which might have been faulty or intentionally biased (so as to report all high-markup sales as "black").[28] To explore this worrisome possibility, I informally audited the raw data comparing the zip code of the purchaser (which was often indicated on the original sale receipt) to the salesperson's recollection of race to see if black and white consumers tended to live in predominantly black and white neighborhoods. While my investigation did not rise to the level of sophisticated geocoding that has been undertaken in other contexts,[29] I did not uncover any tendencies that might taint the data. It may also be worth noting that the purchasers who were reported as being "black" often had first and last names that are particularly common among African Americans (in comparison to the "white" names that were more likely to signal European ethnic origin).[30] In sum, while there are some dimensions on which the Atlanta data is more limited than the CES data and possibly more infected by adversarial bias, on balance it seems to provide data to test for racial disparities in pricing that is at least as informative, and probably much more powerful, than that of the CES.

Table 4.2 reports the results of the simplest regressions testing for racial and gender disparities. The regressions show a consistent pattern that white females receive approximately the same deals as white males while black male and black female testers pay substantially higher profits. The total profits of white female purchasers is only $9 more than that of white males—but unsurprisingly this result is not statistically significant from zero. Total profit paid by black males is $837 more, however, and the total

28. I coded gender based on purchasers' first names. However, because some names (e.g., "Pat") do not reliably indicate sex, there were missing purchaser-gender values for 66 out of 898 transactions. In what follows, I have dropped these missing values from the analysis. But I can also report that none of the results change if the additional observations (and a dummy for the missing gender values) are included in the regressions.

29. See, e.g., Commission for Racial Justice, United Church of Christ, *Toxic Wastes and Race in the United States: A National Report on the Racial and Socio-Economic Characteristics of Communities with Hazardous Waste Sites* 2–3 (1987); Richard Seltzer, John M. Copacino & Diana Roberto Donahoe, Fair Cross-section Challenges in Maryland: An Analysis and Proposal, 25 U. Balt. L. Rev. 127 (1996).

30. See, e.g., Richard Delgado, The Colonial Scholar: Do Outsider Authors Replicate the Citation Practices of the Insiders, but in Reverse? 71 Chi.-Kent. L. Rev. 969 (1996) (relying in part on racial inferences of names).

Table 4.2 Profit and Markup Regressions Detailing Basic Racial–Gender Disparities

Purchaser Type	Vehicle Profit	Finance Profit	Total Profit	Vehicle Markup	Finance Markup	Total Markup
Constant	229.16*	504.69*	526.25*	.0258*	.0431*	.0510*
	(45.84)	(48.95)	(64.43)	(.0064)	(.0052)	(.0079)
White female	−22.94	57.70	9.17	−.0029	.0088	.0027
	(74.14)	(79.32)	(104.21)	(.0103)	(.0084)	(.0128)
Black male	405.04*	470.79*	836.81*	.0534*	.0439*	.0931*
	(72.32)	(72.16)	(101.65)	(.0100)	(.0077)	(.0124)
Black female	504.99*	589.01*	1,018.40*	.0614*	.0566*	.1098*
	(67.73)	(68.18)	(95.21)	(.0094)	(.0072)	(.0116)
N	831	551	831	822	544	822
R²	0.09	0.15	0.17	0.08	.135	.148

Note: Standard errors in parentheses.
* Significant at the 1 percent level.

profit paid by black females is $1,018 more than that of white males. And these results are highly statistically significant (far beyond the 1 percent level). The total markup regressions correspondingly show that black male markups are 9.3 percent higher and black female markups are 11.0 percent higher than the markups for white male purchasers.

The table also shows that the disparate total profits stem from disparities both in vehicle and financing profits. For example, the dealership vehicle profits from black females are $505 higher than their profits from white male purchasers; and the dealership's financing profits (from those five-hundred-odd people who financed) are $589 higher for black female relative to white male purchasers. Again these results are highly significant.[31] Black purchasers were much more likely to pay high profits. Only 2.2 percent of white male purchasers were part of the 10 percent highest profits, while 14.6 percent of black male and 20 percent of black female purchasers were represented in this category of most profitable sales. This means that black males were 6.5 times more likely than white males to pay the highest decile of profits; black females were 8.9 times more likely to do so.

The different distributions of profits for the different purchaser types are graphically displayed in histogram bar charts of figures 4.1. Panel (a) of this figure dramatically illustrates the similarity of the white male and white female profit "bell curves," while panels (b) and (c) show dramatic differences between the white male and both the black male and black female profit distributions.

The data also supports my "anecdotal" assertion of chapter 3 that "at some dealerships up to fifty percent of the profits can be earned on just ten percent of the sales." In this data set, 50 percent of the dealership's profits come from 17.2 percent of its most profitable sales. And the profits stemming from white male and white female purchasers are even more concentrated with 12.5 percent of the most profitable white male purchasers generating 50 percent of the white male profits and with just 11.6 percent of the most profitable white female purchasers generating 50 percent of the white female profits. Black profits are more uniformly elevated and therefore relatively less concentrated with 21.4 percent and 25.0 percent of black male and black female purchasers, respectively, generating 50 percent of the profits coming from that tester type.

The analysis so far has only explored race–gender differences in pricing. It is also possible to assess whether other aspects of the transaction

---

31. Note the total profit coefficients are not merely the sum of the vehicle and financing profit coefficients, because not all purchasers use dealership financing.

Figure 4.1   Distribution of total gross profits for different purchaser types

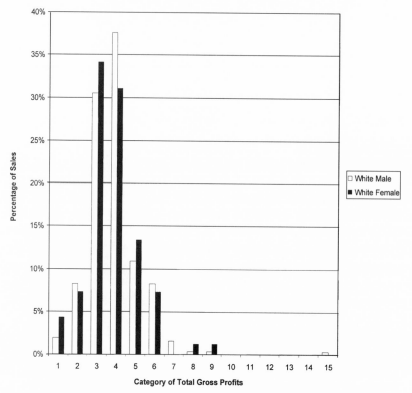

(a) Comparing total gross profits of white male and white female consumers

are "gendered" or "raced." To this end, I ran logit regressions testing whether the race and gender characteristics of the purchaser were correlated with various aspects of the transaction. The regressions indicate that black men and women, respectively, were 55 percent and 37 percent more likely (than white males) to buy a used car, and that black men and black females were 73 percent and 70 percent more likely (than white males) to finance their purchases at the dealership. These differences were statistically significant at (at least) the 5 percent level, while the white female differential in both comparisons was small and statistically insignificant. There were no race or gender differences in purchasers' propensity to trade in a car as part of their purchase transaction. And controlling for the used/ new status of the purchased car, there were no race or gender differences

Figure 4.1 *(Continued)*

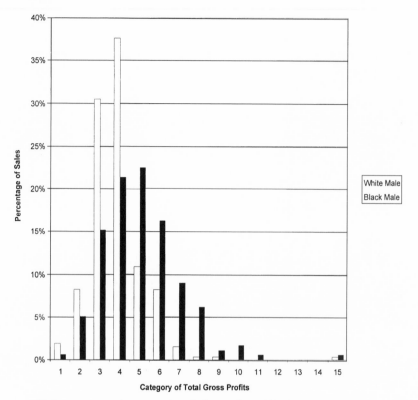

(b) Comparing total gross profits of white male and black male consumers

in the dealership's cost of the cars purchased.[32] So there is no evidence that different types of purchasers were steered to particularly high- or low-cost models.

There was, however, interesting evidence of steering purchaser types to particular sales people. A chi-square analysis with 9 degrees of freedom equaling 42.5 strongly rejects the hypothesis that the race and gender of purchasers is independent of the salesperson's identity. To further investigate a possible motive for such steering I undertook to rerun the total profit regression of table 4.2, adding a "Specialization Percentage" variable that equals the percentage of a particular purchaser type encountered by the

32. Dealer's cost was calculated as "sales price" minus "vehicle profit."

Figure 4.1 *(Continued)*

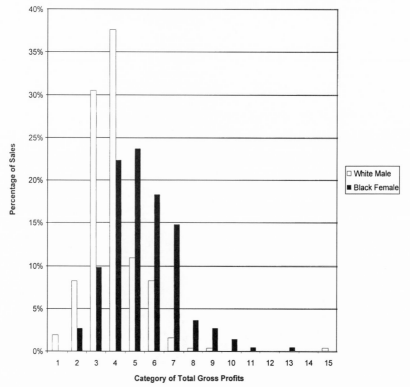

(c) Comparing total gross profits of white male and black female consumers

particular salesperson. For example, if a black female purchased from the second salesperson (referred to in later regressions as "S2") then the "Percentage" variable would take on a value of 41 percent, representing the percentage of that salesperson's customers who were black females. I also created four additional percentage variables—by interacting the purchaser type dummies with the "Percentage" variable. The results are reported in table 4.3.

These regressions suggest that purchasers dealing with a salesperson who specializes in your type of customers produces systematically higher profits for the dealership. The $1,572 coefficient on "Specialization Percentage" in the first regression indicates that if you buy from a salesperson who makes 10 percent more of his sales to purchasers of your race and gender (than the average salesperson) you are likely to pay a $157.2 higher

Table 4.3 Test of Whether Salespeople Who Specialize in Negotiating with a Particular Type of Purchaser Garner Higher Profits

Regressands	Total Profit ($)	Total Profit ($)
Constant	−4.34	372.91
	(220.05)	(431.63)
White female	224.12*	−319.33
	(134.39)	(779.42)
Black male	1094.26***	558.05
	(99.55)	(497.74)
Black female	1016.34***	758.48
	(123.85)	(573.89)
Specialization percentage	1571.83**	—
	(623.50)	
White male × specialization percentage	—	454.26
		(1,264.43)
White female × specialization percentage	—	2399.50
		(3,206.11)
Black male × specialization percentage	—	1037.32
		(1,656.52)
Black female × specialization percentage	—	2,121.29***
		(821.95)
N	831	831
R^2	0.17	0.17

Note: Standard errors in parentheses.
*   Significant at the 10 percent level.
**   Significant at the 5 percent level.
*** Significant at the 1 percent level.

profit.[33] The regression reported in the right-hand column of table 4.3 breaks down the result by specific purchaser type. There we see that the purchaser-specific "Specialization Percentage" coefficients are all estimated to be positive, but that only the steering coefficient for black females is statistically significant.[34]

33.   Because all of the salespeople were African American men, it was impossible to test, as in the original pilot study, whether purchasers are steered to salespeople of their own race and gender who consequently give them systematically worse deals. See Ayres, *supra* note 22, at 833.

34.   The steering result is pronounced and correlates sufficiently with the purchaser's race and gender to render these purchaser-type coefficients statistically insignificant.

To get an even more particularized view of the determinants of dealership profit, I ran a series of nested regressions adding a series of additional variables to the purchaser-type characteristics. In the simpler regressions (reported in columns 1, 3, and 5 of table 4.4), I added variables concerning core transaction characteristics. To test whether dealership profits were related to the dealership's underlying cost (in a potentially nonlinear way), I included both the dealership's cost and the dealership's cost squared.[35] I also included dummy variables indicating whether the consumer was buying a used (=1) or new (=0) car; whether the transaction included a trade-in sale (=1) or not (=0); and whether the purchaser used dealer financing (=1) or not (=0).[36]

In the fuller regressions (reported in columns 2, 4, and 6 of table 4.4), I tested whether the dealership earned different profits on used cars produced by different manufacturers; whether the dealership made different profits on different makes of its new cars; and whether specific salespeople tended to earn different profits. I also included a number of time-related dummies to control for day, week, week of month, and year dummy variables. Following Goldberg, I also included a number of variables interacting the quarter a new car was sold with a dummy variable indicating the car's relative model year. The idea is that new cars of the next model year sold in the fourth quarter might, for example, sell with a higher profit rate than cars of the current or previous model year that are sold in the fourth quarter.

The regressions show that even after controlling for other attributes of the transaction there is a robust tendency for African American customers to pay significantly more than white customers. The coefficients on the black male and black female variables are positive (ranging from $325 to $865) and statistically significant at the 1 percent level in all regressions. The racial disparities are quite robust, but note that the ordering is not. In the fuller regression the black male premium (over white males) exceeds the black female premium, but in the shorter regression (without time and manufacturer controls) this result was reversed. The profits of white female purchasers continue to be statistically indistinguishable from white males.

35. If dealerships charged a fixed markup that was less than 50 percent, then we would expect the coefficient on the squared term to be zero and the coefficient on the linear term to be less than 1.

36. The finance dummy was dropped from the regressions using finance profits as the left-hand-side variable (reported in columns 3 and 4) because these indicators are perfectly correlated with the constant term.

Table 4.4 Determinants of Dealer Profits

Independent Variables	(1) Vehicle Profit ($)	(2) Vehicle Profit ($)	(3) Finance Profit ($)	(4) Finance Profit ($)	(5) Total Profit ($)	(6) Total Profit ($)
Constant	−188.73	−55.95	−13.98	640.60*	−636.53***	25.32
	(142.88)	(327.44)	(177.64)	(361.84)	(183.86)	(427.78)
Purchaser Type						
White female	−12.21	−41.56	48.20	92.16	7.58	−11.67
	(72.92)	(74.35)	(79.81)	(83.59)	(93.83)	(97.13)
Black male	324.76***	459.95***	452.80***	637.05***	632.35***	865.47***
	(71.61)	(70.58)	(73.33)	(74.46)	(92.15)	(92.20)
Black female	450.26***	328.98***	590.48***	433.95***	850.24***	611.43***
	(67.21)	(73.69)	(69.09)	(77.08)	(86.49)	(96.27)
Transaction Characteristics						
Dealer cost	.0082	.0166	.0532***	.0533***	.0397*	.0460**
	(.01584)	(.0178)	(.0195)	(.0228)	(.0204)	(.0233)
Dealer cost squared	−2.26e-08	−3.80e-07	−1.21e-06**	−1.20e-06*	−7.16e-07	−1.06e-06
	(4.34e-07)	(5.12e-07)	(5.14e-07)	(6.21e-07)	(5.59e-07)	(6.68e-07)
Trade-in (= 1)	140.59**	148.30**	37.55	17.49	170.58**	166.56**
	(55.12)	(57.84)	(55.82)	(59.55)	(70.94)	(75.57)
Used (= 1)	416.57**	516.07***	185.73**	189.01*	555.93***	660.83***
	(73.88)	(106.70)	(74.77)	(114.14)	(95.06)	(139.41)
Dealer financing (= 1)	229.22***	192.16***	—	—	959.13***	936.82***
	(55.69)	(58.19)			(71.66)	(76.02)

Table 4.4 (Continued)

Independent Variables	(1) Vehicle Profit ($)	(2) Vehicle Profit ($)	(3) Finance Profit ($)	(4) Finance Profit ($)	(5) Total Profit ($)	(6) Total Profit ($)
Manufacturer Dummies (Mazda Excluded)						
Other Japanese manuf. (= 1)	—	−86.23	—	−222.61	—	−234.80
		(167.13)		(183.11)		(218.36)
Big Three manuf. (= 1)	—	−209.26	—	−4.78	—	−265.03
		(169.61)		(191.86)		(221.60)
Other Make (= 1)	—	166.52	—	512.99	—	430.60
		(329.45)		(350.34)		(430.42)
Model (Miscellaneous Models Excluded)						
Mazda 626 (= 1)	—	−190.93	—	−109.65	—	−257.22
		(157.36)		(177.15)		(205.59)
Mazda 929 (= 1)	—	107.10	—	155.87	—	199.06
		(199.86)		(213.89)		(261.12)
Mazda BXX00 (= 1)	—	−55.95	—	1.01	—	−110.42
		(179.95)		(197.30)		(235.10)
Mazda MPV (= 1)	—	−47.33	—	9.44	—	−42.10
		(184.01)		(204.50)		(240.41)
Mazda MX3 (= 1)	—	−27.33	—	−105.51	—	−120.91
		(193.78)		(203.40)		(253.18)
Mazda MX6 (= 1)	—	−154.46	—	−151.051	—	−204.03
		(200.91)		(221.18)		(262.49)

Mazda Miata (= 1)	−15.98 (184.42)	—	−18.67 (197.62)	—	−49.09 (240.95)	—
Mazda Protege (= 1)	−139.30 (163.56)	—	54.06 (180.50)	—	−114.05 (213.69)	—
Salesperson Dummies (Salesperson 1 Excluded)						
Salesperson 2 (= 1)	26.61 (111.18)	—	−1.22 (106.00)	—	−3.14 (145.26)	—
Salesperson 3 (= 3)	−111.18 (76.74)	—	74.84 (78.37)	—	−80.94 (100.25)	—
Salesperson 4 (= 1)	65.68 (98.25)	—	177.70* (101.29)	—	191.04 (128.36)	—
Salesperson 5 (= 1)	−72.47 (75.39)	—	21.75 (78.30)	—	−48.63 (98.50)	—
Year Dummies (1990 excluded)						
1991 (= 1)	386.39 (355.15)	—	−918.69* (496.515)	—	−125.21 (463.99)	—
1992 (= 1)	158.54 (253.99)	—	−593.67** (256.73)	—	−239.36 (331.83)	—
1993 (= 1)	212.70 (236.01)	—	−627.55** (238.52)	—	−256.99 (308.34)	—
1994 (= 1)	−118.00 (236.89)	—	−556.72** (9.53)	—	−531.42* (309.49)	—
1995 (= 1)	−210.60 (258.01)	—	−345.25 (274.07)	—	−576.63* (337.08)	—

Table 4.4 (Continued)

Independent Variables	(1) Vehicle Profit ($)	(2) Vehicle Profit ($)	(3) Finance Profit ($)	(4) Finance Profit ($)	(5) Total Profit ($)	(6) Total Profit ($)
(Calendar Year) Quarter Dummies Interacted with Relative Model Year (1st Quart. × Same Model Year Excluded)						
1st quart. × prev. model year	—	16.517 (124.83)	—	−59.7282 (129.76)	—	−10.38 (163.09)
2nd quart. × same model year	—	51.15 (89.84)	—	−45.92 (93.10)	—	8.84 (117.38)
2nd quart. × prev. model year	—	137.49 (210.28)	—	208.01 (244.33)	—	196.34 (274.72)
3rd quart. × same model year	—	−101.29 (91.24)	—	14.78 (90.96)	—	−116.46 (119.21)
3rd quart. × prev. model year	—	−48.04 (199.98)	—	180.63 (202.06)	—	37.71 (261.27)
4th quart. × same model year	—	57.00 (103.81)	—	33.83 (110.72)	—	79.75 (135.62)
4th quart. × prev. model year	—	−119.20 (341.37)	—	208.94 (438.00)	—	16.98 (445.99)
4th quart. × next model year	—	121.74 (127.98)	—	169.99 (138.43)	—	220.90 (167.20)
Day of Week Dummies						
Monday	—	−112.28 (92.19)	—	−97.27 (92.26)	—	−187.62 (120.45)
Tuesday	—	70.71 (97.82)	—	−215.37** (104.31)	—	−81.82 (127.80)

	(1)	(2)	(3)	(4)	(5)	(6)
Wednesday	—	−39.96	—	−67.17	—	−115.69
		(95.32)		(98.46)		(124.54)
Thursday	—	−38.98	—	−174.07	—	−129.79
		(105.82)		(111.64)		(138.25)
Friday	—	−43.95	—	−166.61	—	−148.69
		(103.01)		(110.92)		(134.59)
Saturday	—	−50.28	—	−195.21**	—	−168.92*
		(79.56)		(82.60)		(103.94)
Week of Month Dummies						
Week 2	—	−105.50	—	38.27	—	−52.50
		(96.38)		(99.39)		(125.92)
Week 3	—	−34.00	—	87.07	—	19.34
		(90.89)		(94.30)		(118.75)
Week 4	—	−21.15	—	−25.10	—	−32.45
		(92.00)		(94.83)		(120.19)
Week 5	—	−24.89	—	−47.02	—	−29.39
		(97.78)		(101.92)		(127.75)
Week 6	—	−380.46*	—	−232.26	—	−506.06*
		(205.31)		(221.76)		(268.24)
N	818	816	542	541	818	816
Adjusted R²	0.1525	0.1927	0.1629	0.1900	0.3484	0.3598

Note: Standard errors in parentheses.
* Significant at the 10 percent level.
** Significant at the 5 percent level.
*** Significant at the 1 percent level.

The primary picture painted by this data set seems to be that race and not gender is the important determinant of dealership profit. This relative unimportance of gender might, however, be caused by purchasers' bargaining as single-race, heterosexual couples.[37]

The dealership's cost of the vehicle does not have a significant impact on the size of the dealership profit. The linear term suggests that adding an extra $1,000 to the dealer's cost of a car only increases its expected profit by $8.2 to $16.6 (in columns 1 and 2). However, the profits from dealership financing are positively related to the dealership's cost of a car. A car costing the dealership an extra $1,000 leads to an extra profit of more than $50. Although we do not observe the amount of principal borrowed, it may be fair to infer that the larger the principal the larger the expected dealership profit. The squared term on dealership costs in the finance profit regressions is statistically significant and negative, indicating that the effect of cost on profits diminishes as the cost increases. But the effect remains positive for the relevant range of costs in our data set.[38] The final regressions (reported in columns 5 and 6 of table 4.4) show that dealership cost has a positive influence on total dealership profit but this effect is only statistically significant at the 10 percent level and is probably caused by the aforementioned financing effect.

The dealership financing variable is of particular interest. One might expect vehicle profits to be lower on sales that the dealership financed. As Goldberg quite reasonably hypothesized: "One would expect dealers to offer special [vehicle] discounts [on deals which they also financed] since they make additional profits through the higher interest rates charged or the cuts they receive as agents for the loan providers. . . . [T]he dealers have incentives to lower the nominal purchase price of the car in exchange for a higher future return on the loan."[39] However, columns 1 and 2 of table 4.4 indicate that vehicle profits are systematically higher on transactions in which dealers also provide financing.[40] In retrospect, it seems that customers who finance their car purchases are also more willing to pay higher prices. Signaling a willingness to finance at the dealership may also

37. Gender does, however, have some statistical influence. In each of the six regressions, a test of the hypothesis that the black female coefficient and black male coefficient are equal was strongly rejected. But as noted above, the ordering of the gender effect is not stable.

38. The costs are positively related to profit for all costs below $86,000.

39. Goldberg, *supra* note 7, at 634, 638.

40. This is different than Goldberg's finding of larger discounts on transactions with dealership financing.

signal a willingness to pay more for the car itself. But as noted above this result may be related to the customer's race, as black purchasers systematically were more likely to finance.

A similar effect appears with regard to trade-ins and the sale of used cars. Consumers who trade in a car pay systematically higher vehicle profits and higher total profits. Columns 1 and 2 of table 4.4 suggest that vehicle profits are between $140 and $150 higher when there is a trade-in; and columns 5 and 6 indicate that total profits are between $166 and $170 higher. This might be caused by the dealership's giving above-market trade-in allowances in exchange for higher profits on the car sale itself. Or it might be that consumers who trade in their car have a higher willingness to pay. Since we cannot observe the trade-in allowance or the profit on the trade-in transactions, we cannot distinguish between these hypotheses.

The dealership profits on the sale of used cars were systematically higher than those on new cars and surprisingly large—ranging between $556 and $661 more in columns 5 and 6. Moreover, this result is at least marginally significant in all six regressions, suggesting that dealerships earn both higher vehicle profits and higher financing profits when a used car is involved. The financing result might in part be caused by a higher risk of lending to used car purchasers, so that the dealership demands a higher risk-adjusted return. The racial disparities for black male and black female purchasers (and their statistical significance) are robust to dropping all the observations in which a trade-in occurred or in which used cars were sold. In other words, even if we restrict our attention only to purchases without a trade-in or only to purchases involving new cars, we still find that blacks paid significantly higher profits.

Neither the manufacturer (make) nor the model dummies were statistically different than zero in any of the regressions (reported in columns 2, 4, and 6). However, the three manufacturer coefficients in the finance regression (column 4) were jointly different than zero at a 5 percent level of significance—possibly indicating that the dealership disparately matched financing incentives of different manufacturers to remain competitive.[41]

The salesperson indicator variables were not jointly different from each other in any of the three regressions. The total profits of Salesperson 4, however, were significantly higher than those of Salespersons 3 or 5 (respectively, at the 5 percent and 10 percent level of significance). Transactions financed by the dealership produced statistically higher finance profits

41. Other manufacturers, however, predominantly offer finance incentives on their new cars and the non-Mazda observations were predominantly for used cars.

when Salesperson 4 was involved relative to Salesperson 1 or Salesperson 2. This financing result is somewhat surprising since the financing terms are generally not negotiated by the salespeople but by specialists in finance and insurance—"F&I representatives"—in a back office of the dealership.[42]

The year dummies suggest that financing profits were significantly higher in 1990 than in later years but that financial profits were generally increasing over time after 1991.[43] While total profits decreased year by year throughout the data, total profits from observations in the final two years (1994 and 1995) were significantly lower than profits associated with 1990. This suggests a general increase in competition throughout the period under analysis.

An analysis of the calendar quarters indicates, as in Goldberg's analysis, that the total profits earned by the dealership did not vary significantly by quarter or by relative model year. For some quarters, the profits on the "same year models" were higher than profits on the "previous year's model" (as in the first and fourth quarters), but in other quarters the result was the reverse. In the fourth quarter, as predicted, I found that total profits on the next model year were higher than on the same or previous model year, but this difference was not statistically significant. And in each of the regressions, I could not reject the hypothesis that the coefficients were jointly equal to zero.

The day of the week dummies suggest that cars purchased on Sunday had higher total profits than other days of the week (because the incremental coefficients are negative for all other days) and that this difference increased from Tuesday through Saturday, which had estimated profits that were $169 less than Sunday. The Saturday–Sunday increment was the only pairwise difference that was statistically significant.[44] It may be that dealerships concede more when they believe that customers have greater opportunity to search. When negotiating with a potential consumer on a Friday

42. Still, *ex post,* one could hypothesize a number of scenarios that could explain the result. Salesperson 4 might be steered to particular types of customers likely to pay higher profits when financing (i.e., customers of used cars). Or something about the way that Salesperson 4 negotiated for the underlying vehicle might have softened the purchasers for their subsequent financing negotiation.

43. The year dummies were jointly different from each other in all three regressions at the 5 percent level.

44. A joint test failed to reject the hypothesis that day of the week effects were equal to zero.

or Saturday, both the customer and the dealer may realize that the consumer can easily look elsewhere the next day if they do not reach a deal, whereas during Sunday negotiations the customer and dealer may both realize that it will be difficult for the consumer to take time off during the week or negotiate after a long work day.[45]

Finally, I tested whether the dealership was likely to earn different profits during different weeks of the month. The week of month variable was constructed on a Sunday to Sunday basis—so that a month beginning on a Saturday could have six weeks (four full weeks and a partial week at beginning and end). Interestingly the regression suggests that the dealership charged lower prices in the sixth week—more than $506 lower total profit than in the excluded first week of the month. This is consistent with anecdotes that manufacturer incentives sometimes motivate dealers at the end of the month to increase volume to make a particular quota. But this result was only marginally significant (at the 10 percent level) and was not robust to alternative specifications.

While this extended discussion of the right-hand side variables is interesting in itself, these regressions—after controlling for a host of transaction characteristics—underscore that the finding that blacks pay more remains a robust and statistically significant result. While the regressions in table 4.4 are much more controlled than the previous regression comparing the profits of different purchaser types (reported in table 4.2), these regressions cannot be interpreted by themselves as evidence of disparate treatment. It is still possible that black and white consumers behaved differently. But a major goal of the exercise is to show—counter to Heckman's and Epstein's arguments—that disparate behavior by black consumers does not mitigate the harms of disparate treatment uncovered in the audit studies.

Finally, to get a further purchase on the causes of the disparate dealership profits for blacks and whites, I reran the regression from column 6 of table 4.4, adding a number of variables interacting a dummy equal to one if the purchaser was African American with the previously included transaction characteristics (such as dealership cost, financing, trade-in, and used) as well as interacting with the salesperson dummies. The results are reported in table 4.5. A joint test of black interaction terms listed in the right-hand column strongly rejects the hypothesis that the interaction terms

45. The fourth column reveals that financing deals were less profitable on Tuesday. This is unexpected and, even *ex post*, I cannot think of a cogent explanation.

Table 4.5 Regression of Total Profit on Previous Explanatory Variables and Black Interaction Effects

Explanatory Variables	Results	Additional Explanatory Variables	Results
Constant	249.12		
	(461.30)		
White female	−1.77		
	(96.32)		
Black male	347.95		
	(399.05)		
Black female	110.00		
	(399.98)		
Dealer cost	.0345	Black × dealer cost	0.0087
	(.0296)		(0.0426)
Dealer cost squared	−1.01e-06	Black × dealer cost squared	22.88e-07
	(8.04e-07)		(1.18e-06)
Trade-in (= 1)	191.05*	Black × trade-in (= 1)	−74.72
	(105.65)		(150.14)
Used (= 1)	652.89***	Black × used (= 1)	−96.72
	(164.52)		(197.19)
Dealer financing (= 1)	767.18***	Black × dealer financing (= 1)	456.85***
	(98.64)		(149.34)
Salesperson 2 (= 1)	−469.50**	Black × salesperson 2 (= 1)	899.54***
	(206.21)		(286.74)
Salesperson 3 (= 1)	−158.03	Black × salesperson 3 (= 1)	207.75
	(131.47)		(194.81)
Salesperson 4 (= 1)	150.80	Black × salesperson 4 (= 1)	42.32
	(216.39)		(263.13)
Salesperson 5 (= 1)	−9.56	Black × salesperson 5 (= 1)	−125.07
	(128.95)		(193.64)
N		816	
Adjusted R^2		0.3774	

Note: Standard errors in parentheses.
* Significant at the 10 percent level.
** Significant at the 5 percent level.
*** Significant at the 1 percent level.
The make, model, quarter, day of week, and week of month dummies used in table 4.4 were included in this regression but are not reported. As before, they were statistically insignificant.

are equal to zero. This suggests that the purchaser's race does not merely affect the profits as a fixed markup but depends on other aspects of the transaction. Two of the interactions are highly significant (at the 1 percent level). While white customers who finance with the dealership tend to pay $767 more than white customers who do not use dealership financing, the regression suggests that black customers who finance with the dealership pay an additional $457. This suggests, for example, that a black male who financed could expect to pay $1,572 (348 + 767 + 457) more than a white male who did not use dealership financing.

The regression also suggests that Salesperson 2 exhibited the greatest racial disparity in pricing. A white male purchasing from Salesperson 2 could expect to pay total profits that were $1,718 ($900 + 470 + $348) lower than a black male purchasing from the same salesperson. When combined with evidence that blacks were systematically steered toward Salesperson 2 (discussed above), this is consistent with a story that Salesperson 2 specialized in discriminating against black customers.

In an unreported regression, I added to the regression in table 4.5 interactions of a female dummy variable to the same transaction characteristics that had black interactions. The interactions were uniformly insignificant with one exception: the total profits for women who financed were $245 more than for men who financed and this result was marginally significant (at the 10.5 percent level). Still the overall picture for the Atlanta data is nongendered pricing in that white men and women paid similar profits and that black men and black women paid similar profits—at least in comparison with the larger and more robust racial differences.

III. Meta-analysis of Four Studies

There now exist four different data sets to help assess whether blacks are discriminated against in car purchasing. While it is essential to undertake the microanalysis of these data, it is also useful to take stock of their overall message, to step back and assess the broad contours of discrimination. Table 4.6 attempts to do just this by summarizing the race–gender pricing differences. Of course, because the data sets come from such disparate sources, important caveats must be kept in mind:

- The transactions differ: the audit testers solicited offers, but did not purchase cars; the Goldberg and Atlanta data sets include consummated transactions.

- The price measures differ: the audit studies numbers are based on the profits implicit in the dealers' final offers; Goldberg's study is based on imputed differences in discounts from the sticker price; and the Atlanta data is based on differences in total profit (including financing but excluding trade-in profit).
- The controls differ: the audit testers used a uniform bargaining strategy and were controlled on a host of verbal and nonverbal dimensions while the Goldberg and Atlanta studies had no *ex ante* control and we lack basic information about how purchasers bargained, making it impossible to control *ex post* with regressions.
- The racial groups differ: the audit and Atlanta studies are tests of black/white disparities, while the Goldberg study is a test of "minority"/"nonminority" disparities.
- The geographic areas differ: the audit data comes from Chicago; the Goldberg study is based on a nationwide sample; and the Atlanta data is of course from Atlanta.
- The time periods differ: the pilot audit study was completed in 1989; the full audit study was completed in 1990; the Goldberg data covered transactions completed in 1983–87; and the Atlanta data covered transactions completed in 1990–95.

Still, with all these caveats in mind, a global comparison of the race–gender differentials reveals striking similarities. The differentials for both black males and black females (that is, the amount by which their profits exceeded the profits of white males) are uniformly positive and substantial (ranging from $274 to $1,133). Moreover, the black male and black female differentials are highly significant in three of the four data sets, where black women are estimated to pay more then black men. And for heuristic purposes, if we combine the observations from these four different sources, we find that on average black men pay (or are finally asked to pay) $607 more than white men, and that black women are asked to pay $756 more than white men. These weighted average differentials, when compared to the combined standard deviation, are also statistically significant.[46] Thus

46. The combined standard deviation was computed to be:

$$\frac{\sum_{i=1} s_i^2(n_i - 1)}{\sum_{i=1} n_i - 4},$$

where s_i = the standard deviation of the ith data set and n_i = the number of observations of the ith dataset.

Table 4.6 Meta-analysis of Estimated Price Premium over White Males in Four Studies of Markups on New Cars by Demographic Group

Demographic Group	Chicago "Pilot" Audit (Ayres)	Chicago Full Audit (Ayres/Siegelman)	National CES Consummated Sales (Goldberg)	Atlanta Consummated Sales	Weighted Average	Joint Test of Equality of Means (prob =)[a]
White females	220†	216*	129	−11†	85	.0000
	(129)	(116)	(117)	(97)	(113)	
	[21]	[53]	[244]	[164]	[482]	
Black females	1013***†	465**	426	865***†	756**	.0000
	(124)	(103)	(525)	(92)	(181)	
	[23]	[60]	[28]	[224]	[335]	
Black males	283**	$1133***†	$274	611***†	607**	.0000
	(136)	(122)	(263)	(96)	(143)	
	[18]	[40]	[39]	[178]	[275]	
Adjusted R^2	.37	.33	.14	.36		

Sources:
Col. 1   Ian Ayres, Harvard Law Review.
Col. 2   Chapter 2, table 2.1 (col. 2).
Col. 3   Pinelopi Goldberg, Dealer Price Discrimination in New Car Purchases: Evidence from the Consumer Expenditure Survey, 104 J. Pol. Econ. 622 (1996), table 2, col. 1 and table 5. Goldberg tested for differences between "Minority" and "Non-Minority" purchasers. See supra note 16 and accompanying text.
Col. 4   This chapter, table 4.4 (col. 6).
Notes: Standard errors in parentheses. Number of observations in brackets.
*   Significantly different from zero at the 10 percent level.
**   Significantly different from zero at the 1 percent level.
†   Significantly different from CES (Goldberg) estimate at the 5 percent level.
a   Likelihood ratio test of equality of means. See Alexander M. Mood, Franklin A. Graybill & Duane C. Boes, Introduction to the Theory of Statistics 437 (3d ed. 1974).

while the differentials uncovered by Goldberg in the CES data continue to be statistically insignificant, the high standard deviation applied to her small number of observations (28 out of a total of 335 black female observations) is not sufficient to render the global analysis statistically insignificant.

Indeed, one is struck by several results when comparing the Goldberg differentials with the differentials from the other data sets. Goldberg's standard errors for black males and black females are more than twice (and sometimes three and four times the size of) the comparable differentials, and her R-squared is less than half that of all the other regressions. These are strong indications of the noisiness of her data. But the size of the differentials themselves are not so far from at least some of the other data sets. Goldberg's black female differential of $426 is similar to the $465 differential from the full audit study. And Goldberg's black male differential of $274 is similar to the black male differential estimated in the pilot audit.

Still it must be admitted that the sizes of the differentials—while robustly positive—do vary. Two of the black male differentials are near $300 and the two others are more than twice this amount ($611 and $1,133). Two of the black female differentials are in the $450 range, but the other two are twice this amount ($865 and $1013). These higher differentials are not only statistically distinct from Goldberg's estimates, but a joint test (reported in the far right-hand column of table 4.6) rejects the null hypothesis of equal means. Still, given the important differences in the ways these data were produced and analyzed, I believe the similarities of the tables far outweigh the dissimilarities.

The global analysis shows that on net blacks pay substantially more than whites in both audit testing and consummated transactions. Once we appreciate the noisiness of Goldberg's data, her analysis does not so much contradict as add marginal confirmation to this result. Counter to the conjectures of Heckman and Epstein, additional search or alternative bargaining strategies do not eliminate or even importantly mitigate the amounts of discrimination discovered in the initial audits. Customers often do not have sufficient information to take such self-help measures, and given the recalcitrance that dealerships across the board showed in the audit testing, it is not clear that effective self-help measures currently exist.

The results of this chapter concerning racial disparities in financial profits are also supported by yet another litigation-generated analysis. As this book went to press, a class action suit against General Motor's credit division, General Motors Acceptance Corp. (GMAC), uncovered that financing profits for African American borrowers are systematically higher than for white borrowers.[47] The basic facts of the suit can be easily summarized (albeit in a slightly stylized fashion). When a GM dealer approaches GMAC about financing a particular purchaser (and passes on core information about the financial risk of lending to such a car buyer), GMAC responds by telling the dealership the minimum amount of interest rate (the risk-adjusted market rate) that the dealer can charge. But GMAC also allows the dealership to negotiate a higher and more profitable interest rate up to some maximum amount. The dealer and GMAC divide the profits on any excess interest that the dealer can negotiate.

A report of plaintiffs' expert, Marc Cohen, shows that controlling for a host of other variables the excess profit on loans to black consumers is $377 higher than for white consumers. These are not quite as high as the racial differentials uncovered in the Atlanta data set (which as shown in tables 4.4 and 4.5 range from $453 to $637), but are nonetheless highly significant.

The plaintiffs in this litigation are using the Equal Credit Opportunity Act (ECOA),[48] which allows plaintiffs to bring racial disparate impact suits in lending. In this case, the plaintiff class alleges that the financing company's decision to allow dealerships to negotiate has an unjustified disparate impact on black borrowers. We return to this statute in chapter 5 to argue that it provides a new weapon to attack racial disparities not only in excess interest charged but also in the underlying purchase price of the car (the principal of the loan).

Conclusion

Chapter 5 takes up the important issue of what policy makers can do to mitigate the disparate racial pricing detailed to this point—especially focusing on informational reforms that may facilitate consumer self-help. In concluding this chapter, it is appropriate to comment on the catch-22 created by the Epstein/Heckman critique. Discrimination tests are often plagued by difficulties of creating "similarly situated" comparisons. Heckman, for example, has been a leading critic of audits for not adequately controlling for unobserved variables—factors other than race or gender

47. Coleman v. General Motors Acceptance Corp., No. 3-98-0211 (M.D. Tenn. 2000).

48. 15 U.S.C. §§ 1691–1691f (1994 & Supp. IV 1998); see also 12 C.F.R. § 202.1; Interagency Policy Statement, 1994 WL 128417.

(but correlated with these traits) that might offer a nondiscriminatory explanation for the audit results.[49] Defendants in discrimination suits *always* claim that their behavior was not predicated on the plaintiff's race or sex but on some other characteristic.

The catch-22 (or what Margaret Radin calls a "double bind")[50] comes, however, when researchers produce an effective test where blacks and whites (men and women) *do* behave the same. Then enters Heckman claiming that the result is uninteresting because it does not prove that blacks (or women) might not have protected themselves by behaving differently than white men. Thus, as a researcher you are damned if you do and damned if you don't. If you don't adequately ensure uniform tester behavior, you will be criticized for not proving disparate treatment. If you do adequately ensure uniform tester behavior, you will be criticized for not proving that trivial self-help could have mitigated the harms of the seller's disparate treatment. By combining an analysis of both audit testing and consummated transactions, I hope to have at least partially responded to both of these criticisms. While it is still true that controlled testers who undertook slightly more aggressive search or bargaining strategies might have been able to mitigate the types of discrimination found, the empiricism put forward presents a strong prima facie case for the propositions that (1) a broad array of new car dealerships discriminate on the basis of race and (2) consumer self-help does not simply solve the problem.

49. Heckman, *supra* note 2.

50. Margaret J. Radin, The Pragmatist and the Feminist, 63 S. Cal. L. Rev. 1699 (1990).

CHAPTER 5

Legal Implications

The audit tests (buttressed by the consummated transaction analysis) suggest that car dealerships systematically offer higher prices to black customers (male and female) than they offer to white men who use similar negotiation strategies. Whether these findings constitute *actionable* racial discrimination in a traditional legal sense, however, is a separate matter. The different treatment of consumers might be seen as a natural consequence of any bargaining process. Capitalist economies often valorize bargaining by conceiving of such negotiations as the market's working in its purest form. Sellers are free to pursue high-markup sales through a variety of bargaining methods. The precontractual interplay between a potential buyer and seller may seem, in some sense, outside the purview of the law.[1]

---

1. The process of bargaining does not necessitate the disparate treatment of bargainers. A seller could make uniform initial offers followed by uniform concessions—and let the consumers sort themselves at different accepted prices. Sellers could still adopt tough bargaining strategies by refusing to make concessions some proportion of the time. Avoiding disparate treatment would merely require that sellers adopt what game theorists call a uniform "mixed strategy." See Eric Rasmusen, *Games and Information* 69 (1989). A mixed strategy for bargaining would specify the probability that a seller would make a particular type of concession. Under this scenario, the process of bargaining would still have a disparate impact on different consumers—less savvy cus-

This chapter argues, however, that the disparate racial pricing uncovered in the audit tests represents compelling evidence of unlawful racial discrimination under both the civil rights and consumer protection laws. In the first section I explore whether the car sellers' dealings with black testers constitute unlawful disparate treatment in violation of §§ 1981 and 1982.[2] A positive finding does not necessarily imply that sellers dislike black or female customers—only that sellers take their customers' race and gender into account when deciding how to bargain. While such discrimination is actionable, structural impediments—chiefly the difficulty of certifying a racial class of discrimination victims—may make the use of such actions economically infeasible and thus an unlikely method of deterring dealer disparate treatment. In the second section of the chapter I propose legal reforms to strengthen §§ 1981 and 1982 and to extend their coverage to currently unprotected groups. The third section assesses a variety of alternative reforms that might better respond (or at least represent an additional response) to the problem, and in the fourth section I assess the public and academic reactions to the initial publication of the audit data and speculate on the future of car buying in America.

If reform is to be effective in undermining a dealer's incentive to price discriminate, it must reduce the extraordinary concentration of profits—which as we have seen has traditionally allowed dealers to earn a disproportionate share of their profits from a small percentage of their most profitable sales. If we can reduce dealers' dependence on high-markup sales (as a source for such a large percentage of their overall profit), then we can make it profitable for dealerships to commit instead to low-markup, high-volume strategies. The rise of the Internet and "no-haggle" dealerships may be enough by themselves to reduce prospectively the opportunities for race discrimination. But ultimately informational reforms—focused not on transforming average prices into even lower markups but focused instead on deterring "home run" (that is, high-markup) sales—may provide just the nudge that is needed to tip the entire market toward no-haggle (and therefore nondiscriminatory) pricing.

---

tomers or those averse to bargaining would accept the higher initial offers—but there would not be disparate treatment.

2. As stated earlier, §§ 1981 and 1982 do not address discrimination based on gender. See Ian Ayres, Fair Driving: Gender and Race Discrimination in Retail Car Negotiations, 104 Harv. L. Rev. 817, 821.

I. Liability under Sections 1981 and 1982

Sections 1981 and 1982 mandate that all people shall have the same rights "to make and enforce contracts" and to "purchase . . . personal property," respectively, "as is enjoyed by white citizens."[3] There seems little doubt that either of these provisions covers discrimination relating to retail car price bargaining between private parties. In *Jones v. Alfred H. Mayer Co.*,[4] the U.S. Supreme Court emphatically stated that § 1982 (and by implication § 1981) applies to acts of private discrimination.[5] Since *Jones*, courts have applied these sections' prohibitions of private discrimination to contexts similar to retail car price bargaining.[6] And indeed, the Atlanta data discussed in chapter 4 was collected as part of the case preparation for a lawsuit that claimed that a dealership's intentional discrimination violated both §§ 1981 and 1982. The dealership settled the claims of the individual black plaintiffs before its substantive liability was adjudi-

---

3. 42 U.S.C. §§ 1981, 1982 (1988). Although not identical, both sections originated in § 1 of the Civil Rights Act of 1866, ch. 31, 14 Stat. 27, 27. See General Bldg. Contractors Ass'n v. Pennsylvania, 458 U.S. 375, 384 (1982). More important, courts generally treat the two sections identically, at least with respect to the requirements for establishing a claim of intentional discrimination. See Choudhury v. Polytechnic Inst. of New York, 735 F.2d 38, 43 n.5 (2d Cir. 1984). This chapter treats the two sections as interchangeable.

4. 392 U.S. 409 (1968).

5. See id. at 437.

6. Section 1982's prohibition on discrimination in the sale or purchase of property "includ[es] discrimination in modes of negotiation." Newbern v. Lake Lorelei, Inc., 308 F. Supp. 407, 416 (S.D. Ohio 1968). Moreover, although § 1982 is not often used in the context of the sale or purchase of personal property, the text of the statute covers such sales or purchases. See, e.g., Scott v. Eversole Mortuary, 522 F.2d 1110, 1113 (9th Cir. 1975) (finding that § 1982 covers the "attempted purchase of caskets"). Section 1981's prohibition on discrimination in the making of contracts is more extensive, covering "offer[s] to make a contract only on discriminatory terms." Patterson v. McLean Credit Union, 491 U.S. 164, 177 (1989). *Patterson*'s lasting significance, of course, lies in its holding that § 1981 does not prohibit discrimination in postformation relations. See id. at 178. Thus it seems that fair-driving plaintiffs could sue under either § 1981 or § 1982.

Defendants in the present context might try to escape § 1981 or § 1982 liability by distinguishing preliminary offers meant as the starting point for negotiations from later, more authoritative offers. This argument is untenable, however, because earlier offers help determine subsequent offers (and in turn the ultimate terms of the contract). Salespeople surely believe that their actions in the initial rounds of bargaining affect the final contract price; they would hardly be willing to take the time to bargain for several rounds if they thought otherwise.

cated, but after (as discussed below) the court refused to certify a larger class of similarly situated black customers.

Even if car dealership bargaining falls within the scope of §§ 1981 and 1982, a fair-driving plaintiff must overcome a number of hurdles to win a claim under these statutes. The substantive legal standard under §§ 1981 and 1982 is straightforward: plaintiffs claiming disparate treatment must prove that the defendant intentionally discriminated against them and caused them an identifiable injury.[7] Although the Supreme Court has stated that intentional discrimination "can in some situations be inferred from the mere fact of differences in treatment,"[8] no civil rights case has ever concluded that a showing of disparate treatment was insufficient to establish intentional discrimination. A plurality of the Supreme Court has found in the Title VII context that a prima facie case of disparate treatment is made out whenever "gender played a motivating part in an employment decision" and defined this standard to "mean that, if we asked the employer at the moment of the decision what its reasons were and if we received a truthful response, one of those reasons would be that the applicant or employee was a woman."[9] The Civil Rights Act of 1991 reaffirmed this aspect of the plurality opinion.[10] Judge Posner has also addressed the state of mind requirement in a fair-housing disparate treatment case—defining disparate treatment as "treating a person differently because of his race; it implies consciousness of race, and a purpose to use race as a decision-making tool."[11] It thus appears that courts will find intentional

---

7. See, e.g., *Patterson,* 491 U.S. at 185–86; Goodman v. Lukens Steel Co., 482 U.S. 656, 664, 669 (1987); *General Bldg. Contractors,* 458 U.S. at 389, 391; Phillips v. Hunter Trails Community Ass'n, 685 F.2d 184, 187 (7th Cir. 1982). Disparate treatment claims are distinguishable from disparate impact claims under Title VII. Accordingly, the Supreme Court in *General Bldg. Contractors* rejected disparate impact claims under § 1981 as uncognizable. See 458 U.S. at 390–91. Disparate impact claims cover facially neutral (employer) practices that have discriminatory effects. They require no showing of intent to establish a prima facie case. See Griggs v. Duke Power Co., 401 U.S. 424, 430 (1971).

8. International Bhd. of Teamsters v. United States, 431 U.S. 324, 335 n.15 (1977).

9. Price Waterhouse v. Hopkins, 490 U.S. 228, 250 (1989) (plurality opinion).

10. The 1991 Act provided that "an unlawful employment practice is established when the complaining party demonstrates that race, color, religion, sex, or national origin was a motivating factor for any employment practice, even though other factors also motivated the practice." Civil Rights Act of 1991, Pub. L. No. 102-166, § 107(a), 105 Stat. 1075 (*codified at* 42 U.S.C. § 2000e-2(m) [1994]).

11. Village of Bellwood v. Dwivedi, 895 F.2d 1521, 1529–30 (7th Cir. 1990); see also id. (defining conditions when a person would be "guilty of intentional discrimination, or what is the same thing, of disparate treatment").

discrimination whenever the defendant's conduct was conditioned on the plaintiff's race.[12] To establish liability in this context, the typical fair-driving plaintiff would need to show that the specific car dealer with whom he or she had bargained considered the plaintiff's race in deciding how to bargain.

On the other hand, because of the difficulties in obtaining direct proof that a defendant's conduct was race dependent,[13] the law has developed a method for allocating the burdens of proof under §§ 1981 and 1982 that in effect allows intent to be inferred from indirect evidence. In particular, courts hearing § 1981 or 1982 claims have imported from the Title VII context the shifting burdens of proof scheme articulated in *McDonnell Douglas v. Green*.[14] Applying the *McDonnell Douglas* reasoning to fair-driving suits, the plaintiff bears the initial burden of establishing disparate treatment: that sellers took race into account when deciding how to bar-

12. This standard of intent covers not only differential treatment caused by a defendant's animus toward blacks, but also the conscious use of race as a proxy to further some other legitimate goal. *Price Waterhouse*, for example, explicitly rejected the use of gender as a proxy for legitimate employment traits, such as aggressiveness: "[A]n employer who acts on the basis of a belief that a woman cannot be aggressive . . . has acted on the basis of gender." 490 U.S. at 250. See Amy L. Wax, Discrimination as Accident, 74 Indiana L.J. 1130 (1999).

13. An example of such rare, direct evidence is an internal memorandum from the defendant-dealer to his manager explaining that he considered the prospective buyer's race before offering an initial price.

14. 411 U.S. 792 (1973). The *McDonnell Douglas* allocation of the burdens of proof has been applied in subsequent Title VII cases. See, e.g., Texas Dep't of Community Affairs v. Burdine, 450 U.S. 248, 252–56 (1981); see also *International Bhd. of Teamsters*, 431 U.S. at 335 n.15 (1977) (reiterating the underlying rationale of the *McDonnell Douglas* scheme that "[p]roof of discriminatory motive is critical, although it can in some situations be inferred from the mere fact of differences in treatment"). The Supreme Court has distinguished this type of Title VII case from that in which there is direct evidence of subjective discriminatory intent but also direct evidence of other, more legitimate motives (the "mixed motives" case). See *Price Waterhouse*, 490 U.S. at 244–45. Justice O'Connor explicitly distinguished between the two types of cases in her concurrence. See id. (O'Connor, J., concurring in the judgment). The allocation of the burdens of proof are significantly different in the two types of cases. This allocation was unaffected by the Civil Rights Act of 1991. See Civil Rights Act of 1991, Pub. L. No. 102-166, § 107(b), 105 Stat. 1075 (*codified at* 42 U.S.C. § 2000e-5(g)(2)(B) [1994]); Medlock v. Ortho Biotech, Inc., 164 F.3d 545, 551 n.3 (10th Cir. 1999).

The Supreme Court has ruled that "the *McDonnell Douglas/Burdine* scheme of proof should apply in § 1981 cases." *Patterson*, 491 U.S. at 186. For examples of lower federal courts' application of the *McDonnell Douglas/Burdine* standard to both § 1981 and § 1982 claims, see Phiffer v. Proud Parrot Motor Hotel, Inc., 648 F.2d 548, 551 (9th Cir. 1980) (§ 1982 claim); Chauhan v. M. Alfieri Co., 707 F. Supp. 162, 165–66 (D.N.J. 1988) (§ 1981 claim), *rev'd*, 897 F.2d 123 (3d Cir. 1990).

gain.[15] If the plaintiff can establish a prima facie violation of § 1981 or 1982, a burden of production shifts to the defendant "to articulate some legitimate, nondiscriminatory reason" for its differential behavior.[16] Finally, if the defendant can offer such a reason, the burden shifts back to the plaintiff to show that the defendant's response is a mere "pretext."[17]

A black tester from the audit study who wanted to make out a successful prima facie case against a particular dealership would have to persuade the court of two things. First, she would have to persuade the court that the study was sufficiently controlled—that is, that she and the white tester visiting the defendant's car dealership appeared similar in every objective respect except for the color of their skin. If courts' attitudes in housing cases under §§ 1981 and 1982 are any indication,[18] the fair-driving tests conducted in our audit study were more than sufficiently controlled. Although the typical fair-housing test is similarly controlled with respect to timing of the tests, it is less controlled with respect to verbal and nonverbal conduct than was the testing in this study. When a black man suspects that he has been the victim of housing discrimination, he typically complains to a local fair-housing organization. The organization may then dispatch a white tester to observe whether the seller treats him differently. Fair-housing organizations also conduct "audits" in which pairs of trained test-

15. As applied to the fair-driving context, the plaintiff would have to show that she belongs to a racial minority; that she was as ready, willing, and able to buy a car as similarly situated whites; that despite this fact, the defendant offered her higher prices than those offered similarly situated whites; and that the defendant continued to offer lower prices to similarly situated whites. See *McDonnell Douglas,* 411 U.S. at 802. Courts have allowed plaintiffs flexibility in demonstrating disparate treatment. See, e.g., United States Postal Serv. Bd. of Governors v. Aikens, 460 U.S. 711, 714 n.3 (1983); *International Bhd. of Teamsters,* 431 U.S. at 358 n.44 (1977); *McDonnell Douglas,* 411 U.S. at 802 n.13. For example, in fair-housing cases, testers need not seek actual purchase. See Havens Realty Corp. v. Coleman, 455 U.S. 363, 373–75 (1982).

16. *McDonnell Douglas,* 411 U.S. at 802. *Burdine,* 450 U.S. at 252–56, makes clear, however, that the defendant only bears a burden of production.

17. *McDonnell Douglas,* 411 U.S. at 804.

18. See, e.g., Smith v. Anchor Bldg. Corp., 536 F.2d 231, 233 (8th Cir. 1976) (finding a prima facie inference of discrimination "where a black rental applicant meets the objective requirements of a landlord, and the rental would likely have been consummated were he or she a white applicant"); Newbern v. Lake Lorelei, Inc., 308 F. Supp. 407, 417 (S.D. Ohio 1968) (finding a prima facie inference of discrimination "[w]here a Negro offeror . . . meets the objective requirements of a seller-developer . . . and shows further that a substantial number of lots have been sold and none of the buyers is a Negro").

ers target a particular area or seller. The advance preparation for such audits makes them relatively controlled, but fair-housing organizations seldom train and control their testers as rigorously as we did.[19]

Second, a fair-driving plaintiff must persuade the court that the instances of differential treatment are sufficiently numerous that the results cannot be explained by chance.[20] Again, analogy to the fair-housing context suggests that the results of one pair of well-controlled testers should suffice.[21] Under this standard, the present study could theoretically give rise to dozens of actionable instances of discrimination against individual dealers.

Although comparisons with the fair-housing context are generally apposite, courts may be much more reluctant to find the existence of prima facie cases in the fair-driving context because society has differing presumptions about the pervasiveness of the two kinds of discrimination. The long and ongoing history of housing discrimination in the United States is so well known and well documented[22] that courts may require relatively less proof of its occurrence. Race discrimination in car negotiations may have a similarly long and deep-seated history, but the size and nature of such discrimination may be masked by the processes of bargaining. As a result, a court hearing a fair-driving claim may require that the tests be

19. Interview with Ellen Shogan, Executive Director, Fair Housing Council of Greater Washington (Nov. 26, 1990).

20. One might argue that more instances of discrimination are necessary in the car buying context because differences in seller behavior are more subjective than the outright refusals to deal or the steering that is prevalent in fair-housing cases. On reflection, however, this argument cannot be sustained. Quoting two different prices is just as objective a measure of disparate treatment as disparate willingness to deal.

21. See, e.g., Metro Fair Hous. Servs. v. Morrowood Garden Apartments, 576 F. Supp. 1090, 1093 (N.D. Ga. 1983) ("Where a white tester is given substantially different information from that given an otherwise similar black tester, an inference that race was a factor can be drawn."), rev'd sub nom. Watts v. Boyd Properties, Inc., 758 F.2d 1482 (11th Cir. 1985). Of course, a genuine fair-driving plaintiff—one not part of a controlled test—will have a harder time showing that he or she was treated differently from similarly situated whites.

22. See, e.g., George C. Galster, More Than Skin Deep: The Effect of Housing Discrimination on the Extent and Pattern of Racial Residential Segregation in the United States, in Housing Desegregation and Federal Policy 119 (J. Goering ed., 1986); Douglas S. Massey & Nancy A. Denton, Trends in the Residential Segregation of Blacks, Hispanics, and Asians: 1970–80, 52 Am. Soc. Rev. 802 (1987); John Yinger, Measuring Racial Discrimination with Fair Housing Audits: Caught in the Act, 76 Am. Econ. Rev. 881 (1986).

more controlled, that the disparity of treatment be greater, or that there be more instances of disparate treatment by the same dealer.[23]

Once a court finds that a fair-driving plaintiff has made out a prima facie case of disparate treatment, the burden shifts to the defendant-dealer to articulate a legitimate, nondiscriminatory explanation for why it treated white buyers and black buyers differently.[24] The defendant might directly rebut the plaintiff's evidence of disparate treatment by putting forth evidence that the test was not controlled in all relevant respects and that sellers gave different offers not because of race, but because of some other uncontrolled characteristic on which testers differed. Sellers might persuasively argue, for example, that the higher offers received by black women in our audit study do not violate § 1981: because black women were paired with white males, sellers could argue that they were discriminating on the basis of the unprotected characteristic of gender and not the protected characteristic of race.

If the defendant does not directly rebut the plaintiff's evidence of disparate treatment, it might still put forward two distinct arguments that the disparate treatment was not "intentional" discrimination. First, the dealer may argue that the disparate treatment was unintentional because the dealer's motive was to make money, not to harm black people. Under this theory, the dealer might openly admit that its behavior flowed from consciously drawn, economically rational inferences based on the race of prospective buyers—revenue-based inferences, for example, about the proportion of blacks willing to pay a higher markup. It is, however, precisely these sorts of inferences—inferences based on the color of a person's skin—that §§ 1981 and 1982 do not countenance. As Judge Posner has held in discussing the requirements of § 1982: "[d]iscrimination may be instrumental to a goal not itself discriminatory, just as murder may be instrumental to a goal not itself murderous (such as money); it is not any less—it is, indeed, more clearly—discriminatory on that account."[25]

23. Assuming §§ 1981 and 1982 could be expanded to include women, this attitude might be particularly prevalent in cases in which the victims of dealership discrimination are women. I have noted greater resistance among colleagues to the idea of gender than of race discrimination in car sales. In presenting my results, the conclusion that such discrimination exists is more apt to be accepted if I use racial examples; examples based on gender are more often challenged as to whether the testers were uniform.

24. The Supreme Court has clearly indicated that the defendant bears only a burden of production, not persuasion, in rebutting the plaintiff's prima facie case. See *Burdine*, 450 U.S. at 255.

25. *Dwivedi*, 895 F.2d at 1531. Or, to quote another court in a slightly different context: "it is now understood that under § 1982 . . . there cannot in this country be

Alternatively, defendants might claim that their disparate treatment was unintentional in the sense that they were not conscious of it.[26] The D.C. Circuit rejected this argument in *Hopkins v. Price Waterhouse:*[27]

> [Plaintiff demonstrated] that she was treated less favorably than male candidates because of her sex. This is sufficient to establish discriminatory motive; the fact that some or all of the partners at Price Waterhouse may have been unaware of that motivation, even within themselves, neither alters the fact of its existence nor excuses it.[28]

Once a plaintiff has proven that a defendant has treated blacks differently from identically situated whites, it is fair and reasonable to conclude as a matter of law that the dealer at some level of consciousness must have been aware of the testers' race. Such a legal inference conforms with our common moral intuition that a dealer who must consciously decide what initial price to offer every customer who walks through the door must be aware of the skin color of those to whom it consistently offers a higher initial price.[29] Thus, so long as the fair-driving plaintiff can persuade the factfinder that sellers treated blacks differently from similarly situated whites, the disparate treatment discussed in this chapter violates §§ 1981 and 1982.

However, other hurdles loom that may still hinder plaintiffs from receiving the relief. First, if non–bona fide purchasers are used, plaintiffs may have difficulty establishing standing to bring suit and may expose them-

---

markets or profits based on the color of a man's skin." Contract Buyers League v. F & F Inv., 300 F. Supp. 210, 216 (N.D. Ill. 1969), *aff'd sub nom.* Baker v. F & F Inv., 420 F.2d 1191 (7th Cir.), *cert. denied,* 400 U.S. 821 (1970).

26. Cf. Linda Hamilton Krieger, The Content of Our Categories: A Cognitive Bias Approach to Discrimination and Equal Employment Opportunity, 47 Stan. L. Rev. 1161 (1995); Wax, *supra* note 12.

27. 825 F.2d 458 (D.C. Cir. 1987), *rev'd on other grounds,* 490 U.S. 228 (1989).

28. Id. at 468–69. Paul Brest has similarly rejected reading a mens rea requirement into a standard for discrimination: "Race-dependent decisions need not be race-conscious, but may reflect unconscious racially selective indifference. Such indifference violates the antidiscrimination principle when its effect is to deny benefits to minority persons, or impose burdens on them, which would not be denied or imposed if they were white." Paul Brest, The Supreme Court, 1975 Term—Foreword: In Defense of the Antidiscrimination Principle, 90 Harv. L. Rev. 1, 14 (footnote omitted).

29. But see *Dwivedi,* 895 F.2d at 1532 (stating that "since few of the defendants' customers were white, the defendants had little experience with white customers and may therefore have treated the white testers differently out of ignorance rather than design").

selves to paying damages for fraud or trespass. For example, if the actual black testers from the audit study were to bring suit, they would face the additional hurdle of establishing standing under §§ 1981 and 1982 because they lacked a bona fide intent to purchase. In the fair-housing context, the Supreme Court has found that testers need not intend to buy to have standing to bring civil suits under the broad language of Title VIII.[30] The Eleventh and Third Circuits have extended this standing doctrine to fair-housing claims brought under § 1982.[31] At least in the Eleventh and Third Circuits, fair-driving testers would have a strong argument for standing to sue under § 1982; however, the relevant language of §§ 1981 and 1982 is not nearly as broad as that contained in the Fair Housing Act, and courts when asked to interpret standing outside of the housing context may choose a narrower rule.

More alarmingly, the use of non–bona fide testers—in the wake of the recent *Food Lion* opinion[32]—may expose the plaintiffs to a countersuit for fraud or trespass. In 1997, a jury found that ABC television owed the Food Lion grocery chain $5.5 million in punitive damages for fraud, trespass, and breach of employee duty of loyalty because ABC had its agents hired as non–bona fide employees who failed to disclose they were members of the media and then proceeded to surreptitiously film alleged unsanitary meat-handling procedures.[33] Dealerships may argue analogously that they implicitly are only licensing potential customers to enter their stores and that it is fraudulent to bargain with no intention of purchasing (but instead with the intent of potentially exposing the dealership to public ridicule).[34] While to date no damages have been awarded against non–bona fide testers, the specter of *Food Lion* may have a chilling effect on testing.

30. See *Havens Realty Corp.*, 455 U.S. at 373–75.

31. See *Watts*, 758 F.2d at 1485; Meyers v. Pennypack Woods Home Ownership Ass'n, 559 F.2d 894, 898 (3d Cir. 1977).

32. Food Lion, Inc. v. Capital Cities/ABC, Inc., 984 F. Supp. 923 (M.D.N.C. 1997).

33. See Andrew B. Sims, Food for the Lions: Excessive Damages for Newsgathering Torts and the Limitations of Current First Amendment Doctrines, 78 B.U. L. Rev. 507 (1998). The district court denied a motion for retrial on the punitive damages award on the condition that the plaintiff file a remittitur of all punitive damages above $315,000. See *Food Lion*, 984 F. Supp. at 940. Only $2 in nominal damages for trespass and breach of loyalty survived appellate review. See Food Lion, Inc. v. Capital Cities/ABC, Inc., 194 F.3d 505 (4th Cir. 1999).

34. The issues of sending non–bona fide testers are closely related to the ethical issues of testing discussed in chapter 2, note 9, with regard to human subject review.

Enlightened public policy might make clear that a cost of doing business with the public is to be subject to a reasonable amount of testing for invidious forms of discrimination.

Finally, for such litigation to be economically feasible, it may be necessary for plaintiffs to succeed in having a court certify a class action. The common impression that negotiations are necessarily idiosyncratic may make it difficult for plaintiffs to prove the requisite commonality required to establish that a racial class is worthy of certification under Rule 23 of the Federal Rules of Civil Procedure. For example, the Eleventh Circuit in *Jackson v. Motel 6 Multipurpose*[35] refused to certify a class of black plaintiffs alleging that a hotel chain had discriminated against them. This precedent represents a major roadblock to a fair-driving class. The renting of a hotel room would strike most observers by and large as being a less idiosyncratic transaction than buying a car. But the court found that the allegations of racial discrimination in renting a hotel room raised "distinctly case-specific inquiries":

> The issues that must be addressed include not only whether a particular plaintiff was denied a room or was rented a substandard room, but also whether there were any rooms vacant when that plaintiff inquired; whether the plaintiff had reservations; whether unclean rooms were rented to the plaintiff for reasons having nothing to do with the plaintiff's race; whether the plaintiff, at the time that he requested a room, exhibited any non-racial characteristics legitimately counseling against renting him a room; and so on.[36]

Other circuits have been particularly reluctant to certify classes where monetary damages are sought.[37] An important discovery issue involves whether initial testing provides a sufficient basis for forcing a defendant to disclose its sales data as part of plaintiffs' case to certify a racial class. In the Atlanta case alleging that a car dealership violated §§ 1981 and 1982 by discriminating against its black customers, the federal district court not only refused to certify the racial class but earlier refused to force the defendant dealership to disclose its sales data.[38] Even though the plain-

---

35. Jackson v. Motel 6 Multipurpose, Inc., 130 F.3d 999 (11th Cir. 1997).
36. Id. at 1012.
37. See, e.g., Allison v. Citgo Petroleum Corp., 151 F.3d 402, 411 (5th Cir. 1998).
38. Conversation with Edward D. Buckley (Oct. 1999).

tiffs had produced strong evidence of systematic pricing disparities in nearly nine hundred sales at the dealership (which, as discussed in the chapter 4, had been obtained from salespeople who had previously worked for the defendant dealership), the court ruled that such evidence did not provide an adequate basis for forcing the defendant to turn over information on other sales.

In the end, the need to certify classes of black customers is probably the most important hurdle to using civil rights laws to deter disparate treatment in negotiations. But the previous chapters demonstrate that what seems to be the freewheeling and idiosyncratic process of negotiation may mask what in reality is systematic disparate racial treatment. If plaintiffs could succeed in certifying such classes, a profitable new form of civil rights litigation might quickly spread throughout the United States. But if individual plaintiffs must pursue litigation in a piecemeal fashion, the civil rights laws are unlikely to provide a strong deterrent to dealer discrimination.

II. Legal Reform

A. Modernizing Civil Rights Laws

Lawmakers could respond to bargaining discrimination by expanding the current coverage of the civil rights and consumer protection laws. Most important, Congress could amend §§ 1981 and 1982 to extend to women (and other protected classes) the right to be free from discrimination in contracting to buy and sell services as well as goods. California is the only state to have such a law generally prohibiting sex discrimination in contracting.[39] Amended versions of §§ 1981 and 1982 could also allow plaintiffs to bring disparate impact suits, currently actionable under Title VII, which require no showing of intent.[40] Disparate impact litigation would allow suits to challenge the bargaining practices of sellers that are facially neutral (in the sense that they do not consciously take a buyer's race or

39. Unruh Act, Cal. Civ. Code § 51.5 (1999). An indirect way that some local municipalities prohibit retail sex discrimination is by expansive definitions of "public accommodation." See Idaho Code § 18-7301(2) (1987) (guaranteeing "full enjoyment" of any public accommodation); id. § 18-7302(c) (defining "full enjoyment" to include the right to purchase any "article of personal property offered or sold on, or by, any establishment to the public"). See also *infra* note 45 and accompanying text.

40. See, e.g., Griggs v. Duke Power Co., 401 U.S. 424, 432 (1971); cases cited *supra* note 7.

gender into account) but have significant discriminatory effects.[41] More-over, it might be much easier for plaintiffs to have racial class actions certi-fied when claiming disparate impact. While it is harder to show commonal-ity in a disparate treatment suit (because a defendant dealership can claim that the behavior of individual plaintiffs led to their paying higher prices), it is easier to show that a dealership's choice of negotiating instead of com-mitting to a no-haggle sticker had a disparate impact on black consumers by showing—as in the previous chapter—that black consumers were eight times more likely to pay a home run profit.

An indirect way for regulators (possibly including courts without new legislation) to accomplish an expansion of civil rights law both to (1) pro-tect women against disparate treatment in the retail sale of goods and ser-vices and (2) provide disparate impact causes of action is to expand the traditional definition of what constitutes a "public accommodation." Title II of the 1964 Civil Rights Act prohibits sex discrimination in the supply of public accommodations[42] and may allow plaintiffs to pursue disparate impact claims.[43] Public accommodations were traditionally limited to those markets—such as innkeepers and transportation providers—that were subjected to "common carrier" duties to serve the public in a nondiscrimi-natory manner.[44] But increasingly, the concept is taking on a broader and

---

41.   An example of such a facially neutral practice is dealers' giving discounts to any customer—black or white—who lived in areas designated as low-maintenance-cost zones. To the extent that poorer neighborhoods tend to have worse roads that wear down cars, blacks would be disproportionately denied discounts.

Although the practices revealed in this study are anything but facially neutral, fair-driving plaintiffs may have more difficulty establishing disparate treatment than dispa-rate impact. In the Title VII context, the Supreme Court has extended disparate impact analysis to subjective hiring decisions because plaintiffs face similar difficulties in estab-lishing "subconscious stereotypes and prejudices." Watson v. Fort Worth Bank & Trust, 487 U.S. 977, 990 (1988) (plurality opinion). The Court explained:

> [E]ven if one assumed that [subjective] discrimination can be adequately policed through dispa-rate treatment analysis, the problem of subconscious stereotypes and prejudices would remain. . . . If an employer's undisciplined system of subjective decisionmaking has precisely the same effects as a system pervaded by impermissible intentional discrimination, it is difficult to see why Title VII's proscription against discriminatory actions should not apply.

Id. at 990–91.

42.   42 U.S.C §§ 2000a-1 et seq.

43.   Compare Olzman v. Lake Hill Swim Club, Inc., 495 F.2d 1333 (2d Cir. 1974) (suggesting disparate impact claim allowed under Title II), with Arquello v. Con-oco, 1997 WL 446433 (N.D. Tex., July 21, 1997) (dismissing disparate impact claim as "insufficient to establish a Title II violation").

44.   42 U.S.C. § 2000a(b)(1)–(4) (1982) (defining establishments that qualify as public accommodations).

more elastic meaning that basically encompasses all retail sales. For example, the human rights ordinance of the City of Champaign, Illinois, defines a "place of public accommodation" to include

> a business, accommodation, refreshment, entertainment, recreation or transportation facility of any kind, whether licensed or not, whose goods, services, facilities, privileges, advantages or accommodations are extended, offered, sold or otherwise made available to the public, and includes but is not limited to inns, restaurants, eating houses, hotels, soda shops, department stores, clothing stores, hat stores, shoe stores, bathrooms, restrooms, theaters, skating rinks, public golf courses, public golf driving ranges, concerts, cafes, bicycle rinks, elevators, ice cream parlors or rooms, railroads, omnibuses, buses, stages, airplanes, street cars, boats, funeral hearses, crematories, cemeteries, and public conveyances on land, water or air, public swimming pools, retail establishments and other places of public accommodation and amusement.[45]

Under this definition, it would be difficult to identify a retail good or service that was not considered a public accommodation.

Moreover, the Equal Employment Opportunity Commission (EEOC) has explicitly suggested that car dealerships themselves are public accommodations. The EEOC's Technical Assistance Manual for the Americans with Disabilities Act (ADA) requires "a public accommodation . . . to make available appropriate auxiliary aids and services where necessary to ensure effective communication,"[46] and a subsequent illustration expressly contemplates that car dealerships are covered as a public accommodation:

> ILLUSTRATION 2: *H* then stops by a new car showroom to look at the latest models. The car dealer would be able to communicate effectively general information about the models available by providing brochures and exchanging notes by pen and notepad, or perhaps by means of taking turns at a computer terminal keyboard. If *H* becomes serious about making a purchase, the services of a qualified interpreter may be neces-

45. Municipal Code City of Champaign, Illinois, *codified through* Ordinance No. 99-108, adopted April 20, 1999. Supp. no. 27, § 17-3 Definitions <http://www.city.champaign.il.us/government/index.html>.

46. EEOC, *The Title III of the Americans with Disabilities Act Technical Assistance Manual* <http://www.ada-infonet.org/tam3/ III-4.3200>.

sary because of the complicated nature of the communication involved
in buying a car.[47]

But if a car dealership is a public accommodation for purposes of the ADA,
it is not a long step to argue that it is a public accommodation for purposes
of Title II (which prohibits sex and race discrimination by public accommodations). Indeed, even under a more traditional reading of the term *public accommodation,* it is at least arguable that car dealerships are in the
business of providing transportation services in ways that are analogous
to more traditional providers (such as buses or taxicabs). But it should be
emphasized that the ADA has a broader definition of the term than the
1964 Civil Rights Act, so that expansion along these lines might need to
be done legislatively.[48]

The current litigation against General Motors Acceptance Corp.
(GMAC), the credit division of General Motors (discussed in chapter 4),
points to another possible avenue for bringing a disparate impact class
suit. Under the Equal Credit Opportunity Act (ECOA),[49] a plaintiff can
challenge the disparate racial impacts of a lender's finance practices. The
GMAC litigation challenges the lender's willingness to grant dealers discretion to negotiate supracompetitive interest rates. The manufacturer not
only allows the (alleged) disparate impact to occur but directly participates
in the excess profits. But the interest rate is not the only negotiated term
of the loan that might disproportionately disadvantage African American
consumers. The principal amount of the loan also affects the loan profitability. This is not only true as a matter of theory—where profits will increase on loans with excess interest if higher amounts are borrowed. But
as shown in the last chapter, the profitability on the loans was positively
correlated with the profitability on the car sale itself. The manufacturers'
credit division thus may also directly profit from dealers' negotitating
higher transaction prices—which translate into higher loan principals. The
bottom line is that the next wave of finance litigation may challenge the
manufacturer's decision to facilitate haggling over the underlying car price

---

47. Id.

48. Expanding the meaning of public accommodation to include all retail sales
would still leave wholesale contracting and the potential discrimination of retail buyers
on the basis of sex uncovered (while it arguably would cover discrimination on the basis
of race because of the broader contracting language of § 1981).

49. 15 U.S.C. §§ 1691–1691f (1994 & Supp. IV 1998); see also 12 C.F.R.
§ 202.1; Interagency Policy Statement, 1994 WL 128417.

as causing another actionable dimension of racial disparity in finance. Alleging differential loan principals (in addition to disproportionate interest rates) may therefore allow plaintiff classes to use our lending civil rights law to attack the disparate racial impact of haggling over the price of the car itself. The current litigation against GMAC is already indirectly challenging racial disparities in the underlying principal. The plaintiffs' showing of racially disparate loan profits are couched in terms of total dollar profit—which is a product of the heightened interest rate multiplied by the heightened principal amount.

■ ■ ■

Although I have argued that the sellers' search for high-markup consumers causes sellers to discriminate against black males and females, the proposal to extend civil rights protection to the sale of all goods and services is based on the notion that racial- and gender-based disparate treatment may well exist in a broader variety of markets. The problem of disparate treatment in new car sales has been perpetuated by the fact that the bargaining process conceals from black and female consumers the prices received by their white male counterparts. Without such information, blacks and women cannot directly learn of disparate treatment.[50] The 1960s civil rights legislation outlawed discrimination in those markets—most notably housing and employment—in which the seller's disparate treatment was open and notorious. But the absence of a manifest benchmark does not imply the absence of discrimination; there is no reason to think that animus or statistical causes of discrimination manifest themselves only in markets in which interracial comparisons of treatment can be readily made.[51] Indeed, as various overt forms of discrimination have become illegal, more subtle and

50. Disadvantaged consumers need benchmark information in order to realize that they have been harmed. See William L. F. Felstiner, Richard L. Abel & Austin Sarat, The Emergence and Transformation of Disputes: Naming, Blaming, Claiming . . . , 15 Law & Soc'y Rev. 631, 633–35 (1980–81). In the fair-housing context, by contrast, black consumers can more directly infer disparate treatment when advertised apartments are suddenly unavailable.

51. Reinier Kraakman has argued analogously that there is no reason to believe that discounts from fundamental value only occur in those few securities (open-ended mutual funds) for which a benchmark comparison exists. See Reinier Kraakman, Taking Discounts Seriously: The Implications of "Discounted" Share Prices as an Acquisition Motive, 88 Colum. L. Rev. 891, 902 (1988).

covert manifestations have often replaced them.[52] In today's marketplace, disparate racial treatment is most likely to persist in those areas of behavior where information about other consumers' treatment is not readily accessible (especially to the victims of the discrimination). The negotiated prices of new and used cars certainly fit this paradigm, but as discussed in chapter 1 many other salient components of treatment—especially related to service—may also qualify. The existence of disparate racial treatment in the audits test and its persistence in the consummated transaction data analyzed in chapter 4 is not only important in and of itself (concerning as it does what is for most consumers their largest nonhousing purchase) but also provides an opening wedge to justify a fundamental expansion of the domain of our civil rights law.[53]

B.   Reinvigorating Consumer Protection Laws

State and federal governments might also attempt to enforce more rigorously contract common law and consumer protection statutes to reduce the type of discrimination we have been considering. To the extent that consumer protection laws codify common law contract remedies such as fraud and duress, they may provide a viable alternative to civil rights remedies. Thus, although consumer protection laws have not yet been used to attack racial disparate treatment as a "deceptive" misrepresentation, this history does not preclude more extensive governmental intervention in the future.

The Federal Trade Commission (FTC) Act[54] and the myriad "baby FTC acts" enacted by the individual states[55] outlaw the use of "unfair or

---

52.   Lateef Mtima, African-American Economic Empowerment Strategies for the New Millennium—Revisiting the Washington–du Bois Dialectic, 42 How. L.J. 391, 409 (1999).

53.   Another potential target might be race or gender discrimination in intercorporate transactions. Many corporate transactions are individually negotiated because of their idiosyncratic nature. A corporation arguably violates § 1981 if it bargains differently with the agents of other corporations based on the agents' gender or race. Race or gender discrimination against the agents of a corporation may give those agents a cause of action against that corporate "person." Even if such disparate treatment is actionable under current constructions of the civil rights laws, the idiosyncratic nature of corporate transactions makes it difficult for the victims of disparate treatment to infer discrimination.

54.   15 U.S.C. § 45(a)(1) (1988).

55.   See, e.g., Mass. Gen. L. ch. 93A (1988).

deceptive" trading practices.[56] Utilizing such legislation to reach discrimination in bargaining for a new car purchase will require a reconceptualization of what we consider unfair or deceptive. Attacking sellers' disparate treatment in bargaining as being "deceptive" strikes at deeply held beliefs about what is appropriate in the normal course of negotiations. The complexity of these beliefs is demonstrated by contrasting the effect of seller misrepresentation in the context of car sales with seller misrepresentation in housing sales or rentals. Fair-housing cases often gain their moral authority from the egregious nature of seller misrepresentations such as "The apartment is no longer available."[57] In the retail car bargaining context, however, some forms of misrepresentation are broadly accepted. Few would believe, for example, that a seller would be held liable for misrepresenting "I can't reduce the price any further"—even if the seller did reduce the price for another consumer.[58] Seller misrepresentation is present in both the housing market and in the new car market. The distinction in our response turns, if at all, on which types of misrepresentation we deem acceptable.

Nevertheless, both the common law of contracts and consumer protection statutes do provide a framework for attacking disparate treatment in bargaining. Courts have construed consumer protection statutes to prohibit implied as well as express misrepresentation.[59] On this basis, courts could attack disparate treatment in negotiations for new cars by finding an implied representation that the dealer has not discriminated on the basis of race or gender in negotiating the agreement. Or alternatively, courts

56. See S. Chesterfield Oppenheim, Glen E. Weston, Peter B. Maggs & Roger E. Schechter, *Unfair Trade Practices and Consumer Protection* 701–4 (1983).

57. See, e.g., Ann Mariano, Housing Bias Settlement Sets Record, *Wash. Post*, Apr. 13, 1990, at B1 (describing a settlement by a development company that offered white testers apartments but told black testers that "no apartments were available").

58. The degree to which such statements are accepted as a normal aspect of car sales is reflected in cases involving salesperson "puffing." Puffing, or the making of excessive representations by salespeople during their attempts to sell cars, is often treated by courts as inactionable. See Restatement (Second) of Torts § 402B cmt. g (1965) (stating that "puffing," such as the statement that "an automobile is the best on the market for the price," is not a misrepresentation by the seller).

59. See, e.g., Kalwajtys v. FTC, 237 F.2d 654, 656 (7th Cir. 1956), *cert. denied*, 352 U.S. 1025 (1957); see also Richard M. Schmidt Jr. & Robert Clifton Burns, Proof or Consequences: False Advertising and the Doctrine of Commercial Speech, 56 U. Cin. L. Rev. 1273, 1276 (1988) (noting that the U.S. Postal Service and the FTC prohibit implicit misrepresentation).

might find an implied warranty that the dealer will not make better offers in the future because of other buyers' race or gender. In other words, courts may preserve the "essence" of bargaining—by conceding that all consumers should expect idiosyncratic treatment at the hands of car dealers—but refuse to sanction "discrimination" by rejecting regimes in which the seemingly idiosyncratic behavior is in fact systematically predicated on potential customer's race or gender.

Such a finding would be completely consistent with freedom of contract. Sellers could avoid making this implicit representation by expressly reserving the right to bargain differently with customers of different races. A judicial or legislative finding of an implicit representation that race has not played a role in the seller's precontractual behavior (or an implicit warranty that it will not in the performance of this contract or the negotiation of similar future contracts) would simply be "filling a gap" in the parties' contract. Finding an implied representation of no racial disparate treatment is at least as reasonable as finding an implied representation that sellers reserve the right to treat different races differently: few explicit contracts would ever opt for the latter provision.[60] Once lawmakers established a default rule of no disparate treatment, plaintiffs bringing implied misrepresentation cases would then face the same burden as traditional § 1981 plaintiffs: the burden of demonstrating disparate treatment.

Of course, legislative or judicial rules could go beyond such a default rule to establish nonwaivable "mandatory" rules against disparate treatment in bargaining on the basis of gender or race.[61] Mandatory rules may seem superior, but they may be unnecessary because few sellers would contract around a "no-discrimination" default rule by expressly reserving the right to discriminate. If lawmakers instead choose a "discrimination-allowed" default rule for implicit representations, it is possible that some sellers would contract around this presumptive rule in their advertisements by holding themselves out as equal-opportunity sellers. Indeed, this process may be at play in dealership advertisements that proclaim that a particular dealership will not mistreat female customers. For example, the Silver Lake Dodge dealership in Boston ran ads claiming that their dealership was one

60. Contractual theorists have traditionally argued that contractual gaps should be filled with provisions for which the parties would have bargained. See Ian Ayres & Robert Gertner, Filling Gaps in Incomplete Contracts: An Economic Theory of Default Rules, 99 Yale L.J. 87, 88–89 (1989).

61. See id.

"[w]here you don't have to bring a man along to be treated like a customer."[62] At a minimum, sellers that opt for such explicit representations should be held liable under existing consumer protection laws for any disparate treatment that contradicts the advertisement's representation.

The Supreme Court's decision in *Patterson v. McLean Credit Union*[63] strongly supports establishing a no-discrimination default—and may even be read to imply that state contract law already implements such a default. In restricting civil rights protection under § 1981 to discrimination in the formation of a contract, the *Patterson* Court suggested that victims of discrimination should turn to traditional contractual remedies: racial harassment "amounting to a breach of contract under state law is precisely what the language of § 1981 does not cover. That is because, in such a case . . . the plaintiff is free to enforce the terms of the contract in state court."[64] Although the contract at issue was silent as to whether postformation discrimination was permissible, the court implied that nondiscrimination provisions could be read into state contract remedies. Following the *Patterson* rationale, finding an implicit representation that the dealership has not negotiated differently with a consumer because of her race or gender would offer a free market alternative to civil rights interventionism.

III. Structural Reforms

The expansion of traditional civil rights and consumer protection laws is not likely to completely eliminate disparate treatment in bargaining based on race or gender. Victims of disparate bargaining treatment will most likely be restricted to suing individual dealerships rather than manufacturers or groups of dealerships.[65] Even if plaintiffs bring class actions and courts consistently grant testers standing to sue, the piecemeal approach of such suits, combined with the protracted nature of litigation, is unlikely to be sufficient to deter race- and gender-dependent behavior.

---

62. See, e.g., the advertisement for Silver Lake Dodge & Leasing, *Boston Woman*, winter 1990, at 7a.

63. 491 U.S. 164 (1989).

64. Id. at 183.

65. Proof of discrimination would most likely be attributable to individual dealerships unless plaintiffs can find "horizontal" collusion among dealerships or "vertical" pressure from manufacturers to discriminate. Disparate treatment by employees would be attributable to the firm under traditional notions of agency. See, e.g., Miller v. Bank of Am., 600 F.2d 211, 213 (9th Cir. 1979).

In light of these conditions, policymakers might consider structural reforms to improve the workings of the market. Structural changes must, however, reflect an understanding of the cause of disparate treatment in order quickly and effectively to cure it. For example, if animus is inducing price discrimination, a law that outlawed price discrimination might induce some sellers to refuse to bargain. However, if the disparate treatment is caused by inferences about different consumer demand, then outlawing price discrimination should not generate such refusals.[66] Simply put, to formulate effective intervention, policymakers must understand why sellers discriminate.

The analysis of competition in chapter 3 suggested that high-markup customers (and the ensuing concentration of profits) are a central cause of dealer price discrimination. As a result, if policymakers can find a way to reduce significantly the profits on these "home run" sales, individual dealerships would have a stronger incentive to commit to a lower and more uniform pricing. Currently dealerships that commit to uniform "no-haggle" prices must risk sacrificing all the profits that they traditionally extract from "home run" sales—which I showed could be as much as 40–50 percent of their bottom line—in the hopes of making it up on increased sales volume.

The presence of high-markup sales creates a huge negative externality for the rest of car buyers. Dealers are willing to make negotiations unpleasant for all consumers because the dealers are themselves consumed with ferreting out those qualified customers who are going to pay such a large profit. If society could deter the high-markup sales, the rest of consumers would benefit tremendously as dealerships would no longer have an incentive to make car buying such a universally unpleasant experience. Without the pathological effects of highly concentrated profits, dealers would no longer have an incentive to force consumers to expend real and psychic resources in bargaining and car sales might become dramatically more competitive.

My claim here is not that "home run" sales and the high concentration of profits currently allow dealerships to earn supracompetitive profits (or that the barriers to entry in the retail market are high). Instead, my claim is that too many dealerships have entered the market and that the profits from high-markup consumers are dissipated on the needlessly high number of showrooms and the needlessly high numbers of salespeople searching for these "home run" sales. If the market tipped toward lower and more

---

66. After all, airlines would not stop selling to businesspeople if price discrimination on the basis of inferences about willingness to pay were prohibited.

uniform pricing, the number of dealerships and the number of salespeople would decrease—with the profitability per dealership remaining close to current levels (that is, fairly competitive).

Policymakers could use three different strategies to eliminate high-markup sales. Most directly, courts could strengthen current notions of substantive unconscionability to prohibit high-markup sales.[67] This strategy, however, is unlikely to occur: courts in the past have shown extreme reluctance to distinguish conscionable from unconscionable markups. Although courts have voided contracts for unconscionable markups in a handful of cases (for example, *Frostifresh Corp. v. Reynoso*[68] and *American Home Improvement v. MacIver*)[69]—which are favorites among authors of contract casebooks—few courts since the early 1960s have reached similar holdings.[70] The likelihood of courts taking the dramatic step of expanding this rarely used doctrine becomes even smaller in light of the specialized nature of bargaining for retail cars and society's solicitude toward such bargaining.[71]

As a second regulatory strategy, policymakers might restrict the amount of price dispersion permissible in the car market. Regulators might, for example, allow dealerships to engage in bargaining, but void sales with markups that are more than 20 percent above the average markup. Unlike direct unconscionability regulation, firms would retain the freedom to set the average markup for any one model as high as the market would bear, but would be prohibited from selling similar cars at significantly different prices. At its most extreme, this form of regulation would prohibit bargaining and mandate that dealerships sell at advertised prices.[72]

---

67. Under the common law, unconscionable contracts are unenforceable. See, e.g., Williams v. Walker-Thomas Furniture Co., 350 F.2d 445 (D.C. Cir. 1965); U.C.C. § 2-302 (1988). Academics have distinguished between procedural and substantive unconscionability. See, e.g., Richard Epstein, A Critical Reappraisal, 18 J.L. & Econ. 293, 301 (1975).

68. 52 Misc. 2d 26, 27, 274 N.Y.S.2d 757, 759 (Dist. Ct. 1966), *rev'd on other grounds*, 54 Misc. 2d 119, 281 N.Y.S.2d 964 (Sup. Ct. App. Term 1967).

69. 105 N.H. 435, 439, 201 A.2d 886, 889 (1964).

70. See, e.g., Stuart Macaulay, John Kidwell, William Whitford & Marc Galanter, *Contracts: Law in Action* 237 (1995).

71. See Ayres, *supra* note 2, at 857.

72. Currently, similar regulations mandate that common carriers contract at filed rates. All common carriers subject to the Interstate Commerce Act, 24 Stat. 379 (1887) (codified as amended in scattered sections of 49 U.S.C.), are required to sell at the rates filed with the Interstate Commerce Commission. See Richard W. Palmer & Frank P. DeGiulio, Terminal Operations and Multimodal Carriage, 64 Tul. L. Rev. 281, 312–13

Restraining price dispersion is an attractive form of regulation because it might benefit all would-be car buyers. If the number of high-markup sales is reduced, sellers may find that bargaining (and the transaction costs that it imposes on all consumers) is no longer profitable. Once high-markup consumers are protected, sellers may no longer subject their low-markup consumers to costly and unpleasant bargaining.

Finally and least intrusively, regulators might reduce the number of sales with disparately high markups by mandating various types of disclosure from dealerships to consumers. Dealerships, for example, might be required to reveal the average price for which each make of car is sold.[73] Knowing that the dealership is attempting to charge $3,000 more than the average price would allow high-markup consumers to protect themselves. Alternatively, regulation might force dealerships to reveal the size of the markup on each individual transaction. Clay Miller and I have argued elsewhere[74] that markup disclosure could improve both the equity and efficiency of retail car sales: "[M]arkup revelation would truncate the bargaining process at each dealership. The possibility of hoodwinking uninformed buyers into purchasing at a high markup would diminish as the excessive profits would be directly revealed."[75]

Alternatively, we might eliminate the current rule that as a default awards dealerships their lost profit if a consumer breaches her agreement to buy. This rule is inefficient. Buyers don't know how much effort they should take in order to avoid breach because they can't accurately evaluate how much damages are at stake. At a minimum, the sage rule of *Hadley v. Baxendale* (limiting a breaching seller's damages to the foreseeable losses

---

(1989). The Robinson-Patman Anti-Discrimination Act, 15 U.S.C. § 13 (1988), similarly restrains price dispersion among common carriers.

73.   Information about other aspects of how car prices are distributed might also reduce price dispersion. Knowing, for example, the lowest price paid by a consumer (or the prices paid by the lowest 10 percent of consumers) would alert consumers to any overcharging.

74.   See Ian Ayres & F. Clayton Miller, "I'll Sell It to You at Cost": Legal Methods to Promote Retail Markup Disclosure, 84 Nw. U. L. Rev. 1047, 1063–64 (1990).

75.   Id. at 1048. Such a regulatory system would significantly reduce the costs of search for all consumers:

> [B]uying a new car would be easier and more equitable in a world where retailers revealed their true costs. Consumers armed with information about the retailer's markup would not need to search at as many dealerships—for the simple reason that consumers would have a much better idea when they were getting a good deal. Markup information can thus serve as a dramatic substitute for consumer search.

Id.

of the buyer) should be extended to allow breaching buyers to limit damages to lost profits of the seller that were foreseeable to the buyer.[76] A zero-damages default might provide sellers with an even better "information-forcing" incentive to disclose their true profit—because it would encourage sellers to add a liquidated damages clause. A dealership that has negotiated an unusually high price may be reluctant to contract around this zero-damages penalty default. Consumers informed that they are about to sign a high-markup contract might think better of it and continue haggling at this dealership or move on to others. The high-profit sellers might respond to a zero-lost profit by merely contracting for a liquidated amount that was small enough not to distinguish the sale from others sales with more normal profits. But even here the law could make progress by taking more seriously the implicit representations of fact that are made when parties contract around defaults. As Rob Gertner and I recently wrote:

> In using penalty defaults to induce parties to reveal type information, the law intends that by contracting around, one side or the other will implicitly represent information about the profferor's type. Since parties implicitly covenant that their implicit representation will be true, an attempt to contract around a zero-damage default with a liquidated damages clause which substantially understates one's true damages may constitute an implicit misrepresentation of fact. The law might require liquidated damage defaults to be enforceable to accurately state the lost profit of the defendant—or might even hold sellers liable (for breaching their implicit warranty that all implicit representations are true) for negotiating clauses with underliquidated amounts that were not so denominated.[77]

Indeed, one could imagine a regime in which failing to negotiate around a zero-damage default might constitute an implicit (mis)representation that the dealer has zero profits. Thus, merely manipulating the default damage rules (and the rules regulating how they can be contracted around) *might* be sufficient to discourage dealerships from so assiduously pursuing high-markup sales.

Peter Schuck and I have also suggested "reinventing" state depart-

---

76. See Ian Ayres, Three Proposals to Harness Private Information in Contract, 21 Harv. J.L. & Pub. Pol'y 135 (1997).

77. Ian Ayres & Robert Gertner, Majoritarian v. Minoritarian Defaults, 51 Stan. L. Rev. 1591, 1608–9 (1999).

ments of motor vehicles—the dreaded DMVs—to help deter inequitable pricing.[78] The DMVs already require dealers to report the price at which each car actually sold. Our suggestion, put simply, is that the DMVs provide consumers information via the Internet about how particular dealerships price—the average discount from sticker price for each type of car, for example, or the average markup over dealer cost. They could also reveal the relationship between published "blue book" prices for used cars and actual trade-in allowances. The departments or consumer groups could even rank dealerships by their sticker discounts. Yet I worry, given the "racial ravine" in the use of the Internet, that this proposal, while worthwhile, would not be tailored sufficiently to protecting consumers who are currently most in need of protection.

Other minor legal changes that improve consumer information may be sufficient to move the market. In particular, the FTC could more clearly define nonfraudulent uses of the "dealer invoice" amount—so that no-haggle dealerships could speak more credibly about their gross profit.[79] Armed with this information, consumers could protect themselves by patronizing no-haggle dealerships. These types of informational regulation might reduce the dealers' opportunity to extract large profit from a small group of consumers and thus eliminate the primary reasons that dealers like to haggle.

In sum, mandating disclosure and restraining price dispersion are plausible strategies to reduce the importance that dealerships place on high-markup sales. A central prediction of this chapter is that at some point reducing the concentration of dealership profits would rationalize dealership competition by giving individual dealerships an incentive to opt for high-volume, no-haggle selling strategies. Once dealer dependence on high-markup sales decreases, the incentive for *individual* dealerships to break ranks and experiment with more competitive, high-volume marketing becomes much more attractive. And the relatively unintrusive nature of disclosure and price-dispersion regulation makes them politically and administratively more viable.[80]

78. See Peter Schuck & Ian Ayres, Car Buying, Made Simpler, *N.Y. Times*, Apr. 13, 1997, § 3, at 12.

79. In defining the "dealer invoice" amount, the regulation would need to reduce the dealer's cost by any rebates or kickbacks from the manufacturer to the dealer. See Ayres & Miller, *supra* note 74, at 1062.

80. Regulating markup disclosure, after all, would be nothing more than a government-mandated Edmund's service that would more systematically give all consumers the information that many already discover.

Before choosing a strategy to eliminate price dispersion, policymakers should determine whether a single price equilibrium is "sustainable"—that is, whether competitive dealerships that charge a single price could break even and thus survive price dispersion. In markets with high fixed costs, if sellers were required (directly or indirectly through disclosure) to charge a single price, competition might drive that price to a level below sellers' average cost. Such markets have "hollow cores" (because the "core" set of viable single-price equilibriums is empty or "hollow"). [81]

If the retail car market has a hollow core, government intervention to eliminate price dispersion would tend to drive dealerships from the market. In such markets, high-markup sales help dealers cover their fixed costs. In the airline industry, for example, the high-markup sales to business travelers may be necessary to meet industry fixed costs. Indeed, business travelers may benefit from the presence of lower-priced tourist fares because "cheap" seats defray part of these fixed costs. If regulation eliminated price dispersion and mandated a single fare per route, business travelers might have to pay higher prices than under the current regime. Tourist travelers would stop buying, and the airline would then pass its fixed costs along to the smaller group of business travelers.

Regulator concerns should be allayed, however, because the retail car market does not resemble hollow core markets. Retail car dealerships incur some fixed costs, but these costs are not so high that we should worry that single-price equilibria are not sustainable —especially when their fixed costs are compared to those of many other single-price markets such as the market for electronic appliances and stereo equipment. Moreover, it is implausible that white males would (like tourist travelers) stop purchasing in a single-price equilibrium. Mandating a single fare for airlines might lead to an inflated price that only businesspeople could afford, but mandating a single price for automobiles would not leave blacks and females alone to shoulder even higher proportions of the retailers' fixed costs. [82]

Although this discussion of potential regulatory strategies is impres-

81. See John Wiley, Antitrust and Core Theory, 54 U. Chi. L. Rev. 556, 558 (1987).

82. Similar arguments might be directed at the manufacturing level. Although retailers do not incur large fixed costs in selling cars, manufacturers' fixed costs are substantial. Manufacturers may need to extract the profits from retail price dispersion in order to break even. They may be able to extract these dealership high-markup profits through lump-sum franchising fees, credit, or warrantee arrangements. These lump-sum revenues combined with the variable revenues that manufacturers earn on selling additional cars constitute what economists call a "two-part tariff."

sionistic, at the very least it suggests that regulators have a variety of choices beyond traditional civil rights and consumer protection remedies to attack the racial inequalities that are the subject of this book. Naturally, implementing one of these structural interventions would impose enforcement costs that must be weighed against the benefits of regulation. Dealers may attempt to circumvent such regulations in several ways.[83] Nevertheless, in evaluating the efficacy of structural changes, policymakers should pay particular attention to the concentration of profits and the prevalence of high-markup sales.

IV. The Aftermath and the Future

In the years since 1991, when the original pilot study was published, the retail car market has seen a dramatic shift away from haggling. More than 10 percent of new car dealers currently sell all of their cars at nonnegotiable prices and more than 70 percent of dealers sell at least one of their models without dickering.[84] There has also been a dramatic growth in the use of third-party buying services (which bargain on behalf of individual consumers)—with more than a quarter of dealerships selling cars through such services.[85]

A. The Public and Scholarly Reaction

Many newspaper articles have linked this shift away from haggling to a growing frustration of women and minorities with the process and results of negotiation.[86] Indeed, the original pilot study may have played a small

83. Most notably, they might attempt to make up for the loss of concentrated high profits with lower trade-in prices or higher interest fees.

84. See, e.g., James Bennett, Buying without Haggling as Cars Get Fixed Prices, N.Y. Times, Feb. 1, 1994, at A1. Saturn has been successful in prohibiting its dealers from haggling over the sticker price of its cars. But in many cities, so-called no-dicker or one-price dealerships have independently decided to forgo the potential profits of negotiation. The practice is especially prevalent among high-volume sellers: "Fifteen percent of high-volume operators today have at least a single one price dealership." J.D. Powers, No Haggle Study (1994).

85. For example, a nonprofit corporation, Car Bargains (for a fee of $135) solicits offers from at least five dealers in the customer's area. Services Can Save Thousands with No-Haggle Car Buying (CNN television broadcast, July 23, 1994).

86. Bob Storck, American Classics: Trucks with Attitude, Wash. Times, Dec. 24, 1993, at E10 ("The dealership experience is often demeaning to women. It is suggested the one-price, no-haggle concept pioneered by Saturn and Ford Escort should have ap-

role in heightening consumer awareness, particularly about the *extent* of price discrimination: the article was widely reported—literally in hundreds of broadcast (including the three network evening news shows, NBC's *Today,* CNN, *Oprah,* NPR's *All Things Considered*) and print sources (including *Time, Cosmopolitan, Glamour, New York Times, USA Today, Washington Post*).[87] The producers of *PrimeTime Live* contacted me immediately after this coverage and solicited my help in producing three different segments auditing a host of retailers with hidden cameras. Several writers have referred to the finding of the pilot study as an explicit reason why women or minorities might want to buy from no-haggle dealerships or through third-party buying services.[88] Many dealerships themselves have responded by claiming that they (unlike others in the industry) treat women fairly.[89] A few dealers' advertisements have even attempted to ex-

---

peal."); Women Fuel Demand for Sport Utility Vehicles, *St. Louis Post-Dispatch,* May 30, 1993, at 1C ("That's why Saturn has the one price deal. Women don't like the car-lot haggle."); Car Buying Could Be Fairer without the Haggling Hassle: Psst, Have They Got a Deal; One Price Fits All, *Buffalo News,* Feb. 13, 1994, at 8 ("No-haggle pricing could prove a particular hit with the greater number of women who buy cars these days, since so many feel ill at ease in the auto world."); Thousands Due for Saturn Homecoming, *Gannett News Service,* June 23, 1994, at E4 ("[Saturn's] low-pressure approach appeals especially to women."); The Wise Buyer's Car Guide, *Essence,* Nov. 1993, at 119 ("If you're a sister who hates to bargain, try shopping for a car at a "one-price" or "no-haggle" dealership.").

87. White Men Get Better Deals on Cars, Study Finds, N.Y. TIMES, Dec. 13, 1990, at A6; Ellen Goodman, Driving Home a Point about Not Being a Victim, *Chi. Trib.,* Dec. 30, 1990, at C14; Undercover Tests Identify Bias, *USA Today,* Sept. 26, 1991, at 3A; Who Gets the Best Deals on Wheels?; Chicago Study Finds It's White Males, *Wash. Post,* Dec. 14, 1990, at F1; White Men Get Best Car Deals, Study Finds, *Detroit Free Press,* Dec. 14, 1990, at 1A; Women Charged More for Cars, Study Says, *L.A. Times,* Dec. 14, 1990, at D4; Study Offers Proof of Car-Sales Bias, *Boston Globe,* Feb. 14, 1993, at 36.

88. See, e.g., Will Astor, No-Dicker Dealers, *Rochester Business Journal,* Oct. 1, 1993, at 13; The Wise Buyer's Car Guide, *supra* note 86; Shelly Donald Collidge, Purchasing a Car? Using a Buying Service Could Save Big Bucks, *Christian Science Monitor,* Sept. 8, 1994, at 8 ("A 1991 Harvard Law Review study found women and minorities pay prices that give a dealer up to 242 percent more profit than the dealer would get on sales to white males. Because a club buyer negotiates, the dealer doesn't know who the customer is."); Kim Ode, Women Pay Price for Capitalism, *Star Trib. (Minneapolis-St. Paul),* May 25, 1993, at 1E.

89. See, e.g., the advertisement for Silver Lake Dodge & Leasing, *Boston Woman,* winter 1990, at 7a ("Where you don't have to bring a man along to be treated like a customer."). But a *PrimeTime Live* audit of one of Marge Schotz's dealerships in Cincinnati uncovered discrimination against a female tester—even though Schotz explicitly advertises that she treats women fairly. *PrimeTime Live* (ABC television broadcast, May 24, 1993).

plicitly distinguish their practices from the conduct uncovered in the original study.[90] And as discussed in chapter 4, Edward D. Buckley, an Atlanta attorney, remembered the initial media coverage (in interviewing ex-salespeople who complained of being pressured to mistreat black consumers) and ultimately brought the first suit alleging that a dealership's negotiation practice violated §§ 1981 and 1982.

The audit study may also have had a small role to play in Saturn's decision to air a television commercial that portrayed a powerful nonverbal narrative about discrimination. The commercial was composed entirely of a series of black and white photographs. In a voice-over narrative, an African American man recalls his father returning home after purchasing a car and feeling that he had been mistreated by the salesman. The narrator then says maybe that's why he feels good about having become a salesperson for Saturn. The commercial is a remarkable piece of rhetoric. As a visual image, the stark photographic images are devoid of the smiles that normally populate car advertisements. Instead, there is the heartrending shot of a child realizing that his parent has been mistreated because of their shared race and the somber but firmly proud shot of the grown, grim-faced man now having taken on the role of a salesman who does not discriminate. The commercial does not explicitly mention race or Saturn's no-haggle policy—but few viewers would fail to understand that race was a central cause of the father's mistreatment.

This commercial may in fact have been the first national advertisement to put past racial mistreatment by competitors at the core of its message. Individual dealerships have talked about gender discrimination in local advertisements, but racial mistreatment apparently had seemed too controversial an issue to even mention. For example, once while I was discussing the auditing results on NPR's *Talk of the Nation,* a representative of the National Association of Automobile Retailers acknowledged that its members were taking steps to ensure that women were not mistreated when bargaining for a car. I immediately pointed out that the industry spokesman seemed unwilling to even mention the possibility of racial discrimination. The dealer underscored my point by responding with sustained silence.

---

90. See, e.g., the mass mailing from Gerald Lincoln-Mercury, Skokie, IL (Nov. 8, 1993) ("A recent Harvard University research project documents [that] some groups paid over *three times* the amount of dealer mark-up than others were able to negotiate. . . . We believe that no one should have to pay more because of race, gender or negotiation skills.") (emphasis in original).

The Saturn commercial not only raises the issue of race discrimination—albeit nonverbally and by claiming the mistreatment occurred in the past (not by its current competitors)—but also subtly speaks to multiple audiences. The commercial can simultaneously be heard as an argument (1) that minorities should patronize Saturn to avoid being mistreated; (2) that nonminorities who fear mistreatment should patronize Saturn to avoid being mistreated; and perhaps most subtly, (3) that nonminorities whom other dealerships would discriminate in favor of (because of their race) should patronize Saturn because it is immoral to patronize an establishment that discriminates on the basis of race. The last message, probably, has the faintest resonance. While ethical considerations do motivate some consumers (particularly with regard to a company's environmentalism or charitable works), the discrimination track record of a company or its competitors is rarely marketed as a basis for buying or not buying. But Saturn's oblique but nevertheless courageous commercial represented a start.

Of course, with this much publicity there was also a backlash. There were newspaper reports of dealerships pulling their commercials from television stations that covered the story too prominently.[91] And the late *Chicago Tribune* columnist, Mike Royko, denounced the study in no uncertain terms—concluding that "the people who ran these tests . . . should be tapped on their heads to see if they make a sound like a bongo drum."[92] Royko claimed:

> If you've ever bought a new car, you know that there are two ways
> you can go about it. You can be smart, or you can be dumb. . . . [I]f
> the dubious results of this study tell me anything, it is this:
> 1. White males have more experience in new-car shopping than
>   white females, black males and black females.
> 2. White males and white females are better educated than black
>   males and black females, so they're more likely to do the research
>   that helps them get a fair price.[93]

91. Conversation with Kathy Heed (Chicago resident reporting on news coverage of pilot study).

92. Mike Royko, Color Not an Option in Best New-Car Deal, *Chi. Trib.*, Dec. 17, 1990, at p. 3, col. C.

93. Id.

Royko attributed all of the price differential in the audit studies to tester differences. He claimed that "[w]hen it comes to profit, a salesman is without bias."[94] But Royko's criticism glaringly ignored the fact (which was reported in his own newspaper four days earlier)[95] that the testers used a uniform bargaining strategy and so presented identical indicators of car-buying experience (for example, remember that the testers signaled in their initial offer that they knew the dealer's cost by setting the offer equal to this amount).

But to merely criticize Royko for his distortions and borderline racism[96] would be to ignore an important part of the picture. Much of Royko's venting seemed to be caused by a feeling that freewheeling, no-holds-barred haggling is both good and natural and should be left completely outside the ambit of government oversight:

> [The group that made the study] suggest[s] that civil rights laws be
> broadened to somehow make it a crime for a salesman to persuade a
> minority member or a female to pay more for a car than, for example,
> my brother-in-law Gus would pay. Ah, yes, I can see it now—a new
> federal agency with acres of bureaucrats at their desks, listening to peo-
> ple say: "My civil rights were violated; I just found out that I paid $50
> more than my neighbor for a sun roof. And he got better wheel covers
> than I did and tinted glass."[97]

The massive news coverage given the results of the audit study suggests how squarely they struck a chord—but different notes were heard by different groups. While I have not proposed criminalization or "a new federal agency with acres of bureaucrats," I do believe that "paying $50 more . . . for a sun roof" because of your skin color should be actionable. For me, neither the arbitrarily restricted market domain of our civil rights laws nor our tradition of laissez faire car negotiation should be sacrosanct.

---

94. Id.

95. Merrill Goozner, Study Faults Car Sales Tactics: Researcher Finds Women, Blacks Pay Higher Prices, *Chi. Trib.*, Dec. 13, 1990, at 1, col. C.

96. The reference to a "bongo drum" (especially in an article that also characterized the results of the audit studies as "further evidence that being a white guy is terrific, even if we run slow") might be considered a racist reference relating blacks to a primitive jungle object.

97. Royko, *supra* note 92.

B. The Future

The experience of the last few years suggests that the institution of haggling over new car prices may not be immutably entrenched. The time is particularly ripe to consider reform because the industry may be on the verge of tipping almost completely to "no-haggle" sales—needing only a slight nudge from enlightened regulation. Currently 5–10 percent of dealers use a no-haggle approach on at least some of their products.[98] Republic Industries, the nation's largest auto dealer, has used the no-dicker approach in its nationwide chain of AutoNation superstores. And for the first time, the car manufacturers are actively encouraging retailers to adopt no-haggle pricing. Ford Motor Co., in partnership with existing dealers, is buying up dealership networks in medium-sized markets (including San Diego, Oklahoma City, and Tulsa), instituting one-price selling, and earmarking $5 billion to buy dealerships in other markets.[99] Mercedes-Benz is encouraging one-price selling by shrinking the margin between the dealer's cost and the sticker price, thus limiting the abilities of dealers to compete among themselves on sticker discounts.[100]

Commentators have also pointed to the surprisingly widespread use of the Internet as a force pushing toward no-haggle pricing.[101] J.D. Powers estimates that in 1999 more than 40 percent of consumers used the Internet to research and prepare for negotiating, up from 25 percent the preceding year. And nearly 3 percent of all new vehicles are now purchased using the Internet (up from 1.1 percent in 1998).[102] Internet shopping services are particularly popular with women customers. For example, one of the leading services, Auto-by-Tel.com, reports that a majority of its customers are female.[103] The gradual rise of fixed-price dealerships may in the end

98. Donald W. Nauss, No-haggle Sales Policy Is Spreading, but Very Slowly, *Star Trib.* (Minneapolis-St. Paul), May 1, 1999, *available in* 1999 WL 7495839("fewer than 5 percent of the nation's 22,400 new-car dealers could be classified as one-price sellers").

99. Id.

100. Id.

101. Donna Harris, Internet, Republic, Others Push No-haggle Pricing, *Automotive News,* Jan. 18, 1999, at 18, *available in* 1999 WL 7852496 ("Perhaps the biggest push for no-haggle pricing . . . is coming from Internet shoppers. . . . The knowledge that consumers have drives prices down and accelerates the move to one-price selling").

102. Brian S. Akre, Car Buyers Test Drive Internet before Dealing: Survey Finds Many New Auto Purchasers Are Shopping Online, *Detroit News,* July 13, 1999, *available in* 1999 WL 3931664.

103. Eric C. Evarts, Internet Fuels Car-buying Bargains, *Christian Science Monitor,* July 26, 1999, *available in* 1999 WL 5381028. A recent study suggests that the aver-

reinvigorate the Epstein/Heckman conjecture (considered in chapter 4) that consumer self-help may be able to mitigate the worst harms of individual dealer discrimination. Some commentators have explicitly predicted that "[i]n the end, the Internet will narrow the gap between the highest prices people pay for cars and the lowest."[104] But I still worry that the primary impact of the Internet will be to improve the bargaining power of consumers who are already relatively sophisticated. The Internet, by itself, does not seem to be an innovation directed toward protecting those consumers who have been most likely to pay a high markup. There is thus the dark possibility that the advent of the Internet may actually increase the variance in prices paid as negotiated prices would increasingly tend to exhibit a bimodal distribution—with the savvy Internet shoppers getting low prices and the less sophisticated, non-Internet shoppers continuing to pay substantial markups.

The future marketplace may evolve toward no-haggle pricing of its own accord. And there are good reasons to think that the current equilibrium may not be stable. In the coming years, we should expect to see no-haggle market shares either increase dramatically or decline. As one industry representative has put it: "It's very difficult for an individual dealer to implement one-price selling and stay with it."[105] When haggle and no-haggle dealerships of the same manufacturer exist in a single geographic market, there is a strong tendency for the haggle dealerships to systematically cut their price slightly below the no-haggle price of its competitor (at least when a customer signals it knows the posted price). The haggle dealership can retain some of its high-markup sales to unsophisticated consumers and discipline the renegade dealership by systematically stealing its customers. Indeed, Chris Denove, a consulting director for J.D. Power, has stated: "If an entire market for a franchise goes one-price, the system is much more likely to work. . . . It fails if [even] one dealer opts out."[106] Peaceful coexistence between the haggle and no-haggle dealerships of the same manufacturer may not be possible.

The ongoing price wars in Denver between the haggle dealerships and

---

age customer of Auto-by-Tel.com "pays approximately 2% less for her car." Fiona Scott Morton, Florian Zettelmeyer & Jorge Silva Risso, Internet Car Retailing (unpublished manuscript, 2000), at 2.

104. Akre, *supra* note 102.

105. Harris, *supra* note 101, quoting Mike Jackson, president of Mercedes-Benz of North America.

106. Nauss, *supra* note 98.

the seventeen no-haggle John Elway AutoNation stores is instructive. The AutoNation stores have recently entered the Denver market with posted nonnegotiable price policy. The traditional (haggle) dealerships' seeming collective response has been simple and severe. In the words of the president of the Colorado Automobile Dealers Association: "They've pretty much decided they're going to beat AutoNation prices."[107] AutoNation has responded by cutting its nonnegotiable price to "about a 1 percent premium over the estimated invoice price."[108] The no-haggle policy has increased AutoNation's market share by 40 percent, but with such paper-thin margins, it is not clear that its profits have increased. Indeed, the market participants seem to be engaged in a war of attrition waiting to see who will be the first to exit or change its pricing policy. A similar if somewhat less extreme scenario has been played out in other geographic markets with a single or only a handful of no-haggle dealerships. The presence of no-haggle dealers tends to provoke an "emotional response" from the other dealers,[109] with the traditional dealers committing to beat any no-haggle prices for as long as necessary to make the no-haggle dealership rescind its policy.

The recent interest of manufacturers in encouraging no-haggle sales may be sufficient to coordinate a joint move of an entire make toward nonnegotiable pricing.[110] Direct manufacturer coordination may raise resale price maintenance concerns under the antitrust laws, but indirect methods—such as reducing the difference between sticker price and dealer cost or increasing the geographic territory of individual dealerships—can also be effective. B. B. Hollingsworth Jr. (the chairman of Group 1 Automotive Inc., a Houston-based publicly held dealership group) has particu-

---

107. Steve Raabe, Car Wars Prices Fall in No-haggle Auto Battle, *Denv. Post,* May 3, 1999, *available in* 1999 WL 7882197. Antitrust afficionados will note that it might be illegal for competitors to agree ("they've . . . decided") how to respond to a competitor's pricing policy.

108. Id.

109. Bennett, *supra* note 84. See also Tim Martin, No-Dicker Sticker Has Mixed Success, *Nashville Tennessean,* April 12, 1994, at D6 ("The competition between one-price and traditional dealers has changed from a battle to an all-out war."); Santa Fe Ford advertisement, *Gainesville Sun,* June 5, 1993, at 10D ("THE SO-CALLED 'NON-NEGOTIABLE' PRICE AT SOME DEALERS IS *NOT* YOUR BEST PRICE IF YOU DON'T SHOP. . . . Look through this paper at the other Ford dealers' ads, then bring in the ad price on the car or truck you want and WE'LL BEAT IT; NO BULL, NO GAMES, JUST FAIR DEALING!").

110. As Mike Jackson, president of Mercedes-Benz of North America, put it: "It's a whole different story if a manufacturer has embraced it as a principle of its brand and is working systematically with retail partners to implement it." Harris, *supra* note 101.

larly stressed the need for all dealers of a particular manufacturer in a particular geographic market to adopt the no-haggle strategy: "The reason Saturn [nonnegotiable pricing] works is because one dealer controls a large territory. . . . If we owned all seven Toyota stores in Houston, we would be fixed-price dealers, too."[111] It is not so important that dealerships of other manufacturers adopt no-haggle pricing, because the haggle dealerships of, say, Toyota cannot clearly undercut the no-haggle price of Saturn. This individual manufacturer effect suggests that small geographic markets with one manufacturer's dealer per market can more easily sustain no-haggle pricing than larger cities that support multiple Toyota dealerships.

But even given the rise in use of the Internet and the recent support of some manufacturers, there is still a substantial risk that haggling will persist in many geographic markets as a means of extracting high markups from a minority of consumers. The no-dicker sticker has been with us for more than a decade and has still been unable to make substantial inroads (in terms of market share) into the market.[112]

Using the informational interventions outlined above to nudge the retail market toward no-haggle selling would advance both the equity and efficiency of car sales. The dealers' attempts to extract high profits from a small group of consumers create large costs for both dealers and consumers. No-haggle sales require fewer salespeople and fewer dealerships. The possibility that no-haggle price competition has caused some dealerships to go out of business is probably on balance good news, not bad. There are good reasons for Chicago to have ninety-four movie theaters, but it is not efficient for Chicago to have 523 car dealerships.[113] The overhead at many of these dealerships and the salaries of many salespeople are paid for by a few consumers who pay disproportionately high markups. A larger shift to no-haggle sales might thus rationalize the industry structure by reducing the number of dealerships.[114] To be sure, shifting to one-price sales would not

111. Id.

112. Mary Connelly, "One-price" Growth Tapers Off; It's More Than Just a Fad, But It's Not a Revolution, *Automotive News*, Dec. 27, 1993, at 1.

113. These figures are taken from the Chicago area Yellow Pages.

114. In small towns, a shift to fixed-price competition might facilitate anticompetitive collusion because competitors could more easily learn when other dealers were chiseling on the collusive price. But a general move away from no-haggle bargaining might increase consumer choice in all but the most isolated towns. No-haggle sales would make it much easier to purchase a car over the phone or through the mail—so that small-town residents could easily compare their local prices to prices quoted by big-city dealers.

be an economic panacea,[115] but more than efficiency is at stake. Instead of relying solely on traditional civil rights approaches to eliminate race and gender disparities within a larger system of haggling, it may be more appropriate to target the high-markup sales that haggling induces.

Conclusion

The negotiation of contracts occupies a mysterious and somewhat mythical position in the law and in our society. In *The Wealth of Nations*, Adam Smith opined that people have a natural propensity to "truck and barter" over the sale of goods.[116] Law-and-economic scholars at times extend this insight, suggesting that people will tend to negotiate whenever resources are misallocated: if I want to sit on a crowded subway, I will negotiate with the other passengers for a seat.[117]

Common experience indicates, however, that many people in the United States are averse to bargaining.[118] The frustration that many con-

115. Dealerships, for example, could still extract disproportionate profits on trade-ins, financing, and other ancillary terms of trade.

116. Adam Smith, *An Inquiry into the Nature and Causes of the Wealth of Nations* 25 (Roy H.. Campbell & Androv S. Skinner eds., 1981; 1st ed. 1776).

117. Cognoscenti will recognize such bargaining as an application of the Coase theorem. See Ronald H. Coase, The Problem of Social Cost, 3 J.L. & Econ. 1 (1960). However, even Coase recognized that transacting is not costless and that bargaining would not always occur. See John J. Donohue III, Diverting the Coasean River: Incentive Schemes to Reduce Unemployment Spells, 99 Yale L.J. 549, 549 n.2 (1989); Robert C. Ellickson, The Case for Coase and against "Coaseanism," 99 Yale L.J. 611, 612–13 (1989).

Robert Hale, writing long before Coase, understood not only the Coasean impulse to bargain but applied it to a hypothetical of passengers selling their seats on a train:

> At the beginning of the journey there are less than a quarter as many passengers as there are seats. At that time a rule which permitted each passenger to reverse the back of the seat in front of him and occupy both seats to the exclusion of other passengers would operate equally. Any passenger excluded from the seats I occupy suffers no hardship; he can occupy two seats by himself. If the early arrivals are still permitted to exclude others from the extra seats that are occupied, the latter will either have to stand up, or *pay the first passengers for the privilege of occupying even one seat*. And such payments, even though no greater than the value of sitting down, would not reward the recipients for any affirmative act of service, but simply for not forcing the person who pays to stand up.

See Barbara H. Fried, *The Progressive Assault on Laissez Faire: Robert Hale and the First Law and Economics Movement* 93 (1998); Ian Ayres, Discrediting the Free Market, 66 U. Chi. L. Rev. 273 (1999).

118. The vast majority of goods cannot be bargained for: retailers compete for consumers through a "stated price" that they can change from day to day but over which they will not bargain.

sumers experience in bargaining for a car is largely attributable to the ludi-crously inefficient manner in which cars are marketed. Although Smith and others have attached almost mythic qualities to the process of bargaining, this and the preceding chapters have thrown the equity and efficiency of car negotiations into question. The process of retail car negotiations becomes even more problematic when traditionally disadvantaged members of our society effectively pay a bargaining tax whenever they purchase a new car.

Although it is dangerous to extrapolate from the results of even the four (or five) studies discussed in the previous chapters,[119] the amounts of discrimination uncovered, if representative of a larger phenomenon, are truly astounding. A $500 overcharge per car means that blacks annually pay $150 million more for new cars than they would if they were white males. There are substantial reasons to uncover and eliminate such discrimination.

A few years ago, I was speaking about the audit results on a Chicago radio show. A caller identified himself as a black salesman and said it was true that dealers tended to ask black customers to pay more but that it wasn't discrimination because the dealer was motivated by profit, not hatred. I asked him if it would be acceptable for his boss to pay black workers less than whites, not because he hated blacks, but in order to realize larger profits (believing that blacks would be willing to work for less money). The caller answered, "Oh no, that would be discrimination." But he was at a loss for explaining why a profit motive was a legitimate reason to take race into account in one market, but not another.

This story only underscores the deeply market driven views we have about civil rights. The 1960s taught us that disparate racial treatment in employment and housing is contemptible, but we have less certain intuitions about disparate treatment in other markets. In part, this is because we don't think systematic race discrimination is an important problem in other markets. The empiricism in these first chapters, however, gives lie to the notion that race and gender discrimination exists in only a relatively small number of markets in our economy. While the impulse for race and gender discrimination in car markets (for example, the search for high-markup sellers) may not be the same impulse driving discrimination in other markets, the car market probably shares with other markets an important structural aspect that creates an opportunity to discriminate. Just

---

119. The four studies concern the cost of the underlying car, while the fifth concerns exclusively racial disparities in the cost of financing car purchases.

as the car buyer has trouble knowing how other consumers are treated, there are myriad aspects of service and accommodation in which it is difficult for a consumer to know how other consumers are treated. A seller's nondiscrimination along these dimensions of service are a "credence" good that consumers to a large degree must simply take on faith.[120] And these are just the dimensions where discrimination is most likely to persist.

120. See chapter 1, note 2, for a discussion of credence goods.

PART II

DISPARATE IMPACT

This part of the book moves from tests of disparate treatment to tests of disparate impact. Chapter 6 employs a traditional methodology to explore disparate impact in a nontraditional setting—the transplantation of cadaveric kidneys. The traditional empirical approach looks to two different sources of data to show that (1) the federal government's kidney transplant allocation rules disproportionately disqualify black recipients and (2) the allocation rules do not further a compelling medical interest.

In sharp contrast, chapter 7 employs an unconventional methodology to test for an unjustified disparate impact. The setting again is a nontraditional one—the market for bail and bail bonds. But the new methodology uses (1) market prices as a proxy for the probability that individual defendants will skip bail and (2) evidence about the equilibrium probability of flight to assess whether judicial bail setting has an unjustified disparate impact. Instead of using two types of evidence to prove the two elements of a disparate impact case, the chapter uses a unitary test that also has the great advantage of being impervious to the omitted variables problem that often plagues disparate treatment regressions.

CHAPTER 6

Unequal Racial Access to Kidney Transplantation

IAN AYRES, LAURA G. DOOLEY, AND ROBERT S. GASTON

Access to medical care is an issue of acute and increasing importance in the United States, a country in which the most promising of groundbreaking technologies may be available to only the privileged few. Although debate about the problem of unequal access to medical care typically centers on financial obstacles to advanced therapies and the obvious inequity of allowing patients' ability to pay to drive treatment decisions, issues of equitable access for patients of both genders and all racial and ethnic backgrounds increasingly have come into focus.

These concerns about equitable access animate the ongoing debate about how government should regulate the transplantation of kidneys. Over 350,000 people in the United States suffer from kidney failure—what medical professionals call "end-stage renal disease" (ESRD).[1] While kidney failure may be treated with dialysis,[2] kidney transplantation is the preferred treatment: studies show that transplant recipients are more likely to return to work, avoid hospitalization, and enjoy a greater sense of well-being than

---

1. U.S. Renal Data System (USRDS), *2000 Annual Data Report* at 41.

2. Dialysis mechanically purifies a patient's blood. The patient must remain attached to a dialysis machine three times a week for treatments that might take three to four hours each.

patients on dialysis.[3] Kidney transplants constitute more than three-fourths of the solid organ transplants performed in this country and have success rates routinely as high as 80 percent.[4] A severe shortage of transplantable kidneys, however, limits the availability of this preferred treatment.[5] For example, in 1998, while about 40,000 Americans were registered on waiting lists, fewer than 12,300 received renal transplants.[6]

Federal regulations control the allocation of scarce donated kidneys among prospective recipients. Since 1972, Medicare has covered the costs

3. See Roger W. Evans, The Demand for Transplantation in the United States, *in Clinical Transplants 1990*, at 319 (Paul I. Terasaki ed., 1991); Roger W. Evans et al., The Quality of Life of Patients with End-Stage Renal Disease, 312 New Eng. J. Med. 553 (1985); R. J. Fischel et al., Long-term Outlook for Renal Transplant Recipients with One-year Function, 51 Transplantation 118 (1991).

4. James F. Blumstein, Federal Organ Transplantation Policy: A Time for Reassessment?, 22 U.C. Davis L. Rev. 451, 460 (1989); Paul W. Eggers, Effect of Transplantation on the Medicare End-Stage Renal Disease Program, 318 New Eng. J. Med. 223 (1988).

5. Transplantable kidneys come from either "living related" or "cadaveric" donors. In 1990, 1,714 transplants were performed using kidneys from living related donors and 6,443 from cadaveric donors. Potentially many more cadaveric kidneys could be harvested. Up to twenty thousand Americans die annually in circumstances—such as car accidents—that would make their organs suitable for transplantation. Organ Transplants, H.R. Rep. No. 98-769, at 4 (1984); U.S. Dep't of Health & Human Services, Report of the Task Force on Organ Transplantation: Issues and Recommendations (1986); Lloyd R. Cohen, Increasing the Supply of Transplant Organs: The Virtues of a Futures Market, 58 Geo. Wash. L. Rev. 1 (1989); Henry Hansmann, The Economics and Ethics of Markets for Human Organs, 14 J. Health, Pol., Pol'y & L. 57 (1989).

6. UNOS, OPTN Waiting Lists & UNOS Scientific Registry Data as of April 15, 2000, <http://www.unos.org/frame_Default.asp?Category=Newsdata> (visited August 7, 2000). This shortage has intensified in recent years. In 1990, just under 8,200 of the 18,000 Americans waiting for renal transplants received them. UNOS Update (March 1991); USRDS, *supra* note 1; Steven Takemoto et al., A Report of 504 Six Antigen-Matched Transplants, 23 Transplantation Proc. 1318 (1991). The selection process through which ESRD patients are placed on a waiting list is left largely to the discretion of the local transplant team. Developments in the Law: Medical Technology and the Law, 103 Harv. L. Rev. 1519, 1630 (1990). A study has shown that black dialysis patients have a significantly lower chance of being placed on a transplant waiting list, even after controlling for a number of health factors that would affect the likelihood of transplant success. J. Michael Soucie et al., Race and Sex Differences in the Identification of Candidates for Renal Transplantation, 19 Am. J. Kidney Dis. 414 (1992). Compared to white males, the relative likelihoods that black males and females would be placed on a waiting list were .78 and .67, respectively (both statistically significant at .05). The process by which dialysis patients are selected for waiting lists is not the focus of this chapter, yet it may also be a key factor in the disparate access of black patients to kidney transplants. See Developments in the Law: Medical Technology and the Law, 103 Harv. L. Rev. at 1632. See also text accompanying note 241 (discussing new definition of time on waiting list).

of virtually all kidney transplants.[7] To qualify for Medicare reimbursement, transplanting hospitals must abide by rules promulgated by the federal Organ Procurement and Transplantation Network (OPTN).[8] OPTN policies for cadaveric kidney allocation have traditionally given strong preference to potential recipients who are genetically similar to the donor as determined by the identification of antigens located on the surface of cells.[9] For example, if a harvested kidney has all the same antigens as a potential recipient on the waiting list, then that patient will receive the kidney—even if other dialysis patients have waited longer for a transplant.[10]

The rationale for basing kidney allocation on antigen matching is that a recipient who receives a kidney from a donor with similar antigens may be less likely to have her immunologic system reject it. The federal guidelines traditionally have reflected a belief that better antigen matching will lead to a higher rate of kidney graft survival and that this interest in maximizing transplant outcomes should outweigh the equitable claims of patients who must wait longer for a renal allograft.

Mandated antigen matching, however, has made it difficult for black dialysis patients to qualify for the pool of scarce cadaveric kidneys. This chapter reports on the mounting evidence of racial disparity in transplantation that is a result of antigen matching, which we analyzed in a

7. See 42 U.S.C. § 426 (1998). For example, in 1988, Medicare paid for more than 92 percent of the transplants performed. USRDS, *supra* note 1; see also Blumstein, *supra* note 4, at 454; Peter H. Shuck, Government Funding for Organ Transplants, 14 J. Health, Pol., Pol'y & L. 169 (1989).

8. See Blumstein, *supra* note 4, at 463–64.

9. Antigens are proteins that stimulate an immune response. HLA antigens (human leukocyte antigens) are found on the surface of nearly all human cells and are the product of genes located in the major histocompatibility complex (MHC) of human DNA at chromosome six. Michael Owen, Major Histocompatibility Complex, *in Immunology* 4.1 (Ivan M. Roitt et al. eds., 2d ed. 1989). These antigens are the key determinants that enable immunologically active cells to recognize "self" from "foreign" tissues, sparing the former and destroying the latter. While the term *MHC antigens* may be more scientifically correct, the term *HLA* remains in common usage within the transplant community. Efforts to improve tissue compatibility by defining these antigens and allocating donated kidneys among recipients in a manner that minimizes antigenic differences are known as "HLA matching." In this chapter the term *antigen matching* refers to this process.

As discussed below, see *infra* note 240 and accompanying text, recent amendments to the federal point system have reduced the preference for recipients with well-matched antigens.

10. These guidelines are discussed in greater detail in notes 57–61 and accompanying text.

series of articles beginning in 1993.[11] We trace the steps leading to the government's changing the allocation system in the late 1990s to ameliorate the unjustified racial disparities caused by antigen matching. The point system currently in use continues to allocate in part on the basis of antigen matching—and still makes it harder for African Americans to qualify for transplantation. But the revised system at least now arguably imposes only a medically justified disparate impact. While we believe there is more that could and should be done to tailor the point system to further ameliorate unjustified (or at best marginally) justified disparities, it is now more contestable how much more alteration is needed—in large part because the government has laudably responded to our initial scholarship to remove what had become the most capricious aspects of the previous point system.

But this takes us ahead of our story. To better appreciate the information confronting the government regulators, let us return to the early 1990s. Although there was (at that time) a growing awareness in the transplant community of racial disparities in transplantation, antigen matching had not been identified as a cause of this disparity. As to the disparity itself, healthcare researchers understood that blacks waited almost twice as long as whites for their first transplant—13.9 and 7.6 months, respectively.[12] While whites comprised 61 percent of the dialysis population, they received 74 percent of the kidney transplants.[13] In a given year, white dialysis patients had approximately a 78 percent higher chance of receiving a cadaveric transplant than black dialysis patients.[14]

---

11. See Ian Ayres, Robert Gaston, Laura Dooley & Arnold Diethelm, Racial Equity in Renal Transplantation: The Disparate Impact of HLA-Based Allocation, 270 JAMA 1352 (1993); Response to letters-to-the-editors, 271 JAMA 269 (1994); Ian Ayres, Laura Dooley & Robert Gaston, Unequal Racial Access to Kidney Transplantation, 46 Vand. L. Rev. 805 (1993) (hereinafter Unequal Access); Ian Ayres, Robert Gaston & Mark Deierhoi, HLA Matching in Renal Transplantation, 332 New Eng. J. Med. 752 (1995).

12. Office of Inspector General, *The Distribution of Organs for Transplantation: Expectations and Practices* 8 (1991).

13. Health Care Financing Administration, *End-Stage Renal Disease Patient Profile Tables* (1988). In 1988, 33.5 percent of dialysis patients were black, but only 22.3 percent of cadaveric kidney transplants went to black patients.

14. In 1988, 4,865 cadaveric transplants were distributed among 67,778 white dialysis patients (4,865 / 67,778 = 7.17 percent), and 1,486 cadaveric transplants were distributed among 36,951 black dialysis patients (1,486 / 36,951 = 4.02 percent). USRDS, *supra* note 1. Thus, the likelihood that a white dialysis patient will receive a kidney in a given year is 78 percent higher than the likelihood that a black patient will receive a kidney ((7.17 − 4.02)/4.02 = 78.4 percent). More detailed estimates are discussed below in note 64 and accompanying text.

But early in the 1990s the transplant community did not understand that the government's antigen matching rules are a "but for" cause of this racial disparity. Because antigens are distributed differently among racial groups,[15] a white patient is more likely than a black patient to have antigens that match those on a kidney from a white donor. Whites donate almost 90 percent of kidneys in the United States. Because the proportion of blacks on the waiting list is significantly higher than the proportion of kidneys donated by blacks, white patients are more likely to have antigens that match those on donated kidneys. Thus, a disproportionately black waiting list chases a disproportionately white donor pool.

Alternative allocation rules could eliminate the racial disparity in access to donated kidneys.[16] A first-come, first-served rule would, for example, give all patients equal access to the pool of cadaveric kidneys. But such a rule would come at a substantial cost in survivability—because, as argued below, perfectly matched transplants are less likely to be rejected.

Most healthcare researchers during this earlier period believed that the racial disparity in transplantation was caused by lower donation rates by African Americans (relative to whites).[17] Several scholars argued that the

15.   See *infra* note 76 and accompanying text.

16.   To be sure, other factors—including unequal access to waiting lists and a relative inability of blacks to respond when an organ became available—contributed to this racial disparity. Fred P. Sanfilippo et al., Factors Affecting the Waiting Time of Cadaveric Kidney Transplant Candidates in the United States, 267 JAMA 247 (1992).

17.   In 1988, blacks donated only 12 percent of living related transplants and only 8 percent of cadaveric kidneys. Office of Inspector General, *supra* note 12. Studies from New York, Los Angeles, Miami, and Washington D.C. document that blacks were markedly underrepresented in donor statistics. See Clive O. Callender, Organ Donation in the Black Population: Where Do We Go From Here?, 19 Transplantation Proc. 36 (Supp. 2 1987); Luis M. Perez et al., Organ Donation in Three Major American Cities with Large Latino and Black Populations, 46 Transplantation 553 (1988) (saying that black families were two to three times less likely to consent to organ donation than white families).

While the reasons for the historically lower rate of black organ donation were not fully understood, several studies have studied the problem. One found that the most common reasons for donor reluctance were lack of information, religion, distrust of medical professionals, fear of premature death, and a preference to donate only to members of the same race. Clive O. Callender et al., Attitudes among Blacks toward Donating Kidneys for Transplantation: A Pilot Project, 74 Nat'l Med. Ass'n J. 807 (1982); Callender, Organ Donation, *supra*, at 36 (citing Gallup Organization, *Attitudes and Opinions of the American Public towards Kidney Donations* [1983]).

The lower rate of consent by black families to cadaveric donation might have been caused by the failure of healthcare professionals to ask for consent in an effective way. The requests for consent came disproportionately from whites. Researchers investigated whether higher levels of consent could be obtained if the persons making the request were of the same race as the potential donor family. See The Partnership for Organ Do-best solution to racial disparity in transplantation is to increase black donation of both cadaveric and living related kidneys.[18] Increasing black donation rates (they thought) could improve the pool of well-matched kidneys for blacks on the waiting list and thus mitigate the disparate effects of antigen matching rules.[19]

Intensified efforts to increase the donation rates of black Americans, however, proved to have (which remains true today) virtually no chance of eliminating the disparate rates of transplantation for blacks and whites. Because the waiting list for kidney transplants is so disproportionately black, increasing the rate of black donation cannot plausibly equalize the proportions of blacks seeking and receiving kidneys. The incidence of ESRD in the United States is nearly four times greater for blacks than whites: while blacks constitute nearly 13 percent of the general population, 34 percent of ESRD patients are black.[20] To eliminate the disparate impact

---

nation and the Annenberg Washington Program, *Solving the Donor Shortage by Meeting Family Needs: A Communications Model* (Oct. 30–31, 1990). Due in part to such efforts, donation rates of blacks are now equal to those of whites. Clive O. Callender et al., A National Minority Transplant Program for Increasing Donation Rates, 29 Transplantation Proc. 1482 (1997).

18. Callender, Organ Donation, *supra* note 17; Perez et al., *supra* note 17.

19. The relatively low black donation rate does not justify the unequal access that results from the present system. An individual white patient does not have a greater equitable claim to a given cadaveric kidney than a black patient simply because blacks as a class donate fewer cadaveric kidneys than whites, especially given that the lower rates may be an artifact of disparate procurement procedures. See *supra* note 17 (discussing the possibility that black families may encounter substandard requests from medical professionals). Nonetheless, a class-based linking of an allocation scheme to procurement might induce higher donation rates. The possible dependence of procurement success on a localized system of allocation is discussed more fully in the text accompanying note 186. While we favor measures to increase the donation of cadaveric kidneys by blacks, increased donation is unlikely to abrogate unequal racial access to transplantation. Newer research suggests that the black donation rate has recently been increasing toward the white rate. See the third section of this chapter.

20. USRDS, *supra* note 1. In 1977, the incidence rate of ESRD in the United States was 873 per million for blacks and 218 per million for whites. USRDS, Excerpts from the USRDS 1999 Annual Data Report, 34 Am. J. Kidney Dis. S1–S176 (Supp. 1 1999); Dan Gordon, Racial Differences in ESRD, 19 Dialysis & Transplantation 114 (1990). This disproportionate representation defies easy analysis and may be due to several factors. Socioeconomic issues such as diet, accessibility of healthcare, education, and substance abuse surely contribute to it. A. O. Hosten, Kidney Disease in Blacks in North America—An Overview, 19 Transplantation Proc. 5 (Supp. 2 1987). However, the key factor in ESRD among blacks appears to be high blood pressure, or hypertension.

High blood pressure is more common in blacks for poorly defined reasons. Richard F. Gillum, Pathophysiology of Hypertension in Blacks and Whites, 1 Hypertension 468 (1979). Blacks have an incidence of hypertension-related ESRD 6.5 times that of whites.

of antigen matching, blacks would need to donate enough additional kidneys so that the proportion of black donors would approximate the proportion of blacks on the waiting list—34 percent. To accomplish such an increase, the donation rate for blacks—for both cadaveric and living related organs—would have to increase to five times its current rate and more than four times the current rate for whites. Increases of this magnitude are unlikely.[21] It is possible that even a proportionate representation of donated black kidneys would not equalize the rates of antigen matching. Because blacks have more heterogeneous distributions of antigen types, it may be less likely that a black patient will match the antigens on a donated black kidney than that a white patient will match the antigens on a donated white kidney.[22] Efforts to increase black donation are laudable and important, but it is misleading to argue that increasing black donation rates could significantly reduce disparate racial access to transplantation.

■   ■   ■

This chapter explores whether the disparate racial impact of mandated antigen matching was justified by higher overall survival rates of kidney transplants.[23] Advances in the use of drugs that effectively suppress im-

---

In several large series, hypertensive kidney disease has been shown to be the most common cause of ESRD in blacks. See, e.g., Hosten, *supra;* Rafael Oriol et al., Influence of the Original Disease, Race, and Center on the Outcome of Kidney Transplantation, 33 Transplantation 22 (1982). Thus, hypertension in the black population seems either to cause or exacerbate renal disease of all etiologies, hastening the progression to ESRD.

21.   Efforts to spur black donations, including educational funding and the use of blacks to solicit cadaveric donations, have not generated increases of the magnitude required to eliminate the disparity. Paul Delaney, Fighting Myths in a Bid to Get Blacks to Consider Transplants, *N.Y. Times,* Nov. 6, 1991, at C17. Substantial increases in the supply of kidneys might be achieved by governmental purchase of the right to transplant cadaveric organs. *Cf.* Cohen, *supra* note 5; Hansmann, *supra* note 5, at 57; Lori B. Andrews, My Body, My Property, 16 Hastings Ctr. Rep. 28 (Oct. 1986); Chris Hedges, Egypt's Desperate Trade: Body Parts for Sale, *N.Y. Times,* Sept. 23, 1991, at A1. While a market-oriented approach deserves careful consideration, we predict that our government is unlikely to adopt such an approach in the near future. Given the types of public and private initiatives that might plausibly be undertaken, the proportion of blacks on waiting lists almost certainly will continue to be higher than the proportion of cadaveric kidneys donated by blacks.

22.   Regarding polymorphism and the inability to find matched donors for black recipients, see P. G. Beatty, M. Mori & E. Milford, Impact of Racial Genetic Polymorphism on the Probablility of Finding an HLA-Matched Donor, 60 Transplantation 778–83 (1995).

23.   At the outset, it is important to note that for most potential recipients, allocation of kidneys for transplantation is not a matter of life or death due to the alternative

mune responses have dramatically altered the impact of antigen matching: the likelihood of graft survival may now be relatively independent of the degree of antigen matching. These technological advances have made antigen-based allocation less critical to transplant success.

Normatively, we argue that the equitable claims of black dialysis patients for cadaveric kidneys outweigh the marginal improvement in transplant outcomes associated with antigen matching under the old regime. Guido Calabresi and Philip Bobbitt have reasoned:

> [C]orrected egalitarianism . . . plays an unusually influential role in the American concept of equality. It accepts the general premise of formal egalitarianism that discrimination is proper so long as likes are treated alike, but corrects the operation of this premise by rejecting it whenever methods applying it happen to produce results which correlate the permissible category of discrimination—health, for example—with an impermissible one, such as wealth or race.[24]

The federally mandated system for allocating kidneys produced just this impermissible effect based on an increasingly weak correlation with health or transplant survival. Proposals in the early 1990s to expand the influence of antigen matching on organ allocation would have further increased racial disparity in transplantation.[25]

The chapter also serves as a case study of the difficulty of administering regulations in the face of conflicting and evolving empirical data. The increased demand for donor organs has intensified debate over allocation, but the issues are not new. While some within the transplant community

---

treatment offered by dialysis. However, as noted previously, most authorities consider transplantation to be an optimal therapy. See Eggers, *supra* note 4, at 223; USRDS, *supra* note 1. Inexplicably, blacks have lower mortality rates on dialysis than whites. In 1986, for example, blacks on dialysis had a 23 percent lower mortality rate than whites. Gordon, *supra* note 20, at 114. Thus, one might justify the disparate racial impact of antigen matching as a way of decreasing ESRD mortality by taking disproportionate numbers of whites off dialysis, which is relatively more risky for them.

24. Guido Calabresi & Philip Bobbitt, *Tragic Choices* 25 (1978).

25. See David W. Gjertson et al., National Allocation of Cadaveric Kidneys by HLA Matching, 324 New Eng. J. Med. 1032 (1991) (proposing to create a single national waiting list and to allocate every kidney procured within the United States to the potential recipient with best antigen match); see also Steve Takemoto et al., Survival of Nationally Shared, HLA-Matched Kidney Transplants from Cadaveric Donors, 327 New Eng. J. Med. 834 (1992).

argue that allocation based on antigen matching is the most scientifically sound method, others contend that factors such as newer drug therapies, evolving technology, and equitable access are of greater importance.[26] In the absence of firm empirical results, one of the most important normative choices will be allocating burdens of proof, because without certain knowledge about the benefits of antigen matching or new drug therapies, much will turn on presumptions.

The first section of this chapter provides the factual background. We describe in greater detail the federal rules governing antigen matching in the early 1990s and the reasons why these rules cause disparate racial access to cadaveric kidney transplants. We also explore the evolving evidence on the degree to which antigen matching improves the likelihood of successful transplantation—focusing on newer immunological therapies that increasingly have divorced graft survival from antigenic similarity.

The second section explores normative issues of kidney allocation. In our effort to justify a system that devalues antigen matching, we consider the ethical choices that must be made, implicitly or explicitly, in choosing one system of allocation over another. In particular, we pose in concrete terms the trade-off between enhanced graft survival and equitable allocation of available kidneys. We describe specific allocation rules that we proposed in our initial publications (and which in large part have now been adopted)—arguing that these rules strike a more appropriate ethical and clinical balance.

In the final section of the chapter we analyze the aftermath of our original publication in the *Journal of the American Medical Association*.[27] Two scholars have harshly criticized our proposals.[28] But our core suggestion that time on the waiting list should be given more weight in allocative decisions relative to partial matching remains valid. We also show that the most recent medical evidence bolsters our assertion that antigen

---

26.   Both groups can produce scientific evidence to support their respective positions. *Compare* L. G. Hunsicker & Philip J. Held, The Role of HLA Matching for Cadaveric Renal Transplants in the Cyclosporine Era, 12 Seminars in Nephrol. 293 (1992), *with* Gjertson et al., *supra* note 25.

27.   Robert S. Gaston et al., Racial Equity in Renal Transplantation: The Disparate Impact of HLA-Based Allocation, 270 JAMA 1352 (1993).

28.   Richard A. Epstein, *Mortal Peril: Our Inalienable Right to Health Care?* 272–82 (1997); Lloyd R. Cohen & Melisa Michelsen, The Efficiency/Equity Puzzle and the Race Issue in Kidney Allocation: A Reply to Ayres et al. and UNOS, Ann. Rev. L. & Ethics, Band 4, 137 (1996).

matching has declining importance in determining how long transplants will survive.

I. Antigen Matching

A. The UNOS Policies for Mandated Sharing of Well-Matched Kidneys

The National Organ Transplant Act of 1984 (NOTA)[29] provided funds for Health and Human Services (HHS) to establish the Organ Procurement and Transplantation Network (OPTN).[30] The OPTN was to be a nonprofit organization devoted to establishing (1) a national list of people who need organs,[31] (2) a national system to match organs and individuals on the list,[32] and (3) criteria for allocating organs.[33] In 1986 HHS awarded the OPTN contract to a preexisting entity, the United Network for Organ Sharing (UNOS), which had already established a central computer registry of potential kidney recipients.[34]

The 1984 Act also provided grants for qualified organ procurement organizations (OPOs).[35] NOTA required OPOs to have effective agreements "with a substantial majority" of the transplanting hospitals within a service area to acquire and allocate all usable organs "equitably among transplant patients according to established medical criteria."[36] To qualify

29. Pub. L. No. 98-507, 98 Stat. 2339 (1984) (*codified as amended at* 42 U.S.C. §§ 273, 274(a)–(e) (1994)).

30. Id., § 274. An excellent summary of federal regulation of organ transplantation is provided by Blumstein, *supra* note 4, at 461–76.

31. 42 U.S.C. § 274(b) (1994).

32. Id.

33. Id.

34. See Blumstein, *supra* note 4, at 463; Frank A. Sloan et al., Is There a Rationale for Regionalizing Organ Transplantation Services? 14 J. Health Pol., Pol'y & L. 115, 127 (1989). As an overview for understanding HHS's supervision of UNOS, it is useful to introduce the relevant administrative actors that directly or indirectly control transplantation policy. The Division of Organ Transplantation is part of the Bureau of Health Resources Department, which is part of the Health Resources and Services Administration (HRSA, pronounced "her'-sa") which is part of HHS. In addition, the Health Care Financing Administration (HCFA, pronounced "hick'-fa") is responsible for the administration of Medicare and Medicaid coverage for kidney transplants. HCFA is also a part of HHS.

35. 42 U.S.C. § 273(a)(1), (2) (1994).

36. Id., § 273(b)(3).

for grants, OPOs also had to be members of the OPTN, but OPTN membership was not a legal prerequisite for either procuring or transplanting kidneys. As James Blumstein summarized:

> To the extent that the Network was useful and provided a service, transplant centers and their patients could benefit from the system of coordination. To the extent that other avenues of donation and procurement were available and more attractive, transplant centers and their patients were free to utilize those other sources and resources as well.[37]

The voluntary participation in the OPTN changed in 1986, however, with the passage of the Sixth Omnibus Budget Reconciliation Act (SOBRA)[38] and its addition of § 1138 to the Social Security Act.[39] Section 1138 requires that to qualify for Medicare or Medicaid reimbursements, hospitals with transplant programs must be members of the OPTN (that is, UNOS) and abide by its rules. Compliance with the policies of UNOS is a prerequisite not only for Medicare and Medicaid reimbursement relating to transplantation, but for all Medicare and Medicaid payments. Section 1138 thus effectively mandates compliance with UNOS's policies[40] because noncompliance means that the hospital must "forgo Medicare and Medicaid payment for all services, not just transplant services."[41]

37. Blumstein, *supra* note 4, at 464.

38. Pub. L. No. 99-509, 100 Stat. 1874 (1986).

39. Id., § 9318(a), 100 Stat. at 2009–10. Section 1138 of the Social Security Act is *codified at* 42 U.S.C. § 1320b-8 (1988 & Supp. II 1990). See Blumstein, *supra* note 4, at 467.

40. UNOS Policy 1.0 establishes: "By acceptance of membership in UNOS, each member agrees to be bound by all provisions of the UNOS Articles of Incorporation, By-Laws and Policies." UNOS Policy 1.0 (1991).

41. 53 Fed. Reg. 6525, 6529–30 (1988) (to be codified in scattered sections of 42 C.F.R.). Section 1138 gave the OPTN contracting party (UNOS) potentially coercive power that was criticized because it was unchecked by traditional due process protections. See, *e.g.*, Blumstein, *supra* note 4, at 496. The Organ Transplant Amendments Act of 1988, Pub. L. No. 100-607, 102 Stat. 3114, responded in part to these concerns by mandating publication of its policies and providing "members of the public an opportunity to comment." Id. at 3115. HHS has determined that the UNOS policies must be submitted to the HHS Secretary for approval and must follow Administrative Procedure Act (APA) guidelines for proposed rulemaking and ultimate publication in the Code of Federal Regulations. Health Care Financing Administration, Medicare and Medicaid Programs; Organ Procurement and Transplantation Network Rules and Actions, 54 Fed. Reg. 51802, 51803 (1989).

1. An Introduction to Antigen Compatibility

UNOS policies explicitly mandate allocation of cadaveric kidneys to potential recipients with antigens similar to those of the donor. Before examining the specifics of these policies, it is useful to provide a brief introduction to antigen matching. An antigen is a protein on the surface of tissues that can stimulate an immune response. HLA antigens enable white blood cells—the primary immunologically active cells of the body—to distinguish between "self" and "foreign" tissue.[42] Unless suppressed by drug therapy, the immune system will attack tissue that it recognizes as foreign, but ignore "self" tissue. If kidney tissue bearing specific antigens is transplanted into a person whose own tissue does not bear those antigens, then the immune system of the recipient will attack the transplanted tissue in a process known as "rejection." As discussed more fully below,[43] however, the immune system can be suppressed by drugs, enabling transplanted kidneys to survive even in the presence of foreign antigens.

Antigens are the expression, or phenotype, of major histocompatibility complex (MHC) genes. Clinically applicable techniques cannot detect MHC differences at the genomic level in humans; however, phenotypic differences—differing antigens on the surface of cells—are readily detected by a process known as "tissue typing."[44] Sets of antigens at three locations, or loci, on the cell surface have been found to be particularly relevant in transplantation. These three antigen loci are denoted A, B, and DR, and different specificities are commonly labeled by number. For example, at the A locus common antigens include A1, A11, and A25. Each person has

---

42. The white blood cells principally involved in immune response are called lymphocytes. In the human body there are approximately 10^{12} (one trillion) lymphocytes, each of which recognizes a single antigen from among the universe of all possible antigens. As the immune system develops, those lymphocytes that recognize and destroy "self" tissues are deleted. When, however, transplanted tissues with foreign antigens are recognized by lymphocytes, the process of immunologic destruction, or "rejection," is initiated. Rejection is the bane of transplantation: if untreated, it results in the loss of the transplanted organ. Ken Welsh & David Male, Transplantation and Rejection, *in* Immunology 24.1 (Ivan M. Roitt et al. eds., 2d ed. 1989).

43. See section I.C.4 of this chapter.

44. The basic tissue typing technique involves placing the tissue cells into numerous "wells," each with a different type of serum known to contain antibodies to a specific antigen (for example, A2). If the antibodies of a particular serum result in the death of the tissue cells being typed, one can infer that the cells must have that particular antigen expressed on their surface. Michael Steward & David Male, Immunological Techniques, *in* Immunology 25.1 (Ivan M. Roitt et al. eds., 2d ed. 1989).

two antigens at each locus[45]—one inherited from each parent—totaling six antigens altogether. In the absence of immunosuppressive drugs, these antigens strongly affect whether a recipient's immune system will attack a transplanted kidney.[46]

Only identical twins possess identical MHC genes and HLA antigens at all loci; their tissues are thus immunologically interchangeable. Indeed, the earliest successful kidney transplants were between twins. As antigens were identified in the early and mid-1960s, doctors hoped that by matching antigens between donor and recipient as closely as possible, the results achievable in twins could be approximated with minimal immunosuppression. In transplants from living relatives of the recipient this has proven true because genetic inheritance of all antigens makes phenotypic status (antigen matching) a good proxy for the underlying genotypic status. However, with transplantation of cadaveric organs, which are obtained from persons of diverse genetic backgrounds, the use of antigen matching is a poorer proxy for the underlying MHC genes that more directly control the immune response. In order to successfully transplant organs between any nontwin donor–recipient pairs, immune responses must be suppressed in some way, usually by drugs. Thus, while antigen matching has from its inception accurately predicted outcomes in living related transplantation, its role when cadaveric donors are used has been controversial. Another type of antigen matching relevant to transplantation concerns blood group (ABO) compatibility. Antigens that distinguish blood types A, B, and O are also present on the surface of kidney tissue.[47] Blood types A and B, for example, refer to blood cells

45.   An A locus might, for example, have both the A1 and A11 antigens.

46.   In some patients tissue typing is unable to identify six different antigens. For example, tissue typing might identify only the A1 antigen at the A locus. Current techniques would thus define a total of five (1A, 2B, and 2DR) rather than six antigens in such a person, who would be said to have a "blank" at the A locus. Blanks may represent either as yet unidentified antigen specificities or "homozygosity." A person is homozygous on the A locus if both A antigens were, for instance, A11. Such a kidney would be "phenotypically" matched to be transplanted into a recipient who had the donor's five antigens and any additional antigen at the donor's homozygotic locus. Again, as long as the donor kidney does not have antigens present that are absent in the recipient, the recipient's immune response may be weaker.

It is well documented that HLA antigen expression is less well defined in blacks than whites. A. H. Johnson et al., Heterogeneity of the HLA-D Region in American Blacks, 21 Transplantation Proc. 3872 (1989).

47.   The Rh+ or Rh− blood type antigen that distinguishes, for example, blood type O-positive from O-negative is not present in kidney tissue and is not relevant to transplantation.

that have either A or B antigens, respectively. Just as type A blood cannot be transfused into a patient with type B blood, neither will a type B recipient accept a kidney from a type A donor. Donor and recipient must have compatible blood type antigens—regardless of the immunosuppressant drug therapy being used. Blood type O, however, refers to the absence of either the A or B antigens. Hence, type O kidneys can be transplanted into either type A or type B recipients. Persons who are type O are said to be "universal" donors, but can receive kidneys (or blood) only from others of the same blood type. Conversely, a small fraction of persons possess both the A and B antigens—blood type AB—and are universal recipients.[48]

2. Mandatory National Sharing of Six-Antigen-Matched Kidneys

The UNOS policies privileged antigen matching in two separate ways. First, the policies mandated that all "six-antigen-matched" kidneys be shared on a national basis.[49] The policy was implemented in the following manner. When an ESRD patient was placed into the UNOS computer registry, his or her blood type and HLA antigens was also recorded. As a cadaveric kidney became available, blood and tissue typing was immediately performed on the donor and the results were entered into the computer registry. If a donated kidney was a six-antigen match with an ABO compatible dialysis patient on the UNOS waiting list, then "it [was] mandatory that the kidney . . . be offered for the six antigen match patient."[50]

The six-antigen match, however, has been a term of art that has changed over time to include a growing number of harvested kidneys.[51] If

48. David Male, Reactions against Blood Cells and Platelets, *in Immunology* 20.4 (Ivan M. Roitt et al. eds., 2d ed. 1989).

49. The UNOS policies on their face govern the allocation of kidneys from living related donors as well as from cadavers. This means that a kidney donated by the sibling of a dialysis patient could potentially qualify as a six-antigen match with nonrelated recipients. The guidelines mandate that this kidney be offered first to the unrelated six-antigen match. See Blumstein, *supra* note 4, at 486–88. In practice, however, kidneys from family members are considered to be "donated" for a specific recipient and are not subject to allocation guidelines.

50. UNOS Policy 3.3.3 (1992). If there was more than one six-antigen-matched patient, the kidney was offered to the patient with the highest number of UNOS points. Id. The UNOS point system is discussed *infra* note 58 and accompanying text.

51. UNOS defines a "six-antigen match" to be a match between a donor and recipient where the recipient is ABO compatible and matched on all six HLA-A, B, and DR antigens with the donor or there is phenotypic identity between the donor and recipient where at least one antigen is identified at the A, B, and DR loci. UNOS Policy 3.3.1 (1992). See Steve K. Takemoto et al., Twelve Years' Experience with National Sharing of HLA-Matched Cadaveric Kidneys for Transplantation, 343 New Eng. J. Med. 1078 (2000).

tissue typing identifies only one antigen on each of the three loci of the donor—that is, three blanks are present[52]—a donated kidney may still qualify as a six-antigen match.[53] This effective redefinition of a six-antigen match to mean a "zero-antigen mismatch" has important implications for the number of transplants governed by UNOS's mandatory sharing policy.[54] HLA antigens are distributed so that fewer than 10 percent of cadaveric donations go to true six-antigen-matched recipients.[55] This number may be as high as 25 percent, however, if a zero-antigen mismatch standard is used instead.[56]

3. The Mandatory Local Point System

If a cadaveric kidney did not qualify as a six-antigen match for national sharing, then UNOS policies in the early 1990s mandated that the cadaveric kidneys be allocated locally[57] according to the point system set out in table 6.1.[58]

52. The identification of a single antigen on an individual locus can signify two very different things. First, as discussed in *supra* note 46, the presence of a blank might mean that the locus is homozygotic in that both antigens on that locus are the same. Conversely, a blank could signify the presence of an as yet undefined antigen specificity. Current tests cannot distinguish between the two. The rationale for this aspect of the guidelines is that as tissue typing has become more reliable, blanks are more likely to define homozygosity, which would pose less of a barrier to successful transplantation than unidentified antigens.

There are, however, a large number of antigens that still cannot be typed by laboratory serum. In a national study, laboratories were unable to identify antigens on the DR locus for more than 30 percent of the white population and for more than 40 percent of blacks. E. L. Milford et al., Will Transplant Immunogenetics Lead to Better Graft Survival in Blacks?—Racial Variability in the Accuracy of Tissue Typing for Organ Donation: The Fourth American Workshop, 19 Transplantation Proc. 30, 31 (Supp. 2 1987).

53. On January 21, 1991, UNOS extended this definition further to cover blanks discovered on the DR locus as well so that kidneys with only three identified antigens may qualify for six-antigen-matched treatment. UNOS Policy Proposal Statement (Jan. 21, 1991).

54. In the third section of this chapter we show how this definition has been modified in ways that importantly ameliorate the disparate racial impact in transplantation.

55. M. Ray Mickey et al., Recipient Pool Sizes for Prioritized HLA Matching, 47 Transplantation 401 (1989).

56. Id.; see also Paul I. Terasaki et al., A Report on 123 Six-Antigen Matched Cadaver Kidney Transplants, 3 Clinical Transplantation 301 (1989).

57. The cadaveric kidney shall be allocated among the list of local recipients defined to be "either the individual transplant center recipient list or a shared list of recipients within a defined procurement area and shall be no larger than the OPO." UNOS Policy 3.5.1 (1992).

58. UNOS Policy 3.5 (1992). Prior to 1987 each local transplant program could set its own allocation policy. In 1987 UNOS adopted the "Starzl" system, which

Table 6.1   UNOS Point System for Selecting Kidney Transplant Recipients

	Points
HLA Matching	
0—A, B, DR mismatch	10
0—B, DR mismatch	7
0—A, B mismatch	6
1—B, DR mismatch	3
2—B, DR mismatch	2
3—B, DR mismatch	1
Waiting Time	
Patient with longest waiting period (proportionate points for	
shorter periods)	1
Each year on waiting list	0.5
Children	
Age 0–5	2
Age 6–10	1
Presensitization[a]	4

[a] UNOS Policy 3.5.3 (1992). Four points are awarded if the recipient shows a high likelihood of reacting immunologically to more than 80 percent of the potential donors, but displays a negative crossmatch with a particular donor. A positive crossmatch indicates that the recipient already has produced antibodies against the donor's HLA antigens and thus precludes placing a kidney from that donor into that recipient. All persons on a waiting list have their blood tested periodically (usually monthly) for antibodies against HLA antigens in a laboratory test. This is done using a "panel" of cells from approximately forty random donors. If a person's blood reacts with ten of forty donors, he or she is said to have 25 percent panel reactive antibodies (PRA), implying approximately a 25 percent chance of reacting positively with any single donor from the larger population of potential donors. Thus, for patients with high (≥ 80 percent) PRA levels, it is difficult to find a donor with a negative crossmatch. The rationale for this rule is that because the recipient has demonstrated poor compatibility with the larger population of potential donors, but has shown a preliminary compatibility with a particular donor, he or she should receive the kidney. Put simply, extra points are awarded because a better match is not likely to come along. Transplantation to these recipients is privileged in order to provide equitable access, not to maximize success rates. Indeed, patients with high PRA levels may comprise a group at "high risk" for graft loss. Prasad Koka & J. M. Cecka, *Sensitization and Crossmatching in Renal Transplantation*, in *Clinical Transplants 1989*, at 379 (Paul I. Terasaki ed., 1989).

awarded up to ten points for waiting time, twelve for quality of antigen match, ten for presensitization (discussed in the note to table 6.1), ten for "medical urgency," and six for logistical factors such as proximity to the hospital. Thomas E. Starzl et al., A Multifactorial System for Equitable Selection of Cadaver Kidney Recipients, 257 JAMA 3073 (1987). See *generally* J. Michael Dennis, A Review of Centralized Rule-Making in American Transplantation, 6 Transplantation Rev. 130, 132 (1992) (recounting the history of the development of the point system). In 1989, the point system known as the "Terasaki modification" was adopted. In the third section of this chapter we discuss a recent modification of the Terasaki point system that laudably deemphasizes partial antigen matching.

This point system placed heavy weight on the quality of the antigen match, making ten out of approximately seventeen possible points contingent on the number of antigens matched. In contrast, the system gave only one point to the patient who had waited the longest for a kidney; those who had not waited as long received fractions of a point.[59] The point system also awarded an additional one-half point for each additional year on the waiting list after one year.[60] The net result was almost complete emphasis on antigen matching in determining allocation, with time on the waiting list serving largely as a tiebreaker. Thus, in vying for a particular kidney, a patient with only one antigen matched could conceivably be awarded a kidney over someone who had waited up to two years longer.[61]

B. The Costs of Matching: Disparate Access to Cadaveric Kidneys

Here we argue that blacks have disproportionately limited access to cadaveric kidneys and that the mandatory allocation system based on antigen matching contributed to this racial disparity.[62] The first task is relatively straightforward. As discussed above, 33.5 percent of dialysis patients in 1988 were black, but blacks received only 22.3 percent of cadaveric kidney transplants.[63] Detailed studies of national and regional data underscore the fact that white dialysis patients may have had more than a 50 percent greater chance of receiving a transplant.[64] A multivariate analysis conducted by the Urban Institute indicates that even after controlling for

59. UNOS Policy 3.5.2 (1992).

60. Id.

61. For example, a patient with no A locus matches and one out of four B and DR matches and who had just been placed on the waiting list would receive one point for the antigen match (3—B, DR mismatch). A patient with no antigen matches could wait almost two years and receive only one point for his or her relative seniority on the waiting list (additional half points accrue only if the additional year is completed). See D. Norman et al., Cadaveric Kidney Allocation in the United States: A Critical Analysis of the Point System, 27 Transplantation Proc. 800 (1995).

62. This is not to say that other factors did not impede equal opportunities for blacks who needed transplants. A host of socioeconomic factors may also have played a role. See *supra* notes 16–17.

63. See *supra* note 14. See also USRDS, *supra* note 20; UNOS, 1998 Annual Report—Scientific Registry: United Network for Organ Sharing (1999).

64. See, e.g., Carl M. Kjellstrand, Age, Sex, and Race Inequality in Renal Transplantation, 148 Arch. Intern. Med. 1305 (1988). In the United States in 1983, white patients had a 30 percent transplant rate and nonwhite patients had a 20 percent rate: "[N]onwhite patients aged 21 to 45 years had only half the chance of receiving a transplant compared with white patients of the same age and sex." Id. at 1305.

Table 6.2 Distribution of ABO Blood Groups in the United States

ABO Group	White (%)	Black (%)	Average Time on Waiting List (Months)
O	45	49	14.3
A	40	27	6.9
B	11	20	15.7
AB	4	4	4.6

a host of other socioeconomic variables, the likelihood of cadaveric transplants for blacks relative to whites is only 55 percent.[65] This disparity in access to cadaveric kidneys means blacks had to wait almost twice as long as whites for their first transplant (13.9 months for blacks as compared to 7.6 months for whites).[66]

At least a portion of this disparity is attributable to matching ABO blood groups, as required by UNOS policy.[67] ABO compatibility is required for successful transplantation. As table 6.2 demonstrates, the medical requirement of ABO compatibility causes white dialysis patients to receive a disproportionate share of cadaveric kidneys because these antigens are distributed differently in whites and blacks.[68] In particular, the large pool of blood type A donations will go disproportionately to white recipients.[69]

The UNOS rules, however, go beyond the medical requirement of ABO compatibility by mandating that blood type O kidneys, which are universal donors, be transplanted only into patients with blood type O.[70]

65. Philip J. Held et al., Access to Kidney Transplantation: Has the United States Eliminated Income and Racial Differences? 148 Arch. Intern. Med. 2594, 2596 (1988).

66. See *supra* note 12 and accompanying text. The average waiting time for those transplanted in 1998 was 39.5 months for blacks and 20 months for whites. UNOS, *supra* note 63.

67. See UNOS Policy 3.3.1 (1992). The antigenic basis of blood typing is discussed *supra* notes 47–48 and accompanying text.

68. *Technical Manual of the American Association of Blood Banks* (Frances K. Widmann, ed., 9th ed. 1985); Bertrum L. Kasiske et al., The Effect of Race on Access and Outcome in Transplantation, 324 New. Eng. J. Med. 302 (1991).

69. "The fact that whites (40 percent of whom have blood group A) make up the majority of organ donors suggests that cadaver kidneys will more often go to whites than to blacks (27 percent of whom have blood group A)." Id. at 302–3.

70. UNOS Policy 3.4 (1992). An exception to this rule is allowed for "six antigen matched patients who have a blood group other than O." Id. This exception to the O kidney rule is likely to favor whites disproportionately. It is much more likely that white

This "O rule" prohibits types A and B from competing for donated O kidneys. The UNOS O rule was promulgated to provide equal access for O recipients for whom only an O kidney is suitable and who in the past were thought to have waited inordinately long for a transplant.[71] On balance, however, the O rule reduces the ability of blacks to qualify for kidney transplants. Blacks are almost twice as likely as whites to have blood type B (20 percent versus 11 percent).[72] Under the O rule black dialysis patients who have blood type B must wait for a relatively small supply of type B kidneys.[73] If the rule were repealed, these patients could look to the much larger pool of O donors because 45 percent of white donors have blood type O. Although the O rule helps black recipients with blood type O, an analysis of these competing effects using differential equations suggests that the blood type B effect dominates.[74] The likely result of the O rule is to increase the percentage of blacks on the waiting list and the amount of time the average black candidate has to wait.[75]

---

recipients with, for example, blood type A, will meet the six-antigen qualification for a type O cadaveric kidney. As discussed in detail *infra* text accompanying notes 83–86, this results from the higher propensity of white donors to have six-antigen matches with white recipients.

71.   Friedrich K. Port et al., Discrepancies in the Distribution of Renal Allografts Cause Prolonged Waiting Times for Blood Type O Patients, 35 Kidney Int'l 522 (1989); see also Friedrich K. Port et al., The Impact of Nonidentical ABO Cadaveric Renal Transplantation on Waiting Times and Graft Survival, 17 Am. J. Kidney Dis. 519 (1991). Section 3 of this chapter discusses an ingenious argument of Cohen & Michelsen, *supra* note 28, which shows how the O rule might as a theoretical matter have increased efficiency.

72.   See table 6.2.

73.   Again, this is because most cadaveric kidneys come from a white population that has only 11 percent type B kidneys.

74.   See the chapter appendix. An analysis of differential equations suggests that blood type B patients will need to wait much longer for kidneys than blood type A patients—even though under the O rule neither blood type A nor B patients can qualify for donated O kidneys. The reason that the O rule hurts blood type B patients more than blood type A patients is that the donated kidneys are disproportionately white and therefore disproportionately blood type A relative to ESRD patients. ESRD patients with blood type A accordingly have a relatively large pool of cadaveric kidneys even without receiving O type transplants. Blood type B recipients, however, face a very small pool of donated type B kidneys and, accordingly, are dramatically affected by the inability to qualify for type O cadaveric transplants.

75.   The average waiting list times reported above support this analysis. Under the O rule the average waiting time for the predominantly black B recipients is higher than for O recipients (15.7 months > 14.3 months), while the average waiting time for the predominantly white A recipients is lower than for O recipients (6.9 months < 14.3 months). The O rule reduces the waiting time for type O recipients and increases the waiting times for blood type A and particularly for type B recipients. Recent empiricism

Of greater importance, however, were the UNOS policies that mandated organ allocation based on HLA antigen matching. These regulations restricted the availability of cadaveric kidneys for black patients for the simple reason that most donors are white, and white kidneys tend to have different antigens than black kidneys. A study of the American Society of Histocompatibility and Immunogenetics described in detail the racial distribution of HLA antigens. With the participation of eighty-three tissue-typing laboratories, the study showed that twenty-two antigens on the A, B, and DR loci have statistically significant differences in the frequency of appearance in blacks and whites. These disparate frequencies are shown in table 6.3. The differences in frequency of antigen expression are exacerbated by what doctors call "linkage disequilibrium."[76] The expression of certain antigens on one locus is often positively correlated (or "linked") with particular antigens at another locus. This linkage exacerbates these racial differences because a black recipient failing to match a white donor on one locus may be less likely to match at other loci as well.

Not surprisingly, these disparate antigen pools cause blacks to have fewer potential antigen matches with a predominantly white cadaveric donor pool. A study in Illinois calculated how well 352 cadaveric kidneys matched 604 patients on the local UNOS waiting list.[77] The study revealed that while only 52 percent of the overall waiting list was white, whites dominated the class of recipients having four or more antigens matching—with 71.8 percent of these well-matched kidneys.[78] Since the majority of

---

suggests this disparity is increasing. A 2000 article reports that the average waiting time for the predominantly black B recipients has increased to 44 months, while the average waiting time of the predominately white A recipients is only 18.2 months. Carlton J. Young & Robert S. Gaston, Renal Transplantation in Black Americans, 343 New Eng. J. Med. 1545, 1547 (2000).

76.   Owen, *supra* note 9; see also M. R. Mickey & Paul I. Terasaki, The Serological Data of the 8th Workshop and Summary Analyses, *in Histocompatibility Testing* 21 (Paul I. Terasaki, ed., 1980); G. Opelz & A. Engelman, Effect of HLA Matching in Cyclosporine-Treated Black Kidney Transplant Recipients, 21 Transplantation Proc. 3881 (1989).

77.   Velta A. Lazda & M. E. Blaesing, Is Allocation of Kidneys on Basis of HLA Match Equitable in Multiracial Populations? 21 Transplantation Proc. 1415 (1989).

78.   Id. at 1415. Potential black recipients, who made up 39.9 percent of the overall waiting list, constituted only 16.2 percent of the four or more antigen matches. These discrepancies are further exacerbated if the analysis is restricted to matching the cadaveric kidneys from white donors. In that case, white patients would receive 75.2 percent of the four or more antigen matches, and black patients would receive only 14 percent. These latter figures may be more relevant on a nationwide level because the Illinois study contained a relatively elevated proportion of cadaveric kidneys from black donors (13.9 percent).

Table 6.3   Antigen Frequency by Race

	Antigen	White (%)	Black (%)
"AA" Locus Antigens			
Disproportionately white	A1	23.4	9.8
	A11	11.8	3.7
	A24	16.4	6.1
	A25	6.8	0.9
Disproportionately black	A23	5.6	22.3
	A30	7.0	22.0
	Aw33	4.6	16.2
	Aw34	0.8	13.1
	Aw36	0.2	9.1
"B" Locus Antigens			
Disproportionately white	B8	12.4	5.8
	B13	5.1	1.2
	B27	7.5	1.2
	B38	6.9	0.6
	B44	16.4	8.8
	Bw60	7.8	0.9
	Bw62	9.0	2.1
Disproportionately black	Bw42	1.4	14.6
	B45	2.0	8.8
	Bw53	1.4	17.4
	Bw58	1.6	11.9
"DR" Locus Antigens			
Disproportionately white	DR4	20.0	6.1
Disproportionately black	DR9	2.4	4.9

Source: Milford et al., supra note 52, at 31.

donors is white, such disparity in antigen distribution, coupled with an allocation system based heavily on HLA matching, places potential black recipients at a significant disadvantage. Several studies reveal that white patients receive the vast majority of kidney transplants with excellent donor–recipient histocompatibility—more than four antigen matches.[79]

79. Id.; see also Velta A. Lazda, The Impact of HLA Frequency Differences in Races on the Access to Optimally HLA-Matched Cadaver Renal Transplants, 53 Transplantation 352 (1992); Robert S. Gaston et al., Improved Survival of Primary Cadaveric

Another study directly showed that UNOS's emphasis on antigen matching reduced the number of blacks that qualify for transplantation. Velta Lazda analyzed an alternative point system approved by UNOS—termed a "variance"—for the Regional Organ Bank of Illinois (ROBI).[80] Operating under the UNOS variance, ROBI allocated cadaveric kidneys under a point system that, unlike the UNOS system, emphasized time on the waiting list more strongly relative to the quality of the antigen match.[81] Larger numbers of black candidates received transplants under the ROBI variance.[82]

The disparate racial impact is even more extreme with regard to the mandatory sharing of six-antigen matches. The initial study of mandatory sharing of six-antigen-matched kidneys revealed that of 123 transplants, blacks received only 2.[83] Subsequent studies have confirmed this virtual exclusion of blacks from the pool of six-antigen-matched transplants at the national level, although when six-antigen match is redefined as "zero-antigen mismatch," the proportion of kidneys going to blacks rises to 7 percent.[84] A recent study from the University of Alabama at Birmingham, where 65 percent of those waiting for a kidney are black, revealed that of thirty-three mandatorily shared kidneys, only one was transplanted into a black recipient.[85] L. G. Hunsicker and Philip Held have estimated that

Renal Allografts in Blacks with Quadruple Immunosuppression, 53 Transplantation 103 (1992).

80. Velta A. Lazda, An Evaluation of a Local Variance of the United Network for Organ Sharing (UNOS) Point System on the Distribution of Cadaver Kidneys to Waiting Minority Recipients, 23 Transplantation Proc. 901 (1991).

81. As summarized by J. Michael Dennis: "The main difference [between the UNOS and ROBI point systems] is that ROBI gives no points to two of the less match grades (2 and 3 BDR mismatches) and offers slightly more points for length of wait." J. Michael Dennis, American Blacks, Kidney Transplantation & the Politics of Local Inequality (1991) (unpublished manuscript, on file with author).

82. Id. A similar variance in the New England Organ Bank found identical results. F. Delmonico et al., A Novel United Network for Organ Sharing Region Kidney Allocation Plan Improves Transplant Access for Minority Candidates, 58 Transplantation 1875 (1999).

83. Terasaki et al., *supra* note 56, at 303.

84. See Takemoto et al., *supra* note 25. This percentage still is lower than the proportion of cadaveric kidneys donated by blacks—approximately 8 percent—perhaps because the distribution of antigens among blacks is more heterogenous than among whites. See also Takemoto, supra note 51, at 1079 (8 percent of six-antigen-matched recipients were black).

85. Bruce Barger et al., The Impact of the UNOS Mandatory Sharing Policy on Recipients of the Black and White Races—Experience at a Single Renal Transplant Center, 53 Transplantation 770 (1992).

mandatory national sharing of all kidneys with no HLA mismatches would result in a maximum of 8 percent going to black recipients and would reduce the total number of kidneys available to black patients by 3 percent.[86]

C. The Disappearing Benefits of Matching

Given the inherent disparate racial impact of the UNOS antigen matching policies, the desirability of those policies turns crucially on the degree to which matching enhances the probability of transplant survival.[87] This section of the chapter takes up this question and draws four stylized conclusions:

1. Independent of any effect of antigen matching, black kidney recipients have lower survival rates than white recipients.

2. Six-antigen matches may improve transplant survival significantly—by approximately 10 percent.

3. Matching fewer than six antigens has a much less pronounced effect on allograft survival for white recipients and no reliable effect on survival rates for black recipients.[88]

4. The use of new immunosuppressant drug therapies is likely to reduce further the positive correlation between quality of antigen matching and graft survival.

An ancillary goal of this section is to convey the degree to which these empirical conclusions are contested and contingent upon rapidly changing statistical samples. The advent of new drug technologies and new allocation point systems in particular necessitates reevaluating new cohorts of transplantation recipients.

86. Hunsicker & Held, *supra* note 26.

87. Antigen matching might also enhance patient survival. However, numerous studies have found no statistically significant correlation between either race or antigen matching on the mortality rate of transplant recipients. See, e.g., Jane Galton, *Racial Effect on Kidney Transplantation, in Clinical Kidney Transplants* 1985, at 153 (Paul I. Terasaki ed., 1985); H. Krakauer et al., The Recent U.S. Experience in the Treatment of End-Stage Renal Disease By Dialysis and Transplantation, 308 New Eng. J. Med. 1558 (1983). Our analysis of the benefits of antigen matching accordingly focuses on its effects on graft survival.

88. In fact, the article by Takemoto and colleagues implicitly supports this by comparing the success of six-antigen matches to all lesser matches as a group. See Takemoto et al., *supra* note 25.

1. Racial Differences in Transplant Survival

Early analysis of survival rates for kidney transplantation did not mention race as a determinant of graft outcome.[89] In 1977, however, investigators from the U.C.L.A. Kidney Transplant Registry first noted that cadaveric graft survival at both one and three years was 10 percent lower for black transplant recipients than for whites.[90] Although some single-center studies in those early years showed no racial differences in graft survival,[91] other single-center studies[92] and larger multicenter data[93] consistently documented an 8–12 percent advantage in graft survival for white recipients.[94]

The introduction of the drug cyclosporine as an immunosuppressant therapy in 1983–84 dramatically increased the one-year survival rate of kidney transplants and raised hopes of diminishing racial differences in graft survival. Again, small single-center reports suggested no racial difference at one year in survival of first cadaveric transplants and showed vastly

89. See, e.g., Advisory Committee to the Renal Transplant Registry, The Thirteenth Report of the Human Renal Transplant Registry, 9 Transplantation Proc. 9 (1977).

90. G. Opelz et al., Influence of Race on Kidney Transplant Survival, 9 Transplantation Proc. 137 (1977).

91. See, e.g., Paul J. Garvin et al., Recipient Race as a Risk Factor in Renal Transplantation, 118 Arch. Surg. 1441 (1983); Arthur J. Matas et al., Does Race Affect Renal Transplant Results?: A Single Institution Study, 1 Clin. Transplantation 261 (1987); Vijay K. Mittal et al., Influence of Race on Cadaveric Kidney Transplantation, 11 Dialysis & Transplantation 960 (1982).

92. See, e.g., Bruce O. Barger et al., Influence of Race on Renal Allograft Survival in the Pre- and Postcyclosporine Era, in Clinical Transplants 1987, at 217 (Paul I. Terasaki, ed., 1987); Frank P. Stuart et al., Race as a Risk Factor in Cadaver Kidney Transplantation, 114 Arch. Surg. 416 (1979).

93. See, e.g., J. Michael Cecka, The Roles of Sex, Race, and ABO Groups, in Clinical Transplants 1986, at 199 (Paul I. Terasaki, ed., 1986); Galton, supra note 87, at 153; Rafael Oriol et al., supra note 20.

94. These results can be summarized:

			Graft Survival	
Study	Years of Study	Number of Transplants	White (N)	Black (N)
Opelz	1970–75	4,559	47% (3,581)	37% (978)
Oriol	1970–79	10,802	48% (7,984)	36% (2,129)
Krakauer	1977–80	7,202	58% (5,558)	50% (1,624)

One-Year Graft Survival in Primary Cadaveric Transplants by Race in Patients Treated with Azathioprine-prednisone

Source: Krakauer et al., supra note 87; Opelz et al., supra note 90; Oriol et al., supra note 20.

Table 6.4   One Year Graft Survival in Primary Cadaveric Transplants by Race
in Cyclosporine-Treated Patients

Study	Years of Study	Number of Transplants	Graft Survival White (N)	Graft Survival Black (N)
Cecka	1983–85	2,190	77% (1,944)	66% (246)
Kondo	1984–87	6,655	77% (5,126)	68% (1,529)
Barger	1983–86	437	76% (256)	60% (181)

Source: Cecka, *supra* note 93; Kazunori Kondo et al., Racial Effect on Kidney Transplants, *in Clinical Transplants 1987*, at 339 (Paul I. Trasaki ed., 1987); Barger et al., *supra* note 85.

superior overall results using cyclosporine-based protocols.[95] Multicenter data, however, while confirming improved graft survival, have continued to show a racial effect of 8–11 percent—as shown in table 6.4.

Long-term graft survival also varies with race: the half-life of kidney transplants in black recipients has been found to be as much as 50 percent shorter than for white recipients—four and eight years, respectively.[96] These differences in both one-year graft survival and half-life are depicted in figure 6.1. Several explanations have been proposed for this racial disparity in graft survival, including racial differences in (1) original kidney disease and recurrence rate,[97] (2) the quality of antigen matching,[98] (3) the

95. See Matas et al., *supra* note 91; H. J. Ward et al., Outcome of Renal Transplantation in Blacks, 19 Transplantation Proc. 1546 (1987). A study indicates, however, that cyclosporine may not enhance long-term survival of kidney transplants. The half-life of transplants in the cyclosporine and the precyclosporine eras were not statistically different—7.2 and 6.9 years, respectively. Gjertson et al., *supra* note 25.

96. Steven Takemoto & P. I. Terasaki, A Comparison of Kidney Transplant Survival in White and Black Recipients, 21 Transplantation Proc. 3865 (1989); Joyce Yuge & J. M. Cecka, The Race Effect, *in Clinical Transplants 1989*, at 407 (Paul I. Terasaki, ed., 1989). The half-life of mismatched kidneys in blacks transplanted from 1994–99 was 6.9 years compared to 11.7 years for mismatched whites. Takemoto, *supra* note 51, at 1081.

97. It has been suggested that high blood pressure as a cause of kidney failure might also be associated with poorer transplant outcomes. Oriol et al., *supra* note 20. Under this theory, blacks might have lower transplant survival rates because they are six times as likely as whites to have hypertension as the cause of ESRD. Subsequent series have failed to offer support for this original disease hypothesis as a major factor. See Galton, *supra* note 87; Young & Gaston, *supra* note 75, at 1547.

98. As discussed in the text accompanying notes 76–80, blacks are less likely to receive kidneys with equally well-matched antigens. A poorer average antigen match might contribute to poorer survival rates. See Kondo et al., table 6.4 note b, at 339; Opelz et al., table 6.4 note c, at 3918.

quality of the transplanting center,[99] (4) patient noncompliance,[100] and (5) immunologic responsiveness.[101] No consensus exists, however, regarding the validity and relative importance of these factors.

Even though black patients receive kidneys with poorer antigen matching than white recipients,[102] the racial disparity in survival rates persists even among patients receiving kidneys with equally well-matched antigens.

99.   Some authors have argued that black survival rates are lower because black recipients tend to have their operations performed at "poor" transplant centers. Sondra T. Perdue & Paul I. Terasaki, Analysis of Interracial Variation in Kidney Transplant and Patient Survival, 34 Transplantation 75, 75 (1982) (saying that "Negro recipients appear to have essentially the same graft and patient survival rates as Caucasian recipients after analyzing for the center effect"). The cause of widely divergent results across centers is the subject of ongoing investigation. R.W. Evans et al., The Center Effect in Kidney Transplantation, 23 Transplantation Proc. 1315 (1991).

As a statistical matter, however, the direction of causality has proven extremely difficult to determine: Do blacks have poorer survival rates because they receive transplants at poor centers, or do certain centers have poorer survival rates because they perform more transplants on blacks? A report from the U.C.L.A. registry attributes 4.6 percent of the 11 percent racial disparity in one-year survival to the center effect. Kondo et al., table 6.4 note b, at 339.

100.   Two studies have indicated that black allograft recipients are less likely than white recipients to comply with prescribed drug therapies. R. H. Didlake et al., Patient Non-Compliance: A Major Cause of Late Graft Failure in Cyclosporine-Treated Renal Transplants, 20 Transplantation Proc. 63 (Supp. 3 1988) (saying that blacks, comprising 20.7 percent of the transplant population, accounted for 70 percent of noncompliant graft failures); Mary Rovelli et al., Noncompliance in Organ Transplant Recipients, 21 Transplantation Proc. 833 (1989) (finding a noncompliance rate of 30 percent in blacks and 12 percent in whites); see also Donald E. Butkus et al., Racial Differences in the Survival of Cadaveric Renal Allografts—Overriding Effects of HLA Matching and Socioeconomic Factors, 327 New Eng. J. Med. 840 (1992). When these data were reanalyzed, however, there appeared to be no racial differences within socioeconomic strata (blacks were overrepresented in the lower income category). Mary Rovelli et al., Noncompliance in Renal Transplant Recipients: Evaluation by Socioeconomic Groups, 21 Transplantation Proc. 3979 (1989). A higher rate of noncompliance among black recipients may be caused by a host of socioeconomic factors—poverty, inadequate education, and the like—but might also be an artifact of the center effect, discussed in note 99, if inferior resources are devoted to their convalescent therapy.

101.   Studies have indicated that lower kidney survival rates for blacks might be attributable to a tendency for blacks to have a stronger immune response to grafts than whites. R. H. Kerman et al., Influence of Race on Crossmatch Outcome and Recipient Eligibility for Transplantation, 53 Transplantation 64 (1992); R. H. Kerman et al., Possible Contribution of Pretransplant Immune Responder Status to Renal Allograft Survival Differences of Black versus White Recipients, 21 Transplantation 338 (1991); R. H. Kerman et al., Stronger Immune Responsiveness of Blacks vs. Whites May Account for Renal Allograft Survival Differences, 23 Transplantation Proc. 380 (1991).

102.   See *supra* notes 78–80 and accompanying text.

Figure 6.1   Racial differences in (one-year and half-life) measures of cadaveric transplant survival

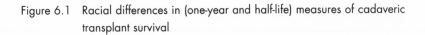

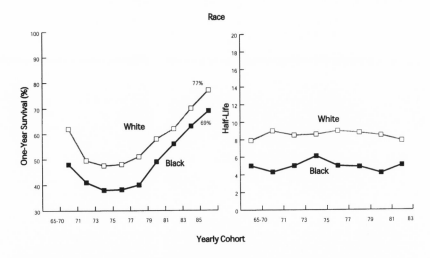

A multivariate regression analysis indicates that after controlling for ten other factors, including the degree of antigen matching, black recipients of white kidneys have a 25 percent greater risk of graft failure than white recipients of white kidneys.[103] With this historical baseline of a significant racial disparity in graft survival, we now consider the incremental effects of antigen matching.

2.   The Benefits of Six-Antigen Matching

Empirical evidence indicates that recipients of six-antigen-matched kidneys experience significantly improved graft survival. An analysis of more than five hundred kidneys transplanted since 1987 under the UNOS mandatory sharing policy of six-antigen-matched kidneys indicates one-year survival rates of 87 percent—a 10 percent improvement over non-matched survival.[104] These results are particularly striking because trans-

103.   John M. Weller et al., Influence of Race of Cadaveric Kidney Donor and Recipient on Graft Survival: A Multifactorial Analysis, 9 Am. J. Kidney Diseases 191 (1987); see also Barger et al., *supra* note 85; G. Opelz & A. Engelmann, Effect of HLA Matching in Cyclosporine-Treated Black Kidney Transplant Recipients, 21 Transplantation Proc. 3881 (1989).

104.   Steven Takemoto et al., A Report of 504 Six Antigen-Matched Transplants, 23 Transplantation Proc. 1318 (1991). To control for the possibility of enhanced kidney

plants occurred at more than sixty centers, with varying degrees of quality, and some of the donor kidneys were preserved for longer periods of time as required to transport them across the nation.[105]

There is more tentative evidence that transplants with zero mismatches have enhanced survival. As discussed, antigen typing might not reveal two different antigens on each of the A, B, and DR loci.[106] A typing blank can result either because the existing sera fail to detect existing antigens, or because the tissue is homozygotic, meaning that its locus expresses two antigens of the same type.[107] If a blank results because the donor is homozygotic, then zero-mismatched transplants might have the enhanced survival characteristics of six-antigen-matched transplants. An initial analysis of forty-two zero-mismatched transplants tentatively found one- and two-year survival rates to be no different from those for six-antigen-matched recipients.[108] These data are particularly relevant to the UNOS amendment that extended national mandatory sharing to this wider class of zero-mismatched transplants.[109]

Six-antigen matching—and possibly zero-antigen mismatching—thus significantly enhances kidney transplant survival. Yet as the foregoing analysis indicated, these well-matched kidneys go disproportionately to white

---

quality, this U.C.L.A. registry study also reported the survival rates of the other donated (contralateral) kidney if one was harvested. The enhanced rate of survival from six-antigen matching is reflected in second-year statistics as well:

Type of Transplant	Survival Rate (%)	
	1 Year	2 Year
6 Antigen	87.2	79.8
Contralateral	75.8	69.6

The effects of six-antigen matching were statistically significant ($P < 0.05$). See also Takemoto et al., *supra* note 25, at 834.

More recent work suggests that six-antigen matches improve survival at one year by only about 5 percent, Takemoto et al., *supra* note 51 at 1078, and much of this difference might be attributable to the disproportionate whiteness of the six-antigen-match pool.

105. Terasaki et al., *supra* note 56, at 304 (saying that "[a]pparently harvest techniques and storage methods have now been worked out sufficiently well to yield uniform high survival rates that are almost independent of harvesting center").

106. See *supra* note 46.

107. A child's locus will be homozygotic if each parent contributed the same antigen to the locus.

108. Takemoto et al., *supra* note 104, at 1318.

109. See *supra* text accompanying notes 53–57. The data are also supported by a recent reexamination of this policy on outcomes. Takemoto et al., *supra* note 51, at 1078.

recipients.[110] Eight percent of these mandatorily shared kidneys now go to black recipients,[111] and early on at least one major center had never received a six-antigen-matched kidney for a black recipient.[112] Thus, although the mandatory sharing policy has been successful for the predominantly white recipients lucky enough to receive six-antigen-matched kidneys, black candidates have not shared propotionally in its benefits.

3. The Attenuated Benefits of Partial Antigen Matching

When one or more antigens are mismatched, there is a much weaker correlation between the quality of matching and transplant survival. In this section, we show that there was evidence of the diminishing effect of partial antigen matching on survivability early in the 1990s—even at a time when the point system continued to award disproportionate points for partial matching. For example, in a 1989 single-center report,[113] while whites and blacks had different survival rates, matching for one or more antigens did not make a statistically significant difference in patient or graft survival at one, two, or three years for either white or black recipients when compared to transplants with no matched antigens.[114] In multivariate analysis of data from Michigan,[115] the presence of three or four antigen mismatches on the A and B loci did not increase risk of graft loss.[116] An analysis of national data indicates that the marginal impact on graft survival of an additional antigen mismatch is greater at the zero end of the scale compared to six mismatches.[117] Graft survival increases more significantly when comparing a change from one to zero mismatches than when comparing six to five mismatches.[118]

110.   See *supra* text accompanying notes 83–86.

111.   Takemoto et al., *supra* note 51, at 1079.

112.   Barger et al., *supra* note 85, at 770.

113.   S. M. Greenstein et al., Does Kidney Distribution Based upon HLA Matching Discriminate against Blacks, 21 Transplantation Proc. 3874 (1989).

114.   Id.

115.   Weller et al., *supra* note 103, at 191.

116.   Id. at 193. The results of this Michigan study are partially contradicted by an Alabama study indicating that matching at least one antigen on both the A and B loci can enhance one- and two-year graft survival by 10 percent. Barger et al., *supra* note 92, at 217.

117.   Hunsicker & Held, *supra* note 26, at 293.

118.   Thus, the study concludes that the aggregate impact on graft survival of a change in the average mismatches depends crucially upon where on the mismatch scale the change occurs. Id.

An article by Hunsicker and Held concluded that recipients of zero-antigen-mismatched kidneys receive most of the benefit from matching, though recipients of single-antigen-mismatched kidneys may also realize some benefit.[119] They found that cadaveric renal transplantation with lesser degrees of matching offered very little gain at all.[120] Indeed, USRDS data demonstrate no statistical relationship of HLA matching to survival of first allografts at five years in the presence of even one or more mismatches.[121]

The data on the effects of partial matching are, however, not monolithic. Multicenter data from the UNOS Transplant Registry and the Collaborative Transplant Study continued to describe marginal improvements in graft survival with improved matching.[122] An analysis conducted by the U.C.L.A. Tissue Typing Laboratory found that the half-life of kidney transplants tended to increase with better antigen matching, but said that this improvement—from 7.2 to 9.4 years—occurred only if there were no mismatches on either the A or the B locus,[123] again suggesting that the most dramatic benefit occurs only with extremely well-matched transplants.

A clearer picture emerges, however, when analyzing the effects of partial matching on graft survival for black transplant recipients: there is virtually no correlation between partial matching and graft survival in black recipients. Two studies from the University of Alabama, which performs a large number of transplants for black recipients, concluded that partial antigen matching did not improve black patients' chances of graft survival.[124] Three reviews from the U.C.L.A. registry failed to note any relationship between cadaveric allograft survival in blacks and antigen

119. Id.

120. Id. The authors also conclude: "The UNOS/UCLA data also show a substantial decrease in the long-term benefits of matching with as few as one mismatched antigen." Id. at 298.

121. Id. at 293.

122. David W. Gjertson, Short- and Long-Term Effects of HLA Matching, *in* Clinical Transplants 1989, at 353 (Paul I. Terasaki, ed., 1989); Gerhard Opelz, In Response to "The Role of HLA Matching in Renal Transplant Patients with Sequential Immunosuppression," 3 Clinical Transplantation 233 (1989). J. Cecka, The UNOS Scientific Renal Transplant Registry, *in* Clinical Transplants 1998, at 1–16 (J. Cecka & Paul Terasaki eds., 1999).

123. Gjertson et al., *supra* note 25, at 1033–34; see also Takemoto et al., *supra* note 25, at 834.

124. Barger, *supra* note 92, at 229 (saying that, for example, one-year allograft survivals for DR matched and nonmatched black recipients were 59 percent and 62 percent, respectively); see also Gaston et al., *supra* note 79, at 103 (finding no beneficial effect of antigen matching on graft survival for black recipients).

matching.[125] Although an article from the Collaborative Transplant Study reported a marginal positive effect of antigen matching, the authors concluded: "[T]he lack of a matching effect in blacks reflects both poorer understanding of HLA antigens in blacks and disparate distribution between races."[126]

The absence of an antigen matching effect for black recipients of white kidneys is likely an artifact of the imprecise nature of antigen typing. The immunologic response of the recipient is actually controlled at the genetic level—that is, by the particular sequencing of DNA—and is only crudely captured by the current antigen typing method.[127] Antigen matching serves as a proxy for the underlying genetic compatibility that directly controls the recipient's immune response. It may be a better proxy for the underlying genetic compatibility when white donors are giving to white recipients. The reduced value of antigen matching for black recipients of a largely white donor population is consequently less surprising because the underlying genetic material does not correlate as well across races.

In sum, the evidence supporting a positive correlation between graft survival and partial antigen matching is dramatically weaker than for six-antigen matching. Moreover, the preponderance of evidence seemed to suggest that partial antigen matching does not enhance transplant success for black recipients. The latter result is particularly important because black recipients, as a practical matter, have access only to less than fully matched kidneys.[128]

125. Yuge & Cecka, *supra* note 96, at 407; Kondo et al., table 6.4 note b, at 339; Takemoto et al., *supra* note 104, at 1318.

126. Opelz et al., table 6.4 note c, at 3918 (finding enhanced one-year graft survival for zero mismatches on the DR locus on the order of 5 percent).

127. See *supra* notes 46–48 and accompanying text.

128. See P. Held et al., The Impact of HLA Mismatches on the Survival of First Cadaveric Kidney Transplants, 331 New Eng. J. Med. 165–70 (1994) (showing small benefit of partial matching); V. Scantlebury et al., Effect of HLA Mismatch in African-Americans, 65 Transplantation 586–88 (1998) (showing small likelihood of blacks receiving well-matched grafts). The implications of these results have not been lost on the transplant community:

> To realize the greatest benefit from scarce cadaver kidneys, it may be appropriate to encourage transplants that have a distinctly superior success rate, such as 6-Ag [antigen] match transplants. However, it is difficult to justify giving a kidney to a patient who has been on the waiting list for a short time while denying it to another who may have waited for years, merely because of a supposedly better match, the value of which has not been demonstrated and continues to be disputed.

Greenstein et al., *supra* note 113, at 3875.

Table 6.5   Graft Survival at One Year

Recipient Race	Standard (N = 276)	Quad (N = 366)
Black	54% (112)	76% (180)
White	74% (164)	73% (186)

Source: Gaston et al., supra note 79, at 103.

4.   The Impact of New Immunosuppressant Drug Therapies

The empirical analyses of the preceding sections—concerning both the racial disparity in graft survival and the impact of antigen matching on graft survival—are based on data accumulated during the "cyclosporine era." This potent immunosuppressive agent, introduced in the United States in 1983, revolutionized transplantation with marked improvements in outcomes compared to previous therapies. Further advances in immuno-suppression are occurring at a dizzying rate. These improved therapies are likely to have a significant impact on both antigen matching and racial differences in graft survival. For example, at the University of Alabama, which for twenty years had experienced 8–19 percent poorer graft survival in black recipients, the use of a modified drug regimen known as "quadru-ple therapy" has completely abrogated the racial disparity in graft survival since its introduction in 1987.[129] In this series of 642 patients, there also was no impact of HLA matching on graft survival in blacks and only mini-mal effects of improved matching in whites. The parity in survival rates induced by quadruple therapy was evident for periods of at least three years. See table 6.5 and figure 6.2.

With quadruple immunosuppression, antibodies are added prophylac-tically to standard cyclosporine-based therapy.[130] Improvement in graft survival for black recipients with this regimen has also been documented

129.   Gaston et al., supra note 79, at 103.

130.   Standard therapy is known as "triple drug" therapy, using cyclosporine along with azathioprine and prednisone in what is thought to be a beneficial combina-tion. Hence, the addition of therapeutic antibodies becomes "quadruple therapy," which is synonymous with "sequential therapy." Antibodies may be extracted from horses or rabbits, and used to attack the lymphocytes of the recipient that initiate a response to a nonmatching antigen of the transplanted kidney. By attacking the cells that initiate the recipient's immune response, antibodies may enhance graft survival. (Human mono-clonal antibodies have emerged in recent years as an alternative to rabbit- or horse-based preparations.)

in a review of data from several centers.[131] The experience of several transplant centers has shown that with quadruple therapy, all recipients—white and black—achieve success rates rivaling those usually associated with six-antigen matches regardless of antigen matching.[132] Available evidence thus suggests that with quadruple therapy neither race nor quality of antigen matching predicts graft survival.

Of potentially greater significance are new drugs on the horizon, which appear to offer more potent immunosuppression, fewer rejections, and less toxicity.[133] These drugs include FK-506, which is extremely effective in liver transplantation;[134] RS-61443, a new agent of high efficacy with few side effects;[135] and rapamycin.[136]

In 1993, several new immunosuppressant drugs (tacrolimus, mycophenolate mofetil, daclizumab, basiliximab, sirolimus) were undergoing clinical trials. Most proved successful, receiving the approval of the FDA for clinical use in the United States between 1994 and 1997. These drugs carried the promise of more effective immunosuppression with fewer toxic effects. This promise has been realized as rejection rates have drop-

131. Donald E. Butkus, Primary Renal Cadaveric Allograft Survival in Blacks—Is There Still a Significant Difference? 5 Transplant Rev. 91 (1991).

132. Ronald M. Ferguson, A Multicenter Experience with Sequential ALG/Cyclosporine Therapy in Renal Transplantation, 2 Clinical Transplantation 285 (1988).

133. Like MALG, many of these agents are antibodies designed to attack the recipient's lymphocytes and thus suppress the recipient's immune response. MALG is a nonspecific "polyclonal" antibody that attacks a broad range of lymphocytes. Unlike MALG, however, many of the new immunosuppressants are "monoclonal"—more specifically targeted to suppress only those lymphocytes that would reject transplanted tissues. OKT3, for example, is a monoclonal antibody that targets only "T cells" for attack. Newer monoclonal antibodies may be even more selective, attacking only T cells that are actively participating in the rejection response. Gideon Goldstein, Monoclonal Antibody Specificity: Orthoclone OKT3 T-Cell Blocker, 46 Nephron 5 (Supp. 1 1987); see also N. Tolkoff-Rubin et al., Immunosuppression with Anti-ICAM-1 (CD54) Monoclonal Antibody in Renal Allograft Recipients, 2 J. Am. Soc. Nephrol. 820 (1991).

134. See A. M. Macleod & A. W. Thomson, FK506: An Immunosuppressant for the 1990s? 337 Lancet 25 (1991); R. Shapiro et al., Kidney Transplantation under FK 506 Immunosuppression, 23 Transplantation Proc. 920 (1991).

135. Hans W. Sollinger et al., RS-61443: Phase I Clinical Trial and Pilot Rescue Study, 53 Transplantation 428 (1992).

136. J. Wang et al., Initial Use of Rapamycin Immunosuppression in Nonhuman Primate Graft Recipients, Am. Soc. of Transplant Surgeons, 17th Annual Scientific Meeting (May 1991), at 49; see also Kozo Tamura et al., 15-Deoxyspergualin (DSP) "Rescue Therapy" against Methylprednisolone (MPSI)-Resistant Rejection of Renal Transplants as Compared with Anti-T Cell Monoclonal Antibody (OKT3), 2 J. Am. Soc. Nephrol. 819 (1991).

Figure 6.2   Racial differences in survival under standard and quadruple therapies

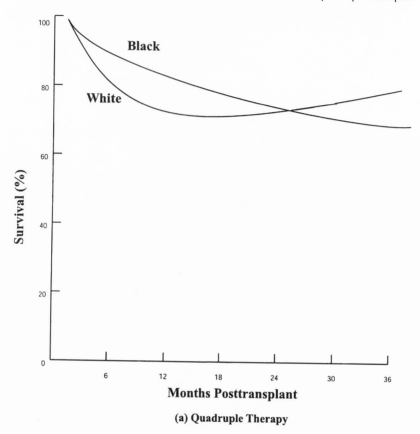

Months Posttransplant

(a) Quadruple Therapy

ped dramatically, graft survival has improved accordingly, and racial disparity in outcomes (despite poor matching in blacks) has diminished further.[137] It seems likely that the continued development and use of these new immunosuppressant therapies has the potential to further enhance graft survival in patients of all races.[138] In short, the new therapies hold

137.   See J. F. Neylan, Immunosuppressive Therapy in High-Risk Transplant Patients: Dose-Dependent Efficacy of Mycophenolate Mofetil in African-American Renal Allograft Recipients, 64 Transplantation 1277 (1997); J. F. Neylan, Racial Differences in Renal Transplantation after Immunosuppression with Tacrolimus versus Cyclosporine, 65 Transplantation 515 (1998); R. S. Gaston, Potential Utility of Rapamycin and Tacrolimus in Long-Term, Low-Toxicity Regimens, 31 Transplantation Proc. S17 (Supp. 8a 1999).

138.   Whether the new therapies will negate the 10 percent improvement in survival associated with six-antigen matching remains to be determined.

Figure 6.2   *(Continued)*

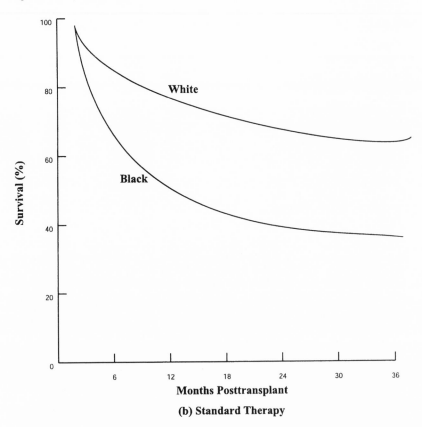

(b) Standard Therapy

the promise of reducing the importance of both race and antigen matching as determinants of transplant outcomes.

II. Tragic Choices

With these stylized facts as a backdrop, we now discuss the difficult policy choices concerning the procurement and allocation of cadaveric kidneys. The choices that society makes concerning the disparate racial impact of antigen matching are, in the end, of the same nature that Guido Calabresi and Philip Bobbitt labeled "tragic."[139] The optimal rules for procur-

139. Calabresi & Bobbitt, *supra* note 24, at 19.

ing and allocating cadaveric kidneys depend not only on social norms but on judgments about the empirical issues raised above. Ultimately, the absence of clear empirical results may make the allocation of burdens of proof the most important normative decision of all.

This section of the chapter begins by analyzing two of the "cleanest" normative objectives of allocation: maximizing transplant survival and minimizing medical cost. We argue that both objectives ultimately lead to allocation schema that would be subjectively unpalatable in our society. This leads us to consider more complicated accommodations between equity and efficiency. We propose a range of allocation alternatives that further these more amorphous goals under both current and future immunosuppressant technologies. Finally, we analyze the political history of kidney allocation in the United States and situate our proposal within the current debate.

A. The Limits of Two Simple Objectives

A straightforward objective in allocating the increasingly scarce supply of cadaveric kidneys would be to maximize transplant survival. Survival maximization furthers one notion of egalitarianism: "[T]reating differently patients in whom the kidney would work from those in whom it would not amounted to treating people equally who were relevantly equal, and discriminating between those groups which were relevantly unequal."[140] This objective would lead to the mandatory sharing of six-antigen-matched kidneys. As discussed, the survival rates of these kidneys are approximately 10 percent better than those of less well-matched kidneys.[141] In addition, maximizing survival rates might also require awarding some preference—at least for whites—to partial antigen matching when the evidence also indicates improved outcomes.

We argue, however, that maximum survival is normatively an incomplete objective because it would lead to the nearly complete exclusion of blacks from kidney transplantation. The evidence from multiple studies is that black kidney recipients have had uniformly lower survival rates than similarly situated whites.[142] Our belief that the wholesale exclusion of

---

140. Id. at 24–25.

141. Recent research finds that six-antigen-match may only increase one-year survival by about 5 percent. See *supra* text accompanying note 104.

142. See *supra* text accompanying note 90. While some of this statistical correlation may result from a tendency for blacks to receive kidneys from inferior transplanta-

blacks would be rejected by society depends on the relatively small size of racial disparity in graft survival.[143] If graft survival in black recipients approached zero percent in the first year, the racial basis for exclusion might be tolerable.[144] Yet, the historical disparity of 8–11 percent in first-year survival rates does not seem sufficiently high to warrant complete exclusion of blacks from the recipient pool.[145]

Indeed, the generic normative question is: How large must the discount be? If, according to the cyclosporine-era statistics, white recipients have a 77 percent first-year survival rate, how much lower must the rate for black recipients be before they are disfavored in the allocation process? Survival maximization yields the straightforward answer that any reliable discount is sufficient for racial exclusion, but this simplicity comes at the sacrifice of other normative values. Our point here is a small one: The social unacceptability of wholesale exclusion of blacks from the transplantation process is strong evidence that our objectives must go beyond simple survival maximization.

A similar analysis applies to arguments that society should minimize the costs of transplantation.[146] One article, for example, has argued for a

---

tion centers, the "center effect" has not been able to explain all of the racial disparity. See *supra* note 99.

143. A pure survival maximization objective would not necessarily exclude all blacks from transplantation, but more precisely would call for a lexicographic system of allocation in which blacks received kidneys only if white recipients were unavailable. Empirically, however, the number of potential white recipients would effectively preclude transplantation to blacks under this system.

Pure survival maximization might even preclude blacks from receiving the cadaveric kidneys of black donors given the perverse empirical finding that black recipients of black kidneys do not have enhanced survival rates. See Opelz et al., *supra* note 90, at 137; Kondo et al., table 6.4 note b, at 339; Harry J. Ward & Martin A. Koyle, The Beneficial Effect of Blood Transfusion and the DR 1 Gene Dose on Renal Transplant Outcome in Blacks, 51 Transplantation 359 (1991). Wholesale exclusion of blacks from transplantation is even supported by an analysis of patient survival because, again perversely, blacks tend to have a slightly lower mortality rate on dialysis than whites. See Barger et al., *supra* note 85, at 770.

144. After all, the exclusion of blood type B recipients from the pool of blood type A cadaveric donations is not problematic given the zero success rates for such transplantation.

145. This analysis could of course proceed upon other measures of survival, each of which itself involves an implicit normative choice. For example, the racial disparity in transplant half-life may be on the order of 50 percent. See figure 6.1.

146. Cost-benefit analysis often is determined by the initial assumptions of what costs and what benefits count. See John J. Donohue III & Ian Ayres, Posner's Symphony No. 3, 39 Stan. L. Rev. 791 (1987).

mandatory national system of partial antigen matching, in part because the authors claim that national matching would save the government $6.5 million a year.[147] Their basic argument is that the additional costs of a national matching system—estimated to be $1,000 per transplant—are outweighed by savings that result from higher survival rates.[148] This type of cost savings, however, clearly is not the sole determinant of our allocation system. The authors' own analysis indicates that the use of cyclosporine increases the cost of transplantation. Even though kidney failure necessitates a costly operation to remove the graft and return to dialysis, the cost savings induced by higher survival rates with cyclosporine and newer drugs are more than offset by the costs of the drugs themselves. Yet, it is hard to imagine that we would eliminate the use of those "wonder drugs" that enhance survival rates by 10–20 percent.

The normatively unacceptable nature of this type of cost calculation is even more striking, however, when extended to issues of race. The exclusion of blacks from the pool of cadaveric transplants would save the government even more money than a mandatory national program of partial antigen matching. We estimated in 1992 that the expected present value of government expenditures for a transplant are $98,300 for a black recipient and $90,700 for a white recipient.[149] Reallocating to whites the approximately 1,400 cadaveric kidneys that currently go to black recipients would consequently save the government more than $10.6 million per year.[150] Analysis of current costs, in an era with better outcomes and greater cost savings relative to dialysis, would be even more striking.

Again our normative conclusion is a limited one. Both pure cost minimization and survival maximization objectives would lead to normatively

147.   Gjertson et al., *supra* note 25, at 1032.

148.   Transplant failure necessitates the removal of the graft, which the authors estimated to cost approximately $10,000, and the return to dialysis, estimated to cost $17,000 per year. Elevated survival rates can reduce the government's expenditures because the government spends only $8,000 per year on cyclosporine therapy for successful transplants after the first year of treatment. Id. at 1035.

149.   For assumptions underlying this calculation, see *supra* note 148. In addition, the authors estimated that the transplantation costs $35,000 and that first-year treatment (including cyclosporine) costs $20,000. Id. To capture the racial difference in survival rates, we have assumed hazard rates for whites of 20 percent in the first year and 6 percent per year thereafter, and for blacks of 28 percent in the first year and 11 percent per year thereafter. See Opelz et al., table 6.4 note c, at 3918.

150.   1400 × ($98,300 − $90,700) = $10,640,000. See also A. Laupacis et al., A Study of the Quality of Life and Cost-Utility of Renal Transplantation, 50 Kidney Int. 235 (1996).

unacceptable results, such as explicit racial exclusions. Consequently, one cannot defend or justify other allocative choices by analyzing these objectives alone. In short, we believe that our society holds these objectives to be morally incomplete. Our argument is not that these objectives are unimportant, but only that our society tempers them with equitable concerns—among them, that government actions should not burden traditionally disadvantaged races.[151]

Two aspects of the UNOS point system—the O kidney rule and the presensitization points—provide especially powerful examples of how the UNOS allocation system rejects a single-minded emphasis on survival.[152] As analyzed above, the O rule prohibits the transplantation of kidneys from O blood type donors into recipients of other blood types unless there is a six-antigen match.[153] Even though the O blood type organs could be transplanted into recipients with A or B blood types, the guidelines reflect a concern that without this prohibition the O blood type recipients would inequitably have to share the pool of O kidneys with too many other recipients.[154] The O rule is an example of equity trumping efficiency because it potentially favors an O blood type recipient with a zero-antigen match over a B blood type recipient with a five-antigen match.[155] This interplay between equity and efficiency has, however, a perverse racial dimension. The O rule favors O blood type recipients over the predominantly black B blood type recipients and thus exacerbates the unequal access of blacks to transplantation.[156]

---

151.   This is what Calabresi and Bobbitt referred to as "corrected egalitarianism." See *supra* text accompanying note 24. J. Michael Dennis refers to this value as "sociological justice." J. Michael Dennis, *supra* note 58, at 130; see also W. B. Arnason, Directed Donation: The Relevance of Race, 21 Hastings Center Rep. 13 (Nov.–Dec. 1991).

152.   In the third section of this chapter, we discuss an alternative, efficiency-promoting interpretation of both the O-rule and the presensitization points.

153.   See *supra* note 70 and accompanying text.

154.   UNOS Policy § 3.4 (1992).

155.   In the third section of this chapter, we concede as a theoretical matter that either the O rule or the presensitization preference could have furthered a more dynamic conception of efficiency, but we continue to maintain as an empirical matter that both the O rule and the presensitization rules are examples of policymaking in which equitable concerns trumped efficiency.

156.   As analyzed *supra* notes 70–73 and accompanying text, the O rule disadvantages predominantly white A recipients and predominantly black B recipients. A recipients may draw from a disproportionately large pool of donated A kidneys in comparison with the pool of donated B kidneys available to B recipients and therefore are not affected as much as B recipients by the removal of O type transplants. A differential equation model of donation and ESRD rates suggests that the advantage to black O can-

Society's willingness to privilege equitable concerns over a simple interest in graft survival is also exemplified by presensitization points. The UNOS system currently awards points to candidates whose blood contains antibodies against more than 80 percent of potential cadaveric donations.[157] Presensitization lowers a candidate's chance of successful transplantation because the recipient's immune system has already produced antibodies to attack a wide array of foreign tissue.[158] The limited goal of graft survival would cause presensitized candidates to receive negative points in an allocation system. However, because presensitized candidates "can wait three or more years for transplant, they have attracted a near-universal sympathy for their plight."[159]

J. Michael Dennis characterizes the treatment of presensitized candidates as consistent with the goal of medical justice: " 'Medical justice' is a principle based on compassion for patients with 'medical bad luck.' Because of their medical condition, these patients have a less-than-average chance to receive treatment. Medical justice dictates that they be given allocative preference."[160] This does not account for the major cause of presensitization: the failure of an initial transplant. When initial transplantations fail, the recipient's body often produces massive numbers of antibodies that presensitize the recipient against further transplantation. The allocative preference for presensitized candidates thus has the perverse effect of rewarding candidates who often already had the opportunity for transplantation. In economic terms, the "medical bad luck" is not completely exogenous.

The "near-universal sympathy" for the plight of presensitized and blood type O recipients, which gave rise to these equitable exceptions to the UNOS allocation system, also might be seen as an instance of effective interest group lobbying. Both of these equitable exceptions respond to the preferences of candidates who are represented on the waiting list long enough to form a powerful political constituency. Indeed, the NOTA ex-

---

didates is outweighed by the disadvantage to black B candidates. Given the current donation rates, the O rule probably decreases the percentage of kidneys transplanted into black Americans. See the chapter appendix.

157. See table 6.1, note a.

158. See M. Aprile et al., Effect of Peak PRA's on the Outcome of Cadaver Kidney Transplants, 21 Transplantation Proc. 735 (1989). There is a greater likelihood that immunosuppressant drugs can prevent an unmatched recipient from producing antibodies.

159. Dennis, *supra* note 58, at 134.

160. Id. at 133.

plicitly mandates that allocative preference be given to presensitized patients.[161] The strength of the presensitization lobby is such that UNOS turned down an application for a variance to deemphasize sensitization at a single transplant center. The organ procurement organization (OPO) in question argued that because presensitized patients have worse medical outcomes, giving them priority wastes resources.[162] Yet UNOS, in compliance with its federal contract, affirmatively rejected the survival goal to promote the equitable interests of presensitized candidates. As in other contexts, one person's equity is another person's private interest.

B. The Relevance of Race

The above analysis may demonstrate that our allocation systems are not determined solely by the goals of transplant survival or cost minimization, but it has not directly addressed why society should respond to allocation strategies that have a disparate impact on blacks. This section attempts to provide such a rationale. One of the strongest rationales for disparate impact liability in the law is to prohibit actions that might be motivated by racial animus.[163] Such suspicions are, however, virtually absent in the transplantation context. All participants in the area believe that the original point system and its subsequent modifications were developed in good faith to accommodate the goals of graft survival and other equitable concerns.

We believe, however, that race is relevant for two reasons. First, ignoring the disparate impact of blacks represents selective indifference.[164] The UNOS guidelines privileged equity over efficiency when presensitized or blood type O patients receive smaller numbers of transplants, but are indifferent to the equitable claim of blacks. If the roles were reversed and white patients had lower chances of matching antigens, we believe that the point system might have given less weight to matching. Even for those who believe that the best allocation should simply try to maximize survival rates, the willingness of the system to respond selectively to other equitable claims might argue for considering the claims of blacks as well. In a world where

161. NOTA § 372, 98 Stat. at 2344; see also Dennis, *supra* note 58, at 133; R. Mendez, A National Allocation System, 20 Transplantation Proc. 1014 (Supp. 1 1988).

162. Dennis, *supra* note 81, at 11.

163. Paul Gewirtz, Remedies and Resistance, 92 Yale L.J. 585 (1983).

164. Paul Brest, The Supreme Court, 1975 Term—Foreward: In Defense of the Anti Discrimination Principle, 90 Harv. L. Rev. 1, 6 (1976).

the equitable claims of other discrete groups are heard, UNOS's failure to respond to the equitable claims of black patients becomes suspect.

Second, responding to this disparate racial access can be justified as an attempt to eliminate the effects of past discrimination.[165] Kidney failure is associated with a number of other factors that may be exacerbated in black communities because of past discrimination—including poverty, stress, alcohol use, and poor medical care. To the extent that past discrimination[166] has left blacks disproportionately poor and that poverty induces higher rates of kidney failure,[167] these lingering effects of discrimination also support society's corrective concern. At a minimum, we believe it is incumbent on society not to ignore the equitable claims of blacks in favor of other possibly less pressing equitable claims such as those of presensitized or blood type O recipients.

165. Government has constitutional authority to remedy even private discrimination if it does so with the (narrow tailoring) specificity required by the Fourteenth Amendment. Ian Ayres & Fredrick E. Vars, When Does Private Discrimination Justify Public Affirmative Action? 98 Colum. L. Rev. 1577 (1998); see also Paul Gewirtz, Choice in the Transition: School Desegregation and the Corrective Ideal, 86 Colum. L. Rev. 728 (1986).

166. Research by Clarence E. Grim suggests that blacks may have higher rates of hypertension and kidney failure because of the quintessential expression of discrimination—slavery. "[B]lacks living in the United States today may owe their higher hypertension rate to a genetic trait that helped their ancestors survive the grueling conditions of slavery. That trait is an inherited tendency to conserve salt within the body. . . ." Kathy A. Fackelmann, The African Gene? 140 Sci. News 254 (1991).

Grim's provocative hypothesis is that Africans with a salt-conserving gene or genes were less likely to die of dehydration during transport across the Atlantic by slave-traders. Id. at 254. The ability to hold onto salt—and thus water—also helped them to survive the harsh conditions they encountered in the New World. Seventy percent of African slaves died within the first four years of their capture. This devastating fatality rate might have radically accelerated the process of genetic selection. The same genetic ability to retain salt that may have conferred a temporary survival advantage on slaves may now be responsible for a higher level of hypertension and kidney failure.

It should be stressed that while this causal hypothesis is supported by some indirect evidence, id., it is quite controversial. For example, even though West Africans consume a high salt diet, they have much lower rates of high blood pressure than among American blacks. Id. at 255. Yet the possibility that the elevated renal failure among blacks is a vestige of the slave trade makes concrete the causal link between past discrimination and the current demand for renal transplantation. Even if we conclude that the theory has only a 50 percent chance of being true—or only explains 50 percent of the elevated black demand—the mere possibility that slavery increased the kidney failure rate among blacks provides a conceivable rationale for restructuring allocation systems that disfavor blacks.

167. Id. at 254 (saying that "the stress of poverty or racism may evoke a hormonal 'fight or flight' response that boosts heart rate and blood pressure").

In making this case for privileging race, difficult issues of framing need to be addressed. For example, one might persuasively argue that federal funding of virtually all renal transplants represents tremendous governmental largess to the disproportionately black ESRD population and that, when considered as a whole, the program disproportionately favors blacks—even though the antigen matching aspect of the allograft allocation disproportionately excludes blacks.[168] Moreover, even if the disparate racial impact of antigen matching is a concern, blacks—and society—might benefit more from corrective efforts that address other health issues such as high blood pressure, smoking, or even prenatal care.

Guido Calabresi and Philip Bobbitt argue that no single perspective can capture all of society's concerns. They speak of "the motion that is composed of the succession of decision, rationalization, and violence as quiet replaces anxiety and is replaced by it when society evades, confronts, and remakes the tragic choice."[169] In making tragic choices, societies inevitably oscillate between different perspectives. In this chapter we have framed the issue around the ongoing debate about how to allocate cadaveric kidneys and have implicitly left aside the thorny issues of whether government should continue its subsidy of kidney transplantation and whether attempts to remedy past discrimination are better accomplished by other forms of compensation. To the extent that the proper allocation of cadaveric kidneys remains a discrete public concern, the medically unjustified disparate impact on blacks is a relevant concern of policymakers.

C. Proposal to Revise the UNOS Point System

1. Accommodating Equity and Efficiency

This tension between equity and efficiency concerns[170] is reflected implicitly in the language of the NOTA, which requires organ procurement organizations to "allocate donated organs equitably among transplant pa-

---

168. This framing argument parallels the issue in Connecticut v. Teal, 457 U.S. 440 (1982). In that case, the Supreme Court considered whether an employment test that disparately excluded blacks violated Title VII even though the employer had hired proportionate numbers of protected workers. The Court rejected the employer's "bottom line" defense and held that Title VII plaintiffs had discretion on how to frame their disparate impact claim.

169. Calabresi & Bobbitt, *supra* note 24, at 19.

170. A classic discussion of these concerns can be found in Arthur M. Okun, *Equality and Efficiency, The Big Tradeoff* (1975).

tients according to established medical criteria."[171] We do not claim that a consensus exists concerning the appropriate balance between equity and efficiency objectives. Instead, we suggest that there is a spectrum of allocative systems representing different accommodations of these conflicting objectives.

At one extreme is the traditional system, which places almost exclusive emphasis on antigen matching. At the other extreme would be allocation purely by length of time on a waiting list. Giving cadaveric kidneys to the dialysis patients who had waited longest would ensure that persons of each race would receive a share of transplants proportional to that race's representation on the waiting list. A pure waiting list achieves this equity, however, at the cost of reduced graft survival. By giving no weight to recipients who have even six-antigen matches, allocating available organs on a first-come, first-served basis sacrifices increased probability of graft survival for at least a portion of the transplanted kidneys.[172] At least in the current cyclosporine era of drug therapy, we ultimately reject this type of queueing allocation for reasons analogous to those that led us to reject the extreme efficiency-based allocation schemes.[173] We conjecture that our society cares about equity, but equitable goals, like efficiency goals, are themselves incomplete.

Our preferred accommodation of these competing goals of equitable access and graft survival is (1) to give allocative preference to antigen matching in proportion to its effectiveness in enhancing graft survival, and also (2) to give patients with rare antigens, and who are therefore harder to match, a preference in receiving those unmatched kidneys when enhanced graft survival is not at issue. This modified allocation system would continue the mandatory sharing of six-antigen-matched kidneys and might

171. 42 U.S.C. § 273(b)(3)(E) (1994). Originally, the Act mandated that kidneys be allocated equitably "between patients and centers." But in 1988, Congress amended the Act deleting the reference to transplant centers, thus further focusing the allocation issues on patient equity.

172. There is an argument that pure waiting lists sacrifice equitable concerns because dissimilar people are treated similarly. Thus, among the class of white recipients, a waiting list would be inequitable because recipients with lower expected graft survival might be given priority in transplantation. We conjecture, however, that pure waiting lists would not be as immediately objectionable to society as allocations that include racial exclusions. Other countries, for example, have used pure waiting lists to allocate kidney transplants in the past. See Calabresi & Bobbitt, *supra* note 24.

173. See section II.A of this chapter; see also Developments in the Law: Medical Technology and the Law, *supra* note 6, at 1642 (saying that first-come, first-served allocations "are ethically bankrupt: society would be choosing not to choose").

Table 6.6   Modified Point System for Selecting Kidney Transplant Recipients
(Additions are in brackets; deletions are struck through)

	Points
HLA Matching	
0—A, B, DR mismatch	~~10~~[Mandatory sharing]
[1—A, B, DR mismatch	7]
~~0—B, DR mismatch~~	~~7~~
~~0—A, B mismatch~~	~~6~~
~~1—B, DR mismatch~~	~~3~~
~~2—B, DR mismatch~~	~~2~~
~~3—B, DR mismatch~~	~~1~~
Waiting Time	
Patient with longest waiting period (proportionate points for shorter periods)	~~1~~ [2]
Each year on waiting list	~~.5~~ [1]
Children	
Age 0–5	2
Age 6–10	1
Presensitization	4
Rare antigens	4

possibly give some preference to recipients with only one antigen mismatch as this degree of partial matching may enhance graft survival.[174] Unlike the traditional UNOS system, however, recipients who mismatched two or more antigens of a donated kidney would receive no points. Our proposed system also would give patients with relatively rare antigens at least the same number of points that are given for other equitable concerns such as presensitization. Although the exact values are open to debate, table 6.6 provides a redacted version showing how our proposal would change the traditional UNOS point system.

Patients whose combination of antigens would give them less than a 10 percent chance of qualifying for one of the antigen matching preferences could receive "rare antigen" points. Awarding rare antigen points would be consonant with the equitable exceptions already in place. Just as the presensitization points promote medical justice by elevating the chances of

174.   See *supra* text accompanying note 123.

those with medical bad luck,[175] recipients with the poor fortune of having rare antigens would receive a preference. And, indeed, that preference is even more defensible than the one for presensitized patients because a patient's antigens are an immutable characteristic, while presensitization often is the result of a previous transplant opportunity that failed. Awarding points for rare antigens thus would increase the *ex ante* equality of opportunity.[176] While the criterion of having less than a 10 percent chance of matching five or six antigens is an arbitrary cutoff, it is no more arbitrary than the current criteria for who qualifies as presensitized (greater than 80 percent reactivity).

Most important, rare antigen points, combined with a deemphasis on partial matching, could substantially reduce the disparate racial impact of the current point system without resorting to race-conscious points. Because black ESRD patients only rarely qualify for six-antigen-match transplants,[177] disproportionate numbers of rare antigen points would go to blacks. Awarding points on the basis of rare antigen type would also avoid problems that might accompany a race-conscious preference. If blacks received race-conscious points to remedy this disparate impact and possible past discrimination, the rate of white cadaveric donations might decrease.

175. Dennis, *supra* note 58, at 133.

176. Before being antigen typed (*ex ante*), each ESRD patient theoretically could have the same probability of transplantation. Typing would then reveal which recipients had nonrare antigens—and hence an elevated chance of qualifying for antigen matching preference—and which recipients had rare antigens—and hence an elevated chance of qualifying because of the rare antigen preference.

Equalizing *ex ante* opportunity is not universally reflected in our discrimination law. Imagine, for example, that an employer needs to hire one hundred people. Ninety-five of the jobs can be performed by any worker, but five jobs require sufficient strength so that hiring only men constitutes a bona fide occupation qualification (BFOQ) under Title VII. In economic parlance, *ex ante* equal employment opportunity would mean that an applicant would have an equal opportunity of being hired regardless of gender. A commitment to *ex ante* equality of opportunity would therefore require employers to give women preference in competing for the remaining jobs; fifty of ninety-five would need to go to women to counterbalance the five BFOQ jobs for which women could not compete. Title VII imposes no such requirement upon employers to employ preferences to counterbalance BFOQ hiring.

We suggest, however, that the government regulations concerning kidney transplantation should reflect a concern for *ex ante* racial equality. Employers under Title VII are not required to consider equity when hiring employees, and individual employers are not required to eliminate the vestiges of past societal discrimination. In the kidney context, the government does mandate other forms of equitable allocations, and the possible connection between kidney failure and slavery heightens society's responsibility for disparate racial access to this scarce commodity.

177. See *supra* text accompanying notes 83–86.

In addition, race-conscious points awarded on the basis of a patient's declaration might induce whites to misrepresent their race in order to qualify for these additional points.[178]

At a minimum, the traditional UNOS point system needed to be amended to award more points for time on the waiting list relative to partial antigen matching. As discussed above, the point system used time on the waiting list largely as a tiebreaker.[179] The practice of awarding points for as few as one or two antigen matches cannot be supported absent reliable evidence that recipients with two or three matching antigens have higher success rates than patients with zero or one matching antigen. The system, therefore, needlessly sacrificed equity for a minimal increase in graft survival. Eliminating the points for two or more mismatches and increasing the points for time on the waiting list could mitigate both the disparate racial impact and the caprice of the allocation rules.[180]

Moreover, our proposal is consonant with the variances in place at several OPOs throughout the country. The Regional Organ Bank of Illinois (ROBI) allocates cadaveric kidneys under a UNOS-approved variance that already employs two of our proposed changes. The ROBI point system gives more weight to time on the waiting list relative to antigen matching and gives no points for two or three B, DR mismatches.[181] Indeed, virtually all of the alternative allocation rules put less emphasis on antigen matching relative to time on the waiting list.[182] Thus, when individual transplant centers seek to vary UNOS rules, they almost invariably move away from antigen matching toward the kind of allocation rules that we propose.

178.   A race-conscious allocation system, however, does have some merits. The traditional point system gave black recipients an arbitrary preference for partial antigen matching even though partial matching has no empirical relation to survival rates in black recipients. See *supra* text accompanying notes 124–26. Moreover, giving black ESRD patients a fixed number of points could directly counterbalance the disparate racial impact of mandatory six-antigen sharing and partial antigen points, so that cadaveric kidneys would be allocated to blacks in proportion to black representation in the ESRD population.

179.   See *supra* note 61 and accompanying text.

180.   Granting more points for time on the waiting list would enhance equity while retaining some of the benefits of antigen matching. Due to relatively poor matching, however, black ESRD patients would be able to overcome the racial impact of antigen matching only by waiting for longer periods. Thus, enhancing the relative importance of waiting list points would mitigate but not extinguish the disparate racial impact.

181.   See Lazda, *supra* note 80, at 901.

182.   See Dennis, *supra* note 81.

2. Defining the Geographic Scope of the Point System

We have focused on modifying kidney allocation by changing the relative weights given to different factors under the UNOS point system. The choices involved in constructing a scheme for allocating cadaveric kidneys, however, also include the appropriate geographic scope of the point system. Defining the geographic scope establishes the pool in which the point system operates. A kidney harvested in an Alabama hospital, for example, could go to the recipient who had the most points on that hospital's waiting list, on that OPO's waiting list, or on a national waiting list. The choice of the appropriate pool size is analytically distinct from the question of the appropriate bases for awarding points.

Advocates of increased antigen matching have proposed extending the geographic scope of the partial antigen matching pool.[183] Instead of the current system, which applies the point system to those on local waiting lists, the proposal would pool recipients nationally and transport each kidney to the recipient who had accumulated the most points for that kidney based on HLA matching. A national point system is consistent with an emphasis on enhanced survival through better antigen matching because the larger the pool of recipients, the greater the probability of finding a good match. The choice of a national system might also be consistent with an emphasis on equity. If a pure waiting list were used to allocate kidneys, it would be inequitable to apply the points on a local basis because under this normative view the dialysis patients who had waited the longest should have a prior claim to kidneys harvested in any part of the country. Thus, a national scope for the point system is supportable on both equity and efficiency rationales.

The strongest arguments in favor of a local scope for point systems concern issues of procurement.[184] The mode of allocating cadaveric kidneys may alter the number of kidneys that are harvested. The incentives of the harvesting doctor may be particularly important.[185] Beyond the often ardu-

183. Gjertson et al., *supra* note 25, at 1032.

184. A local allocation system provides the added benefits of lower cost and quicker transplantation. National allocation, however, has been estimated to entail an increased expenditure of only $1,000 per transplant. Id. While national allocation causes longer delays between harvesting and transplantation, better techniques and new drug therapies have reduced the importance of preservation time as a determinant of graft survival.

185. See Blumstein, *supra* note 4, at 490:

In light of the . . . strong condemnation of commercializing organs and its advocacy that property rights of donors be eliminated, it is ironic that the ideology of "national reous task of removing organs at the time of death, which may often be at night, the harvesting OPO must first gain the consent of the donor family. Making more than perfunctory efforts to accomplish these tasks requires a committed and sometimes tireless altruism. Much of the incentive to procure kidneys aggressively derives from the knowledge that local patients will benefit. Local allocation may increase procurement rates by enabling centers to transplant patients on their own waiting list[186] and aggressive OPOs to reap rewards for their efforts.

Conversely, mandatory sharing of all kidneys may discourage procurement in an era when the donor shortage is clearly the limiting factor in renal transplantation. Expanding the scope of the UNOS point system to the national level would decrease the likelihood of transplanting kidneys that were harvested locally. While there are no direct empirical data on the magnitude of this procurement effect, its existence is widely acknowledged in the literature[187] and implicit in the UNOS guidelines, which require OPOs that receive a six-antigen-matched kidney from another center to return the next suitable kidney with the same ABO type.[188] In sum, because of this possible procurement effect,[189] we tentatively propose retention of local geographic allocation, but suggest that more empirical work is necessary.

D. Adapting Allocation to New Drug Therapies

The previous sections have been concerned primarily with discussing how we should allocate kidneys in the current cyclosporine era. But as we advance these tentative proposals, the postcyclosporine era is rapidly tak-

---

source" for organs confronts and must respond to the territoriality or property rights perspective—not of donors or patients, but of transplant centers and their surgical teams.

186. See Starzl et al., *supra* note 58, at 3073.

187. See id.

188. UNOS Policy § 3.5.11 (1992) ("Payback for Six Antigen Match Kidneys"); see also id. § 3.5.12 ("Payback of Voluntarily Shared Kidneys with Extra-Renal Organs"); id. § 3.5.13 (1992) ("Payback of Kidneys Shared for Highly Sensitized Recipients").

189. In reaching this conclusion, we should note that one of the authors is a nephrologist at the University of Alabama. Because of the high procurement rates of the Alabama Regional Organ and Tissue Center, a national point system—whether based on pure antigen matching or a pure waiting list—would inevitably reduce the number of transplants performed at the center and increase the waiting time for those on the local waiting list. Consequently, readers may want to probe our analysis because of a possible conflict of interest. For a more detailed discussion of various interests of participants in the current allocation debate, see *infra* note 195 and accompanying text.

ing shape as new therapies become available. These new therapies not only have increased survival rates, but also have simplified the normative dilemmas outlined above. Inasmuch as the new drugs successfully eliminate recipient race and antigen matching as determinants of graft survival, allocation schemes can begin to treat time on the waiting list as the determinative factor.[190] Under this scenario, the trade-off between equity and efficiency would largely disappear.

At the very least, the current empiricism is sufficient to suggest that immunosuppressant therapies should be sensitive to racial differences. There is growing evidence that black patients have heightened immunologic responsiveness[191] and may require more intense drug therapies.[192] Indeed, quadruple immunosuppression, which has been shown to resolve racial disparity in graft survival over three years, originated not because of a special concern for race, but rather to alleviate cyclosporine toxicity. The improvement in black allograft survival was noted only as an ancillary benefit. Therefore, with the evidence of immunologic differences between races evolving, the medical community now must define parameters of immune responsiveness that may differ between races. Failing to account for such potential racial differences would be another form of selective indifference, paralleling the unfortunate practice of extrapolating the results of white or male cohorts in other areas of science.[193]

The more difficult normative question may concern the degree of empiricism that is required to justify a change in allocation policies. At a minimum, we argue that such policies should not be static, but should continue to evolve. The emergence of new drug therapies only underscores this conclusion. In the absence of authoritative empiricism, administrative agencies should consider whether it is advantageous to wait for more information.[194] While deemphasizing partial antigen matching may reduce survivability, retaining or expanding the antigen-based allocation will almost certainly perpetuate or worsen the racial disparity in transplantation. Weighing these speculative costs against certain equitable benefits might militate for changing the allocation rules without waiting for further con-

190. It may be that six-antigen-matched transplants would retain significance and therefore should be included in the revised point system. See Takemoto et al., *supra* note 51, at 1081.

191. See, e.g., Kerman et al., *supra* note 101, at 380.

192. See Gaston et al., *supra* note 79, at 103.

193. See, e.g., Carol Gilligan, *In a Different Voice* (1982).

194. See, e.g., International Harvester v. Ruckelhaus, 478 F.2d 615 (D.C. Cir. 1973).

firming data. In the postcyclosporine era the heavy preference for partial matching relative to time on the waiting list is normatively untenable. Even if our prior understanding justified privileging partial antigen matching, newer empiricism indicates that those benefits are small and potentially decreasing, with a decidedly adverse impact on blacks.

E. A Political History of Antigen Matching and Immunosuppression

These pressing allocative decisions are not made in an esoteric or ahistorical setting. Indeed, we argue that the history of kidney transplantation has powerfully framed the normative issues that policymakers now confront. The transplantation community has itself been sharply divided between those who would extend antigen matching even further and those who would deemphasize antigen matching in the face of superior therapeutic regimens. In this section we sketch the history of renal transplantation and outline the current positions of the major players in the policy debate.[195]

The first successful kidney transplant in the United States was performed in 1953 by Joseph Murray at Boston's Peter Bent Brigham Hospital with a kidney donated by an identical twin of the recipient.[196] The early history of transplantation was shaped by the use of living related donors, particularly twins, whose kidneys could be transplanted in the absence of immunosuppressant drugs. Until the late 1960s, chronic dialysis treatments were not widely available, and kidney failure was a fatal disease. In those years, surgeons were willing to attempt transplants without firm evidence of the likelihood of success because the alternative for the patient was almost certain death. Thus, transplants from a variety of living related donors—including fraternal twins, siblings, and parents—were attempted. At that time, the only immunosuppressant drugs were cortisone derivatives, which were highly toxic and poorly tolerated. In the absence of effective immunosuppressive therapies, research focused on genetic determinants of graft survival. Initially, it was observed that some transplants from siblings were quickly rejected while others survived for long periods of time. In the early 1960s, Jean Dausset and others discovered HLA antigens and developed the techniques of tissue typing. The discovery of the antigen

195. For a more detailed history of the politics of transplantation, see Dennis, *supra* note 58, at 130.

196. See James B. Nelson, *Human Medicine Developments in the Law* (1984); Developments in the Law: Medical Technology and the Law, *supra* note 6, at 1614.

loci and the ability to identify different antigen types furthered the genetic emphasis in kidney transplantation. Tissue typing for antigens among potential living donors became the accepted method for choosing donors, and results of tissue typing studies predicted transplant outcomes with a fair degree of reliability.

This emphasis on genetics and antigen matching was in some ways a historical artifact of the early days of kidney transplantation. In contrast, liver and heart transplantation developed a radically different therapeutic ethos. Transplantation from living related donors obviously is not a consideration for hearts and livers. In addition, short preservation times for these organs when obtained from cadaveric donors did not allow doctors to use tissue typing results in the selection of recipients.[197] As a result, transplantation of these organs did not evolve along the same genetics-oriented route as for kidneys, and thus far, tissue typing plays a very minor role.

The introduction of cyclosporine in 1984 revolutionized transplantation, markedly improving results in renal transplantation, and for the first time making heart and liver transplants practical.[198] Since the beginning of the cyclosporine era, however, the kidney transplant community has been divided about whether survival of cadaveric grafts is determined more by antigen matching or by immunosuppressant therapies.

Paul Terasaki of the U.C.L.A. Tissue Typing Laboratory, a pioneer in the development of tissue typing, has been particularly effective in championing allocation based on antigen matching.[199] As noted earlier, he and his associates called for an expanded emphasis on matching and advocated mandatory national allocation of cadaveric kidneys on the basis of hierarchical antigen matching in order to maximize transplant survival rates.[200] Others, with supportive data, have opposed such a system. Philip Held and coauthors, using data from the U.S. Renal Data System, concluded that even with a sevenfold increase in the number of six-antigen matches, there would be only a 2–3 percent increase in the overall graft survival

197. Hearts and livers, until quite recently, required transplantation within six to eight hours of harvest. Kidneys, by comparison, may be preserved for thirty-six to forty-eight hours.

198. See Organ Transplantation: Hearing Before the Senate Committee on Labor and Human Resources, 98th Cong., 177, 179 (1983) (statement of Nancy L. Ascher, transplant surgeon); Barry D. Kahan, The Impact of Cyclosporine on the Practice of Renal Transplantation, 21 Transplantation Proc. 63 (1989).

199. See Terasaki et al., *supra* note 56, at 301.

200. Gjertson et al., *supra* note 25, at 1032.

of all transplants.[201] Proponents of mandatory antigen matching programs usually downplay any relationship between antigen matching and racial access to transplantation.[202]

At the beginning of the 1990s, the time was ripe administratively for a reconsideration of the kidney allocation program (as HHS was in the process of bringing the UNOS rules under the procedures of the APA),[203] but the division between the two camps (the antigen matchers and the immunosuppression therapists) seemed, if anything, to be widening. Tissue typers continued to demand broader application of antigen matching and were actively involved in research to define more precisely the genetic origins of HLA antigens.[204] Many clinicians, however, remained committed to retaining local control of harvested kidneys and were involved in the development of immunosupression therapies that had the potential to minimize the impact of antigen matching. Neither side appeared to be listening to the other.[205] However, as discussed in the next section, by the late 1990s, as the transplant community became increasingly aware of the ways in which antigen matching increased racial transplant disparities (in part because of our published research), there had been a shift away from antigen matching as an allocative criteria—not just by the most ardent defenders of antigen matching (the tissue typers) but in the revised UNOS point system itself.

201. See Hunsicker & Held, *supra* note 26, at 293. These data have been disputed by Terasaki and associates, who, using data voluntarily submitted to the U.C.L.A. Transplant Registry, contend that a national allocation program that included partial antigen matches could increase overall five-year survival rates by 5 percent. Gjertson et al., *supra* note 25, at 1032.

202. For example, as one article states:

Some contend that HLA matching would discriminate against blacks. . . . [Currently] [p]atients forced to wait for long periods, presumably because they are difficult to match, receive an allowance in the form of points allocated for waiting time. When kidneys were allocated according to a point system rather than a center-driven system in a local two-year trial, transplantation in patients with longer waiting times and those with high levels of HLA antibodies were performed more frequently. . . . Therefore, a change to a national system will not suddenly decrease the number of black recipients undergoing transplantation; rather, it may increase it.

Id. at 1035.

203. See Ayres et al., *Unequal Access, supra* note 11, at 812.

204. Aida A. Barbetti et al., HLA Serologic Epitopes, *in Clinical Transplants 1989*, at 477 (Paul I. Terasaki ed., 1989). However, as emphasized in the third section of this chapter, there is some evidence that even tissue typers are slowly recognizing the limits of antigen matching.

205. A. R. Hull, Editorial, 5 Nephrology News & Issues 42 (1991).

III. The Scholarly and Public Reaction

Since the publication of our first article on the disparate impact of antigen matching in the *Journal of the American Medical Association* in 1993,[206] there have been important developments in both science and policy. This section briefly reports on the scholarly reactions to our initial analysis, on the new medical evidence, and on the laudable efforts of UNOS to deemphasize antigen matching.

A. Scholarly Reaction

Our original publication has been criticized in two publications, a book by Richard Epstein[207] and a responsive article by Lloyd Cohen and Melisa Michelsen.[208] In particular, Cohen and Michelsen are vehement in their opposition to our aforementioned proposals, asserting that "Ayres' proposal is not merely thoroughly incorrect but [it is] evil and pernicious as well."[209] Their primary criticisms concern our argument that race was relevant both because of regulators' "selective indifference" and as a way to remedy past discrimination.

The most persuasive point—made originally by Cohen and Michelsen and picked up as well by Epstein[210]—concerns our assertion that UNOS's concern with equity in adopting the O rule and the presensitization preference evidences a selective indifference to the equitable claims of African Americans. Cohen and Michelsen argue, however, that our selective indifference argument is based on a faulty assumption. They argue that the O Rule and the presensitization preference might have been adopted solely to promote efficiency. Their basic idea is that in a dynamic analysis we might on average have better matches if we were to give a preference for hard-to-match recipients whenever a relatively well-matched kidney is available. For example, imagine there are only two people waiting for transplants: one who is presensitized and the other who is not. And let us imagine, counterfactually, that we are living in a time prior to the improvement of immunosuppression drugs when the degree of partial antigen

---

206. Gaston et al., *supra* note 27.

207. Epstein, *supra* note 28.

208. Cohen & Michelsen, *supra* note 28.

209. Id. at 138.

210. See Epstein, *supra* note 28, at 279; Cohen & Michelsen, *supra* note 28, at 162.

matching was an important determinant of transplant success. And finally, imagine that a kidney becomes available for transplantation that is a four-antigen match with the presensitized recipient and a five-antigen match with the non-presensitized recipient. While static survivability considerations would counsel toward planting the kidney into the better-matched recipient, a consideration of the future might suggest giving a presensitization preference. Specifically, if we think it is unlikely that another kidney will be donated in the future that will have even a two-antigen match with the presensitized recipient, but that it is likely that we will find another donor who has at least a four-antigen match with the non-presensitized recipient, then it might enhance expected survivability to transplant the first kidney in the poorer matched, but hard-to-match presensitized recipient. Better to have a four-match transplant followed by a three- or four-match transplant, rather than a four-match transplant followed by a one- or two-match transplant. We readily concede this point and hereby retract our earlier assertion that the preferring blood type O or presensitized recipients can, as a theoretical matter, only be rationalized as a regulatory attempt to further equity.

However, there are still strong empirical reasons to believe that equitable considerations influenced the adoption of each of these rules. As an empirical matter, the presensitization preference is unlikely to increase the overall survivability of transplants. Presensitized patients have a considerably greater likelihood of rejecting a new organ than nonsensitized patients,[211] and there are so many potential recipients waiting for a relatively small number of donated kidneys that preferring a presensitized recipient would almost certainly lower the overall survivability. From a survivability standpoint, it would be better simply to write off the presensitized recipients, even taking into account the dynamic argument mentioned above. There are so many non-presensitized patients waiting that there is likely to be a fairly well-matched, non-presensitized recipient for all the kidneys that are donated over time. Thus, Cohen and Michelsen conclude, "Ayres is probably correct that points for pre-sensitization can not be justified on pure efficiency grounds *at current levels of supply and demand.*"[212]

But appreciating that the stock of demand is more than fifteen times greater than the yearly flow of supply also cuts against the theoretical efficiency-enhancing effect of the O rule. While it is true that giving an

211. Aprile et al., *supra* note 158, at 735.
212. Cohen & Michelsen, *supra* note 28, at 166.

initial kidney to a poorly matched zero-recipient might avoid being forced to give this patient an even more poorly matched kidney in the future, in a world with so many dialysis patients waiting for a transplant, it is not necessary ever to transplant to blood type O recipients. And even if an efficiency goal (in the sense of enhanced survivability) justified some preference for blood type O recipients, it certainly does not justify the current categorical requirement that blood type O kidneys can only be transplanted in blood type O recipients.

In the end, the existence of any presensitization preference and the particularly extreme form that the O rule preference takes are strong evidence that they were not merely motivated by a desire to maximize overall survivability. We are still confident that equitable considerations played a role in adopting these rules and hence our claim about "selective indifference" still stands. In passing these preferences, UNOS acted on the equitable concerns of some recipients and not others.

Indeed, Cohen and Michelsen's fine observation that the O rule and presensitization preference might advance the cause of survivability should ultimately be viewed as an additional argument *in favor* of our proposal for rare antigen points. Giving a preference for recipients with rare antigens can be justified on the same efficiency rationale: A patient with rare antigens relative to the donor pool will be a more difficult match, and thus overall efficiency might be heightened if that patient gets a preference as to a particular kidney that is not well matched to anyone else on the recipient list.[213] Cohen and Michelsen's argument thus shows that our rare antigen proposal can be defended on the grounds of efficiency as well as equity. Recognizing the efficiency rationale for rare antigen points also deepens our original "selective indifference" criticism. We now see that UNOS was moved by the dynamic efficiency argument with regard to the O rule and the presensitization preference but does not act when an efficiency-enhancing preference disproportionately favors African Americans.

To be clear, we believe the point about dynamic efficiency to be a neat theoretical insight. But because demand for transplants far exceeds supply, we do not believe that any of these rules is likely to increase survivability. So our original equity-based analysis stands unscathed. But even if these rules did promote efficiency, there may be an even stronger selective indifference argument for adopting our rare antigen proposal.

In rejecting the relevance of race, both Epstein's and Cohen and Mi-

213. See Laura G. Dooley & Robert Gaston, Stumbling toward Equity: The Role of Government in Kidney Transplantation, 1998 U. Ill. L. Rev. 703, 712.

chelsen's writings largely ignore our remedial justification. If past government discrimination has caused elevated African American demand for kidney transplantation, could this not justify race-conscious efforts to mitigate the injury? Cohen and Michelsen are particularly willing to latch onto any bit of empiricism to justify antigen matching, but they imply that they would impose much higher requirements of proof before admitting that public or private discrimination contributed to racial disparities in ESRD.

Both writings harshly criticize our race-neutral "rare antigen" proposal because it has the explicitly race-conscious motive of increasing African American participation in kidney transplantation. Cohen and Michelsen choose to label the underlying race consciousness of this proposal not just as "morally grotesque and abhorrent" and "evil and pernicious," but as "racist" as well, and Epstein analogizes our rare antigen points to "Jim Crow's neutral rule limiting the eligibility to vote to individuals whose grandfathers had voted before the Civil War."[214]

But the traditional remedy in *every* disparate impact case is a race-neutral adjustment undergirded by a race-conscious motive to enhance minority participation. For example, consider a *Griggs*-like setting where an employer demands that unskilled workers must have a high school diploma. If the court finds that the employment rule has an unjustified disparate racial impact, the remedy is to require the employer to change its hiring practice in a race-neutral way—dropping the diploma requirement—so as to *enhance minority participation* in the workforce. This is exactly what we do with regard to partial antigen points. We show that they have an unjustified disparate impact and we suggest dropping them so as to increase minority participation.

So it cannot be that all race-neutral changes to a decisionmaking process that attempts to increase minority participation are wrong (evil, racist, and so on) unless Epstein and Cohen and Michelsen wish to subsume their personal criticisms in a larger criticism of all disparate impact law. No doubt these authors would. But our point is that our rare antigen proposal falls squarely within the traditional remedies for disparate impact violations—and therefore is no more (nor less) morally grotesque than *Griggs* (as subsequently codified by the Civil Right Act of 1991).[215]

214. Epstein, *supra* note 28, at 277; Cohen & Michelsen, *supra* note 28, at 178, 138, 173.

215. See Civil Rights Act of 1991, Pub. L. 102-166, § 105(a), 105 Stat. 1075, *codified at* 42 U.S.C. § 2000e-2(k) (1994). There is a possible difference between forcing

Indeed, in both *Croson*[216] and *Adarand*,[217] Justice O'Connor explicitly states that "race-neutral means to increase minority business participation" are constitutionally preferable to non-race-neutral means.[218] If the federal government is moved by our arguments to adopt a remedy for past and present discrimination, our race-neutral implementation is unambiguously more consonant with the Supreme Court's favored approach. Besides the valuable insight that the equitable preferences might also enhance a dynamic conception of survivability, Epstein and Cohen and Michelsen ultimately do little more than rehearse why they are against attempts to remedy disparate impact violations.

B. New Medical Evidence

While conservative legal scholars have criticized our proposals—largely on theoretical grounds—the intervening years have produced new evidence that antigen matching has an unjustified disparate impact on African Americans. This new evidence strengthens our previous claims that antigen matching disproportionately excludes African American transplant recipients and that points given for partial antigen matching do not appreciably increase expected allograft survival. Moreover, there are strong indications that the transplant community is now sensitive to the impact of allocation rules on racial disparities, with explicit discussion and tailoring of new allocation systems to mitigate the problem.

First, there is a growing consensus in the medical community that partial antigen matching does not appreciably increase graft survival. For example, Philip Held and his coauthors, in a comprehensive overview published in the *New England Journal of Medicine*, conclude:

---

a decisionmaker to repeal a rule and forcing it to adopt a new race-neutral rule, but this is certainly not a difference in the underlying motive of enhancing minority participation.

It should also be emphasized that our proposal to deemphasize partial antigen matching need not be undergirded by a race-conscious motive. A motive merely to reduce the capriciousness of allocation rules could counsel toward deemphasizing matching points once those points are shown to be increasingly unrelated to transplant outcomes.

216. 488 U.S. 469 (1989).

217. 515 U.S. 200 (1995).

218. See id., 515 U.S. at 238, quoting *Croson*, 488 U.S. at 507. I have, however, criticized this reasoning in Ian Ayres, Narrow Tailoring, 43 UCLA L. Rev. 1781 (1996).

[P]rogressive increases in the number of mismatches from one to six have only a small effect on survival as compared with the the large benefits afforded by the use of a graft with no mismatches.[219]

Thus, while giving zero-mismatched recipients preferences continues to be medically justified, improvements in immunosuppression increasingly reduce the benefits of partial antigen matches.

Moreover, recent evidence on the high success of mismatched live donor transplants strongly suggests the declining importance of antigen matching.[220] Conventional wisdom held that transplants from mismatched family members or unrelated live donors would result in very low success rates, such that only complete or half matches were considered sufficient to justify the risk of removing a kidney from an otherwise healthy donor. More recent data published by researchers (known in the past for their resolute commitment to the importance of antigen matching) demonstrates, however, no ascertainable difference in outcomes at three years posttransplant between completely mismatched, unrelated donor–recipient pairs and most family member pairs. This striking research is capsulized in figure 6.3, which shows that donations from living spouses with the poorest matches do better than the best matched transplants from cadaveric donation. The authors of the study conclude: "The survival of grafts from unrelated donors was comparable of that of parental-donor grafts despite the average of 4.1 HLA mismatches in the former group, as compared with 2.3 HLA mismatches in the latter group."[221] Nonantigen factors today easily swamp the effect of antigen matching in predicting survivability.

The declining impact of partial antigen matching is also observable in recent studies that simulate the impact of extending the current national sharing of perfectly matched kidneys to mandatory national sharing of partial antigen matches. For example, one article concludes that mandatory national sharing of transplants with four or more antigen matches pro-

219. Philip J. Held et al., The Impact of HLA Mismatches on the Survival of First Cadaveric Kidney Transplants, 331 New Eng. J. Med. 765, 768–69 (1994). See also Steven Katznelson & J. Michael Cecka, *Immunosuppressive Regimens and Their Effects on Renal Allograft Outcome in Clinical Transplants* (Michael Cecka & Paul Terasaki eds., 1996).

220. See Paul I. Terasaki et al., High Survival Rates of Kidney Transplants from Spousal and Living Unrelated Donors, 333 New Eng. J. Med. 333 (1995).

221. Id. at 334.

Figure 6.3 Survival of first cadaveric grafts according to urine flow on first day. The grafts were further grouped on the basis of the number of HLA–A, B, and Dr mismatches.The spousal-donor group is included for comparison.

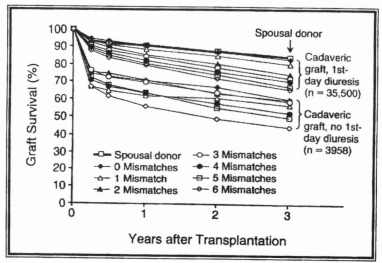

Copyright © 1995 Massachusetts Medical Society. All rights reserved, reproduced with permission.

duced estimated survival rates that were "less than 2% better" than the current system.[222] While there may not be unanimity on the issue, there is certainly a consensus that the impact of partial antigen matching in the wake of new immunosuppression techniques is small and declining.

Second, recent research incontrovertibly shows that the UNOS points for partial antigen matches made it harder for African Americans to qualify for transplantation. There is increasing evidence that blacks not only have different antigens than whites but that their antigens are more heterogeneous (polymorphic), meaning that African Americans will have a harder time even matching each other.[223] Moreover, analysis of the equilibrium effects of the UNOS point system show the startling impact of the partial antigen preference. To begin, 75 percent of cadaveric transplants have

222. Harold I. Feldman et al., National Kidney Allograft Sharing: A Decision Analysis, 64 Transplantation 80, 80 (1997).

223. Patrick G. Beatty et al., Impact of Racial Genetic Polymorphism on the Probability of Finding an HLA-Matched Donor, 60 Transplantation 778 (1995).

three or more HLA mismatches—so in equilibrium partial antigen matching is a common occurrence.[224] And the magnitude of the preference for partial antigen matching relative to time on the waiting list can be seen by the fact that, with regard to non-presensitized recipients, 88.8 percent of the total UNOS points were given for antigen matches vs. only 11.2 percent of the points given for waiting time.[225] Forty-five percent of minorities receiving transplants received no HLA points, while overall only 10.4 percent of recipients received no antigen points. The disparate racial impact of these rules can be directly inferred as well from the fact that, in equilibrium, minorities were overrepresented in the group of recipients with at least three BDR mismatches while minorities were underrepresented in the group of recipients with only one BDR mismatch.[226]

Researchers in the wake of our original publication have also simulated the effect of alternative antigen matching regimes on black participation. As our analysis would suggest, mandating maximal national matching would reduce the proportion of recipients who are black by more than 25 percent (from 22.2 percent to a projected 15 percent).[227] Reducing the points for partial antigen matching would increase black participation. One study concluded:

> If points for 0ABmm and 3BDRmm grades were eliminated 41% of patients would have no HLA points and if points for 2BDRmm were also dropped 76.6% of patients would have no HLA points. For these patients the driving force would then be waiting time, and minorities who have the longest waiting times would be given an advantage.[228]

While some may still contest whether basing allocation decisions on partial antigen matching is medically justified, it is now beyond dispute that antigen matching has a disparate impact on African Americans.[229]

---

224. Steven K. Takemoto, *HLA Amino Acid Residue Matching in Clinical Transplants* (Michael Cecka & Paul Terasaki eds., 1996).

225. D. J. Norman et al., Cadaveric Kidney Allocation in the United States: A Critical Analysis of the Point System, 27 Transplantation Proc. 800 (1995).

226. Id.

227. Held et al., *supra* note 219, at 768–69.

228. Norman et al., *supra* note 225.

229. There has also been additional confirmation of what we earlier referred to as the "salty gene" hypothesis. There is new evidence of a strong genetic link between low-renin hypertension and kidney failure in blacks. See generally Suzanne Bergman et al., Kidney Disease in the First-Degree Relatives of African-Americans with Hypertensive End-Stage Renal Disease, 27 Am. J. Kidney Dis. 341 (1996); James K. Bubien et al., Lid-

The medical and scientific community has responded to our original publication and this newer evidence of disparate racial access with a variety of proposals to reduce disparate impact of partial antigen matching. One cannot currently discuss allocation rules without assessing the question of racial access. And more recent research seems to support our view that it is possible to achieve more equitable allocation (in terms of evening out the waiting times for all demographic groups) without appreciably sacrificing expected graft survival.[230] A simulation-based policy study using data obtained from both UNOS and the U.S. Renal Data System has demonstrated that an "equity-based" algorithm that assigned priority to African American recipients achieved the smallest difference in median waiting time while achieving the second-highest score for efficiency as measured by a quality-adjusted life expectancy.[231]

Even the tissue-typing community—which in the past has championed ever-increasing antigen matching allocation rules—has recently begun to embrace a new type of matching that has as an explicit goal the mitigation of the disparate racial access caused by antigen matching. The new approach is to match not on the basis of antigens but on the basis of similar amino acid residues.[232] Evidence suggests that even if two antigens are not perfect matches, their molecular structure may be sufficiently similar that a transplantation (with appropriate drug therapy) can occur without in-

---

dle's Disease: Abnormal Regulation of Amiloride-Sensitive Na+ Channels by [β]-Subunit Mutation, 270 Am. J. Physiol. C208 (1996). See also Stephen G. Rostand et al., Renal Insufficiency in Treated Essential Hypertension, 320 New Eng. J. Med. 684 (1989) (documenting link between hypertension and renal failure in blacks). The hypothesis that slavery tended to select black Africans who could retain salt and water continues to be tested with a variety of different data. See Clarence E. Grim et al., High Blood Pressure in Blacks: Salt, Slavery, Survival, Stress, and Racism, in Hypertension: Pathophysiology, Diagnosis, and Management (J. H. Laragh & B.M. Brenner eds., 2d ed. 1995); P. D. Curtin, The Slavery Hypothesis for Hypertension among African Americans: The Historical Evidence, 82 Am. J. Public Health 1681 (1992). While far from conclusive, the salty gene hypothesis gives an extreme example of why race might be relevant for policymakers. If there is just a 10 percent chance that slavery caused elevated black ESRD, then it might be reasonable for the victims of slavery to be given a preference. Less dramatically, if elevated black ESRD is caused by other vestiges of our country's public and private racial discrimination, it might be cognizable as a policy concern.

230. See generally Stefanos A. Zenios et al., Allocation of Kidneys to Patients on the Transplant Waiting List: Assessing the Trade-Off Between Equity and Efficiency, 8 J. Am. Soc. Nephrol. 708A, 708A (1997) (program presentation abstract).

231. Id. See also Stafanos A. Zenios, Evidence-based Organ Allocation, 107 Am. J. Med. 52 (1999).

232. Takemoto, supra note 224.

ducing an immunologic reaction in the recipient. This new approach is called cross reactive epitope-group (CREG) classification, or amino residue matching.[233] Residue matching represents a ninefold decrease in the number of factors to match from almost ninety HLA-A and -B antigens to only ten residues.[234] Research has shown that blacks and whites have much greater overlap in the distribution of these ten residues than in the distribution of the underlying ninety antigens.[235] As a consequence, allocating kidneys on the basis of residue matching is less likely to disparately exclude blacks. And, indeed, simulations have shown that a new allocation scheme that adds points for two new categories of residue matching would increase black participation.[236]

This new-found sensitivity of the tissue-typers—heretofore the most ardent supporters of antigen matching—to the issue of racial access shows how salient this issue has become. And even the issue of which residues to count in a point system could become somewhat politicized in that the decision might turn on a mixture of expected medical benefit and expected impact on minority participation.[237]

C. The Revised UNOS Point System

In the wake of our original publication (and the mounting evidence that antigen matching causes an unjustified racial disparity), UNOS itself has been remarkably responsive. A report issued by the UNOS Histocompatibility Committee in 1995 concluded that "black recipients wait longer due to biologic factors" including sensitization, blood type, and "some HLA antigen types that are common in blacks but may not be common

233. Id. at 521.

234. Id. at 415.

235. Id.

236. Id. at 417. See also Steve Takemoto et al., Equitable Allocation of HLA-Compatible Kidneys for Local Pools and for Minorities, 331 New Eng. J. Med. 760 (Sept. 22, 1994). However, as with the present matching scheme, the reality is that excellent outcomes with cadaveric transplants only accrue to extremely well-matched pairs, regardless of the way one defines "matching." See Takemoto et al., supra note 25, at 834; Yoshinobu Hata et al., HLA Matching, in Clinical Transplants 1996 (J. Cecka & Paul Terasaki eds., 1997).

237. Including in a point system a residue that has a larger overlap in its appearance in whites and blacks is less likely to produce a disparate racial impact in transplant allocation.

in the donor population."[238] The report further notes that "even though blacks donate organs in proportion to the general population, the fact that most donors are Caucasian may disadvantage those black patients who have HLA antigens that are rare in the Caucasian population."[239]

Most important, UNOS in 1995 modified its point system. The new point system enacted two of our three proposals. It deemphasized the significance of partial antigen matching—eliminating the points for zero AB mismatches and three BDR mismatches;[240] and it doubled the points for time on the waiting list (from 0.5 points per year to 1.0 point per year). And while UNOS did not adopt our proposal for "rare antigen" points, it made two other changes that predictably enhanced minority participation. First, it expanded the mandatory share program to include not just phenotypically identical matches but also to include zero antigen mismatches. Since potential black recipients—with rare antigens—are much more likely to have antigens that cannot be identified with current typing assays, the move to mandatory matching of zero antigen mismatches benefits candidates with extremely rare antigens—who are disproportionately black. Second, the new point system defined time on the waiting list to begin at the time of dialysis (instead of when one first registered for transplantation). This change eliminated the disadvantage from delays in being placed on the list that blacks disproportionately encountered.[241]

The UNOS changes have resulted in an appreciable increase in the percentage of transplants that African Americans receive.[242] The expanded (zero mismatched) definition of who qualifies for mandatory sharing seems to have been particularly important.[243] More African American candidates

238. UNOS Histocompatibility Committee, The National Kidney Distribution System: Striving for Equitable Use of a Scarce Resource, *UNOS Update*, Aug. 1995, at 31, 32.

239. Id. at 32. Another study found that in a system in which quality of HLA match accounted for roughly 90 percent of allocation points, points were being assigned for partial match levels associated with graft survival equal to or worse than the national average. See Norman et al., *supra* note 225.

240. The modified system did, however, increase the number of points (from three to five) given for one BDR mismatch. But this is not so inconsistent with our proposal to give seven points for one ABDR mismatch.

241. Bertram L. Kasiske et al., Race and Socioeconomic Factors Influencing Early Placement on the Kidney Transplant Waiting List, 9 J. Am. Soc. Nephrol. 2142 (1998).

242. Andrea A. Zachary et al., Local Impact of 1995 Changes in the Renal Transplant Allocation System, 63 Transplantation 669 (1997).

243. Id.

now receive well-matched kidneys (from 1.9 percent in 1994 to 4.7 percent in 1995),[244] though white recipients continue to be the overwhelming beneficiaries of the points given for excellent matches.[245] Meanwhile, transplants of partially matched kidneys declined in both the black and white populations.[246] Although the vast majority of transplants for African American patients are still poorly matched, the success rates continue to improve.[247]

There is, however, more that might be done to mitigate the unpalatable impact of antigen matching, an issue that still seems to be salient for UNOS. For example, in 1998 UNOS announced a pilot study to examine the effect of a more sophisticated matching system on the availability of cadaveric kidneys for racial minorities.[248] And since 1996, UNOS Region 1 (comprising most of the northeastern states) has been allocating kidneys under a system that awards no points for partial antigen matching and awards increased points for time on waiting list (eight points for three years).[249] Predictably, "removing partial antigen points increased the proportion of kidneys going to African Americans and Hispanics from 17 to 22%."[250]

Conclusion

The severe and growing shortage of transplantable kidneys necessitates "tragic" allocative choices regarding the competing social objectives of graft survival, graft procurement, and equity. This chapter has presented a series of stylized conclusions related to the disparate racial impact of antigen matching. Because blacks and whites have different distributions of antigens and because blacks have almost four times the rate of kidney

244. See Hata et al., *supra* note 236, at 388.

245. Over 14 percent of white candidates receive well-matched kidneys. See id.

246. See id. at 391.

247. J. Michael Cecka, The UNOS Scientific Renal Transplant Registry, *in Clinical Transplants 1996, supra* note 236, at 1, 2.

248. UNOS Press Release, New Method of Matching Donated Kidneys May Mean More Transplants for Minorities (visited Mar. 11, 1998) <http://www.unos.org/Newsroom/archive_newsrelease_062597b.htm>.

249. Francis L. Delmonico et al., A New Allocation Plan for Renal Transplantation, 67 Transplantation 303 (1999).

250. Id. at 307.

failure, allocation schemes based on antigen matching make it more difficult for black patients to qualify for transplantation. Under the traditional UNOS point system, blacks received a disproportionately small percentage of cadaveric transplants and had to wait almost twice as long as whites for transplantation. In short, a white dialysis patient may have had a 50 percent higher chance of receiving a transplant in any given year. Some contended that this problem could be solved merely by increasing organ donations by blacks. While efforts in this regard are desirable, it is implausible to believe that black donation rates for both cadaveric and living related kidneys could be increased fivefold in order to eliminate the disparate impact of antigen matching rules. Antigen matching is a "but for" cause of blacks' unequal access to renal transplantation.

The disparate racial impact of the antigen matching rules was not justified by offsetting medical benefits. The benefits of partial antigen matching are small and declining. Although in the current cyclosporine era white recipients do have enhanced survival rates of up to 10 percent in the first year for six-antigen-matched kidneys, no persuasive evidence exists that partial antigen matching enhances transplant survival—especially for recipients who match fewer than four HLA antigens. Moreover, the use of new immunosuppressant therapies further reduces the impact of antigen matching on graft survival. The emphasis on partial antigen matching relative to time on the waiting list sacrifices equitable access to transplantation without any corresponding medical benefit.

These stylized conclusions suggested that the traditional federal system of allocating cadaveric kidneys had become capricious and outmoded. In 1993, we proposed allocation rules that would (1) eliminate points for patients with two or more mismatched antigens, (2) increase the points for time on the waiting list, and (3) award points for patients with rare antigens.[251] While the exact point values might be debated, our proposal gave preference to antigen matching that demonstrably increases graft survival while promoting *ex ante* equal opportunity for transplantation. The new UNOS point system, by awarding more points for time on the waiting list and by awarding fewer points for partial antigen matching, adopted two of our three proposals. And while our proposal for rare antigen points has not yet been adopted by UNOS, the movement toward residue matching in the scientific community may ultimately move the government toward a kind of rare antigen preference—albeit by a different means—by

251. See *supra* notes 174–80 and accompanying text.

allowing rare antigen recipients to match with nonrare antigen, but similar residue kidneys. All is not right in the world, but the developments of the last five years are heartening.

Appendix 6.A: Estimating the Disparate Impact of the O Rule

As described above,[252] the UNOS O rule mandates that blood type O kidneys may be transplanted only into blood type O recipients. This rule favors blood type O recipients over blood type A and B recipients. Because the blood type A population is disproportionately white and the blood type B population is disproportionately black, it is initially unclear whether the reallocation of cadaveric kidneys toward blood type O patients decreases the total number of kidneys going to black patients.

Using stylized facts about the different racial distribution of blood types[253] and the disparate racial rates of donation and kidney failure, it is possible to analyze a differential equation model to predict the likely effect of the O rule on the composition and size of the waiting list. Let R = a constant rate at which ESRD patients sign on to the waiting list. Combining the facts that 34 percent of the recipient group is black, 49 percent of blacks are blood type O, and 45 percent of whites are blood type O, we can derive the rates at which blood type O patients join the waiting list:

$$R[O] = \text{rate of new blood-type O recipients}$$
$$= [.45(1 - .34) + (.49)(.34)]R = .46R.$$

Similarly, we can derive:

$$R[A] = [.40(1 - .34) + (.27)(.34)]R = .36R$$
$$R[B] = [.11(1 - .34) + (.2)(.34)]R = .14R$$
$$R[AB] = .04R.$$

Let N = the constant rate at which kidneys are being donated. Because 8 percent of donors are black, the rates at which specific blood types are being donated can be calculated in an analogous fashion:

$$N[O] = .45 N; N[A] = .39N; N[B] = .12N; \text{ and}$$
$$N[AB] = .04N.$$

<hr/>

252. See *supra* note 70 and accompanying text.
253. See table 6.2.

Finally, let G = the rate at which the waiting list is growing [R = N + G], then a differential equation describing the rate at which the number of O type people on the waiting list changes is as follows:

$$dO / dt \; = \; R[O] - N[O] \; = \; .46\,R - .45N \; = \; (.01 + .46G)N,$$

which can be solved in terms of an initial position O[O]:

$$O(t) \; = \; O[O] + (.01 + .46G)Nt.$$

Analogous solutions for the other blood types yield.

$$A(t) \; = \; A[O] + (-.03 + .36G)Nt$$
$$B(t) \; = \; B[O] + (.02 + .14G)Nt$$
$$AB(t) \; = \; AB[O] + (.04G)Nt.$$

For the special case in which the donation rate matches the ESRD rate (G = 0), these solutions clearly reveal that blacks are disadvantaged by the O rule. Over time, more than 44 percent of the waiting list would be black even though only 34 percent of ESRD patients are black. This result is because two-thirds of the waiting list would be comprised of blood type B patients, who are disproportionately black. The disproportionately white blood type A recipients are disadvantaged by the rule, but the donor pool is predominantly white and therefore provides a rich source for blood type A kidneys.

The model predicts that the O rule also has a disparate effect against blacks when the waiting list is growing through time (G > 0), but that the disparate effect diminishes as the waiting list growth rate increases. For the past several years, the waiting list has grown at an annual rate of about 20 percent. In setting G = 1.2, the model predicts that under the O rule, 38 percent of the waiting list would be black even though only 34 percent of ESRD patients are black.

CHAPTER 7

A Market Test for Race Discrimination in Bail Setting

IAN AYRES AND JOEL WALDFOGEL

Judge Skelly Wright expressed the feeling of many in writing that the "professional bondsman system . . . is odious at best. The effect of such a system is that the professional bondsmen hold the keys to the jail in their pockets."[1] These words capture the disdain often shown to bail bond dealers,[2] who are widely thought to be corrupt and to assert too much control over pretrial release decisions.[3] Commentators offering

---

1. Pannell v. United States, 320 F.2d 698, 699 (D.C. Cir. 1963) (Wright, J., concurring).

2. We refer to the people who post bail bonds as "bond dealers" instead of the more prevalent "bondsmen," in part because we believe that language not only describes the world (in our data, all persons providing this service were male) but also establishes normative categories.

3. Ronald Goldfarb's characterization is typical:

> Many, too many, agents are undesirable persons, former felons, and generally repugnant characters. Some bondsmen are colorful Runyonesque characters. Some are legitimate businessmen. But too many are "low-lifes" whose very presence contaminates the judicial process. . . . [V]ery frequently, if not generally, the bail bondsman is an unappealing and useless member of society.

Ronald Goldfarb, *Ransom: A Critique of the American Bail System* 101–2 (1965); see also Arthur L. Beeley, *The Bail System in Chicago* 40 (1927) ("The moral standards of these bond-runners and their agents are very low."); The Cleveland Foundation, *Criminal Justice in Cleveland* (Roscoe Pound & Felix Frankfurter eds., 1922) (identifying the real evil in bail bonding as disreputable professional bond dealers who exploit the poor

bail reform proposals often advocate eliminating private bail bonding entirely.[4]

This chapter suggests, however, that the bail bond market may have an unforeseen usefulness. If competition induces bond dealers to charge fees equal to their average costs, the pricing behavior of bond dealers can be used to assess whether states discriminate on the basis of race or gender in setting bail. This chapter uses empirical evidence from the bail bond market in Connecticut to evaluate the determinants of bail setting.[5]

Chapter 6 applied a traditional disparate impact method to a nontraditional market: one type of data was used to show that antigen matching disparately disqualifies black transplantation applicants and another type was used to show that partial antigen matching is not medically justified. In contrast, this chapter uses a method for proving an unjustified disparate impact that is nontraditional in two senses. First, we use the rate that bond dealers charge defendants as evidence of the individual defendant's expected probability of flight (given the bail amount). And second, we use this flight probability proxy to test whether the judicial criteria for setting bail have an unjustified disparate impact on minorities. The latter aspect of our methodology is similar to other "outcome" tests of discrimination. As argued below, a major advantage of these outcome tests is that they

---

and prostitute the administration of justice); Daniel J. Freed & Patricia M. Wald, Bail in the United States: 1964, at 34 (National Conference on Bail and Criminal Justice Working Paper) ("Regular payoffs by bondsmen to police have sometimes been described as essential to survival in the bonding business."); John S. Goldkamp & Michael R. Gottfredson, *Policy Guidelines for Bail: An Experiment in Court Reform* 18 (1985) ("Bondsmen seemed to invite corruption of jailors, police, and judges."); Charles E. Ares, Anne Rankin & Herbert Sturz, The Manhattan Bail Project: An Interim Report on the Use of Pre-Trial Parole, 38 N.Y.U. L. Rev. 67, 67 (1963) ("The final decision as to whether a defendant is to be kept in jail usually rests in the hands of the professional bondsman. . . .").

4. The American Bar Association concludes, for example, that "reliance on money bail should be reduced to minimal proportions" and that "compensated sureties should be abolished." American Bar Association, Standards Relating to Pretrial Release 1.2(c), *quoted in* State of Connecticut, Pretrial Commission, Report of the Connecticut Pretrial Commission to the General Assembly 34 (1981).

5. Existing empirical research on bail setting typically either focuses directly on the determinants of bail setting or analyzes the impact of bail on flight and pretrial crime. For examples of bail analyses, see Goldkamp & Gottfredson, *supra* note 3; John S. Goldkamp, Questioning the Practice of Pretrial Detention: Some Empirical Evidence from Philadelphia, 74 J. Crim. L. & Criminology 1556 (1983); William M. Landes, Legality and Reality: Some Evidence on Criminal Procedure, 3 J. Legal Stud. 287 (1974); Ilene H. Nagel, The Legal/Extra-Legal Controversy: Judicial Decisions in Pretrial Release, 17 L. & Soc'y Rev. 481 (1983). See also Samuel L. Myers Jr., The Economics of Bail Jumping, 10 J. Legal Stud. 381 (1981) (providing an analysis of bail jumping).

are not as susceptible to the omitted-variable bias critique as traditional regression-based tests of disparate treatment. As researchers, we do not need to observe and control for all the variables that judges considered in setting bail as long as we can observe the outcome of their decisionmaking. Or in this context, we do not need to observe all the decisionmaking criteria as long as the bond dealers can set the bond rates in reaction to these observables plus the judicially imposed bail amount.

Connecticut law has traditionally mandated that bail be set at the smallest amount that will "reasonably assure the appearance of the arrested person in court."[6] Implicit in this statutory command is the notion that higher bail tends to reduce the probability that a defendant will flee. If the defendant posts bail herself, the potential forfeiture of the bail gives the defendant a direct financial incentive to appear at trial. If the defendant contracts with a bond dealer, however, the incentive to appear is indirect. A bond dealer charges the defendant a nonrefundable fee, and in return assumes the risk of paying the bail amount to the state should the defendant flee. Because the bond dealer's fee is nonrefundable and therefore is a "sunk cost," the size of the fee should not affect the likelihood of the defendant's appearance.[7] Nevertheless, a higher bail amount can reduce

6. Conn. Gen. Stat. Ann. § 54-64a (1985 & West Supp. 1993); cf. Freed & Wald, *supra* note 3, at 8 (generalizing that "bail in America has developed for a single lawful purpose: to release the accused with assurance that he will return at trial"). In Connecticut, bail traditionally could not be used to prevent suspects from committing pretrial crimes. If the prosecution believed "there existed a danger that the defendant would commit a serious crime, or would seek to intimidate witnesses, or would otherwise unlawfully interfere with the orderly administration of justice," it had to petition the court separately to additionally restrict pretrial release. Conn. Ct. R. 667 (1990). The Connecticut statute, however, was amended to allow courts to set bail amounts designed to reasonably ensure "that the safety of . . . other persons will not be endangered." Conn. Gen. Stat. Ann. § 54-64a(b) (West Supp. 1993) (effective 1990). See note 60 *infra* for a more detailed discussion of this amendment. In future research, we plan to investigate whether this revision has affected how courts set bail.

7. Commentators have reasoned that the nonrefundable nature of bond dealer fees counteracts any possible deterrent value of bail:

> [I]t was strongly argued [by critics of the bail system] that use of the bondsman defeated the rationale that defendants released on cash bail would have an incentive to return. Any deterrent value associated with the use of financial bail to protect against possible defendant flight was seen to be destroyed when defendants lost the fee paid to the bondsman whether or not they returned to court.

Goldkamp & Gottfredson, *supra* note 3, at 19; see also *Pannell*, 320 F.2d at 702 (Bazelon, C.J., concurring in part and dissenting in part) ("If [the bond dealer] does not [require collateral], then appellant has no real financial stake in complying with the conditions of the bond, regardless of the amount, since the fee paid for the bond is not refundable under any circumstances.").

the probability of flight because it credibly commits the bond dealer to expend more resources on (1) monitoring the defendant's whereabouts before a scheduled appearance and (2) searching to reapprehend any defendant who flees.[8] The foregone forfeiture is a bounty the bond dealer is paid for bringing back a fleeing defendant. Thus, if a defendant fails to appear, a bond dealer with $20,000 at risk would likely search more extensively than a bond dealer with only $2,000 at risk. Anticipating bond dealers' incentive to monitor and search more aggressively, defendants might perceive a lower likelihood of successful flight when the court sets a high bail amount.[9] Even when defendants use bond dealers to secure release, high bail amounts can thus reduce the probability of successful flight and even deter flight attempts. Connecticut courts can therefore "reasonably assure the appearance" of defendants by setting bail amounts high enough to reduce the defendants' flight probability to an acceptable level.[10]

Bail setting in Connecticut came under fire in 1991 amid allegations of racial bias. The *Hartford Courant* reported that bail amounts for black defendants were, on average, more than 70 percent higher than for white defendants.[11] Reports such as this are consistent with prior evidence of

8. Indeed, bond dealers can exercise "power over an accused [that] may exceed the power of the state." Note, Bailbondsmen and the Fugitive Accused—The Need for Formal Removal Procedures, 73 Yale L.J. 1098, 1100 (1964). For example, bond dealers "may seize the accused in a foreign jurisdiction without the slightest compliance with extradition requirements in the foreign jurisdiction." Id.; see also Freed & Wald, *supra* note 3, at 22 ("As a bailor, [a bond dealer] enjoys a private power to arrest his bailee. He can even surrender him to the court before trial if he suspects that flight is imminent.").

9. Commentators have been divided over whether, as an empirical matter, higher bail amounts deter flight when the defendant uses a bail bond dealer. Compare Landes, *supra* note 5, at 320–25 (finding deterrence effect) and Caleb Foote, Compelling Appearance in Court: Administration of Bail in Philadelphia, 102 U. Pa. L. Rev. 1031, 1066–67 (1954) (finding deterrence effect likely), with Stevens H. Clarke, Jean L. Freeman & Gary G. Koch, Bail Risk: A Multivariate Analysis, 5 J. Legal Stud. 341, 375 (1976) (finding that "cash bond releasees probably differed little from bondsmen releasees with regard to actual rates of nonappearance"). Using bail bonding data, this chapter independently concludes that higher bail amounts deter pretrial flight. See note 115 *infra* and accompanying text.

High bail amounts may also deter flight if bond dealers require defendants with higher bail to post more personal collateral. The prospect of forfeiting personal belongings would create the same flight deterrence as directly posting bail. We examine the effect of collateral at notes 126–29 *infra* and accompanying text.

10. Implicit in this statement is the assumption that those who set bail disregard the rates set by bond dealers. For arguments justifying this point, see notes 66–68 *infra* and accompanying text.

11. Brant Houston & Jack Ewing, Blacks and Hispanics Must Pay More to Get Out of Jail, *Hartford Courant*, June 16, 1991, at A1.

race discrimination in Connecticut[12] and in other states.[13] For example, Malcolm Feeley's classic analysis of the New Haven Court of Common Pleas found that black defendants were more often subject to monetary bail and were less likely to flee when released on bail than were white defendants.[14]

12. See, e.g., Noreen L. Channels & Sharon Hertzberger, The Effects of Offender Characteristics on Progress through the Criminal Justice System (May 1988) (unpublished manuscript, on file with authors) (concluding from 1983–84 Connecticut bail commission interviews that blacks and Hispanics were more likely to be required to post bail and more likely to receive higher bail amounts); Justice Education Center, Court Disposition Study: Criminal Offenders in Connecticut's Courts in 1991 (1993) (unpublished manuscript, on file with authors) (Latinos and African Americans are more likely than whites to receive bail); Catherine M. Sharkey, The Economics of the Bail System in New Haven: An Examination of Judicial Bail Setting and the Market for Bail Bonds 27–30 (Apr. 1992) (unpublished manuscript, on file with authors) (finding that, after controlling for measures of community ties and offense severity, race has a significant effect on bail amounts in Connecticut). But see Mwangi S. Kimenyi, Thomas J. Miceli & Subhash C. Ray, Race and Justice: An Economic Analysis of the Bail System (April 1993) (unpublished manuscript, on file with authors) (finding that racial discrimination in bail setting is due to imperfect information rather than prejudice).

13. Empirical evidence of race discrimination has been documented in New York state, see 2 New York State Judicial Commission on Minorities, Report 141–55 (1991); Florida, see Florida Supreme Court Racial and Ethnic Bias Study Commission, Where the Injured Fly for Justice (1991); and New Jersey, see New Jersey Supreme Court Task Force on Minorities, Interim Report (1989).

Anecdotal evidence of race discrimination has also been reported by academics. See Freed & Wald, *supra* note 3, at 33 (citing reported difficulties of Puerto Ricans and civil rights demonstrators as evidence that bond dealers may refuse to post bail for unpopular minority groups); Goldfarb, *supra* note 3, at 84–85 ("It is fairly common knowledge that bondsmen in various cities were subject to severe pressures against writing bonds for persons arrested during civil rights protests during the last decade."). But see James Eisenstein & Herbert Jacob, *Felony Justice: An Organizational Analysis of Criminal Courts* 199 (1977) ("In [Chicago, Detroit, and Baltimore], when bonds rather than personal recognizance were required, the offense charged was more important in determining the bail amount than the defendant's race, his police record, the kind of attorney (if any), or the courtroom workgroup that processed his case."); Nagel, *supra* note 5, at 506 ("The defendant's race has no effect on the decision to release on recognizance and small effects on the bail amount decision and on the decision to offer a cash alternative.").

14. Malcolm M. Feeley, *The Process Is the Punishment: Handling Cases in a Lower Criminal Court* (1979). In a multivariate regression, Feeley found that blacks were 15 percent more likely than whites to be required to post bail but were 6 percent less likely to flee. Id. at 207, 231. Even though the first result was statistically significant at the 95 percent confidence level, Feeley concluded that these results did not support a finding of significant discrimination:

[A]s suggested here, there is some evidence to support charges of racial discrimination. On the whole, however, no strong evidence demonstrates any significant or even measurable amount of racial discrimination in outcomes. The fast pace and standardized routines of the court probably minimize the importance of race. But offhand racial slurs by court personnel are occasion-

Nevertheless, providing unequivocal evidence of racial discrimination in bail setting has proven elusive to scholars and lawyers alike. The traditional way to statistically test for discrimination in bail setting is to estimate in a regression how factors that are both permissible (that is, related to a defendant's flight risk) and observable (that is, seen by the judge at the time of bail setting) affect the size of bail, and then to determine whether, after controlling for these factors, race is still a significant determinant[15] of the bail amount. Despite its popularity, this regression methodology is dogged by the problem of "omitted variable bias": race may be correlated with unobserved variables that are not controlled for in the regression but that legitimately increase bail size. If this is the case, the race effects estimated by regression analysis might not be caused by disparate racial treatment.

For example, our analysis of 1,118 New Haven arrests reveals that after controlling for eleven variables relating to the severity of the alleged offense, bail amounts set for black male defendants were 35 percent higher than those set for their white male counterparts.[16] By itself, this result does not constitute very powerful evidence of race discrimination because the regression does not control for many other variables that might explain the racial disparity. For example, black male defendants might be less likely to

---

ally overheard in courtroom and corridors; and it is these remarks, coupled with the disproportionately high numbers of Black defendants in an otherwise "white" courtroom, that give the impression of pervasive racial discrimination by the court. This belief is widespread among Blacks and many whites. Here court personnel are more guilty of fostering the appearance of discrimination than of fostering its actual practice.

Id. at 312 n.10. Feeley's analysis of race discrimination in New Haven in 1973 is particularly relevant to our study because our data comes from the same court.

15. For further discussion of the use of regression analysis to prove discrimination, see Thomas J. Campbell, Regression Analysis in Title VII Cases: Minimum Standards, Comparable Worth, and Other Issues Where Law and Statistics Meet, 36 Stan. L. Rev. 1299 (1984). Another traditional test of race discrimination is the "audit" methodology discussed extensively in part 1 of this book, whereby auditors who are identical except for race attempt to rent an apartment or purchase a car. See Ian Ayres, Fair Driving: Gender and Race Discrimination in Retail Car Negotiations, 104 Harv. L. Rev. 817 (1991); Ian Ayres & Peter Siegelman, Race and Gender Discrimination in Bargaining for a New Car, 84 Am. Econ. Rev. 304 (1995); James J. Heckman & Peter Siegelman, The Urban Institute Audit Studies: Their Methods and Findings, in *Clear and Convincing Evidence: Measurement of Discrimination in America* 187 (Michael Fix & Raymond Struyk eds., 1993); John Yinger, Measuring Racial Discrimination with Fair Housing Audits: Caught in the Act, 76 Am. Econ. Rev. 881 (1986). In regression methodology, the researcher attempts to control for differences among racial groups after the fact (that is, after the potentially discriminatory treatment has taken place), whereas in audit methodology, the researcher attempts to eliminate differences among racial groups before collecting data.

16. See notes 79–86 *infra* and accompanying text.

be employed or to have other community ties, which might justify a higher bail amount.[17] Judges might have set higher bail for black male defendants not because they were black, but because other characteristics we did not observe indicated that these defendants had a higher propensity to flee.

The omitted-variable problem has made it exceedingly difficult to use regression analysis to demonstrate racial discrimination.[18] For example, in *McCleskey v. Kemp*[19] the U.S. Supreme Court rejected a regression study that, after controlling for 230 variables, indicated that black defendants charged with killing whites were more likely to receive the death penalty than white defendants charged with killing blacks.[20] While assuming that the regression study was "valid statistically,"[21] the Court nonetheless concluded that "at most, the . . . study indicates a discrepancy that appears to correlate with race."[22]

In contrast to the traditional disparate treatment regression, this chapter presents a test for discrimination in bail setting based on the rates bond dealers charge after bail is set. Underlying our approach is the familiar economic concept of competitive pricing. In a competitive market, the bail

17. Alternatively, one might argue that the courts rationally infer from statistical information that black defendants were more likely to flee and thus required higher bail. Each of these two explanations for racial disparity (omitted variables and statistical discrimination) turns on what kinds of information may be observed and who is able to observe them. The omitted-variable explanation posits that courts and bond dealers observe variables that we did not account for. The statistical discrimination theory suggests that courts use race as a proxy for variables related to flight but unobservable to either the courts, the bond dealers, or to us.

These two explanations for the racial disparity have very different legal significance: if the racial disparity is caused by omitted variables then the bail setters are not discriminating on the basis of race. But statistical discrimination (even if based on valid statistical inferences) would constitute disparate racial treatment and would violate the Equal Protection Clause unless the state could show under the strict scrutiny test that the disparate treatment furthered a compelling state interest.

18. See Campbell, *supra* note 15, at 1305–12 (suggesting that "goodness-of-fit" measures can be used to evaluate whether relevant variables have been omitted); Michael O. Finkelstein, The Judicial Reception of Multiple Regression Studies in Race and Sex Discrimination Cases, 80 Colum. L. Rev. 737, 742–45 (1980) (discussing the exclusion of relevant job qualification variables).

19. 481 U.S. 279 (1987).

20. The study in question was David C. Baldus, Charles Pulaski & George Woodworth, Comparative Review of Death Sentences: An Empirical Study of the Georgia Experience, 74 J. Crim. L. & Criminology 661 (1983).

21. 481 U.S. at 291 n.7.

22. Id. at 312. The district court specifically criticized the study's treatment of unknown variables. McCleskey v. Zant, 580 F. Supp. 338, 357–59 (N.D. Ga. 1984).

bond rate (that is, the bond fee divided by the bail amount) should approximate the market's assessment of the defendant's probability of flight: the bond dealer's expected cost of writing a bond is simply the amount of the bond multiplied by the probability that the defendant will flee.[23] For instance, if there is a 10 percent chance that a defendant will fail to appear, bond dealers in a competitive market should charge a 10 percent bond rate.

Our core finding is that bond dealers in New Haven charged significantly lower rates to minority defendants than to whites. Among black male defendants, rates were almost 19 percent lower than those charged to white male defendants.[24] This race differential in the bond market, we argue, raises the specter of unjustified racial discrimination at the bail-setting stage. The lower minority rates indicate that bail reduced the probability of flight for minority males below the flight probability for white males. Our results showing significantly lower bond rates (alongside a traditional regression showing significantly higher bail amounts for black defendants in our sample) constitute powerful market evidence of unjustified racial discrimination in bail setting. The market evidence indicates that judges in setting bail demanded lower probabilities of flight from minority defendants. Judges could have reduced bail amounts for minority males without incurring flight risks higher than those deemed acceptable for white male defendants.

Moreover, our analysis avoids the problem of omitted-variable bias. Bond rates provide a market-disciplined assessment of a defendant's probability of flight, given her bail amount. As a result, bond rates obviate the need to observe and measure defendant characteristics that, in traditional discrimination studies, serve as indirect proxies for the defendant's flight probability.[25] Knowledge about bond prices substitutes for the traditional requirement that the researcher control for everything that might have affected courts' decisions. Specifically, evidence that bond dealers charge blacks lower rates makes it implausible to contend that the black defendants in our sample had a higher propensity to flee and therefore needed higher bail amounts to induce a sufficiently low probability of flight. Put

23. Possible exceptions to this proposition are addressed in notes 116–35 *infra* and accompanying text.

24. See note 103 *infra* and accompanying text.

25. Our market test assumes that bond dealers have the same information as the bail setter. We explore the possibility that bond dealers have access to additional information in our discussion of sample selection at notes 168–72 *infra* and accompanying text.

simply, evidence of lower market bond rates for blacks suggests that courts could set lower bail for black defendants without incurring abnormally high risks of flight.

We emphasize, however, that the racial disparity in bail amounts and bail bond rates is not evidence of disparate racial treatment. These disparities might be explained by a number of alternative, nondiscriminatory rationales.[26] But the presence of market information, at the very least, shifts the grounds of debate. In the face of this evidence, one cannot plausibly argue that our failure to control for certain variables induced the racial disparity, nor can one argue that this disparity serves the purpose of the law.[27]

Thus, while observers of the criminal justice system have traditionally regarded bond dealers with scorn, their pricing behavior, when disciplined by competition, is useful in evaluating government bail setting procedures. Moreover, our study suggests that bond dealers in competitive markets may provide an additional service of mitigating the effects of state discrimination. Although bail amounts for black male defendants are on average 35 percent higher than for white male defendants, the bond fees that black males pay are only 16.5 percent higher.[28] For all its faults, this pariah industry may be responsible for mitigating more than half of the effects of racially disparate bail setting.[29]

This chapter has four main sections. The first describes the bail bonding system in Connecticut and provides a theory for the actions of courts,

26.   In the third section of this chapter, we explore three types of nondiscriminatory explanations. See notes 116–72 *infra* and accompanying text.

27.   The lower bond rates are inconsistent with a statistical discrimination explanation because competition should force bond dealers to rely on the same racial inferences that any court might use. Even after making statistical inferences about race, however, bond dealers consistently offer lower rates to blacks. This indicates that judges demand a higher certainty of appearance from black defendants than from whites.

28.   See text accompanying note 107 *infra*.

29.   The results for Hispanic males are even more dramatic. While bail levels for Hispanic males are 19.4 percent higher than for white male defendants, their bond dealer fees are only 4.6 percent higher. See text accompanying note 107 *infra*.

As discussed below, perfect competition among bond dealers need not necessarily eliminate all effects of discrimination. See text accompanying notes 108–10 *infra*. For example, if raising bail amounts by 10 percent only reduced the probability of flight by 3 percent, then minority defendants would still expect to pay higher fees because competition would eliminate only 30 percent of any judicial discrimination. It is also possible that bond dealers themselves discriminate against minorities. This would suggest that but for bond dealers' discrimination even more of the judicial discrimination would be eliminated by bond dealer competition.

bond dealers, and defendants. The second section discusses the outcome test in more detail. To infer an unjustified disparate impact in bond setting from disparate bond rates, we needed to make three crucial assumptions:

1. *Proportionality Assumption:* Defendants' bond rates are proportional to their probability of flight.
2. *Equalization Assumption:* The only legitimate goal of bail setting is to equalize the probability of appearance for all defendants who are released.
3. *Representativeness Assumption:* Defendants who are released on bail bonds constitute a representative sample of those receiving bail as a condition of release.

The proportionality assumption ensures that lower minority bond rates actually indicate a lower risk of flight. The equalization assumption permits us to conclude that the disparate impact against minority male defendants is not justified by alternative permissible bail setting goals. And the representativeness assumption allows us to assume that the selected sample of defendants posting bail is representative of the larger population of defendants for whom bail is set. If these three crucial assumptions are valid, the market test of discrimination provides evidence that bail setting has an unjustified disparate impact on minority males.

We find evidence that:

1. The bail bond market in New Haven, Connecticut, is reasonably competitive.
2. Bail amounts for black and Hispanic male defendants are significantly higher than for white male defendants.
3. Bail bond rates for black and Hispanic male defendants are significantly lower than for their white counterparts.

The first result suggests that the proportionality assumption may be reasonable (because in competitive markets bail rates will tend to be proportional to defendants' risk of flight). The second result provides by way of comparison the traditional regression-based test of judicial disparate treatment. And the third result—of lower bail bond rates for minority defendants—is the core market-based evidence of an unjustified disparate treatment.

In the third section of this chapter we explore several ways that each of these three assumptions (regarding proportionality, equalization and sample selection) might fail and provide alternative, nondiscriminatory explanations for the disparate bond rate. The fourth section argues that, while market competition may help to mitigate unjustified judicial bias, complete reliance on remedial market correction places too much confidence in the resilience of competitive forces, given the evidence currently available. In the concluding section, we suggest some of the broader implications of our findings and methodology, along with possible applications to other market settings.

I. A Theory of Bond Dealers, Defendants, and Court Behavior

An empirical study is only as good as the structural theory underlying it. Thus, we first examine the institutional features of the Connecticut bail system, and then construct a theory of strategic interaction between the defendant, the court, and the bond dealer.

A. Institutional Features of Connecticut Bail Setting

In Connecticut, defendants have opportunities to gain pretrial release at several stages after arrest. When police arrest a defendant, they must either release her on a written promise to appear (PTA) or set a money bail amount. If they set monetary bail, the defendant may then arrange terms with a bail bond dealer. If a defendant does not arrange for immediate release, a bail commissioner reviews her bail and has discretion to change (usually lower) the bail amount set by the police. At this point, the defendant may once again attempt to arrange terms with a bail bond dealer. If the defendant is still unable to secure release, a judge reviews (and may lower) her bail.[30] Once again, the defendant can arrange terms with a bail bond dealer.[31]

30. Judicial review must normally occur within forty-eight hours of arrest. See County of Riverside v. McLaughlin, 500 U.S. 44 (1991) (holding that jurisdictions combining probable cause determinations with other pretrial proceedings must make these determinations within forty-eight hours of arrest).

31. This multistage process could be modeled as a series of three offers to sell pretrial freedom. Such a model is particularly apt because the state's offers almost inevitably decline at each subsequent stage, as is common in bilateral bargaining. In future work, we will attempt to derive the state's optimal concession curve given a variety of objectives. We hope to use our estimates of the actual concession curve of the state to assess what objective function best describes the state's bail setting practices.

This suggests another nondiscriminatory explanation for the higher bail amounts

In 1990, the year for which we analyzed New Haven bail data, 217,539 individuals were arrested in Connecticut (30 percent of whom were black).[32] Sixty-five percent of those arrested were released on PTAs or accepted the bail amount set by the police and were released before being interviewed by a bail commissioner.[33] Of those defendants appearing before bail commissioners prior to arraignment, 7.5 percent made bail using the services of a bond dealer, and another 33 percent secured release on either a nonsurety bond or a PTA.[34] Of those defendants still in detention at arraignment, 16 percent had their cases disposed, 37 percent made bail

---

set for black defendants: black suspects may more readily accept earlier (and higher) offers made by the police or the bond commissioner. Under this explanation, the state may offer similar concessions to all suspects—but black suspects may simply be more likely to accept the higher early offers. This selection effect would violate the statutory mandate that bail be set at the lowest level that reasonably ensures appearance. The state's concession strategy—which produces lower bail for those defendants who wait—could only be justified if impatient suspects (those more likely to accept the first offer) are also more likely to flee. However, if the acceptance of higher initial offers is what produces the higher bail figures for blacks, then we should not find that blacks receive lower bond rates, since bond dealers presumably would also be aware that these impatient defendants pose higher flight risks. In addition, a uniform concession strategy that adversely affects minorities might raise disparate impact concerns similar to those that frequently arise in employment cases.

32. Division of State Police, Connecticut Department of Public Safety, *Connecticut Uniform Crime Reporting Program—1990*, at 33 [hereinafter *Uniform Crime Reporting Program*] (reporting that 66,350 out of 217,539 arrestees were black). These state data do not distinguish between Hispanic and non-Hispanic whites.

33. Id.; Superior Court Bail Commission, State of Connecticut Judicial Department, *Annual Report*, at table A (1990) [hereinafter *Commission Report*] (reporting that 74,675 arrestees, or 35 percent of the total number of arrestees (217,539) were interviewed by a bail commissioner during 1990). Although this chapter focuses solely on discrimination in setting bail, discrimination could also affect the probability of being released on a promise to appear (PTA). For example, while 75.1 percent of white (including Hispanic) defendants were released before a bail commissioner interview, only 44.7 percent of black defendants were released at this early stage. See *Uniform Crime Reporting Program*, supra note 32, at 33 (reporting a total of 150,519 white and 66,350 black arrestees during 1990); *Commission Report*, supra, at table B (26,827 white arrestees, or 24.9 percent of total, were interviewed by bail commissioner, while 30,655 black arrestees, or 55.3 percent of total, received such interviews). Our interviews with the bail commission suggest that many of these early releases were costless PTAs.

34. *Commission Report*, supra note 33, at table A (16,441 of the 49,561 persons interviewed by bail commissioners were released on PTAs or nonsurety bonds; 3,715 used bond dealers). With a nonsurety bond, a defendant need not post any assets as a condition of release, but incurs a monetary penalty if he or she fails to appear. A PTA release is similar but imposes no monetary penalty at all. In either case, however, a defendant who chooses to flee may incur new criminal liability for the independent crime of failing to appear.

using a bond dealer, and 40 percent secured release on either a nonsurety bond or a PTA.[35]

During that same year in New Haven alone, police arrested 8,540 individuals (55 percent black, 32.4 percent Hispanic, and 12.6 percent white).[36] While our data for New Haven do not identify when defendants were released, they do identify the conditions of release. Of those arrested, 83.5 percent secured release on a PTA, and 0.6 percent secured release on a nearly equivalent nonsurety bond;[37] 1.8 percent posted bail themselves, 10.9 percent posted bail using the services of bond dealers, and 3.2 percent remained in jail.[38]

The bonds studied below were written by "professional" bond dealers.[39] In essence, these bond dealers sell the state "flight insurance." If they agree to write a bond for a defendant—or to "take him out," in industry parlance—they promise to pay the state the bail amount in the event the defendant fails to appear in court.[40] Bond dealers incur no up-front capital

35. Id.

36. State of Connecticut, Judicial Branch, *Criminal/Motor Vehicle Statute File* (1991) (computer tape, on file with author) [hereinafter *Connecticut Justice Department Tape*].

37. Id. Surprisingly, the state apparently does not prefer using nonsurety bonds even though the state can garner higher forfeitures from such bonds. Officials suggested that, for many defendants who were judgment proof, nonsurety and PTA releases were often monetarily equivalent.

This 1990 data resembles Malcolm Feeley's 1973 analysis of the same New Haven court. He found that 52 percent of defendants were released on a PTA, 37 percent were released on bail, and 11 percent were detained until trial. Feeley, *supra* note 14, at 202. However, the trend has been for defendants to post their own bail less frequently and for the percentage of PTA releases to increase.

38. *Connecticut Justice Department Tape, supra* note 36.

39. There are two types of bond dealers in Connecticut. Professional bond dealers are licensed and regulated by the Commissioner of State Police. Insurance bond dealers are licensed as insurance agents by the state Insurance Commissioner and write bond contracts for insurance companies specializing in this type of surety bond. Paul Rice, Bail and the Administration of Bail in the State of Connecticut, 4 Conn. L. Rev. 1, 26 (1971). The state permits insurance bond dealers to charge somewhat higher rates than professional bond dealers. Id. at 26–28.

40. Bond dealers forfeit approximately 50 percent of a bond's face value when a defendant fails to appear. See note 125 *infra* and accompanying text. The 50 percent forfeiture rate effectively increases the maximum rate that bond dealers may legally charge. Even though bond dealers, by statute, cannot charge more than a 10 percent fee on a $5,000 bail, see note 42 *infra*, the 50 percent forfeiture rate allows bond dealers to charge a $500 fee when they only have $2,500 at risk.

Because the 50 percent forfeiture rate does not apply to defendants who personally post bail, this forfeiture rate is a great inducement to use professional bond dealers. A defendant with a $5,000 bail may either risk that entire $5,000 or pay a bond dealer to

costs on bonds. They do not post any money in advance, and while the total amount of bonds a given bond dealer may have at risk must not exceed a bond dealer's total capital, this capital can remain invested in interest-bearing assets.[41]

Bond dealers may refuse to write bonds for particular defendants. Should they choose to accept a defendant's business, however, the fees they charge are subject to regulation. For bail amounts up to $5,000, a professional bond dealer may charge fees of no more than 10 percent of the bail amount. For bail amounts in excess of $5,000, a bond dealer may charge up to 10 percent for the first $5,000 and up to 7 percent of the portion that exceeds $5,000.[42]

In the next two subsections we present a theory of how bond dealers and state officials interact to determine a defendant's pretrial release status. We first analyze how, given the bail amount for a particular defendant, a bond dealer sets fees in a competitive market. We then examine how a court (or other bail setter) goes about choosing the minimum bail amount that will "reasonably assure" the defendant's appearance.

B. Determinants of Bond Dealers' Fees in a Competitive Market

Competition among bond dealers in New Haven is critical to our analysis. Competitive theory suggests that the individual rates charged by bond dealers[43] should reflect the flight risk of the defendant. Our evidence shows that the rates charged by bond dealers are inversely related to the number of dealers competing in a city. In cities with little competition, bond dealers simply charge the maximum statutory rate. In cities like New Haven, where there are several bond dealers, the bail bonding rate is well below

---

risk a mere $2,500. At text accompanying notes 124–25 *infra*, we explore the impact of the 50 percent forfeiture rate on our discrimination tests. Given the 50 percent forfeiture rate and the uncorrelated nature of bond risks, it is puzzling that the value of professional bond dealers' total outstanding bonds may not exceed their capital. A 100 percent reserve ratio is much higher than the rate required for commercial banks.

41.   See Conn. Gen. Stat. Ann. §§ 29-145 to -146 (West Supp. 1993).

42.   Id., § 29-151 mandates that no professional bond dealer

shall charge for his commission or fee more than fifty dollars for [any amount of bail] up to five hundred dollars, nor more than ten percent of the amount of bail . . . from five hundred dollars to five thousand dollars, nor more than seven percent of the amount of bail . . . in excess of five thousand dollars.

43.   Recall that the bond rate is the ratio of the bond dealer's fee to the bail amount. See text accompanying note 23 *supra*.

the statutory maximum, suggesting that competition depresses rates to reflect bond dealers' true costs.[44]

Our market test of discrimination assumes that competition in New Haven drives the bail bonding fees to equal the bond dealers' expected costs, and that the bond rates will consequently be proportional to flight risks for each defendant. Absent competition, bond dealers may charge what they believe the market will bear—discriminating based on the defendant's willingness to pay. Competition may eliminate price discrimination because a competitor has an incentive to undercut any discriminatory price charged by competitors that is above expected cost.[45]

In appendix 7.A, we derive a technical model of competitive fee setting.[46] We present a simplified version here to illuminate the intuition that, in a competitive market, bond dealers' rates are likely to be proportional to the probability that a defendant will flee. Our model uses the following notation:

B = bail amount set by the state
f = forfeiture rate (fraction of B forfeited if the defendant fails to appear)[47]
p = probability of flight[48]
R = total nonrefundable fee paid to the bond dealer
r = R/B (bond rate the defendant pays to the bond dealer)
C = value of the defendant's available collateral[49]

---

44. See text accompanying notes 75–76 *infra*.

45. For elaboration of this argument in the employment context, see Gary S. Becker, *The Economics of Discrimination* (1957).

46. See text accompanying notes 189–91 *infra*.

47. The forfeiture rate in New Haven during this period was approximately 50 percent. See note 125 *infra* and accompanying text.

48. The bond dealer's payoff turns on whether a suspect flees and avoids recapture for six months. One can interpret p as the probability of flight minus the probability of recapture. In the more complicated model presented in appendix 7.A, we explicitly include the costs of search and probability of recapture to reflect the fact that bond dealers are more likely to try to recapture suspects as the bail amount increases. See text accompanying notes 189–91 *infra*.

49. Collateral serves two distinct purposes: (1) it deters flight, and (2) it compensates bond dealers if suspects flee. The value of the collateral to the suspect determines its value as a flight deterrent, while its value to the bond dealers usually determines its usefulness as compensation. Bond dealers might accept collateral with little market value if it has significant personal value to the suspect—and hence would deter the suspect from flight. See Oliver E. Williamson, Credible Commitments: Using Hostages to Support Exchange, 73 Am. Econ. Rev. 519 (1983).

The bond dealer's expected profit on any individual bail bond equals the fee paid, less the money forfeited when a defendant fails to appear discounted by the probability of such an occurrence,[50] plus any proceeds the dealer derives from sale of bond collateral.[51] The expression for profit (π) is thus:

$$\pi = R - p(fB - C).$$

Under the traditional assumption that competition drives profits toward zero, we can derive the market rate for a bail bond (r) by setting the above profit expression equal to zero and solving for r. This calculation yields:[52]

$$r = p(f - C/B).$$

The collateral term (C/B) in the expression above poses a problem for our theory because it indicates that defendants with higher bail amounts (B) could face higher rates (r) even though they do not pose greater flight risks.[53] If we make the plausible assumption that the value of the collateral

50. Note that interest costs are zero because bond dealers do not actually post bond; rather, they promise to pay should their customer fail to appear. In the interim, bond dealers continue to earn interest on their invested capital. See text accompanying notes 40–41 *supra*.

51. A more complete bond dealer model might:

1. Include the bond dealer's fixed administrative costs of doing business. Below, we estimate the size of fixed costs and their impact on our results. See notes 130–35 *infra* and accompanying text.
2. Allow for differences between the market value and the defendant's personal valuation of collateral. If personal and market values differ, p would be a negative function of the defendant's personal valuation, while C would equal the market value of the collateral. We discuss the empirical importance of collateral below. See notes 126–29 *infra* and accompanying text.
3. Include the costs of *ex ante* monitoring and *ex post* search. We include these costs in the model derived in the appendix 7.A. See text accompanying notes 189–91 *infra*.

52. Setting the profit expression equal to zero yields:

$R - pfB + pC = 0$.

Dividing this equation by B (and remembering that $r = R/B$) yields:

$r - pf + pC/B = 0$.

Solving for r yields the expression in the text.

53. For example, consider two defendants who post $200 in collateral. Assume that the first defendant has a higher flight propensity and therefore needs a higher bail amount to deter flight. By setting bail at $2,000 for the first defendant and at $1,000 for the second defendant, the judge can ensure that each has only a 10 percent chance of flight. Finally, assuming a forfeiture ratio of 50 percent, the first defendant will be charged a bond rate of:

required by bond dealers is proportional to the bond amount ($C = \alpha B$), it is possible to preserve the proportionality of bond rates and flight risk.[54] Substituting this value for C in the rate equation, yields:

$$r = p(f - \alpha).$$

Because the term $(f - \alpha)$ is a constant and does not depend on the bail amount, the bond rate remains proportional to the probability of flight.[55]

To reiterate, our market test of discrimination relies on the assumption that the bond rate is proportional to the probability of flight regardless of the size of bail. A more direct test of whether judicially imposed bail over-deters minority defendants would be to examine the actual probability of flight for different racial groups. Despite our best efforts, however, we were unable to obtain this data from the State of Connecticut. In the absence of this direct "outcome" evidence, the bond rates actually charged by market participants with their own money at risk might provide a powerful proxy for the expected probability of flight.

Even if strict proportionality does not hold,[56] the intuition remains that

---

$$r = p(f - C/B) = 0.1\ (0.5 - 0.1) = .04$$

while the second defendant will be charged a bond rate of:

$$r = 0.1\ (0.5 - 0.2) = 0.03.$$

Although the judge has succeeded in equalizing the flight probabilities of the two defendants, the first defendant is forced to pay a higher rate. This is because, compared to his bail amount, his collateral is relatively smaller.

Later, we present empirical evidence that collateral does not affect the pricing of bail bonds. See text accompanying notes 126–29 *infra*. For our proportionality assumption to hold, however, we need not assume that dealers' proceeds from disposing of collateral are zero.

54. The possibility that collateral does not bear a constant relationship to the bail amount—so that it differs across demographic groups—does not necessarily invalidate our test for race discrimination. Because African Americans are, on average, poorer than whites, one might conjecture that black defendants would post less collateral. This would suggest that bond rates for blacks should be higher, on average, than for whites. This would make our finding that bond dealers charge blacks lower rates even stronger evidence of discrimination.

55. If the defendant does not offer the bond dealer any collateral, this expression simplifies even further:

$$r = pf.$$

In this case, the bond rate is simply a market estimate of the defendant's probability of flight multiplied by the forfeiture rate.

56. For reasons why strict proportionality may not hold, see notes 117–25, 189–91 *infra* and accompanying text.

Figure 7.1   Flight schedule relating flight probability to bail amount

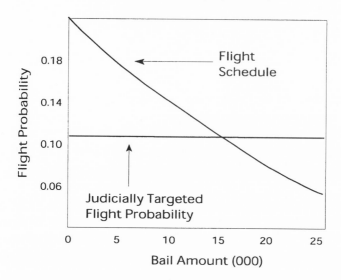

defendants with higher probabilities of flight will be charged higher bond rates to compensate the dealer for the greater risk. As we pointed out earlier,[57] higher bail amounts might deter flight even in the presence of bond dealers because defendants know that higher bail encourages enhanced monitoring and search efforts by bond dealers. Figure 7.1 illustrates the notion that probability of flight decreases if the bail is set higher for any particular defendant.[58]

The downward sloping curve in figure 7.1 represents a hypothetical defendant's flight schedule (the relationship between bail amount and probability of flight). It also is proportional to the bond dealer's rate schedule for a hypothetical class of defendants who differ only by their bail amount. Because competition causes the bond dealer's rate to be proportional to the defendant's flight probability, dealers serving defendants who differ only by the amount of bail will tend to charge lower rates to those with higher bail.

57. See text accompanying notes 6–10 *supra*.

58. William Landes's pathbreaking study of bail setting found this inverse relationship. See Landes, *supra* note 5, at 322. Other scholars have argued, however, that higher bail does not reduce the probability of flight. See Clarke et al., *supra* note 9, at 376.

C.   Determinants of Bail Amount

Given the flight schedule hypothesized above, the next step is to analyze how bail is set. Our analysis of the bail setting process relies on a second assumption, mentioned earlier—the equalization assumption— which states that the only legitimate purpose of bail is to reduce the probability of flight to a uniformly low level for all defendants. Such a rationale excludes other purposes, even if nondiscriminatory (punishment, incapacitation, retribution, and so on). While we discuss these possible alternate rationales in a subsequent section,[59] Connecticut law supports the assumption that flight risk equalization is the sole permissible use of bail.

Until October 1, 1990, Connecticut General Statute 54-64a required courts setting bail to choose the minimum bail amount that would "reasonably assure the appearance of the arrested person in court."[60] A reasonable interpretation of the statute is that courts should set bail for each defendant so as to reduce his or her flight probability to some acceptably low uniform level. For example, the statutory mandate could mean that judges should set bail high enough to ensure that there is no more than a 10 percent chance that any defendant will flee. Figure 7.1 depicts this goal as a horizontal line intercepting the "flight probability" axis at $p = 0.10$. To set bail in accordance with the statute's mandate, a judge would thus select a bail amount represented by the intersection of the flight schedule with the horizontal line representing the targeted flight probability. In figure 7.1 this intersection occurs at approximately $15,000.

---

59.   See notes 135–62 *infra* and accompanying text.

60.   Conn. Gen. Stat. Ann. § 54-64a(a)(1) (West 1985). The statute and accompanying court rules explicitly detail the factors that courts may consider in setting bail.

On October 1, 1990, amendments to § 54-64a took effect which mandated that courts set bail for certain felonies "sufficient to reasonably assure . . . that the safety of any other person will not be endangered." Conn. Gen. Stat. Ann. § 54-64a(b)(1) (West Supp. 1993). Bail set after this date may reflect this additional criterion. Limiting our data to the period before October 1, 1990, however, did not affect our results. Our discussions with Connecticut bail commissioners indicate that judges rarely used this "safety of any other person" criterion. This may be because the amended statute arguably permits use of this criterion only when judges determine that the released defendant may commit another crime "based upon the expressed intention of the" defendant. Id., § 54-64a(b)(2)(L). Moreover, even if judges had begun inflating bail amounts based on the "safety" criterion, the purpose would have been to set bail high enough to force defendants to remain incarcerated pending trial, so it is not surprising that any such defendants would not have appeared in our data set (which only includes defendants released on bail bonds). For a judicial gloss on these amendments, see State v. Ayala, 222 Conn. 331, 342–54, 610 A.2d 1162, 1169–74 (1992).

Figure 7.2   Flight schedules depicting different flight propensities

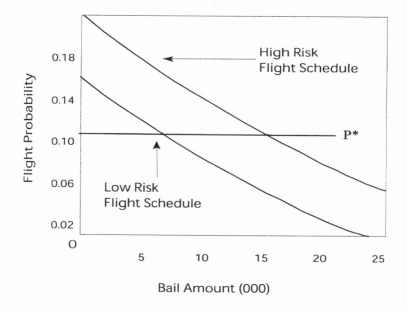

Bail Amount (000)

Different defendants will often have different flight propensities, however. For instance, defendants facing serious charges or those who have weak community ties might be less likely to appear.[61] Judges may therefore need to vary the amount of bail to produce a uniform probability of appearance for defendants with unequal propensities to flee.[62] To see this, suppose that (as depicted in figure 7.2) two defendants have differing flight propensities for every bail amount. To induce a uniform 90 percent probability of appearance, the court must set bail for the high-risk defendant at $15,000 and for the low-risk defendant at only $6,000.

Thus, the empirical observation that courts set widely varying bail amounts for different defendants is consistent with the judicial goal of equalizing flight probability. As William Landes notes, "one might observe

61.   See Myers, *supra* note 5 (analyzing factors that may influence a defendant's propensity to flee).

62.   By varying the bail amount, the judge can influence the effort that the bond dealer will expend on (1) monitoring a defendant's whereabouts before a scheduled appearance and (2) searching for a defendant who has failed to appear. See text accompanying note 8 *supra*.

identical probabilities of disappearance across defendants with different size bonds."[63]

Before proceeding with the empirical analysis, we must take note of three caveats to our equalization assumption. First, while we interpret the Connecticut statute to require a uniform probability of appearance for all defendants, we recognize that bail setters may in fact consider a variety of other nondiscriminatory criteria (both consistent and inconsistent with the statute). We directly address a number of these alternative criteria and their impact on tests of discrimination in a later section.[64]

The second caveat is that we have interpreted the statute to mandate equalizing the probability of appearance conditioned upon the defendant's release from jail. This is an important qualification because conditional and unconditional probabilities of appearance may diverge significantly. Our interpretation requires the judge to ask, "If this defendant makes bail, what bail amount would produce a 90 percent likelihood that she will appear in court?" An alternative interpretation (which we reject) focuses on unconditional probabilities of appearance and requires judges to ask, "What bail amount will ensure a 90 percent appearance rate by deterring flight (if the defendant makes bail) or by precluding flight (if the defendant remains in jail)?" The language of the statute supports the conditional interpretation in that it emphasizes "conditions of release" necessary to ensure appearance.[65] By implication, the statute does not contemplate incarceration as a method of ensuring appearance. Moreover, an unconditional probability criterion can lead to anomalous results. For instance, even if a judge following an unconditional probability criterion is certain that a particular defendant will skip bail, the judge would be compelled to set bail sufficiently low to allow a 10 percent chance that the defendant will be able to make bail.

The third caveat concerns the interplay between judges and bond dealers. Under our equalization assumption, when judges set bail to equalize the probability of flight, they should ignore how dealers set their fees. One might expect judges to predict the size of bond dealers' fees, and adjust bail to compensate for the workings of the bail bond market. Such behavior would, however, violate their statutory mandate to do no more than

63. See Landes, *supra* note 5, at 321 n.46.

64. See notes 135–62 *infra* and accompanying text.

65. See Conn. Gen. Stat. Ann. § 54-64a(a)(1) (West Supp. 1993).

induce a reasonable assurance of appearance.[66] Because the bond dealer's fee is a nonrefundable "sunk cost" to the defendant,[67] it should not influence the defendant's probability of flight, and thus is not a factor judges should consider.[68]

Subject to these qualifications, our analysis of bond rates allows us to test whether minority defendants in our sample deserved the higher bail amounts we observe because these defendants had a higher propensity to flee. If courts set bail levels solely to equalize flight probabilities, then the rates charged by bond dealers should be equal for all defendants. If bail was set too high for black defendants, then the average risk of flight would be lower for blacks than for whites, and thus our data would show that black defendants pay bond dealers lower rates.

II. Testing the Theory

A. A Description of the Bail Bonding Data

Our study is based on data concerning defendants who were arrested and processed in the Court of Common Pleas in New Haven, Connecticut, during 1990, and who secured release using the services of bond dealers. We derived the data from Connecticut State Police records on professional bond dealers, and Connecticut Justice Department court records.[69] We

66. See id. For a discussion of other factors that might cause a judge to consider the size of bond dealer's fee, see notes 157–62 *infra* and accompanying text.

67. A sunk cost is one which a person has previously incurred; because it cannot be recovered or changed, its magnitude should not affect future behavior. See Richard A. Posner, *Economic Analysis of Law* 7 (4th ed. 1992).

68. A judge attempting to equalize flight probabilities across defendants would consider how bail size affects dealers' efforts to monitor and search (since these efforts do affect the probability of flight), but monitoring and search effects depend only on bail size and not on how bond dealers have previously decided to price their services.

An analogous "sunk cost" argument applies to the behavior of bond dealers: because the bond fee is a "sunk revenue," it should not affect a rational bond dealer's propensity to monitor or search for the defendant. Only the prospective threat of forfeiting the bail amount would influence the bond dealer's incentives. Thus, while a judge attempting to equalize flight probabilities across defendants would consider how bail size affects dealers' incentives to monitor and search (since these efforts affect the probability of flight), the judge need not consider any effect of fee levels on monitoring and search incentives.

69. *Connecticut Justice Department Tape, supra* note 36. Connecticut requires professional bond dealers to submit monthly and annual reports to the state

linked bond data (using defendant names and arrest dates) with the more detailed court data. Each court record included the defendant's race and gender, as well as offense and judge identifiers.[70] Table 7.1 summarizes the data for the 1,366 felony defendants whose records we were able to match in this manner.

The average bail amount in the sample is $3,466, and the average bond fee is $177. The average age of the defendants is twenty-seven years. Seventeen percent of the defendants are female, two-thirds are black, and 12 percent are Hispanic. The most common offenses are drug offenses (24 percent), assault (20 percent), disorderly conduct (13 percent), and larceny (10 percent).

B.   Evidence of Market Competition

The model we designed to examine the relationship between bond rates and flight probabilities hinges on the existence of competitive pressures in the bail bond market. Thus, before we can assume that bond rates reflect the expected costs of flight, we must first establish that bond dealers in New Haven behave competitively. By comparing market concentration and bond dealer rates in nine Connecticut towns, we find that towns with multiple bond dealers, such as New Haven, have average rates far below the statutory maximum. This suggests that competition is indeed driving down rates to reflect expected costs.

The market for bail bonds in New Haven shares some, but not all, of the features of a competitive market. On the one hand, the New Haven market has unrestricted entry. More than twenty bond dealers wrote at least one bond on defendants arrested in New Haven in 1990. The Herfindahl index of market concentration in New Haven—a traditional measure of market competition—was 1,674. This level of concentration is analogous to the concentration of a market with six equally sized competitors.[71] On the other hand, the market may not be perfectly competitive because

---

police. These records include defendant names and arrest dates, as well as the defendants' bail amounts and fees paid to the bond dealers.

In addition, we collected reports directly from professional bond dealers operating in New Haven and several other Connecticut towns. We used these reports solely to compare the average rates paid in different towns.

70.   The offenses were classified as A, B, C, D, and U misdemeanors and felonies. Judges were identified by numeric codes.

71.   For a discussion and application of the Herfindahl index, see Ian Ayres, A Private Revolution: Markovits and Markets, 64 Chi.-Kent L. Rev. 861, 865–68 (1988).

Table 7.1 Sample Characteristics (N = 1,366)

	Mean	Std. Dev.
Bail amount (B)	3466.23	6651.3
Fee paid	177.37	237.02
Age	27.10	8.60

	Percent of Sample
White male (WM)	0.187
White female (WF)	0.045
Black male (BM)	0.533
Black female (BF)	0.115
Hispanic male (HM)	0.106
Hispanic female (HM)	0.014
Kidnapping	0.004
Prostitution	0.007
Rape	0.001
Assault (ASLT)	0.197
Gun Offense	0.071
Disorderly conduct (DISOR)	0.129
Fraud	0.019
Failure to appear (FTA)	0.074
Forgery	0.009
Larceny (LARC)	0.100
Arson	0.002
Burglary	0.021
Drug	0.236
Robbery (ROB)	0.008
Class A or B felony (CLASABF)	0.038
Class C or D felony (CLASCDF)	0.144
Class U felony (CLASUF)	0.323
Class A or B misdemeanor (CLASABM)	0.411
Class C or C misdemeanor (CLASCDM)	0.063

Table 7.2   Market Structure and Bond Dealers' Rates

Town	Number of Active Bond Dealers[a]	Avg. Rate Paid[b]	Percent of Max. Rate Paid	Poverty Rate[c]	Per Capita Income[d]
New Haven	8	4.1	64	23.2	9,378
Bridgeport	10	7.3	78	20.4	9,427
Norwalk	3	4.8	54	7.0	15,907
Meriden	2	9.1	98	7.4	11,952
Ansonia	2	7.9	99.6		
Wallingford	1	9.4	99		
Stamford	1	9.0	99	7.7	18,246
New London	2	10.0	98	16.9	10,629
Plainville	1	8.3	99		

Source: Adapted from Sharkey, supra note 12, appendix I.
[a] Derived from Yellow Pages listings.
[b] Ratio of the amount paid to the bond dealers to the bail amount set by the state, in percent.
[c] Percent of persons below the poverty line, from Bureau of the Census (1988), at 628.
[d] Per capita income in 1985, from Bureau of the Census (1988), at 628.

some defendants may be poorly informed about competitive pricing among bond dealers or face significant costs in searching for competitive bids.[72]

Table 7.2 compares bond market data from nine Connecticut towns. For each town, the table lists the number of active bond dealers,[73] the average bond rate paid, and bond fees as a percentage of the statutory maximum.[74] Where data are available, the table also lists the percent-

72.   Defendants' limited access to information about bond dealers is dramatized by the inaccurate, but widely repeated, adage that prisoners are limited to "one phone call." In fact, jails normally allow multiple calls, and a defendant's lawyer, relatives, and friends often help arrange bond services. Several other factors, however, may still impede competitive pricing. As a practical matter, multiple bond dealers may not be available at all hours of the night. Moreover, even markets with many sellers may not be perfectly competitive, as shown for example in chapter 2's analysis of new car sales in the Chicago area, finding that a large degree of price discrimination can persist even in a market with a large number of sellers. See Severin Borenstein, Price Discrimination in Free-Entry Markets, 16 Rand J. Econ. 380 (1985) (examining brand preference as a possible explanation for the persistence of price discrimination in consumer markets with many sellers).

73.   The number of active bond dealers was derived from local telephone book listings.

74.   Because bond rate ceilings vary according to the size of the bond, the average maximum statutory rate for a particular town depends on the distribution of bail bond amounts in that town.

age of persons below the poverty line in 1979, and per capita income in 1985.

Three towns—New Haven, Bridgeport, and Norwalk—have three or more active bond dealers. Bond rates in New Haven, with eight active bond dealers, average 64 percent of the statutory maximum. Bond rates in Bridgeport and Norwalk are similarly low, averaging 78 and 54 percent of the maximum, respectively. The remaining six towns, by contrast, have only one or two active bond dealers, and their rates average 98 percent or more of the allowable rate. The higher rates in these towns comport with traditional antitrust and industrial organization theories, which predict that prices should drop with the number of viable competitors.[75] At a minimum, table 7.2 suggests that the New Haven bail bond market is more competitive than the monopoly and duopoly markets in nearby cities.[76]

An alternative explanation for the lower rates observed in New Haven and certain other cities might be that defendants in these cities are poorer, and that bond dealers price discriminate, charging what individual defendants can afford. However, a closer look at the data summarized in table 7.2 casts doubt on this hypothesis: while rates vary systematically with the number of bond dealers, rates are apparently not correlated with average incomes. Norwalk, for example, has high per capita income and a relatively low poverty rate, suggesting that defendants there might have a greater ability to pay for bond services. Yet bond rates in Norwalk, which has three active bond dealers, average only 54 percent of the maximum. In New London, by contrast, where per capita income is low, the two dealers charge an average of 98 percent of the statutory maximum. We conclude that the number of bond dealers per town, rather than the defendants' ability to pay, better explains the rate variation across towns.[77]

75. See, e.g., Jean Tirole, *The Theory of Industrial Organization* 220–21, 226–28 (1988) (providing a mathematical demonstration of this effect and citing further literature). The bond rates in table 7.2 do not decline monotonically as the number of bond dealers increases: three bond dealers in Norwalk charged only 54 percent of the statutory maximum, while the eight bond dealers in New Haven charged 64 percent of the maximum. It is possible that Norwalk's relative affluence is correlated with attributes of bail setting that might explain this result.

76. The data in table 7.2 may also reflect higher average costs per bond for dealers in small geographic markets with high fixed costs.

77. Anecdotal evidence from interviews we conducted with bond dealers in New Haven and Meridian, Connecticut, indicate that New Haven dealers undercut each other's rates more frequently than do dealers in other Connecticut towns, further supporting this conclusion. See also Freed & Wald, *supra* note 3, at 24. ("Within the legal maximums . . . bondsmen frequently bargain for special rates, particularly in high volume, low risk offenses like gambling. Disputes between bondsmen over price cutting are not

This evidence leads us to conclude that the New Haven bond market is relatively competitive, and that the lower rates charged in New Haven are not the result of price discrimination based on defendants' ability to pay. In a subsequent section of this chapter, we consider whether bond dealers price discriminate on the basis of other factors, such as the defendant's information or search costs and whether the keener competition in New Haven is sufficient to drive bond prices all the way down to dealers' expected cost.[78]

C.   A Market Test for Discrimination in Bail Setting

We derive our market test for discrimination in bail setting from a regression of the bond rate against offense and defendant characteristics, including the defendant's race and gender. The test simply asks whether minority defendants are charged bail rates that are significantly lower than those charged whites. If minorities and whites pay bond dealers the same rates, then interrace differences in bail amounts may be justified by unobserved factors correlated with both race and flight risk. On the other hand, if minorities face higher bail amounts but pay lower rates than whites, then the higher bail amounts for minority defendants may reflect racial disparity in bail setting.

This disparate rate test relies on three distinct assumptions, two of which we have discussed above. First, we assume that bond rates are proportional to expected flight probabilities.[79] Second, we assume that bail setters impose bail amounts designed to equalize flight risks across defen-

---

uncommon."); Forrest Dill, Discretion, Exchange and Social Control: Bail Bondsmen in Criminal Courts, 9 Law & Soc'y Rev. 639, 647 (1975) ("Like many small businessmen, the bondsman operates in an environment offering neither steady demand for his services nor reliable means for guarding against incursions by competitors. In other business settings such conditions foster highly competitive modes of behavior.").

If price discrimination based upon defendants' ability to pay were profitable, we would expect the greatest degree of price discrimination (and thus the greatest rate variance) to arise in towns with only one or two bond dealers, since bond dealers who face little or no competition are most likely to have sufficient market power to price discriminate. But the bond rates in towns with only one or two dealers are almost always at the statutory maximum. The example of New London is particularly striking: despite the substantial poverty rate in the town, the dealer duopoly apparently engages in virtually no price discrimination.

78.   See text accompanying notes 117–21 *infra*.

79.   If our proportionality assumption fails, then we cannot infer that the judges failed to equalize the probability of appearance from our evidence of disparate rates. For a full discussion of this assumption, see notes 46–57 *supra* and accompanying text.

dants, and that flight probabilities decrease as bail increases.[80] The final assumption, which we address more explicitly later,[81] is that our data do not suffer from "sample selection" effects. In other words, we assume that the defendants who use bond dealers to post bail constitute a representative sample of all defendants. Given these three assumptions, rates should not vary systematically across different classes defendants. If, however, average bond rates for minorities are lower than average rates for whites, we can infer that bail set for minorities exceeds the level necessary to equalize the probability of flight across defendants.

Examining how a competitive bail bond market responds to the judicial selection of bail is an example of an "outcome" test of discrimination. Gary Becker has proposed analogous tests of discrimination in mortgage lending.[82] Becker suggested that if banks discriminate against minorities we should expect that minorities would have lower default rates. Similarly, this chapter suggests that if minorities have a lower default rate on their bail bonds (that is, a lower probability of flight), we can infer a type of discrimination by judges in setting bail.

The outcome approach that Becker suggested with regard to mortgage defaults has been justly criticized for ignoring the difference between marginal and inframarginal default rates. Under Becker's theory, if lenders dislike lending to minorities, then the least qualified minority to which they would be willing to lend (the marginal minority borrower) should have a lower expected default rate than the least qualified nonminority to which they are willing to lend (the marginal nonminority borrower):

> Unfortunately, marginal default rates are unobservable and the average default rates often subjected to examination are inappropriate proxies. The equality of average default rates for minorities and whites, there-

---

80. See notes 59–68 *supra* and accompanying text. If the bail amount did not affect the probability of flight, then judges could not use bail to equalize the probability of flight. Judges would set zero bail for those defendants who were reasonably likely to appear, and arbitrarily large bail for those who were not. Our empirical observation that judges set intermediate bails (that are consistently higher for minorities) would thus indicate a failure to follow the Connecticut bail statute's mandate to choose the minimum bail amount that is effective in deterring flight.

81. See text accompanying notes 163–72 *infra*.

82. Becker first proposed this approach in a *Business Week* op-ed, Gary S. Becker, The Evidence against Banks Doesn't Prove Bias, *Business Week*, 1993 WL 2142407 (April 19, 1993), and detailed his suggestion in his Nobel Prize lecture. Gary S. Becker, Nobel Lecture: The Economic Way of Looking at Behavior, 101 J. Pol. Econ. 385, 389 (1993).

fore is irrelevant to the discussion of disparate treatment in the application process.[83]

Lenders might still discriminate against minority lenders—in the straightforward sense that the lending cutoff for minorities might be more stringent than for nonminorities—and we might still see that the average rate of minority default (conditional on being above the minority lending cutoff) is higher than the average rate of nonminority default (conditional on being above the nonminority lending cutoff). As long as inframarginal nonminority borrowers have lower expected default rates (than inframarginal minority borrowers), a comparison of average defaults may mask disparate treatment by lenders in setting the minimum thresholds for granting loans.

This inframarginal criticism does not, however, apply to the outcome test at issue in this chapter. Unlike lending, the bail bond context has a nondichotomous, noncensoring decision variable and under the null hypothesis the decisionmaker's goal is to equalize the probability of flight across all defendants. In the mortgage context, better than average loan applicants will be granted loans and have reduced (inframarginal) probabilities of default. In contrast, better than average bail applicants (that is, defendants) can have lower bail amounts set so as to induce any probability of flight. Judges can vary the bail amount to induce the same maximum probability of flight (minimum probability of appearance) for all defendants. The judges' ability to individually vary the bail amount in a sense *makes every defendant marginal*—and thus avoids the inframarginal problem that has plagued the application of outcome tests to the mortgage context.[84]

Chapter 9 discusses "outcome" tests more generally, but for now we stress that unlike Becker we believe outcome tests are not direct tests of disparate treatment but can provide powerful evidence of an unjustified disparate impact (which constitutes a cognizable claim of "discrimination"

83.   James H. Carr & Isaac F. Megbolugbe, The Federal Reserve Bank of Boston Study on Mortgage Lending Revisited, 4 J. Housing Res. 277, 309 (1993). See also George C. Galster, The Facts of Lending Discrimination Cannot Be Argued Away by Examining Default Rates, 4 Housing Pol'y Debate 141 (1993).

84.   As discussed in chapter 9, we (writing separately with different coauthors) have an analogous nondichotomous decision (the order in which editors decide to publish articles) to help identify whether the marginal publication decisions of editors produced unjustified disparate impacts. See Scott Smart & Joel Waldfogel, A Citation-Based Test for Discrimination at Economic and Finance Journals (NBER Working Paper 5460 1996); Ian Ayres & Fredrick E. Vars, Determinants of Citations to Articles in Elite Law Review, 27 J. Legal Stud. 427 (2000).

in many civil rights contexts). A finding of racially different bond rates (or, for that matter, a finding of different flight probabilities) is not sufficient to infer disparate treatment.[85] Such an outcome test is both over- and underinclusive. It is underinclusive, because it would not capture "statistical" disparate treatment. For example, if judges were correctly inferring among groups of observationally equivalent defendants that minority defendants had a higher flight propensity and set higher bail amounts for these minorities, then in equilibrium we might not see differences in the rates charged by bond dealers (or differences in the probability of flight). Even though the judges are engaging in a type of disparate racial treatment—a type of racial profiling, if you will—the outcome test might show no racially disparate outcome.

If underinclusion were the only problem, an outcome test might still provide a valuable "one-tailed" test of the existence of disparate treatment. But the outcome test is also overinclusive as a test of disparate treatment. As discussed below,[86] judges' unwillingness to engage in disparate treatment itself might induce disparate racial outcomes. For example, if observationally equivalent minority defendants have a lower propensity to flee than similarly situated nonminority defendants, then judges unwilling to discriminate between these groups in setting bail will necessarily produce lower rates of flight for the minorities.

In contrast, it is our claim that if our three assumptions (of proportionality, equalization, and representativeness) hold, an outcome test based on a comparison of bail bond rates charged different racial and gender groups provides a powerful test of whether judges' bail setting criteria impose an unjustified disparate impact on minority defendants. Under the null hypothesis, that judges are setting bail so as to equalize the probability of flight (induce a minimum expected probability of appearance), no observable defendant characteristic should in equilibrium be systematically related to higher or lower probabilities of flight.

The outcome regressions described below are unique in not being embarrassed by omitted-variable bias, because under the null hypothesis there should be no observable variables that affect the probability of flight (or the charged bond rates) once judges have made individualized bail assess-

85. Such evidence, however, may be introduced as part of the evidence in a disparate treatment case. Evidence of disparate racial outcomes, absent evidence to the contrary, can be probative of disparate treatment and, for example, might be sufficient to shift the burden in a disparate treatment case to the defendant.

86. See *infra* text accompanying note 143.

ment so as to equalize this very probability. Indeed, perversely the outcome test intentionally harnesses omitted variable bias to test whether any excluded (unjustified) determinant of decisionmaking is sufficiently correlated with the included racial characteristics to produce evidence of a statistically significant racial disparity.[87] Any finding that the bail given to a set of defendants with a particular characteristic (such as minority status) induces a systematically lower probability of flight suggests that judges were failing at inducing a uniform minimum probability of appearance.

At a minimum, a finding that minority defendants are charged lower rates (or have a lower probability of flight) suggests that some of the judges' bail setting criteria must be correlated with defendants' race without being correlated with defendants' propensity to flee. It still might be the case that the judges' bail setting criteria are valid with respect to the full population of defendants, but a finding that bail induces racially disparate probabilities of flight (as evidenced by racially disparate bond rates) at a minimum suggests that the bail setting criteria are not valid with regard to the individual subgroups. For example, imagine that white defendants with common law spouses have an elevated propensity to flee, while the presence or absence of a common law spouse is not correlated with the propensity of minority defendants to flee. If the white proportion of defendants with common law spouses is sufficiently high, a judge's decision to use this characteristic as the basis for setting higher bail might be valid with regard to the populations of defendants as a whole but would not be valid with respect to the minority subgroup. In this example, minority defendants with common law spouses receiving enhanced bail would be overdeterred from flight (relative to their white counterparts) and thus would likely show up in our analysis receiving systematically lower bail rates. As discussed below,[88] while it is controversial whether the disparate impact law does (or should) require subgroup validation, in the penal context a finding that bail setting is not valid with regard to minorities is strongly indicative that it is not valid overall. Minority defendants made up over three-quarters

---

87. Stephen Ross and John Yinger have noted that the default approach attempts to identify mortgage discrimination by purposely omitting variables from the regression. Stephen L. Ross & John Yinger, The Default Approach to Studying Mortgage Discrimination: A Rebuttal, in *Mortgage Lending Discrimination: A Review of Existing Evidence* 107,112 (Margery Austin Turner & Felicity Skidmore eds., 1999). But they emphasize that because not-accepted loan applicants are marginal—in the sense just discussed in the text—omitting variables from the analysis may continue to bias the racial regression coefficients. Id. at 113.

88. See *infra* at note 143; chapter 9.

of our sample (76.8 percent). It is difficult to believe that criteria that are not valid with regard to the overwhelming majority of observations would nonetheless be valid with regard to the entire population.

The outcome approach thus combines in a single test both elements of a disparate impact inquiry: a showing that decisionmaking disproportionately disfavors minorities together with a showing that the decision's disparate impact is not justified by some countervailing furtherance of the decisionmaker's legitimate objectives. Normally, these elements are proven with very different types of data, but racially disparate bond rates by themselves suggest that judges could have charged minority defendants less without unduly sacrificing the legitimate goal of ensuring court appearance.

While we base our market test for discrimination on bond rates alone, we jointly estimate both a bond rate equation and a bail equation for purposes of comparison and efficient estimation. We thus estimate the following equations using the "seemingly unrelated regressions" (or SUR) technique:[89]

$$\ln B_i = \alpha_b + X_i\beta_b + \epsilon_{ib} \tag{7.1}$$

$$\ln r_i = \alpha_r + X_i\beta_r + \epsilon_{ir} \tag{7.2}$$

The regression equations above state that for each defendant i, the natural logs of both the bail amount (B_i) and the bond rate (r_i) are equal to a constant (α_b and α_r, respectively), plus a linear combination of defendant and offense characteristics ($X_i\beta_b$ and $X_i\beta_r$, respectively) and an error or "noise" term (ϵ_{ib} and ϵ_{ir}, respectively).[90]

---

89. While a thorough review of econometric theory is beyond the scope of this chapter, a few concepts may be of use to the reader. The SUR technique is a way to estimate two different regression equations that, though seemingly unrelated to one another, are in fact related through their error terms. By estimating the equations jointly rather than separately, one can improve the precision of the estimates of the regression coefficients. For large data sets, the consequence of increased precision is a lower variance of the estimator. Thus, it is possible that coefficients that appear statistically insignificant under standard techniques will test significant under the SUR technique. Indeed, the SUR technique is always more precise than the standard ordinary least squares (OLS) technique for large data sets. Hence, the SUR estimator is often referred to as an asymptotically efficient estimator. See, e.g., William E. Griffiths, R. Carter Hill & George G. Judge, *Learning and Practicing Econometrics* 456–57, 550–55 (1993).

90. Note that for each defendant i, X_{ib}, and X_{ir} are vectors of coefficients. This is a shorthand way of expressing rather lengthy linear functions.

The variables in the vector X_i fall into three categories: defendant characteristics, offense severity, and offense category. Defendant characteristics include five race and gender dummy variables (for black women, black men, white women, Hispanic women, and Hispanic men), while white men form the benchmark (omitted) category.[91] We divide offense severity into six categories and designate a dummy variable for each of the first five: class A and B felonies, class C and D felonies, class U felonies, class A and B misdemeanors, and class C and D misdemeanors. Class U misdemeanors are the omitted category. Finally, we include dummy variables representing six offense categories: assault, failure to appear (FTA), larceny, drug-related offenses, gun offenses, and disorderly conduct. The omitted offense category includes the other offenses listed in table 7.1.[92]

The left-hand columns of table 7.3 report the bail regression results produced by equation (7.1). This regression constitutes the traditional test for discrimination. It suggests that race strongly influences bail levels. Specifically, average bail amounts for black and Hispanic men are 35 and 19 percent higher, respectively, than those for white men, and these differentials are statistically significant.[93] White and Hispanic women appear to face lower bail amounts on average than do white men, and black women

91. A "dummy variable" resembles an on-off switch; it assumes a value of one if the defendant falls into a designated category, and zero if the defendant falls outside that category. By assigning dummy variables to all but one category, we can compare differences between any two categories. Thus, for a group of n mutually exclusive and exhaustive categories, we assign a dummy variable to $(n - 1)$ of these categories, and the regression provides us with the estimated coefficients for each variable. The estimated dummy coefficient represents the amount by which membership in the associated category increases or decreases the dependent variable (that is, the bail or bond rate) as compared to the nondummy (or "omitted") category.

92. The data set includes 1,118 observations that satisfy the following criteria. First, we include only those observations with judge identifiers. This allows us to use judge identifiers as instruments in later instrumental variables estimations. This restriction excludes about 5 percent of the sample. Second, we include only observations with positive rates paid to bond dealers. We include only these observations for two reasons: to avoid the results on rates paid being driven by nonpayment alone, and because it is more convenient to conduct the analysis in terms of logarithms. Neither our sample selection decisions nor the choice of logarithms affects the results reported below.

93. The differential between black and white defendants' bond rates is statistically significant from zero at the 99 percent significance level. The same is true of the differential between Hispanic and white rates at the 90 percent level. The race–gender coefficients approximate the percentage effect of belonging to a given race–gender category. Interpreting regression coefficients as percentage effects is standard in studies of this kind. See, e.g., Jacob Mincer, On-the-Job Training: Costs, Returns, and Some Implications, 70 J. Pol. Econ. 50 (Supp. Oct. 1962).

Table 7.3 Determinants of Bail and Rates Paid to Bond Dealers

| | SUR Estimation | | | | | |
| | Log Bail Amount | | Log Rate Paid | | Effect on Log Fee Paid | |
	Coeff.	t-stat.	Coeff.	t-stat.	Est.	t-stat.
Constant	6.673**	29.85	−2.615**	−27.04		
Defendant Characteristics						
BM	0.352**	4.67	−0.188**	−5.76	0.165**	2.58
HM	0.194*	1.79	−0.148**	−3.16	0.046	0.50
WF	−0.057	−0.38	0.030	0.47	−0.026	−0.21
BF	0.075	0.71	−0.114**	−2.48	−0.039	−0.43
HF	−0.234	−0.96	−0.068	−0.65	−0.302	−1.47
Offense Severity						
CLASABF	1.587**	6.23	−0.186*	−1.69	1.401**	6.50
CLASCDF	0.926**	4.13	−0.039	−0.41	0.886**	4.66
CLASUF	0.683**	3.43	−0.069	−0.80	0.615**	3.64
CLASABM	−0.207	−0.97	0.162*	1.75	−0.045	−0.25
CLASCDM	−0.300	−1.28	0.146	1.44	−0.154	−0.78
Offense Category						
ASLT	0.062	0.67	0.045	1.14	0.107	1.38
FTA	−0.118	−0.93	0.058	1.07	−0.059	−0.55
LARC	−0.043	−0.37	0.083	1.64	0.040	0.41
DRUG	0.519**	4.03	−0.035	−0.62	0.485**	4.44
GUN	0.339**	2.20	0.073	1.09	0.412**	3.16
DISOR	−0.367**	−3.50	0.115**	2.54	−0.252**	−2.84
R^2	0.387		0.141			
N	1,118		1,118			

* Significant at the 90 percent level.
** Significant at the 95 percent level.
Note: Effect on log fee paid is the sum of effects on log bail and log rate paid.

appear to face bail amounts that are 7.5 percent higher than those faced by white men, but these differences are not statistically significant.

We find that crime severity has a large effect on bail. Bail amounts increase steadily with the severity of the offense, with Class A or B felony defendants (CLASABF) facing average bail amounts 158 percent higher than those faced by Class U misdemeanor defendants.[94] Finally, we find that certain offense categories have a significant effect on bail size. In particular, bail for drug-related offenses averages 52 percent higher than bail for the benchmark category of offenses.[95]

By itself, this regression does not provide a very powerful test of race discrimination. Bail setters likely consider a number of factors that do not appear in our data set. In fact, the amended Connecticut bail statute explicitly allows courts to consider up to eight distinct factors when determining the bail level necessary to reasonably ensure court appearance.[96] The offense category variable included in the bail regression crudely controls for only one of these eight factors.

Without more, we cannot dismiss the possibility that the higher bail amounts for minority defendants reflect the courts' response to legitimate omitted factors. Courts may, for instance, set higher bail for unemployed defendants. If minority defendants are disproportionately unemployed, our inability to control for employment status will bias the race coefficient.[97] Thus, while the bail regression indicates that bail setting has a disparate

---

94. For additional evidence that crime severity and defendants' prior records predict harm and thus affect bail amounts, see Landes, *supra* note 5, at 298–99.

95. The negative coefficient for the failure to appear offense indicates that the average bail amount set for defendants charged with failing to appear is lower than that set in the omitted-offense categories. While this result is somewhat surprising because the prior failure to appear might itself be evidence of a higher propensity to flee, the result is not statistically significant. Moreover, some arrests in this category may only indicate a negligent failure to appear on a particular court date, rather than a genuine propensity to flee.

96. These factors include (1) the nature and circumstances of the offense insofar as these are relevant to the risk of nonappearance; (2) the weight of the evidence against the defendant; (3) the defendant's record of previous convictions; (4) the defendant's past record of appearance in court after being released on bail; (5) the defendant's family ties; (6) the defendant's employment record; (7) the defendant's financial resources, character, and mental condition; and (8) the defendant's community ties. See Conn. Gen. Stat. Ann. § 54-64a(a)(2), (b)(2) (West Supp. 1993).

97. William Landes found that in New York, a defendant's employment and earnings have a significant impact on bail, although they are not related to the probability of appearance or the tendency to commit pretrial crimes. Landes, *supra* note 5, at 326 n.54.

impact on minority males in our sample, the possibility of omitted-variable bias prevents us from ruling out that this disparate impact is justified by observable factors affecting defendants' propensity to flee.[98]

Using bail bond data potentially eliminates the need to control for the numerous other variables that might have influenced courts. Bond rate data make it possible to test for race discrimination in bail setting by running a simple regression of the bond rate (r) on the race dummy variables. A regression yielding statistically significant negative coefficients for the minority variables would constitute powerful evidence of discrimination in bail setting. This is true even if the regression excludes all other variables that might influence the riskiness of flight, and even if the regression "fits" the data poorly (that is, produces a low R^2 ratio). Unlike a traditional bail regression, omitted-variable bias does not undermine the probative value of the rate regression for civil rights purposes.

The lower minority rates are still probative of the two elements necessary to establish a disparate impact claim. First, the coefficients indicate that judges set bail based on criteria that have a disparate impact on minority defendants. Second, these criteria are unjustified relative to the stated goal of limiting flight risk.[99] The ability of this disparate rate test to overcome the problem of omitted-variable bias makes it, at least in this respect, much more powerful than the traditional test of discrimination.[100] So long as our assumptions about proportionality, equalization, and representativeness hold, this disparate rate test establishes evidence of unjustified racial disparate impact even in the presence of omitted-variable bias.

At a minimum, then, the bond rate test indicates whether judges use criteria that have disparate racial impact without the offsetting justification

98. The 0.387 R^2 coefficient itself suggests omitted-variable bias, since it indicates that more than 60 percent of the variance in the amount of bail across defendants is not explained by variables included in the regression. This R^2 does represent, however, the best goodness-of-fit found to date in a bail regression. For example, William Landes's regression model of bail setting explained only 23–27 percent of variation in bail amounts. Id. at 297.

99. In the employment context, Title VII mandates that employers justify employment practices that have disparate impact by showing that they are "consistent with business necessity." 42 U.S.C. § 2000e-2(k) (1988 & Supp. IV 1992).

100. The most extreme example of omitted-variable bias would be to estimate the regression using only the race variables to explain the bond rate. This regression would be equivalent to estimating whether the means for different defendant race–gender types are statistically different. (They are.) While omitted-variable bias would undermine any confidence that race caused the disparate rate, the finding that the average rate paid by minorities was significantly lower than the average white rate would be probative of some unjustified disparate impact.

of equalizing flight risks.[101] If the omitted variables do not bias the race coefficients, then the bond rate regression is probative of actual disparate racial treatment, not just of unjustified disparate impact. We reemphasize that these conclusions hinge on our earlier assumptions of proportionality, equalization, and representativeness. In a later section, we explore several other nondiscriminatory explanations for the results that may pertain if these assumptions do not hold.[102]

The center columns of table 7.3 contain the coefficient and t-statistic estimates for the rate regression, which provide our prime evidence of racial discrimination. Most notably, after controlling for offense type and severity, black men, Hispanic men, and black women paid rates that are 18.8, 14.8, and 11.4 percent lower, respectively, than the rates paid by white men.[103] Moreover, these differences are statistically significant. Because bond dealers are consistently willing to charge blacks and Hispanic men lower rates for putting their bonds at risk, we can reject the possibility that black and Hispanic men pose higher flight risks justifying higher bail.

The coefficients for black female defendants also illustrate the limitations of the traditional bail regression test. Our bail regression indicates that bail set for black women is not significantly different from that set for white males. The traditional test therefore provides scant evidence of racial bias against black women. The bond rate regression, on the other hand, shows that bond dealers charged black women significantly lower rates (11.4 percent lower) than they charged white men. The statistical significance of the lower rate charged black women suggests that judges should have set lower bail for black female defendants in order to equalize flight risks.[104]

101. Unjustified racial impact is caused anytime a court raises bail based on factors that are not correlated with propensity of flight, but that are correlated with a defendant's race. For example, a judge might mistakenly estimate the impact of prior arrests on the defendant's flight probability and select a bail level that is higher than that necessary to obtain a "reasonable assurance of appearance." If these factors are disproportionately associated with minority defendants, then the minority coefficients in the bond rate regression could be negative and statistically significant.

102. See notes 116–72 *infra* and accompanying text.

103. For instance, the bond rates for defendants charged with the misdemeanors falling within the omitted-offense category were as follows: white males 7.32 percent; black males 6.06 percent; Hispanic males 6.31 percent; white females 7.54 percent; black females 6.53 percent; and Hispanic females 6.84 percent.

104. In fact, while bail amounts for black women were slightly higher than those for white men, these amounts were considerably higher than those for other women. The bond dealer data reveal no systematic discrimination against white and Hispanic

Table 7.3 indicates another striking phenomenon. The results show that variables with a positive effect on bail tend to have a negative effect on rates paid to bond dealers. For example, as the severity of the offense increases, the bail amount increases, but the rate paid by the defendant decreases. Defendants charged with drug-related offenses (the offense with the highest average bail amount) pay bond dealers the lowest rates. This suggests that variance in bail is too high along dimensions other than race.[105]

D. The Price of Pretrial Freedom

While bail is the symbolic price of pretrial freedom, the actual price that most defendants must pay for pretrial release is the bond dealer's fee. This section uses data on bond dealers' fees to estimate the extent to which competition in the bail bonding market mitigates racial discrimination in bail setting.

The far right-hand column of table 7.3 reports the effects of defendant characteristics on dealers' fees. The actual fee paid to the bond dealer is a product of the rate charged and the bail amount.[106] Because dealers charge minority defendants lower rates when a judge has set excessive bail, the bail bond market can soften the impact of disparate bail setting on the price of pretrial freedom. Although bail levels for black and Hispanic men are 35.2 and 19.4 percent higher than for white men, the bond fees are only 16.5 and 4.6 percent higher, respectively.[107] These statistics suggest that the bail bond market eliminates over half of the effect of the bail disparity for black men, and virtually all of the effect for Hispanic men.

Bond market competition cannot totally eliminate the impact of race discrimination, however, unless a 1 percent increase in bail results in a 1 percent decrease in the bond rate. Stated more generally, competition will

---

women, as the rates charged to these two groups are not significantly different from the rates charged to white males.

105.   One possibility is that courts wish to ensure higher probabilities of appearance for more severe offenses. See notes 139–43 *infra* and accompanying text.

106.   Because the regression equations (1) and (2) are estimated in natural logs, the percentage impact of a variable on the fee is the sum of the impact on log rate and the impact on log bail. For instance, the black male bond estimate (0.165) is sum of the black male bail effect (0.352 from left-hand column) and the rate effect (−0.188 from the center column).

107.   In fact, only black men pay a fee premium over white men that is statistically significant.

fully mitigate the effect of discrimination only if the function relating bond rates to bail amounts displays what economists call "unitary elasticity."[108] Because we find that bond rates are actually fairly inelastic,[109] however, we conclude that the bond market can only partially alleviate the impact of discriminatory bail setting.[110]

E. Estimating the Extent of Discrimination in Bail Setting

The disparate rate test indicates the presence, but not the extent, of race discrimination in bail setting. In order to estimate the extent of discrimination—the amount by which actual minority bail exceeds the bail necessary to achieve the maximum flight probability apparently targeted for white males—we must determine the relationship between bail amounts and flight probabilities for white and minority defendants. In essence, we need to determine the position of the defendants' flight schedules. Flight schedules are not directly observable, but we can estimate the position of the rate schedule, that is, the relationship between rates paid to bond dealers and bail amounts. If we continue to assume that the bond rates are proportional to the probability of flight, then knowing the relative position of the rate schedules for different race and gender types allows us to infer the relative positions of the corresponding flight schedules. In short, by estimating rate schedules we can test whether the minority defendants in our sample had higher propensities to flee and thus deserved somewhat higher bail amounts. We refer to this comparison of rate schedules as the "rate schedule

---

108.   See note 197 *infra* for a discussion of the elasticity concept.

109.   See table 7.8 *infra* (estimating a bond rate elasticity of −0.527).

110.   In theory, it is easy to present pathological examples of flight probabilities that are extremely elastic with respect to the amount of bail. The degree of elasticity depends on the effectiveness of bond dealers' efforts to monitor and search, because these efforts determine the deterrence effect of additional bail. Suppose that a bond dealer has two methods of searching for a defendant who failed to appear. The first method costs $500 and has a 10 percent chance of recapturing the defendant. The second method costs $10,000 but has a 100 percent chance of recapture. If bail is set at $9,000, the bond dealer would be unwilling to use the second method, and, consequently, the bond dealer would charge a fee that reflects some possibility that the defendant will flee. However, if bail is set at $11,000, the bond dealer will use the expensive search technology, and because of the 100 percent recapture rate, defendants will be strongly deterred from fleeing. If defendants are rational and respond to these probabilities to maximize their welfare, there would be a zero probability of flight, so the bond dealer would be able to charge a negligible fee since there is little risk. This kind of example could easily generate elastic flight schedules. It is implausible to suppose that flight schedules are elastic, however. If they were, defendants would clamor for higher bail amounts in order to reduce their fees.

test." Estimating the relationship between bail and the bond rate paid (that is, the rate schedule) is difficult because the amount of bail is not independent of the flight risk. In appendix 7.B, we discuss how we statistically control for the endogeneity of bail using an "instrumental variables" technique, and actually estimate rate schedules for different defendants.[111]

The rate schedules estimated in appendix 7.B indicate that race is not related to flight propensity. After accounting for bail, bond rates paid by minority men are not significantly different from rates paid by white men.[112] The insignificance of the race dummies for men suggests that race is not related to the propensity of a defendant to flee: minority men have roughly the same flight schedule as do white men.

Since white and minority males appear to have the same rate schedule, we can infer that they have the same average flight propensity and should be given equal bail. If rate schedules are identical, the entire bail disparity between minority and white males is unjustified. The difference between white and minority bail amounts thus directly indicates the extent of racial discrimination. Even if judges could constitutionally make racial inferences about flight propensity, such inferences should not lead to higher bail amounts for minorities.[113]

Our analysis in appendix 7.B further indicates that flight schedules for black and Hispanic women are significantly lower than for white males. This suggests that the bail amount that equalizes flight probabilities is lower for minority women than for white men. This result roughly justifies the lower bail amounts set for Hispanic women. It also suggests that the 7.5 percent higher bails black women receive were 15 percent too high.[114]

Our estimates of the rate schedules also provide evidence that bail deters flight. The elasticity of the bond rate with respect to the bail amount is -0.527, which indicates that bond fees increase as bail increases. For

111. See text accompanying notes 192–98 *infra*.

112. The fourth column in table 7.8 in appendix 7.B indicates that the t-statistics associated with the race coefficients are not statistically different from zero. This means that race has a statistically negligible effect on bond rates once bail amounts are included in the regression.

113. These regressions were constrained to estimate a single flight elasticity for all defendant race–gender types. We investigated whether the rate schedules for minority defendants had different slopes than for white defendants. In separate regressions we found no statistical difference in the slopes (or intercepts) of the rate schedules of white and minority defendants.

114. Recall from table 7.3 that black women face bail amounts that are 7.5 percent higher than for white men (although this result is not statistically significant). See text accompanying note 93 *supra*.

example, if bail is increased 10 percent, the bond rate should only fall by about 5.3 percent, causing the fee amount (the product of bail amount and bond rate) to rise.[115]

III. Nondiscriminatory Explanations

To reach our conclusion that the disparate bond rate test provides evidence that bail setting subjects minority male defendants to an unjustified disparate impact, we needed to make three crucial assumptions:

1. *Proportionality Assumption:* Defendants' bond rates are proportional to their probability of flight.
2. *Equalization Assumption:* The only legitimate goal of bail setting is to equalize the probability of appearance for all defendants who are released.
3. *Representativeness Assumption:* Defendants who are released on bail bonds constitute a representative sample of those receiving bail as a condition of release.

The proportionality assumption ensures that lower minority bond rates actually indicate a lower risk of flight. The equalization assumption permits us to conclude that the disparate impact against minority male defendants is unjustified.[116]

The third and final assumption concerns representativeness. The population of defendants who obtain release using bail bonds is only a subset of all defendants for whom bail is set. Some defendants who receive bail as a condition of release never make bail and remain in jail pending trial. Others gain release by posting their own assets. If the defendants who se-

---

115. The sign and statistical significance of the offense severity and offense category variables imply that defendants with more serious offenses receive higher bond rates, indicating that serious offenders have higher flight propensities. For instance, drug, gun, and larceny have significantly higher flight schedules than the omitted category. This suggests that judges are rational in setting higher bail for more serious crimes. Judges do seem to overshoot, however, increasing bail more than the underlying offense characteristics merit.

116. For example, if judges could legitimately set higher bail for defendants they suspect might commit further crimes pending trial, then our evidence that bail setting does not equalize flight probabilities across defendants would not rule out the possibility that disparate bail levels were justified by this alternative goal (which the bail bond market does not "price").

cure release by employing the services of bond dealers do not constitute a representative sample of all defendants receiving bail, our inference of discrimination may not be valid.

This section critically examines each of these three assumptions and the variety of ways in which they might fail. Specifically, we examine possible market distortions affecting the proportionality assumption, possible alternative judicial goals, and possible selection biases. We offer three classes of alternative hypotheses that could provide nondiscriminatory explanations for the results summarized in table 7.3. We conclude, however, that these nondiscriminatory explanations cannot completely account for the racial disparities in bail setting and bond rates.

A.   Market Forces That Might Cause Bond Rates Not to Reflect Flight Probabilities

Factors that undermine the proportionality of bond rates and flight probabilities could provide an alternative (nondiscriminatory) explanation for the lower bond rates black males receive. If bail rates diverge from flight probabilities, then minority defendants might receive lower bond rates even if judges set bail amounts so as to equalize the probability of flight. Here we examine whether competition forces bond prices to reflect expected cost and whether expected cost is proportional to the probability of flight. Competition may not force bond prices to reflect costs if bond dealers engage in various forms of price discrimination. Furthermore, costs might not be proportional to the probability of flight because of differences in the forfeiture rates and collateral for various types of defendants, as well as because of the effect of dealer search and monitoring costs.

1.   Price Discrimination

A possible alternative explanation for the lower bond rates we observe for minority bailees is that bond dealers in New Haven engage in price discrimination. If bond dealers have sufficient market power to charge supracompetitive prices, they might find it profitable to charge higher fees to richer defendants. Under this theory, minority defendants might encounter lower rates simply because they are more likely to have a lower ability to pay.[117]

---

117.   Note that if bond dealers discriminate against minority defendants on the basis of race, our market evidence is particularly powerful, because minority bond rates would have been even lower if blacks had encountered nondiscriminatory pricing.

Table 7.4   Average Rates for Different Bail Sizes

Bail Range	White	N	Minority[a]	N	Adjusted % diff.[b]
0–1,000	8.86%	164	8.68%	463	−7.1%*
	(2.08)		(3.14)		
1,001–2,500	7.53%	54	6.78%	157	−9.9%*
	(2.24)		(2.29)		
2,501–5,000	7.82%	30	5.85%	106	−27.7%**
	(2.32)		(2.02)		
5,001+	5.69%	12	4.27%	132	−3.2%
	(2.43)		(1.59)		

Test of independence of race and bail amount: $\chi_{(3)}^2 = 21.68$.*
Standard deviations in parentheses.
*   Significant at the 90 percent level.
**   Significant at the 95 percent level.
[a]   All nonwhites are aggregated to maintain adequate cell sizes.
[b]   Coefficient on nonwhite dummy in rate regression, using the same offense and severity controls as in table 7.3.

We conclude, however, that bond dealers in New Haven did not discriminate on the basis of defendants' ability to pay. As observed earlier, low bond rates in towns like New Haven are more closely associated with a town having many dealers than with a town having significant poverty,[118] and monopolist and duopolist bond dealers in other Connecticut towns find it unprofitable to price discriminate based on the ability to pay.[119] The first finding suggests that bond dealers may not have sufficient market power to raise price above cost, while the second suggests that even bond dealers who do have market power do not choose to discriminate based on ability to pay.

If bond dealers did price discriminate on the basis of defendants' ability to pay, we would expect the difference between white and minority bond rates to be more marked with large bail amounts for which the bond dealer's fee is more substantial. Yet, racial differences in rates persist over the entire range of bails. Table 7.4 shows average rates paid by white and minority defendants, the raw differences between the rates, and the adjusted percent rate differences, sorted by size of bail. As the adjusted percent difference column indicates, nonwhites generally pay lower rates in

118.   See text accompanying notes 75–76 *supra*.
119.   See text accompanying note 77 *supra*.

all bail ranges. For bail amounts of $1,000 or less, for which the maximum fee is $100, white men pay an average of $63 and black men pay an average of $52. It is unlikely that black men can pay bond dealers $52, but not $63. The persistence of the racial discount for even small bail amounts indicates that racial disparity in bond rates cannot be fully explained by differences in ability to pay.[120]

The racial disparity in bond rates might, however, be caused by a different type of price discrimination. Bond dealers may charge higher prices to defendants who have higher search costs or poor information about competitive offers. If white defendants have disproportionately high search costs, bond dealers may have de facto monopoly power over any white defendant who solicits a bond dealer. This difference in search costs could lead bond dealers to charge lower rates to minority defendants, who would be more likely to search for better offers.[121]

While we have presented evidence that tends to disprove "ability to pay" discrimination, we cannot exclude the possibility that dealers discriminate based on differences in search costs or information. Indeed, if minority defendants in our sample have more prior experience with the criminal justice system, then minority defendants may have better information about competitive pricing and may be able to search more easily for competitive bail fees.

120. An analysis of bonds written by individual bond dealers also indicates that New Haven bond dealers compete for the business of all defendants—regardless of race. A chi-squared test showed white and minority defendants were distributed randomly among bond dealers, suggesting that individual bond dealers did not specialize in serving defendants of a particular race.

121. The possibility of search cost- or information-based price discrimination is an important concern. Chapter 2 indicates that these types of price discrimination can persist even in markets with very large numbers of competitors. Chapter 2 found that car dealerships in the Chicago area routinely charge blacks and women higher prices, despite the existence of about five hundred competing dealerships in the area.

Black male defendants may have lower search costs than white defendants if black males in New Haven are more likely to have experience with the criminal justice system. This possibility is suggested by studies showing that nationally 23 percent of black men between the ages of twenty and twenty-nine are either in prison, jail, on probation, or on parole on any given day, compared to only 6.2 percent of whites in the same age group. Mark Mauer, *The Sentencing Project, Young Black Men and the Criminal Justice System: A Growing National Problem* 3 (1990). A search–cost explanation is consistent with our earlier finding in table 7.2 that bond dealers charged uniformly high prices in poor Connecticut towns such as New London. Even if minority defendants had lower costs of search, they would not receive lower rates in duopoly markets (where all search is in vain).

2. Dealer Search and Monitoring Costs

Even if competition forces bond dealers to set their fees equal to their expected costs, the presence of search and monitoring costs could prevent bond rates from being proportional to flight probabilities. As shown in appendix 7.A, competitive prices might reflect not only the risk of bond forfeiture, but also the expected costs of monitoring defendants and attempting to recapture defendants who flee.[122]

Search and monitoring costs might provide an alternative explanation for disparate bail rates. If bond dealers believe that white defendants would be more costly to monitor or search for, then the minority defendants may be offered lower bond rates than white defendants with equal flight probabilities. Several factors diminish—but do not eliminate—the plausibility of this alternative type of explanation. First, as an empirical matter, bond dealers report that search costs are not an important determinant of bond fees.[123] Thus, it is unlikely that differences in search costs could explain the widely disparate bond rates. Second, it is unlikely that it is significantly easier for bond dealers to monitor the whereabouts of minority defendants because the bond dealers in our sample, all of whom are white, reported reluctance to drive into some of the predominantly minority neighborhoods (for example, to pick up and escort defendants to a court date). Thus, even though monitoring and search costs could potentially undermine our proportionality assumption, these costs, as an empirical matter, are not significant enough to account for the racial disparity in bond rates.

3. Forfeiture Rates

The forfeiture rate is the proportion of bail that the bond dealer forfeits when a defendant fails to appear. If the forfeiture rate were lower on average for black defendants than for white defendants, then bond dealers might charge black defendants lower bond rates because bond dealers would incur relatively less risk. In particular, if the percentage forfeiture declines with the bail size, then black male defendants may have lower

---

122. For example, if *ex ante* monitoring were completely efficient in deterring flight, then competitive bond rates would only reflect expected monitoring costs and would have no relation to the constant (zero percent) probability of flight.

123. See text following notes 189–90 *infra*. Moreover, in appendix 7.A, we show that the proportionality assumption continues to hold if *ex ante* monitoring is proportional to the amount of bail at risk.

forfeiture rates and therefore lower bond rates, because they face higher
bail amounts on average than do white males.[124]

Accordingly, we investigated whether the size of the forfeiture rate
varies with the bail amount. We found that the forfeiture rate is a constant
55 percent, regardless of the bail amount.[125] This result is consistent with
reports from local prosecutors, who indicated that the forfeiture rate was a
uniform 50 percent. Thus, differences in forfeiture rates apparently cannot
explain the lower bond rates charged to black and Hispanic males.

4. Collateral

Because the value of the collateral posted by the defendant reduces a
bond dealer's risk, racial differences in posted collateral could, in theory,
account for differences in bond rates. However, we find that differences
in collateral also fail to account for the racial disparities in bond rates. As
an initial matter, racial differences in posted collateral might easily
strengthen our confidence in our findings of race discrimination. Because
racial minorities are more likely to be poor, we might expect minority defendants to post less collateral than white defendants. If this is so, bond
rates for white defendants should be lower than bond rates for minority
defendants. This would indicate that our findings actually understate the
true amount of discrimination.[126]

124. The average bail amounts, by race and gender, in our sample were as follows:

Average Bail Amounts by Race and Gender			
Defendant Type	Mean	Std. Dev.	N
White male	1,978.1	2755.3	210
Black male	4,446.8	8117.3	596
Hispanic male	3,624.2	6486.0	118
White female	1,780.0	2345.6	60
Black female	2,271.5	4201.4	128
Hispanic female	1,421.9	2549.1	16

If the fraction forfeited declines with the bail amount, there will also be a negative
relationship between the rate paid and the bail amount, even if bail has no deterrence effect.

125. The forfeiture rate is set by the prosecutor. We have 1990 data on thirty-
one bond forfeitures in New Haven. Using regression analysis, we estimated the relationship between the amount forfeited and the bail amount to be:

$$F_i = 0.55 \, (B_i)$$

where F_i is the amount forfeited on defendant i's bail (B_i). Because the exponent 1.01 is
not statistically different from 1, the equation is linear in B_i.

126. Criminal defendants do not, however, represent a random cross section of
the population. While minorities are generally more likely to be poor, it is possible that,

Our data set does not contain information on collateral amounts. However, both anecdotal and ancillary empirical evidence indicate that collateral effects are not a serious concern. Bond dealers in New Haven often write bonds without any collateral requirements. According to a major New Haven bond dealer, the most common form of "collateral" is the signatures of the defendant's relatives.[127] Although some defendants deposit titles to cars and houses and occasionally jewelry and other personal objects as collateral, this particular bond dealer claims that his net proceeds from collateral are close to zero. Bond dealers almost never foreclose on collateral: collection is costly, and collateral may have private value to the defendant but lack sufficient market value to warrant collection.[128]

Table 7.4 provides further evidence against the hypothesis that differences in collateral induce the disparate pattern of bail and bond rates. Even in the subsample of defendants with bail of $1,000 and below, we find that the average rate for minority defendants is 7 percent less than for white defendants. The fact that collateral is rarely collected for small bail amounts suggests that differences in collateral cannot explain the results.[129]

5. Fixed Costs

In theory, bond dealers might charge lower rates to minority defendants because a dealer's fixed cost of writing a bond could be amortized over the larger fees charged minority defendants with higher bail amounts. But fixed costs are unlikely to figure prominently in bond pricing, because unlike other professionals, bond dealers do not maintain offices dedicated

---

within the class of criminal defendants, minorities could happen to have a greater ability to pay. If, under this scenario, minority defendants post proportionately more collateral than whites, then minorities would pay lower rates, not only because they may be less likely than whites to disappear, but also because their disappearance costs bond dealers less.

127.   Interview with Robert Jacobs.

128.   See note 49 *supra*. Freed and Wald report several anecdotes of idiosyncratic collateral:

> A D.C. bondsman [once took] a lap dog as collateral. A story current among bondsmen in Florida is that one of their number used to carry a collateral box in which he collected items of sentimental value, such as wedding rings, or of practical value, such as false teeth. On one occasion he is supposed to have kept the child of the accused.

Freed & Wald, *supra* note 3, at 27.

129.   One study found that bond dealers collected collateral in only 5–10 percent of their cases and concluded: "These are probably cases involving more serious offenses and thus higher bail amounts." Dill, *supra* note 77, at 663.

to their businesses.[130] Consequently, we expect that bond dealers' average fixed costs are not high enough to significantly affect the rates they charge, even for relatively small bail amounts.

Moreover, allowing for fixed costs actually strengthens our finding of disparate impact. After accounting for the presence of fixed costs,[131] we find that the percentage racial rate disparity actually becomes larger and more significant.[132] Therefore, while bond dealers may incur fixed costs, these costs do not provide an alternative explanation for the racial disparity in bond rates.[133]

While the preceding consideration of market forces casts doubt on a variety of factors that might cause the bond rate to diverge from the defendant's probability of flight, our analysis has not been exhaustive. For example, even if bond dealers accurately price the defendant's flight risk, judges may be more concerned about a different contingency: judges may care about inducing a timely appearance at a scheduled court date, while bond dealers may care only about whether the defendant will remain at large for six months—because only then do they risk forfeiture.[134] Even though we have presented a number of arguments to support our general contention that bond rates will broadly reflect a defendant's probability of flight, we are most concerned with the possibility that bond dealers discriminate on the basis of the defendant's ability to search for a competitive price, or that bond dealers have racially disparate costs of monitoring a

130. Bond dealers may, however, bear fixed administrative costs (for example, paperwork) in taking on each defendant.

131. If the fee includes a fixed cost component, we can estimate fixed costs (FC) from a rate regression as the coefficient on $(1/B)$: $r_i = X_i + FC(1/B) + \epsilon_i$. Running this regression, we estimate FC to be $18.87 (with a standard deviation of $0.87). Using judge dummies as instruments to correct for the endogeneity of bail in $(1/B)$ (as we did in obtaining the results summarized in table 7.8), we estimate FC to be $32.22 (with a statistically significant t-statistic of 5.95).

132. This is not surprising, because minorities pay lower bond rates than whites. If we subtract a fixed amount from all fees, the racial disparity (in percentage terms) becomes even larger.

133. Furthermore, assuming that white and minority defendants may impose differing fixed costs on dealers cannot account for this finding. In fact, we estimate that minorities have higher fixed costs (although the difference is insignificantly small when we instrument for $(1/B)$), which suggests that minorities should pay somewhat higher rates than whites with the same flight probabilities. If anything, this strengthens our finding of discrimination against minorities.

134. The possibility that judges and bond dealers might have divergent concerns figured prominently in Malcolm Feeley's study of the New Haven courts. See Feeley, *supra* note 14, at 224–29 (describing continuances and other accommodations that could attenuate the relationship between failure to appear and bond forfeiture).

defendant's whereabouts or searching for a defendant after a failure to appear. In sum, our results should only be relied upon with appropriate caution.[135]

B.   Alternative Judicial Goals

While we have assumed that the only legitimate criterion judges may consider in setting bail is equalizing the probability of appearance for all defendants, a number of commentators have suggested that judges apply other criteria.[136] Here we consider four alternative motivations for bail setting:

1. Targeting higher probabilities of appearance for more severe offenses.
2. Avoiding racially based inferences.
3. Deterring pretrial misconduct.
4. Targeting a desired bond fee instead of a desired probability of appearance.

It should be emphasized that only the first two of these criteria were even arguably consistent with Connecticut state law as of the time our data was collected.[137] Consequently, even if courts set bail to deter pretrial misconduct or to induce a desired bond fee, our disparate rate test still provides

135.   Before leaving this section, we note that although the disparate rate test hinges on the proportionality of bond rates paid and flight probabilities, the rate schedule test remains valid even if the factor of proportionality between cost and flight probability varies with the bond amount, as long as this variation is the same for whites and minorities. For example, if the ratio of required collateral to bail varies with the bail amount, bond rates will not be proportional to flight probabilities. However, if bond dealers require the same relationship between collateral and bail for all defendants, the rate schedule test (discussed in appendix 7.B) remains valid. While minority and white defendants with the same flight probabilities could have different rates because of differing bail amounts, the estimated rate schedule controls for differences in bail amounts. Thus, the rate schedule test would show whether blacks and whites have different underlying flight tendencies warranting different bail treatment regardless of the effect of differing bail amounts.

136.   See, e.g., Freed & Wald, *supra* note 3, at 9–21.

137.   During the last three months of our sample period, an amendment to the Connecticut bail statute permitted courts to set higher bail amounts to deter certain types of pretrial misconduct, but this option was almost never used. See note 60 *supra* (discussing the amendment and why it did not affect the data). The second criterion, as discussed below, might flow from the state or federal Equal Protection Clauses. See text accompanying notes 144–49 *infra*.

evidence of unjustified disparate impact during that period. Under these alternative assumptions, minority males in our sample were injured by bail setting criteria that contravened existing state law.[138]

1. Targeting Higher Probabilities of Appearance for More Serious Offenses

Although the Connecticut statute mandates that bail be set to "reasonably assure the appearance of the arrested person in court,"[139] courts may interpret the statute to demand a higher degree of assurance for more serious offenses. Judges may feel that a reasonable assurance of appearance in a murder case mandates no more than a 5 percent chance of flight, while a 7 percent chance of flight may be tolerable in a simple larceny case.[140] Our finding that bond rates are lower for more serious offenses may be consistent with such an interpretation of the Connecticut statute. If courts in fact demand a higher probability of appearance for more serious categories of crime, the fact that minorities pay lower bond rates might be explained by a tendency of black defendants to commit more serious crimes.[141]

138. Our assertion that equalizing flight probabilities was the only legitimate goal of bail setting puts tremendous weight on the supremacy of the statute. Preventive detention is a constitutionally permissible objective for bail setting. Some might argue that it is legitimate for judges to set bail on this basis even though that would contravene a statutory mandate.

139. Conn. Gen. Stat. Ann. § 54-64a(a)(1) (West Supp. 1993).

140. This interpretation might be consistent with the traditional notion that more serious crimes must be deterred with harsher penalties or a higher probability of punishment. Achieving a higher likelihood of appearance enhances the probability that the defendant will be punished.

141. There is no clear evidence, however, that minority defendants are more likely to commit more serious offenses. The distribution of offense severities for minority and white defendants was as follows:

Offense Severity	Minority	White
Class A or B felony	4.0%	3.5%
Class C or D felony	12.2%	15.0%
Class U felony	40.8%	32.7%
Class A or B misdemeanor	6.6%	41.5%
Class C or D misdemeanor	2.1%	5.0%
Other	2.1%	2.3%
Total	858	260

Although minority defendants are somewhat more likely to have committed Class A and B felonies, they are less likely than white defendants to be charged with other types of felonies. However, none of these differences is statistically significant. An analysis of par-

To control for this possibility, we tested for racial disparities in bail and bond rates within individual offense categories.[142] Table 7.5 reports the results for the two largest offense categories: assault and drug offenses. These results indicate that, even within individual offense categories, minority men (and for drug offenses, black women as well) pay lower bond rates. Judges seem to demand lower flight probabilities for more serious offense categories, but even controlling for this propensity, bail set for minority defendants is unjustifiably high.[143]

2. Color-Blind Bail Setting

Attempts to comply with the equal protection provisions of the Connecticut and federal Constitutions might also provide a nondiscriminatory explanation for disparate bond rates.[144] If these constitutional mandates

---

ticular offense types similarly reveals that, with the exception of firearm offenses, minority defendants do not commit serious offenses more frequently than whites.

142.   This approach ensures that results are not skewed by overrepresentation of minority defendants in serious offense categories.

143.   The bond rate disparities within offense categories might still have been caused by our failure to adequately control for aspects of offense severity that are correlated with minority status. It is also possible that judges care not only about their estimate of a defendant's flight probability but also about their confidence in this estimate. In statistical parlance, the bail setters might legitimately take into account not only their estimate of a defendant's flight probability, but also the variance of this estimate. In particular, judges might legitimately target a lower expected flight probability if they are less confident about their estimate. If judges are more uncertain about minority defendants' propensity to flee, they might demand a higher probability of appearance, much as investors demand higher expected returns on assets that bear high risks.

Bond dealers are likely to be just as uncertain about minority defendants' flight propensities under this scenario. However, because some dealers write hundreds of bonds each year, they may be able to diversify away the additional risks associated with minority defendants. Uncertainty will not contribute to rate disparity if judges are also able to diversify away risks.

144.   The Equal Protection Clause of the Fourteenth Amendment reads: ". . . nor [shall any state] deny to any person within its jurisdiction the equal protection of the laws." U.S. Const. amend. XIV. The Connecticut state constitution reads: ". . . all men when they form a social compact, are equal in rights; and no man or set of men are entitled to exclusive public endowments or privileges from the community." Conn. Const. of 1965 art. I, § 1. There is still some uncertainty as to whether racially contingent state decisionmaking in the criminal context (including various forms of racial profiling) are impermissible under strict constitutional scrutiny or under what conditions they might be narrowly tailored to further compelling state interests. See, e.g., Brown v. City of Oneonta, 1999 WL 973532 (2d Cir. Oct 26, 1999) (giving police considerable latitude to consider race when identifying specific suspects), but see United States v. Armstrong, 517 U.S. 456 (1996) (prohibiting police from considering race in making stops unconnected to racial description of a particular suspect).

Table 7.5 Bail and Rate Regressions by Offense

	Drug Offense (SUR Estimate)			
	Log Bail Amount		Log Rate Paid	
	Coeff.	t-stat.	Coeff.	t-stat.
Constant	6.440**	20.442	−2.499**	−21.835
Defendant Characteristics				
BM	1.109**	6.40	−0.439**	−6.97
HM	0.704**	2.62	−0.166*	−1.70
WF	−0.175	−0.46	0.026	0.18
BF	0.495	1.60	−0.225**	−1.99
HF	−0.195	−0.34	−0.065	−0.31
Offense Severity				
CLASABF	NA	NA	NA	NA
CLASCDF	0.164	0.20	0.457	1.52
CLASUF	0.958**	3.26	−0.076	−0.71
CLASABM	0.569	0.91	0.051	0.22
CLASCDM	−0.869	−1.51	0.607**	2.90
R^2	0.219		0.219	
N	264		264	

	Assault			
	Log Bail Amount		Log Rate Paid	
	Coeff.	t-stat.	Coeff.	t-stat.
Constant	6.756**	50.42	−2.437**	−45.43
Defendant Characteristics				
BM	−0.093	−0.62	−0.148**	−2.47
HM	0.121	0.57	−0.150*	−1.77
WF	−0.541	−0.63	0.135	0.39
BF	−0.091	−0.41	−0.060	−0.68
HF	−0.284	−0.64	0.010	0.06
Offense Severity				
CLASABF	2.095**	7.84	−0.439**	−4.10
CLASCDF	1.272**	8.52	−0.195**	−3.26
CLASUF	1.010**	3.92	−0.158	−1.53
CLASABM	NA	NA	NA	NA
CLASCDM	NA	NA	NA	NA
R^2	0.375		0.130	
N	220		220	

* Significant at the 90 percent level.
** Significant at the 95 percent level.

Figure 7.3   Color-blind bail setting induces lower minority bond rates

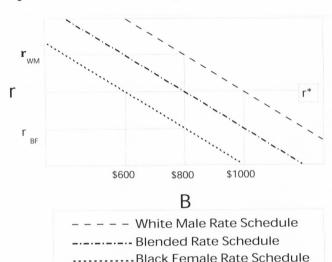

force courts to ignore racial inferences that would indicate lower flight propensities (for black women, for example), courts would be compelled to set bail higher than these defendants deserve under a pure equalization standard.

Figure 7.3 illustrates the possible impact of color-blind bail setting. The figure depicts our earlier evidence that black female defendants have a 7.5 percent lower flight propensity than white male defendants.[145] A judge forced to ignore racial inferences for equal protection reasons would have to set bail only on the basis of the average or blended flight propensity for the entire population of defendants of all races and genders.[146] The judge would thus have to set the bail at a level that would induce the requisite probability of appearance for the average defendant, which in figure 7.3 is depicted as $800.[147] The effect of setting the same bail for all defendants

145.   See table 7.8. This result was only significant at the 90 percent level. Table 7.8 also indicates that Hispanic female defendants had a 19 percent lower propensity to flee (with 95 percent significance).

146.   The average flight propensity would depend on the relative proportion of black, Hispanic, and white defendants of each gender in the population of defendants.

147.   The judge in this scenario is analytically in the same position as an issuer of pension annuities after City of Los Angeles v. Manhart, 435 U.S. 702 (1978). Because Title VII prohibits discrimination in the pricing of annuities, an issuer cannot charge women more than men on the grounds that women live longer. Accordingly, the issuer must price annuities based on the blended life expectancy of men and women in the an-

(even though black females have a lower propensity to flee) is that black females will be overdeterred from flight and white males will be underdeterred.[148] This example shows that the unwillingness or inability of judges to set race-contingent bail amounts—that is the unwillingness to engage in a form of racial profiling—may itself perversely produce a disparate impact on minority defendants that is not justified by the group's true propensity to flee. However, if bond dealers can develop race specific bail setting criteria so as to equalize probabilities of flight, they can charge black female defendants lower rates than white male defendants, as depicted in figure 7.3 by the equilibrium rates r_{BF} and r_{WM}.[149]

Two important pieces of evidence contradict the theory of color blindness, however. First, table 7.8 in appendix 7.B indicates that the flight schedule for minority male defendants is not statistically different than the flight schedule for white males, suggesting that, as an empirical matter, race is not a valid predictor of defendants' propensity to flee. Color-blind adjudication therefore cannot explain the disproportionately low bond

---

nuity pool. See George J. Benston, The Economics of Gender Discrimination in Employee Fringe Benefits: *Manhart* Revisited, 49 U. Chi. L. Rev. 489, 536–37 (1982).

John Goldkamp describes a similar difficulty with ignoring race and gender effects when constructing other criminal guidelines:

> Guidelines critics have noted instances when attempts were made to eliminate the effects of status variables merely by dropping the obnoxious factors from the equation and then rerunning the new equation. . . . The effects of the status variables will not be removed in this fashion because the remaining predictors in the new equation will change their weights; in effect, the weight of the purged variables will be redistributed among other seemingly neutral variables.

John S. Goldkamp, Prediction in Criminal Justice Policy Development, *in* 9 *Prediction and Classification: Criminal Justice Decision Making* 103, 138 (D. Gottfredson & M. Tonry eds., 1987); see also Franklin M. Fisher & Joseph B. Kadane, Empirically Based Sentencing Guidelines and Ethical Considerations, in 2 *Research on Sentencing: The Search for Reform* 184, 192 (Alfred Blumstein, Jacqueline Cohen, Susan E. Martin & Michael H. Tonry eds., 1983).

148. Figure 7.3 indicates that, in order to induce equal probabilities of appearance, judges would need to set bail at $600 for the black females and at $1,000 for white males.

149. As in the *Manhart* context, discussed in note 147 *supra,* prohibiting the decisionmaker from acting upon relevant predictors causes one group to subsidize another. In this bail example, color-blind bail setting forces the judge to set the bail too high for black females and too low for white males. As discussed above, since the bond rate is almost always inelastic with respect to the bail amount, color-blind bail setting would increase the cost of pretrial release for black female defendants and lower the cost for white male defendants. See note 103 *supra* and accompanying text. The black females' lower flight propensity would subsidize the cost of white males' pretrial release, because the presence of black females in the population lowers the average bail that white male defendants would need to post.

rates for minority males. Second, color-blind bail setting should cause black females and white males to receive the same bail amount. Table 7.3 indicates, however, that after controlling for several other variables, bail is set significantly higher for black females than for white males. Thus, the available empirical evidence is not consistent with the hypothesis that judges' attempts to ignore race in setting bail caused disparate bond rates.

3. Deterring Pretrial Misconduct

A third alternate goal that courts may be pursuing in setting bail is reducing the incidence of pretrial crime. Such a goal might further the traditional aim of specific deterrence, but would clearly violate the governing state statute.[150] In the 1980s, however, the U.S. Supreme Court significantly expanded the power of states to use pretrial detention to prevent arrestees from committing crimes before trial.[151] The Connecticut Supreme Court subsequently suggested that preventive detention is as a matter of state law constitutionally permissible,[152] and the Connecticut legislature amended the statute governing bail setting procedures to authorize courts to use bail to "reasonably assure . . . that the safety of another person will not be endangered."[153]

While courts in setting bail may be concerned about the risk of pretrial crime, this risk will not be reflected in bond rates because the bond dealers' payoffs do not depend on whether the defendants commit additional

---

150. See State v. Menillo, 159 Conn. 264, 269, 268 A.2d 667, 670 (1970) (the "fundamental purpose of bail is to ensure the presence of an accused throughout all proceedings"). However, the state constitution permits the court to withhold bail for capital offenses, indicating that courts may legitimately take preventive measures. Conn. Const. of 1965 art. I, § 8 (1988).

151. See, e.g., United States v. Salerno, 481 U.S. 739 (1987); Schall v. Martin, 467 U.S. 253 (1984); see also Marc Miller & Martin Guggenheim, Pretrial Detention and Punishment, 75 Minn. L. Rev. 335 (1990).

152. In State v. Ayala, 222 Conn. 331, 610 A.2d 1162 (1992), the Connecticut Supreme Court wrote:

> Consideration of the customary purposes of bail prior to the adoption of the constitution of 1818 supports the conclusion that while ensuring the appearance of the defendant is a primary purpose of bail in this state, it is not necessarily the sole purpose. The statutory right to bail in Connecticut is traceable to a 1672 legislative enactment declaring that "no mans person shall be Restrained or Imprisoned by any Authority whatsoever, before the Law hath sentenced him thereunto if he can put in sufficient security, bail or mainprize for his appearance and good behaviour. . . ."

610 A.2d at 1172.

153. Conn. Gen. Stat. Ann. § 54-64a(b)(2) (West Supp. 1993); see also note 60 *supra* (discussing the negligible impact of this amendment on our data).

crimes.[154] At first glance, however, using the bail amount to prevent pretrial crime is only likely to be successful if the defendants cannot afford the bond dealer's fee. Even if judges use high bail to induce preventive detention for some high-risk defendants, this practice would not affect our sample of defendants who gained release using the services of a bond dealer.[155] Only if courts failed in their attempt at preventive detention would we observe some defendants with unreasonably high bail amounts obtaining release using bond dealers. Thus, while a goal of preventive detention could clearly affect who makes bail, it does not necessarily affect the bail amounts of those people who do use a bond dealer. Moreover, even if judges set bail on the basis of this criterion, our conclusion that minority males are subjected to a disparate impact not permitted under Connecticut law stands.[156]

154. Indeed, if bond dealers believe that a defendant is likely to commit a crime while out on bail and be rearrested, it might lead the bond dealers to offer a lower rate because after rearrest the risk of forfeiture on the initial bond would be eliminated. Thus, if both judge and bond dealer believe that, if released, a defendant will ineptly rob a convenience store, the judge may be inclined to set a high bail to prevent the defendant's release, while the bond dealer may charge a lower fee because of the low risk that the defendant will not be returned quickly to jail.

It might be useful to make forfeitures contingent on pretrial crime as well as failure to appear. If courts force bond dealers to offer "pretrial crime insurance" as well as "flight insurance," bond dealers would have a greater interest in deterring pretrial misconduct. Such a reform would cause bond rates to more fully price the correct judicial goals.

155. It is theoretically possible that a higher bail amount that failed to induce preventive detention could still deter pretrial crime. For example, a defendant considering committing a pretrial crime and then fleeing might be deterred if her bond dealer has posted a higher bond, on the theory that the bond dealer would make a greater effort to recapture her. This would enhance the likelihood that the defendant will be caught and punished for the pretrial offense. But this kind of attenuated argument has been rejected by most commentators. See, e.g., Goldkamp & Gottfredson, *supra* note 3, at 96 ("Any deterrent effect of bail on rearrest seems a priori less plausible, and thus the data do not seem to suggest much correspondence between the assignment of cash bail amounts and rearrest.").

156. Our theory of legal legitimacy, based as it is on the provisions of the Connecticut bail setting statute, differs from most economic theories of legitimacy, which recognize the benefits of deterring pretrial misconduct. See, e.g., William M. Landes, The Bail System: An Economic Approach, 2 J. Legal Stud. 79 (1973); Myers, *supra* note 5.

In United States v. Salerno, 481 U.S. 739 (1987), the Supreme Court upheld the constitutionality of the Bail Reform Act of 1984, which permits pretrial detention to "reasonably assure the safety of any person and the community." Justice Rehnquist, writing for the majority, reasoned that under federal law, the government has a "legitimate and compelling interest . . . in preventing crimes by arrestees." Id. at 799.

We were able to construct a crude indication of whether defendants in our sample misbehaved while out on bail. Using judicial identifiers to instrument for the bail amount as previously done to obtain the results summarized in table 7.8, we found that

4. Targeting Desired Bond Fee Instead of Desired Probability of Appearance

Courts might also disregard the Connecticut bail setting statute's mandate by setting bail at levels sufficient to force defendants to pay particular bond fees. As emphasized above,[157] a judge targeting a minimum probability of appearance for defendants released on bail should ignore the size of the bond dealer's fee: the fee is a sunk cost that affects neither the bond dealer's monitoring and search efforts nor the defendant's incentives to appear. Judges, however, might attempt to increase the defendant's bond fee for two reasons: first, in order to punish the defendant (the "punishment theory"),[158] or second, to maximize bond dealers' profits (the "capture theory").[159]

The punishment theory has wide support among commentators. Most notably, the title of Malcolm Feeley's groundbreaking analysis of the New Haven Court of Common Pleas heralded that "The Process Is the Punishment."[160] Earlier New York City and Philadelphia studies concluded that "high bail is sometimes set to 'punish' the defendant."[161] In extreme cases,

---

minority males had a lower propensity to misbehave while released on bail. However, our confidence in this result is significantly weakened by our estimate in the same regression that raising the size of bail actually increases the probability of misbehavior. If this latter result were true, it would be particularly irrational for judges to increase the amounts of bail to deter pretrial misconduct unless the judges could ensure that the targeted defendants would remain in jail. Because we are highly skeptical of the estimated bail effect, we are also reluctant to place much faith in our estimate that minority males have a lower propensity to misbehave before trial.

157. See notes 67–68 *supra* and accompanying text.

158. One could also imagine that judges manipulate bail amounts to counteract noncompetitive pricing by bond dealers. Thus, if judges believed that bond dealers discriminated against white defendants, they might be moved to reduce the average bail of these disfavored clients. This "reverse discrimination" explanation of lower minority bond rates, however, seems at odds with our finding that minority male defendants received higher bail amounts and the fact that all the bond dealers in our sample were white.

159. Theories of "regulatory capture" predict that participants in regulated industries capture the "hearts and minds" of public officials, particularly those officials who are directly responsible for regulating industry participants. See Ian Ayres & John Braithwaite, *Responsive Regulation: Transcending the Deregulation Debate* 54, 63–71 (1992). Besides providing "flight insurance" to the state, bond dealers in various jurisdictions also provide various courtroom services. See Feeley, *supra* note 14, at 102–8 (bond dealers answer questions of prosecutors and defendants in court and facilitate case flow); Dill, *supra* note 77, at 653–56 (bond dealers advise judges about acceptable bail, give defendants legal advice, and often encourage guilty pleas).

160. Feeley, *supra* note 14.

161. Ares et al., *supra* note 3, at 71.

this punishment motive might cause judges to target a bond fee beyond the means of the defendant, punishing the defendant not by forcing him to pay a higher nonrefundable fee, but with pretrial incarceration.[162]

The capture theory is in direct conflict with our assumption that the bond market is competitive. Participants in a competitive market would have little to gain by having the bail setter raise the bail amount, because competition would bid away any supracompetitive profits, regardless of the bail amount. If the bond market is not perfectly competitive, however, bond dealers might benefit from influencing judges. For example, by setting bail above the liquid wealth of the defendant, the judge could compel a defendant to use a bond dealer to secure pretrial release (instead of posting bail personally).

Setting higher bail in a noncompetitive market might also allow bond dealers to charge higher fees. This form of capture, however, is much more likely to exist in smaller Connecticut cities with only one or two bond dealers—where the bond dealers are already charging rates close to the statutory maximum. If bond dealers in New Haven had the market power to charge supracompetitive prices, they would not need higher bail amounts; they could simply raise their rates.

Neither the punishment nor the capture theory of fee targeting lends itself to vigorous testing. Nonetheless, neither theory can adequately explain the disproportionately low rates charged to minority males. Recall that in table 7.4, when considering only specific offenses and controlling for offense severity, we found that bond dealers continued to charge minority males disproportionately low fees. Thus, even among defendants that judges might want to punish equally, we still find evidence of discrimination. The capture theory is also inconsistent with our finding that racially disparate bond rates persist for even bail amounts less than $500.

C. Representativeness

As noted above,[163] our results are reliable only if our sample of defendants is representative of the underlying defendant population. Our sample contains only defendants who obtained pretrial release through the use of a bond dealer. It does not include two types of defendants who received bail as a condition of release: those who failed to post bail and remained

162. The Manhattan Bail project observed this motive. See id. (noting bail was used to "break crime waves or to keep the defendant off the street until trial").

163. See text following note 116 *supra*.

in jail, and those who were released after posting their own assets. Here we explore how these two types of sample selection affect our interpretation of the discrimination test. A defendant who seeks pretrial release faces three constraints that influence her ability and inclination to seek the aid of a bond dealer. The relationship among these constraints is depicted in figure 7.4.

The first constraint is produced by regulations that cap the maximum allowable bond rates.[164] The rate caps imposed by Connecticut law are denoted by a curve in figure 7.4 ("Regulatory Constraint"). If, for a given defendant and bail amount, bond dealers believe that the defendant's flight risk is greater than the maximum allowed rate, they will refuse to serve the defendant.[165]

Even if a bond dealer is willing to offer a bail bond at a rate below the statutory maximum rate, the defendant may not be able to accept the dealer's offer if she has limited wealth. This constraint is represented by the hyperbola $rB = W$, where W is the defendant's wealth (denoted in figure 7.4 as the "Bond Wealth Constraint"). Thus, if the competitive bond rate for a given defendant's bail exceeds either the bond wealth constraint or the regulatory constraint, the defendant will not be offered or will not be able to accept bail bonding. Such a defendant will remain in jail and therefore be excluded from our sample. The set of defendants who remain in jail is represented by the right-hand shaded area in figure 7.4.

The third constraint is the defendant's willingness and ability to post bail personally. This constraint is denoted by the vertical line in figure 7.4 (denoted as the "Posting Wealth Constraint"). If the bail amount is less than the defendant's wealth, she can (but need not) post bail personally. If she plans to appear in court, she should prefer to post bail herself so long as her opportunity cost of foregone interest is less than a bond dealer's nonrefundable fee—that is, $iB < rB$, where B equals the bail amount, i equals the percentage return that could be earned during the period preced-

---

164. See note 42 *supra*.

165. In this way, rate regulations ensure that a defendant released on bail bond will fail to appear no more than a certain percentage of the time. It is tempting to conclude that the rate regulations ensure that a defendant's probability of flight will never exceed 10 percent. However, because bond dealers forfeit only approximately 50 percent of the bail amount if a defendant fails to appear, the rate regulation may ensure no more than a 20 percent probability of appearance. See text accompanying note 124 *supra*. Moreover, we have only claimed that bond rates are proportional to the probability of flight, so it is difficult to infer the maximum probabilities implied by the maximum rates.

Figure 7.4   Regulatory and wealth constraints that can limit defendants' ability to
purchase bail bonding services

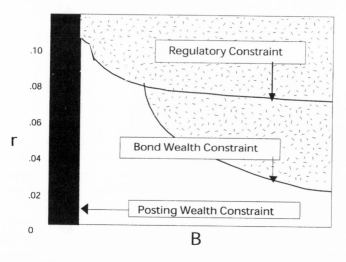

Defendant Remains in Jail (Jail Selection Effect)

Defendant Posts Bail Personally (Personal Bail Selection)

ing the defendant's court appearance, and r equals the bail bond rate.[166]
This expression reduces to a determination of whether the rate of return
is less than the bond rate—$i < r$. As a practical matter, bail is normally
posted for less than six months and the foregone interest is almost always
less than a bond dealer's nonrefundable fee.[167] In figure 7.4, when a defendant is assigned a bail amount that falls to the left of (is less than) her
personal wealth constraint, she should choose to post bail personally.
These defendants "select" themselves out of our data set (this selection
effect is depicted in figure 7.4 by the shaded rectangular area).

   Thus, defendants may be omitted from our sample by remaining in

   166.   More generally, if the defendant is not sure that she will appear in court,
personal bonding will be less costly if:

$pB + (1\ p)iB < rB + pC.$

In interpreting this equation, note that the probability of flight (p) may be endogenous
to the suspect's choice, because posting personal bail may more strongly deter flight.

   167.   For example, suspects will normally lose less interest by posting $5,000 bail
personally for six months than by paying a bond dealer a typical $400–500 fee, espe-
cially if the foregone interest would have been taxable.

jail or by posting bail personally. We now explore whether either of these two selection effects might generate racially disparate bond rates.

1. Defendants Who Remain in Jail

Defendants who cannot afford the bond dealer's fee remain in jail and thus are excluded from our sample. If minority defendants are more frequently unable to pay such a fee, it is possible that the minority defendants who use bond dealers will pay lower rates than white defendants. To see this, suppose that a judge sets bail at $1,000 for a racially diverse group of defendants who on average have the desired probability of flight (say, 10 percent). The competitive bond market responds to these $1,000 bails by offering a range of bond rates that average 10 percent.[168] This scenario is depicted in figure 7.5. If minority defendants are generally poorer than white defendants, only those minority defendants who receive low rate offers may have sufficient resources to accept, whereas white defendants may be able to accept the entire range of offers, even those with the highest rate. As shown in figure 7.5, this selection effect may cause minority defendants to have lower bond rates than white defendants.

This type of "jail selection" is a serious empirical concern. As shown in table 7.6, in 20 percent of the cases where judges required bail, the defendants remained in jail pending disposition of their cases, and minority defendants were more than twice as likely to remain in jail as white defendants. Because our sample only includes defendants who accepted bond dealer offers, our analysis of bond rates may misstate the true relationship between rates offered and defendants' race. The size of this "jail selection effect" may be large enough to produce the bond rate disparities that we found.[169]

Because this form of jail selection is caused by a wealth constraint, one would expect this effect to induce the largest differences between white and minority rates at the high bail levels where affordability plays the greatest role. Yet table 7.4 indicates lower bond rates for minority defendants over the entire range of bail amounts. It is unlikely that defendant wealth constraints can explain the large white-minority rate differentials

---

168. Even a competitive bail bond market might offer a range of different rates either because some bond dealers have better information about defendants or because bond market offers are generated with some kind of random error.

169. The most direct way of assessing whether jail selection affects our results would be to include bona fide bond rate offers for defendants who remained in jail and assess whether the bond rates for incarcerated minorities are higher than bond rates for those using bond dealers.

Figure 7.5 Jail selection

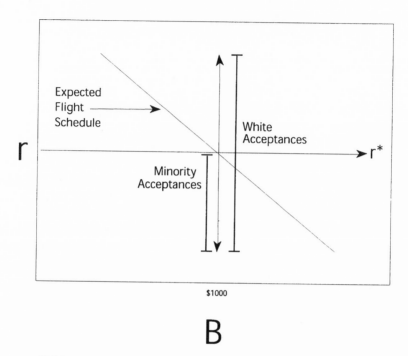

B

Range of Offers to Both Minority and White Defendants

Table 7.6 Release Status of All New Haven Defendants (N = 1,358)

	All (%)	Race		
		Black (%)	White (%)	Hispanic (%)
Defendant posted cash	11.2	7.9	17.5	12.0
Bail bond	68.6	68.2	73.3	62.5
Defendant retained in jail	20.0	3.95	1.27	4.76

observed for bail fees of less than $1,000. Nevertheless, it remains plausible that the jail selection effect could provide a nondiscriminatory explanation for part of the observed racial disparity in bond rates.[170]

2. Posting Bail Personally

The inability of some defendants to accept bond offers may produce a jail selection effect. We now examine the possible effects of defendants choosing to reject bond offers and post bail personally.

Because posting one's own bail is generally cheaper then paying bond fees when the defendant intends to appear, it is reasonable for a bond dealer to infer that affluent defendants would want to use a bond dealer only if they are considering flight.[171] Thus, any defendant who has sufficient assets to post bond personally and yet chooses to go to a bond dealer is immediately suspect. This heightened tendency of high-risk defendants to choose bond dealers over personally posting bail is called "adverse selection."

The impact of adverse selection is depicted in figure 7.6, in which the flight schedule for a particular class of defendants is shown in relation to the various statutory and wealth constraints previously examined in figure 7.4. The flight schedule for bail amounts to the right of defendants' posting wealth constraint are unaffected by adverse selection because bond dealers know that for these bail amounts this class of defendants does not have the option of posting bail personally. However, the adverse selection effect is visible in figure 7.6 for bail amounts less then the defendants' wealth, that is, to the left of the posting wealth constraint, where defendants could afford to post bail themselves. For these lower bail amounts, defendants choosing to post their own bail are less likely to flee because their own money is at risk. As for defendants seeking bond dealer services when they could post their own bail, bond dealers may rationally assume that such defendants have a higher propensity to flee. Dealers are therefore likely to demand higher rates of these defendants. The adverse selection effect

---

170. The standard deviations of the white and minority rates provide some evidence of a jail selection effect. As figure 7.5 indicates, if jail selection leads to racially disparate bond rates, we would expect there to be a lower variance in minority rates than in white rates for any given bail amount. Table 7.4 shows that the standard deviation for minority rates was lower than for white rates (2.02 versus 2.32 for bail amounts between $2,501 and $5,000; 1.59 versus 2.43 for bail above $5,000).

171. Defendants who intend to flee would naturally prefer to pay the nonrefundable fee to avoid having to post and forfeit the much higher bail amount.

Figure 7.6   Adverse selection

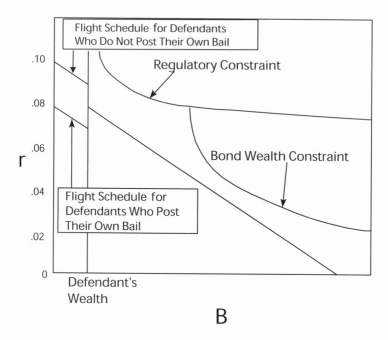

Flight Schedule for Defendants
Who Do Not Post Their Own Bail

.10

Regulatory Constraint

.08

.06

r

Bond Wealth Constraint

.04

Flight Schedule for
Defendants Who Post
Their Own Bail

.02

0

Defendant's
Wealth

B

therefore produces two different rate schedules for bail amounts that fall below defendants' wealth, as depicted in figure 7.6.

This adverse selection effect might explain why, in our bail bonding sample, minority defendants received lower rates than whites. Suppose that white defendants are wealthier and therefore more likely to be able to post bail themselves without using a bond dealer. Then a white defendant's decision to hire a bond dealer, rather than post his own bond, is more likely to signal a tendency to jump bail.[172] As a result, bond dealers may

172. It is not clear how courts should fulfill their statutory mandate to reasonably ensure appearance if adverse selection is of concern. Suppose that judges face one hundred defendants, each with the flight schedule depicted in figure 7.6. Suppose further that the judge knows that historically 50 percent of these defendants will use bond dealers if bail is set below their individual wealth. If the maximum acceptable flight probability is 8 percent, should the judge set bail just above the defendants' wealth (to ensure that no released defendant has more than an 8 percent probability of flight) or should the judge set bail below their wealth (to ensure that the average defendant has an 8 percent probability of flight)? If the statute mandates the former interpretation, then adverse selection should not be a concern. We assume, however, that the latter interpretation is justified and that the adverse selection effect could theoretically arise even among judges who legitimately attempt to induce a uniform probability of appearance.

charge whites higher rates. Since minority defendants are less likely to be able to self-post, a greater proportion of those who do not intend to flee will seek bond dealers' services. Consequently, the "average" expected flight probability for a minority member would be lower.

As with the jail selection effect, we are concerned that adverse selection might explain the racially disparate rates. Table 7.6 indicates that in 11 percent of the cases where judges require bail, defendants choose to post bail personally, and that whites are twice as likely to self-post as are blacks. Adverse selection, however, should not be expected to cause racially disparate bond rates for bail amounts where bond dealers might have confidence that white and minority defendants can either both afford or both not afford their own bail. But contrary to this expectation, we find that minority defendants pay lower rates even for bail amounts less than $1,000 or more than $5,000. As with the jail selection effect, we conclude that adverse selection seems an unlikely explanation for the full range of racial disparities in bond rates.

To summarize, the preceding section set forth what we think are the most critical nondiscriminatory explanations for our findings. We laid out the three major assumptions on which our conclusions depend and tested them against these nondiscriminatory alternatives. While we uncovered inconsistencies and weaknesses in some of these alternative explanations, we continue to approach our original assumptions of proportionality, equalization, and representativeness with caution and a fair amount of skepticism.

IV. Harnessing the Market in the Bail Setting Process

If racial discrimination in bail setting is indeed prevalent, what can be done to mitigate its effect? In this section, we consider a somewhat unorthodox proposal to harness the competitive forces of the bail bond market to produce an auction system of setting bail.[173] Determining the size of bail by private auction would substantially reduce the influence of judges in setting bail. While we ultimately reject the proposal, our analysis of bond dealer auctions forces us to reevaluate our assumptions about market competition. If we trust market competition as a premise for our finding of judicial discrimination, then we must examine why we do not trust competition enough to allow market forces to set bail.

---

173. This idea was originally suggested to us by Professor Stephen G. Marks.

The proposed auction mechanism would allow bond dealers' competitive bids to determine a defendant's bail. Imagine that lawmakers want to ensure that defendants are released on bail only if there is no more than a 10 percent chance they will fail to appear. Bond dealers who wished to compete for a chance to write a bond for a particular defendant would enter a bid for the nonrefundable fee, and the lowest bid would win the right to bail the defendant. The crucial feature of this proposed system is that the bond dealer who wins the bid would have to pay ten times the winning bid if the defendant failed to appear.[174]

Because lower bail amounts induce higher probabilities of flight, a bond dealer would want to avoid entering too low a bid. If, for example, bond dealers believed that a particular defendant had the flight schedule depicted in figure 7.1, no bond dealer would bid below $1,500.[175] In a perfectly competitive market, bond dealers would bid down the asking fee until there was exactly a 10 percent probability of flight, thus producing the legislative goal.

However, several considerations lead us to doubt that a low-bid auction would have this desired effect. First, defendants would have a tremendous incentive to make hidden side payments to bond dealers to induce lower bids. For instance, in the previous example where the equilibrium fee bid was $1,500, the defendant might offer the bond dealer a $600 bribe in order to induce the bond dealer to make a $50 bid. The bond dealer would make $650 from the bribe and the fee and yet have only $500 at risk. Meanwhile, the defendant would reduce her costs of making bail from $1,500 to $650.[176]

---

174. More generally, if the maximum allowable probability of flight were q, then the auction mechanism should mandate that the bond dealer forfeit [fee/q].

175. Under that flight schedule, a $1,000 bid would be unprofitable because it would expose a bond dealer to a 15 percent chance of a $10,000 forfeiture. The bond dealer would have an expected cost of $1,500, which is higher than the bail fee of $1,000. In contrast, a $1,500 bid would expose a bond dealer to a 10 percent chance of a $15,000 forfeiture, which generates the competitive zero-profit equilibrium.

176. This side payment problem could be mitigated to a certain extent by adopting a second-bid auction structure, wherein the bond dealer with the lowest bid also receives a fee equal to his bid, but is forced to risk forfeiting ten times the second lowest bid. This second-bid alternative, at a minimum, would force the defendant to make side payments to two bond dealers in order to induce an artificially low bid.

Second-price auctions have been widely analyzed in the economic theory of auctions and have been used in several market contexts. See, e.g., James D. Dana Jr. & Kathryn E. Spier, Designing a Private Industry: Government Auctions with Endogenous Market Structure, 53 J. Pub. Econ. 127 (1994) (suggesting that government agencies use

Second, while it is plausible to argue that higher bail amounts deter flight by inducing greater *ex ante* monitoring and *ex post* search (indeed, we have estimated downward sloping flight schedules in table 7.8 in appendix 7.B), the low-price auction mechanism tests our faith in the deterrence effect of bail. There is reason to doubt the assumption that lower auction bids would induce higher probabilities of flight.[177] Even without side payments, bond dealers might well have an incentive to substantially decrease their bids for a large class of defendants who, regardless of bail, are relatively likely to appear in court. The possibility that bond auctions would produce low fees for a large class of defendants is not an embarrassment for the proposal, however. For this class of defendants, an auction system would actually produce more equitable results than the current system, which now increases the costs of pretrial release without deterring flight.[178]

Our biggest concern with a private auction for bail is not that bids will be too low but that they will be too high. Bond dealers may have the traditional incentive of auction competitors to collude and fix bids to increase the size of their fees. While competition is the traditional antidote to collusion, we fear that the market structure of cities such as New Haven (and certainly those of smaller towns) is not sufficiently competitive to make collusion impossible.

These visceral concerns about the competitiveness of the bail bond market raises troubling questions about our original results. If bail does not deter flight and bail bond markets are insufficiently competitive, our inference of discrimination may not be valid. Our market test of discrimination should not by itself form the basis for this kind of radical market-based reform.

---

second-bid auctions in allocating production rights); Gabrielle Demange, David Gale & Marilda Sotomayor, Multi-Item Auctions, 94 J. Pol. Econ. 863 (1986) (contending that dynamic second-bid auctions may often result in prices approximating the minimum price equilibrium).

The possibility that defendants may bribe bond dealers is a serious concern, but before rejecting the auction mechanism on this ground we would need to compare the relative susceptibility of police, bail commissioners, prosecutors, and judges to the same type of bribery abuse under the current system.

177. As discussed at note 9 *supra*, several scholars have argued that bail does not deter flight.

178. Moreover, the auction mechanism could deter arbitrarily small fee bids by mandating a minimum forfeiture amount. In the end, the qualified evidence of discrimination that we have presented militates toward reducing judicial discretion in bail setting and instituting a more standardized procedure based on relatively rigid guidelines.

Conclusion

In this chapter, we have used data on the pricing of bond dealers' fees to assess whether judges discriminate on the basis of race or gender in setting bail. Our market test for race discrimination represents an attractive alternative to traditional regressions, which infer disparate racial treatment from unexplained residuals produced by multivariate regression studies. Because the traditional approach requires controlling for all variables that are possibly related to the probability of flight, this approach is often vulnerable to alternative explanations of the regression results based on omitted-variable bias.

Our analysis of bond dealers' pricing behavior eliminates the need to control for all relevant variables because bond dealers are able to observe and price everything about a defendant's flight propensity that the courts observe. Our analysis of the bond rates indicates that bail setting produces lower probabilities of flight among minorities. This is inconsistent with the statutory mandate that bail be set to limit flight probability to a constant maximum level for all bailees.

Our bond rate regressions, by themselves, do not provide credible evidence that courts engage in disparate racial treatment. However, unlike traditional regression analysis, our market test does provide evidence that bail setters in our sample used criteria inconsistent with the statute—criteria that disproportionately burden minority males. Specifically, the statistically significant tendency of bond dealers to charge lower bond rates to minority males shows (1) that courts increase bail for some characteristic unrelated to defendant flight propensity, and (2) that minority male defendants are most likely to have this characteristic.

These inferences provide the two core elements of a traditional disparate impact case: a showing that a criterion has a disparate impact and a showing that that criterion does not further legitimate goals of the decisionmaker.[179] Normally, these two elements require different kinds of evidence, but our rate regression provides evidence of both elements in a single test. The market test represents an important methodological innovation not only because of its unified nature, but also because it is the first regression-based test that remains valid even when there are omitted variables. Our market evidence shifts the grounds of the debate away from the traditional arguments about omitted-variable bias.

179. See, e.g., Wards Cove Packing Co., Inc. v. Atonio, 490 U.S. 642, 656–59 (1989).

Our test, however, is premised on three crucial assumptions, whose validity is difficult to demonstrate. We have shown that the failure of any of these assumptions might give rise to numerous nondiscriminatory explanations for our results. We are most confident of our assumption that the only legitimate criterion for bail setting under the Connecticut bail setting statute at the time our data were collected was to create equal flight probabilities for defendants charged with offenses of equal severity. Although courts might reasonably demand a higher probability of appearance for more serious crimes (indeed, we found strong empirical evidence of this tendency), we showed that minority males are charged significantly lower bond rates than white males even after controlling for offense severity.

The proportionality and representativeness assumptions do not stand on equally strong footing. Our assumption that the bond rates are proportional to the probability of flight could fail for several reasons, which we explored in detail. Most basically, bond markets may not be sufficiently competitive to drive bond fees to equal bond dealers' expected costs. Even though we found significant evidence of competition in the New Haven bond market, bond dealers may have discretion to charge higher fees to defendants who have poor information or lack opportunities to search for lower bids—and these defendants may be disproportionately white. And even if the market fees reflect bond dealers' costs, it is possible that costs unrelated to the probability of disappearance may undermine the correlation of bond rates and flight risk. In the final analysis, however, we are still confident that the probability of flight is a major component of a bond dealer's expected cost and therefore a major determinant of a bond dealer's fee.

We also examined the possibility that the selection process by which defendants either remain in jail or post bond personally distorts our data. If, for example, only low flight-risk minorities can afford bond dealer fees, or if bond dealers infer that wealthier whites who seek bail bonds are higher risks, then the sample of defendants on which we based our results would not be representative of the entire population of defendants who receive bail as a condition of release. While we have argued that disparate rates persist even for bail amounts where sample selection is less likely, the possibility of selection bias remains a concern, further qualifying our confidence in the rate regression.

While we have tried to interpret the rate regression cautiously, we should not overlook the startling nature of our results. We may have uncovered one of the only markets in the United States in which minorities pay lower prices.[180] While price discrimination based on ability to pay can theoretically create favorable pricing for minorities, researchers have never been able to document its existence.[181] The uniqueness of the result itself suggests a nonmarket cause.

A more direct test of discrimination would explicitly measure the likelihood of flight for various types of defendants. If we had direct evidence that minority men had a higher probability of appearance, we could draw stronger inferences of an unjustified disparate impact. In the absence of such data, however, we have relied on a classic economic axiom: in competitive markets, price is a good proxy for expected cost. This insight permits us to evaluate how bond dealers price the risk of flight—the major cost of providing bail bonds.

Our outcome test is an example of reactive institutional analysis, assessing the operation of one institution by evaluating the reactions of another institution.[182] For the secondary reactions to be illuminating, one needs a predictive theory about how the reactive institution will behave. This chapter has strongly relied on the premise that competition forces bond dealers to price the probability of a defendant's flight. While it might seem that this methodology could only be used under the unique circumstances of bail setting, this idea of testing for discrimination by looking at the consequences or outcome of a particular type of decision has already been used in a variety of contexts—from professional sports hiring, to journal editors' deciding to accept a submitted manuscript for publication, to mortgage lending.[183] While chapter 9 discusses more extensively the appropriate (and inappropriate) uses of this analysis, for now imagine how the market reaction in the secondary pricing of securitized assets might be

180. Nonmarket pricing in the form of educational scholarships and certain housing prices depressed by "block busting" or white flight might provide other examples.

181. To the contrary, wealth effects tend to disproportionately disadvantage minorities. See, e.g., David Caplovitz, *The Poor Pay More* (2d ed. 1967); Ayres, *supra* note 15.

182. In the state corporate law context, one of this chapter's authors has explored how the reactions of courts to legislative initiatives (and the reactions of legislatures to common-law decisions) can be used to assess the race-to-the-top and common-law efficiency theories. Ian Ayres, Judging Close Corporations in the Age of Statutes, 70 Wash. U. L.Q. 365 (1992).

183. See, e.g., Anthony H. Pascal & Leonard H. Rapping, The Economics of Racial Discrimination in Organized Baseball, *in Racial Discrimination in Economic Life* 119 (Anthony H. Pascal ed., 1972); Benjamin Zycher & Timothy A. Wolfe, Mortgage Lending, Discrimination, and Taxation by Regulation, *Regulation*, No. 2, 1994, at 61; Ian Ayres & Fredrick E. Vars, Determinants of Citations to Articles in Elite Law Review, 27 J. Legal Stud. 427 (2000).

used to assess discrimination in the initial issuing market.[184] For example, if banks discriminate against minorities in making house or car loans, we might expect that loans would only be made to minorities with lower probabilities of default than average white debtors. If this were true, competition should cause secondary purchasers of securitized "paper" to pay a premium for minority loans.[185] A finding that the secondary market pays more for minority paper may indicate that the primary lenders used lending criteria that have an unjustified and disparate impact on minorities.

In this chapter, we have not attempted to explain why courts might discriminate on the basis of race. This is in part because our results are not evidence of conscious discrimination, only that courts use unjustifiable criteria that disproportionately burden minority males. Racial animus is only one possible example of an unjustified criterion. Moreover, because police, bail commissioners, and judges all set bail, it is difficult to identify the source of the racial disparity. Following Gary Becker's insight that employment discrimination could be caused by customer animus,[186] it is also possible that judicial discrimination is caused by voter animus. If voters disproportionately punish judges when minority defendants flee or engage in pretrial misconduct, then elected judges may raise the size of minority bail to reduce the possibility of "Willie Horton"–style attacks.[187] This voter animus theory would probably demand a more informed voter and a smaller incumbency advantage than we typically observe, but the theory illustrates the variety of possible causes of bail discrimination.[188]

Given the variety of alternative theories that might at least theoretically

184.   For an overview of the world of securitized assets, see, e.g., Steven L. Schwarcz, *Structured Finance: A Guide to the Principles of Asset Securitization* (2d ed. 1993).

185.   Implementing this test, however, may suffer from the same inframarginal problem that has undermined the power of Becker's suggested default test of mortgage discrimination. See *supra* text accompanying note 83. While it may seem intuitively unlikely that the Fannie Mae market (or its automobile counterpart) would pay more for loan packages that include disproportionate numbers of minority loans, we thought it no more likely that we would find evidence that the bail bond market favors minority defendants prior to attempting this study. Our results are all the more surprising because they confound prior intuitions about market preferences.

186.   Becker, *supra* note 45, at 57.

187.   During the 1988 presidential campaign, an independent organization supporting Vice President George Bush used Willie Horton, a black convict, as a symbol of the dangers of the parole system.

188.   Racial animus by decisionmakers might be weakly inferred by testing whether white decisionmakers discriminate more than minority decisionmakers. See chapter 3. We cannot perform this test in our sample, however, because all of the judges in our sample are white.

explain our findings, this study cannot be taken as a definitive demonstration of race discrimination. Several of these alternative explanations, however, are themselves capable of empirical refutation (and where possible we have provided some evidence bearing on their validity). The results of this study can thus be regarded as a first step toward analyzing the bail system using market data. Given the daunting problems with traditional race regressions, we believe that we have outlined a promising new approach to analyzing the bail system. Our market-based approach used in conjunction with traditional methodologies offers the possibility of a more powerful test of discrimination. At the very least, our results lend added empirical support to widespread concerns that the State of Connecticut in setting bail may discriminate on the basis of race. Policymakers should continue to investigate whether the bail setting process unduly disadvantages minority defendants.

Appendix 7A: *Ex Ante* Monitoring and *Ex Post* Search

In the text of this chapter, we developed a simple model of bail pricing that accounted for the effects of both collateral and the bond forfeiture rate. In the model that we develop here, we suppress these aspects of bond pricing (by assuming that $C = 0$ and that $f = 1$)[189] and instead examine the effects of *ex ante* monitoring and *ex post* search. Modeling the effects of monitoring and search allows us to demonstrate (1) that higher bail amounts can reduce the probability of flight, and (2) that monitoring and search costs can potentially undermine the proportionality between the probability of flight and the bond rate.

1. Demonstrating How Monitoring and Search Can Deter Flight

In this revised model, the expected profits (π) of a bond dealer can be expressed as:

$$\pi = R - M - pS - p(1 - p_r)B$$

where:

B = the bail amount;
R = the bail bond fee;

---

189. Incorporating collateral and forfeiture rates effects into this model does not qualitatively change the results. As long as the fraction of bail taken as collateral and the portion of bail that is forfeited remain constant, the proportional relationship between the bond rate and the probability of flight will not be affected.

M = the costs of monitoring the defendant to ensure that she
appears at trial;

p = the probability that the defendant will flee;

S = the costs of searching if the defendant flees; and

p_r = the probability that the defendant will be recaptured if
she flees.

The bond dealer bears the cost of monitoring each defendant plus the cost of search (if a defendant flees) plus the cost of bond forfeiture (if the defendant flees and is not recaptured). The bond dealer must choose how much to monitor and search. We assume that increased monitoring decreases the probability of flight ($\delta p/\delta M < 0$) and that increased search increases the probability of recapture ($\delta p_r/\delta S > 0$), but that there are diminishing returns to each type of expenditure ($\delta^2 p/\delta M^2 < 0$, $\delta^2 p_r/\delta S^2 < 0$). We can derive the profit maximizing amount of monitoring and search by examining the first-order conditions (FOCs) for profit maximization.[190] The FOC for monitoring is:

$$1 = -(\delta p/\delta M)\,[S + (1 - p_r)B]$$

and the FOC for search is:

$$1 = (\delta p_r/\delta S)B.[191]$$

Each of these optimizing conditions can be interpreted to show that it will be profitable for a bond dealer to increase the amount of monitoring and searching until the marginal cost (expressed on the left-hand side of each equation) equals the marginal benefit (expressed on the right-hand side).

Most important, these FOCs imply that, as the bail amount increases,

---

190. The first-order conditions for monitoring and search are derived by taking the derivative of profits with respect to S and M and setting this expression equal to zero.

191. Although expectation of (*ex post*) search reduces the (*ex ante*) probability of flight, bond dealers cannot credibly commit to a level of search until after the defendant flees. Accordingly, the bond dealer chooses the level of search that minimizes $[S + (1 - p_r)B]$. The indirect effect of search on the probability of flight $[(\delta p/\delta p_r)\,(\delta p_r/\delta S)]$ does not affect the bond dealer's choice. Because the level of search is determined after the fact, the bond dealer has already determined that the defendant has disappeared ($p = 1$).

bond dealers will find it in their interest to increase both monitoring and search efforts. Increasing the bail increases the marginal benefit of these activities, and bond dealers will increase their expenditures until the marginal impacts on the probabilities of flight ($\delta p/\delta M$) and recapture ($\delta p_r/\delta S$) are reduced to fulfill the first order conditions. Increased monitoring directly reduces the probability of flight, because the bond dealer keeps closer tabs on the defendant's whereabouts [$\delta p/\delta M < 0$]; increased search in the event of flight indirectly reduces the probability of flight, because defendants know that there is an increased probability that they will be recaptured (and received an enhanced punishment) [$(\delta p/\delta p_r)(\delta p_r/\delta S) < 0$].

2. Investigating the Effects of Monitoring and Search Costs on the Bail Rate

The bail rate in a competitive (zero-profit) equilibrium can be derived by setting the profit equation equal to zero and dividing the equation by B. Solving the resulting expression in terms of r yields:

$$r = p[1 - p_r + (S/B)] + (M/B).$$

The monitoring effect [M/B] and search effect [$-p_r + (S/B)$] on the competitive bond rate create two independent sources of concern because each of these two terms could vary as the bail amount changes. If either one varies, the bond rate might not remain proportional to the probability of flight as we assumed for our discrimination test.

Our initial assumption of proportionality (between r and p) will still hold if we assume both that *ex post* search costs are negligible and that *ex ante* monitoring expenditures are proportional to the amount of bail. The former assumption may well be justified. As an empirical matter, the search effect is not likely to have a large impact on the bail rate; bond dealers have reported that *ex ante* monitoring is a much more important determinant of defendants' appearance than ex post efforts at recapture. The simplifying assumption that $S = 0$ may therefore approximate current dealer practices. The latter assumption is akin to saying that bond dealers spend proportionately more time keeping tabs on defendants as bail amounts increase. This assumption can be expressed algebraically as:

$$M = \beta B.$$

Making these assumptions, we can reexpress the market bail rate as:

$$r = (1 - p_r + \beta)$$

in which r is once again proportional to the probability of flight regardless of bail amount.

Appendix 7B: Estimating Rate Schedules

Estimating the relationship between bail amounts and the bond rates is difficult because both bail amounts and bond rates are dependent on flight risk. In econometric parlance, both the bail amount and the flight risk are "endogenous" variables. In order to obtain an unbiased estimate of the causal relationship running from bail amounts to bond rates (and, subsequently to flight risk), we must statistically control for the endogeneity of bail.

Endogeneity bias, if not controlled for, can result in an underestimate of the deterrence effect of bail. Because bail is based in part on flight factors that are observable to both the court and the bond dealers but not to the researcher, such factors should mitigate any true negative correlation between r and B.[192] Accordingly, we should expect that the endogeneity bias would cause simple ordinary least squares (OLS) regressions to understate the deterrence effect that increases in bail would have on the probability of flight. In mathematical terms, the endogeneity bias would cause us to underestimate $\delta r/\delta B$.

In the analysis below, we control for the endogeneity of bail by looking at the bail amounts set by different judges for similar defendants. If defendants are similarly situated, then interjudge differences in average bail amounts are unrelated to defendants' flight risks. These differences in bail are thus free from the flight risk endogeneity problem, and can therefore be used to identify the relationship between bail amounts (B) and bond rates (r).

This technique for estimating equations that have endogenous variables is called the "instrumental variables" technique. Intuitively, an "instrument" provides a truly exogenous source of variation in the data. By regressing the endogenous variable against a set of instruments, we can

---

192. See Griffiths et al., *supra* note 89, at 585–602. Because the bail amount appears in the denominator of the left-hand side bond rate variable (r = F/B) and as a right-hand side variable (B) in this regression any errors in measuring variables would lead to predictable ratio bias in underestimating the true coefficient on bail. Id. However, since the size of bail is well measured in our data, the possibility of ratio bias is not a substantial concern.

generate an exogenous proxy for the endogenous variable, which, in turn, can be fed into the original regression to obtain unbiased estimates.[193]

Table 7.7 reports the results of an OLS regression of log bail on judge identifiers and defendant and offense characteristics. As the table indicates, judges do in fact tend to set bail at significantly different levels (for random sets of defendants). For example, two of the judges set bail 50.3 and 37.7 percent higher, respectively, than the baseline judges, after controlling for observable defendant and offense characteristics.[194] Therefore dummy variables for judge identification can be used to "instrument" for bail.

To estimate the position of various rate schedules, we estimated equations (7.3) and (7.4) by means of a three-stage least squares regression:[195]

$$\ln B_i = \alpha_b + X_i\beta_b + \epsilon_b, \tag{7.3}$$

$$\ln r_i = \alpha_r + X_i\beta_r + \theta \ln B_i + \epsilon_r. \tag{7.4}$$

Note that the only difference between these equations and equations (7.1) and (7.2) (in section III.C of the chapter) is the inclusion of B_i in the rate equation. We will refer to equation (7.4) as the "rate schedule equation," since it estimates the rate charged for any bail amount.

Assuming that the bond rate is proportional to flight probability, the rate schedule shows how various characteristics affect the propensity of flight.[196] In particular, the rate schedule allows us to test whether a defendant's race or gender affects her propensity to flee.

The parameter θ is the elasticity of rate paid with respect to bail amount. Because under our assumptions the rate paid is proportional to

193. For a rigorous explanation of this technique, see id. at 458–65. The strategy of using interjudge differences in decisionmaking tendencies as instruments has been employed elsewhere. See, e.g., Joel Waldfogel, The Selection Hypothesis and the Relationship between Trial and Plaintiff Victory, 103 J. Pol. Econ. 229 (1995); Orley Ashenfelter & Joel Waldfogel, Bargaining in the Shadow of the Judge: Empirical Tests (Apr. 24, 1993) (unpublished manuscript, on file with authors).

194. These differences are particularly reliable since they are based on large numbers of cases. Judges 3 and 7 were assigned 164 and 184 cases, respectively.

195. Three-stage least squares regression (3SLS) amounts to nothing more than using instrumental variables to help estimate a system of seemingly unrelated regressions (SUR). See note 89 *supra* for a brief discussion of the SUR technique.

196. Under the proportionality assumption, the rate schedule is proportional to the flight schedule such that variables that shift the latter would also shift the former. Shifts in the flight schedule reflect different flight propensities.

Table 7.7   Judge Effects on Bail

	Log Bail Amount	
	Coeff.	t-stat.
Constant	6.551*	25.64
Defendant Characteristics		
BM	0.289*	3.80
HM	0.134	1.23
WF	−0.091	−0.61
BF	0.044	0.41
HF	−0.282	−1.16
Offense Severity		
CLASABF	1.457*	5.69
CLASCDF	0.867*	3.86
CLASUF	0.636*	3.19
CLASABM	−0.203	−0.95
CLASCDM	−0.329	−1.40
Offense Category		
ASLT	0.120	1.30
FTA	−0.081	−0.64
LARC	−0.018	−0.16
DRUG	0.530*	4.12
GUN	0.348*	2.26
DISOR	−0.299*	−2.83
Judge Identifiers		
1	0.051	0.27
2	0.011	0.07
3	0.503*	3.51
4	0.157	0.78
5	0.057	0.34
6	0.076	0.55
7	0.377*	2.66
8	0.083	0.56
9	−0.024	−0.12
10	−0.083	−0.36
11	−0.002	−0.01
R^2	0.410	
N	1,118	

* Significant at the 95 percent level.

Table 7.8 Bail Equation and Rate Schedule (Estimated by 3SLS[a])

	Log Bail Amount		Log Rate Paid (Rate Schedule)	
	Coeff.	t-stat.	Coeff.	t-stat.
Constant	6.673**	29.85	0.900**	2.33
Defendant Characteristics				
Black male	0.352**	4.67	−0.002	−0.06
Hispanic male	0.194*	1.79	−0.046	−1.05
White female	−0.057	−0.38	0.000	0.01
Black female	0.075	0.71	−0.075*	−1.78
Hispanic female	−0.234	−0.96	−0.191**	−1.99
Offense Severity				
Class A or B felony	1.587**	6.23	0.650**	4.85
Class C or D felony	0.926**	4.13	0.448**	4.39
Class U felony	0.683**	3.43	0.291**	3.35
Class A or B misdemeanor	−0.207	−0.97	0.053	0.63
Class C or D misdemeanor	−0.300	−1.28	−0.012	−0.13
Offense Category				
Assault	0.062	0.67	0.078**	2.16
Failure to appear	−0.118	−0.93	−0.004	−0.07
Larceny	−0.043	−0.37	0.061	1.32
Drug	0.519**	4.03	0.239**	4.10
Gun	0.339**	2.20	0.251**	3.97
Disorderly conduct	−0.367**	−3.50	−0.078*	−1.70
Natural log of bail			−0.527**	−9.32
N	1,118		1,118	
R^2	0.387		0.356	

* Significant at the 90 percent level.
** Significant at the 95 percent level.
[a] All right-hand side variables except log bail are treated as exogenous. Judge dummies are used as instruments.

the flight probability, θ is also the elasticity of the flight probability with respect to bail amount.[197]

The results of these regressions appear in table 7.8. As discussed in the text,[198] the rate schedules for minority male defendants are not statistically different from those of white males (and the rate schedules for black and Hispanic females are significantly lower than those of white males). This suggests that minority defendants do not have a higher propensity to flee. Judges wishing to equalize the probabilities of flight would therefore not have to set higher bail amounts for minority men than for white men.

197. The elasticity of an endogenous variable Y with respect to some endogenous variable X is simply the percentage change in Y induced by a change in X divided by the percentage by which X changes. For small changes in X, this is $\delta Y/\delta X \, (X/Y)$, which is equivalently $\delta \ln(Y)/\delta \ln(X)$. From the rate schedule equation in the text, θ is simply $\delta \ln(r)/\delta \ln(B)$ and therefore θ is the elasticity of the bond rate with respect to the bail amount. Additionally, under the proportionality assumption that $r = \alpha p$, the elasticity of the bond rate with respect to the bail amount is the sum of the elasticity of α and the elasticity of flight probability p (both with respect to bail amount B). Since α is constant, its elasticity with respect to B is zero—so the bond rate elasticity equals the flight probability elasticity.

198. See text accompanying notes 112–13 *supra*.

PART III

AFFIRMATIVE ACTION

The preceding chapters are concerned with testing for disparate treatment and disparate impact. In the following chapter we turn our attention to a surprising effect of affirmative action. Instead of testing for disparate treatment, we analyze whether a particular type of government disparate treatment—namely, affirmative action—might improve the competitiveness of government's attempt to buy (procurement) or sell (licenses). While the procompetitive effect of affirmative action is not constitutionally sufficient to justify race-conscious state action, chapter 8 shows that nontraditional methods (game-theoretic auction models) can illuminate policy-relevant effects that have heretofore gone unnoticed.

How Affirmative Action at the FCC Auctions

Decreased the Deficit

IAN AYRES AND PETER CRAMTON

Introduction

Congress first authorized the Federal Communications Commission (FCC) to auction licenses for slices of the radio spectrum in 1993.[1] Since then, FCC auctions have raised nearly $22.8 billion.[2] As part of these auctions, Congress requires the FCC to "ensure that . . . businesses owned by members of minority groups and women are given the opportunity to participate in the provision of spectrum-based services, and, for such purposes, consider the use of tax certificates, bidding preferences, and other

---

1. 47 U.S.C. § 309(j) (Supp. 1995). The FCC previously awarded licenses by lottery or by comparative hearing. See text accompanying notes 179–80 *infra*.

2. See Peter C. Cramton, The PCS Spectrum Auctions: An Early Assessment, 6 J. Econ. & Mgmt. Strategy 431 (1997); Peter C. Cramton & Jesse Schwartz, Collusive Bidding: Lessons from the FCC Spectrum Auctions, 17 J. Reg. Econ. 229–52 (May 2000). The auctioned frequencies were made available to personal communication services (PCS) providers. The FCC auctioned ten nationwide narrowband PCS licenses in July 1994, thirty regional narrowband licenses in October and November 1994, and ninety-nine broadband licenses for major trading areas (MTAs) from December 1994 through March 1995. Id. A second broadband auction for 493 licenses was scheduled for the spring of 1995 but was delayed by litigation over the FCC's bidding preferences for small businesses, women, and minorities. The auction ultimately was rescheduled for December 18, 1995. See note 134 *infra*.

procedures."[3] Relying on this statutory mandate, the FCC has at times granted substantial bidding preferences to firms controlled by women or minorities ("designated bidders").

This chapter focuses on the 1994 "regional narrowband" auction of thirty licenses for use in advanced paging services (which might, for example, both transmit and receive messages).[4] Designated bidders in the regional narrowband auction were allowed to pay for any of the licenses in installments over ten years at a favorable interest rate[5] and, on ten of the thirty narrowband licenses, were granted a 40 percent bidding credit.[6] The combination of these preferences resulted in favored bidders having to pay the government only 50 percent of a winning bid.[7]

The FCC's affirmative action has been criticized as a huge giveaway,[8] but in this chapter we show that the bidding preferences increased the government's revenue by more than 12 percent—an increase in total revenues of nearly $45 million. Although at first blush it seems that allowing designated bidders to pay fifty cents on the dollar would necessarily reduce the government's revenue, we show that subsidizing designated bidders created extra competition in the auctions and induced the established, unsubsidized firms to bid higher.

The unsubsidized firms bid more both because there were fewer licenses for which they could compete (once the substantial designated preferences effectively set aside ten of the thirty licenses) and because they had to compete against the subsidized designated bidders crossing over to bid

3. 47 U.S.C. § 309(j)(4)(D) (Supp. 1995).

4. Because of their narrow bandwidth, however, these licenses are ill suited for cellular or other real-time voice services. Cellular services require broadband (30 MHz) transmission, up to six hundred times wider than the spectrum assigned to narrowband (50 kHz), while narrowband transmission is sufficient for delayed voice or data services. For example, downloading phone messages to a pager for later playback only requires a narrowband license. See Cramton, *supra* note 2, at 432.

5. See notes 51–55 *infra* and accompanying text for a description of the installment subsidy.

6. For example, due to the bidding credit, a designated bidder who won a license with a bid of $10 million would only owe the government $6 million. See text accompanying notes 47–50 *infra* for a detailed description of the specific frequency blocks to which these bidding credits applied.

7. See note to table 8.1 and notes 61–62 *infra* and accompanying text for a calculation of the combined subsidies. If a designated bidder prevailed on one of the twenty licenses to which the 40 percent bidding credit did not apply, the government would receive an estimated 84 percent of the winning bid. Id.

8. See, e.g., Jonathan Rauch, Color TV, *New Republic,* Dec. 19, 1994, at 9.

on licenses that were not set aside. The regional narrowband auction is a vivid example of how subsidized bids by a minority- or female-controlled firm can substantially increase the price that the government receives from a nondesignated firm. Early in the auction, a nondesignated firm (PageMart), attempting to aggregate a national license by bidding for all five regional licenses on a particular frequency block, had succeeded in outbidding all of its nondesignated rivals by offering to pay a total of $76 million.[9] However, a minority-controlled bidder, PCS Development, entered the fray, upping the ante more than a dozen times and forcing PageMart ultimately to bid $93 million to win the licenses. The additional competition from the minority-controlled firm increased the government's revenue by $16 million.[10] The extra revenue the government earned from unsubsidized winning bidders, such as PageMart, more than offset the subsidy to the designated bidders. Far from being a giveaway, affirmative action bidding preferences induced competition that prevented established firms from buying the airwaves at substantial discounts.

Our positive thesis is that affirmative action can enhance bidding competition and thereby increase revenue. Of course, this can only occur where competition among unsubsidized bidders would otherwise fail—for example, if there were a shortage of serious unsubsidized bidders or if bidders were to collude, explicitly or tacitly. Moreover, affirmative action's capacity to enhance competition is not limited to situations where the government is a seller. Indeed, the government buys far more than it sells, and affirmative action bidding preferences may reduce the cost of government acquisitions for the same reasons. When competing against subsidized bidders for government contracts, unsubsidized suppliers may lower their bids to increase their chances of winning the new contract.

More broadly, this analysis reveals a potential profit motive for private affirmative action. Just as competition among unsubsidized bidders may not maximize the auction organizer's revenue, competition among workers in some labor markets may not maximize employer profits. If competition among the strongest job applicants is not sufficient for the employer to extract all the gains of trade from the employment relationship, then em-

9. Even though no other firm raised PageMart's bids for several rounds, the simultaneous auction was designed to remain open until there were no new bids on any of the thirty licenses. See notes 45–46 *infra* and accompanying text. The final results of the auction appear in table 8.3.

10. See text accompanying notes 82–83 *infra*.

ployers may have an incentive to subsidize weaker candidates, thereby inducing stronger applicants to work harder or for a lower wage.[11]

While we show that affirmative action at the FCC's regional narrowband auction decreased the budget deficit (and might plausibly be used to reduce government procurement costs or to increase private profits), we do not argue that this revenue enhancing effect is sufficient to normatively justify race- or gender-conscious decisionmaking. Indeed, using affirmative action to reduce the budget deficit would not satisfy either prong of *Adarand*'s strict scrutiny analysis:[12] raising additional revenues is not a "compelling governmental purpose," and race-conscious means are not "narrowly tailored" to further that goal—race-neutral subsidies of small bidders would also likely be able to enhance the government fisc.

The revenue enhancing effect, however, shows that affirmative action may cost the government less than previously thought. Demonstrating that such measures need not drain the Treasury might be imperative for garnering legislative support. Thus, even if the revenue effect is not constitutionally sufficient to justify affirmative action, it may establish a necessary condition for politically justifying it.

The relevance of showing that affirmative action subsidies do not burden the Treasury was apparent in the debates surrounding the California Civil Rights Initiative to end state-sponsored affirmative action.[13] Proponents of this initiative trumpeted the nonpartisan estimates of the legislative analyst office that the state could save tens of millions of dollars annually by eliminating affirmative action.[14] These estimates assumed that affirmative action increases the state's procurement costs whenever the state rejects a low bid to contract with historically disadvantaged firms.[15]

11. The troubling aspects of describing beneficiaries of affirmative action as "weaker candidates" are discussed *infra* at note 20.

12. Adarand Constructors v. Pena, 515 U.S. 200 (1995) (holding that federal government affirmative action measures must pass strict scrutiny).

13. Several constitutional amendments concerning affirmative action were filed with the California attorney general for potential inclusion on the 1996 ballot. See, e.g., Carl Ingram, Affirmative Action Measures Threaten to Confuse Voters, *L.A. Times,* July 3, 1995, at A3. The California Civil Rights Initiative—banning affirmative action in public employment, education, and contracting—ultimately passed and survived a constitutional and statutory challenge. See Coalition for Economic Equity v. Wilson, 122 F.3d 692 (9th Cir. 1997).

14. William F. Buckley, California's New Fight over Civil Rights, *Fresno Bee,* Jan. 12, 1994, at B7.

15. For example, 16 percent of prime contractors responding to a 1986 survey by the California Construction Industry Research Board reported submitting the lowest bid on a federal project within the previous year but losing that project because of failure to

But the take-home lesson of this chapter is that affirmative action may not cost nearly as much as such crude estimates. In the procurement context, there is anecdotal evidence that affirmative action bidding subsidies have destabilized tacit collusion among unsubsidized bidders and have thereby reduced the average cost of procurement. The all-too-familiar story of a few government suppliers entering inflated, collusive bids can be rewritten by affirmative action initiatives that subsidize new entrants and thereby spur more competition. An unidentified source at the California Department of Transportation reports that affirmative action has forced the price of winning construction bids to approach independent estimates of construction costs.[16]

But in emphasizing the normative relevance of enhanced bidding competition, it is also important to recognize that increased government revenue (or decreased government cost) does not imply that affirmative action subsidies promote efficiency. Indeed, the beneficial impact on the government's revenue from bidding subsidies may often come at a cost of some economic inefficiency—in equilibrium some contracts will be awarded to lower-valuing buyers (or higher-cost producers). While enhancing market competition usually increases efficiency, enhancing bidding competition through affirmative action subsidies simply allows the government to capture more of the gains of trade, often at the cost of some allocative inefficiency.

The potential inefficiencies of not allocating licenses to the highest valuer may, however, be offset by affirmative action's improving the efficiency of either (a) generating government revenue or (b) producing PCS aftermarket services. To the extent that affirmative action increases government revenue, the cost due to an inefficient assignment may be more than offset by the efficiency gain from raising revenues in a nondistortionary way. Governments need revenue, which is normally raised by taxation. Taxation, however, is distortionary. Economists estimate that the welfare loss from increasing taxes is in the range of 17–56 cents per dollar of extra revenue raised.[17] Hence, even if the subsidies cause substantial inefficiencies

---

meet affirmative action goals. These contractors reported that the winning bids were on average 5.3 percent higher than their own low bids. See Charles Oliver, Making California Colorblind? *Investor's Bus. Daily,* Mar. 21, 1995, at A1, A2.

16. Confidential conversation with Ian Ayres (1995).

17. See Charles L. Ballard et al., General Equilibrium Computations of the Marginal Welfare Costs of Taxes in the United States, Am. Econ. Rev., Mar. 1985, at 128; Michael H. Rothkopf & Ronald M. Harstad, Reconciling Efficiency Arguments in Taxation and Public Sector Resource Leasing 1 (RUTCOR Research Report No. 66-90, 1990).

in assignments, the welfare loss may be more than offset by a reduction in distortionary taxes. Governments should care about the revenue consequences of the auction design.

Moreover, as discussed below, particular bidders may value a set of licenses most not because they are most efficient producers of the aftermarket product, but because they are more likely to be able to charge a supracompetitive price. Affirmative action may be effective in enhancing the aftermarket competition. The inefficiency of preferring lower-valuing bidders may be short term if affirmative action promotes a new entry that stimulates subsequent, unsubsidized market competition. Finally, there may be no efficiency loss if lower designated bids simply reflect inability to pay (possibly caused by discrimination in credit markets) rather than less prospective ability to supply paging services.[18]

This chapter is divided into four sections. The first analyzes a series of game-theoretic examples to show how bidding preferences could enhance government revenue. In the second section, we illustrate how this occurred in the FCC's regional narrowband auction. We consider (and reject) alternative hypotheses and we consider whether the experience from subsequent auctions qualifies our results. The third section then identifies a limited set of other contexts where affirmative action might be profitable. Finally, the fourth section explores the normative and legal implications of affirmative action's revenue enhancing effect.

I. Theory

An auction with few bidders can generate selling prices substantially below the highest bidders' valuations. Foreclosure sales, for example, are notorious for this type of competitive failure: if only two bidders show up to bid on a single piece of property, the bidder with the higher valuation will only have to outbid her counterpart—even if the lower bid is only a fraction of the property's true market value.[19] Giving bidding preferences

18. A final normative implication of using affirmative action to enhance competition concerns the legality of affirmative action by private employers under Title VII. That some private employers may institute affirmative action programs solely to increase profits may cause courts to scrutinize private affirmative action more closely, in order to distinguish plans that seek to remedy past discrimination from those motivated solely by a desire to increase profits. See notes 173–76 *infra* and accompanying text.

19. Similarly, in bankruptcy, secured creditors are interested in generating enough income to cover their debt, rather than in maximizing the debtor's residual value. In liquidating or reorganizing debtors, creditors have no incentive to sell corporate assets for

to weak bidders[20] can increase auction revenues by inducing stronger bidders to bid more aggressively. Bidding preferences can enhance both "intragroup" and "intergroup" auction competition: bidding preferences that reduce the quantity available to strong bidders may cause them to bid more aggressively among themselves (intragroup competition); subsidizing weak bidders may allow them to challenge strong bidders (intergroup competition).[21]

Giving bidding preferences to relatively weak bidders, however, is likely to enhance expected revenue only if (1) there is insufficient competition among the highest valuing bidders, and (2) the seller is able to identify stable classes of bidders who are likely to have relatively low valuations. The first of these conditions is likely to be met where there are few bidders relative to the number of goods auctioned. The auction price is determined by the value of the last bidder to drop out, and the reservation price of this last bidder is likely to be lower when fewer bidders participate in an

---

more than the value of their claims. See Philippe Aghion et al., The Economics of Bankruptcy Reform, 8 J.L. Econ. & Org. 523, 525–28 (1992) (discussing obstacles to attainment of full market value for assets auctioned pursuant to a bankruptcy proceeding).

20. A "weak" bidder is a bidder who has a lower expected "reservation price," which is the highest amount that a bidder is willing or able to pay. See Jennifer Gerarda Brown & Ian Ayres, Economic Rationales for Mediation, 80 Va. L. Rev. 323, 331 n.26 (1994). In this chapter, we assume that a bidder knows its own reservation price, but that sellers and other bidders are imperfectly informed and can only form expectations of the bidder's reservation price.

In the regional narrowband auction, affirmative action subsidies were premised on the FCC's belief that firms controlled by women and minorities had a lower ability to pay for licenses, in part because of discrimination in credit markets. Implementation of Section 309(j) of the Communications Act—Competitive Bidding, 9 F.C.C.R. 2941, 2968–71 (1994) (Third Report and Order, PP Docket No. 93-253) [hereinafter Third Report & Order].

Our description of designated firms as relatively weak bidders is intended only to connote that these bidders may have lower expected reservation prices. Making this assumption without sufficient empirical support risks a disabling type of stereotype. As Justice Clarence Thomas has written: "It never ceases to amaze me that the courts are so willing to assume that anything that is predominantly black must be inferior." Missouri v. Jenkins, 515 U.S. 70, 114 (1995) (Thomas, J., concurring). However, the FCC's difficulties in promoting diverse participation and the results of the narrowband auction themselves support the inference that designated bidders had lower reservation prices. See table 8.3.

21. By granting designated bidders a 40 percent subsidy on two frequency blocks, the FCC effectively excluded nondesignated bids, thereby forcing nondesignated bidders to bid more aggressively on the remaining blocks (intragroup competition). See notes 49–50 *infra* and accompanying text. In addition, the FCC fostered intergroup competition by giving designated bidders a 16 percent subsidy on the four other frequency blocks. Id.

Table 8.1   Effect of Excess Bidders on Seller's
            Expected Payoff

Number of Bidders	Expected Percentage of Gains from Trade Accruing to Seller
1	0.0
2	0.0
3	0.0
4	0.0
5	28.5
6	44.4
7	54.5
8	61.5

auction. Conversely, if there are a large number of relatively high-value bidders active in an auction, then competition among these bidders by itself will allow the seller to extract most of the gains from trade, obviating the need for bidding subsidies.[22]

But even having as many as four excess bidders may not be sufficient to extract all of the gains of trade. For example, assume that four widgets are being auctioned to a group of bidders who have reservation prices uniformly distributed between $0 and $100 (and that the seller's reservation price is $0). The percentage of the gains of trade that the seller captures crucially depends on the number of bidders in excess of the number of items being sold. As shown in table 8.1,[23] even with eight bidders the seller

22.   See R. Preston McAfee & John McMillan, Auctions and Bidding, 25 J. Econ. Literature 699, 703 (1987). Formally, if the valuations for a group of high valuers is drawn from the same probability distribution, then the expected auction price will asymptote to the highest bidder valuation as the size of the group becomes arbitrarily large. Id. at 711.

23.   Because the seller's reservation price is $0, the expected gain from trade is simply the expected high value among a certain number of bidders. Statisticians call this value the "first-order statistic." The expected price in an auction of four items is the "fifth-order statistic." To derive table 8.1, we simply calculated the first- through fifth-order statistics for different numbers of bidders (which are well defined for the uniform distribution); we then divided the fifth-order statistic by the sum of the first- through fourth-order statistics and multiplied the result by the number of items being auctioned, which yielded the expected percentage of gains from trade accruing to the seller (as auction revenue). For example, with n = 9 bidders, the expected value of the first- to fifth-order statistics are 0.9, 0.8, 0.7, 0.6, and 0.5. Revenue is equal to $4 \times (0.5) = 2$ and the expected gains from trade are $0.9 + 0.8 + 0.7 + 0.6 = 3$, so the seller's share is $2/3 = 66.7$ percent. For a technical discussion of expected bids, see Jeremy Bulow &

will only capture 61.5 percent of the expected gains from trade. Our analysis shows that subsidizing weak bidders can increase the seller's yield by inducing the highest valuers to bid more.

The second condition for profitably subsidizing weak bidders does not require that sellers know either the bidders' reservation prices or their expected reservation prices. But sellers must be able to estimate the expected difference between the reservation prices of at least two stable groups of bidders in order to identify the weaker group and to calculate the size of the subsidy that might enhance revenue.[24] Sellers would want to distinguish between expected high- and low-value bidders because subsidizing high-value bidders would normally reduce the expected auction revenues.[25]

The narrowband PCS auctions likely satisfied both conditions: an insufficient number of higher-value bidders and a readily identifiable class of weak bidders. Because the demand for, and the supply of, these advanced paging services are unproven, capital markets shied away from financing companies that did not already have significant prior industry ex-

---

John Roberts, The Simple Economics of Optimal Auctions, 97 J. Pol. Econ. 1060, 1086–89 (1989).

24. Game theorists use the term *private valuation* auction to refer to auctions in which each bidder knows her private valuation, but the seller and the other bidders know only the probability distribution from which this valuation is drawn. Private valuation models are usually contrasted with "common valuation" models, in which all bidders have a single, common value for the good being auctioned, but have imperfect information about what this value will turn out to be. See Peter Cramton & Alan Schwartz, Using Auction Theory to Inform Takeover Regulation, 7 J.L. Econ. & Org. 27, 28–29 (1991) (distinguishing between common value and independent private value auctions). While the narrowband auctions certainly have some aspects of a common valuation game, bidders' idiosyncratic entrepreneurial abilities inject a private valuation component that can give rise to a revenue enhancing effect—that is, bidders "derive different surplus from winning." Id. at 29 n.4.

25. Giving bidding subsidies to a bidder who is likely to have a high valuation would *reduce* auction competition and lead to lower expected revenues because such a subsidy would entrench the strong/subsidized bidder and reduce the amount that this bidder would likely have to pay to win the auction.

If the seller believes that bidders' demand for multiple items to be auctioned is sufficiently inelastic, then the seller may want to set aside one or more of the items even if she cannot distinguish between higher- and lower-valuing bidders. Indeed, increased revenue from quantity reduction on the auctions without set-asides might be greater than the reduced revenue that the seller would expect to receive from the set-aside license. Where the seller cannot identify relatively weak bidders—from the seller's perspective all bidders are symmetric *ex ante*—arbitrary preferences will not maximize expected revenue. Under these conditions, the revenue-maximizing multiobject auction is symmetric. See generally Eric Maskin & John Riley, Optimal Multi-Unit Auctions, *in The Economics of Missing Markets, Information, and Games* 312 (Frank Hahn ed., 1989).

perience. This capital market constraint by itself could explain why competition among nonpreferred firms would be insufficient to drive bidding toward the highest bidders' reservation prices. Since designated bidders are disproportionally underrepresented in communications technology markets, the government could reasonably expect that these capital market constraints would bind designated bidders all the more. Thus, the FCC could reasonably conclude that designated bidders would have lower reservation prices. Nonetheless, the government's informational problem was far from trivial: while the government could reasonably expect that designated bidders would be weaker, it is not clear that they knew how much weaker. And knowing the magnitude of the difference in reservation prices between strong and weak bidders is critical to calculating the size of the subsidy necessary to increase expected revenue.

To underscore how difficult it is to meet these two conditions, the reader should keep in mind that few real-world sellers find it worthwhile to subsidize weak bidders to increase their expected revenue.[26] For example, one would think in the context of art auctions that subsidizing museums (which are often thought to have constrained budgets) might be a way to induce private collectors to bid more. But auction houses normally do not subsidize weak bidders. The FCC, however, has several advantages over private sellers.[27] Most important, the FCC can prohibit subsidized bidders from reselling to unsubsidized firms.[28] The resale possibility greatly exacerbates the private seller's informational problem: it is much more difficult to identify a class of weak bidders because a weak bidder may in effect just be purchasing on behalf of the stronger, unsubsidized bidders.

26. Sellers often do establish minimum auction bids (often referred to as the "reserve price") above their own value, which has the effect of subsidizing themselves as a particular type of weak bidder. See note 35 *infra* and accompanying text (discussing effect of seller reserve prices). We revisit this informational problem when we assess the analogous use of affirmative action by private employers. See notes 152–57 *infra* and accompanying text.

27. The Robinson-Patman Act's (rarely enforced) prohibition against price discrimination may deter sellers from subsidizing weak bidders—especially as here when bidders subsequently compete with each other. Robinson-Patman Act, 15 U.S.C. § 13a (1994).

28. The FCC rules do not specifically address the leasing of licenses from a designated bidder to a nondesignated bidder. See Third Report & Order, *supra* note 20, at 66–89. This failure may increase the possibility of a sham designated bidder. However, if the lease was structured in a way that the designated bidder effectively lost control of the license, then presumably the FCC would prohibit the arrangement, since it would amount to a change in control.

By prohibiting (or restricting) resale of the designated bidders' licenses to nondesignated firms, the government by fiat can eliminate the unraveling effects of resales. The FCC's decision to sell more licenses than a profit-maximizing monopolist also increased the chance that affirmative action would raise revenue. If the FCC were only interested in maximizing the auction revenue, it would have only auctioned one license per region because firms bidding for the right to have a monopoly would pay much more than firms bidding for the right to compete with many other firms. While there may have been enough established firms to create a competitive auction for single licenses, the FCC's decision to sell six narrowband licenses in each of the five regions, in addition to the ten nationwide, created the need to bring more bidders to the table to enhance auction competition.

To illustrate how affirmative action can enhance bidding competition, we begin with a series of examples showing how a particular set-aside or bidding credit might increase expected revenue, without addressing whether the seller has adequate information to choose the right subsidy. In section I.D we explain how an imperfectly informed seller could calculate revenue enhancing subsidies.

In the initial series of examples, we assume that four firms are bidding to purchase two licenses and that each bidder is only interested in purchasing a single license.[29] The four bidders have different reservation prices: the two strong bidders ($Strong_1$ and $Strong_2$) are willing to bid up to $110 and $90, respectively, and the two weak bidders ($Weak_1$ and $Weak_2$) are willing to bid up to $60 and $40, respectively.

Using a traditional English (or open ascending) auction, in which the price rises until a single buyer remains, the government should expect to earn slightly more than $120. The two strong bidders only need to slightly outbid the $60 weak bidder in order to win licenses. Even though the strong bidders would have been willing, if needed, to bid more, they have no reason to compete against each other; the supply of licenses at this price is sufficient to satisfy their own demand. Using this auction as a benchmark, we now consider a series of examples in which bidding credits and set-asides generate more than $120 in government revenue by inducing the strong bidders to bid more aggressively.

---

29. We assume that a single license will give the bidder sufficient capacity to serve all of the demand in the geographic area. Alternatively, we might have assumed that the FCC prohibits any firm from owning more than one license in a geographic area.

A. Set-Asides Can Enhance Intragroup Competition among Strong Bidders

Sellers can induce more competition among strong bidders, and therefore increase auction revenues, by reducing the number of items available to the strong bidders. This is accomplished simply by setting aside one of the licenses to be auctioned only among the weak bidders. The set-aside license will be auctioned for just over $40, as $Weak_1$ will bid slightly more than $Weak_2$'s reservation price. After the set-aside, there are no longer enough licenses to satisfy strong-bidder demand, and these bidders accordingly will bid more aggressively for the remaining license. This remaining license will be auctioned for slightly more than $90, as $Strong_1$ will bid slightly more than $Strong_2$'s reservation price, and $30 more than it would bid absent the set-aside. Setting aside one license thus raises the government's expected revenue to slightly more than $130, an increase of $10. Despite increasing government revenue, the set-aside also reduces the efficiency of the license allocation—as one of the licenses ends up in the hands of a $60 valuer instead of a $90 valuer.[30]

B. Bidding Credits Can Create Effective Set-Asides

Like explicit set-asides, bidding credits can enhance government revenues by effectively reducing the quantity available to strong bidders. Consider a bidding credit that allows weak bidders to pay only 50 percent of their winning bids. Because of this 50 percent bidding credit, $Weak_1$ would be willing to bid up to $120. Therefore, $Strong_1$ and $Weak_1$ would each win a license by bidding slightly more than $90 ($Strong_2$'s reservation price).[31] The government revenue from this auction would be approximately $135: $Strong_1$ would pay slightly more than $90, and $Weak_1$ would pay 50 percent of its bid, or slightly more than $45. The bidding credit

---

30. The set-aside correspondingly reduces the *profits* or, in game-theoretic terms, *payoffs* that the strong bidders would earn in the absence of a set-aside. The set-aside reduces the payoffs to the strong bidders by $60. $Strong_1$'s payoff decreases from $50 to $20: without the set-aside, $Strong_1$ pays $60 for a license it values at $110 ($110 − $60 = $50) whereas with the set-aside $Strong_1$ must pay $90 ($110 − $90 = $20). But as emphasized in this chapter's introduction, affirmative action may simultaneously enhance other dimensions of efficiency, making it difficult to "sign" the ultimate efficiency effect.

31. $Weak_2$ would not bid more than $80, because winning at more than this price would force it to pay more than its reservation price of $40.

reduces the quantity available to the strong bidders. Because neither strong bidder will bid up to $Weak_1$'s \$120 subsidized reservation price, they will compete with each other for one license, driving its price to \$90. The bidding credit generates more government revenue than the set-aside because $Weak_1$ must compete with $Strong_1$ rather than $Weak_2$ to win a license. Like the set-aside, the 50 percent bidding credit induces inefficiency by allowing $Weak_1$ to win a license instead of $Strong_2$; nonetheless, the government realizes more revenue than it would either with a traditional English auction or with a set-aside.

C. Bidding Credits Can Create Intergroup Competition

Properly calibrated bidding credits can simultaneously cause strong bidders to bid more aggressively and avoid inefficiency. With a 25 percent credit (rather than the previous 50 percent), $Weak_1$ will bid \$80,[32] and the strong bidders will each win a license by bidding slightly more than this amount. The total auction revenue will be slightly more than \$160. The 25 percent bidding credit induces intergroup competition as weak bidders raise the amounts that strong bidders must pay to win licenses. Absent any bidding preference, the strong bidders pay only \$60 per license, but the bidding credit forces each strong bidder to increase its bid \$20.[33]

D. Affirmative Action Can Increase Expected Revenue When the Government Is Imperfectly Informed about Bidder Valuations

The foregoing examples make clear that bidding preferences can enhance government revenues when the seller knows the reservation prices of the individual bidders. Imputing this knowledge to sellers, however, is unreasonable, not only because they seldom have this information, but also because if they did, knowledgeable sellers would maximize revenue by setting firm-specific reservation prices. For example, if the government knew the reservation prices of the strong firms, it would simply make $Strong_1$ and $Strong_2$ take-it-or-leave-it offers of slightly less than \$110 and \$90, respectively.

32. Bidding more than \$80 would force $Weak_1$ to pay more than its \$60 reservation price if it won a license (\$80 $\times$ (1 − 0.25) = \$60).

33. Giving the weak bidders a 33.33 percent bidding credit would further increase the government's revenue—$Weak_1$ would force strong bidders to bid at least \$90 to win the auction. $Weak_1$ would bid \$90 because \$90 $\times$ (1 − 0.3333) = \$60.

In this section, we show how bidding preferences can enhance revenue even when sellers are imperfectly informed about bidder valuations. When sellers do not know bidders' exact valuations, subsidizing weak bidders may allow a low-value bidder to buy a license for a low price, resulting in reduced revenue and lost efficiency. Nonetheless, the expected benefits of more aggressive bidding by strong bidders may outweigh this cost:

> There is a trade-off. By favoring the low-valuation type of bidders, the
> seller raises the probability of awarding the item to someone other
> than the bidder who values it the most and receiving a relatively low
> payment. The benefit from this policy, however, is that the favoritism
> forces the bidders from the high valuation class to bid higher than they
> otherwise would, driving up the price on average.[34]

The intuition behind this result explains why sellers in an auction sometimes set a reserve price above their actual valuations. With an inflated reserve price, the sellers in effect are subsidizing themselves as bidders. Although an inflated reservation price can induce more aggressive bidding by unsubsidized bidders, sellers also increase the risk that they will sell the item back to themselves.[35]

To see the effect of affirmative action in a specific imperfect information example, consider a seller auctioning a single good between two potential risk-neutral buyers.[36] Assume that the reservation price for the first potential buyer (Strong) is drawn from a uniform probability distribution that is equally likely to take on any value between $100 and $300 million, and that the reservation price for the second potential buyer (Weak) is drawn from a distribution that is equally likely to take on any value between $0 and $100 million. Also assume that the seller's reservation price is known to be $0.

---

34. McAfee & McMillan, *supra* note 22, at 715.

35. Id. at 715 n.19 ("The optimal reserve-price policy . . . can . . . be seen to be a special instance of this optimal discriminatory policy, with the seller discriminating between himself, as an implicit bidder, and the actual bidders."); see also Robert C. Marshall et al., The Private Attorney General Meets Public Contract Law: Procurement Oversight by Protest, 20 Hofstra L. Rev. 1, 8 (1991) ("The . . . reserve . . . force[s] vendors to bid more aggressively to ensure that they exceed the reserve. When a reserve has been optimally set, the potential *ex post* inefficiency from making no award is more than offset, in an expected sense, by the higher surplus generated from more aggressive bidding.").

36. This example is adapted from one found in Bulow & Roberts, *supra* note 23, at 1061. Uniform distribution examples also can be found in Roger B. Myerson, Optimal Auction Design, 6 Math. Operations Res. 58, 59 (1981).

With only these two bidders in a traditional English auction with open ascending bids, Strong will always win, paying an expected price of $50 million (the price where on average Weak would stop bidding). In this simple auction, the weak bidder offers little competition to the strong one. As suggested above, the seller can encourage more aggressive bidding by entering a bid above its own $0 valuation: setting a reserve price of $150 million increases the seller's expected revenue from $50 million to $112.5 million.[37]

A revenue-maximizing seller can do still better. The seller can induce even more bidding competition by subsidizing both itself and the weak bidder. As originally derived by Myerson,[38] the optimal English auction

37. Three-quarters of the time, Strong will bid $150 million; the other quarter of the time, Strong will bid between $100 and $150 million, and the seller will retain the good (($150 × 0.75) + ($0 × 0.25) = $112.5). Setting a reserve price of $100 million would increase the seller's expected revenue from $50 to $100 million, because, under our assumptions, Strong will always be willing to bid at least $100 million. But our example shows that setting a reserve price above both the seller's and Strong's minimum value can be a revenue maximizing strategy. See Bulow & Roberts, *supra* note 23, at 1064–69.

38. See Myerson, *supra* note 36. Myerson employed mechanism design techniques to derive the optimal auction design. He assumes there are *n* bidders and a single good being sold. (The analysis applies to multiple goods, so long as their values are not interdependent.) Bidder *i*'s valuation v_i is known only to *i*, but it is commonly known among bidders that each v_i is drawn independently from the distribution F_i with density f_i.

In the symmetric case, where each valuation is drawn from the same distribution ($F_i = F_j = F$), the seller optimally treats the bidders the same, and the good goes to the bidder with the highest valuation v_i. Moreover, any of the standard auction forms (with the optimal reserve) maximizes revenue for the seller. Myerson shows that the seller optimally awards the good to the bidder with the highest value of $J(v_i) = v_i - [1 - F(v_i)]/f(v_i)$ (assuming J is increasing in v_i and J is positive for the bidder with the highest valuation v_i). See id. at 66. The second term, $[1 - F(v_i)]/f(v_i)$, represents the information rent going to the winning bidder. This is equal to the expected difference between the highest and second highest valuation.

In the asymmetric case, ($F_i \neq F_j$), the seller optimally treats bidders differently. In this case, the seller does not always award the good to the bidder with the highest valuation v_i. Rather, the seller manipulates bidders' incentives to increase competition among the bidders at the auction. More precisely, the seller optimally awards the good to the bidder with the highest value of $J_i(v_i) = v_i - [1 - F(v_i)]/f(v_i)$.

For example, if bidder *i*'s valuation is uniformly distributed between a_i and b_i, then $F_i(v_i) = (v_i - a_i)/(b_1 - a_i)$, $f_i(v_i) = 1/(b_i - a_i)$, and $J_i(v_i) = 2v_i - b_i$. See Bulow & Roberts, *supra* note 23, at 1067. Suppose there are two bidders, Weak and Strong. Weak's maximum valuation, b_w, is less than Strong's maximum valuation, b_s. According to the rule above, the seller awards the good to Weak if $2v_w - b_w > 2v_s - b_s$, or $v_w > v_s - (b_s - b_w)/2$. Since $b_s > b_w$, Weak is favored in the optimal auction because Weak will sometimes win even when Strong values the good more than Weak. In an ascending bid auction, the seller implements this preference by giving similarly situated weak bidders a bidding credit of $(b_s - b_w)/2$.

should take the following form: the seller should set a $150 million reserve price, that is, the minimum acceptable bid, and give Weak a $100 million bidding credit.[39] With the bidding credit, Weak competes more vigorously with Strong because, for example, if Weak's value were $60 million, it would be willing to bid up to $160 million. Even though it is common knowledge that Weak's valuation is lower than Strong's valuation, the seller can use Weak to extract higher bids from Strong. In this revenue-maximizing auction, the seller's expected revenue rises to $120.83 million; the bidding preference for the weak bidder raises the expected revenue by more than $8.3 million.[40]

These enhanced expected revenues come at the expense of allocative efficiency: As before, subsidizing weaker bidders creates the possibility that lower-valuing owners will purchase the good. For example, if Weak's value is $80 million and Strong's value is $170 million, then Weak would win the auction with a bid slightly above $170 million (and would pay only slightly above $70 million).

In general, the size of the bidding that will maximize revenue depends on the seller's beliefs about the strong and weak bidders' relative valuations.[41] But this example has shown that a seller cannot do as well by merely establishing minimum acceptable bids. When a seller has imperfect

39. For an explanation of this form of auction, see Bulow & Roberts, *supra* note 23 at 1069–77.

40. In equilibrium, the payoffs for Strong and Weak average $47.92 million and $4.17 million, respectively. The bidding preference, however, induces inefficiency, because the weaker bidder wins the auction three-sixteenths of the time (and because the reserve price prevents trade one-eighth of the time). Without the bidding preference or the reserve price, Strong always wins and produces average "gains of trade" equaling $200 million. Without the bidding preference but with the $150 million reserve price, the seller inefficiently retains the good 25 percent of the time—the total gains of trade therefore fall to $168.75 million ((300 + 150) / (2 × 0.75) + (0 × 0.25)). With both the $100 million bidding preference and the $150 million reserve price, the average "gains of trade" are $172.92 million (gain from optimal auction = 120.83 + 4.17 + 47.92 = $172.92)—which represents 13.54 percent inefficiency; the gain from an English auction would be $200 million (50 + 0 + 150). See Bulow & Roberts, *supra* note 23, at 1064–69 (discussing construction of an optimal auction). Bidding credits improve efficiency, holding the $150 million reserve price constant, because the auction without the bidding credit completely ignores Weak and instead promotes competition by subsidizing an even weaker bidder (the seller). The bidding credit allows the seller to use Weak to induce Strong to pay more. Trade occurs seven-eighths of the time with the bidding credit, rather than just six-eighths of the time with the optimal reserve price alone.

41. Whenever the valuation distributions have the same shape but different means, sellers seeking to maximize expected auction revenue will subsidize bidders with the lower mean. See McAfee & McMillan, *supra* note 22, at 715.

information about the buyers' values, subsidizing weak bidders may be necessary to maximize the seller's expected returns.

E. Affirmative Action Can Destabilize Tacit Collusion

Fostering additional competition by subsidizing weaker bidders may also destabilize incentives for bidders to collude tacitly. The incentives for tacit collusion are particularly acute where multiple products are being auctioned: rational bidders consider how bidding on one product may affect the price that they will pay on other products—and might accordingly bid less.

To see how tacit collusion occurs, imagine that Sprint and AT&T are competing for two licenses, one in Philadelphia and the other in Boston. To keep things simple, assume that it is commonly known that AT&T has a reservation price of $10 million for each license and that Sprint's reservation prices for the Philadelphia and Boston licenses are $8 and $7 million, respectively. Also assume that without affirmative action, no other bidder would bid more than $2 million for either license.

How much money should the government expect to make from the simultaneous auctioning of these two licenses? If both AT&T and Sprint ignore the impact of their bidding on the other license's price, then the government should earn slightly more than $15 million—as AT&T would outbid Sprint to win both licenses.

Rational bidders, however, will consider how bidding on one license may affect the other license's price. Specifically, AT&T may decide to bid only slightly above $2 million for the Boston license and to refrain from bidding for the Philadelphia license. This strategy would be an implicit offer to Sprint to divide the markets: "We'll let you buy the Philadelphia license cheaply, if you let us buy the Boston license cheaply." Coupled with this implicit invitation comes an implicit threat: if Sprint bids to increase the price of the Boston license, AT&T will retaliate by bidding up the Philadelphia license's price.[42]

If Sprint accepts this implicit offer, AT&T and Sprint will each pur-

---

42. Sprint, rather than AT&T, might just as easily have made the tacit "offer" to collude by initially refraining from bidding on the Boston license. Tacit "offers" and "acceptances" were especially easy to implement in the regional narrowband auction because the licenses for different regions were auctioned simultaneously, allowing any colluder to monitor its counterparty's compliance with the "agreement." Collusive behavior is more difficult to coordinate during sequential auctioning of individual licenses, because there is a stronger incentive for the early auction winner to breach the agreement and to bid in the subsequent auctions.

chase a license for slightly more than $2 million. Both parties have an incentive to abide by this market-division agreement, because they earn higher profits by coordinating their bidding behavior rather than by competing. AT&T does better by buying one license for a low price than by buying two licenses for relatively high prices. Without the tacit market division, AT&T's expected profit would be $5 million (because it would pay $15 million for licenses that it valued at $20 million). Dividing the market, however, increases AT&T's payoff to $8 million (because it buys a $10 million license for only $2 million).[43]

Affirmative action can destabilize this collusive equilibrium. If the government gave weak bidders a 67 percent bidding credit, weak bidders (with $2 million reservation prices) would be willing to bid up to approximately $6 million. Facing subsidized competitors, AT&T would no longer want to divide the market. Tacit collusion would now allow AT&T to realize only a $4 million payoff on the Boston license, while AT&T would earn $5 million by bidding aggressively on both licenses (buying one $10 million license for $8 million and the other for $7 million).

The moral of these reductive economic fables is quite simple: subsidizing weak bidders can enhance a seller's auction revenue by forcing strong bidders to bid more aggressively. Bidding subsidies for weak bidders, far from being "giveaways," can prevent giveaways by forcing relatively strong bidders to bid closer to their reservation prices. Nonetheless, the subsidies often cause inefficiency whenever the good is actually sold to a weak bidder. But this is a cost that revenue-maximizing sellers are willing to bear. Such sellers might consider the windfall that occasionally accrues to a weak bidder as a fee for enhancing the auction competition.

II. Empiricism

A. Describing the Regional Narrowband Licenses and the Auction Rules

The FCC offered thirty licenses for sale in the regional narrowband auction. Six narrowbands of the radio spectrum (Frequency Blocks 1

---

43. The market division also clearly helps Sprint because it would win neither license without the tacit restraint but earns $6 million by cooperating with AT&T (as it pays $2 million for a license that it values at $8 million). Tacit collusion therefore reduces the government's revenue by $11 million (from $15 to $4 million) and creates inefficiency by allowing Sprint to win the Philadelphia license even though its valuation of that license is lower than AT&T's.

through 6) were offered in each of five regions (Northeast, South, Midwest, Central, and West). Thus, each of the thirty licenses authorized transmission on a particular frequency block in a particular region.

Each frequency block was divided so that licensee pagers could both send and receive information. Two of the six licenses in every region (Blocks 1 and 2) were allocated 50 kHz for both incoming and outgoing messages ("50/50 blocks"), while the remaining four licenses (Blocks 3–6) were allocated 50 kHz for incoming transmissions and 12.5 kHz for outgoing transmissions ("50/12 blocks").[44]

The thirty licenses were sold in a simultaneous multiple-round auction, which is similar to a traditional English auction except that, rather than selling each license in sequence, a group of licenses is auctioned simultaneously.[45] In any round a bidder may bid on any of the licenses being offered, and the auction does not close until bidding has ceased on all licenses—that is, until a round goes by in which no one raises the prevailing bid on any license.[46]

The FCC changed the rules governing designated subsidies just before the regional auction. In the July 1994 auction for nationwide licenses, the FCC had granted designated bidders 25 percent bidding credits on three

44.   Licenses of the same bandwidth that cover the same region should be perfect demand substitutes, with two qualifications. First, owning licenses with adjacent bandwidths within a particular region may be particularly valuable because a small guard band that prevents interference between adjacent licenses can be used for transmission by a single owner to increase its effective capacity. See Peter C. Cramton, Money Out of Thin Air, 4 J. Econ. & Mgmt. Strategy 267, 275 (1995). Second, owning licenses in adjacent regions on the same frequency may allow a company to reduce disruption along the geographic border of the two regions. See id.

45.   Some core aspects of the auction form were proposed by auction experts Paul Milgrom and Robert Wilson of Stanford University and Preston McAfee at the University of Texas. See John McMillan, Selling Spectrum Rights, J. Econ. Persp. summer 1994, at 145, 154. The simultaneous, open ascending bid format allowed bidders to switch among licenses. With sequential auctions, bidders must predict future prices when determining current bids. See id. at 153–54. The FCC's choice of the simultaneous, open ascending bid format is an extraordinary example of reliance on economic theory in the absence of empirical data. And the FCC's willingness to innovate probably increased government revenue by millions of dollars. See Cramton, supra note 2, at 435.

46.   Paul Milgrom, Putting Auction Theory to Work: The Simultaneous Ascending Auction, 108 J. Pol. Econ. 245–72 (2000). To ensure that the auction would end within a reasonable time, the FCC imposed several ancillary rules, including minimum bid increments and an activity rule, which reduced a bidder's eligibility to bid in later rounds if it were inactive in early rounds. For details about the auction rules, see Implementation of Section 309(j) of the Communications Act—Competitive Bidding, 9 F.C.C.R. 5532, 5541–53 (1994) (Fifth Report and Order, PP Docket No. 93-253) [hereinafter Fifth Report & Order].

of the ten narrowband licenses.[47] The 25 percent credit, however, proved to be insufficient to allow any designated bidders to win a license, and most designated bidders dropped out after the first round of bidding.[48] The FCC responded by increasing the bidding credit in the regional narrowband auction from 25 percent to 40 percent.[49] The bidding credits could be used on ten of the thirty regional licenses: the five Frequency Block 2 licenses (a 50/50 block) and the five Frequency Block 6 licenses (a 50/12 block). Although the ten licenses subject to the designated bidding credit were not de jure set aside for designated bidders, the credit was large enough to create de facto set-asides.[50] Thus, we refer to these ten licenses on Blocks 2 and 6 as "effectively set aside" or simply "set aside."

The FCC also allowed any designated bidder that qualified as a small business to pay for its license over ten years at an attractive interest rate.[51]

47. Third Report & Order, *supra* note 20, at 2968.

48. Results of the nationwide narrowband auction are located on the Internet at ftp://ftp.fcc.gov/pub/Auctions/PCS/Narrowband/Nationwide/finalbid.txt. Although bidder identities were supposed to be confidential, most designated bidders physically left the auction site early in the bidding. Because it was relatively easy for big, established bidders to identify each other, the FCC made bidder identities public for the second auction.

49. Implementation of Section 309(j) of the Communications Act—Competitive Bidding Narrowband PCS, 10 F.C.C.R. 175, 201 (1994) (Third Memorandum Opinion and Order and Further Notice of Proposed Rulemaking, PP Docket No. 93-253) [hereinafter Third Memorandum & Order]. The FCC also expanded the definition of what constitutes female or minority "control." In the nationwide auction, 50.1 percent equity ownership by women or minorities was required, but in the regional auction, women and minorities could create control groups that owned as little as 25 percent of equity as long as the group owned more than half of the voting stock. Implementation of Section 309(j) of the Communications Act—Competitive Bidding, 9 F.C.C.R. 5306, 5307 (1994) (Order on Reconsideration, PP Docket No. 93-253) [hereinafter Order on Reconsideration]. The relaxed requirements for acquiring designated bidder status made it easier for designated firms to partner with existing paging companies, which solved the second major problem facing designated entity bidders: acquisition of technical knowledge. PCS Development partnered with A-Plus, Arch and USA Mobile; Benbow partnered with Westlink; and Shearing partnered with Adelphia. These partnerships brought essential knowledge in addition to capital to the designated entity firms.

50. See Milgrom, *supra* note 46, at 27. A designated bidder willing to pay $100 million for a license could bid as much as $167 million.

51. The installment plan was available to all "small businesses, including small businesses owned by minorities and/or women, on all regional licenses." Order on Reconsideration, *supra* note 49. The FCC announced the small business installment plan prior to the nationwide auction. See Third Report & Order, *supra* note 20, at 2978–79. After the nationwide auction, the FCC allowed designated bidders that did not qualify as small businesses to pay by installments at an interest rate "equal to the rate for ten-year treasury obligations, plus 2.5 percent." Order on Reconsideration, *supra* note 49.

While nondesignated bidders were required to pay 20 percent of their winning bids within five business days of the auction's close, and the remaining 80 percent within five business days of the licenses' award,[52] the FCC required a winning small designated bidder to pay 10 percent at the auction close and only 10 percent more upon the award of the license.[53] The remaining 80 percent would be financed by the government at the ten-year Treasury Bill rate of 7.5 percent. The designated bidder would only owe interest for the first two years and then would make equal quarterly installments for the next eight years to pay off the remaining interest and principal.[54]

Like the bidding credit, this installment program represented a significant bidding subsidy because designated bidders could not borrow from private lenders on such favorable terms. The size of the subsidy can be calculated by discounting the installment payments to present value using a risk-adjusted interest rate. Finance economists equate the risk-adjusted interest rate with the market rate—in this case, the rate designated bidders would have to pay private lenders. Since private lenders possibly discriminate against designated bidders,[55] the rate they are forced to pay in the market may not represent the true risk of nonpayment.[56]

Determining the appropriate risk adjustment with any kind of preci-

---

In the regional narrowband auction, however, the only serious bidders that qualified as small businesses were also designated bidders (namely, Benbow PCS Ventures, Constant Touch Communication, InstaCheck Systems, PCS Development, and Lisa-Gaye Shearing).

52. The FCC typically awards licenses within three months of the auction's close. See Cramton, *supra* note 2, at 437.

53. Third Report & Order, *supra* note 20, at 2978.

54. Order on Reconsideration, *supra* note 49, at 5307.

55. When considering an installment subsidy for designated bidders, the FCC found that Congress, in passing the Small Business Credit and Business Opportunity Enhancement Act of 1992, Pub. L. No. 102-366 (1992),

> recognized that these funding problems are even more severe for minority and women-owned businesses, who face discrimination in the private lending market. For example, Congress explicitly found that businesses owned by minorities and women have particular difficulties in obtaining capital and that problems encountered by minorities in this regard are "extraordinary." A number of studies also amply support the existence of widespread discrimination against minorities in lending practices.

Fifth Report & Order, *supra* note 46, at 5573.

56. This suggests that the interest rate subsidy benefits the designated bidders more than it costs the government. This would be true if lenders demanded a risk premium of 8 percent even though true nondiversifiable risk would only justify a four-point premium.

sion is extremely difficult. At most, we know that the government was extending credit as a secured lender with a 20 percent equity cushion.[57] If a designated bidder defaulted, the government could foreclose and resell the licenses, but their resale value would be uncertain. Therefore, the government's primary risk as lender is that the licenses may be worth less than 80 percent of the auction price and that the proceeds of subsequent resale would not repay the government's loan. Much of this risk, however, may be diversifiable and therefore does not justify a higher risk premium.[58] In order to estimate crudely the installment subsidy, we assume that the risk-adjusted market rate for designated bidders would have been 12 percent—4.5 percentage points higher than the 7.5 percent ten-year Treasury rate that the government actually charged.[59] We chose 12 percent because it approximates the actual cost of secured financing for two of the narrowband bidders (as well as the cost of funds for broadly similar high technology organizations).[60]

To illuminate the effect of this assumption regarding the size of affirmative action subsidies, figure 8.1 presents estimates of the present value of the installment and of bidding credit subsidies for a range of possible risk-adjusted interest rates. The top line depicts how the installment subsidy alone affects the present value of designated bidders' payments, while the lower line depicts the combined effect of the installment subsidy and the 40 percent bidding credit.[61] At a 12 percent risk-adjusted rate, the present value of the installment payments equals 84.2 percent of the amount financed. This is the proportion of a winning bid that the government would receive if a designated bidder won any of the twenty regional licenses to which only the installment subsidy applied (namely, Frequency Blocks 1,

57. As discussed below, however, the government in the subsequent C-block auction has lacked both the political will and the legal ability to quickly foreclose and reauction licenses on which winning bidders had defaulted. See section II.E of this chapter.

58. The Capital Asset Pricing Model suggests that risk premia should only compensate owners for risk that they cannot avoid by diversification. Richard A. Brealey & Stewart C. Myers, *Principles of Corporate Finance* 161–66 (4th ed. 1991).

59. The ten-year Treasury note rate itself overstates the risk-free rate: Treasury notes pay interest only at maturity, while the auction installment plan requires higher repayment levels in earlier years, when a lower risk-free rate would obtain.

60. At the time of the auction, PageNet, a substantial paging firm, had a bond maturing in 2002 with a yield of 11.75 percent. See Moody's Investor Service, Corporate Bonds (U.S.), Moody's Bond Record, June 1995, at 81. The largest bidder's approximate cost of debt was 12 percent. Telephone interview with Steve Lerner, financial analyst for PCS Development, 15 November 1994.

61. The lower line is simply 60 percent of the upper line.

Fig. 8.1   Present value of installment and bidding credit subsidies

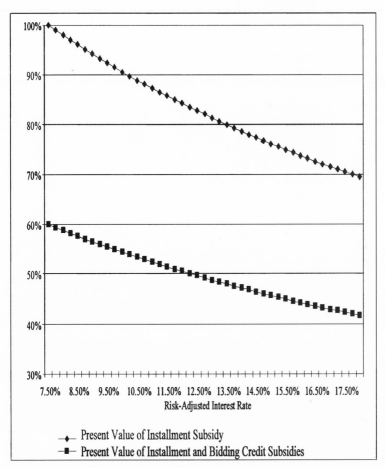

Note: The present value of an installment subsidy for a particular risk-adjusted interest rate was calculated assuming that the government received 20 percent of the nominal bid immediately, 7.5 percent of the nominal bid after both the first and second year, and 8.125 percent of the nominal bid in each of the remaining eight years. This cash flow was then discounted to present value for particular interest rates using the formula: present value of year n cash flow = (year n cash flow)/(1 + risk − adjusted interest rate). The present value of all cash flows was then expressed as a percentage of the nominal bid. The line representing the present value of the installment subsidy and the bidding credit (expressed again as a percentage of the nominal bid) is simply 40 percent of the previous calculation.

Table 8.2   Bidders after Round 12 in Regional Narrowband Auction

Nondesignated Bidders	Designated Bidders
Advanced Wireless Messaging (Advanced Wireless)	Benbow PCS Ventures, Inc. (Benbow)
AirTouch Paging (AirTouch)	Constant Touch Communications, Inc. (Constant)
Ameritech Mobile Services, Inc. (Ameritech)	Insta-Check Systems, Inc. (InstaCheck)
MobileMedia PCS, Inc. (MobileMedia)	PCS Development Corporation (PCSD)
PageMart II, Inc. (PageMart)	Lisa-Gaye (Shearing)
Radiofone Nationwide Paging Service (Radiofone)	
Westlink Licensee Corporation (Westlink)	

3–5). As for the ten set-aside licenses (Blocks 2 and 6), because of the combined effect of the installment subsidy and the 40 percent bidding credit, the government only receives 50.5 percent of the winning bids.[62]

B.   The Impact of Affirmative Action

1.   Comparing the Nationwide and Regional Results

Twenty-eight bidders participated in the regional narrowband auction; by the twelfth round, only the twelve firms listed in table 8.2 remained.[63] Of these twelve, nine won licenses when the auction ended after 105 rounds.

Two aspects of the auction outcome (table 8.3) stand out: (1) four of the six frequency blocks were sold as nationwide aggregates, and (2) eleven of the thirty licenses were sold to designated bidders. Not only did designated bidders win all ten of the "effectively set aside" licenses, but Insta-Check prevailed on the Block 5–South license, even though the 40 percent bidding credit did not apply.

The present value of the government revenue—after taking into account both the bidding credits and installment subsidies—was approxi-

62.   As shown in figure 8.1, if the appropriate risk-adjusted interest rate were 18 percent, the present value of the installment payments would be 69.4 percent and the value with both installment and bidding subsidies would be 41.6 percent.

63.   The installment and bidding credits induced a substantial amount of designated entity interest. Of the twenty-eight bidders who initially took part in the auction, twenty had some kind of designated entity preference and nearly one-half of the upfront payments came from designated entity bidders. See Cramton, *supra* note 2, at 442.

Table 8.3 Final Outcome in Regional Narrowband Auction

Freq Block	Type (kHz)	Winning Bidder by Region					Present Value (in $M) of Winning Bids by Block	$ per MHz-pop	Premium over Nationwide ($)
		Northeast	South	Midwest	Central	West			
1	50/50	PageMart won all regions					92.56	3.67	15.7
2**	50/50	PCS Development* won all regions					76.56	3.06	−4.3
3	50/12	MobileMedia won all regions					53.67	3.40	13.3
4	50/12	Advanced Wireless won all regions					53.62	3.40	13.2
5	50/12	AirTouch	InstaCheck*	Ameritech	AirTouch	AirTouch	49.56	3.14	4.7
6**	50/12	Shearing*	Shearing*	Shearing*	Benbow*	Benbow*	44.78	2.84	−5.4
						Total	370.89	3.26	6.2

* Designated (woman/minority) bidder.
** Designated bidders received a 40 percent bidding credit on Blocks 2 and 6.

mately $371 million. Bidders paid an average of $3.26 per MHz-pop,[64] but as in the earlier nationwide auction, the 50/50 licenses were worth more per MHz-pop than the 50/12 ones.[65] Not surprisingly, after taking into account the bidding credit and the installment subsidy, the cost per MHz-pop of licenses purchased by designated bidders was lower than that of analogous licenses purchased by unsubsidized bidders.

The regional auction did, however, produce one surprising result: the price per MHz-pop was 6.2 percent higher than the price paid by bidders in the nationwide auction that occurred just three months earlier. This increase in the regional narrowband auction represents more than a $21 million increase in government revenue.[66] If the nationwide prices per MHz-pop had been realized in the regional auction, the two 50/50 frequency blocks would have each sold for $80.0 million and the four 50/12 frequency blocks would have sold for $47.3 million, which would have generated a total revenue of $349.3 million. The total revenues in the actual auction, however, were $21.6 million more than this benchmark. PageMart, MobileMedia, and Advanced Wireless paid significantly more for national aggregations than winners paid for identical licenses in the earlier auction. The increased prices in the regional auction are surprising because it is difficult to understand why the winners did not bid more when they participated in the national auction three months earlier.

Indeed, evidence from other auctions suggests that, when similar items are sold in sequence, the later items usually sell less than the earlier items.[67] This "declining price anomaly" has been observed in auctions for wine,

64. "Dollars per MHz-pop" is calculated by dividing the total revenue ($370.9 million) by both the population (252.6 million) and the number of megahertz auctioned (0.45). Population as of April 1, 1990, from FCC, Bidder's Information Package for the Regional Narrowband PCS Auction 3 (1994) (citing Bureau of the Census, U.S. Department of Commerce, Statistical Abstract of the United States: 1993, at 822 [113th ed. 1993]). For a given bandwidth, the "dollars per MHz-pop" measures how much a bidder is willing to pay per potential customer for a MHz license. For example, since Frequency Block 1 had a total width of 0.1 MHz (50 kHz incoming + 50 kHz outgoing = 100 kHz), a $3.67 price per MHz-pop suggests that PageMart was willing to pay approximately 37 cents per potential customer for 50/50 nationwide coverage.

65. In the nationwide narrowband auction, the 50/50 licenses sold for $3.17 per MHz-pop and the 50/12 licenses sold for $3.00 per MHz-pop. Nationwide auction data is located at ftp://ftp.fcc.gov/pub/Auctions/ PCS/Narrowband/Nationwide/finalbid.txt.

66. The actual regional revenues are shown in table 8.3.

67. Orley Ashenfelter, How Auctions Work for Wine and Art, J. Econ. Persp., summer 1989, at 23, 29–30 (describing the price decline anomaly at wine auctions).

timber, cattle, and satellite licenses.[68] Game theory provides three different reasons why we should have expected prices in the regional auction to be lower than in the earlier national auction: risk-averse bidders, marketing advantages, and the difficulty of aggregating regional licenses. First, risk-averse bidders prefer the sure gains of winning today to the uncertain prospects of winning tomorrow. Such bidders, therefore, would be willing to bid more in the first auction than the expected sale price in the later auction.[69] Second, early resolution of uncertainty regarding a firm's spectrum capacity provides a tremendous marketing and development advantage. Being first to market in an unproven industry with substantial network externalities and significant switching costs has enormous value.[70] Third, because the later licenses were regional, a firm wanting to create a national paging system would probably pay a premium to avoid the aggregation difficulties presented by buying five individual regional licenses on a single frequency block.[71]

Based on the above, we would expect prices in the regional auction to be lower than those in the nationwide auction. What, then, explains the $21 million increase in regional prices? We contend that the rise in prices was caused by the FCC's unexpected announcement after the nationwide auction that a substantial increase in the affirmative action subsidy would apply to subsequent auctions. As discussed above,[72] affirmative action can create more bidding competition by enhancing both intergroup and intragroup competition, and it can thereby increase the seller's expected reve-

68.   See R. Preston McAfee & Daniel Vincent, The Declining Price Anomaly, 60 J. Econ. Theory 191, 192 (1993). There are exceptions to declining prices: prices tended to increase in the sequential sale of Israeli cable television licenses. See Neil Gandal, Sequential Auctions of Interdependent Objects: Israeli Cable Television Licenses, 45 J. Indus. Econ. 227–44 (1997). Apparently, firms were willing to pay more for later licenses because of complementarities. Id.

69.   McAfee & Vincent, *supra* note 70, at 193 (noting that "[f]or a risk averse bidder . . . the randomness of utility from the final auction reduces his value and therefore increases the bid he is willing to make in the first period").

70.   Fast resolution of spectrum allocation is so important that designated bidders have even petitioned the FCC to eliminate certain prospective affirmative action subsidies, which were to apply to the second broadband auction, in order to avoid litigation over the subsidies' constitutionality. Text of "Affirmative Action Review" Report to President Clinton Released July 19, 1995, 1995 Daily Lab. Rep. (BNA) No. 139, § 11.1.1 (July 20, 1995).

71.   See text accompanying notes 113–17 *infra* (discussing partial aggregation risk at regional auction).

72.   See text accompanying notes 20–23 *supra*.

nue.[73] The increase in affirmative action is an attractive hypothesis because it alone is a key variable that changed in the interim between the nationwide and regional auctions.[74]

A simple comparison between nationwide and regional prices, however, does not provide very powerful evidence that affirmative action alone effected the price change, because other factors might have caused the regional prices to increase. For example, regional prices may have been higher not because of designated bidder competition, but rather because of the presence of nondesignated bidders with regional strategies. Bidders that only sought regional licenses would not have provided direct bidding pressure in the nationwide auction, but would have been able to bid up the winning prices in the regional auction.[75] However, since three of the four regional frequency blocks not set aside were sold as nationwide aggregations, it is apparent that many of the nondesignated firms that won in the regional auction could have purchased comparable licenses in the nationwide auction at lower prices.[76] Indeed, PageMart, MobileMedia, and Advanced Wireless did participate in the nationwide auction, but dropped out at prices well below those they were willing to pay three months later in the regional auction.[77] Thus, for regional demand adequately to explain

73. For affirmative action to have caused the price increase, however, its existence or magnitude must have been unanticipated. If the increased demand for licenses caused by increased affirmative action in the regional narrowband auction had been anticipated, bidders who sought nationwide aggregates of regional licenses (for example, PageMart, MobileMedia, and Advanced Wireless) would have bid more aggressively in the nationwide auction. Some auction participants might have anticipated that the FCC would enhance the affirmative action subsidies in the subsequent auction after designated bidders exited en masse following the early rounds of the nationwide auction, but we believe that, even if that were the case, they did not anticipate the *extent* of the subsidy increase.

74. After considering affirmative action's effect on revenue, we describe and critique three alternative explanations for the increased revenue—none of which proves satisfactory. See section II.C of this chapter.

75. For an example of how regional demand can enhance bidding competition, see McMillan, *supra* note 45, at 156 n.10.

76. In the nationwide auction, 50/50 licenses sold for an average of $80 million, and 50/12 licenses cost an average of $47.3 million. In the regional auction, the non-set-aside 50/50 aggregations sold for $92.6 million, while the non-set-aside 50/12 aggregations sold for an average of $52.3 million.

77. See Cramton, *supra* note 44, at 296–317. Tables VIIA-D and VIIIA-G give the national auction bids of PageMart (bidder ID 9683), Advanced Wireless (alias American Portable, bidder ID 5403), and Mobile Media (bidder ID 1666). See id. PageMart dropped out of the 50/50 bidding at $79.0 million, but paid $92.6 million in the regional auction; Advanced Wireless dropped out of the 50/12 bidding at $45.9 million,

the increased regional prices, it must be that these firms did not anticipate the higher regional prices.

Another possibility is that bidders paid more in the regional auction because they were capital constrained in the nationwide auction—that is to say, since the nationwide prices exceeded government estimates, it is possible that bidders failed to bring enough capital to the nationwide auction. Under this theory, prices were higher in the regional auction simply because bidders amassed larger war chests. This capital constraint hypothesis, however, is inconsistent with the bidding behavior of some relatively liquid corporations who dropped out of the national auction, yet paid more for a national aggregation in the regional auction. In particular, AirTouch, with equity worth more than $10 billion, had substantial resources at its disposal,[78] and in all likelihood could have bid more in the nationwide auction, but chose not to.

While neither the regional demand nor the capital constraints theories adequately explain the higher prices in the regional auction, we still do not wish to base our affirmative action theory on the simple comparison between the regional and national auctions. In the next subsection, therefore, we provide direct evidence from an analysis of designated and nondesignated bidding behavior in the regional narrowband auction that affirmative action increased government revenue.

2. The Impact of Designated Crossover Bidding

A simultaneous auction is somewhat like a game of musical chairs. The auction continues as long as there are more bidders than items to be auctioned. If three identical goods are being simultaneously auctioned, the price at which the fourth highest valuer drops out determines the price that the top three valuers will pay. For example, consider five bidders (A, B, C, D, and E) who have reservation prices of $50, $40, $30, $20, and $10, respectively. If we held an ascending simultaneous auction with $1 bid increments for three identical chairs, we would expect that bidders A, B, and C would each win a chair for $21. D's willingness to bid $20 creates excess demand at prices less than $21. If D were not present at the auction, E would be the fourth highest valuer, and the three chairs would sell for only $11 each. In this example, then, D's willingness to pay increases the

---

but paid $53.6 million in the regional auction; Mobile Media dropped out of the 50/12 bidding at $44 million, but paid $53.7 in the regional auction.

78. On March 20, 1995, AirTouch's stock was worth $13.5 billion. See http://www.streetnet.com/airtouch.

total auction revenues by $30 (from $33 to $63). Identifying the "marginal excess demand"—that is, the last bidder to drop out—allows us to infer how the presence of certain bidders affected price.[79]

The bidding data from the regional auction provide strong evidence that designated bidders caused the excess demand responsible for increasing government revenues by approximately $45 million. By the twelfth round (of the 105 rounds), when bidders had reached 70 percent of the ultimate price, all of the ultimate nondesignated winners (PageMart, MobileMedia, Advanced Wireless, AirTouch, and Ameritech) held high bids on the licenses that they would ultimately buy,[80] and virtually all other nondesignated bidders had dropped out of the auction.[81] Because the nondesignated bidders that were still eligible held high bids for the licenses they desired by round twelve, they had no incentive to raise prices any more.

The dramatic exit of the excess nondesignated entity demand is illustrated in figure 8.2, which shows the average excess demand for both 50/50 and 50/12 licenses for different auction prices (expressed as a percent of the final price). The step function shows how the excess demand by nondesignated bidders was gradually extinguished as prices rose. When the auction prices had reached 20 percent of their final level, there were two excess nondesignated bidders for each license type in each region. When the prices rose above 30 percent of the final price, excess demand by nondesignated bidders fell from two to one for each license type (50/50 or 50/12). Most important, when prices rose above 70 percent of the final prices, there was no excess demand by nondesignated bidders for any license. Figure 8.2, then, shows that designated bidders were responsible for the last 30 percent of auction revenue for the simple reason that none of the remaining nondesignated bidders had an incentive to increase prices.

All of the excess demand came from designated bidding. The two fre-

79. Milgrom uses a similar analysis to identify the marginal bidders who determined the prices of the first broadband auction. See Milgrom, *supra* note 46, at 45–46.

80. The one exception to this was AirTouch, a nondesignated bidder that held prevailing bids in Frequency Block 5 in the Northeast, South, and West regions but ultimately won licenses for Frequency Block 5 in the Northeast, Central, and West regions. See table 8.3. However, as discussed at notes 85–86 *infra* and accompanying text, *shifting* demand from the South to the Central regional licenses would not increase the auction price.

81. The only nondesignated bidders that were still active, but would not ultimately purchase a license, were Westlink, which made its last new bid in round fifteen, and Radiofone, which made its last new bid in round forty-four.

Fig. 8.2 Excess demand by nondesignated entities

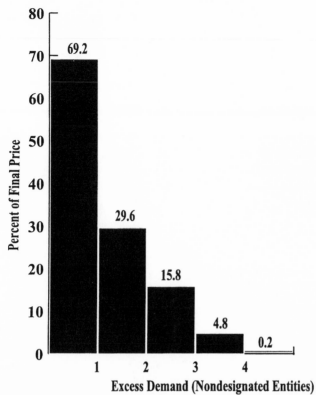

Excess Demand (Nondesignated Entities)

Note: Figure 8.2 is derived as follows. First, for each region and type of license (50/50 and 50/12), the highest bids that each nondesignated bidder placed on the license(s) are identified and sorted in decreasing order. For example, consider the Northeast Block 1 license. The highest bids by the final two nondesignated firms to bid on this 50/50 license were $17.5 million (PageMart) and $12.6 million (McCaw). From these bids, we conclude that at a price of $12.6 million there is excess demand for one Northeast 50/50 license by a nondesignated bidder. This identifies the top step of the excess demand function.

To aggregate the excess demand curves across license type and region, we state the price dimension as the fraction of the final bid. In the case of the Block 1 Northeast 50/50 license, the top step then occurs at 12.6/17.5 = 72 percent. That is, when the price is above 72 percent of the final price, there is no excess demand by nondesignated bidders. For prices below 72 percent of the final price, there is nondesignated excess demand of at least one. These individual demand curves are then aggregated in the usual way.

Figure 8.2 shows the average excess demand where the licenses are weighted by revenue. When only aggregated across regions, but not across license type (50/50 or 50/12), the excess demand curves are nearly identical to the curve in the figure. Excess demand by nondesignated bidders falls to zero (on average) when prices are greater than 70 percent of the final price. Hence, by this measure, 30 percent ($70 million) of the revenue collected in the auction comes from bidding by designated bidders. This number is higher than the $45 million number we determine in Table 8.4, because here the assumption is that by placing a highest bid of $12.6 million, McCaw is expressing a willingness to pay $12.6 million, but no more. In Table 8.4, the alternative assumption applies—that McCaw is willing to bid all the way up to the response to the $12.6 million that caused McCaw to drop out. In fact, since bids increase in a discontinuous fashion, it is impossible to know how high McCaw would be willing to go. The only known fact is that McCaw dropped out after placing a final bid of $12.6 million. The actual increase in revenue caused by the designated firm bidding is probably between the overly conservative figure of $45 million and the overly optimistic figure of $70 million.

quency blocks effectively set aside for designated bidders by the 40 percent bidding credit (Blocks 2 and 6) were insufficient to satisfy the demands of the five designated bidders still in the auction: PCSD, Shearing, Benbow, InstaCheck, and Constant. These designated bidders upped the price of the ten set-aside licenses to the point where it became attractive for them to cross over and bid on the licenses for which only the installment subsidy was available. Specifically, in round eighteen (after Benbow and PCSD had bid up the prices on Frequency Block 2), PCSD crossed over and bid against PageMart for Frequency Block 1 licenses.[82] PCSD hiked the price on the Block 1 licenses thirteen times before dropping out. PageMart ultimately won all the Block 1 licenses, but PCSD's bidding raised the final price on Block 1 licenses by $16.4 million, as shown in table 8.4. PCSD could afford to push the bidding on Block 1, even without the 40 percent bidding credit, because it still would receive the installment subsidy, permitting payment of only 84 percent of a winning bid. Moreover, the 40 percent bidding credits, which effectively set aside the Block 2 licenses, allowed PCSD to cross over and bid against PageMart without fear that PageMart would retaliate by bidding up the price of Block 2 licenses.[83] Our inference that designated crossover bidding caused the price increase is particularly strong because designated bidders were the only firms to bid against PageMart for Block 1 licenses after round twelve.[84]

Although InstaCheck also bid for Block 1 licenses, we attributed the price increase to PCSD's crossover because InstaCheck did not ultimately drop out of the bidding for the licenses not set aside. Instead, at various times in the auction, InstaCheck merely shifted its constant demand for a single license by bidding on a variety of licenses one at a time.[85] Accordingly, InstaCheck's crossover bidding did not represent excess demand but merely shifted demand: InstaCheck never reduced its demand for a license that was not set aside as it ultimately purchased a South license for Fre-

82. *Compare* ftp://ftp.fcc.gov/pubs/Auctions/PCS/Narrowband/Regional/Round_018/s3_18.txt *with* Round_017/s3_17.txt. The competition between Benbow and PCSD had increased the combined price of Frequency Block 2 Northeast and South licenses to $49.94 million by round seventeen, which, even after deducting the 40 percent bidding credit, was still more than PCSD's $29.64 million bid on the same two regional Frequency Block 1 licenses in round eighteen ($29.64 < (49.94 \times 0.6) = 29.97$).

83. See Milgrom, *supra* note 46, at 33.

84. PCSD raised PageMart thirteen times, and Instacheck raised PageMart three times.

85. InstaCheck was active in crossover bidding raises in each of the frequency blocks not set aside: three times in Block 1, four times in Block 3, three times in Block 4, and ten times in Block 5.

quency Block 5. However, PCSD's crossover demand for licenses not set aside was excess in the sense that PCSD reduced its demand (to zero) before the auction's end. As in our earlier example of musical chairs, it is only excess demand that drives up auction prices.[86]

PCSD's crossover bidding was therefore crucial in driving up the ultimate sale price of Block 1 licenses because it was the last bidder to reduce its demand for the licenses that were not set aside. PCSD's crossover bidding on Frequency Block 1 also predictably led to price increases for the other frequencies not set aside (Blocks 3–5). PageMart, facing unexpected competition from PCSD on Block 1 licenses (and unable to retaliate by bidding up prices of Frequency Blocks 2 or 6), responded by repeatedly shifting its demand to Blocks 3–5. As shown in table 8.4, PageMart shifted its demand from the Frequency Block 1 50/50 licenses to the 50/12 licenses in Frequency Blocks 3, 4, and 5, raising the bid on these latter licenses sixty-one times and increasing their final price by $28.5 million.[87] PageMart's shifted demand was the only bidding that raised the prices of the 50/12 licenses in the last sixty rounds of the auction (all other firms bidding on 50/12 licenses during the last sixty rounds ultimately purchased 50/12 licenses),[88] and PageMart only shifted its demand to the 50/12 licenses because of PCSD's crossover bidding on the Frequency Block 1 50/50 licenses.

Table 8.4 shows that the only excess demand for the last $44.9 million of the auction increases came from designated bidders. As shown in the

86. In the earlier example, see text accompanying note 79 *supra,* even though the fourth highest valuer (*D*) controlled the auction price, we would expect to observe "shifted" demand from the ultimate winners (*A, B,* and *C*). For example, if in the middle of the auction *A, B,* and *C* each held a high bid of $15 on one of the chairs, *D* might raise the price of Chair 1 to $16, displacing *A*'s previous high bid. Instead of bidding $17 on Chair 1, *A* might temporarily shift its demand and bid $16 on Chair 2, thereby displacing *B*'s previous high bid. Likewise *B* might shift its demand and bid $16 on Chair 3, displacing *C. C* might in turn raise the price of any one of the chairs to $17. Shifting demand would continue until *D* finally dropped out of the market after bidding its reservation price of $20.

87. From table 8.4, 10.9 + 10.8 + 6.8 = $28.5 million. The "Maximum Region Bids by Nondesignated Bidders Who Ultimately Dropped Out" was calculated by identifying the ultimate winner's response to the highest bid from a nondesignated bidder who ultimately dropped out or reduced the number of licenses that it demanded. A license-by-license breakdown of table 8.4 appears in table 8.5.

88. As shown in table 8.4, designated bidders on two occasions raised the price of non-set-aside 50/12 frequency blocks: Constant once raised the bidding on a Block 3 license (in round seventeen), and PCSD once raised the bidding on a Block 4 license (in round twenty-eight). This crossover bidding by designated bidders who ultimately reduced their demand shows even more directly how affirmative action raised prices.

Table 8.4 Effect of DE Crossover Bidding on Raising Revenues

Nondesignated Bidder Block	Maximum Region Bid by Nondesignated Bidders Who Ultimately Dropped Out ($M)	Number of Subsequent Crossover Raises by Designated Bidders Who Ultimately Dropped Out	Number of Subsequent Raises by Nondesignated Bidders Who Ultimately Dropped Out	Number of Subsequent Raises by PageMart on 50/12s after Designated Crossover Bidding	Final Bid ($M)	Increase in Revenue Caused by Crossover Bidding ($M)
Block 1	76.2	16	0		92.6	16.4
Block 3	42.8	1	0	26	53.7	10.9
Block 4	42.8	1	0	25	53.6	10.8
Block 5	42.8	0	0	10	49.6	6.8
Total	204.6	18	0	61	249.5	44.9

column labeled "Number of Subsequent Raises by Nondesignated Bidders Who Ultimately Dropped Out," none of the bidding that gave rise to the last $45 million in revenue came from nondesignated bidders who ultimately dropped out. Had affirmative action not created excess designated bidder demand, the ultimate winners would not have needed to bid above the levels listed in the "Maximum Region Bids by Nondesignated Bidders Who Ultimately Dropped Out" column.

InstaCheck's purchase of a license not set aside is also strong evidence that designated bidding determined the final price of those licenses.[89] Once excess demand for the set-aside licenses drove up their prices to the point where crossover bidding became attractive, the excess designated demand started setting the prices for licenses both set aside and not set aside. Our theory that excess designated demand determined pricing of licenses not set aside is confirmed by the similarity of the prices paid for the licenses that were set aside (net of the 40 percent bidding credit).[90]

The crossover bidding effect on the regional auction can be summarized as follows:

1. Excess demand by designated bidders for the set-aside frequency blocks (2 and 6) drove PCSD to cross over and bid up the price of Frequency Block 1.

2. Crossover bidding by PCSD on Frequency Block 1 caused PageMart to bid up the price of Frequency Blocks 3, 4, and 5.

3. The auction ended when the bidding on Frequency Block 2 finally extinguished excess designated demand, allowing PCSD to create a national aggregation of regional licenses on Frequency Block 2 so that it no longer needed to cross over and bid on Frequency Block 1.

89. See table 8.3; see also Milgrom, *supra* note 46, at 30 ("The fact that a minority-owned bidder was able to acquire a license for which no discount was offered indicates that there was excess demand for the reserved licenses."). If excess nondesignated demand had been determinative in pricing the non-set-aside licenses, designated bidders would have been able to buy set-aside licenses more cheaply than licenses that had not been set aside.

90. The prices of the set-aside bands net of the 40 percent bidding credit were 1.7 percent higher than those of the nondesignated bands and represented the minimum bid increment by which the nondesignated bidders needed to exceed the designated bidders. Net revenue for the designated band/MHz = $(90.9 + 53.2)/(0.1 + 0.0625)$ = $887/MHz. Net revenue for the nondesignated band/MHz = $(92.6 + 53.7 + 53.6 + 50.8)/(0.1 + (3 \times 0.0625))$ = $872/MHz. Comparing the designated and nondesignated bands: $(\$887 - \$872)/\$872 = 1.7$ percent. The price-setting effect of the excess designated demand does not mean that designated bidders were not weaker bidders. Indeed, the installment subsidy by itself was substantial, reducing the present value of the designated bidders' payments to 84 percent of these net bid.

By round 104, the bids were high enough to squelch the excess designated demand and, therefore, the impetus for crossover bidding, but only after this crossover bidding had increased the government's revenues by approximately $45 million—or 12 percent of the government's total auction revenue. In short, PCSD's crossover bidding, and the shifted bidding it inspired, made the government a substantial sum of money.

3. The Impact of the Set-Aside Licenses

The preceding subsection demonstrated how crossover designated bidding on Frequency Blocks 1 and 3–5 increased auction revenue, but it did not discuss how affirmative action affected the price on the frequency blocks that were effectively set aside by the 40 percent bidding credit. To analyze these de facto set-asides, we need to estimate not only the effect of the set-asides on the prices designated bidders ultimately paid for Frequency Blocks 2 and 6, but also how the reduced supply affected the prices nondesignated bidders ultimately paid for the frequencies not set aside.

One might initially suspect that affirmative action would have decreased the auction revenues for the set-aside licenses because the 40 percent bidding credits effectively precluded nondesignated bidder competition. But, in the absence of affirmative action, allowing the excluded nondesignated bidders to compete for the set-aside licenses would not have increased the winning bids for these licenses. Table 8.4 shows that the final excess demand by nondesignated firms was extinguished when the bidding for the 50/50 block went above $76.2 million and the bidding for the 50/12 blocks went beyond $42.8 million. Allowing these excluded nondesignated bidders to compete for the set-aside licenses would not have raised the price of set-aside licenses for the simple reason that, even after deducting the bidding credit and installment subsidy, the set-aside frequency blocks sold for more (Block 2 for $76.6 million and Block 6 for $44.8 million) than the excluded nondesignated bidders were willing to pay. On these facts, it does not appear that setting aside Frequency Blocks 2 and 6 reduced their equilibrium price.

The 40 percent bidding credit acted as a safety net to ensure a minimum amount of designated entity participation, but in the end this safety net was not needed. The designated demand was sufficient to compete away virtually all of this bidding credit—as the nominal prices on Blocks 2 and 6 were approximately 40 percent higher than on their non-set-aside counterparts. Indeed, the final auction bids superficially suggest that the installment subsidy did all the work—meaning that if only the installment credit had been granted, designated bidders would have still been strong enough to win eleven licenses and would still have pushed the bidding of the nondesignated firms to the same level.

Yet this superficial analysis ignores how the "safety net insurance" of the 40 percent bidding credit may have induced designated entities (and their passive nondesignated partners) to form and prepare for the auction. Knowing that there were at least ten licenses effectively set aside may have induced many designated firms to undertake the fixed costs to organize, investigate, and finance auction participation. Having incurred these fixed costs, the designated firms created enough demand that they bid away virtually all of the 40 percent bidding credit, but the bidding credit may have played an important role in encouraging the firms to incur these costs.[91]

There is an important lesson here. The government can offer very substantial bidding credits to ensure minimal minority or female participation often without increasing the cost of the subsidy.[92] Guaranteeing a minimum amount of participation may induce stronger designated firms to form so that in the end the government need not pay off on the guarantee.[93]

In sum, the bidding data suggest that the 40 percent bidding credit did not reduce the price of the effectively set-aside licenses and, if anything, this large credit, by providing a type of insurance, may have induced stronger designated demand to form. The designated demand was so strong that even after taking account of both the bidding credit and the installment subsidy, the designated firms paid more for the set-aside blocks than the nondesignated firms were willing to bid. Since affirmative action did not reduce the government's revenue on the set-aside licenses, the evidence that crossover designated entity bidding raised the price of the other licenses by $45 million therefore constitutes our combined estimate of the revenue enhancing impact of affirmative action.[94]

---

91. In section II.C.3 we consider whether the 40 percent bidding credit deterred nondesignated firms from bidding.

92. This analysis is extended in Ian Ayres, Narrow Tailoring, 43 UCLA L. Rev. 1781 (1996).

93. If the designated entities had not formed, the final bids on the block not set aside would almost surely have been lower. Although table 8.4 estimated that without crossover bidding the twenty non-set-aside licenses would have sold for $204.6 million—the price where excess nondesignated demand stopped pushing up the bidding—if 50 percent more licenses were offered to nondesignated firms, then the prices on all the licenses that were not set aside would undoubtedly have been lower. Rather than the twenty-first highest valuer determining license prices, the thirty-first highest valuer would have determined the final price.

94. One may be tempted to reduce the revenue increase by the effect the higher revenue has on tax receipts. For example, the Congressional Budget Office routinely ap-

4. Robustness of the Revenue Enhancement Estimate

Our conclusion that affirmative action raised the government's revenue by $45 million is, however, contingent on our discount rate assumption. If the appropriate risk-adjusted interest rate to use for discounting the future promised payments of the designated bidders is greater than our assumed 12 percent rate, then the present value of the amounts to be received on the licenses won by designated bidders would be smaller and could, at least on these licenses, produce lower revenues than nondesignated bidders might have been willing to spend.

Indeed, for interest rates just slightly higher (above 12.15 percent), the present value of future designated bidder payments on Block 2 would be smaller than the $76.2 that nondesignated bidders were willing to pay on the identical Block 1 50/50 licenses. Therefore, to estimate the net impact of affirmative action on revenue for higher interest rates, it is necessary to subtract the amounts lost on the licenses won by designated bidders (relative to the amounts that nondesignated bidders would have been willing to pay) from the amounts gained on the licenses won by nondesignated bidders (as detailed above in table 8.4). This subsection examines the extent to which our finding of a revenue enhancement effect is robust to assuming a higher risk-adjusted interest rate.[95]

---

plies an offset of 25 percent, which is the average marginal corporate tax rate. See Congressional Budget Office, *Budget Estimates: Current Practices and Alternative Approaches* 8–9 (1995). (The 25 percent offset is specifically mentioned in Emil M. Sunley & Randall D. Weiss, The Revenue Estimating Process, Tax Notes, June 10, 1991, at 1302.) This would be the right thing to do if the larger amounts paid by firms reduced corporate taxes by 25 percent of the extra revenue. However, according to David P. Gamble, vice president of PageNet, "The amount paid to the government does not change our tax position at all." Telephone interview with David P. Gamble (Feb. 9, 1996). Because of the enormous outlays in building a paging network, the paging companies rarely, if ever, show a profit that would be taxed. PageNet, the largest and most established paging company in the United States, has never paid corporate income tax. Hence, in the paging business the appropriate offset for lost corporate taxes should be much less than 25 percent.

95.   The FCC's experience of defaults on licenses won in the C-block auction (discussed in section II.E of this chapter) make it particularly appropriate to assess whether assuming a higher discount rate undermines our results. However, it should be stressed that the C-block installment plan was substantially riskier for the government lender than the regional narrowband installment play. The winning bidders only had to pay 10 percent down (as opposed to 20 percent) and were allowed to make interest-only payments for the first six years (as opposed to the first two years). Thus it is appropriate to assume a smaller risk premium for the narrowband installment plan. See Cramton, *supra* note 2 (assuming a 10 percent risk premium instead of the 4.5 percent premium used in our primary estimates).

We find that the auction continues to have a revenue enhancing effect for substantially higher discount rates. If the appropriate risk-adjusted interest rate were 18 percent (instead of 12 percent), the affirmative action would have caused losses of over 18 million on the Block 2 and 6 licenses, but still would have produced a net revenue enhancement of $24.7 million (more than a 7 percent increase in revenue).

Indeed, we find that the auction would have a revenue enhancement effect for any discount rate up to 28.8 percent. At this rate, the present value of a dollar bid with the installment subsidy would be only 53.12 cents, and the present value of the installment and bidding credit combined would be a 68.13 percent credit. Thus, for truly substantial increases in the interest rate (more than double our initial assumption) we still find a modest revenue enhancement effect.

As an alternative robustness check, we analyzed the revenue enhancing effects of affirmative action using the amounts paid in the nationwide auction as the benchmark for what nondesignated bidders would have been willing to pay. The nationwide prices per MHz-pop imply a $80 million price for the 50/50 licenses and a $47.3 million price for the 50/12 licenses.[96] These nationwide benchmarks are slightly higher than amounts to which the nondesignated excess demand was driven from the regional narrowband auction ($76.2 and $42.8 million dollars for the 50/50 and 50/12 licenses, respectively, as shown in table 8.4). Therefore, calculating the revenue enhancement effect assuming that nondesignated bidders would have been willing to pay the nationwide prices will predictably produce more conservative estimates.

Using the nationwide price benchmarks (and returning to our 12 percent discount rate assumption), however, we still estimate that affirmative action increased the government revenue by $21.6 million. Moreover, this finding of a revenue enhancement is robust to any discount rate up to 17.6 percent.

We ultimately will argue that the central normative insight of this chapter is that affirmative action is not as costly to the government fisc as is commonly assumed. Thus, it is not essential for affirmative action actually to enhance revenues. But this section shows that our estimates of a revenue enhancing effect are robust to alternative assumptions about the appropriate risk-adjusted interested rate and to alternative assumptions about the demand of excess nondesignated bidders.

96. See *supra* note 76.

C. Alternative Hypotheses

Before accepting our enhancement estimate, however, we consider three alternative hypotheses that might explain the auction's outcome. Our estimate is based on a crucial assumption that, in the absence of affirmative action, no bidder would have bid above the final price where the excess nondesignated bidders dropped out of the auction. This assumption, however, might fail for three reasons:

1. *Nondesignated Bidders Hid in the Grass:* The reservation prices of the nondesignated bidders that dropped out may have been higher than their observed highest bids, so that in the absence of affirmative action, these nondesignated bidders may have forced up the bidding.

2. *Designated Bidders Would Have Bid Anyway:* In the absence of affirmative action, the winning designated bidders may still have bid more than the prices at which the nondesignated bidders dropped out.

3. *Affirmative Action Chilled Nondesignated Bidder Participation:* In the absence of affirmative action, the reservation prices of the non= designated bidders that did not participate may have been increased.

If any of these explanations are true, then our estimate of revenue enhancement would be inflated because our benchmark of what the winning prices would be in the absence of affirmative action would be too low.

Before considering each of these alternative hypotheses, it is important to emphasize that our $45 million estimate does not depend on the earlier comparison with the nationwide auction. As suggested above, even though unexpected regional demand or capital constraints might explain why the regional prices were higher than the nationwide prices, these theories do not refute the evidence that all the excess demand responsible for the last $45 million of bidding came from designated bidders. Our benchmark, the price at which nondesignated bidders dropped out of the auction, already takes into account the possibility that these bidders had unexpected regional demand[97] or were less capital con-

97. Only four nondesignated firms—AirTouch, Ameritech, Radiofone, and Westlink—showed any regional demand. Our $45 million estimate already takes into account the pressure that Radiofone and Westlink exerted on the bidding by setting the pre-cross-over designated bidding benchmark at the prevailing prices when these firms dropped out of the bidding. And because the demand of AirTouch and Ameritech was

strained.[98] We now, however, consider the three reasons listed above why our excess demand benchmark may have understated the prices that would have prevailed in the absence of affirmative action.

1. Hiding in the Grass

Recall that PCSD crossed over to bid on licenses that had not been set aside when the set-asides proved insufficient to satisfy its demand. If PCSD had not provided the excess demand, it is possible that a nondesignated bidder would have stepped in at the lower prices and created excess demand by bidding on more licenses. If this were true, the excess demand of nondesignated bidders would have been greater than we observed in the auction bidding; one or more of the nondesignated bidders would have been "hiding in the grass"—bidding on fewer licenses than it actually preferred to buy at a given price. If nondesignated bidders were hiding in the grass, then our inference that crossover designated bidding caused the $45 million increase would be overstated. In the absence of affirmative action, some of the nondesignated bidders may have bid on a greater number of licenses and driven the prices at least part of the way toward those achieved through crossover bidding.

Hiding in the grass strategies usually assume that rivals have limited capital budgets: hiding in the grass in early rounds may let a bidder buy a license more cheaply if its rivals commit too much of their limited budgets to other licenses and thereby lose the ability to bid as much against the hidden demand when the "snake" surfaces by bidding in later rounds.[99] For example, consider an auction in which a forthright bidder has a limited budget of $100 million and early in the auction holds high bids for three licenses at $20 million per license. Under these assumptions, a snake bidder might delay revealing its interest in one of these licenses—even if its reservation price is $30 million. By hiding in the grass for a number of rounds, the snake may induce the forthright bidder to commit more than $70 million in bids on the other two licenses; the snake can then enter the bidding

---

ultimately satisfied, the regional demand of these bidders was not the excess demand that caused the last $45 million in bidding.

98. Even if limited capital constrained prices in the nationwide auction, bidders in the regional auction would not have used their increased liquidity unless necessary. Our previous analysis of regional bidding indicates that prices were not increased by competition among large, liquid nondesignated bidders in the last rounds of the auction; instead, PCSD's subsidized crossover bidding drove prices up.

99. There is some evidence that GTE employed this strategy in the initial rounds of the broadband auction. See Milgrom, *supra* note 46, at 47.

knowing that it can outbid the incumbent. Hiding in the grass is a rational strategy when a rival faces a firm budget constraint, and higher bids on one license by the rival necessarily reduce its ability to bid on other licenses.

The FCC designed the auction eligibility rules to discourage hiding in the grass. To maintain eligibility in the first stage of the auction (which the FCC ended in round twenty), each bidder needed to remain "active," by holding or raising the prevailing bid, on at least one-third of the bandwidth it ultimately sought to buy.[100] In the second stage (which the FCC ended in round seventy-three), each bidder needed to remain active on two-thirds of the bandwidth it ultimately sought to buy.[101] By round twelve, nearly all of the excess nondesignated bidder eligibility came from ultimate license winners.[102] These eligible nondesignated bidders represent the only potential sources of unobserved excess demand.

The observed bidding behavior of these eligible nondesignated bidders, however, was not consistent with a hiding in the grass strategy. A snake holds back in early rounds, intending to increase demand in later rounds. But no bidder increased its demand for licenses after round twelve.[103] To the contrary, as prices rose, bidders reduced demand.[104] For example, MobileMedia began by demanding three nationwide aggregations, and PageMart demanded two. After round one, MobileMedia reduced its demand to two nationwide aggregations, and after round six, further reduced it to one band. By the seventh round, PageMart had also cut its demand to a single nationwide aggregation.[105]

100. See note 46 *supra*.

101. Id.

102. The only other bidders who remained eligible were Constant, Radiofone, and Westlink. See table 8.2.

103. The only exception is PageMart's bidding for multiple 50/12 licenses, as in rounds seventy-two and seventy-four. This behavior, however, was not hiding in the grass: before round seventy-three, PageMart tested multiple bidders in a single round, which was consistent with its behavior in the nationwide auction. After round seventy-three, Stage 3's heightened activity rules required multiple license bidding—PageMart needed to bid on two 50/12 licenses to retain the option of later bidding on a single 50/50 license.

104. The early rounds of the auction were characterized by aggressive, jump bidding to stake out large claims. See Milgrom, *supra* note 46, at 32.

105. These reductions in demand are consistent with the behavior of these firms in the nationwide auction, where no bidder increased demand after the first few rounds of bidding. Even if the crossover designated bidding ultimately outstripped the amounts that possible snake bidders were willing to pay, snake bidders should have emerged before the bids went above their reservation price, hoping to bid just as the designated bidders were dropping out. However, these interim increases in nondesignated demand never materialized.

That individual nationwide bidders controlled three of the four non-set-aside frequency blocks by round twelve makes us particularly confident that hiding in the grass would not have been a rational strategy. As discussed below,[106] bidders that hold the prevailing bid for a national aggregation are willing to pay a premium in order to retain the aggregation. Breaking up a bidder's national aggregation can expose the bidder to significant losses if it must buy a subset of the regional licenses; thus, any snake that waited until later rounds to show its demand would confront an opponent whose fear of suffering significant losses would bolster its willingness to compete. Hiding in the grass appears irrational as it creates more hardened national rivals that need to defend their aggregations.[107]

Not only would it be unprofitable to hide in the grass in hopes of outbidding an entrenched nationwide bidder, but the strategy would also be unlikely to provide an advantage against a rival bidding on only a single license. The strategic rationale for hiding in the grass—that the competitor may commit too much of its budget to another license—does not apply to single license bidders. Excluding nationwide and single license bidders as potential targets of a hiding in the grass strategy eliminates virtually all nondesignated bidders. While it is impossible to prove that in the absence of crossover bidding additional nondesignated demand would not have surfaced, the observed bidding behavior, as well as partial aggregation risk, strongly discounts this hypothesis as a plausible reason to question our excess demand benchmark.

2.   The Designated Bidders Would Have Bid Anyway

Our excess demand benchmark might also fail if designated bidders (or their passive nondesignated partners) still would have raised prices without affirmative action. Our $45 million estimate implicitly assumes that, without affirmative action, no bidder would have increased the price beyond the point at which the excess nondesignated bidders dropped out. But if the designated bidders or their passive nondesignated partners would have bid up the price even without affirmative action, then all price increases could not be attributed to the presence of affirmative action.

We think it unlikely that either the designated bidders or their passive

---

106.   See notes 113–17 *infra* and accompanying text.

107.   Likewise, national aggregate bidders become more vulnerable to retaliation as the amounts at stake increase, and they therefore are much more likely to test the waters by revealing their increased demand before they commit to defending their aggregations. The high cost of partial aggregation suggests that the national aggregate bidders would not have chosen to hide in the grass and risk retaliation.

partners would have enhanced competition in the absence of affirmative action. None of the designated bidders or their partners appears to have had the resources to bid successfully without affirmative action—indeed, none of these firms was a serious contender in the earlier nationwide auction. The installment payment subsidy was especially important in inducing the designated bids. Without government financing, designated bidders would have needed five times as much liquid capital to pay for the licenses.

Even if designated bidders would have been willing to pay the same present value in the absence of affirmative action, the government revenue would still have been much less because of the interest rate subsidy increasing the nominal designated bids and forcing nondesignated firms to pay 16 percent more. Table 8.3 estimated that in present value terms designated entities paid $76.7 and $44.8 million, respectively, for the set-aside 50/50 and 50/12 blocks.[108] Even if we made an assumption more unfavorable to our thesis—that in the absence of affirmative action, there would be sufficient designated demand to buy all six blocks at these prices—we still find that affirmative action would have increased the auction price by more than $38 million.[109] But given our strong belief that designated bidders would not have been willing to bid as much (or at all) in the absence of the 80 percent government financing,[110] we are also confident in rejecting this criticism of our excess demand benchmark.

3. Affirmative Action Might Have Chilled Nondesignated Bidder Participation

Finally, it is possible that affirmative action deterred some nondesignated bidders from participating in the regional auction. Given the effective set-aside of Blocks 2 and 6, some nondesignated bidders may have calculated that it was not worth the fixed costs of preparing for an auction—including the substantial expense of amassing a war chest to pay quickly for any purchased licenses.

This theory would undercut our excess demand benchmark, because, in the absence of affirmative action, these additional nondesignated bidders

---

108. See table 8.3.

109. If, in the absence of affirmative action, designated demand pushed up the price that the designated winners were willing to pay with affirmative action, then the six blocks would have sold for $332.4 million—(76.6 × 2) + (44.8 × 4)—which is $38.5 million less than the auction with affirmative action produced.

110. See text accompanying notes 54–56 *supra*.

may have driven up the prices beyond the amounts at which the participating nondesignated bidders dropped out. This theory seriously qualifies our reliance on the excess demand methodology. We note, however, that there were no conspicuous "no shows" at the regional auction. All of the nationwide bidders that could legally purchase additional licenses made substantial up-front payments and then actively bid in the regional auction.[111] This is not surprising: The nationwide auction bidders would have incurred most of the fixed costs necessary to participate in the regional auction. And as noted earlier, even if we assume that the nondesignated bidders would have been willing to pay the nationwide prices, we still find a revenue enhancement effect of $21.6 million. Thus, while we cannot guarantee that without affirmative action other nondesignated bidders would not have entered to provide additional competition (or that those who did bid might have been willing to bid more), no direct evidence of deterred participation exists.[112]

D. Strategic Perversities: Bidding Above Atomistic Reservation Prices

The preceding analysis assumed that bidders' reservation prices for particular licenses were independent of who won other licenses. In this section, we show how simultaneously auctioning multiple licenses might lead bidders to pay more for a license than they would pay if the license were offered in isolation.

---

111. Pagenet could not purchase additional licenses because the FCC prohibits firms from owning more than three licenses.

112. While the text has focused primarily on the possibility that affirmative action might have deterred nondesignated bidders from incurring fixed costs of participation, it is also possible that affirmative action might have deterred nondesignated bidders from incurring nonfixed costs, such as investigating the value of licenses (as much as they would have in the absence of affirmative action). Spending less on such investigations might then exacerbate the "winner's curse" (to the extent that the auction had a common value element, see note 24 *supra*) and consequently reduce the reservation prices of even those nondesignated bidders that participated in the auction. See Cramton, *supra* note 44, at 279–82. While reducing the quantity of licenses available would seem to induce less investigation on the margin, the strategic interaction of bidders is not so straightforward. Game theorists have shown that reducing the quantity of items being auctioned may, for a variety of subtle reasons, induce greater bidder investigation. Id. at 269. Because it is difficult even to "sign" the effect of affirmative action on how much bidders will investigate and because many of the investigations would have already been incurred in preparation for the nationwide auction, we believe this possibility is of secondary importance.

1. Risk of Partial Aggregation

In an auction for regional licenses, a bidder that values a national aggregation more than its constituent parts risks winning a subset of regional licenses. Because the cost of an incomplete aggregation may be greater than its synergistic reservation price, an auction participant may be willing to place a total bid that exceeds its reservation price for the aggregation.

This perverse overbidding is analogous to the bidding behavior observed in simple classroom demonstrations of a "both pay" auction in which the professor offers to auction a prize of $10 to two students. The prize goes to the student who bids the most, but the game also requires each bidder to pay the amount of her last bid. Requiring both the winner and the loser to pay often induces each of the students to bid more than $10—because a bidder about to lose the auction with a $9 bid would prefer to win with an $11 bid (and thereby lose $1 instead of $9).[113] The crucial feature of this game is that making the loser pay can induce both bidders to bid above their reservation prices—this is the core aspect of all "war of attrition" or "escalation" games.[114]

To see how the risk of partial aggregation induces similar overbidding as a "both pay" game, consider an "incumbent" bidder that values owning a national aggregation of five licenses at $100 ($20 per license) but values owning four of the five at only $40 ($10 per license). If it held high bids of $15 on all five ($75 total) and then an "attacker" bid up the price of individual licenses, a rational incumbent would worry that if it were to lose one license, it would be stuck paying $60 (at $15 per license) for the other four licenses that it valued at only $40. To avoid losing the fifth license, the incumbent would be willing to spend up to $120 to win all five licenses.[115] This might mean, for example, that if the bidder thought it could win all five for $23 each, it would prefer bidding above its reservation price rather than winning four for $15 each.[116]

---

113. See Barry O'Neill, International Escalation and the Dollar Auction, 30 J. Conflict Resol. 33 (1986); Martin Shubik, The Dollar Auction Game: A Paradox in Noncooperative Behavior and Escalation, 15 J. Conflict Resol. 109 (1971).

114. See, e.g., John G. Riley, Strong Evolutionary Equilibrium and the War of Attrition, 82 J. Theoretical Biology 383, 383–85 (1979).

115. If the attacker were bidding only on a particular license, the incumbent might bid up to $60 to retain the license—meaning that it would pay $60 for four licenses and $60 for the attacked license. However, an attacker will often switch its bidding among the five licenses, increasing the price of each.

116. If the incumbent miscalculates and later finds that $23 per license is not sufficient to win all five, her predicament deepens. Having high bids of $23 on four licenses

The risk of partial aggregation may induce a firm to bid more than its reservation price, including the synergistic value, for a national aggregation of licenses. As in the "both pay" auction, the prospect of a negative payoff leads to higher bidding. The cost of defending their national aggregations may explain why PageMart, MobileMedia, and Advanced Wireless were willing to pay so much more after PCSD began its crossover bidding: The PCSD crossover might have surprised them and disrupted PageMart's national aggregation.[117] Yet the possibility that partial aggregation exposure induced higher bidding does not undermine our positive thesis. The bidding pattern shows clearly that PCSD's crossover bidding started the chain of events that disrupted PageMart, Multimedia, and Advanced Wireless' national aggregations. Thus, even under this theory, affirmative action was a but-for cause of these higher prices (indeed, partial aggregation risks enhanced the effect of designated bidder crossovers).

2. Raising Rivals' Costs and Predatory Strategies

Not only does the risk of partial aggregation affect incumbents' bidding behavior, it may also have secondary effects on other auction participants. Anticipating that aggregate bidders will pay inflated prices to avoid being stuck with partial aggregations, a firm may strategically choose to bid up the price of a rival's individual license in order to weaken the rival's market positions (for example, requiring the rival to charge higher use fees to cover its interest payments).

While such behavior is theoretically possible, it is probably not rational for a firm to engage in this strategy because the risk of actually buying one of the rival's regional licenses, should the rival drop out of the bidding, likely outweighs any advantage. Additionally, money spent on licenses is sunk and therefore should not affect a rival's subsequent pricing decisions.[118] Finally, engaging in this strategy may induce the rival to retaliate, especially if the initial bidder is itself trying to form a national aggregation.

---

means that the incumbent now stands to lose $52 ($40 − $92), which means she should now be willing to bid up to a total of $152 to win all five, or more than $30 per license. Just as in the simple "both pay" auction and other "war of attrition games," a bidder's belief that she can win at an intermediate value determines her willingness to continue.

117. See notes 120–22 *infra* and accompanying text for a discussion of PageMart's motivation for bidding against MobileMedia and Advanced Wireless when Frequency Block 5 (50/12) licenses were cheaper.

118. See, e.g., Thomas G. Krattenmaker & Steven C. Salop, Anticompetitive Exclusion: Raising Rivals' Costs to Achieve Power over Price, 96 Yale L.J. 209 (1986) (emphasizing that only strategies that raise a rival's marginal costs are likely to weaken its ability to compete).

As an alternative, a bidder may engage in an even more extreme "predatory" strategy. Whereas the goal of raising a rival's costs is just to make it pay more for its licenses, predation seeks to stop the rival from forming a national aggregation. Breaking up a rival's national aggregation might increase the marginal cost of providing certain nationwide paging services (and thus satisfy Salop's marginality requirement). But given bidders' aforementioned willingness to defend their national aggregation "turf," we doubt that reducing the number of national competitors from nine to eight would be worth the amount of money needed to outbid an entrenched firm.[119]

Nonetheless, there is some evidence that, in shifting its demand from 50/50 licenses to the 50/12 licenses after PCSD's crossover, PageMart targeted MobileMedia and Advanced Wireless' national aggregations even though AirTouch's licenses were then cheaper.[120] While it is possible to interpret these episodes as evidence of either a "raising a rival's costs" or a "predatory" strategy, we think it more likely that PageMart was engaged in a "temporizing" strategy in which PageMart attempted to retain eligibility by remaining active on the 50/12 licenses so that it could later return to bid against PCSD for the Block 1 national aggregation.[121] Thus, PageMart bid against the national aggregators despite the higher prevailing bids in these markets, because PageMart had greater confidence that these bidders would defend their national aggregation and ultimately outbid PageMart. This provides a nonpredatory explanation for why PageMart might have been willing to bid on Blocks 3 and 4 when AirTouch's comparable Block 5 licenses were cheaper.[122]

Regardless of PageMart's motivation, it is clear that PageMart's 50/12 bidding was caused by PCSD's crossover. PageMart showed no interest

119. The nationwide auction produced ten nationwide competitors and the regional auction added four more. See table 8.3. The number of nationwide competitors may increase further when the FCC auctions subsequent narrowband blocks.

120. AirTouch also bid against MobileMedia and Advanced Wireless but only when the prevailing bids on Blocks 3 and 4 were cheaper than AirTouch's Block 5 bid. Rather than engaging in predation, AirTouch was arbitraging a price difference.

121. This term and this interpretation of PageMart's strategy were developed by Milgrom. See Milgrom, *supra* note 46, at 31–34 (describing the bidding strategy of PageMart).

122. Indeed, there is some evidence that at times PageMart might have been trying to win one or more of the 50/12 licenses. For example, in round seventy-two, PageMart entered jump bids of $14 million in the West region on all three 50/12 frequency blocks (Blocks 3–5). PageMart's message appeared to be that it preferred a 50/12 in the West at $14 million to a 50/50 at nearly $21 million. PageMart was challenging each of the nondesignated 50/12 bidders in the West to top $14 million or leave it to PageMart. See ftp:// ftp.fcc.gov/pub/Auctions/PCS/Narrowband/ Regional/Round_072 /s3_72.txt.

in the 50/12 licenses until PCSD repeatedly bid up the price of the Block 1 (50/50) licenses. Moreover, PCSD's disruption of the Block 1 licenses both gave PageMart an excuse for bidding on the 50/12 licenses and made PageMart less susceptible to retaliation from Advanced Wireless and MobileMedia.[123]

3.   Reduced Retail Competition

Because firms were bidding for the right to provide paging services in competition with other license winners, auction rules that affected the identity of the ultimate retail competitors, such as affirmative action, also might have affected how much a firm was willing to bid. Specifically, if affirmative action reduced the expected competitiveness in the paging services market, then nondesignated bidders might have been willing to pay more to enter the market.[124] If nondesignated bidders perceived that their designated competitors would have higher marginal costs or limited capacity, they might be willing to bid more for a license because they would expect to earn higher oligopolistic profits in the paging market.

We do not, however, believe that this hypothesis provides a plausible explanation for the narrowband bidding. In most regions, designated bidders hold only two of seventeen narrowband licenses (and there are thirteen nationwide nondesignated bidder aggregations). Even if the designated bidders were less effective competitors,[125] the reduction from seventeen to fifteen strong competitors should not substantially affect pricing.

123.   Retaliation would be harder to accomplish because PageMart was no longer defending a national aggregation of the 50/50 licenses. PageMart's bidding on Blocks 3 and 4, when Block 5 licenses were cheaper, led to final bids on Blocks 3 and 4 that were $4.1 million higher than the final Block 5 bids. Even if PageMart were not a predator, MobileMedia and Advanced Wireless would have had to pay at least what Block 5 winners paid because the Block 5 winners (AirTouch, InstaCheck, and Ameritech) switched whenever there was an arbitrage opportunity. Final bids for Blocks 3 and 4 each totaled approximately $53.6 million, and the final bid for Block 5 was $49.6, which included the $2.1 million PageMart penalty. See table 8.4. Thus, even if the instances of PageMart's bidding on the more expensive 50/12 licenses were not caused by affirmative action, "predation" would only reduce our $45 million estimate for the aggregate effect of affirmative action by a few million.

124.   At the extreme, if firms expected that without affirmative action, nondesignated bidders would win all of the licenses and compete the price of paging services down to its marginal cost, then firms would only have been willing to bid very little.

125.   We are skeptical that designated bidders will prove to be less efficient. First, the "build out" costs of exploiting a narrowband license are small (approximately $2.5 million) compared with the cost of the licenses. See Third Report & Order, *supra* note 20, at 2969 n.40. Second, the designated bidders, together with their partners, have sufficient capital and expertise to bring PCS paging services to market.

Reduced competition also does not explain why designated bidders and their passive nondesignated partners were willing to pay such substantial sums for licenses if they expected difficulty in succeeding in the subsequent marketplace.[126] We nonetheless highlight this possibility to underscore the point that producing more government revenue is not the same as allocating licenses to the most efficient users.[127]

This section of the chapter has shown how affirmative action in the FCC's regional narrowband auction increased government revenues. While game theorists have long understood as a matter of theory that subsidizing weaker bidders can enhance a seller's expected payoff, we have presented the first empirical demonstration that subsidies can increase revenue.[128] We do not claim that the FCC intended this effect. Nor do we claim that affirmative action increased revenues in other FCC auctions where designated bidder subsidies were smaller, less comprehensively designed, or nonexistent.

E. Lessons from Subsequent Auctions

While this chapter has focused primarily on the national and regional narrowband auctions, the FCC completed more than twenty subsequent

126.   If there were fewer licenses for sale, however, it would be possible to construct an example in which a designated bidder would be willing to pay a substantial sum for a license. For example, if the FCC sold only two licenses, setting one aside for a designated bidder, then a designated bidder that could commit to limiting its capacity might expect to earn supracompetitive profits. The nondesignated bidder would then find it profitable to charge a supracompetitive price and might not find it worthwhile to drive the less efficient designated bidder from the market. See Judith R. Gelman & Steven C. Salop, Judo Economics: Capacity Limitation and Coupon Competition, 14 Bell J. Econ. 315 (1983) (outlining strategies for smaller firms to compete effectively with larger firms).

127.   Game theorists analyzing the "success" of the FCC auctions may tend to equate the highest willingness to pay with the most efficient user. Regulators, however, may worry that the firms that can most easily collude would be willing to bid the most. Also, large bidders have a strong incentive to reduce demand to keep auction prices low. See Lawrence M. Asubel & Peter C. Cramton, Demand Reduction and Inefficiency in Multi-Unit Auctions, (Univ. of Md. Working Paper, 1995). Hence, small bidders (like InstaCheck) may inefficiently win licenses when the large bidders (like AirTouch) have higher valuations.

128.   Controlled experiments have shown similar results. See Andrew Schotter & Keith Weigelt, Asymmetric Tournaments, Equal Opportunity Laws, and Affirmative Action: Some Experimental Results, 107 Q.J. Econ. 511 (1992) (finding that affirmative action may lead to increased employee effort and employer revenue); see also Allan Corns & Andrew Schotter, Can Affirmative Action Be Cost Effective? An Experimental Examination of Price-Preferences, (N.Y.U. Working Paper, 1996).

spectrum auctions before the millennium. (See table 8.6 at the end of this chapter.) In this section, we analyze the experience from two of these subsequent auctions: the 1994 broadband auction for the A and B blocks, and the 1996 broadband auction for the C block. These two auctions are disproportionately important in economic terms (90 MHz of the radio spectrum were sold in these broadband auctions compared to only 1.2 MHz sold in the two narrowband auctions). The A-block and B-block auction provides further evidence that unsubsidized auctions may fail to produce sufficient bidding competition and that the presence of even a few additional marginal bidders who are not subject to retaliation can substantially increase the auction revenue. But the C-block auction also suggests that it is difficult for government to tailor subsidies to produce a revenue enhancement effect. Together they suggest that the decision to sequentially auction the three broadband blocks likely cost the government hundreds of millions of dollars.

1. Lessons from the A-Block and B-Block Broadband Auction

Competition in the first broadband auction (for the A and B blocks) was severely diminished by bidding "alliances." Because the licenses in this auction covered fifty-one relatively small geographic areas—so-called major trading areas or MTAs—the FCC allowed bidder alliances so that licensees could offer more efficient regional or national service aggregations. Just before the auction, there was a frenzied rush for alliances among the largest telecommunication companies. In the end, two large alliances formed: WirelessCo, a limited partnership between Sprint (40 percent) and three large cable companies (TCI [30 percent], Comcast [15 percent], and Cox [15 percent]), and PCS PrimeCo, a collection of three Bell Operating Companies (BOCs) (Bell Atlantic, Nynex, and USWEST) and AirTouch, the wireless spinoff of Pacific Telephone (another BOC).

These alliances reduced auction competition because an alliance could not bid in any market in which one of its members held a significant cellular interest. The BOCs and Airtouch had substantial assets and technical knowledge and could have mounted serious independent bids. But by law the PrimeCo alliance was excluded from bidding on licenses in which 64 percent of the nation's population resided. Hence the alliance eliminated three deep-pocketed bidders in nearly two-thirds of the United States and turned four bidders into one in the remaining third. The prices on individual licenses were strongly influenced by alliance eligibility. For example, the price/MHz-pop was much higher in Chicago ($30.4) where all three national bidders—WirelessCo, AT&T, and PrimeCo—were eligible than in New York ($16.5) or San Francisco ($16.10) where only WirelessCo was eligible.

There were substantial indicia of poor competition in the auction itself. Only thirty bidders made up-front payments to participate in the auction. And the initial eligibility ratio (the total eligibility in pops divided by total pops being auctioned) was only 1.9. In comparison, the eligibility ratios in the nationwide and regional narrowband auctions were 8.8 and 6.1, respectively. The bidding was consistently restrained and cautious. Bids were rarely much above the minimum bid increment. And jump bids, rather than being the norm, were the exception. The auction strongly suggests that the combination of alliances and bidding prohibitions can undermine the competitiveness of an auction.

The bidding of Craig McCaw, however, further substantiates our prior finding that small "value seeking" bidders can dramatically increase the government's revenue. McCaw, bidding as Alaacr Communications, put up just $33 million as an up-front payment.[129] Unlike many other bidders who pursued either a national strategy (à la PrimeCo) or a "must have" local license strategy (à la PacTel in Los Angeles), McCaw simply sought to buy individual licenses anywhere in the country on the cheap. "Value seeking" bidders of individual licenses like McCaw were not subject to retaliation or other strategic considerations that might dampen the incentive to bid up an underpriced license. Multi-license bidders, especially those with a "must have" national or local strategy, are particularly susceptible to retaliation if they decide to bid on additional licenses. There are thus strong incentives for multi-license bidders to reduce the number of licenses on which they bid because they worry that bidding on other licenses will ultimately raise the price of core licenses that they want to win. Although McCaw in the end failed to win a single license, he was a wonderful government agent—substantially driving up the winning bids. Replicating our previous marginal bidder analysis, we see that in the five markets where McCaw was the marginal bidder, his bidding was responsible for increasing the government's revenue by $825 million.[130] But McCaw's presence,

129. See Peter C. Cramton, The FCC Spectrum Auctions: An Early Assessment, 6 J. Econ. & Mgmt. Strategies 431 (1997).

130. Most of the revenue enhancement came from two markets: New York, where GTE dropped out at $150 million, and Los Angeles, where no one else ever bid against PacTel. Due to underbidding, this may overstate McCaw's effect on revenues. For example, even though McCaw was the only bidder to compete with PacTel in Los Angeles, someone else may have stepped in if McCaw was not there. But bidders who were pursuing either a national or a local "must have" strategy had little to gain and

while an important palliative, was not sufficient to cure the competition problems in the auction overall—in part because McCaw (as the largest shareholder in AT&T) refused to bid in markets where AT&T was eligible. There is substantial evidence to suggest that lack of competition in the A-block and B-block broadband auction allowed some bidders to win licenses far below their reservation price.

2. Lessons from the C-Block Auction

The government's decision to sell the C-block licenses in a distinct and separate auction probably cost the government hundreds of millions of dollars in reduced auction revenues. The great value of simultaneously auctioning subsidized and nonsubsidized licenses in the regional narrowband auction was that subsidized designated bidders could crossover and bid up prices on the less subsidized licenses without fear of retaliation by the unsubsidized bidders. This was the crucial strategy that created much of the revenue enhancing effect that we uncovered in the regional narrowband auction. But by segregating the subsidized and unsubsidized bidders, the FCC eliminated any potential that subsidized bidders could have further driven up the price of the A-block and B-block licenses.

The FCC, however, decided to segregate the subsidized and unsubsidized auctions because it feared that a simultaneous auction of the three blocks (A, B, and C) with a procedure that included some racial preferences for designated bidders would delay the start of auction or even affect the validity of the awards to unsubsidized bidders. "Quarantining" the designated licenses allowed the unsubsidized A-block and B-block auction to take place without delay or risk of legal challenge.

The FCC's fears were not unfounded. The C-block auction, which was initially designed to be open only to small businesses and which had race-conscious bidding credits for designated bidders, was in fact stalled in the courts. On March 15, 1995, the U.S. Court of Appeals for the District of Columbia stayed the auction until it could hear the case brought by Telephone Electronics Corporation (TEC), a rural telephone company. TEC claimed that it was unfairly excluded from the auction and questioned the constitutionality of bidder preferences for women and minorities.[131] On

---

much to lose by bidding against PacTel in Los Angeles because, unlike McCaw, they were much more subject to retaliation. See Cramton, *supra* note 2, at 435–44 (describing the bidding in the broadband auction).

131. See Edmund L. Andrews, Court Stalls FCC Program for Women and Minorities, *N.Y. Times,* Mar. 16, 1995, at A22.

April 18, TEC unexpectedly withdrew its lawsuit in a settlement with the FCC.[132] The auction, which was scheduled to begin in June 1995, was postponed until early August, and then again when the June 12 Supreme Court decision in *Adarand Constructors v. Pena*[133] announced that racial preferences would be subjected to strict scrutiny. The FCC modified the rules to give all small businesses, regardless of the race or sex of its owners, the same 25 percent price preference and attractive payment terms previously available only to women- or minority-controlled firms. After two more stays challenging the revised preferences,[134] the auction finally began on December 18, 1995.

In the ultimate design, all bidders were granted not only a 25 percent bidding credit but a much more generous installment credit than had been extended to designated bidders in the regional narrowband auction. The government only required the winners to pay 5 percent at the end of the auction and 5 percent at the time of the license award (usually within three months); it then allowed them ten years of quarterly installment payments at the ten-year Treasury note rate (of 6.5 percent), and for the first six years these quarterly installments covered interest only.

The minimal down payment and initial "interest only" financing gave bidders a tremendous incentive to speculate in their bidding. Winners of licenses in the C block were purchasing important options with their licences. The back-loaded installment plan gave them the option to default at relatively low cost if the value of the spectrum turned out to be less than anticipated. The license holders also foreseeing that there might be massive defaults gained the option to renegotiate the terms of their payment directly with the FCC or as mediated by bankruptcy courts.

The results of the auction show how difficult it is to narrowly tailor installment credits. The speculation induced by the installment subsidies caused the bids on the C block to soar. Even after deducting the 25 percent

132. See Gautan Naik, Firm Plans End to Challenge of PCS Auction, *Wall St. J.,* Apr. 19, 1995, at A3.

133. 515 U.S. 200 (1995)

134. The auction was rescheduled for August 29. However, it was postponed yet again when the D.C. Circuit stayed the auction in response to a suit filed by Omnipoint, a New York provider that claimed the new rules would allow large companies to dominate the auction by making it too easy for small companies to serve as fronts for large ones. See Edmund L. Andrews, FCC Is Ordered to Delay an Auction for Wireless Licenses, *N.Y. Times,* July 28, 1995, at D4. The D.C. Circuit again lifted the stay, and the auction was rescheduled for December 11. The Sixth Circuit then granted another stay, but the Supreme Court lifted that stay on October 30. See FCC v. Radiosonde, Inc., 516 U.S. 938 (1995); FCC v. Radiosonde, Inc., 516 U.S. 1301 (Stevens, C.J., 1995).

bidding credit and 40 percent as the effective value of the installment subsidy,[135] the revenues were still 50 percent higher than in the A-block and B-block auction ($15.5 versus $27.7 per pop). While some of this difference is undoubtedly due to the lack of competition previously described in the A-block and B-block auction itself, the low-cost option to default induced fierce bidding competition.

Unfortunately, most winners in the C-block auction have not only exercised their option to default but have litigated through the bankruptcy courts for the right to retain their licenses without paying the obligation. Almost as soon as the auction closed, the FCC realized that major defaults were in the offing. It first allowed bidders to defer their payments but ultimately, on October 16, 1997, issued a restructuring order that offered troubled C-block license holders three mutually exclusive restructuring options, ranging from amnesty—return of the licenses in exchange for forgiveness of debt obligations—to a plan that allowed bidders to keep as many of their licenses as they could pay for by converting 70 percent of their down payment into a prepayment of the full bid price of a smaller number of licenses.[136] Most large license holders have decided, however, to reject these options and instead pursue bankruptcy as a means of retaining their licenses.[137] The three largest winners in the auction (NextWave, Pocket, and GWI) have defaulted on licenses on which the winning bids were more than $7.6 billion.[138] Of course, this does not reflect the government's lost revenue. These licenses will likely be re-auctioned and

135. See Cramton, *supra* note 2, at 442.

136. See In the Matter of Amendment of the Commission's Rules Regarding Installment Payment Financing for Personal Communications Services (PCS) Licensees, Second Report and Order, FCC 97-342, 12 F.C.C.R. 16436 (Oct. 16, 1997), 1997 WL 643811 (F.C.C.).

137. For example, NextWave convinced a bankruptcy judge that the FCC's grant of sixty-three C-block licenses to NextWave, for which it had bid $4.74 billion, was a constructively fraudulent conveyance. The bankruptcy court voided $3.7 billion of NextWave's $4.74 billion obligation to the FCC, allowing NextWave to keep the licenses while it reorganized in bankruptcy. The Second Circuit has reversed this decision and prohibited bankruptcy interference with the FCC allocation of the radio spectrum. See In re Nextwave Personal Communications, Inc., 200 F.3d 43 (2d Cir. 1999). The Second Circuit's opinion goes far toward resolving legal uncertainty surrounding the defaults, but the opinion itself clings to a romanticized, noneconomic notion of license auctions—as, for example, when the court held: "The radio (or electromagnetic) spectrum belongs to no one. It is not property that the federal government can buy or sell. It is no more government-owned than is the air in which Americans fly their airplanes or the territorial waters in which they sail their boats." Id. at 50.

138. See Shawn Zeller, Plenty of Static over Cell Phone, Nat'l J., 2000 WL 6436726 (Jan. 29, 2000).

put to use. But the speculative bidding and bankruptcy negotiations have severely delayed the utilization of the C block. As the twentieth century closed, very few of the C-block licenses were actively used.

The C-block defaults have chastened the FCC. As shown in table 8.7, none of the subsequent auctions has granted bidders an option of government financing. The C-block experience suggests that the bidding credits should be preferred to installment subsidies. The government is a poor banker that often lacks the political will to enforce installment obligations, and seems to lack the legal power to perfect a security interest in the licenses. The only counterstory in favor of continued government financing concerns the possibility of imperfect capital markets. If the cost of capital for small or designated bidders is higher than the government's cost of lending to such bidders, then it may be more efficient to use installment rather than bidding credit subsidies. But the C-block auction shows that the government's cost of lending to small firms can be high and that it is hard to tailor the installment subsidy to be large enough to induce small firm participation without being so large as to induce wanton speculation. Indeed, the difficulty in setting a single financing or bidding credit that does not provide too little or too large a subsidy also suggests that bidding credits should be contingent on the number of licenses (or MHz per pop) that are won by designated bidders: more substantial credits would be awarded if few licenses were being allocated to designated bidders.[139]

But the largest mistake of the FCC in aucting the C block was not the excessive installment subsidy, but instead was the decision to quarantine the C-block competition from the A-block and B-block competition. The decision to hold a separate auction meant that the government bore the costs of default by subsidized bidders without the substantial procompetitive benefits these bidders might have brought to bear on the unsubsidized competition. Given that sluggish bidding in the A-block and B-block auction produced more than $7 billion in revenue, it is not difficult to imagine that the FCC may have raised hundreds of millions more in revenues in the broadband auctions if the auctions for the A, B, and C blocks were combined into one auction and C-block bidders had been given modest bidding credits on the A and B blocks and more substantial preferences on the C block. The broadband results illustrate an important disadvantage

139. A declining credit schedule could, for example, be implemented by establishing *ex ante* a fixed number of subsidy dollars that would be split (pro rata per MHz pop) among any designated bidders who ultimately won licenses. A more detailed analysis is provided in Ayres, *supra* note 92.

of using sequential set-asides, namely, that they do not permit the crossover bidding between designated and nondesignated bidders that can be so important to enhancing auction competition.

A final, but important, lesson from the C-block auction concerns the FCC's wrongheaded rules concerning "unjust enrichment." The FCC, concerned that bidders who receive bidding credits would turn around and sell their licenses at a profit to unsubsidized bidders, passed unjust enrichment regulations that require the original licensee upon resale to pay the initially credited amount. The rule is wrongheaded because it fails to see that competition among the subsidized bidders may bid away part or all of the nominal bidding credit. For example, imagine that the unsubsidized value of a license is $100 and that subsidized bidders have enough cash to pay $80 for the license. Then if there is a 50 percent bidding credit, we should expect these bidders to bid up to $160 for the license. The subsidy costs the government $20, but the unjust enrichment rule would force the initial licensee to pay the government $80 if it ever resells the license. Turning to the C-block auction, it would seem that giving a 25 percent bidding credit to every bidder in an auction would be an economic nonevent. But once we appreciate the perverse effects of the unjust enrichment rules, we can see that the 25 percent subsidy is likely to hamper severely the ability of C-block winners to resell their licenses. The failure to calibrate the unjust enrichment penalty to the unsubsidized price (per MHz pop) instead of the subsidized bidder's nominal bid suggests that the FCC still does not fully appreciate the ways that bidding credits interplay with auction competition.

III. Applications to Government Procurement and Private Employment

FCC auctions are not the only arena in which affirmative action subsidies might enhance competition. This section of the chapter illustrates how an analogous effect could reduce government procurement costs or increase private employer profits. As we emphasized in our discussion of affirmative action's effect on auction revenue,[140] affirmative action is likely to increase competition only if

1.   absent affirmative action, there would be insufficient bidding competition; and

140.   See notes 19–25, *supra* and accompanying text; section I.D of this chapter.

2. the decisionmaker is able to estimate the expected difference between the reservation prices of preferred and nonpreferred bidders.

While these conditions would not apply to most employment and procurement settings, the strength of the FCC data suggests that affirmative action
could enhance competition in a limited set of circumstances.

A.   Government Procurement

While our finding that affirmative action enhanced bidding competition in the FCC's sale of telecommunication licenses is itself significant,
affirmative action may also enhance bidding competition when the government is a buyer. Inducing bidders to sell goods and services to the government at lower prices could affect a significant portion of the economy:
procurement by federal, state, and local governments accounts for "about
10 percent of the GNP or approximately $450 billion per year."[141]
There is ample evidence that the current procurement process is not
always sufficient to guarantee the government a good price. Even beyond
the hype of anecdotal $450 hammers,[142] relatively few firms bid for major
contracts. For example, Steven Kelman's detailed case studies of computer
procurement found an average of only 4.2 bidders per contract.[143] Furthermore, procurement officers "often demonstrate a preference for a familiar
product or an incumbent firm. This kind of firm-specific favoritism is well
known in procurement circles and has led to such expressions as, 'No one
was ever fired for buying from IBM.' "[144] Favoritism for incumbent firms
reduces bidding competition by entrenching the market power of either
one or a small number of firms.
Affirmative action can enhance bidding competition and reduce the

141.   Marshall et al., *supra* note 35, at 3 n.1, citing Steven Kelman, *Procurement
and Public Management* 2 (1990).
142.   See Jerry Mashaw, The Fear of Discretion in Government Procurement, 8
Yale J. Reg. 511, 511 (1991) (discussing media distortions in coverage of government
procurements).
143.   See Marshall et al., *supra* note 35, at 8 n.23, citing Kelman, *supra* note 141,
at 109–83).
144.   Id. at 13–14 n.49; see also Jean-Jacques Laffont & Jean Tirole, Auction Design and Favoritism, 9 Int'l J. Indus. Org. 9 (1991) (discussing effects of auction favoritism on seller's ability to maximize profits).

government's cost of procurement in the same ways that it increased the government's revenue from selling narrowband licenses. The nonpreferred private firms competing to sell the government goods and services are likely to bid more aggressively (that is, offer lower prices) both because they might have to compete against subsidized bidders and because they might have to compete for fewer contracts.

While our earlier examples demonstrated the revenue enhancing effect of affirmative action in multiple-round, open-bid auctions, affirmative action in single-round, sealed-bid auctions, commonly used in government procurement, can produce the same results.[145] A private bidder who knows it must compete against a large number of subsidized bidders may reduce the markup in its sealed bid to increase its chances of winning the contract. Giving traditionally disadvantaged groups bidding subsidies may be especially effective in destabilizing tacit collusion for the very reason that bidders from different social networks may have more difficulty coordinating behavior.

Set-asides may also create lower overall procurement costs because the reduced quantity of contracts available to nonpreferred firms can induce them to bid more aggressively. For example, if four incumbent construction firms were bidding to build four different playgrounds, they might be able to coordinate their bidding (either tacitly or explicitly) to divide the contracts among themselves. Setting aside one of the bidding contracts for traditionally disadvantaged, nonincumbent firms may enhance intragroup competition, as the four incumbents must now compete for just three contracts. Any incumbent that believes it may end up empty handed is likely to reduce the markup in its sealed bid. While the government may pay more on contracts set aside for traditionally disadvantaged bidders, reduced costs for non-set-aside contracts can lower overall procurement costs.

Failing to recognize how affirmative action can be used to enhance procurement competition grossly overstates the cost of affirmative action subsidies. For example, nonpartisan state legislative analysts estimated the California Department of General Services spent an additional $9.9 million in 1995 by rejecting low bids from firms that failed to comply with affirmative action requirements. Unfortunately, these estimates ignore how affirmative action may have driven down the low bids that were used as the

---

145. See generally Kelman, cited *supra* note 141 (describing common procurement methods).

benchmark.[146] Without the enhanced bidding competition created by affirmative action, these low bids and the low bids on other bidding contracts may have been substantially higher. While we do not have access to sufficient data to claim reliably that affirmative action reduced California's procurement costs, the procompetitive effects of subsidizing weak bidders (and the evidence from the FCC's regional narrowband auction itself) suggest that affirmative action is much less costly than appears from simply comparing the low bids to the winning bids of traditionally disadvantaged firms.

There is even a sense in which affirmative action promotes the "full and open competition" mandated by the Competition in Contracting Act of 1984.[147] The government procurement process seeks to balance three competing goals of "equity (fair access to competing bidders), integrity (reduction in opportunities for corruption) and economy, (obtaining goods or services required at the lowest possible price)."[148] Although the main thrust of our argument has concerned economy, affirmative action may also increase fairness and integrity. When affirmative action increases auction competition, it inevitably diminishes firms' opportunities to bilk the government. The privilege of participating in a noncompetitive auction could be recharacterized as unfair access to the public fisc. And affirmative action may promote fairness by redressing past and present instances of either private or governmental discrimination. To the extent that well-organized incumbents are more likely to capture or corrupt the purchasing process,[149] affirmative action subsidies counteract both possibilities by forcing favored incumbents to bid closer to their reservation prices.

Moreover, the enhanced bidding competition induced by affirmative action need not reduce efficiency in government procurement. While selling to higher cost producers decreases productive efficiency (as in the FCC auctions), creating lower overall prices may increase allocative efficiency by inducing the government to make more efficient choices about the quantity and mix of its purchases. Absent the bidding competition affirmative action

146.   Indeed, a strategic bidder who knows that it is not in compliance with state affirmative action requirements might have an incentive purposefully to enter a low-ball bid to exacerbate the perceived cost of affirmative action.

147.   10 U.S.C. § 2304 (1994). The Competition in Contracting Act of 1984 attempted to discourage sole-source procurement partly by raising the status of procurement by competitive proposals. See Mashaw, *supra* note 142, at 513.

148.   Mashaw, *supra* note 142, at 512.

149.   See generally Ian Ayres & John Braithwaite, *Responsive Regulation: Transcending the Deregulation Debate* 54–100 (1992) (discussing factors conducive to regulatory capture).

fosters, the government may face inflated procurement prices that distort its choice of inputs. In efficiency terms, the increase in allocative efficiency may outweigh or at least mitigate the decrease in productive efficiency caused by selling to disadvantaged firms with higher production costs.[150]

Although the preceding analysis suggests that the procurement context satisfies the first precondition (the revenue enhancement effect), the government still faces a substantial information problem in calculating the size of the affirmative action subsidy. Even if the government is confident that disadvantaged contractors are likely to be weaker bidders, it would still need to estimate the expected difference in reservation prices to know how much of a subsidy or set-aside would lower costs. This is not a straightforward calculation, but the government makes just this kind of calculation when it subsidizes small businesses. For example, the Department of Defense sometimes reimburses small bidders for certain bidding costs if it anticipates that greater competition will lower the government's price.[151] Even if the government does not have the requisite data to ensure that affirmative action actually decreases procurement costs, it may have sufficient information (for example, data concerning the effects of past bidding) to be confident that affirmative action is less costly than the direct cost of the subsidy.

B. Private Employment

To explore the limits of our analysis, this section considers whether affirmative action could induce workers to "bid" more aggressively for their jobs. Although employees do not literally bid for their jobs, their decisions over how hard to work or what level of pay to accept might be analogized to an auction bid. Workers may commit to work harder or for less money if they face subsidized competition from preferred job applicants or have to compete for fewer jobs because some are set aside for a preferred class.

150. This enhancement in allocative efficiency would not apply to the government's sale of FCC licenses unless the government's choice of what or how much to sell were influenced by artificially deflated revenues.

The importance of allocative efficiency is at the core of Henry Manne's justification for legalizing insider trading: If insider trading drives stock prices more quickly toward their true value, better investment and consumptive choices might follow legalizing its exchange. See Henry G. Manne, *Insider Trading and the Stock Market* (1966).

151. See Jerome S. Gabig & Richard C. Bean, A Primer on Federal Information Systems Acquisitions: Part Two of a Two-Part Article, 17 Pub. Cont. L.J. 553, 580–81 (1987) (discussing Department of Defense proposals to subsidize benchmarking costs for small information systems firms).

While our goal for the moment is to assess whether as a positive matter private employers would have a profit motive for engaging in this type of affirmative action, we emphasize that the translation of our theory from firm-based preferences to individual-based preferences raises two troubling normative problems. First, the premise that women or minority workers have lower expected productivity is a more invidious stereotype than the FCC's assumption concerning designated bidders' ability to compete. Even if the choice to subsidize disenfranchised groups were based on the disadvantages to which the individuals had been subjected, this profit motive for affirmative action lacks the moral coherence of standard diversity theory, which presumes not that traditionally disadvantaged workers are less productive, but that they bring different life experiences to their jobs, which synergistically enhance corporate decisionmaking.[152] Second, the goal of extracting additional surplus from white or male workers is more problematic than extracting additional surplus from nondesignated firms.[153] Nondesignated bidders have no right to make supracompetitive profits from our nation's finite radio spectrum, but workers have a normative claim to some of the surplus from their employment. The problem is that employers would use affirmative action to extract additional surplus from nonpreferred workers.

We return to these normative issues in the final section of this chapter, but even at a positive level, we believe that, in the labor markets, the two preconditions for affirmative action to enhance competition rarely both

152. See, e.g., Taylor Cox Jr., The Multicultural Organization, 5 Acad. Mgmt. Exec. 34 (1991) (contending that diversity enhances decisionmaking, creativity, and marketing to foreign communities); Duncan Kennedy, A Cultural Pluralist Case for Affirmative Action in Legal Academia, 1990 Duke L.J. 705 (arguing that affirmative action would improve the quality and social value of legal scholarship).

153. In a sense, the employer would be using affirmative action to induce a "rat race." See George Akerlof, The Economics of Caste and of the Rat Race and Other Woeful Tales, 90 Q.J. Econ. 599, 603–5 (1976). The rat race effect results from workers' increasing their efforts to distinguish themselves from other coworkers without considering that their extra efforts would inspire others to work harder. The rat race effect might intensify where workers with higher expected productivity had to work even harder to exceed the subsidized output of workers with lower expected productivity.

The rat race effect underscores how affirmative action's possible profit motive will usually reduce social efficiency. While reducing workers' market power may lead to more efficient use of labor, see text accompanying note 151 *supra*, it is just as likely that employees' disutility of work will exceed employers' enhanced profitability.

obtain. Employers do not need to resort to affirmative action to extract surplus from white or male employees because competition among these employees is sufficient to drive the wage to the marginal product. Until recently, the persistent unemployment in the United States meant the number of job applicants usually far exceeds the number of openings. Under such conditions, voluntary affirmative action would not be necessary for employers to gain bargaining power: Affirmative action is most likely to be able to spur additional competition only if there are relatively few bidders compared to the number of items being auctioned.

Nonetheless, we see a possibility that employers could benefit from using affirmative action to enhance their bargaining power when, because of private information or contracting costs, employers are unable to extract all of the gains from trade.[154] Andrew Schotter and Keith Weigelt experimentally tested whether affirmative action subsidies could spur employees to work harder.[155] They found that overall effort of their subjects increased when weak "employees" were favored. While there is only indirect empirical evidence that affirmative action enhances productivity,[156] our enhanced-competition theory may provide a causal explanation for two of the most

154. Most important, employers often receive only a noisy signal about the expected productivity of a particular applicant. The heterogeneity in expected productivity reduces the competitive pressure that employees with the strongest resumes face from other applicants with less scintillating resumes. Because applicants may know more about their prospective productivity than employers, employers cannot simply extract the surplus by tailoring the contractual terms of employment to each employee's actual abilities. For example, consider an employer that wishes to promote a small proportion of its entry-level employees based on the employees' observed productivity during a long probationary period. If the employees exhibit different expected productivities, then the strongest workers might be able to shirk without fear that they will be passed over for promotion. Because the employees' exact capabilities are unknown to the employer, simply requiring employee-specific minimum output would not allow the employer to extract all of the expected gains from trade. Instead, the employer might be able to do better by subsidizing some of the weaker applicants in this competition. Faced with this subsidized competition, the employees with the highest expected productivity may work harder.

155. See Schotter & Weigelt, *supra* note 128. For groups with a severe disadvantage, affirmative action significantly increased effort and firm profits. Without the affirmative action, the disadvantaged parties tended to supply no effort, since their chance of promotion was so small. Id.

156. One intriguing study of stock market "events" shows that when the Department of Labor announced awards for companies that had exemplary affirmative action programs, the companies' stock prices increased. See Peter Wright et al., Competitiveness through Management of Diversity: Effects on Stock Price Valuation, 38 Acad. Mgmt. J. 272 (1995).

important changes during the last two decades in entry level hiring for law teaching: (1) an increase in the perceived amount of affirmative action, and (2) an increase in the number of publications candidates must write before application.

We remain skeptical, however, that employers would subsidize disadvantaged applicants solely to maximize profits. Even if affirmative action subsidies or set-asides could profitably enhance employers' bargaining power, few employers have sufficient information to risk subsidizing workers with lower expected productivity when profit-maximization is their sole motivation.[157] However, when employers are motivated by other factors to offer affirmative action subsidies, our overarching conclusion still pertains: private employment subsidies may not be nearly as costly as commonly assumed if they enhance the employer's terms of trade with nonpreferred employees.

IV. Legal Implications

The central thesis of this chapter has been positive rather than normative: affirmative action can (and in the FCC auction did) increase government revenues by enhancing bidding competition. But at some level this fact is insignificant unless it informs normative legal issues. Accordingly, this section addresses the normative relevance of the revenue enhancing effect.

A. Public Affirmative Action

An expected increase in government revenue or decrease in government procurement costs is an inadequate constitutional rationale for race- or gender-conscious subsidies. But, in cases where there are independent constitutional justifications, the simple fact that affirmative action subsidies may not be as costly as is commonly thought may help demonstrate that affirmative action is cost justified.

---

157. We can think of few examples where private employers explicitly subsidize weaker applicants to spur competition, but "second-sourcing"—where a firm profitably subsidizes a higher cost second-source to enhance its bargaining power with the primary input supplier—may be analogous. See Ayres & Braithwaite, *supra* note 149, at 134.

1. Revenue Enhancement Is Constitutionally Insufficient

After *Croson*[158] and *Adarand*,[159] to withstand an equal protection attack, a racial subsidy must be "narrowly tailored" to further a "compelling government interest."[160] Reducing the federal government's budget deficit is unlikely to qualify as a "compelling government interest" for disparate racial treatment.[161] Even if increasing government revenue were a constitutionally permissible goal, the means of achieving this goal would not be "narrowly tailored," because there is a strong possibility the government could find a racially neutral means of substantially achieving the same goal. Specifically, if the FCC had simply subsidized small firms,[162] similar revenue enhancing effects might have been achieved.

Whether a small-firm subsidy would create more or less revenue than a race–gender subsidy depends in part on the government's ability to identify a stable, nonracial class of "weak" bidders. While many critics of affirmative action have complained that "sham" corporations have falsely qualified for minority status,[163] this problem might be even more intracta-

---

158. City of Richmond v. J. A. Croson Co., 488 U.S. 469 (1989) (requiring that a city affirmative action plan satisfy a compelling governmental interest and be narrowly tailored to remedy the past effects of discrimination).

159. Adarand Constructors v. Pena, 515 U.S. 200 (1995) (holding that all governmental racial classifications must withstand strict judicial scrutiny).

160. Id. at 235. Gender-based subsidies may be more likely to pass constitutional muster because they need not satisfy strict scrutiny. See Mississippi Univ. for Women v. Hogan, 458 U.S. 718, 724 (1982) (subjecting gender-based discrimination to intermediate scrutiny). Even under the relevant "heightened scrutiny," however, it may be difficult for the government to justify revenue enhancement as a substantial government purpose.

161. The Court would likely require the government to show that there was no equally effective race-neutral means to achieve the same result. See *Adarand*, 515 U.S. at 237–38. In *Adarand*, two justices even wrote that there could be no compelling government purpose for race-based subsidies. Id. at 239–41 (Scalia and Thomas, JJ., concurring separately).

162. Although in the regional narrowband auction the FCC subsidized firms with annual gross revenues of less than $40 million in the last two years, the subsidies were not as significant as those given to designated bidders. Small firms received no bidding credit, but they were able to pay in installments at the ten-year Treasury note rate. The installment payments applied to all licenses. See Order on Reconsideration, *supra* note 49, at 5306–7.

163. See, e.g., Mark I. Pinsky, FCC Takes Trinity TV Station: Religious Broadcaster Illegally Used Minority Status, U.S. Says, *Sun-Sentinel*, Nov. 16, 1995, at 1D, available in LEXIS, News Library, Curnws File (" '[T]he findings establish that TBN and Crouch created a sham corporation to take advantage of the minority preference' policies of the FCC.").

ble if preferred status were determined simply by a corporation's revenue or financial structure. Strong bidders might be able to redefine their corporate structure to qualify for small business subsidies. Thus, while it is possible that racial or gender classifications are the best means to enhance bidding competition, we think it clear that the current Supreme Court would not accept revenue enhancement by itself as a sufficient justification for affirmative action set-asides.

2. Did the FCC's Rules Enhance Minority or Female Control of the Airwaves?

To underscore our agnosticism about whether the FCC's affirmative action was consistent with the Constitution's equal protection requirement, we digress for a moment to consider whether the FCC's designated bidder regulations enhanced minority or female control of the airwaves. The FCC designed the designated bidder regulations to avoid two problems: (1) unjust enrichment and (2) sham designated bidders. The unjust enrichment problem was created in response to public concern generated when previous lottery winners quickly resold their licenses for huge profits.[164] The FCC responded by promulgating detailed unjust enrichment rules aimed at stopping unjust minority enrichment. These rules restricted designated bidders' ability to resell or lease licenses in the short term to nondesignated bidders, and required repayment both of the 40 percent bidding credit and the installment subsidy if the license were resold in the long term.[165] These rules should stop unscrupulous designated bidders from capitalizing on the affirmative action subsidies. Indeed, because the 40 percent bidding credit did not mean that designated bidders actually paid 40 percent less than nondesignated bidders for comparable licenses, the payback rules may discourage even legitimate resale.[166]

The FCC also attempted to deter corporations from trying to get desig-

164. See, e.g., Edmund L. Andrews, Airwave Auction Bill Advances, N.Y. Times, May 12, 1993, at D1, D13; Edmund L. Andrews, Senate Plan To Sell Radio Frequencies, N.Y. Times, May 28, 1992, at D1, D9.

165. See Implementation of Section 309(j) of the Communications Act—Competitive Bidding, 9 F.C.C.R. 2348, 2394–95 (1994) (Second Report and Order, PP Docket No. 93-253) [hereinafter Second Report & Order].

166. The extensive crossover bidding and the designated bidder purchase of a non-set-aside license suggest that the effective bidding credit was 0 percent (not including the installment benefit). Thus, making the designated bidders pay back the full 40 percent actually penalizes resellers. Although designated bidders presumably take this illiquidity into account when valuing designated licenses, requiring overpayment of the bidding credit will tend to increase the inefficient holding of designated licenses.

nated status by using minority or female entrepreneurs as fronts, without allowing them any actual control over the corporation. The FCC therefore required that women or minorities own a majority of the voting stock and at least 25 percent of the total (voting and nonvoting) equity.[167]

The greatest weakness of the FCC's approach was its failure to limit the amount or terms of designated bidder leverage. While nonvoting stock could represent no more than 75 percent of total equity, designated bidders were allowed to borrow unlimited amounts from their passive equity holders. In fact, female or minority entrepreneurs did not have to pay in any capital in return for their majority control; some designated bidders financed 100 percent of their auction payments with debt and capital contributions from nonvoting shareholders. Moreover, while designated bidders were required to file a "long-form" application to qualify for designated status, they never had to disclose the amount or terms of debt financing.

The lack of leverage regulation created a strong likelihood of extreme separation of ownership from control. The FCC did not limit the amount of free cash flow passive financiers could take from the corporation. The FCC's regulations thus permitted a leaky bucket where many of the benefits of affirmative action ultimately flowed to people who were not members of the disadvantaged group. FCC apologists might respond that capital markets are sufficiently competitive to protect designated entrepreneurs and that the goal of the program is to let designated entrepreneurs control part of the telecommunications spectrum. However, the complete lack of leverage regulation threatens to undermine the more limited goal of giving women and minority entrepreneurs effective control of the designated firms.

Passive financiers in these ventures must have been sorely tempted to control the bidding strategies when millions of dollars of their own money were at stake. The FCC regulations failed to specify the amount of control that passive debtholders and nonvoting stockholders were allowed to ex-

---

167. See Third Memorandum & Order, *supra* note 49, at 212. In addition, if the designated bidder control group owned less than half of the total equity, then no single nondesignated investor could own more than 25 percent of the total equity or more than 15 percent of the voting stock. Id.

The FCC's rules, however, did not prohibit designated bidders from adopting supermajority voting requirements that might undermine the effective control of the control group. For example, while a woman owned 85 percent of Benbow P.C.S. Ventures, Inc., her dominant ownership share was insufficient to make many major corporate decisions, because any such decision required approval from 86 percent of the voting shares. See Long Form Application of Benbow P.C.S. Ventures, Inc., FCC Form 401, Exh. VI at 1 (Nov. 23, 1994).

ert. Quite possibly, these so-called passive financiers might have made round-by-round bidding decisions, with the ultimate threat of withholding financing should the controlling shareholders act otherwise. In other instances, exerting this type of influence has exposed passive debtholders to various types of control liability.[168]

While we cannot assess who controlled the bidding strategies of the prevailing designated bidders in the regional auction, an analysis of their long-form applications for designated status indicates extreme forms of leverage. For example, Lisa-Gaye Shearing disclosed that its passive partner financed 100 percent of the more than $3 million spent for auction prepayments.[169] Moreover, some of the designated bidders seemed to cede control of the bidding process to their white male financiers.[170] For example, the female controlling shareholder of Benbow seemed detached during important parts of the bidding, and one of us observed her reading a novel for several rounds while her white male team decided how to bid.[171]

Because the entrepreneurs who own the designated firms did not face the same threats of ouster by proxy contest or merger as those who run typical corporations, it strains the imagination to think that nonvoting shareholders and debtholders would extend virtually all of the firm's working capital without retaining substantial influence over its most important decisions. Race- and gender-conscious subsidies must do more than merely

168. See, e.g., A. Gay Jenson Farms Co. v. Cargill, Inc., 309 N.W.2d 285, 294 (Minn. 1981) (holding lender vicariously liable to other creditors because its financial and managerial control over the principal created an agency relationship); see also Restatement (Second) of Agency § 14(o), cmt. a (1957) (security holder may be considered principal of debtor where security holder takes over management of debtor); Daniel R. Fischel, The Economics of Lender Liability, 99 Yale L.J. 131 (1989).

169. See Long Form Application of Page Call, Inc., FCC Form 401 Exh. IV at 5, 7 (Nov. 23, 1994). Benbow similarly disclosed: "Westlink has advanced funds to Benbow to make the necessary down payments to the Commission." Long Form Application of Benbow, P.C.S. Ventures, Inc., *supra* note 167, at 2.

170. Shearing's long form states that she "had an oral agreement [with her passive partner, Adelphia] that they would consult with each other on bidding strategies during the auction and, to the extent Lisa-Gaye Shearing chose not to be present at the auction, she would direct what bids to place in what markets and an Adelphia employee would act as her agent in placing those bids." Long Form Application of Page Call, *supra* note 169, at 5.

171. While controlling shareholders might rationally delegate many corporate decisions, it seems odd that the controlling shareholder would delegate how the corporation invests the vast majority of its capital. Benbow's observed behavior is all the more disheartening if one of the goals of affirmative action is to create role models for future disadvantaged entrepreneurs.

enhance government revenues to pass constitutional muster, and we remain agnostic about whether the FCC subsidies achieved these additional requirements.

3. Affirmative Action Costs the Government Less Than Is Commonly Assumed

Notwithstanding the fact that a revenue enhancing effect is not constitutionally sufficient to justify affirmative action, our finding that affirmative action can enhance government revenue has normative relevance. The cost of affirmative action is significant as a matter of public policy. Affirmative action may appear more attractive if it costs the government very little to redress past discrimination. Even if race- and gender-based subsidies further a compelling government purpose, the amount of affirmative action must turn, at least in part, on the cost of the subsidy.[172]

From this perspective, it is not crucial that the FCC's affirmative action subsidy actually increased government revenue; it is only important that the subsidy cost the government less than is commonly assumed. The government cost of affirmative action is exaggerated if one considers only the shortfall on contracts that go to minorities. A more accurate view takes account of the ways in which subsidized minority bidders drive traditional players to surrender more of the gains of trade on the contracts they win. The naive analysis wrongly assumes as a benchmark that unsubsidized bidders would have bid as aggressively in the absence of competition from preferred bidders. The naive benchmark also wrongly assumes that minority bidders only compete with unsubsidized bidders and therefore that competition among minority bidders does not compete away any of the subsidy. But in the narrowband auction, designated competition was sufficient to do just this: it competed away virtually all of the 40 percent bidding credit. What naively seems like a huge giveaway ended up costing the government nothing. As our examination of the FCC auction reveals, subsidizing discrete classes of bidders can increase both intergroup and intragroup competition, invalidating both of the naive assumptions.

While we have shown that the affirmative action subsidies increased revenues in comparison to an auction without any bidder subsidies, some critics might argue that we have not chosen the appropriate benchmark and in particular that we should use for comparison an auction with the

---

172. Assessing the cost of affirmative action will also turn on a variety of other factors, including the cost of excluding white males and the amount of social inefficiency.

most effective race- and gender-neutral subsidies. We emphasized above
that small business subsidies might have been able to generate more government revenue than the affirmative action subsidies did.[173] Yet even if
giving small business subsidies could have extracted higher bids from the
dominant bidders, our central finding would still hold: affirmative action
subsidies cost much less than we would have estimated if we merely multiplied the eleven licenses that designated bidders acquired by the effective
50 percent (or in one case 16 percent) subsidy.[174]

This naive method would estimate that affirmative action cost the government $125.6 million. A small business subsidy may have succeeded in
extracting even more from the established bidders, and in comparison with
this benchmark, affirmative action may still have cost the government some
revenue. But this shortfall in revenue would only be a fraction of the naive
cost estimate.

Even if the race and gender subsidies had not increased government
revenues, the take-home lesson of this chapter is that the fiscal cost of affirmative action may be much less than the facial expense of a fifty-cents-
on-the-dollar subsidy. In a sense, the legal significance of our finding is
captured by the simple idea that "demand curves slope downward"—
meaning the discovery that affirmative action has a lower price should, on
the margin, induce society to demand more of it.

B. Private Affirmative Action May Deserve Higher Scrutiny

Our discovery that affirmative action subsidies can enhance bidding
competition does not unambiguously militate for an increase in all types
of affirmative action. The theoretical possibility that employers may adopt
race-conscious hiring or promotion standards solely to make money suggests that private affirmative action may deserve higher scrutiny than currently given in Title VII litigation.

A bedrock principle of Title VII is that there is no profitability defense
for disparate treatment on the basis of race or gender.[175] Particularly with
regard to disparate racial treatment, the statute explicitly excludes racial

173. See note 162 *supra* and accompanying text.
174. See text accompanying note 62 *supra*.
175. See City of L.A. Dep't of Water & Power v. Manhart, 435 U.S. 702, 716–
17 (1978) (noting that "Title VII [does not] contain . . . a cost-justification defense comparable to the affirmative defense available in a price discrimination suit.").

classifications as a possible "bona fide occupational qualification."[176] Unlike equal protection jurisprudence, which requires the symmetrical treatment of laws favoring and disfavoring racial minorities,[177] Title VII distinguishes between race-conscious employment standards that favor minorities and those that disfavor them. Thus, even though "there is no BFOQ for race" when disfavoring minorities, the Supreme Court has said that race-conscious disparate treatment (in the form of an employer's voluntary affirmative action program that favors minorities) does not violate Title VII if it is intended to "eliminate a manifest racial imbalance" and does not unduly burden or absolutely bar the advancement of white employees.[178]

Our enhanced-competition theory suggests, however, that employers might engage in affirmative action solely to extract more surplus from their white or male employees. While the Supreme Court has not yet treated race-conscious employment practices that favor and disfavor minorities symmetrically, we suspect that the Court would require symmetric application if it thought that a private employer adopted a voluntary affirmative action program solely to increase profits. The Supreme Court may therefore require employers to prove more than a statistical imbalance—that is, to make some showing that they are motivated by more compelling factors than making money.[179]

Yet the need for heightened scrutiny turns in large part on how often private employers would likely implement voluntary affirmative action solely to make money. In our previous analysis, we sketched how racial and gender preference might enhance a firm's profits, but concluded that in practice employers would seldom have the information necessary to calculate the appropriate subsidy with any confidence.[180] Accordingly, heightening the employer's standard of justification because of the possibility of enhanced employee competition seems unwarranted.

176. 42 U.S.C. § 2000e-2(e)(1) (1994).

177. See, e.g., 42 U.S.C. § 1981 (1994).

178. Johnson v. Transportation Agency, Santa Clara County, 480 U.S. 616, 630 (1987), citing United Steelworkers of Am. v. Weber, 443 U.S. 193, 208 (1979).

179. Our interim conclusion that Title VII should prohibit affirmative action programs adopted solely to increase an employer's profits, however, has broader application: namely, the more conventional "diversity" justification for affirmative action—improving decisionmaking by increasing the diversity of decisionmakers—would also violate Title VII unless the employer could offer a sufficient nonprofit-based motive.

180. See text accompanying notes 152–58 supra.

Conclusion

In undertaking this study, we set out to estimate how much the bidding subsidies cost our government. Our first intuition was that allowing firms controlled by women or minorities to pay just 50 percent of their winning bids would lower the government's auction revenue. Only after analyzing the bidding data through the lens of game theory did it become clear that the FCC's affirmative action increased narrowband prices by forcing non-preferred firms to bid more aggressively. In a simultaneous auction, the last bidders to drop out determine final prices—and in the regional narrowband auction the subsidized designated bidders dropped out last, but only after they drove up final prices by 12 percent or $45 million.

Our results demonstrate how law-and-economics can illuminate otherwise counterintuitive behavior. The game-theoretic explanation does not come naturally to those unschooled in strategic thinking. Civil rights advocates have implicitly conceded that affirmative action subsidies burden the public fisc. They argue instead that the social benefits of remedying past discrimination or of promoting diversity justify the cost of the government subsidies. Showing that the subsidies cost much less than previously thought—or indeed that the subsidies may reduce the federal deficit—makes it easier for affirmative action programs to pass cost-benefit analysis.

Opponents of affirmative action might contend that the effect on the public fisc should not be dispositive. But for those who believe that there is an appropriate role for affirmative action in remedying past discrimination or in furthering diversity, then the results of this chapter, by illuminating the size of the public subsidy, will help policy makers select the appropriate scope of the remedy.

The United States has a long history of giving away the radio spectrum.[181] From 1927 until 1982, radio spectrum licenses were assigned by a process known as "comparative hearings" in which the FCC evaluated competing requests for broadcast licenses. The licenses were simply given away—once applicants had paid their lawyers significant sums to construct arguments explaining why they would best serve the nebulous "public interest." By 1982, the volume of new cellular telephone licenses began to overwhelm the FCC's ability to conduct comparative hearings, so Congress authorized the agency to assign the licenses by lotteries, again without

---

181. This history is detailed in Milgrom, *supra* note 46, at 2, 12–13.

charge. Hundreds of thousands of firms applied for the giveaway—many only with the desire to resell their lottery winnings for a profit.[182]

Congress' decision to auction licenses went a long way toward ending these blatant giveaways, but even in an auction, entitlements can be sold on the cheap if there are not enough bidders. The FCC auctions created just this risk. Had large telecommunications companies reaped windfalls by purchasing licenses at prices substantially below their valuations, the auctions would have continued the trend of giving away the spectrum. Though requiring disadvantaged firms to pay just 50 percent of their winning bids struck many commentators as an unjustifiable giveaway,[183] we have shown that besides promoting diverse ownership of the broadcast spectrum, the FCC's affirmative action actually prevented an even larger corporate gratuity.

Appendix 8.A

Table 8.5 shows on a license-by-license basis how we calculated the information in table 8.4. The full names of the relevant bidders appear in table 8.2, with the exception of the nondesignated bidder, KDM Messaging Co. (McCaw), which is a wholly owned subsidiary of McCaw Cellular, now owned by AT&T. The information contained under the heading "Last Nondesignated Entity Bidder Excess Demand" reports the last time an unsuccessful nondesignated bidder entered a bid on a particular license. For example, for the Midwest Region/Block 1 license, McCaw placed the last unsuccessful nondesignated bid of $12.6 million in round 6. The next column, "Response to Final Bids By Nondesignated Entity Bidders Who Ultimately Dropped Out," simply reports how the ultimate winners responded to this excess nondesignated demand. For example, in response to McCaw's Midwest/Block 1 bid, PageMart bid $16 million. We assume that, without the crossover designated bidding, prices for the licenses would have risen to this level, because there was demonstrated excess nondesignated demand at lower prices. While it would be tempting to use this

---

182.   Milgrom gives the example of a sham telephone company—one formed solely for the purpose of filing lottery applications—that won the right to supply cellular services to Cape Cod and promptly resold its license to Southwestern Bell Telephone Company for $41 million. See id. at 13.

183.   See, e.g., Rauch, *supra* note 8, at 9, 12 (discussing "discriminating for the sake of discriminating" in interactive video and paging licenses).

Table 8.5 Analysis of DE Crossover Bidding on Individual License Basis

Freq Block	Region	Last Nondesignated Bidder Excess Demand			Response to Final Bids by Nondesignated Bidders Who Ultimately Dropped Out ($M)	Maximum Response within Region ($M)	Final Bid ($M)	Increase in Revenue Caused by Crossover Bidding ($M)
		Final Nondesignated Bidder Who Ultimately Dropped Out	Last Nondesignated Bidder's Bid	Round Placed				
1	NE	McCaw	12.6	7	13.2	13.2	17.5	4.3
1	South	Advanced Wireless	10.0	4	5.0	15	18.4	3.4
1	Mid	McCaw	12.6	6	16.0	16	16.8	0.8
1	Cent	Westlink	15.0	8	16.0	16	17.3	1.3
1	West	Westlink	15.0	6	16.0	16	22.5	6.5
3	NE	Mobile Media	7.5	4	8.3	0.3	9.5	1.2
3	South	Mobile Media	7.5	4	8.3	8.3	11.8	3.5
3	Mid	Mobile Media	7.5	4	8.3	0.5	9.3	0.8

3	Cent	Mobile Media	7.5	4	8.3	0.3	8.3	-0.1
3	West	Mobile Media	7.5	4	8.3	0.4	14.9	5.5
4	NE	Mobile Media	7.4	5	7.8	0.3	8.9	0.6
4	South	Advanced Wireless	7.8	6	0.3	8.3	11.5	3.2
4	Mid	Advanced Wireless	7.8	6	8.5	8.5	10.1	1.6
4	Cent	Mobile Media	7.4	5	7.8	0.3	8.8	0.5
4	West	Mobile Media	7.4	5	7.8	0.4	14.3	4.9
5	NE	PageMart	7.0	3	7.4	8.3	8.7	0.4
5	South	McCaw	7.7	7	8.1	8.3	8.9	0.6
5	Mid	McCaw	7.9	7	8.5	8.5	9.5	1.0
5	Cent	Radiofone	8.1	44	8.3	0.3	8.3	0.0
5	West	Westlink	8.9	15	9.4	0.4	14.3	4.9
		Block 1 Total			76.2	76.2	92.6	16.4
		Block 3 Total			41.5	42.8	53.7	10.9
		Block 4 Total			40.2	42.8	53.6	10.8
		Block 5 Total			41.7	42.8	49.6	6.8
		Grand Total			199.6	204.6	249.5	44.9

Table 8.6 Summary of FCC Spectrum Auctions

Auction Number[a]	Auction	Licensing Scheme[d]	Date Opened	Number of Rounds	Number of Bands	Number of Markets	Number of Licenses	Net High Bids ($M)	Bidders without Bidding Credits	Small Bidders	Very Small Bidders	Bidders without Bidding Credits	Small Bidders	Very Small Bidders
1	Nationwide Narrowband PCS	Nationwide	25-Jul-94	47	10	1	10	617	100	0	NA	100	0	NA
2	IVDS	MSA	28-Jul-94	Oral Outcry	2	297	594	213.9	NA	NA	NA	NA	NA	NA
3	Regional Narrowband PCS	Regional	26-Oct-94	105	6	5	30	392.7	61	39	NA	61	39	NA
4	A & B Block PCS[b]	MTA	5-Dec-94	112	2	51	99	7019.4	100	NA	NA	100	NA	NA
5	C Block PCS Broadband[c]	BTA	18-Dec-95	184	1	493	493	9197.5	0	100	NA	0	100	NA
6	MDS	BTA	14-Nov-95	181	1	493	493	216.2	38	62	NA	46	54	NA
7	900 MHz SMR	MTA	5-Dec-95	168	20	51	1020	204.3	73	15	13	81	10	9
8	DBS (110 W)	Nationwide	24-Jan-96	19	1	1	1	682.5	100	NA	NA	100	NA	NA
9	DBS (148 W)	Partial	25-Jan-96	25	1	1	1	52.3	100	NA	NA	100	NA	NA
10	C Block PCS Re-auction[c]	BTA	3-Jul-96	25	1	18	18	904.6	NA	100	NA	NA	100	NA
11	D, E & F Block PCS Broadband[c]	BTA	26-Aug-96	276	3	493	1479	2517.4	69	2	29	57	3	40
12	Cellular Unserved	MSA/RSA	13-Jan-97	36	1/1	13/1	14	1.8	100	NA	NA	100	NA	NA
14	WCS	MEA/REAG	15-Apr-97	29	2/2	52/12	128	13.6	83	0	17	72	0	28
15	DARS	Nationwide	1-Apr-97	25	2	1	2	173.2	100	NA	NA	100	NA	NA

#	Auction	Type[d]	Date											
16	800 MHz SMR	EA	28-Oct-97	235	3	175	525	96.2	95	1	4	99	0	1
17	LMDS	BTA	18-Feb-98	128	2	493	986	578.7	37	15	48	28	13	59
18	220 MHz	NW/EAG/EA	15-Sep-98	173	3/5/5	1/6/175	908	21.65	49	5	46	41	6	53
20	VHF Public Coast	VPC	3-Dec-98	44	1	42	42	7.45	79	0	21	85	0	15
21	LMS Auction	EA	23-Feb-99	54	3	176	528	3.4	NA	0	100	NA	—	100
22	C, C2, E & F Block PCS Reauction[c]	BTA	23-Mar-99	78	1[e]	339	347	412.8	6	14	80	7	27	66
23	LMDS Reauction	BTA	27-Apr-99	43	2	121	161	45.1	41	6	54	26	5	69
24	220 MHz Re-auction	EAG/EA	8-Jun-99	71	2-3/1-5	4/87	225	1.9	61	0	39	56	0	45
25	"Closed" Broadcast Auction	FM/FMT			1/1	95/1								
		PST/SST	28-Sep-99	35	1/1	12/11	119	57.8	NA	NA	NA	NA	NA	NA
27	Broadcast Auction	FM	6-Oct-99	15	1	1	1	0.17	NA	NA	NA	NA	NA	NA
	Total						8224	23431.57	67.98	22.36	40.92	66.24	23.79	44.07

Source: FCC. See <http://www.fcc.gov/wtb/auctions/>.

a Auctions 13 (IVDS) and 19 (GWCS) postponed; Auction 26 (929 and 931 MHz Paging Service) scheduled for Feb. 24, 2000.

b A Blocks in Washington, New York, and Los Angeles were not auctioned.

c C and F-Block license bidding limited to entrepreneurs (2 yr avg. annual revenue <$125m, assets <$500m); no bidding credits or installment payments available in D and E-Block auctions.

d MTA = Major Trading Area; BTA = Basic Trading Area; EA = Economic Area; MEA = Major Economic Area; REAG = Regional Economic Area Grouping; MSA = Metropolitan Statistical Area, RSA = Rural Service Area; VPC = VHF Public Coast Area; FM = FM Broadcast; FMT = FM Translator; PST = TV Broadcast; SST = TV Retransmit or TV Translator.

e Eight BTAs were auctioned with two bands—one C or C2 block and one E or F block.

Table 8.7 Summary of Affirmative Action Provisions in FCC Spectrum Auctions

Auction Number	Auction	Bidding Credits[a]	Unjust Enrichment Penalties[h]	Tax Certificates	Special Gov't Financing Provisions	Down Payment Provisions[i]	Installment Payments[i]	Interest Rate on Installment Payments
1	Nationwide Narrowband PCS	25% to DEs on 3 licenses[b]	Yes	for DEs	No	none	none	NA
2	IVDS	10% to SBEs, 15% to DEs, 25% to small DEs[b]	Yes	for DEs	Yes	SBEs pay 20% down	SBEs pay int. only for 2 yrs	5 yr note rate
3	Regional Narrowband PCS	40% to DEs on 10 licenses (2 entrepreneurs' blocks)[c]	Yes	for DEs	Yes	Des pay 20% down	DEs pay int. only for 2 yrs	10 yr note rate +2.5%
4	A & B Block PCS	none	No	none	No	none	none	NA
5	C Block PCS Broadband	25% ot SBEs[d]	Yes	none	Yes	All winning bidders pay 10% down	Each licensee pays int. only for 6 yrs	10 yr note rate
6	MDS	15% to SBEs	Yes	none	Yes	SBEs pay 10% down	SBEs pay int. only for 2 yrs	10 yr note rate +2.5%
7	900 MHz SMR	10% to SBEs, 15% to VSBEs[e]	Yes	none	Yes	SBEs pay 10% down	VSBEs pay int. only for 5 yrs, SBEs for 2 yrs[e]	10 yr note rate +2.5%
8	DBS (110 W)	none	No	none	No	none	none	NA
9	DBS (148 W)	none	No	none	No	none	none	NA

						All winning bidders pay 10% down / F-Block winning bidders pay 20% down	Each licensee pays int. only for 6 yrs / SBEs pay int. only for 2 yrs, entrepreneurs[f] for 1 yr	10 yr note rate / 10 yr note rate[k]
10	C Block PCS Re-auction	25% ot SBEs[d]	Yes	none	Yes	All winning bidders pay 10% down	Each licensee pays int. only for 6 yrs	10 yr note rate
11	D, E & F Block PCS Broadband	15% to SBEs, 25% to VSBEs[d]	Yes	none	Yes	F-Block winning bidders pay 20% down	SBEs pay int. only for 2 yrs, entrepreneurs[f] for 1 yr	10 yr note rate[k]
12	Cellular Unserved	none	No	none	No	none	none	NA
14	WCS	25% to SBEs, 35% to VSBEs	Yes	none	No	none	none	NA
15	DARS	none	No	none	No	none	none	NA
16	800 MHz SMR	25% to SBEs, 35% to VSBEs[e]	Yes	none	No	none	none	NA
17	LMDS	25% to entrepreneur[f], 35% to SBEs, 45% to VSBEs	Yes	none	No	none	none	NA
18	220 MHz	25% to SBEs, 35% to VSBEs[e]	Yes	none	No	none	none	NA
20	VHF Public Coast	25% to SBEs, 35% to VSBEs[e]	Yes	none	No	none	none	NA
21	LMS Auction	25% to SBEs, 35% to VSBEs[e]	Yes	none	No	none	none	NA
22	C, C2, E & F Block PCS Re-auction	15% to SBEs, 25% to VSVEs[e]	Yes	none	no	none	none	NA

Table 8.7 (Continued)

Auction Number	Auction	Bidding Credits[a]	Unjust Enrichment Penalties[h]	Tax Certificates	Special Gov't Financing Provisions	Down Payment Provisions[j]	Installment Payments[j]	Interest Rate on Installment Payments
23	LMDS Reauction	25% to entrepreneur[e], 35% to SBEs, 45% to VSBEs	Yes	none	No	none	none	NA
24	220 MHz Re-auction	25% to SBEs, 35% to VSBEs[e]	Yes	none	No	none	none	NA
25	"Closed" Broadcast Auction	new entrant bidding credit[g]	Yes	none	No	none	none	NA
27	Broadcast Auction	new entrant bidding credit	Yes	none	No	none	none	NA

Source: See table 8.6.

ᵃ SBE = Small Business Enterprise (3 yr avg. annual revenue <$40m); VSBE = Very Small Business Enterprise (3 yr avg. annual revenue <$15m); DE = Minority- or woman-owned Business Enterprise.

ᵇ A business owned by minorities and/or women is one that has a control group composed 100 percent of minorities and/or women that owns 50.1 percent of the voting interests and 50.1 percent of the total equity.

ᶜ A business owned by minorities and/or women is one that has a control group composed 100 percent of minorities and/or women that owns 50.1 percent of the voting interests, and (A) 50.1 percent of the total equity; or (B) 25 percent of the total equity, if no single other investor owns more than 25 percent.

ᵈ C and F-Block license bidding limited to entrepreneurs (2 yr avg. annual revenue <$125m, assets <$500m); no bidding credits or installment payments available in D and E-Block auctions.

ᵉ For this auction, SBE = business with 3 yr avg. annual revenue <$15m; VSBE = business with 3 yr avg. annual revenue < $3m.

ᶠ For this auction, entrepreneur = business with 3 yr avg. annual revenue <$70m, but >$40m.

ᵍ The new entrant bidding credit depends on the number of the bidder's ownership interests in other media of mass communications. The credit is 35 percent if the bidder has no attributable interest in any other media and 25 percent if bidder has an interest in no more bidding credit.

ʰ During the initial license term, licensees utilizing bidding credits and seeking to transfer control of a license to an entity that does not meet the eligibility criteria for bidding credits will be required to reimburse the government for the amount of the credit plus interest.

ⁱ This includes the amount due upon receiving the license. The default provisions for winning bidders are that they must pay a down payment of 20 percent of the winning bid and pay the remaining 80 percent upon receiving the license.

ʲ Principal and interest amortized over ten years at the specified interest rate.

ᵏ Ten-yr U.S. Treas. note rate for SBEs, note rate + 2.5 percent for entrepreneurs⁶, note rate + 3.5 percent for others.

response as the benchmark estimate as the price for which each license would sell, this method ignores the fact that 50/12 licenses within the same region are close to perfect substitutes (for any bidder not seeking a national aggregation). To calculate a more conservative estimate of the effect of crossover bidding, we assumed a bidder expressing demand of $12 million on a Block 3 regional license would have been willing to bid as much for the similar regional license on Blocks 4 and 5. Accordingly, we calculated, for each region, the maximum response on three 50/12 licenses (to the final bids by nondesignated bidders that ultimately dropped out). We used this higher figure as our benchmark for expected revenue in the absence of affirmative action. For example, we assume that Westlink would have been willing to replicate its bid of $8.941 million on the West Block 5 license on all of the West 50/12 licenses, and used the response of $9.4 million as the relevant benchmark for each of the three licenses. The bottom of the table aggregates the increase in revenue by block—the overall increase of $44.9 million.

CHAPTER 9

Expanding the Domain of Civil Rights Empiricism

The previous chapters documenting disparate treatment in retail car sales and unjustified disparate impacts in kidney transplantation and bail setting suggest that discrimination is neither a thing of the past nor is it confined to the traditional core markets of employment, housing, and public accommodations. In this concluding chapter, I argue that government should expand the domain of civil rights empiricism along four dimensions. Specifically, government should sponsor (1) more testing, (2) in more markets, (3) with more types of testing, and (4) with more attention to cause.

Knowing the actual incidence of disparate treatment is particularly relevant to the ongoing debate about affirmative action—for the simple reason that race-conscious remedies are most easily justifiable as a response to *current* discrimination. Identifying the extent and cause of discrimination is a necessary first step to formulating an efficacious remedy. Widespread discrimination auditing could serve not only as a basis for disparate treatment suits but more provocatively might provide powerful evidence that traditionally disadvantaged groups continue to be subject to inferior treatment and thus help sustain the government's use of race-conscious affirmative action.

I. More Auditing in More Markets

Government should more systematically test for disparate treatment across a wide variety of markets. Such testing could provide valuable information to private individuals and public officials. Private individuals qua consumers may want the choice not to patronize stores that discriminate on the basis of race or gender. This might be true not only of minority or female consumers who seek to avoid being victims, but also true for the supposed beneficiaries of the discrimination (nonminority or male consumers) who might be averse to shopping at a store that is publicly known to discriminate. Civil rights consumerism is still in its infancy. But this may in large part be because consumers do not have ready access to reliable information about which sellers discriminate and which do not. The dramatic antidiscrimination Saturn commercials (discussed in chapter 5) suggest that consumers may value this type of information. It is not hard to imagine that consumers would deliberately avoid patronizing a retailer (think, for example, of Denny's)[1] who has been found to systematically engage in disparate racial treatment of its employees or customers. Nondiscrimination is often a credence good, because consumers often cannot tell whether a retailer is systematically engaging in disparate racial or gender treatment, especially regarding discretionary aspects of their behavior. Providing consumers information about credence aspects of quality is a standard and well-recognized role of government.[2] Giving consumers this information—without more—might help to drive out important types of disparate treatment by giving corporations a stronger profit motive to monitor their agents on just this dimension.[3]

---

1. See Denny's Manager Accused of Racial Bias, *L.A. Times,* Jan. 8, 1998.

2. See generally Howard Beales, Richard Craswell & Steve Salop, The Efficient Regulation of Consumer Information, 24 J.L. & Econ. 491, 525 (1981); Ian Ayres & F. Clayton Miller, "I'll Sell It to You at Cost": Legal Methods to Promote Retail Markup Disclosure, 84 Nw. U. L. Rev. 1047 (1990).

3. Providing such information also creates benefits of a quasi-constitutional dimension insofar as it gives individuals better information on which to exercise their associational rights. Knowing whether a particular (economic or noneconomic) organization discriminates facilitates individuals' ability to make a more informed choice about whether to associate with such an organization. Cf. Buckley v. Valeo, 424 U.S. 1, 66–67 (1976) (upholding mandatory disclosure of donor identity, in part, because it gives voter's better information about whether they should associate with particular candidates); Boy Scouts of America v. Dale, 120 S. Ct. 2446 (2000) (finding that Boy Scout Oath's injunction to be "clean" and "morally straight" was sufficient to give potential mem-

This information would also be valuable to private individuals in their roles as citizen voters. As Jody Armour has pointed out:

> A recent survey found that sixty-eight percent of white respondents believed that blacks enjoy the same or more opportunity as whites to be "really successful and wealthy." A majority of the poll's white respondents believed that, educationally, the average black American is just as well-off or better off than the average white American; nearly half of the whites polled (forty-seven percent) believed that blacks enjoy the same standard of living as whites. Another poll by People for the American Way found that most Americans believed that the predominant type of discrimination today is "reverse discrimination" . . . .[4]

Given this view of the world on the part of the public, it is not surprising that there is increasing resistance to remedial affirmative action. More systematic data detailing the extent and pervasiveness of current discrimination might be crucial to informing the current debate about what shape our government's efforts to end discrimination should or should not take.

That there should be more government auditing of the status of civil rights is similar to the Urban Institute's call for a "National Report Card on Discrimination."[5] But my suggestion is for an even broader and systematic program of ongoing auditing of disparate racial and gender treatment. The tests should focus on those terms and conditions of consumption that are least comparable across consumers—aspects of discretionary treatment that might easily mask disparate treatment. The results of this book are not sufficient to establish that disparate treatment is pervasive in discretionary

---

bers notice that they were associated with an organization that reserved an ability to discriminate against homosexuals).

4. Jody David Armour, Hype and Reality in Affirmative Action, 68 U. Colo. L. Rev. 1173 (1997), quoting Mollyann Brodie, *The Four Americas: Government and Social Policy through the Eyes of America's Multi-Racial and Multi-Ethnic Society* (1995). A 1995 *Newsweek* poll found that twice as many respondents believed that whites were losing out because of affirmative action than believed blacks were losing out because of discrimination. David Benjamin Oppenheimer, Understanding Affirmative Action, 23 Hastings Const. L.Q. 921, 958–59 & n.217 (1996)

5. *A National Report Card on Discrimination in America: The Role of Testing* (Michael Fix & Margery Austin Turner eds., 1999). See also Christopher Edley Jr., Color at Century's End: Race in Law, Policy, and Politics, 67 Fordham L. Rev. 939 (1998).

aspects of retailing, but the results when combined with the empirical studies of others[6] are at least sufficient to reject the notion that race and gender discrimination is confined to employment, housing, and public accommodations.

Indeed, there is no reason that testing must be limited to the retail level. A substantial amount of government affirmative action in procurement attempts to remedy discrimination against minority-owned businesses. Audit findings of racial discrimination might provide important support for the use of affirmative action. Fred Vars and I have recently argued that government may constitutionally remedy private discrimination as long as it narrowly tailors its remedy.[7] An audit finding that either private suppliers or customers discriminate against minority firms would accordingly provide powerful evidence under *Adarand* and *Croson* that the government has a compelling interest to enhance minority utilization.[8] Of course, to satisfy the constitutional requirements of strict scrutiny, the government would also need to show inter alia that merely enforcing a § 1981–like prohibition against discrimination in contracting would not be sufficient to deter discrimination. But the audit information could be valuable to governments deciding whether to introduce (or maintain) affirmative action programs or attempting to defend these programs from constitutional attack.

Auditing of individual applicants for affirmative action benefits might also provide valuable information about whether they are subjected to systematic social disadvantage. In the rare instance where the racial status of a potential affirmative action beneficiary is at issue,[9] auditing information

6. See, e.g., Peter Siegelman, *Race Discrimination in "Everyday" Commercial Transactions: What Do We Know, What Do We Need to Know, and How Can We Find Out* (1998); John Yinger, Evidence of Discrimination in Consumer Markets, 12 J. Econ. Persp. 23 (1998).

7. Ian Ayres & Fredrick E. Vars, When Does Private Discrimination Justify Public Affirmative Action? 1998 Colum. L. Rev. 1577 (1998).

8. Id.; Adarand Constructors, Inc. v. Pena, 515 U.S. 200 (1995); City of Richmond v. J.A. Croson Co., 488 U.S. 469 (1989). In *Croson*, Justice O'Connor, concluded that the City of Richmond "can use its spending powers to remedy private discrimination, if it identifies that discrimination with the particularity required by the Fourteenth Amendment." Id. at 492.

9. Two much publicized (but nonrepresentative) instances of "whites" seeking to pass as minorities in order to qualify for affirmative action benefits concern the Malone brothers and the Liberman family. Extrinsic evidence suggests that Paul and Philip Malone—who were fair-skinned but nevertheless claimed African American status as part of an effort to join the Boston fire department—had not been subjected to disparate ra-

on whether third parties treat the applicant differently could provide a much stronger basis for resolving the dispute rather than arcane and objectionable proof regarding sanguinity. If an applicant's self-reported racial identity is disputed, the agency administering the program might test to see whether the applicant is subjected to systematically worse treatment in a variety of different settings. It might even be possible to include the applicant (or the applicant's photograph) in the implicit attitude tests described below to see if subjects systematically treat the applicant differently than whites (whose race is not disputed).

One can even imagine using the results of audit studies of minorities more generally as a prerequisite (necessary but not sufficient) for race-contingent affirmative action remedies. It would be much easier to defend affirmative action programs that were explicitly triggered by a finding of disparate treatment *and* that automatically suspended the race-contingent remedy if future tests failed to find further disparate treatment. Just as federal highway subsidies to a particular state can be extinguished if ongoing radar testing were to reveal systematic speeding by that state's drivers,[10] a remedial affirmative action program might be suspended (at least after some period to remedy prior discrimination) if future audits were to show

---

cial treatment by society. See Christopher Ford, Administering Identity: The Determination of "Race" in Race-Conscious Law, 82 Cal. L. Rev. 1231, 1272–76 (1994). The status of the Liberman family (which claimed Hispanic status as Sephardic Jews to qualify for an FCC affirmative action program) stands, however, on a much firmer footing. While the FCC's finding that the Libermans qualified as Hispanic has been decried as a racial hoax by commentators and judges, see Metro Broadcasting, Inc. v. FCC, 497 U.S. 547, 633 n.1 (1990) (Kennedy, J., dissenting) ("The [FCC], for example, has found it necessary to trace an applicant's family history to 1492 to conclude that the applicant was "Hispanic" for purposes of a minority tax certificate policy."); Ronald D. Rotunda, *Modern Constitutional Law* 544 (4th ed. 1993) (the Liberman family "qualified as Hispanic because they traced their family to Jews whom the King had expelled from Spain in 1492. If you assume 20 years to a generation, there were over 24 generations from 1492 to the [present]. That means that Mr. Liberman was as closely related to 16,777,216 ancestors."), the FCC found that Adolfo Liberman and his sons Jose, Elias, and Julio were "regarded by both themselves and their community as being Hispanic." Their native language was Spanish, which "they still speak a majority of the time." The family members had lived together in Mexico, Guatemala, and Costa Rica before coming to the United States and becoming naturalized citizens. See In re Storer Broadcasting Co., 87 F.C.C.2d 190, 190 (1981). I hypothesize that if we tested the Malones and Libermans in a variety of retail setting (including say car dealerships), we would find that the Libermans received systematically poorer treatment than most self-described whites but that the Malones would not receive poorer treatment. Audit testing provides an objective way of resolving the relatively rare, but sensational question of who qualifies as a minority.

10. See 23 U.S.C. § 154 (1986).

that minority contractors were no longer subjected to disparate treatment in purchasing inputs or selling output.

There are increasing indications that a majority of the Supreme Court will require sunset provisions for affirmative action programs.[11] But sunset remedies are only logically implicated if discrimination is a thing of the past. We do not think about sunsetting tort remedies for assault because it is clear that assaults continue to happen today.[12] A showing that racial torts also continue today would analogously provide an important rationale for a continued remedy. Auditing sunsets are much more tailored than arbitrary temporal measures (ending a program after, say, some fixed number of years).

Because audit tests necessarily have an aspect of deception (in that the auditors do not reveal their underlying purpose to the subject of the audits), they raise ethical concerns of government as Big Brother invading our privacy. Indeed, according to Alan Greenspan, concerns over deception were the primary reason why the Federal Reserve in 1991 rejected racial audits of banks' willingness to make home mortgage loans.[13] But concerns with the aspect of deception can at least be minimized. First, at the retail level, there is already a large amount of deceptive auditing of retailers. Retailers regularly audit the prices of their competitors. Franchisors regularly audit a variety of behaviors of the franchisees. Second, it is no longer deceptive for a brokerage firm to tape-record a phone call as long as they warn in advance that "this call may be recorded." Our concerns with deception may be similarly allayed if at the time of licensing, government puts retailers on notice that a condition of doing business is that a retailer consents to being audited. The testing is still deceptive at the level of the individual transaction, but is no longer deceptive at a broader level (and to a degree the retailer has even consented to it as a condition of doing business). It seems particularly appropriate to test in heavily regulated industries—such

---

11. See, e.g., *Adarand*, 515 U.S. 200 at 237 (affirmative action program " 'will not last longer than the discriminatory effects it is designed to eliminate,' " quoting Fullilove v. Klutznick, 448 U.S. 448, 513 [1980] [Powell, J., concurring]); *Metro Broadcasting*, 497 U.S. at 596 ("[S]uch a goal carries its own natural limit. . . . The FCC's plan, like the Harvard admissions program discussed in *Bakke*, contains the seed of its own termination."); *Fullilove*, 448 U.S. at 489 ("The MBE provision may be viewed as a pilot project, appropriately limited in extent and duration, and subject to reassessment and reevaluation by the Congress prior to any extension or re-enactment.").

12. This argument is fleshed out more explicitly in Ian Ayres, Narrow Tailoring, 43 UCLA L. Rev. 1781 (1996).

13. Steven A. Holmes, U.S. Is Asked to Expand Undercover Bias Testing, *N.Y. Times*, Sept. 26, 1991, at A18.

as banking or taxicabs—where regulatory conditions of doing business are accepted (and where the government, because of its regulation, bears a particularly high burden to smoke out and remedy discrimination). Finally, and most pragmatically, the testing could be structured to impose relatively minor costs on retailers. As an equitable matter, the costs of the audits would fall disproportionately upon discriminatory firms who would more likely be subject to follow-up audits to determine the validity of initial findings.

II. More Types of Testing

Expanding the use of tests for discrimination should not involve only the traditional audit methodology. In this section, I will further describe the strengths and weaknesses of the outcome tests used in chapter 7's discussion of discrimination in bail bond setting. But first, I want to recommend the use of a new type of testing that I call the "principal" audit, which can be used whenever there is an intermediary or agent (or, in the more traditional parlance, a "middleman") who metaphorically stands between potential discriminators and potential victims of discrimination. This is a type of testing that is ready-made for use in either housing or employment contexts in which real estate agents or employment agencies serve just this intermediating function for principals (employers/real estate sellers) who may wish their agents to discriminate.

A central advantage of both principal audits and outcome tests is that neither is susceptible to the concern with what econometricians call "omitted-variable bias"—which is recurrently raised with regard to traditional audits. Civil rights defendants confronted with adverse auditing evidence almost always claim that their disparate treatment was not based on the testers' race (or sex) but on some other characteristic for which the testing organization failed to control. By circumventing the omitted-variable bias, principal audits and outcome tests thus provide strong new forms of evidence to complement traditional audit testing.

A. Principal Audits

The basic idea of the principal audit is that instead of using two testers who pretend to be applicants for a job, the testing group uses a single tester who pretends to be an employer seeking employees. If the employment agency being audited offers to discriminate on the tester's behalf, the test produces conclusive evidence of the agent's willingness to violate the statute. A recurrent problem with the traditional (two-person) audit is that the employment agency almost always claims that its disparate treatment of the testers was not based on the testers' racial difference but on some nonracial characteristic. This omitted-variable defense, however, is not available with a principal audit when the agency that is the subject of the test expressly volunteers to discriminate on the basis of race in sorting potential job applicants (or potential real estate buyers or renters in the context of fair housing).

I should confess, however, that the idea for "principal audits" did not come to me in a moment of inspiration. It rather was thrust upon me soon after my first child Henry was born as I (with bleary eyes) made some initial calls to find out how much it would cost to hire a nanny. I first called "Thank Goodness I've Found," a New Haven nanny agency. The agency representative ignored my question about cost and launched into what sounded like a canned sales spiel, during the course of which the representative said:

> Tell me your prejudices. We'll only send you *pink* polka dotted nanny's if that's what you want. If you're not comfortable with a older or a younger girl, we'll make sure that you only have to interview candidates that you like.

The representative expressly offered to discriminate on the basis of age, but I am highly confident that had I responded by saying "I'm not really comfortable dealing with Hispanics," the representative would have agreed to only send non-Hispanic applicants.

While I did not challenge the representative on the phone, I did file a complaint with Connecticut's Human Rights Commission, which is required to investigate allegations of discrimination. In my affidavit, I suggested that they could undertake a five-minute investigation by merely having someone call the agency pretending to be a potential employer. (To my knowledge the commission never acted on my complaint).

To be sure, such principal audits raise important ethical issues. As with traditional audits there is unavoidable deception. Pretending to be an employer or a real estate seller can also raise concerns of government "entrapment." While as a legal matter the entrapment defense only immunizes criminal defendants, a civil suit analogue might arise especially if a government official went further and directly asked if the real estate or employment agent would be willing to discriminate against minorities. The entrapment concern that the audit lured an otherwise innocent agent to discriminate could be reduced if the audits were only used in response to consumer complaints that they had encountered discrimination (as in my nanny incident). But even in such instances, principal audits might unwittingly send a false signal that there is demand by principals for such behavior. Accordingly, it would be important for the faux principal (that is, the tester) to announce at the end of the test (whether or not the agent had acceded to the discrimination request) that an audit had just occurred.

Even given these important ethical issues in implementation, the principal audit has important advantages. My nanny narrative suggests that intermediaries may have their guard down when speaking with principals. Testing both sides of the intermediary market would let real estate and employment agents know that there is no safe harbor for openly talking about race discrimination. Just making it more difficult for potential employers and real estate sellers to communicate their discriminatory preferences might on the margin drive some discrimination out of the market. Indeed, a useful analogue to principal audits might be a requirement that real estate and employments agents have a duty to report to the appropriate commission on human rights any instance in which a potential principal solicits their discrimination. Under such a regime, an agent who hears a solicitation for discrimination would either have to report it or fear that she would be disciplined for failure to report (if the soliciting principal turned out to be a tester).

B. Outcome Tests

As discussed in chapter 7, outcome tests can provide powerful evidence of when a particular kind of decisionmaking has an unjustified disparate impact. Outcome tests can produce a single statistic indicating both traditional elements of a disparate impact case—that decisionmaking disproportionally burdens minorities and that this disproportionality is not justified by heightened institutional productivity. Moreover, as discussed below, the outcome tests (while having some limitations of their own) are not susceptible the traditional concern with omitted-variable bias.

The basic idea of the outcome test is to analyze whether the outcomes (about which the decisionmaker cares) are systematically different for minorities and nonminorities. If we find that in distributing benefits the decisionmaker effectively demands better outcomes from minorities than from whites, we may infer there to be a class of minorities that might have received benefits and produced the same quality of outcomes for the decisionmaker. Thus if we find

- lending decisions produce higher profits on loans to minorities than to whites, we might infer that the lending decisions have an unjustified disparate impact in excluding qualified minority lenders;[14]
- bail bond setting decisions produce higher appearance rates for minorities than for whites, we might infer that bond setting decisions have an unjustified disparate impact on minority defendants;[15]
- editorial acceptance decisions produce higher citation rates for articles written by minorities than by whites, we might infer that acceptance decisions have an unjustified disparate impact in excluding qualified minority articles;[16] and
- hiring decisions produce higher productivity for minority workers than for white workers, we might infer that hiring decisions have an unjustified disparate impact in excluding qualified minority workers.[17]

Outcome tests can also be effective in analyzing a decisionmaker's allocation of detriments. If we find that in distributing a detriment that the decisionmaker effectively accepts poorer outcomes from minorities than from whites, we may infer there to be a class of minorities that might have avoided the detriment. For example, if we find

14. Becker suggested that if banks discriminate against minorities we should expect that minorities would have lower default rates. Becker first proposed this approach in a *Business Week* op-ed, Gary S. Becker, The Evidence Against Banks Doesn't Prove Bias, *Business Week*, 1993 WL 2142407 (April 19, 1993), and detailed his suggestion in his Nobel Prize lecture. Gary S. Becker, Nobel Lecture: The Economic Way of Looking at Behavior, 101 J. Pol. Econ. 385, 389 (1993).

15. This type of test of course was the basis of chapter 7.

16. See Scott Smart & Joel Waldfogel, A Citation-Based Test for Discrimination at Economic and Finance Journals (NBER Working Paper 5460 1996); Ian Ayres & Fredrick E. Vars, Determinants of Citations to Articles in Elite Law Review, 29 J. Legal Stud. 427 (2000).

17. See James Gwartney & Charles Hayworth, Employer Costs and Discrimination: The Case of Baseball, 82 J. Pol. Econ. 873, 876 (1974); Jack F. Williams, Title VII and the Reserve Clause: A Statistical Analysis of Salary Discrimination in Major League Baseball, 52 U. Miami L. Rev. 461, 509 (1998).

- police search decisions are systematically less productive with regard to minorities than with regard to whites, we might infer that search decisions have an unjustified disparate impact in subjecting undeserving minorities to being searched.[18]

Because outcome testing is an especially useful tool in assessing allegations of racial profiling by police, the following discussion will focus on "police search" outcome tests as a primary example to illuminate the strengths and weaknesses of this methodology.

The *ex post* probability that a police search will uncover contraband or evidence of illegality is strong evidence of the average level of probable cause that police require before undertaking a search. A finding that minority searches are systematically less productive than white searches is accordingly evidence that police require less probable cause when searching minorities. To be sure, such a finding does not require that we infer that police engaged in disparate treatment—but, at a minimum, it is evidence that whatever criteria the police employed produced an unjustified disparate impact.[19] Such evidence would suggest that if police required the same level of probable cause when searching minorities as when searching whites, there would be fewer minorities searched (or proportionally more whites searched).

A major advantage of these outcome comes tests is that they are not susceptible to the omitted-variable bias critique that has plagued traditional regression-based tests of disparate treatment. Researchers do not need to observe and control for all the variables that police considered in deciding whether to search as long as they can observe the outcome of their decisionmaking. The outcome tests are not embarrassed by omitted-variable bias because, under the null hypothesis, there should be no observable variables that systematically affect the probability of success once the decisionmaker has made an individualized assessment so as to equalize this very probability. Indeed, the outcome test intentionally harnesses omitted-variable bias to test whether any excluded (unjustified) determinant of decisionmaking is sufficiently correlated with the included racial character-

18. For an example of this type of testing, see John Knowles, Nicola Persico & Petra Todd, Racial Bias in Motor Vehicle Searches: Theory and Evidence, J. Pol. Econ. (forthcoming 2000).

19. Evidence of an unjustified disparate impact can be used to show intentional discrimination (disparate treatment); and under current law unjustified disparate racial impacts of police action can be challenged under federal law. See 28 C.F.R. § 42.203(3), *implementing* 42 U.S.C. § 3798d(c).

istics to produce evidence of a statistically significant racial disparity.[20] Any finding that the police searches of individuals with a particular characteristic (such as minority status) induce a systematically lower probability of uncovering illegality suggests that police search criteria unjustifiably subject that class of individuals to the disability of being searched.

This point about omitted variables can be restated in more legalistic terms. The outcome test is not susceptible to the "qualified pool" problem that plagues both traditional disparate impact and disparate treatment issues of proof. The decisionmaker in an outcome test defines by her own decisions what she thinks the qualified pool to be, and the outcome test then directly assesses whether the minorities and nonminorities so chosen are in fact equally qualified. A finding that chosen minorities produce better outcomes than chosen whites suggest that the decisionmaker unfairly excluded some qualified minorities from benefits (or subjected them to unjustified detriments). As applied to police searches, a finding that the search success rate (that is, the probability of finding evidence of illegality) is systematically lower for searched minorities than for searched whites suggests that minorities less deserved (that is, were less "qualified") to be searched. A defense that police searching decisions were driven by the underlying criminality of those searched—and that minorities make up a larger proportion of those deserving to be searched—would be contradicted by systematically lower success rates when such searches were in fact completed.

But while the outcome test methodology has important strengths, it has limitations as well. First and foremost the methodology is primarily a test of whether decisionmaking criteria have an unjustified disparate impact. While such evidence can be quite probative of disparate treatment, there are ways that the outcome test can be both under- and overinclusive as a test of disparate treatment.

Because they are not well structured to capture disparate racial treatment motivated by rational statistical inference—so-called statistical discrimination—outcome tests can be underinclusive as tests of disparate treatment. In his Nobel Prize lecture, Gary Becker extolled outcome tests as being the "direct" approach to measuring discrimination. His definition of "discrimination," however, does not capture all race-contingent

20. Stephen Ross and John Yinger have noted that the default approach attempts to identify mortgage discrimination by purposely omitting variables from the regression. Stephen L. Ross & John Yinger, The Default Approach to Studying Mortgage Discrimination: A Rebuttal, *in Mortgage Lending Discrimination: A Review of Existing Evidence* 107, 112 (Margery Austin Turner & Felicity Skidmore eds., 1999).

decisionmaking. Analyzing bank lending, Becker concluded: "If banks discriminate against minority applicants, they should earn *greater* profits on the loans actually made to them than on those to whites."[21] But this is true only if the discrimination is caused by associational animus and is not necessarily true if, instead, the discrimination is caused by statistical inference.

As applied to police searching criteria an outcome test would likely capture efforts by police to arbitrarily target and harass a minority population. But it might not capture express racial profiling that was based on valid statistical inference. For example, if police were correct in inferring among some group of otherwise observationally equivalent suspects that minority suspects had a higher likelihood than whites of possessing contraband and therefore used race expressly as a part of their criteria for searching, then in equilibrium we might not observe lower search success rate for minorities than for whites. Even though the police were engaging in a type of disparate racial treatment—express racial profiling—the outcome test might show no racially disparate outcomes.

If underinclusion were the only problem, an outcome test might still provide valuable "one-tailed" test of the existence of disparate treatment. But certain forms of the outcome test may also be overinclusive as a test of disparate treatment—particularly with regard to what I will call problems of "inframarginality" and "subgroup validity."

1.   The Inframarginality Problem

A potential problem with outcome assessments as tests of disparate treatment arises if researchers are only able to measure the average outcome and not the outcomes associated with the marginal decision. In the mortgage context, a test of disparate treatment would want to ask whether the least-qualified whites to which banks were willing to lend had a higher default rate than the least-qualified minorities to which banks were willing to lend. If lenders dislike lending to minorities, then the least-qualified minority to which they would be willing to lend (the marginal minority borrower) should have a lower expected default rate than the least-qualified nonminority to which they are willing to lend (the marginal nonminority borrower). Unfortunately, marginal default rates are unobservable and researchers are often only able to estimate the average default rates condi-

---

21.   Becker, *supra* note 14, at 389.

tional on being above this marginal lending threshold.[22] Lenders might still discriminate against minority borrowers—in the straightforward sense that the lending threshold for minorities might be more stringent than for nonminorities—but we might still see that the average rate of minority default (conditional on being above the minority lending cutoff) is higher than the average rate of nonminority default (conditional on being above the nonminority lending cutoff). As long as inframarginal nonminority borrowers have lower expected default rates (than inframarginal minority borrowers), a comparison of average defaults may mask disparate treatment by lenders in setting the minimum thresholds for granting loans.

A similar inframarginality problem could also limit the use of outcome analysis as a measure of disparate racial treatment in police search decisions. As discussed above, a finding that police have systematically lower success rates when searching minorities than when searching whites might raise concerns that police were using race contingent search thresholds. But observing that the average search success rate for minorities was lower than for whites does not necessarily prove that the threshold (or marginal) expected success rate was lower for minorities than for whites. Disparate treatment tests are normally tests of decisionmaking on the margin, but real-world data at times only allows researchers to assess inframarginal effects.[23]

This problem of inframarginality does not, however, equally undermine all outcome tests. If either the decision or the outcome is nondichotomous, it may become easier for the researcher to identify the marginal effects. For example, in the bail bond setting context, the fact that judges were setting continuous (nondichotomous) bail amounts allowed us to directly test the marginal impact of their decisions. The judges' ability to individually vary the bail amount in a sense makes every defendant marginal—and thus avoids the inframarginal problem that has plagued the

---

22. James H. Carr & Isaac F. Megbolugbe, The Federal Reserve Bank of Boston Study on Mortgage Lending Revisited, 4 J. Housing Res. 277, 309 (1993). See also George C. Galster, The Facts of Lending Discrimination Cannot Be Argued Away by Examining Default Rates, 4 Housing Pol'y Debate 141 (1993).

23. It should be emphasized that this inframarginality problem can also cause outcome analysis to be underinclusive as a test of disparate treatment. For example in the policing context, we might as a theoretical matter observe minority search success rates to be higher on average even though police require less probable cause on the margin to search when searching minorities. As argued before, however, underinclusiveness would not undermine the test's use as a one-sided test for disparate treatment.

application of outcome tests in the mortgage context (where lenders make a much more dichotomous decision about whether to lend or not). Similarly, if the outcome itself is nondichotomous, it may be easier to identify whether the threshold decisionmaking is discriminatory. Thus, for example, in the citation studies mentioned above, by measuring the number of citations given to articles written by minorities and nonminorities, researchers can assess not just the average level of success (as with a dichotomous outcome variable, such as nondefault on a loan) but they can estimate the entire distribution of success. By analyzing this distribution, it may be possible to identify whether the editors in making acceptence decisions systematically demand more or fewer expected citations in accepting the marginal (least likely cited) articles of minority authors.

The most daunting problem for research using outcome tests concerns those contexts in which both the decision and outcome are dichotomous. This might well describe both mortgage lending (where the bank decides to lend/not lend, and the outcome is default/nondefault) and police searches (where the police decide to search/not search and the outcome is contraband found/not found). In such circumstances, the basic structure of the data does not allow the researcher to go beyond observing averages. But even in these contexts, I believe that outcome tests may still be of use for two reasons.[24]

First, in some contexts evidence of racial disparities in the average outcome is strong evidence of disparities on the margin. Here it is useful to contrast mortgage lending and police searches. In the mortgage context, evidence about average defaults may not provide strong evidence of marginal expected default rate. Because white borrowers, as an empirical matter, are likely to control more wealth, it should not be surprising if whites are disproportionately inframarginal borrowers (with a low default rate). Observing lower average white default rates should accordingly not give us confidence that the expected default rate of the marginal white is less than that of the marginal minority borrower.

In contrast, in the context of police searches, it is harder to articulate why the average search success rates would not be a credible proxy for the marginal success rate. If researchers found that the average white search success rate was systematically higher than that for minorities, it would be difficult to explain why whites were more likely to be inframar-

24. Knowles et al., *supra* note 18, have recently suggested a third reason. The strategic actions of those subject to a decision may systematically move the average success rate toward the marginal success rate thus making the average a better proxy.

ginal searchees. To argue that this finding was not evidence of discrimination, the police would need to say that they searched every one with a minimum probable cause but that of those meeting this standard whites for some reason had a systematically higher chance of possessing evidence of illegality. The difficulty is articulating a particular reason why the inframarginal white would have a higher probability of possessing contraband even though the marginal white did not.[25] The core issue is whether evidence of average (inframarginal) racial outcomes difference is probative of marginal (or threshold) outcome differences. When there are not compelling reasons to suspect the inframarginal effects to differ from the marginal—which I have suggested is much more the case with police searches than with mortgage lending—the outcome tests can still provide valuable information about the probable existence of discrimination.

Second, while the inframarginality problem can limit the usefulness of outcome analysis as a test of disparate treatment, it is not as much of a problem when interpreting the outcome analysis merely as a test of unjustified disparate impact. For example, imagine researchers find that the average white search uncovers contraband 15 percent of the time, while the average minority search uncovers contraband only 10 percent of the time. The police could raise inframarginality as a defense to the claim that this finding proves disparate treatment: for example, they might argue that they stop all people who display at least a 5 percent probability of having contraband (and of this group, it just so happens that 15 percent of whites have contraband while only 10 percent of minorities do). In essence, the police would be arguing that they apply a uniform (5 percent) threshold to all suspects regardless of race—so that at the margin there is no disparate treatment. But this would not be a defense to the claim that police search criteria impose a disparate impact on minorities. The finding of an average racial disparity must mean that there exists some higher uniform probable cause threshold (between 5 and 15 percent) that would have subjected disproportionately fewer minorities to search. In other words, the finding that white searches are systematically more successful than minority searches suggests that choosing a low uniform threshold had a disparate impact of disproportionately exposing minorities to unsuccessful searches. But while

25. Disproportionate minority recidivism might begin to provide such a theory. If recidivists are more skilled in secreting contraband and if recidivists are disproportionately minorities, then we might think of nonrecidivists as being the inframarginal searchees (whose search would produce a higher probability of uncovering contraband). If nonrecidivists are disproportionately white, then the average search success rates of whites might be higher than that of minorities.

a finding of disparity in the average search success rates would be evidence of a disparate impact, it might—taking into account the inframarginality—no longer imply evidence of an *unjustified* disparate impact. Under the previous hypothetical, as long as the uniform probable cause threshold (5 percent) was not unreasonably lowed, the police could argue that their searching criteria had a justified disparate impact. So ultimately, outcome analysis can still provide strong evidence of a disparate racial impact. But in this instance, whether the impact is justified or not may turn on whether evidence of racial disparities in the average outcomes is evidence of racial differences in the threshold (or marginal) decisionmaking.

2.   The Subgroup Validity Problem

A second limitation on the use of outcome tests as evidence of disparate racial treatment concerns what I term the "subgroup validity problem." Put simply, when a particular observable characteristic is valid for some races but not for others, it is possible that a decisionmaker conditioning her decisions on this characteristic generally might induce racially disparate outcomes. To put the matter provocatively, when a particular observable characteristic is only a valid proxy of desert for some races, then a decisionmaker's *unwillingness* to engage in disparate racial treatment may induce just the racial disparities in outcomes that are generally a concern.

For example, imagine that wearing a particular type of baseball cap is strong evidence of drug possession when worn by whites but not when worn by minorities. In the extreme, imagine that 100 percent of whites wearing this cap possess drugs, and zero percent of minorities wearing this cap possess drugs. And finally imagine that if the police stopped all people wearing such a baseball cap, that 75 percent of those stopped would be white (possessing illicit drugs) and 25 percent would be minorities (not possessing illicit drugs). These stylized examples suggest that the baseball cap is a valid indicator of illicit activity for whites but it is not valid for the minority subgroup. Moreover, because 75 percent of the baseball cap wearers are white, we might claim that the characteristic is valid overall for the entire population—after all there is a 75 percent chance that a cap search will uncover illicit drugs.

But under these stylized facts, what is a police department likely to choose as its search criteria? In today's politically charged environment, the department might want to avoid just searching whites wearing the cap—fearing that such decisionmaking would constitute illegal racial profiling. As an alternative, it might choose to stop all those who wear the cap (minorities and nonminorities alike). The result of such a color-blind criterion, however, would be to produce systematically poorer outcomes for minority searches than for white searches. While I argued above that lower search success rates for minorities might be indicative of the most blatant type of police attempts of racial harassment, in this hypothetical the systematically lower minority search success rate is caused by the police department's unwillingness to engage in disparate racial treatment—its unwillingness to engage in racial profiling.

This cap hypothetical provides a cautionary tale for overdefining what constitutes racial profiling. If, given our nation's painful history of minority oppression, we are more concerned with the possibility of invidious discrimination by police against minorities (than in favor of minorities), then we should more stringently scrutinize race-contingent decisionmaking in which minority status makes it *more* likely that a search will occur, than decisionmaking in which minority status makes it *less* likely that a search will occur. This is merely an implication of what legal scholars sometimes refer to as the "antisubordination principle"—which argues that courts should more strictly scrutinize government actions that burden a traditionally subordinated group than ones that burden a nonsubordinated group.[26]

The outcome test still can provide strong evidence (putting aside for the moment the inframarginality problem) that the criteria for minority searches are less valid than the criteria for nonminority searches—and hence might still show that police demand less probable cause when searching minorities than whites. But the cap hypothetical vividly illustrates that an unwillingness to engage in disparate treatment can itself have a disparate impact that is unjustified (when judged from the perspective of subgroup validity). As applied to police searches, a finding that the minority search success rate was systematically lower than that of whites would at a minimum indicate that the search criteria were less valid when applied to minorities than to whites.

However, such a showing (that particular decisionmaking criteria is systematically less valid for minorities) might not be sufficient to make out a case that the disparate impact was unjustified. It is far from clear whether disparate impact law does (or should) require a showing that particular criteria are valid for racial subgroups.[27] In the cap hypothetical, police

26. Unfortunately, this principal has been explicitly rejected by the Supreme Court. See *Adarand,* 515 U.S. at 224 (explaining that "consistency" requires the same strict standard of review apply no matter "the race of those burdened or benefited by a particular classification," quoting *Croson,* 488 U.S. at 494 [plurality opinion]).

27. Vicki Schultz has informed me that the 1966 and 1970 EEOC guidelines required evidence of subgroup racial validity (so-called differential validation), requiring

might succeed in arguing that the search criteria imposed at worst a *justified* disparate impact because 75 percent of all cap searches uncovered illicit contraband.

The foregoing analysis suggests, then, that the outcome analysis tests relative subgroup validity of decision criteria and not whether the criteria are valid with respect to the full sample of people being searched. While this is an important theoretical concern, as applied in a criminal context (where in many jurisdictions minorities comprise a majority of those who are searched), it is highly unlikely that police search criteria could be valid overall without being valid to minorities. For example, as applied to the outcome test of bail bond setting in chapter 7, our finding that bail setting criteria were not valid with regard to minorities strongly indicated that these criteria were not valid overall—for the simple reason that minorities made up over three-quarters of those for whom bail was set. It is difficult to believe that criteria that are not valid with regard to the overwhelming majority of observations would nonetheless be valid with regard to the entire population.[28]

■   ■   ■

In sum, the principal audits and the outcome tests both have important strengths in comparison to traditional auditing tests of disparate treatment.

---

employers to conduct separate validation studies for different racial groups. See United States v. City of Chicago, 549 F.2d 415, 433 (7th Cir. 1977) (requiring differential validation). The Supreme Court even endorsed it in Albermarle Paper Co. v. Moody, 422 U.S. 405, 435 (1975). But the guidelines eliminated the requirement for differential validation and replaced it with something called "unfairness studies." See 29 C.F.R. § 1607.14B(8). Subgroup validation is still required with language, see Mark Kelman, Concepts of Discrimination in General Ability Job Testing," 104 Harv. L. Rev. 1157, 1192 (1991). And as Christine Jolls has recently noted, see Christine Jolls, Accommodation Mandates (unpublished manuscript, 2000), a disparate racial impact decision invalidating an employer's "no beard" policy (as having an unjustified disparate impact on African Americans) has expressly endorsed race-contingent remedies. Bradley v. Pizzaco of Nebraska, 7 F.3d 795, 799 (8th Cir. 1993) ("injunction shall be carefully tailored to place Domino's under the minimal burden of recognizing a limited exception to its no-beard policy for African American males who suffer from PFB and as a result of this medical condition are unable to shave"). Such decisions suggest that decisionmakers may have a duty to remedy racial disparate impacts by resorting to express racial disparate treatment. However, the performance of such a duty may run afoul of the 1991 Civil Rights Act's ban on race norming. See 42 U.S.C. § 2000e-2(l) (Supp. IV 1992).

28. However, in other contexts where minorities comprise only a small proportion of those subject to a particular type of decision, there remains a stronger possibility that criteria which were subgroup invalid might still be valid overall.

Most importantly, these new tests avoid the recurrent omitted-variable bias or "qualified pool" problems that plague attempts to show disparate treatment on the basis of traditional audits or with disparate impact evidence. But these new tests also have limitations: the principal audits raise ethical concerns of entrapment, while the outcome tests may be over-inclusive because of problems of inframarginality or subgroup validity. But because there are, in particular contexts, adequate responses to each of these problems, these two new types of tests deserve to be part of the accepted arsenal of civil rights empiricism. They can provide credible evidence especially when combined with other (more traditional) types of evidence that decisionmaking subjects minorities to an unjustified disparate impact.

III. More Attention to Cause

Establishing the continuing fact of disparate treatment is important in and of itself, but empirical studies should also strive to assess the causes of discrimination. As stressed in the analysis in chapter 3 of car-buying negotiations, different causal theories can militate toward the use of dramatically different remedial measures. For example, mandating nondiscriminatory car pricing (the so-called no-dicker sticker) is more likely to bring about refusals to deal if cost-based statistical inferences are causing the discrimination than if revenue-based discrimination or consequential animus is driving the discrimination. That is, dealers who believe that it costs more to sell to African Americans are more likely to react to a mandated no-dicker sticker by refusing to deal than are dealers who initially offer higher prices because they think African Americans have a higher willingness to pay.

Some civil rights advocates seem to worry that even acknowledging the possibility that discrimination may have a variety of causes undermines the moral claims that discrimination is wrong. This seems particularly true with regard to what economists call "statistical" discrimination—that is, the idea that disparate treatment might be caused by rational statistical inferences about race (in contrast to discrimination caused by a decisionmaker's animus). There seems to be a concern that we will lose the moral high ground if we concede that rational inference instead of animus might drive certain types of discriminatory behavior. I take this to be a grave mistake. Instead, I believe an ultimately firmer ground on which to base the proscription against disparate racial treatment is to acknowledge the possibility of multiple causes and to show that even the relatively benign statistical causes are properly prohibited.

In this regard, I particularly admire the work of Stuart Schwab and Jody Armour, who have separately pointed out ways that even rational statistical inference may be socially inefficient because of the external costs that it imposes on the class of people subjected to the negative inference.[29] But Armour, who does an admirable job distinguishing several types of disparate treatment that cannot be morally justified, in the end fails to acknowledge that as a conceptual matter there might still exist types of statistical discrimination that are cost justified. That is, as a conceptual matter, there may exist types of rational statistical inference where, even taking into account the negative externalities of the statistical inference, the social benefits outweigh the social costs. For example, it is now fairly well settled that police can explicitly use race as a criteria for stopping suspects in response to a particularized racial description of a suspected offender by a victim of a crime.[30] This rule might not seem to be as much a type of statistical inference as a nonstatistical response to the *fact* that we know that a particular criminal has a particular race. But from the prospective of the police, victim descriptions of an offender's race are not incontestable facts—at most the police can infer that such descriptions are highly correlated with an offender's actual race. "Victims" such as Susan Smith and Charles Stuart sometimes intentionally misdescribe the race of the offender (to divert attention from themselves as the real criminal), and there is good reason to suspect that unintentional mistakes will systematically tend to "darken" the true offender's racial identity.[31] Thus, allowing

29. Stewart Schwab, Is Statistical Discrimination Efficient? 76 Am. Econ. Rev. 228 (1986); Jody David Armour, Race Ipsa Loquitor: Of Reasonable Racists, Intelligent Bayesians, and Involuntary Negrophobes, 46 Stan. L. Rev. 781 (1994). See also Jody David Armour, *Negrophobia and Reasonable Racism: The Hidden Costs of Being Black in America* (1997).

30. See Brown v. Oneonta, 1999 WL 973532 (2d Cir. Oct. 26 1999).

31. See Don Terry, A Woman's False Accusation Pains Many Blacks, *N.Y. Times,* Nov. 6, 1994, at 32; Fox Butterfield, Boston Tries to Minimize Racial Anger, *N.Y. Times,* Sept. 28 1995, at A16; Jody David Armour, Hype and Reality in Affirmative Action, 68 U. Colo. L. Rev, 1173 (1997). See also Sheri Lynn Johnson, Cross-Racial Identification Errors in Criminal Cases, 69 Cornell L. Rev. 934, 950–51 (1984), citing Gordon W. Allport & Leo Postman, *The Psychology of Rumor* 75 (1965): "White witnesses expect to see black criminals. This expectation is so strong that whites may observe an interracial scene in which a white person is the aggressor, yet remember the black person as the aggressor."

racial profiling in response to particularized victim descriptions can at best be defended as a type of cost-justified statistical discrimination—in which the statistical inference is highly valid and the social benefits from such disparate treatment outweigh the social harms.

Instead of treating cost-justified statistical discrimination as though it were a null set, we would do better to raise public consciousness that most types of so-called statistical discrimination are not based on rational statistical inference or are not cost justified. To concede that a type of cost-justified statistical discrimination exists far from suggests that all or even most forms of statistical discrimination are morally palatable. Indeed, a main point of chapter 3 was to show that there are a rich set of potential causal theories that might explain disparate treatment in car negotiations and that these causal theories may be normatively distinguishable. That chapter subdivided both statistical and animus theories of discrimination: distinguishing on the statistical side between cost-based and revenue-based statistical inference, and on the animus side between associational and consequential animus. While some may cling to the notion that inferences about the relative costs of supplying different races necessitates charging different prices, it is much harder for them to argue that inferences merely about a dealership's ability to extract additional revenue from a particular race justifies disparate treatment.[32]

Economists in particular have been wedded to an overly narrow theory of animus. Following in Gary Becker's large footsteps, the vast majority of economists have been content to model prejudice as a type of "associational" animus—whereby the decisionmaker required compensation for having to associate or spend time with members of particular (racial) groups.[33] But as elaborated in chapter 3, animus might alternatively take nonassociational forms. Instead of not wanting to associate with minorities, a decisionmaker might take pleasure in hurting or disadvantaging members of such groups. I called this alternative motive a kind of "consequential" animus, because the decisionmaker does not mind spending time (associating) but cares instead about the consequences of the decisions. Associational animus is much more likely to lead to refusals to deal, while consequential animus is likely to lead toward continuing relationships so

32. Ian Ayres, Alternative Grounds: Epstein's Discrimination Analysis in Other Market Settings, 31 San Diego L. Rev. 67 (1994).

33. But see Richard H. McAdams, Cooperation and Conflict: The Economics of Group Status Production and Race Discrimination, 108 Harv. L. Rev. 1003 (1995).

that the decisionmaker might take additional pleasure in continually mis-treating the object of his hatred. Failing to test for the possibility of conse-quential animus has seriously limited economists' ability to see possible forms of discrimination.

Yet even this expanded causal list is severely limited in not sufficiently accounting for whether the particular cause is prompted by a conscious or unconscious cognitive processes. Any of these four explanations (revenue-based statistical, cost-based statistical, associational animus, or consequential animus) might be produced unconsciously. For example, a salesperson might have either a conscious aversion to associating with blacks or an unconscious predisposition that leads her to act as if she consciously were averse to such association. Or a salesperson either may consciously believe that women im-pose higher (say, unreimbursed repair) costs or may make similar inferences not consciously because of the consumer's gender but instead because of some more free-floating gestalt impression about the likely cost of trans-acting. Recent work in social science suggests that unconscious causes (even by people espousing strong commitments against race-contingent action) are increasingly important determinants of disparate treatment.[34]

So, increasingly, a commitment to teasing out the possible causes of discrimination will have to contend with the difficulties of testing for un-conscious causes and attempting to tailor appropriate remedies. These are not tasks at which economists normally excel. Following Milton Friedman, economists normally are not concerned whether sellers consciously at-tempt to set the price of their goods equal to their marginal cost—as long as competition drives them to act "as if" this is what they were consciously

---

34. See Samuel L. Gaertner & John F. Dovido, *The Aversive Form of Racism in Prejudice, Discrimination and Racism* (1986); Margo J. Monteith, Self-Regulation of Prejudiced Responses: Implications for Progress in Prejudice-Reduction Efforts, 65 J. Per-sonality & Soc. Psychol. 469 (1993).

A great deal of legal scholarship has been recently produced on the issue of uncon-scious discrimination. See Armour, *supra* note 29, at 68–80; Martha Chamallas, The Ar-chitecture of Bias: Deep Structures in Tort Law, 146 U. Pa. L. Rev. 463 (1998); Barbara J. Flagg, "Was Blind, But Now I See": White Race Consciousness and the Requirement of Discriminatory Intent, 91 Mich. L. Rev. 953 (1993); Sheri Lynn Johnson, Uncon-scious Racism and the Criminal Law, 73 Cornell L. Rev. 1016 (1988); Linda Hamilton Krieger, The Content of Our Categories: A Cognitive Bias Approach to Discrimination and Equal Employment Opportunity, 47 Stan. L. Rev. 1161 (1995); Charles R. Law-rence III, The Id, The Ego, and Equal Protection: Reckoning with Unconscious Racism, 39 Stan. L. Rev. 317 (1987); David Benjamin Oppenheimer, Negligent Discrimination, 141 U. Pa. L. Rev. 899 (1993); Jessie Allen, Note, A Possible Remedy for Unthinking Discrimination, 61 Brook. L. Rev. 1299, 1311–15 (1995).

doing.[35] Similarly, economists normally do not distinguish (accord chapter 3) between conscious and unconscious causes of discrimination as long as they can identify whether decisionmakers are acting as if they were consciously discriminating for a certain reason. The weakness with this "as if" approach is that there are good reasons to think that different remedial policies are appropriate depending on whether a particular form of discriminatory decisionmaking is deliberately (that is, consciously) race contingent or rather is based on some form of unconscious cognitive process. Jody Armour in particular has powerfully argued that courts should use different strategies to counteract disparate treatment that grows out of different degrees or forms of conscious belief.[36] Most basically, it may be easier to reduce disparate treatment by bringing unconscious predispositions for discrimination to the attention of potential discriminators—especially when these potential discriminators simultaneously espouse sincere commitments against discrimination.

In this regard, I am particularly attracted to the Implicit Association Test (IAT), a straightforward test of unconscious disparate treatment that can be taken quickly (in approximately five minutes) on the Internet—at www.yale.edu/implicit/.[37] If you have a computer handy, I recommend that you pause in your reading and take this test now. The IAT asks the subject to complete four different sorting tasks. In the first task, the subject is asked to simply sort photographs into two categories labeled "African American" and "European American." (On the Internet version of the test, you might be asked to press the "e" key [on the left side of your keyboard] to indicate that a photograph is of an African American and to press the "i" key [on the right side of your keyboard] to indicate that a photograph is of an European American.) In the second task, the subject is asked to sort words (such as "love," "war") into two categories labeled "Good"

35. See Milton Friedman, The Methodology of Positive Economics, *in Essays in Positive Economics* 3–43 (1953).

36. Jody Armour, Sterotypes and Prejudice: Helping Legal Decisionmakers Break the Prejudice Habit, 83 Calif. L. Rev. 733 (1995). Amy Wax, however, has recently argued that employers cannot effectively deter unconscious discrimination. Amy L. Wax, Discrimination as Accident, 74 Ind. L.J. 1129, 1206 (1999).

37. The IAT is not the only method of testing for unconscious bias. See, e.g., Eric J. Vanman et al., The Modern Face of Prejudice and Structural Features That Moderate the Effect of Cooperation on Affect, 73 J. Personality & Soc. Psychol. 941, 944–45 (1977) (describing lie-detector-type process measuring tiny movements in affective face muscles).

and "Bad." These first two tasks allow the test to establish a baseline metric of the subject's ability (measured by speed and accuracy) to sort photographs and words.[38] The third task then asks the subject to sort combinations of photographs and words into two categories. One of the categories is labeled "African American *or* Good" and the other category is labeled "European American *or* Bad."[39] And the final task asks the subject to sort the categories into the two categories "African American *or* Bad" and "European American or Good."

The test centrally measures whether a subject can identify African Americans photographs more quickly when these images are associated with "good" or "bad" words. A finding that it is easier to group African American photographs and bad words than it is to group African American photographs and good words suggests that subjects may harbor unconscious negative associations of African Americans.[40] As a general matter, it is easier to sort disjunctive categories that we normally associate with each other.[41] Thus, we might expect it would be easier to group together the disjunctive categories of "red flowers or red balls" relative to "red flowers and green balls"—because our minds can more naturally associate "things red." If the racial status of the photographs and the good/bad valence of the words were truly orthogonal to each other in our cognitive processes, we would not expect to be able to group together items that were "African American photographs or Bad words" more quickly than items that were "African American photographs or Good words."

---

38. Subjects are told: "The test gives no results if you go slow—Please try to go fast. Expect to make a few mistakes because of going fast. That's OK." http://www.yale.edu/implicit/race/race2.html. A better controlled test might more explicitly tell subjects how to trade off additional speed versus accuracy (as in typing tests) and in certain of the implementations suggested below (such as in the sensitivity training or the affirmative action testing) it might be appropriate to incentivize subjects with compensation or prizes to give them appropriate inducements to sort quickly enough to capture unconscious reactions.

39. For example, on the Internet version, a subject might be asked to press the "e" key whenever either an African American photograph or a good word (for example, "love") appeared, and to press the "i" key whenever either a European American photograph or a bad word (for example, "war") appeared.

40. Analogously, a finding that it is easier to group European American photographs and good words than it is to group European American photographs and bad words suggest that subjects may harbor unconscious positive associations of European Americans.

41. See Anthony G. Greenwald et al., Measuring Individual Differences in Implicit Cognition: The Implicit Associaiton Test, 74 J. Personality & Soc. Psychol. 1464 (1998).

Table 9.1   Implicit (Racial) Association Test

	All Subjects (N = 27,676)	White Subjects (N = 24,557)	Black Subjects (N = 3,119)
Strong automatic preference for whites	49%	52%	23%
Moderate automatic preference for whites	13%	13%	10%
Slight automatic preference for whites	12%	12%	12%
Little or no automatic preference	12%	11%	16%
Slight automatic preference for blacks	6%	5%	10%
Moderate automatic preference for blacks	4%	3%	9%
Strong automatic preference for blacks	6%	4%	19%

Source: B. A. Nosek et al., Measuring Implicit Attitudes on the Internet (poster presented at the 2000 conference for the Society of Personality and Social Psychology, Nashville, Tenn., February 2, 2000). Data is based on Internet tests (September 1999–February 2000). An important caveat: race of subjects is self-reported via the Internet—so some subjects might have misreported their true race.

It is interesting to note that a truly color-blind subject would be unable to sort photographs into racial categories—being unable by definition to even see race. Such a complete inability to sort would of course prevent the subject from being able to discriminate on the basis of race. But even among the much larger group of the population (verging on 100 percent) that is able to accurately identify and sort photographs by race, a subject could avoid a finding of disparate treatment if he or she could sort good and bad words with equal success regardless of the racial attributes with which they are disjunctively paired.

Unfortunately, as shown in table 9.1, the results of the IAT suggest that the majority (62 percent) of subjects have a moderate to strong automatic preference for whites (a proportion that is six times greater than the just 10 percent that have a moderate to strong preference for African Americans). And reminiscent of the doll empiricism cited in *Brown v. Board of Education*,[42] table 9.1 shows some evidence that at least a substantial proportion of African Americans find it easier to sort "bad" words when they are associated with black photographs than when they are associated with white photographs. Forty-five percent of black subjects exhibited at least a slight automatic preference for whites, while 38 percent of black subjects exhibited at least a slight preference for blacks. But the distribution of black responses while skewed toward a white preference is

42.   Brown v. Board of Educ., 347 U.S. 483, 495 n.11 (1954), citing K. B. Clark, *Effect of Prejudice and Discrimination on Personality Development* (1950). Professor Clark's experiments and testimony at trial are discussed in Gordon J. Beggs, Novel Expert Evidence in Federal Civil Rights Litigation, 45 Am. U. L. Rev. 2 (1995).

still much less skewed toward a white preference than the white responses. As shown in table 9.1, 77 percent of white subjects exhibited at least a slight automatic preference for whites, while only 12 percent of white subjects displayed at least a slight preference for blacks.

The IAT has potential application in a number of different legal settings. In the most adversarial of uses, the test might be used as part of the examination in a Title VII disparate treatment case. Imagine, for example, the following cross-examination of the defendant decisionmaker:

Q: Mr. X, do you ever treat African Americans differently than whites because of their race?
A: No.
Q: Are you sure that you don't have any unconscious thought processes that might lead you to treat blacks differently than whites?
A: Yes.
Q: You're confident that you could refrain from treating blacks differently than whites in a controlled setting?
A: Yes.

Whereupon the counsel for the plaintiff might then attempt to have the defendant complete the IAT on the stand (or, less dramatically, this exchange might take place in the defendant's initial deposition).

This examination game of "gotcha" should certainly not be dispositive. Evidence that the defendant treats blacks differently than whites when attempting to sort individuals (literally photographs of individuals) of different races paired disjunctively with different types of words does not mean that the defendant engaged in disparate treatment in making employment decisions. The IAT is intentionally structured to require such quick (unmediated) decisionmaking so as to bypass more conscious deliberative thought processes. It is possible that in making less time-constrained decisions—where more deliberative controls can be brought to bear—that the decisionmaker would be able to purge from his decisionmaking any tainted unconscious associations.

But the IAT at least shows that the decisionmaker may entertain unconscious negative associations for blacks relative to whites and may in at least some contexts (contrary to his testimony) be unable to control the impact of these associations on his decisionmaking. The IAT's probative value is admittedly limited by being a test of decisionmaking (sorting) far removed from the decision at issue, but its probative value is enhanced by the fact that (unlike the employment decisions) the defendant is put on explicit notice that his decisionmaking will be scrutinized for disparate racial treatment and that he should make every effort to avoid race-contingent behavior.

Some will even deny that the IAT is a test of disparate treatment. But surely it tests whether the subject *treats* black photographs differently than similarly situated white photographs. While photographic images are not people, one would strongly suspect that the results would not change if images of live people were briefly shown to subjects instead of their photographic images. And while the IAT's decisionmaking does not replicate employment decisions, evidence that a defendant engages in disparate treatment in nonemployment contexts might certainly be probative of whether the defendant might engage in disparate treatment in employment as well. In the end, the IAT result might not be excluded on pure grounds of relevance, but more likely (under Rule 403 of the Federal Rules of Evidence) if the court believed the probity of the evidence was outweighed by its prejudicial effect. Appropriate judicial or expert testimony might properly frame the relevance of the result, and the ultimate decision might also turn in part on whether the defendant categorically denied (as in the foregoing hypothetical examination) that he ever engaged in disparate treatment. But many alternative types of evidence currently admitted to help prove disparate racial treatment are also troubling (such as the "gotcha" evidence concerning a decisionmaker's use of racial slurs).[43]

In other adversarial contexts, the probity of the IAT evidence would be much less attenuated. Imagine, for example, in the recent criminal prosecution of the New York City police officers who were charged with the February 4, 1999, killing of Amadou Diallo,[44] if the prosecution introduced evidence showing that the defendant officers when under a time constraint could much more easily group African Americans together with pejorative words than nonpejorative words. Here the test's attempt to force a decisionmaker to quickly sort visual images into one of two categories comes much closer to the defendants' need as police officers to quickly categorize a suspect as "good" or "bad."

The IAT might also be applied in a so-called *Batson* challenge as part of a defendant's evidence that the prosecution may have at least unconsciously been motivated by race in its preemptive challenge of black ju-

43. See, e.g., Beth J. Harpaz, First Lady Denies Using Antisemitic Slur in '74, *Wash. Post,* July 17, 2000, at A6; Witnesses Tell Jury of Fuhrman's Racial Epithets, *L.A. Times,* Sept. 6, 1995, at 1.

44. See Jerome H. Skolnick, Code Blue, 11 American Prospect 49 (2000).

rors.[45] Or the IAT might be used in the voir dire itself in an attempt to assess whether individual jurors would treat a defendant in a racially charged case fairly. Again, I do not claim that an IAT finding of even a strong disparate treatment should by itself be dispositive in either of these contexts. I only claim that the results might usefully enrich the factual record. Introducing evidence of unconscious predispositions even of those who sincerely espouse a distaste for disparate treatment is not a subterfuge but a way to make increasingly clear the likely causes of disparate treatment.

Finally, the IAT may play a useful role in less adversarial proceedings. Racial sensitivity programs (whether or not conducted pursuant to consent decrees) might include the IAT as one of the exercises to make decisionmakers aware that their actions might be tainted by unconscious predispositions or associations.[46] Or more proactively, governments might require systematic implicit association testing of its employees as part of an effort to determine whether a race-based affirmative action remedy is necessary. For example, a finding that government procurement officers harbor systematically negative associations regarding minorities might play a small role in government's efforts to show that the exercise of procurement officers' discretion might unconsciously disadvantage minorities. Governments are often at pains (both politically and as a matter of the evidence) to produce any direct evidence of disparate racial treatment by its procurement officers—so the IAT may at least show that government actors might be prone to discriminating against minorities in their discretionary decisionmaking.[47]

Implicit attitude testing might also itself be used as a criterion for hiring both governmental and nongovernmental actors. It might be valuable

45. In Batson v. Kentucky, 476 U.S. 79 (1986), the Supreme Court held that the Equal Protection Clause prohibits prosecutors in exercising their peremptory challenges from striking jurors because of their race. In essence, the Court found that a criminal defendant is entitled to a jury selected without racial discrimination.

46. Deana Pollard has written an excellent article suggesting ways that employers might use the IAT to sensitize their managers and employees to the possibility of bias and arguing that the the results of such self-critical assessment be privileged in subsequent civil rights litigation. Deana A. Pollard, Unconscious Bias and Self-critical Analysis: The Case for a Qualified Evidentiary Equal Employment Opportunity Privilege, 74 Wash. L. Rev. 913 (1999).

47. It should be stressed that direct evidence of government disparate treatment is not constitutionally necessary. See Ayres & Vars, *supra* note 7. But audit and IAT evidence of disparate treatment against minorities by governmental and nongovernmental actors participating in the same market may play an important role in making out that the government has a "compelling interest" in remedying race discrimination and that the affirmative action is "narrowly tailored" to remedy the effect of the discrimination.

to hire police who exhibit fewer racially charged predispostions. As the Amadou Diallo case painfully reminds us, split-second decisionmaking is a necessary part of the job, and police that have an easier time associating particular races with pejorative meanings may be expected to make systematically poorer life and death decisions about when to use force. Implicit attitude testing might itself constitute a race-neutral means of enhancing minority participation in the workforce. Even if minorities also tend to exhibit an IAT bias against themselves, as long as this bias is not as strong as the white bias against minorities, then screening on the basis of the IAT would likely have a disparate impact in qualifying minorities for employment. For example, using the data in table 9.1, consider the effect of a hiring criterion that rejected any applicant who showed a moderate or strong automatic preference for either whites or blacks. Such a screening device would leave 38 percent of black applicants qualified compared to only 28 percent of whites. Indeed, in the police context, John Lott has found that black male police officers are systematically less likely to be involved in an accidental shooting.[48] While there may be many alternative explanations for this result, IAT testing as one part of the application process holds the tantalizing prospect of enhancing minority workforce participation and reducing the unconscious discrimination of institutional actors.[49]

Conclusion

This chapter has argued that we should resituate the civil rights debate on a more quantitative basis. The empirical studies reported throughout this book have given some concrete examples of this effort. But we still do not know the current ambit of race and gender discrimination in America. Many whites think that disparate treatment against minorities is by and large a thing of the past. If we are going to retain a commitment

---

48.   John R. Lott, Does a Helping Hand Put Others at Risk?: Affirmative Action, Police Departments, and Crime, Econ. Inquiry (forthcoming 2000) (finding that accidental shooting rate went down significantly as percentage of black males on police force increase; but also finding increase in general crime rate).

49.   As Clark Freshman has recently emphasized, people who discriminate on one ground (say, against homosexuals) are more likely to discriminate on others (say, against African Americans). Clark Freshman, Whatever Happened to Anti-Semitism? How Social Science Theories Identify Discrimination and Promote Coalitions between "Different" Minorities, 85 Cornell L. Rev. 313 (2000).

to racial justice, we must further document whether discrimination is still a problem.

I have emphasized a strong preference for quantitative evidence of discrimination and its causes. But qualitative narratives of discrimination are also valuable. Researchers in particular should increasingly videotape the decisionmaking. My quantitative study of car discrimination was widely reported, but *PrimeTime Live*'s visual images of disparate treatment—whether it be in the form of vividly different degrees of retail friendliness or different dealership prices for the same car—have had a greater impact on just those people who wrongly think that disparate racial treatment is a thing of the past. Pictures and numbers are the key to convincing whites that unjustified race-contingent behavior persists in the modern marketplace.

To be clear, what I am suggesting would constitute a relative deemphasis on evidence of unjustified disparate impacts (often referred to more broadly as "institutional discrimination") as a justification for civil rights intervention. While I still believe (as evinced in chapters 6 and 7) that unjustified disparate impacts are an appropriate concern for law and policy, I do not believe that they provide as firm a moral basis for political organizing. There may come a time when race-contingent behavior as an empirical matter recedes to such an extent that institutional discrimination becomes the dominant source of racial disability. But it is my sense that that time has not yet come.

Finally, in expanding the domain of civil rights empiricism, we should not be content with testing others. Civil rights empiricism should begin at home. If I wish to truly talk about the pervasiveness of prejudice, I should be willing to open myself to potentially uncomfortable findings. The IAT researchers are particularly fond of a quotation that they attribute to Fyodor Dostoevsky:

> Every man has reminiscences which he would not tell to everyone but only his friends. He has other matters in his mind which he would not reveal even to his friends, but only to himself, and that in secret. But there are other things which a man is afraid to tell even to himself, and every decent man has a number of such things stored away in his mind.[50]

50. http://www.yale.edu/implicit/learn1.html. Fyodor Dostoyevsky, *Notes from Underground* 35 (Ralph E. Matlow trans., Dutton 1960). This quotation may also be found in Tim O'Brien's novel, *In the Lake of the Woods* 145 (1994).

In this spirit, I'm saddened to report that after taking the implicit attitude test several times, I have consistently been rated as having a "moderate" to "strong" automatic preference for whites relative to blacks. It is one thing to believe in the abstract that our collective conscious and unconscious dispositions are the by-product of a highly racialized society; it is quite another to be confronted with the impact of this socialization in your own decisionmaking. It is easy to think that socialization affects the other guy, but harder to acknowledge that it affects yourself. I find my IAT results jarring not because I am surprised that growing up in this society almost necessarily racialized my perceptions, but because I was mistakenly confident that my nondiscriminatory ego could stamp out any unconscious discriminatory predispositions. Apparently not. The evidence of my uncontrollable unconscious racial predisposition does more than let me close the book on a trendy note of personal confession: to my mind it suggests that I am less qualified for holding certain types of employment. Now gentle reader, what about you? An answer is a few clicks away.